THE HARVEST OF
MEDIEVAL THEOLOGY

Gabriel Biel and Late Medieval Nominalism

Heiko Augustinus Oberman

THE LABYRINTH PRESS

Durham, North Carolina

1983

For information contact:
The Labyrinth Press, P.O. Box 2124
Durham, N.C. 27702-2124

Library of Congress Cataloging in Publication Data

Oberman, Heiko Augustinus
    The harvest of medieval theology.

    Reprint. Originally published: Cambridge, Mass.:
Harvard University Press, 1963. (The Robert Troup
Paine prize-treatise ; 1962)
    Bibliography: p.
    Includes indexes.
    1. Theology, Doctrinal — History — Middle Ages,
600-1500. 2. Biel, Gabriel, d. 1495. 3. Nominalism.
I. Title. II. Series: Robert Troup Paine prize-
treatise ; 1962.
[BT26.02 1983]   230'.2'0924   82-20896

ISBN 0-939464-05-5

Praeceptori meo
MAARTEN VAN RHIJN
in gratitudine
dedicatus

PREFACE TO THE THIRD EDITION

In the postscript to the first edition of this book (1963), I expressed the hope that a subsequent study would explore the relation of nominalistic thought to the beginnings of the Reformation movement. A plethora of events intervened and disrupted the original time schedule. My decision, however, to deal with late medieval nominalism in its own right, for its own sake, and, first, in an independent study, now proves more apposite than could then have been foreseen. Three potent intellectual forces must be confronted if nominalism is to be extricated from the quagmire in which it has been submerged.

As presented by Martin Grabmann, Étienne Gilson, and their many students, the history of medieval philosophy seemed to culminate in the High Middle Ages, reaching its pinnacle in the works of Thomas Aquinas and in the *via antiqua* which hearkened to his voice. Accordingly, fourteenth and fifteenth century thought was evaluated by this standard and found wanting. The later Middle Ages became the "journey's end"; nominalism and its *via moderna* were no more than the "tired" and "sceptical disintegration" of the formidable medieval synthesis, the inspiring *summa* achieved in the thirteenth century.

Renaissance studies pointed in the same direction and tended to harden these assumptions. Those scholars who prefer to designate the later Middle Ages as "Renaissance" have overcome, under the leadership of Paul Oskar Kristeller, the misconception of a programmatic opposition between scholasticism and Renaissance humanism. Nevertheless — and notwithstanding assertions to the effect that "humanism" is neither Platonic nor Aristotelian — the long-standing preoccupation with Florence and the fascination with the Platonic Academy of Ficino and Pico have continued to highlight, onesidedly, the connection of Italian Renaissance thought with medieval Thomism. Charles Trinkaus has done much to redress the balance, and Ficino is no longer the Saint Thomas of Renaissance scholarship. But a parallel and equivalent treatment of the intriguing connections and rivalries between Renaissance humanism and nominalism is only now beginning to find its way into textbooks for college students.

In regard to the question of nominalism, the state of Reformation studies is even less encouraging. Confessional forces have done more than medieval and Renaissance studies combined in devising impediments to a comprehensive grasp of the term and its real implications. Roman Catholic historians have tended—and still tend—to shun nominalism as the contaminated cradle of Protestantism. European historians, particularly German Luther scholars, have encouraged a rift between the late Middle Ages and the Reformation in order to present Martin Luther and early Reformation thought as unprecedented phenomena: a radically new beginning, heralding "modern times." Where in one or two studies Gabriel Biel and nominalism are in fact taken seriously, the movement is first limited to its theological dimension and next reduced to tenets criticized and rejected by the young Luther. When the roots of the Reformation in the later Middle Ages are severed in such a way, the impressive originality of Luther is obscured rather than established.

If confessionalism prevails, then Protestants and Catholics alike—in a rare and unfortunate display of ecumenicity—will go on "working over" (literally and figuratively) the later Middle Ages until the period is finally defaced beyond recognition.

In view of the intransigence of such vested interests, I decided to convert my planned two-volume study into a trilogy. Rather than embarking at once on the development of the Reformation movement from Luther to Calvin, I chose to devote a second, and separate, volume to the evolution of nominalism since the days of Gabriel Biel (†1495) and its impact on the incipient Reformation in Wittenberg and the cities. This second volume, *Werden und Wertung der Reformation* (Tübingen, 1977; 2nd edition, 1979), was translated and published in English under the title *Masters of the Reformation* (Cambridge, 1981). Although *Masters* involves a range of concerns which fall within the province of what is loosely construed as social history, it remains nonetheless a close companion to the *Harvest of Medieval Theology* and is developed upon foundations laid in the earlier book.

The 1965 revised edition of *The Harvest of Medieval Theology* being no longer available, it gives me great satisfaction that before the third and final volume of the trilogy has appeared its indispensable foundation and point of departure will once again be placed within reach of students and scholars.

Heiko A. Oberman
Tübingen, September 1982

viii

CONTENTS

CONTENTS

CONTENTS

CONTENTS

CONTENTS

CONTENTS

INTRODUCTION

It is a curious — and dangerous — coincidence that the late medieval period is one of the least known in the history of Christian thought *and*, at the same time, a period in the interpretation of which there are a great many vested interests. The former is primarily the result of the fact that — while one can no longer call late medieval thought *terra incognita* — for too long a time it has been regarded solely as a part of the history of philosophy. Consequently its theological contributions have been largely neglected. The latter is undoubtedly due to the fact that this period forms the frontier between the so-called high middle ages and the Reformation. This has certainly made it difficult for scholars to come to a reasonably unbiased evaluation of the place and function of the late medieval period in the history of Christian thought.

One can substantiate this observation by pointing to at least three significant schools of interpretation. Reformation scholars have been inclined to view the later middle ages merely as the "background of the Reformation" and have too often been guided in their evaluation by statements of the Reformers — especially Martin Luther — which by their very nature tend to be informed by a conscious departure from particular developments in the medieval tradition. There is a tendency in this school to stress contrasts between Luther and late medieval theologians and in general to assign Luther more to the tradition of St. Paul and St. Augustine than to that of William of Occam and Gabriel Biel.

There is, secondly, what one may loosely call the Thomistic school of interpretation which holds that in the thought of Thomas Aquinas, the middle ages reached its apex. It states that the thought of the succeeding period, beginning with Duns Scotus and culminating in nominalism — the work of Occam, Biel, and their disciples — is characterized by the disintegration and rapid collapse of the Thomistic synthesis. The

I

idea that nominalism is an essentially anti- or at least a non-catholic movement leading up to the Reformation, and that, for example, Luther, however catholic in intention, became a heretic unwittingly because of his distorted, nominalistic training, is very often connected with this hypothesis. In this school late medieval thought is merely seen as the "aftermath of high scholasticism."

Finally, there is a third school which can be called the Franciscan school of interpretation. This school is apt to stress the orthodoxy and theological contribution of "new" Franciscans such as Scotus and Occam. And since this is a relatively young, and, until recent years, a decidedly less vocal school of interpretation, it is not as yet clearly committed to one particular approach. There are, however, signs which indicate that this group is willing to defend the orthodoxy of nominalism; it explains the theology of Luther as an erroneous interpretation of the theology of such a nominalist as Gabriel Biel, due to other elements in Luther's thought unrelated to the nominalistic tradition. While the Thomistic school locates the break in the medieval catholic tradition somewhere between Aquinas and Scotus, this third school searches for the decisive rupture somewhere between Biel and Luther.

It does not seem to be a far-fetched conclusion that the results of the study of the later middle ages have been too often determined by ulterior motives, especially those motives at stake in the controversy between Protestantism and Roman Catholicism. Confronted with these conflicting and often emotionally or denominationally colored presuppositions, we have felt the need to investigate the theology of Gabriel Biel in such a way as to take with the utmost seriousness his position *between* Thomas and Luther. Hopefully this will avoid treating late medieval thought, in general, and the theology of Gabriel Biel, in particular, either as the "aftermath of high scholasticism" or merely as "the background of the Reformation." Our aim is to view Gabriel Biel within the context of the tradition which he himself acknowledges to be authoritative, and thus to train our eyes to discern the emerging shape of a theological school of late medieval nominalism. This must be evaluated according to its own intention and according to its own peculiar contribution to medieval thought.

To succeed in this endeavor, we cannot restrict our analysis to either the philosophical departures of nominalism from Thomism or to the contrast between the nominalistic doctrine of justification and that of the succeeding Reformation theology, the two aspects usually treated. We shall not only analyze all those aspects of Biel's thought which appear from his own viewpoint to be important, but we shall also investigate all the Biel sources that are available. Hitherto, selected passages of his *Sentences* and *Exposition* have been discussed, but there have not been more than a handful of quotations from his *Sermons*, which comprise almost half his total opus, in circulation. Of course, it is conceivable that there could have been a development in Biel's thought from his early sermons to his late academic works; but as we have found no evidence for such a development, it is clear that the sermons must be taken seriously as documenting his thought. The discrepancies which we shall note between Biel's homiletic and his academic works can be explained as due to the different audiences to which they were directed.

This volume is part of an over-all plan to come to a reassessment of the impact of nominalism on sixteenth-century thought, especially of the elusive relation — both negative and positive — between Gabriel Biel and Martin Luther. Precisely because of the sharply contrasting interpretations of this period in Christian thought indicated above, it seems mandatory to treat Biel and Luther in two separate volumes. This will make it possible to deal with Biel for his own sake, not merely as a point of departure for a description of the theology of Martin Luther. For this reason Luther will seldom appear on the following pages; we shall enter into a discussion with Luther scholars only insofar as they have dealt with Biel.

The footnotes in this volume, again in view of the differing interpretations, are of particular importance. We have tried to provide such extensive documentation, by full-length quotations from Biel and elaborate cross references to the various works of Biel, that the reader is permitted not only to follow the argumentation by reading over our shoulder, but also to come to an independent evaluation. We hope in this way to present a description of Biel's thought which may perhaps have its own significance regardless of whether this interpretation finds general recognition. Because of the limited accessibility of the works of Biel, his sermons in particular, we are preparing a third volume which will reproduce a selection of Biel's most significant sermons in their entirety, along with representative examples of late medieval preaching.

In view of the limited use made of the sources to date, it is fair to say that the case of Gabriel Biel has been prejudged. This may also be true of William of Occam. Since, as we shall see time and again, the *Sentences* commentaries of Occam and Biel manifest parallel theological structures, we must at least consider whether Occam's interests would not also prove to be more theologically oriented if we had pastoral literature by Occam of the same genre as Biel's sermons and letters at our disposal. Although we shall stress that Biel must no longer be seen exclusively as a spokesman for Occam, future interpreters of Occam can profitably take into account the pastoral-theological potentialities inherent in the structure of Occam's thought which were actualized by Biel.

With respect to the question of the influence of Occam on the Reformation, we cannot ignore the form which Occam's thought has received in its restatement by Gabriel Biel, a form to which almost any other epithet better applies than the usual verdicts of "pure logic," "scepticism," and "disintegration." Furthermore we should at least call attention to the problem of the relation of "Occamism" and "nominalism." The present state of scholarship simply does not permit us to draw firm lines of relation or dependence within the period. Elsewhere [1] we have suggested that at least four "schools" within late medieval nominalism can be discerned. These are the Occam-Biel school, to which we add Pierre d'Ailly and Jean Charlier Gerson; the English left-wing school represented by Robert Holcot and Adam Woodham; the right-wing school centered around Gregory of Rimini; and a syncretistic school, particularly vocal at Paris, where the influence of Scotus and of Occam converge. In this study, which may be considered to be the first test of our hypothesis, there is further corroboration for an emphasis upon the essentially theological cohesion of the various schools within nominalism that transcends the philosophical presuppositions which originally gave the movement its name.

The analysis of the thought of Gabriel Biel necessarily leads us to investigate medieval thought as a whole. The indebtedness of Biel to Duns Scotus and Jean Gerson at the one hand, and the obedient discipleship of Bartholomaeus von Usingen, professor at Erfurt — and in this function teacher of Luther — at the other, mark the time span of our more detailed investigation.

[1] "Some Notes on the Theology of Nominalism with Attention to its Relation to the Renaissance," *HTR* 53 (1960), 47–76.

Chapters One to Five are primarily intended as descriptions of basic structures in Biel's thought. Building on this foundation, the second half of the book represents an effort to interpret the major systematic issues of the post-Avignon period in the light of our analysis of the position of Gabriel Biel.

At certain points we believe we have brought new perspectives to the study of late medieval thought, not so much because we proclaim Biel to be a great innovator, but because in Biel we are provided with a strategic vantage point. From here we see spread out before us, not the barren wastelands of sterile debates which we had been led to expect by traditional late medieval scholarship, but a richness of deep pastoral and searching theological concern. Through Biel's eyes we see the Church threatened by a rising tide of Donatism and the costly rivalry between the theologians of the Dominican and Franciscan orders. With a profound respect for the period before the rise of rival traditions growing out of thirteenth-century developments, Biel marks the spirit of late medieval nominalism in conscientiously probing all the great theological traditions, harvesting those fruits which seemed ripe enough to nourish the Christian faith in search of understanding, to heighten the quality of Christian life, and to undergird the unity of the Church under Christ and his vicar. Deeply indebted as we are to Johan Huizinga's *The Waning of the Middle Ages*, the image of "harvest" in our title is intentionally opposed to the connotation of "decline" carried by the French and English translations of the Dutch "Herfsttij," which literally means "harvest-tide."

Biel's vast knowledge of medieval theology in all its variety appears from the fact that apart from his great debt to Occam, he listens throughout his works most intently to the voices of other medieval theologians — among whom should be mentioned especially Bernard of Clairvaux, Peter Lombard, the old Franciscan school (Alexander of Hales and Bonaventura), Albert the Great, Thomas Aquinas, and Duns Scotus.

We have been particularly impressed by the fact that Biel throughout his works acknowledges Gerson along with Occam as a great authority. This has led us to explore particular aspects of Gerson's thought in order to establish the extent of Biel's systematic dependence on him. It is most revealing to see that Biel does not find it necessary to sacrifice his allegiance to Occam while obviously respecting the judgment of Gerson, particularly in respect to Mariology, the authority of the Church, and the mystical aspects of the Christian's existence. This study has led us to place Gerson more squarely within the nominalistic tradition than has been customary.

To present the rich diversity of the nominalistic tradition, we have dedicated special sections to those two intriguing figures who stand farthest apart, Gregory of Rimini, O.E.S.A. and Robert Holcot, O.P.

Biel's eloquent Marian piety has led us to include a chapter on late medieval Mariology. We found it most illuminating to see how this important flowering of medieval devotion and theology is systematically related to Christology and to the doctrine of justification.

An examination of Biel's mariological corollaries proved to be a natural test of the significance of the *pro nobis* theme in his Christology. We have also found it necessary to investigate the common claim that nominalistic Christology manifests Nestorian debilities. In fact, the defense of the Chalcedonian interpretation of the relation between the two natures in Christ is not only genuine, but is explicitly directed against Nestorian interpretations.

Here again Biel reveals the nominalistic search for the catholic *via media*. One can only comment regretfully that in a striking parallel to the failure of the efforts of the Council of Pisa to reunite divided Christendom, resulting only in the formation of a third faction, nominalistic theology was unable to succeed in the mediating role which it envisioned for itself.

Most surprising has been the discovery that Biel's own understanding of the Christian faith incorporates both the essence of nominalistic theology and traits which one cannot avoid classifying as mystical. The usual assumption that nominalism and mysticism are mutually exclusive would therefore seem no longer tenable.

The analysis of the polemic regarding the relative authority of Scripture and Church has not only suggested that this problem is for Biel and his school one of the more crucial theological questions; it also appears that new tools of interpretation are necessary in order to unravel the complexities of this problem in the later middle ages. The traditional contrast between *sola scriptura* and Tradition does not admit of sufficient subtlety to lay out sharply the issues underlying this polemic.

In fact two opposing currents of thought — the line from Thomas Bradwardine via John Huss to Wessel Gansfort over against the line from Occam via Gerson to Biel — are both concerned with the authority of Tradition, but Tradition conceived in two radically differing fashions.

Finally in the postscript which concludes this book, we have taken up explicitly the general claim that late medieval theology represents a period of disintegration and decay. This discussion is the natural context within which the hotly contested "catholicity of nominalism" can be assessed.

Due to the highly controversial nature of the subject matter, we have felt ourselves obliged — all too often for our own liking — to take issue with respected scholars in the field. Since this impression does not by any means convey an awareness of our indebtedness, we wish to acknowledge explicitly the meticulous and stimulating research of which we have readily availed ourselves.

Although bibliographical indications in the footnotes will call attention to a wide range of scholars, we should like to mention especially our grateful appreciation for the wisdom and the fresh insight brought to bear on the period by Otto Scheel and Paul Vignaux.

In order to assist those who may wish to find their way into the field of late medieval scholarship, which is gradually taking shape as a field in its own right, we have appended a glossary of the most crucial technical terms of the period along with a bibliography which is meant to be representative of contemporary scholarship in the field.

Chapter One

CURRICULUM VITAE GABRIELIS

Our first step, before turning to an analysis of Gabriel Biel's thought, will be to examine the outer course of his life, and to survey his writings. This prefatory discussion cannot be extensive, however, for the historical sources yield but few scattered references to the "last of the scholastics." Furthermore, many aspects of Biel's biography have already been satisfactorily described.[1] Hence, we shall simply outline the life of Gabriel

---

[1] Among the more comprehensive biographies are: F. X. Linsenmann, "Gabriel Biel und die Anfänge der Universität zu Tübingen," *Theologische Quartalschrift* 47 (1865), 195–226; H. Hermelink, *Geschichte der Theologischen Fakultät in Tübingen vor der Reformation 1477–1534* (Tübingen, 1906), pp. 204–207; C. Feckes, "Gabriel Biel, der erste grosse Dogmatiker der Universität Tübingen in seiner wissenschaftlichen Bedeutung," *Theologische Quartalschrift* 108 (1927), 50–76; J. Haller, *Die Anfänge der Universität Tübingen, 1477–1537*, I (Stuttgart, 1927), 153–172; II (Stuttgart, 1929), 54–64; M. Cappuyns, "Biel, Gabriel," in *Dictionnaire d'histoire et de géographie ecclésiastique*, vol. VIII (Paris, 1935), cols. 1429–1430; W. M. Landeen, "Gabriel Biel and the Brethren of the Common Life," *CH* 20 (1951), 23–36; "Gabriel Biel and the *Devotio Moderna* in Germany," *Research Studies, Washington State University* 27 (1959), 135–176, 214–229; 28 (1960), 21–45, 61–78.

Studies dealing with particular aspects of Biel's life include: G. Krätzinger, "Versuch einer Geschichte des Kugelhauses zu Butzbach," *Archiv für hessische Geschichte und Altertumskunde* 10 (1861), 48–93; G. Plitt, *Gabriel Biel als Prediger* (Erlangen, 1879), pp. 1–19; O. Meyer, *Die Brüder des gemeinsamen Lebens in Württemberg 1477–1517* (Stuttgart, 1913), pp. 13–42; W. M. Landeen, "Das Brüderhaus St. Peter im Schönbuch auf dem Einsiedel," *Blätter für Württembergische Kirchengeschichte*, 60–61 (1960–1961), 5–18.

Studies dealing with Biel's works include: K. Steiff, *Der erste Buchdruck in Tübingen, 1498–1534* (Tübingen, 1881); C. Ruch, "Biel, Gabriel," in *DThC*, vol. II, cols. 814–816, 825; Hermelink, *Geschichte der Theologischen Fakultät*, pp. 88–91; F. W. E. Roth, "Ein Brief des Gabriel Biel, 1462," *Neues Archiv der Gesellschaft für ältere deutsche Geschichtskunde* 35 (1910), 582–585; Cappuyns, cols. 1430–1432, 1435; F. Stegmüller, "Literargeschichtliches zu Gabriel Biel," *Theologie in Geschichte und*

Biel and dwell at length only on the points that are pertinent to the background and understanding of his inner development and thought.

I. The Early Years

Gabriel Biel was born at Speyer during the first quarter of the fifteenth century.[2] Sources impart no information concerning his family,[3] youth, or primary education and only fragmentary information regarding his early manhood and university training. From these fragments the following outline of Biel's early adult life can be constructed.

At some unknown date, in or before 1432, Biel was ordained to the priesthood, and while still serving as a matinal priest at the Chapel of the Ten Thousand Martyrs at St. Peter's in Speyer, he entered the faculty of arts of the University of Heidelberg, July 13, 1432. There he received the baccalaureate degree on July 21, 1435,[4] and the master's degree three years later on March 21, 1438, under Magister Conrad Gummeringen.[5] Remaining at the University of Heidelberg for at least three subsequent years, the young *magister* served as an instructor in the faculty of arts.[6] Thus, we see that his first nine years of university life were spent exclusively within the faculty of arts.

In 1442 or 1443 Biel attended the University of Erfurt, but he apparently remained there only a short time. It was perhaps during this sojourn that Biel first met Eggeling Becker von Braunschweig, the *famosissimus*

Gegenwart: Michael Schmaus zum sechzigsten Geburtstag (Munich, 1957), pp. 309–316. This last article is particularly helpful for the dating of the four books of the *Collectorium.*

[2] Biel himself mentions Speyer in *Lect.* 89 P: "Et ego Gabriel ex Spira . . ." and again in the prologue to the *Def.*: "Ego Gabriel Biel de Spira." His birth date is unknown. However, his ordination before 1432, his entry into the University of Heidelberg (1432), and his death at Schönbuch (1495), suggest a date in the early decades of the fifteenth century. It is Hieronymus Wigand Biel's conjecture that Biel was born while the Council of Constance was in session. See *De Gabriele Biel celeberrimo papista anti-papista* (Wittenberg, 1719), p. 5.

[3] Cappuyns suggests (col. 1429) that the Johannes Bihel cited by G. Töpke, *Die Matrikel der Universität Heidelberg*, vol. I: *von 1386–1553* (Heidelberg, 1884), 191, was a brother of Gabriel. We have no documentary evidence to support this suggestion.

[4] Töpke, I, 190 f.
[5] Töpke, I, 384 f.
[6] Töpke, I, 386.

magister to whom he felt himself so deeply indebted.[7] Returning to the University of Erfurt in 1451, Biel probably matriculated in the faculty of theology.[8] In the spring of 1453 the wandering scholar was enrolled at yet a third university, the University of Cologne, there to study in its then famous faculty of theology.[9]

It should be noted that no document states explicitly that Biel studied in the faculty of theology at the University of Erfurt. Furthermore, the matriculation lists at the University of Erfurt give no graduation dates. Consequently we cannot be sure when or if Biel received a degree from Erfurt. At any rate, he must have received his licentiate before 1475, since in a letter dated December 3, 1474, from Pope Sixtus V addressed to Biel and the chapter of St. Mark's in Butzbach, Biel is called *Licentiatus in Theologia*.[10] It is possible, of course, that Biel received the licentiate of theology degree from the University of Cologne or Tübingen.

One significant fact concerning Biel's inner development and thought during the years 1442–1453 ought not to be overlooked, namely, his association in these early years with both the *via moderna* and the *via antiqua*. Whereas Erfurt favored Occam to the exclusion of both Thomism and Scotism, Cologne granted a place of honor only to Thomas and Albert. Already in his student years, then, Biel acquired not only an intimate knowledge of Occam's thought, but also acquainted himself with the thought of Thomas and with the thought of others who, by the mid-fifteenth century, had come to represent the *via antiqua*. Hence, it is not strange to find that Biel is both an articulate spokesman of the *via*

[7] *Lect.* 89 P. Cf. A. Franz, *Die Messe im deutschen Mittelalter* (Freiburg i. Br., 1902), p. 537 ff.

[8] J. C. H. Weissenborn, *Akten der Erfurter Universität* (Halle, 1881), p. 224; Plitt, p. 4 f.; Haller, II, 55.

[9] Cf. F. Benary, "Via antiqua und via moderna auf den deutschen Hochschulen des Mittelalters mit besonderer Berücksichtigung der Universität Erfurt," *Zur Geschichte der Stadt und der Universität Erfurt am Ausgang des Mittelalters* (Gotha, 1919), p. 35. H. Keussen, *Die Matrikel der Universität Köln*, vol. I: *1389 bis 1559* (Bonn, 1928), 559–561.

[10] "Sixtus Episcopus servus servorum Dei dilectis filiis Gabrieli Biel preposito et capitulo ecclesie sancti Marci in Butzbach salutem et Apostolicam benedictionem. . . . Quare pro potestate sua, Preposite, qui Licentiatus in Theologia et Magister in artibus existis . . . ," Johann Just Winckelmann, *Gründliche und warhafte Beschreibung der Fürstenthümer Hessen- und Hersfeld* (Bremen, 1711), fol. 189. We are indebted to Mrs. Harriet C. Jameson, Rare Book Librarian of the University Library of the University of Michigan, for photo-copies of this work.

moderna and a critic of narrow school rivalry, as well as a discerning user of the thought of the *via antiqua*, most elaborately so of Duns Scotus and, in his sermons primarily, of Thomas.[11] The authority of Thomas is, thus, by no means nullified or disregarded. But Biel, nevertheless, regards as one of the signs of progress in his time that Thomas can now be openly contradicted in the universities.[12]

II. Pastor and Frater

If Biel's early life centered in the university and was characterized by a diversified education, then the middle years of his life (c. 1460–1484) found their locus in the Church and were remarkable because of their concern for the practical problems of church life. This concern was manifest in his three major activities during the middle years: in his position as cathedral preacher and vicar in Mainz, in his support of Adolph von Nassau in the latter's struggle with Diether von Isenburg and in his association with the Brethren of the Common Life. Likewise this concern for the practical life of the Church was exhibited in his two major literary products of the period: the Mainz *Sermones* and the *Defensorium obedientie apostolice*. It is certainly extraordinary that Biel did not pursue his academic career but became instead a priest and preacher. In order to understand more clearly this phase of Biel's life, we shall examine each of these activities more closely.

During the early years of the sixties, Biel served as cathedral preacher and vicar in Mainz.[13] The exact date of his appointment and the extent of his tenure in these offices is unknown. However, in his letter to a friend in Mainz dated 1462, Biel speaks with obvious familiarity about Mainz and its ecclesiastical problems. He also indicates that he is well known

---

[11] The association that Biel had with both Erfurt and Cologne was by no means an uncommon occurrence. Benary notes that, ". . . 400 Männer . . . zwischen 1392 und 1466 in Erfurt und Köln studiert haben" (p. 35).

[12] "Licet beatus thomas sanctus credatur et ab ecclesia canonizatus . . . hodie in scholis publice sibi contradicitur," *Lect.* 41 K.

[13] Cf. "The Annals of the Wolf Brethren House," abt. 701, nr. 92, fol. 20ᵛ: "Fuit antea secularis sacerdos et predicator maioris ecclesie Moguntine. . . ." The entry is dated 1495. See also prologue to the *Def.* wherein Biel modestly refers to himself as: "ecclesie Moguntine vicarius, inter orthodoxes predicatores minimus." Excerpts of the records were kindly made available to me by the Staatsarchiv, Coblenz.

to his "gutten Frunde" as a preacher. These passing references suggest that Biel had not come to Mainz only recently; his ministry there may thus well have considerably predated the year 1462.[14] Concerning his ministry in Mainz, we know only that later sources remember him as a famous preacher and a well-respected pastor.[15]

Biel was actively engaged during these same years in the struggle of Adolph von Nassau, papal appointee to the see of Mainz, against Diether von Isenburg.[16] On the death of Dietrich I (May 6, 1459), the cathedral chapter of Mainz elected Diether von Isenburg as Archbishop of Mainz. With the assistance of Albert, Margrave of Brandenburg, Diether received papal confirmation on the condition that he pay the required annates to the papal treasury and appear before the Pope in person within the year. But failing to live up to these conditions, Diether was placed under a lesser ban, deposed and finally put under a major ban on January 8, 1462. In the meanwhile, two significant developments took place. In order to protect himself from the attacks of Pope Pius II, Diether appealed to the antipapal parties within the Holy Roman Empire; soon he emerged as their spokesman. This gave the conflict a quality of gravity it might not have had had it remained simply an ecclesiastical dispute. Secondly, on August 21, 1462, Pius II secretly sent a personal representative to Mainz armed with a bull deposing Diether and granting papal confirmation to Adolph von Nassau, Diether's rival in the election of the Mainz chapter in 1459. The situation became more complex when on November 11, 1461, Diether signed a peace agreement with Adolph, only to deny soon thereafter that such a treaty had ever existed.

Biel's role in this struggle was unequivocal; he fully supported Adolph

---

[14] *Epist.* I; Haller, II, 55; Cappuyns, col. 1429.

[15] F. J. Bodmann, *Rheingauische Alterthümer. Landes- und Regimentsverfassung des Westlichen- oder Niederrheingaues im mittlern Zeitalter* (Mainz, 1819), p. 212; Keussen, p. 561, n. 44. "The Annals of the Wolf Brethren House," fol. 20ᵛ, record that Biel while at Mainz "edidit sermones quosdam predicabiles."

[16] On this struggle see: Karl Menzel, *Diether von Isenburg, Erzbischof von Mainz 1459–1463* (Erlangen, 1868); Karl Hegel, *Die Chroniken der deutschen Städte vom 14. bis ins 16. Jahrh.*, XVIII (Leipzig, 1882), 87–100; Ludwig von Pastor, *Geschichte der Päpste seit dem Ausgang des Mittelalters*, II (Freiburg i. Br., 1886), 164–211; Heinrich Schrohe, *Mainz in seinen Beziehungen zu den deutschen Königen und den Erzbischöfen der Stadt bis zum Untergang der Stadtfreiheit* (1462). Beiträge zur Geschichte der Stadt Mainz, IV (Mainz, 1915), 184–224. Biel is not specifically mentioned in any of these studies.

von Nassau and the papal cause. We do not know exactly when he became actively engaged in the conflict, but judging from the content of Biel's letter to his friend in Mainz,[17] he was forced to flee Mainz sometime during the reign of Diether, that is, between June 1459 and September 1462. While the traditional historical treatment of this controversy stresses Diether's simony and failure to pay the annates which he owed to the Pope as the reason for his excommunication, in Biel's judgment the crucial issue was a quite different one. For Biel, Diether's guilt resided primarily in his failure to seek ordination, or at least proper dispensation, in the three years that had elapsed since his election as Archbishop of Mainz. Biel apparently does not contest the legality of the election itself.[18]

During the time of his flight from Mainz, Biel lived in the Rheingau, actively preached on behalf of Adolph, and wrote his *Defensorium*.[19] After Adolph's conquest of Mainz in October 1462, Biel apparently returned to Mainz and resumed his former duties.[20]

Biel joined the Brethren of the Common Life sometime in the sixties and remained active therein the rest of his life. It is by no means clear when Biel first came into contact with the *Devotio Moderna*, but according to an entry in "The Annals of the Wolf Brethren House," Biel was actively engaged in the internal life of the Brethren "while yet a preacher at the cathedral church in Mainz." [21] However, according to another entry in the "Annals," his actual involvement with the Brethren postdated his term as cathedral preacher and vicar and his participation in the struggle of Adolph and Diether.[22] This suggests that his entry into the

[17] See F. W. E. Roth, p. 584.

[18] *Def.* II 1 col. 2: "Notorium vero est dominum Dietherum nec sacerdotalem nec alium sacrum ordinem post electionem suam ante triennium factam suscepisse nec dispensationem quesisse nec impedimentum ante statutum terminum allegasse quod nec ipse negat nec sui defensores."

[19] "The Annals of the Wolf Brethren House" say in this connection: "Item cum maximo conatu in schismate Moguntino defendit obedientiam apostolicam ut patet in tractatu suo qui dicitur Defensorium obedientie apostolice," fol. 20ᵛ.

[20] There is no conclusive evidence that Biel resumed his former position as preacher and vicar, nor did we find evidence to substantiate Cappuyns' claim that subsequent to the termination of the struggle "le pape Pie II reconnaissant des services rendus, l'appela à Rome avec quelques autres savants" (col. 1430). This same suggestion appears without documentation in Plitt, p. 8.

[21] "Annals of the Wolf Brethren House," fol. 30ᵛ.

[22] "Fuit antea secularis sacerdos et predicator maioris ecclesie Moguntine, ubi

community came after the fall of 1462. According to all reports, Biel seems indeed to have decisively furthered the cause of the Brethren.[23]

Until 1468 Biel lived in the Brethren House at Marienthal in the Rheingau.[24] While Biel was there the chapter attained an intellectual and spiritual life never before or afterward known.[25] In 1468 at the invitation of Count Eberhard III of Eppstein and other noblemen of Eppstein and Koenigstein,[26] Biel moved to Butzbach to become the first provost of the new Brethren House at St. Mark's.[27] Here for nine years under his leadership the Brethren grew in number and name. Noteworthy among Biel's accomplishments at Butzbach was the reorganization of the local school. By making character-building the aim of the educational process and by insisting that the master be a model of virtue, the ideas of Brethren piety were built into the educational fabric.[28] It is interesting to note that Wendelin Steinbach, Biel's student who edited his later works and eventually became his successor at the University of Tübingen as professor and at the Brethren House at Schönbuch as provost, was from Butzbach and was probably schooled in this town school.[29] Also noteworthy was Biel's role in the establishment of a general chapter of the Brethren Houses on the Upper Rhein in 1471 (June 25).[30]

---

edidit sermones quosdam predicabiles. Item cum maximo conatu in schismate Moguntino defendit obedientiam apostolicam ut patet in tractatu suo qui dicitur Defensorium obedientie apostolice. Postmodum factus frater et hinc electus in patrem in Butzbach." *Ibid.*, fol. 20ᵛ.

[23] "Vom Butzbacher Hause aus beginnt Gabriel Biel die vierte süddeutsche Gründungszeit," Ernst Barnikol, *Studien zur Geschichte der Brüder vom gemeinsamen Leben* (Tübingen, 1917), p. 11.

[24] The exact dates of Biel's sojourn at Marienthal are not known. Bodmann says that Biel was at Marienthal "das Ende des XV. Jahrh." (p. 212). By process of elimination we can date his stay there sometime between September 1462 (the date of Biel's letter to his "Gutten Frunde") and late 1468 (the date of the beginning of his sojourn in Butzbach).

[25] Bodmann, p. 212.

[26] Cf. Haller's publication of a facsimile copy of a letter from Biel to Count Eberhard III dated 1470, II, 152 f.

[27] "Annals of the Wolf Brethren House," fol. 20ᵛ.

[28] A copy of a contract between the Brethren and the headmaster of the school dated 1481 is to be found in W. Diehl, *Monumenta Germaniae Paedagogica* XXVII (Berlin, 1903), 485–487.

[29] See in this regard Krätzinger, p. 66. For a survey of the available data on Steinbach, see Haller, I, 187 ff.; II, 67 ff.

[30] A copy of the proceedings is to be found in Bodmann, pp. 217 f.; Krätzinger, pp. 58–59.

On July 10, 1477, at the request of Count Eberhard I, the Bearded, of Württemberg, the General Chapter of the Rhein Brethren Houses commissioned Biel and Benedict of Marienthal to go to Württemberg and to establish the first chapter of the Brethren of the Common Life in that province.[31] Arriving at Urach on August 16, the two religious together with four other Brethren converted St. Amandus Church into a Brethren chapter house. Benedict was elected provost, and when in 1479 he returned to Marienthal, Brother Gabriel was elected in his place.

His treatise on the life of the Brethren [32] witnesses to the fact that his association with the movement of organized, often mystical piety is not to be understood as a break with scholastic — and in his case primarily nominalistic — training but rather in conjunction with his life as a theologian and pastor.

III. Professor and Prepositus

On November 22, 1484, Gabriel Biel was appointed to the theological faculty of the newly founded University of Tübingen.[33] Yet, significant though this association proved to be, it would be wrong to suggest that the later years of Biel's life ought to be interpreted simply in terms of this association with Tübingen; all the primary sources pertinent to this period mention Biel in two regards, that is, "in Urach prepositus" and "ordinarius theologie in hac universitate." [34]

The nature of his *Exposition of the Canon of the Mass* and of its compendium suggests that the interest in the university and education which characterized Biel's early years and the concern for piety and the practical life of the Church which dominated his middle years were in his later years brought together in a harmonious coherence. His appointment to the University of Tübingen enabled Biel to combine the virtues of

---

[31] "Annals of the Wolf Brethren House," fol. 20ᵛ.

[32] Biel, *De Communi vita.*

[33] R. Roth, *Urkunden zur Geschichte der Universität Tübingen aus den Jahren 1476 bis 1550* (Tübingen, 1877), p. 495 f. The citation reads as follows: "Intitulati sub rectoratu venerabilis viri domini *Conradi Bömlin* decani ecclesie collegiate huius loci a festo S. Luce ev. a.d. 84. . . [22.] M. *Gabriel Byel* s. theologie licentiatus, in Urach prepositus et ordinarius theologie in hac universitate."

[34] "Annals of the Wolf Brethren House," fol. 20ᵛ; R. Roth, p. 499; H. Hermelink, *Die Matrikeln der Universität Tübingen* I (Tübingen, 1906), 59, 75.

piety and rigorous scholarship. It is in these terms that one best understands Biel's later life.

Only gradually did the theological faculty of the University of Tübingen take definite form.[35] Though made up from the outset of representatives of the *via antiqua,* the *via moderna,* and humanism, the faculty came clearly under the domination of representatives of the *via antiqua* during its early years.

Biel's association with the faculty of theology effected a profound reversal of this trend in two ways. First, he succeeded in bringing the *via moderna* to a place of preeminence;[36] and second, he gathered about himself a group of young, enthusiastic students, thus securing his accomplishments for the future. Best known of his followers is perhaps Wendelin Steinbach who was in later years a highly regarded professor of theology at Tübingen.

In 1485 and again in 1489 Biel was elected rector of the university. We know nothing of Biel's association with the University of Tübingen after his last term as rector. Undoubtedly his retirement from academic life was dictated by his age, for in 1489 Biel may well have been more than 75 years old.[37]

Apart from the doctrinal continuity between Biel and Bartholomaeus von Usingen, which we will discuss in the relevant chapters, a few more things should be said about Biel's disciples. The brief poems at the beginning of the Tübingen and Hagenau editions of the *Sermones dominicales* are dedicated to Biel and his editor-disciple Wendelin Steinbach.[38] They are not particularly beautiful, but for other reasons they are important enough to be mentioned here. Their author is Henry Bebel who had been teaching poetics and rhetoric since 1497 at the University of Tübingen, an enthusiastic humanist with great admiration for Lorenzo Valla who furthered with all his power the study of classical antiquity and the purification of the Latin in current use.[39] As the *poeta laureatus* of Tü-

---

[35] For a discussion of the history of the University of Tübingen and Biel's relation to it, see Hermelink, *Geschichte der Theologischen Fakultät,* pp. 78 ff., 191 ff.

[36] Among the earlier exponents of the *via moderna* were Christian Wolmann and Elias Flick. See Hermelink, *Geschichte der Theologischen Fakultät,* p. 193.

[37] See Cappuyns, col. 1430.

[38] Hermelink, *Geschichte der Theologischen Fakultät,* pp. 81, 195 ff.

[39] K. Hagen, *Deutschlands literarische und religiöse Verhältnisse im Reformations-*

17

bingen he made a lasting impression on Johannes Altenstaig whom we shall meet time and again as the author of the *Vocabularius theologie*, in which he surveys late medieval theological terminology.[40]

It is this theological dictionary which is one of the most important witnesses to the great authority and central position of Biel in the ranks of late medieval theologians. Biel is not only quantitatively one of the most quoted — and most explicitly quoted — authorities, but also qualitatively for Altenstaig the most persuasive voice of tradition. It is clear from the selection of sources adduced that Altenstaig stands in the nominalistic tradition. Biel heads the list of theological authorities when Altenstaig surveys in a concluding section of his theological dictionary the cloud of witnesses to whom he had directed his questions.[41]

Also included in this list is Johann Eck, who not only came from the same part of the country as Altenstaig and received at the same time his degree as *magister artium*, but who was also a disciple of Bebel and member of the *bursa modernorum* in his Tübingen student years.[42] It is no mere coincidence or chauvinism on the part of Altenstaig that Eck is mentioned here together with Biel. Later professor at Ingolstadt and Luther's principal opponent from the moment of the publication of his *Obelisci* (1518) and his participation in the Leipzig Debate (1519), Eck had started his academic career in Freiburg in the same year as Luther, 1509–1510. There is a further parallel with Luther in that Eck as *sententiarius* interpreted the *Sentences* of Lombard according to the commentaries of Occam and Biel. As late as 1539 Eck proudly states in a fervent attack on Andreas Osiander that he can still vividly recall his teachers at Tübingen, among whom was Wendelin Steinbach. Thus,

---

zeitalter, I (Erlangen, 1841), 381 ff. A selection of poems is published by Gustav Bebermeyer, *Tübinger Dichterhumanisten: Bebel, Frischlin, Flayder* (Tübingen, 1927), p. 17 ff. See further on Bebel: Haller, I, 212 ff.; II, 76 ff.

[40] We have used the first (Hagenau 1517) edition. For other editions and works of Altenstaig, see the helpful essay of Friedrich Zoepfl, *Johannes Altenstaig: Ein Gelehrtenleben aus der Zeit des Humanismus und der Reformation* (Münster i.W., 1918), p. 47 ff.

[41] ". . . imitatus sum precipue auctores quos cum diligentia legi vel pro maiore parte Gabrielem Byel prepositum primum in Schonbach. . . ," *Vocabularius theologie*, postscriptum.

[42] "Videatur Eckius doctor germanus non incelebris, mihi notissimus et intimus qui preter ceterorum theologorum morem, eloquentiam cum theologie sapientia coniunxit," Altenstaig, fol. 218ᵛ. See also Zoepfl, p. 15.

there is abundant evidence for the contention that Biel had a profound influence on this important protagonist of the Counter-Reformation.[43]

With respect to the question of the extent to which we may expect Johannes Staupitz, who studied from 1497 until 1500 in Tübingen, to be familiar with the works of Biel, it is important to note that Altenstaig dedicated — in a letter dated October 4, 1517[44] — his dictionary to Staupitz, in which Biel as in the *Vocabularius* itself is singled out as "noster illustri gratia theologus Gabriel Biel."

If one further considers the fact that another disciple of Bebel and friend of Altenstaig, Johann Brassican who came in 1489 to Tübingen,[45] was the teacher of Philip Melanchthon, we may well conclude that around the turn of the century at Tübingen nominalism and humanism were apparently more compatible than we have long been inclined to believe. Whereas Augustin Renaudet has pointed to the great tensions at the

[43] In 1538 Eck mentions in his *Epistola de ratione studiorum suorum*: ". . . G. Ocham et Gabrielis commentaria prelegendo in Ianuario anni noni," *CC* II, ed. Johann Metzler (Münster i. W., 1921), 45 f. ". . . ihm [Biel] folgten die Lehrer Ecks, deren Namen er noch 1540 [1539] mit Stolz nannte; und wie diese so hat auch der Schüler sich später als "Occamist" bezeichnet, und seine Vorlesungen via moderna gehalten," Joseph Schlecht, "Dr. Johann Ecks Anfänge," *Historisches Jahrbuch* 36 (1915), 3. He also observes that "Biel . . . auf Ecks Denkrichtung bestimmend eingewirkt hat." Eck refers to Steinbach in *Schutzred Kindtlicher unschuld wider den Catechisten Andre Hosander* . . . Aichstet (1539) fol. LIII. On this discussion see W. Möller, *Andreas Osiander* (Elberfeld, 1870), p. 218 ff. On the relation between Eck and Bebel see J. Greving, *Johann Eck als junger Gelehrter: Eine literar- und dogmengeschichtliche Untersuchung über seinen Chrysopassus Praedestinationis aus dem Jahre 1514* (Münster i. W., 1906), p. 12 f. For Eck as "Occamist" see Greving, p. 99. Erwin Iserloh, who does not mention Schlecht's article in his important *Die Eucharistie in der Darstellung des Johannes Eck: Ein Beitrag zur vortridentinischen Kontroverstheologie über das Messopfer* (Münster i. W., 1950), plans to compare Biel and Eck as regards the doctrine of the Eucharist (p. 344, n. 1). For a further understanding of the wide range of Biel's impact it is important to note the words of the influential Jesuit theologian and participant at the Council of Trent, Jacob Lainez: "Haec ille quae Gabriel Biel lectione 3 supra canonem missae item clare et docte explicat," *Disputationes Tridentinae*, ed. H. Grisar, S. J., I (Oeniponte, 1886), 137.

[44] Altenstaig, fol. IV[r].

[45] Hermelink, *Die Matrikeln der Universität Tübingen*, I, 76, 199. According to the author of "De Wesselo Groningensi," Biel was for a number of years in close contact with Wessel Gansfort, as is pointed out by Maarten van Rhijn, *Wessel Gansfort* (The Hague, 1917), p. 73. Cf. "Aliquot annos etiam [erat?] cum Gabrieli Byel ab Urach, viro doctissimo, ut ejus monumenta testantur," van Rhijn, appendix A, p. v. See also Zoepfl, p. 14 f.

19

turn of the century between the Parisian humanists and the nominalistic circle centered around Johann Maior and later Jacob Almain, editor of Biel's *Collectorium*, we find that Biel — who himself proves to be familiar with the work of Pico della Mirandola — is intimate with Geiler von Kaysersberg and through him is in contact with a prestigious circle of German humanists.[46]

After his retirement from the University of Tübingen, Biel served as provost of the new Brethren House, St. Peter's at Einsiedel in Schönbuch. Here under his leadership an unusual rule and institution was established wherein the three estates of the nobility, clergy, and burgesses dwelled together according to the ideals of Brethren piety. All vowed upon admission to the house to take upon themselves the common life of the canons, yet there remained for each group certain privileges characteristic of that particular estate. Such an arrangement was to be found in no other Brethren House in Germany. By eliminating extremes in fasting and prayer Biel laid emphasis on the simple life and piety characteristic of the *Devotio Moderna*. From the few documents extant, it is clear that the house prospered spiritually and financially under his leadership until it was secularized in 1517.

Gabriel Biel died at St. Peter's on December 7, 1495.[47] We can well

[46] A. Renaudet, *Préréforme et Humanisme à Paris pendant les premières guerres d'Italie 1494–1517*, 2 ed. (Paris, 1953), pp. 385; 404 ff.; 464 ff.; 594, n. 3; 658, n. 3; 659, n. 2. Apparently it has not yet been noted that Biel quotes Pico della Mirandola twice: III *Sent.* d 1 q 2 art. 1 A; and *ibid.* art. 2, ad 5. Biel cites Pico, *Opera Omnia* I (Basiliae, 1572), *Apologia*, p. 160. A searching discussion of Pico is found in Engelbert Monnerjahn, *Giovanni Pico della Mirandola* (Wiesbaden, 1960).

Geiler expressed repeatedly his high regard for Biel. See Adolf Vonlanthen, "Geilers Seelenparadies im Verhältnis zur Vorlage," *Archiv für elsässische Kirchengeschichte* 6 (1931), 282 ff. Charles Schmidt reports two occasions on which Biel assisted Geiler with advice in his *Histoire littéraire de l'Alsace à la fin du XVe et au commencement du XVIe siècle*, I (Paris, 1879), 342, 357. For references to Peter Schott and Trithemius, see Haller, II, 60.

[47] His obituary recorded in the *Annals* speaks in simple and appreciative terms of Biel's important contribution to the *devotio moderna*: ". . . septimo die mensis decembris (1495) obiit feliciter eximius et venerabilis magister Gabriel . . . et suppultus in Swevia in domo Schoenbuech; multum fideliter laboravit pro statu nostro" (fol. 20ᵛ). "Et multos labores pro statu nostro subiit habere merito memoria cuius perpetuo apud nos habetur" (*ibid.*). On the statutes of Schönbuch, drawn up by Biel, and the final dissolution of the Brethren House, see Landeen, "Das Brüderhaus St. Peter," pp. 7 ff., 16 f.

understand that Biel wished to spend the last years of his life among the Brethren who exemplified the piety he had preached and taught throughout his life, and whose good name he had so successfully propagated in central and south Germany.

Thus, we have before us the main events of the life of Gabriel Biel. This image of a man actively engaged at once in the doctrinal and practical life of the Church will emerge time and again when in succeeding chapters we turn to analyze his thought.

IV. Character of Biel's Sermons

It is clear that in their published form the sermons are *sermones predicabiles*;[48] a series of directions — of which at least part are from the hand of Biel — is provided to help other preachers make the best use of these homiletical examples.[49]

At one place Biel criticizes three kinds of preachers: (1) those who incite disobedience and criticize their superiors; (2) those who are lazy in their preparation and try to preach without paying sufficient attention to the relevant authorities, especially the sayings of the Fathers;[50] (3) those who show off with their knowledge, trying to impress their congregations by endless quotations from concordances.[51]

Even a cursory glance indicates that Biel is not in danger of belonging to one of the first two groups. It would also be wrong to classify him with "the vain quoters." His extensive use of scholastic authorities, however, has led some scholars to the conclusion that his sermons were not aimed *ad populum* but *ad clerum*.[52]

There are, however, too often explicit exhortations meant for laymen to be satisfied with this classification.[53] Sometimes special groups are envisaged, such as widows who should not despair because of bereave-

---

[48] *S* II 1, intr.

[49] "Si vero non placet . . . abbrevia eandem materiam succincte prout placet et deinde sic procede," *S* I 99 B. Compare *S* II 26 S; *S* II 36 J; *S* IV 30 E.

[50] "Garriunt et effundunt quicquid in buccam venerit: ceci cecos alloquentes. . . ," *Lect.* 77 R.

[51] ". . . non deum sed se sed scientiam suam ostentare volentes. . . ," *Lect.* 77 R.

[52] See Haller, II, 56. "His [Biel's] sermons were long, involved and probably intended for the cathedral clergy rather than for the public," William M. Landeen, "Gabriel Biel and the Brethren of the Common Life in Germany," *CH* 20 (1951), 24.

[53] "Secundo . . . exhortatio et pastorum et populi elicietur," *S* I 40 A.

ment,[54] or women who are criticized for coming to confession all dressed up, painted, and with artificial curls.[55] It is fair to say that notwithstanding the elaborate citation of scholastic authorities, the general content of Biel's sermons is extremely simple. The refrain of almost all of them, so often repeated, can be summed up in two typical statements which are parallels at that: "Arbor non faciens bonum fructum excidetur," and "Si vis ad vitam ingredi, serva mandata." [56]

The structure of the sermons manifests the usual order of text authorities, *postilla*, moral application, to which sometimes the *sensus mysticus* is added.[57] Before the *postilla* Biel almost always inserts "pro gratia, ave Maria." On several occasions Biel speaks about the vital role of preaching in the life of the congregation. In his open letter of 1462 to the Christians at Mainz living under the interdict, he calls for abstention from all the sacraments except, in emergency, the sacrament of baptism, since the sacraments are administered by priests who opted for the cause of Diether and have therefore separated themselves from the Church.[58] But the preaching of the Word is an act Biel wishes to continue under any circumstances. The wickedness of a priest as such is no obstacle for God working through the words of this priest.[59]

This does not imply that the Word preached is for Biel the redemptive Word of God; rather it is a "consilium," exhortation that prods the sinner onto the path of righteousness. The preached Word is the seed of Luke 8:4 ff., but man has to provide the proper disposition which will enable the seed to root and flourish.[60] Nevertheless, this "consilium" is not so anthropocentrically understood that the moral standing of the preacher is the decisive factor. Moral guidance, even when coming from a wicked priest, has to be viewed as coming from God, the author of Holy Scripture.[61]

---

[54] *S* III 25 L.

[55] *S* I 26 K. On abstention from sexual intercourse before Communion see *S* II 23 E.

[56] *E.g. S* I 64 F; *S* I 44 G [Matt. 19:18].

[57] Cf. *S* I 39 A.

[58] *Epist.* I; cf. pp. 26–29.

[59] "Nolite ergo causari vos derelictos: dum etiam per mercenarios pascit vos deus, qui solus est pastor bonus. . . ," *S* I 40 G.

[60] *S* I 22 D. See also *S* I 21 D ff. and Oberman, "Preaching and the Word in the Reformation," *Theology Today* 18 (1960) 16 ff.

[61] "Nec tamen spernendum est consilium etiam eorum qui male sunt vite, dum

Twice Biel asks the question whether the Word of God is more important than the Body of Christ. His answer is most interesting. From a negative point of view there is no difference; one is as guilty when he does not pay proper attention to the preached Word of God as when he carelessly drops the Body of Christ.[62] From a positive point of view, however, Biel feels that the preached Word is more important insofar as it can bring about conversion since faith is the beginning of salvation and faith is the fruit of preaching — *fides ex auditu*! The sermon can provide the foundation of the Christian life, while one receives in Holy Communion only an increase of the saving grace already granted to the sinner when he had proceeded from faith to sincere contrition.[63]

As we will see later in the context of the discussion of the process of justification, the very connection of the sermon with contrition is indicative of the importance for Biel of the preached Word as the new Law.

---

non ex suis sed ex scriptura loquuntur quoniam talia non quasi sua sed quasi dei consilia scripturam inspirantis sunt imitanda," *S* II 17 G. Compare *S* I 40 G and also Mauritius of Leyden: "Praedicatio non est aliud quam verbi Dei conveniens et congrua dispensatio" (UB Basel, A VII, 45, 169ʳ) as quoted by D. Roth, *Die mittelalterliche Predigttheorie und das Manuale Curatorum des Johann Ulrich Surgant* (Basel, 1956) p. 120.

[62] "Interrogo vos fratres vel sorores: dicite mihi, quid vobis plus esse videtur, verbum dei quam corpus christi . . . quoniam non minus erit reus qui verbum dei negligenter audierit quam ille qui corpus christi sua negligentia in terram cadere permisit," *S* I 59 D. Compare *Lect.* 71 G. The same observation is made by Ulrich Surgant in *Manuale Curatorum*, book I, cons. 4, probably dependent on canon law. See *CIC*, canon 94 q 1. Cf. L. Dacheux, *Un réformateur catholique à la fin du XVe siècle: Jean Geiler de Kaysersberg* (Paris, 1876), p. 12. See also J. Geffcken, *Der Bilderkatechismus des fünfzehnten Jahrhunderts und die catechetischen Hauptstücke in dieser Zeit bis auf Luther* (Leipzig, 1855), p. 196 ff. as quoted by Johannes Janssen, *Geschichte des deutschen Volkes seit dem Ausgang des Mittelalters*, vol. I: *Deutschlands allgemeine Zustände beim Ausgang des Mittelalters* (Freiburg i. Br., 1878), p. 27 f. For a clear survey of the present state of scholarship on late medieval preaching see Eduard Langwiler, *Die vorreformatorischen Prädikaturen der deutschen Schweiz von ihrer Entstehung bis 1530* (Fribourg, 1955), pp. 1–17; bibliography, p. ix ff.

[63] "Nam multos convertit ad fidem sine qua nulli est salus . . . peccatores ammonet et compungit ad penitentiam et conversionem et sic tollit in eis omne peccatum et mortale et veniale. Corpus autem christi quamvis vis [sic] augeat gratiam, non tamen tollit nisi venialem culpam, et si mortalem, tunc solum oblitam. . . Et ideo si homo nunquam audiret verbum dei . . . tunc . . . negligeret totam salutem suam, quia quomodo sciret precepta dei et multa facienda necessario et cavenda . . . contemnit aliquid sine quo non est salus." *S* I 59 D. Compare *S* IV 8 E and *S* I 21 A.

V. Internal Evidence on the Chronology of Biel's Writings

When we turn to the chronology of Biel's works, the following points should be made:

(1) The date of the *Defensorium*, 1462, is apparent from the Steinbach indication in the table of contents of the *Sermones dominicales* to which it was appended at its Hagenau, 1510, publication.[64]

(2) From the same period stems the letter of exhortation sent by Biel to his friends in Mainz to encourage them in their resistance against Diether von Isenburg.[65] It directs itself to the same issue, that is the removal of Diether, and is like the *Defensorium* a request for an open debate on the matter.

(3) In the mariological sermons Biel mentions the 1476 indulgences grant of Pope Sixtus IV.[66] This not only proves that this group of sermons must be of a later date but also that they are later than November 4, 1488. On that day Biel finished his *Exposition* but had not yet acquainted himself with the statement of Pope Sixtus of 1476.[67]

(4) A cross reference in one of the *Sermones de sanctis* which does not seem to be an insert by the editor, Steinbach, indicates that these sermons postdate the *Sermones de festivitatibus gloriose virginis Marie*; the same can be noted with regard to the *Sermones dominicales*.[68]

(5) *The Passionis dominice sermo historialis* may well have been one of Biel's first publications. This appears not only from the fact that Steinbach informs us that it was "quite some time ago" published by Biel himself,[69] but also from its style which suggests more an exercise in homiletics than the kind of sermon we have come to expect from Biel.

(6) It is most revealing with respect to the amount of attention paid

[64] ". . . ad romanum pontificem Pium secundum, anno incarnationis 1462 transmissus . . . ," *Registrum Sermonum de tempore*, fol. 17ʳ, dated by Biel himself on fol. 166ʳ as finished Oct. 22, 1462.

[65] *Epist. I.* In view of the relevance of this letter, we include a translation of it at the end of this chapter.

[66] "Facit ad idem decretum Sixti pape . . . 1476 dotavit festum illud omnibus et singulis indulgentiis . . . ," *S* III 1 F.

[67] For a more detailed discussion see Chapter Eleven, section II.

[68] "Ad primum responde ut patuit annunciationis marie sermone quarto. Et applica ad propositum." *S* IV 6 C, referring to *S* III 12 C. *S* IV 36 E. refers to *S* I 18.

[69] "Olim impresso," *S* II fol. 169. *S* II 24 is a selection from *S* V.

to Biel that — while there has been quite some effort made to establish the years in which Biel was writing his *Collectorium* — no one has noticed that he himself indicates the year in which he wrote Book III. It proves to be the same year in which he finished his *Exposition*, 1488.[70]

Friedrich Stegmüller has called attention to the existence of a copy of Occam's commentary on the first book of Peter Lombard's *Sentences* which was already in Biel's possession in 1453.[71] This scholar has further conclusively shown that Book I was written in or before 1486 and Book II in or before 1488.[72]

In view of the adduced reference from distinction 4 of Book III, one may well wonder whether it is as clear as Stegmüller seems to imply that Biel's *Collectorium* for the better part has grown out of his teaching responsibilities in Houses of Brethren of the Common Life in pre-Tübingen days.[73] Stegmüller refers to the remark in the description of the *Collectorium* made by Steinbach indicating that part of the *Collectorium* had been delivered as lectures in these Houses.[74] This observation of Steinbach could, however, also refer to Biel's post-Tübingen period since before 1492 he left Tübingen for Schönbuch. Book IV must have been written in this South German Brethren House, since Biel introduces this writing with an explanation as to why he breaks the silence he had planned: due to the insistence of his Brethren and aided by their prayers, he undertakes a task which seems to him to be otherwise beyond his powers.[75]

[70] ". . . verum esset quod homo 1488 annorum inciperet esse naturalis filius marie; tot enim anni fluxerunt a nativitate christi usque ad diem dum hec scribimus," III *Sent.* d 4 q 1 art. 3 nota 2 corol. 6.

[71] UB Giessen, cod 773, fol. 330ʳ; F. Stegmüller, "Literargeschichtliches zu Biel," p. 316.

[72] *Ibid.*, p. 312 ff.

[73] "Biel's Collectorium ist also ein langsam gereiftes Werk, das weitgehend aus seinen Vorlesungen in den Häusern der Brüder des gemeinsamen Lebens gewachsen ist," *ibid.*, p. 316.

[74] ". . . partim ordinarie in theologorum scholis, partim in edibus ab eodem lectum et elucidatum . . . ," *Sent.* Prol. CCIII.

[75] "Nimia tamen fratrum meorum (quibus meipsum debeo) precum instantia devictus opus supra vires (divina confisus gratia) fratrumque meorum orationibus adiutus aggredior . . . ," IV *Sent.* d 1 q 1 intr. Biel appends to IV *Sent.* d 16 q 3 art. 3 LL ad 5, which deals with the question whether housefathers and landlords commit mortal sin when they serve food on official fasting days "mane et sero indifferenter," the consensus of Conrad Sumerhart, Frater Andreas O.E.S.A., Martinus Plansch, Wendelin Steinbach, Conrad Ebinger, Martinus Wanius, Hierony-

(7) From the Prologue to the abbreviated version of the *Exposition*, it appears that we have to count this summary with the works of Biel. It is meant for "the simple priests less familiar with scholastic subtleties and therefore unable to cope with traditional expositions, and also for those who are bored by long lectures." For a more explicit treatment, Biel refers to his *Exposition* which he describes as "novissime . . . ordinarie lectam"; [76] this would therefore suggest a date soon after 1488.

(8) It is hard to say whether the *Monotesseron* [sic] which is the basis for the *Sermo historialis* and is published by Steinbach with the christological sermons is a work of Biel or merely Steinbach's choice from one of those in circulation. Half a century earlier Jean Gerson had written a *Monotesseron*; according to L. E. Du Pin, Gerson was the first to do so in the middle ages.[77] In view of the now emerging medieval *Monotesseron* tradition,[78] it is unlikely that Gerson's edition would stand thus unprecedented; still the number of differing types in circulation must have been small. Since the *Monotesseron* used by Biel is clearly independent from that of Gerson, it may be true that it stems from Biel's own hand.

VI. Biel's Letter to the Church at Mainz under Interdict

To you, first of all, a friendly greeting — grace and enlightenment of the Holy Spirit to confess Christian truth and to live steadfastly for the same in these troublesome days without being afraid of the erring world.[79]

---

mus de Croacia, Conrad Wesseler: "Viri doctissimi Tubingensis gymnasii subscripserunt huiusmodi sub tenore." Added is the approval of the theological faculty of Mainz, dated Oct. 5, 1495. Since the last addition is not explicitly identified as Biel's own work, we cannot use this passage to show that Book IV was still uncompleted in October 1495. There is no reason to agree with Haller that Biel himself rests his case on "die erbetenen Äusserungen von Summenhard . . . und der theologischen Fakultät in Mainz," since this "Gutachten" may have been inserted later by editor Steinbach. See Haller, II, 60.

[76] *SCE*, Prologus, A 3.

[77] "Post veteres scriptores primus Joannes de Gerson quatuor evangelistarum historiam ipsis eorum verbis connectendum suscepit," "Monitum" in *Opera omnia* ed. L. E. du Pin (Antwerpen, 1706). For Gerson's text, see vol. IV, 101–202. Biel's *Monotesseron* is published between *S* II 23 and *S* II 24.

[78] Cf. G. Quispel, "L'Evangile selon Thomas et le Diatessaron," *Vigiliae Christianae* 13 (1959), 98–117.

[79] *Epist.* I. Mrs. Helmut Koester and Professor Joachim Bumke of the German Department of Harvard University have made it possible to present this letter in English translation. Mr. Ernest L. Lashlee assisted in assembling the known data on Biel's life.

Very beloved friend and brother in the Lord Christ! I have great sympathy for you and those who are yours because you are so heavily oppressed and burdened with the deprivation of the divine office and holy sacraments; not because their celebration has been discontinued, but because no lover of God may avail himself of them nor be present when they are distributed without the loss of his soul. For to hear the divine office from the disobedient who are under the ecclesiastical ban or to have fellowship with them in the sacraments is damnable blasphemy of God.

The holy sacraments have flowed mightily out of the wounded heart of our Lord Christ and have been established out of the inexpressible love of Christ who is our Savior for the salvation of souls. To touch the sacraments in grievous sin, against the ordinance of God and His holy Church — what is this other than to nullify along with the accursed Jews and heathen the precious blood of our beloved Lord, so far as this lies within their power, to spill it, to contaminate it, and to transform the work of salvation and life into a work of death and eternal damnation? And therefore, I warn you, by the love of the Lord Jesus, not to make yourselves in any way accomplices to these grievous sins, but rather for God's sake to withdraw entirely from spiritual fellowship with those under the ban.

As dearly as you love your souls, receive no sacraments from them. In case it should become necessary to baptise anyone belonging to you, and it would not be possible to delay baptism without trepidation, let such a one be baptised in your homes by a layman or a laywoman who is not excommunicate. And if it is not possible for you to have anyone else to administer this sacrament, then it is permissible for you to baptise your own children. Should it be so, however, that neither you nor anyone else who has not been excommunicated were at hand and one feared for the death of the child, then one would of necessity have to allow it to be baptised by someone under the ban.[80] But the other sacraments, that of Confession, of Holy Communion and of Extreme Unction, you shall not receive under any circumstances from one who has been excommunicated, not even in the extremity of death. For should it be so that God would take you or anyone of yours hence — may God in his mercy forbear to do so — it is sufficient that the sinner have contrition and sorrow over his sins, and that he confess these to God by pouring out his soul before God with the intention to confess these sins to an authorized priest as soon as possible, after the interdict of the holy Church is removed.

Do not allow yourselves to be burdened by the fact that you are deprived

[80] Decretum pro Armenis, Bulla *Exultate Deo*, Nov. 22, 1439: "In causa autem necessitatis non solum sacerdos vel diaconus, sed etiam laicus vel mulier, immo etiam paganus et haereticus baptizare potest, dummodo formam servet Ecclesiae et facere intendat, quod facit Ecclesia" (Denz. 696). Denzinger points out that this decretum should not be seen as a definition but — in places — as practical instruction (695, n. 1). Cf. also Pierre d'Ailly, *Sacramentale seu Tractatus Theologicus de Sacramentis* (Lovanii, 1487), cap. 6 P ff. and cap. 11 L.

of the sacraments, since it is to be hoped that you are not robbed thereby of the grace of the holy sacraments which you would gladly receive, but from which for the sake of God's will you abstain. For God who gives grace through the sacraments to those who receive them worthily has not knit His almighty power to the sacraments so closely that He may not, apart from the sacraments, give such and even greater grace to those who do not despise them.

Good friend, remain steadfast in obedience to the Holy Church outside of which no one can be saved, whose Head and Ruler on earth in the place of God is, not by human but divine ordinance, the pope, the successor to St. Peter. . .

Also, do not allow yourself to be upset, should the disobedient have good fortune and those who are obedient be oppressed. For if temporal fortune and welfare were a sign of righteousness, and temporal suffering and persecution were a sign of unrighteousness, then nothing would be more unrighteous than the Christian faith and the Christian life. For in no faith under heaven has so much duress and shedding of blood taken place as among the holy martyrs for the sake of the Christian faith. The Lord, who was the first to suffer and die, did not promise his followers on earth fortune, tranquility, and temporal peace, but oppression, persecution, abuse, and torture.

Therefore, blessed are those to whom it is given to suffer for the sake of God and of righteousness, be it in body, goods, honor, children, or friends. They shall rejoice and be glad, for abundant is their reward in heaven. Now is the time for judgment to begin in the house of God, that is, with the true Christians and followers of God. But if God the Lord chastises even his friends, how unbearable will be the chastisement of His enemies! Therefore, give yourselves willingly into the hand of God to suffer whatever his divine will may inflict; for in suffering he is near to those who are his and does not leave them comfortless. These are, good friends, the days of the harsh punishment of the sinners I have always opposed. . .

Consider, dear friend, and mourn with me, the sorrowful and dreadful state of your fellow citizens and inhabitants of Mainz; for all external help through which the poor sinner should come to grace and confession [this] has become the cause of great sin. Oh! what a lamentable state this is, where to read the Mass, to hear Mass, or to receive the holy sacraments is nothing other than to become guilty of the shed blood and death of our Lord. Where to confess is to sin, where the spiritual medicine of the sacrament becomes poison, where the voice of the preacher leads astray, where the shepherds rob and rend even as wolves. I pity with my whole heart, as is proper, both the town council and the congregation, and especially the simple ones who are so miserably led astray.

Let us earnestly beseech all holy friends of God and good people that on our behalf they may ask God to withdraw His wrath, that He chastise us to repentance and not allow the hellish enemy to attract so lamentably the

Christian people whom Christ has redeemed at so great a cost with His precious blood.

Good friend, I would gladly have written to you long ago, although I did not do so for special reasons. But I can no longer be silent for true brotherly fidelity and love. Therefore, you may of course have this letter read wherever you think it might bring help. For I will uphold and justify it point by point if anyone should speak against it, wherever it is proper. And I desire that it might be seen by our preachers, who, as I hear, falsely strengthen the people in their errors; they neither want nor dare to give account of their preaching except within the safety of their own circle. For should they wish to come forth to defend their erroneous doctrine with which they stiffen the necks of the people against obedience to the Church of Rome, or concerning all that I have preached with regard to this issue, and all therewith connected, as it behooves me, I will be prepared to stand against them in the strength of God almighty, even unto fire.

I desire also that the majors and the council of the city should see and read this letter, and that they may grant me safe conduct so that I may preach against the pervertors of the Christian truth; so that the people of the city of Mainz, whose salvation I desire with all my heart, be not so sorely led astray. And in the event that I should preach, I would desire, as is my right, not to stand alone, but also before all Christian bishops who are in harmony with the Holy Church and the universities whose churches or possessions do not belong to one of the parties and whom this matter does not affect with temporal harm or gain, and who, notwithstanding an adverse judgment, would not betray their duty.

God the Almighty be with you unto all good. In the name of God I implore your prayers on my behalf, poor sinner that I am.

Given in the Rheingau on Saturday in the holy autumn fast in the year of our Lord, 1462.

/s/ Gabriel Byel

Chapter Two

PROLEGOMENA

༚‒

I. *Potentia absoluta* and *potentia ordinata*

1. Traditional interpretations

WE shall present first, in outline form and condensed to a summary, some key terms and central points which will help the reader orient himself in what might otherwise seem to be the bewildering world of thought of Gabriel Biel and of late medieval nominalism in general.

Study of the primary and secondary sources makes it clear that it is vital, in a proper presentation and evaluation of Biel's theology, to ascertain first of all the content of the terms *potentia absoluta* and *potentia ordinata*. More precisely, we must ask what Biel means with the distinction between and the relation of the two orders *de potentia absoluta* and *de potentia ordinata*. And secondly, subordinate to this, we must know the meaning of the term *ex puris naturalibus*. These terms appear at all the decisive junctures of Biel's theology — *formaliter* in the relation of faith and understanding, philosophy and theology — *materialiter* in such central theological issues as original sin, redemption, and reconciliation.

For this very reason these terms could not and have not been ignored by students of late medieval thought. Yet the results of several important contributions in this field have been seriously impaired by misinterpretations of their meaning. It appears that the sharp contrasts between the conclusions of studies in nominalistic thought are largely reducible to a difference in the interpretation of these terms.

In his analysis of Biel's doctrine of justification, Carl Feckes finds that what is said *de potentia absoluta* reflects Biel's real intentions and deepest convictions. As a grudging concession to ecclesiastical authority, every statement Biel would really like to make *de potentia ordinata* is made *de potentia absoluta* in order to evade and forestall inquisitional interference.[1] For this reason Feckes concludes that while nominalism erected two virtually independent and even mutually exclusive systems, one should take the system *de potentia absoluta* as the only true measure of the theology of nominalism.[2]

The conclusions of Reynold Weijenborg sharply contrast with those of Feckes. He speaks about "la distinction assez innocente des deux puissances"[3] and affirms that it would be difficult to find anything unusual or dangerous in this distinction. In Weijenborg's rather eclectic presentation of Biel's doctrine of charity, therefore, he limits himself to what is said *de potentia ordinata* and takes these statements as the true teaching of the "last" scholastic. Whereas, for example, Biel declares that *de potentia absoluta* God can accept a sinner who is not first informed by created grace, Weijenborg feels that, nevertheless, in view of the requirements actually set by God *de potentia ordinata*, infusion with created grace is as essential to Biel as to the traditional systems of high scholasticism.[4]

---

[1] "Darum retten sich die Nominalisten gern auf das Gebiet der potentia absoluta hinüber, wenn die Konsequenzen ihrer Prinzipien mit der Kirchenlehre in Konflikt zu geraten drohen," *Die Rechtfertigungslehre des Gabriel Biel und ihre Stellung innerhalb der nominalistischen Schule*. Münsterische Beiträge zur Theologie, VII (Münster i.W., 1925), 12. Erwin Iserloh states that Occam "gewagte Thesen entwickelt . . . und sich selbst dann durch ein Bekenntnis zur Autorität der Kirche gleichsam ein Alibi verschafft. . ." *Gnade und Eucharistie in der philosophischen Theologie des Wilhelm von Ockham: Ihre Bedeutung für die Ursachen der Reformation*, Veröffentlichungen des Instituts für europäische Geschichte Mainz, VIII (Wiesbaden, 1956), 283.

[2] Feckes, *Die Rechtfertigungslehre des Gabriel Biel*, p. 22: "Schon in der Grundlage aller Rechtfertigungslehren hebt demnach im Nominalismus bereits ein zweifaches System an: das eine nach der potentia absoluta, d.h. letzthin nach den richtigen nominalistischen Prinzipien. . . Das andere nach der potentia ordinata, die bekannte Kirchenlehre." Cf. p. 139.

[3] "La charité dans la première théologie de Luther," *RHE* 45 (1950), 617. Extensive excerpt reprinted in *Sylloge excerptorum e dissertationibus*, XXI (Louvain, 1950), 615–669. Cf. E. Iserloh's evaluation of and response to Weijenborg, "Luther-Kritik oder Luther-Polemik," in *Festgabe Joseph Lortz*, ed. E. Iserloh and P. Manns (Baden-Baden, 1958), I, 16–22. An incisive answer is given by Gordon E. Rupp, *The Righteousness of God: Luther Studies* (London, 1953), pp. 94–101.

[4] "Cet appel à la théorie des deux puissances, ou plutôt des deux modes de concevoir l'oeuvre du salut n'apporte en somme rien de neuf. Elle a été empruntée aux scolastiques classiques. Elle ne supprime pas la charité infuse ni l'amour rationnel

This leads him, of course, to a criticism of Joseph Lortz, who in the tradition of Carl Feckes has characterized the Occamistic program as one of extreme naturalism with a definite tendency to suppress the doctrine of grace.[5]

While Feckes and Weijenborg had each selected one of the two orders as that one within which the nominalists came into their own, Paul Vignaux was the first to warn seriously against such a rigid classification of these two orders: "La *potentia absoluta* ne représente pas la raison et le droit, ni la *potentia ordinata* une pure donnée de fait: toute interprétation de ce genre trahirait la pensée de Gabriel Biel." [6]

Vignaux repeatedly attacks the thesis that the order *de potentia absoluta* is a product of the arbitrariness of God's will; and he finds rationality also in the established order, which, however, can be brought to light not with necessary but only with probable arguments.[7]

For Vignaux the deepest significance of the distinction between *potentia ordinata* and *absoluta* is that by contrasting the established order with the one required by logic, the given order is shown to be "un ordre de miséricorde" ruled by a "volonté toute gratuite par laquelle Dieu entre en relation de justice avec la créature raisonnable." [8] God has made himself a debtor of all those who possess infused grace. In this way, Vignaux defends the religious significance of the teaching of such men as Occam, d'Ailly, and Biel.[9]

In Bengt Hägglund's study of the nominalistic understanding of the relation between theology and philosophy,[10] there is no explicit analysis

qui restent essentiels à l'amitié entre Dieu et l'homme" (p. 626). Weijenborg supports his interpretation with a reference to II *Sent.* d 17 q 1 concl. 2 C [intended is I *Sent.* d 17 q 1 art. 2 concl. 1 C]. The use of the term "essentiels" is unfortunate in view of Biel's statement that acceptation ". . . non dependeat essentialiter ab illa forma [habitus of love]," I *Sent.* d 17 q 1 art. 2 concl. 1 C.

[5] *Die Reformation in Deutschland*, 2 ed., 2 vols. (Freiburg i. Br., 1941), I, 173.

[6] *Luther Commentateur des Sentences* (Paris, 1935), p. 78.

[7] "Nous croyons que le nominalisme veut seulement montrer dans la doctrine classique de l'habitus de charité l'expression d'un fait et non d'une nécessité," *Justification et prédestination au XIVe siècle: Duns Scot, Pierre d'Auriole, Guillaume d'Occam, Grégoire de Rimini* (Paris, 1934), p. 132.

[8] *Ibid.*, p. 127 ff. See Paul Vignaux, "Sur Luther et Ockham," *FS* 32 (1950), 25.

[9] See the discussion of the dialectics of the *potentia absoluta* and *ordinata* in Oberman, "Some Notes on the Theology of Nominalism," p. 50 f.

[10] *Theologie und Philosophie bei Luther und in der occamistischen Tradition: Luthers Stellung zur Theorie von der doppelten Wahrheit*, Lunds Universitets Årsskrift, vol. LI, no. 4 (Lund, 1955).

of the distinction under consideration. In two ways, however, we become aware of the unstated presuppositions of the author. First, Hägglund uses the term *potentia absoluta* in analyzing the nominalistic conception of the middle ground between strictly philosophical and strictly theological knowledge. He wants to prove that, whereas *de potentia absoluta* it is possible to understand theological truths which *de potentia ordinata* have to be revealed, there is no essential difference — according to Occam — between the understanding of, for example, the doctrine of the Trinity by way of revelation or by way of natural reason.[11] This conclusion leads Hägglund to identify *scientia* and *sapientia* to such a degree that he can find in Occam an absolute harmony between theology and philosophy.[12]

When he has described Biel's concept of acquired faith it becomes even more apparent that Hägglund has discarded the difference between the *potentia absoluta* and *ordinata*. Comparing faith acquired through natural capacities with supernatural faith infused by God, Hägglund draws the conclusion that while infused faith without acquired faith cannot produce assent to creedal statements, and therefore is not sufficient, *fides acquisita*, however, is not only necessary but also sufficient. At this point he refers to Biel's words: "Et licet fides acquisita actum producere posset sine infusa, et non econverso. . ."[13] When we put this sentence in its proper context, we discover that what Biel actually stresses is: "*Non potest naturali ratione probari* fidem infusam ad credendum fidei articulos esse necessariam,"[14] thereby assigning the conclusion quoted by Hägglund to the order possible only *de potentia absoluta*. Biel makes his position *de potentia ordinata* quite clear: "Fidem infusam poni preter acquisitam creditum est et expressum per scripturam."[15] Since Hägglund had

[11] *Ibid.*, p. 34. Cf. p. 36: "Zwar setzt diese Erkenntnis die potentia absoluta voraus, die ihren Mangel an intuitiver Erkenntnis ausgleicht, in der Hauptsache ist sie aber von gleicher Art wie die rationale Erkenntnis."

[12] "Hier . . . waltet eine ungestörte Harmonie zwischen Theologie und Philosophie, zwischen Glaubenserkenntnis und rationaler Erkenntnis," *ibid.*, p. 40. Cf., however, Biel in III *Sent.* d 23 q 2 art. 1 GH: ". . . fides dicitur esse cognitio ex parte et in enigmate et obscuritate . . . quia habens fidem non credit articulum verum esse ex evidentia obiecti, sed ex hoc quia assentit veracitati dei asserentis."

[13] III *Sent.* d 23 q 2 art. 1 GH *in fine.*

[14] III *Sent.* d 23 q 2 art. 2 concl. 2.

[15] *Ibid.*, concl. 3; the necessity of infused faith is "proved"; "Quod enim illa [fides infusa] requiritur, signum est quia duo audiunt eundem predicantem, vident et eadem miracula facientem, unus credit, alius non, ut patet in predicatione Christi et apostolorum. Cuius ratio est quia ille recipit donum fidei desuper alius non."

not seen the dialectics of the two orders, his misinterpretation of an essential element in Biel's thought was unavoidable.

Before we draw our own conclusions as to the proper interpretation of the distinction between the two orders, we must consider Erwin Iserloh's criticism of Occam bearing exactly on this point. Iserloh feels that so many words and so much "theological energy" are spent by Occam on the possibilities *de potentia absoluta* that sufficient attention cannot be given to the theologian's real task which is to deal with God's actual revelation. This necessarily results in an "Als/ob" theology which does not seem to be interested any more in the traditional theological enterprise: ". . . die Darstellung der Heilsgeschichte weicht der Erörterung blosser Möglichkeiten." [16]

Is the heavy charge which Iserloh makes against Occam also applicable to Biel? [17] To answer this latter question — relevant inasmuch as Iserloh several times moves from Occam to "Occam and his school" and so implies Biel [18] — we will have to pay equal attention to Biel's sermons and to his strictly academic works. His sermons may well prove to be an excellent standard with which to judge the religious quality implicit in his dogmatic speculations.

2. Relation of philosophy and theology

With these viewpoints in mind, we shall now turn to Biel himself to try to define the theological and philosophical significance and application of the distinction between the *potentia absoluta* and *ordinata*. This offers us an opportunity to look at the same time into Biel's theory of knowledge, his metaphysics, and his concept of the natural knowledge of God. These subjects will be dealt with in the next chapter in more detail, but considering them here has the advantage of linking philosophical to theological presuppositions in exactly the same way in which they are found in *perichoresis* in the primary texts themselves.

It has become traditional in the treatment of medieval theology in gen-

---

[16] Iserloh, *Gnade und Eucharistie . . . Ockham*, p. 77; cf. pp. 35, 74, 78, 100, 105, 135 f and 179 ff.

[17] "Dabei geht dem Theologen das Bewusstsein von dem unabdingbaren Ernst des in der Menschwerdung von Gott beschrittenen Heilsweges . . . weitgehend verloren," *ibid.*, p. 74.

[18] *Ibid.*, p. 130.

eral, and of late medieval theology in particular to devote the first part of the discussion to philosophical issues and the second part to theological problems. This order is entirely acceptable so long as we recognize the danger that with such an ordering it is tempting to apply a form-matter concept, according to which either Platonic or Aristotelian philosophical doctrines serve as a determining factor for the "implied" theological propositions. While this concept often seems to be applicable in high scholasticism, it should not be taken for granted that this is necessarily true in the case of late medieval nominalism.

Carl Feckes had argued, and he has been echoed time and again, that nominalistic philosophy has such a very low opinion of man's power to know that the whole world of knowledge necessarily starts to slide. For this reason, according to Feckes, the nominalist turns to faith as the only means of security in an uncertain, unknowable world.[19] This conclusion should be regarded as a fabrication, be it true or not; it is not derived from the sources themselves. There are two other possible explanations for the faith of the nominalist which are equally viable insofar as his academic works are concerned. It may well be typical for the nominalist and the late medieval religious atmosphere that the sovereignty and the all-overriding importance of faith is taken as a point of departure so that a philosophy must be found which is truly *ancilla theologiae*. But there is still a third option in this case. The issue of certitude and security, for all kinds of nontheological reasons, may have become so central that this has led to the questioning of the reliability of traditional physics, metaphysics, and theology. Theology and philosophy *both* may have been "formed" by such extraneous motives.

Therefore, let us beware of taking it for granted that a particular philosophy forced Biel or any other nominalist to particular theological conclusions, a view which is implied, for example, in the widespread thesis that the philosophy of nominalism corrupted its theology. If any corruption took place, theology itself or some exterior force may be primarily responsible.

As a matter of fact, wherever we move within nominalistic thought,

[19] "Weit kommt also das menschliche Erkennen nicht. Für einen konsequenten Denker muss die Welt des Wissens, wenn er sich auf Biels Universalienlehre stützen will, stark ins Wanken geraten. Darum sucht der Nominalismus um so mehr den Glauben, der allein Sicherheit bringt, zu betonen," Feckes, *Die Rechtfertigungslehre des Gabriel Biel*, p. 11.

we find, as a result of its unusual stress on the dialectics of the two orders, a constant oscillation between philosophy and theology. In view of this, it is clear that we should neither limit ourselves to a presentation of Biel's philosophy or metaphysics nor forgo the conclusion that the theology of nominalism may be as central a pillar of its structure of thought as its philosophy.[20]

3. Biel's definition of the two orders

Before we assess the application of the distinction between the *potentia absoluta* and *ordinata* of God, we want to outline briefly how Biel himself understands these terms. But we do not for a moment want to suggest that Biel is original here, since actually Biel defines them in exactly the same way as Duns Scotus and Occam had before him. Although these terms had been employed since the beginnings of scholasticism,[21] they had been more or less peripheral. Only in Duns Scotus,[22] and after him in the nominalistic tradition, did the terms become key words for theological method and for the understanding of an increasing number of dogmatic *loci*.

Apart from many cursory references, Biel writes explicitly on God's double *potentia* only in two places: once in the context of justification and

[20] Primarily because of the great interest the "Inceptor Venerabilis" took in philosophical issues, we must point here to the inherent danger in studies of Occam which tend to lead to exactly this limitation. Without qualifying the great contribution of Philotheus Boehner to the modern understanding of Occam, we must be most careful not to regress to the pre-Vignaux period when late medieval thought was only dealt with as part of the history of philosophy. See P. Boehner, *Collected Articles on Ockham*, ed. E. M. Buytaert (St. Bonaventura, N. Y., 1958). Gerhard Ritter called attention to the fact that the significance of the nominalistic criticism has been stressed out of all proportion, *Studien zur Spätscholastik* (Heidelberg, 1922) II, 8. See also his "Romantische und revolutionäre Elemente in der deutschen Theologie am Vorabend der Reformation" *Deutsche Vierteljahrschrift* 5 (1927), 348 ff.

[21] Cf. A. Lang, *Die Wege der Glaubensbegründung bei den Scholastikern des 14. Jahrhunderts*, in *BB*, vol. XX, pts 1–2 (Münster i.W., 1930).

[22] "Fere omnes doctrinas theologicas Scotus considerat non solum respectu Dei potentiae ordinatae, sed etiam respectu potentiae absolutae . . . Eiusmodi dissertationes quid de potentia Dei absoluta . . . sit possibile, partim valde extensae sint, ita ut Scotus fere obliviscatur docere quid de potentia dei ordinata seu de facto tenendum sit. . ." Parthenius Minges, *Ioannes Duns Scoti doctrina philosophica et theologica*, 2 vols. (Quaracchi, 1930), I, 578 f.

infused grace and once in the context of the sacraments and their effects.[23] Concerning Biel's statement that God, *de potentia absoluta*, can accept someone who does not possess the habit of grace, the question arises: does the term not seem to imply that God can alternate between ordinate and inordinate behavior? To this Biel answers with the words of Occam that the *potentia ordinata* and *absoluta* should not be understood as two different ways of divine action, as God's actions *ad extra* are undivided.[24] Nor is it to be understood that God can act sometimes with, sometimes without order — this would contradict God's very being. But the distinction should be understood to mean that God can — and, in fact, has chosen to — do certain things according to the laws which he freely established, that is, *de potentia ordinata*. On the other hand, God can do everything that does not imply contradiction, whether God has decided to do these things [*de potentia ordinata*] or not, as there are many things God can do which he does not want to do. The latter is called God's power *de potentia absoluta*.[25]

The words of Christ to Nicodemus[26] serve as a clarification of this distinction: under the new law only those baptized by water and the Spirit can enter heaven. Under the old law, however, circumcised children could enter heaven without baptism. This proves that this is possible in an absolute sense, though not true now, *de facto*, *de potentia ordinata*. Revelation then, is seen as an historical, non-metaphysical category.

When we compare Biel's definition with Occam's *Quodlibet* VI statement, it appears that, apart from some insignificant variations, Biel makes one change that tends to broaden this definition. Instead of Occam's "posse deum aliquid quandoque accipitur secundum leges ordinatas . . . ,"

[23] I *Sent.* d 17 q 1 art. 3 H and IV *Sent.* d 1 q 1 art. 3 [K.] dub. 2; compare Occam, *Quodl.* VI q 1 and Gregory of Rimini, I *Sent.* d 42–44 q 1 art. 2 [fol. 162 P].

[24] "Hec distinctio non est sic intelligenda quod in deo realiter sint due potentie, quarum una sit ordinata, alia absoluta, quia unica est potentia in deo ad extra, que omni modo est ipse deus," I *Sent.* d 17 q 1 art. 3 H.

[25] *Ibid.*, ". . . posse aliquid aliquando accipitur secundum leges ordinatas et institutas a deo. Et illam sic deus dicitur posse facere de potentia ordinata. Aliter accipitur posse pro posse facere omne illud quod non includit contradictionem fieri, sive deus ordinavit se hoc facturum sive non, quia deus multa facere potest quod non vult facere secundum magistrum [I *Sent.* d 43]. Et illa dicitur posse de potentia absoluta."

[26] John 3:5; ". . . unless one is born of water and the Spirit, he cannot enter the Kingdom of God."

Biel lays his foundation with the slight change "posse aliquid quandoque accipitur secundum leges ordinatas. . ." Although in this context the change does not make sense and seems to be a simple misquote, the reason for it becomes clear from IV *Sent.* d 1 q 1 K, where Biel takes over Peter d'Ailly's further application of this distinction to created man himself. This does not introduce a new element so far as any principle is involved, but shows that, *de potentia absoluta*, natural laws can be suspended to such an extent that a created cause can produce effects[27] radically different from what they can now, *de potentia ordinata*. Miracles are the reminders that nature is not a self-contained reality — nature is creation.[28]

Finally, we should not overlook a noteworthy variant on the first definition in the parallel passage of I *Sent.* d 17 in *Lectura* 59. As Biel here defines the order *de potentia ordinata* as the order of God's wisdom, this additional reference may well warn us not to conclude hastily the arbitrariness of the given order,[29] as is so often done on the strength of I *Sent.* d 17 alone.

With these data in hand we can turn now to the question of the theological and philosophical significance and influence of this distinction between the two orders. And repeatedly we will touch upon issues which form the subject matter of later chapters.

II. The Theological Significance of the Dialectics of God's Power
Its Significance for Man's Intellectual Powers

God acts contingently in his *opera ad extra* — therefore human reason could not have predicted the course God would take. God alone is without beginning or end, eternal and incorruptible, and therefore God alone

[27] IV *Sent.* d 1 q 1 art. 3 dub. 2 M: ". . . etiam creatura potest aliquid de potentia ordinata que videlicet potest secundum ordinem a deo nunc institutum. Potest etiam aliquid de potentia absoluta . . . secundum ordinem institui possibilem. Et ita natura aliqua potest in effectus contrarios effectibus quos modo potest. Sicut de cataplasmate ficuum apposito vulneri regis ezechie per esaiam prophetam quo sanatus est." Cf. II Kings 20: 7. The example is taken from d'Ailly, IV *Sent.* q 1 art. 2 B.

[28] "Potest etiam aliquid de potentia absoluta sive obedientiali secundum quam potest quicquid mediante ipsa deus potest producere. . . Posset deus creare aliqua per aliquem non per eum tanquam auctorem sed ministrum cum quo et in quo operetur." IV *Sent.* d 1 q 1 art. 3 dub. 2 M *in fine*.

[29] *Lect.* 59 O: "Statuit siquidem deus secundum ordinem sue sapientie nullum fore glorificandum in patria nisi fuerit prius gratificatus in via."

is necessary in an absolute sense. Everything aside from God exists only with a hypothetical necessity: God could also *not* have wanted it to come into being. In this sense everything except God's own essence is contingent.

We have chosen the word "predicted" because Biel identifies the present with the established order, *de potentia ordinata*, which is in no sense less real or dependable because of the fact that God could have chosen another possibility; on the contrary, its dependability is guaranteed by God's eternal, immutable will, that is, God himself. "Could *have* predicted" because Biel writes from within the Christian era, addressing himself to all *viatores existentes in gratia aut in culpa*.

This is not the same as saying that Biel's anthropology presupposes the true Christian in a state of grace, as Weijenborg has suggested.[30] To what this confusion of the *viator* with the just can lead appears most clearly in the context of the doctrine of justification, where Weijenborg concludes that Biel's moral optimism refers only to the justified who are able to love God above everything else.[31] Though so far as Biel's doctrine of justification is concerned we cannot go into detail here, this single example warns us to take this matter seriously.

Biel's theological anthropology is not one of the just but of the *viator*, who stands in between the beatified and the damned,[32] — that is to say — in between those who cannot sin and those who ultimately cannot act meritoriously. Biel's anthropology refers to the traveler on his way to his eternal destiny, at once *damnabilis* and *beatificabilis*. Though the *viator* cannot enter into eternal bliss so long as he is in mortal sin, and though he needs God's acceptation, he can freely choose between the two final alternatives.[33]

Except for the events leading up to and connected with the "last things," the *potentia ordinata* is concerned with past events which shaped the present — creation, preservation, fall, and redemption. Explicit faith

[30] "Car Biel construit toute son anthropologie du point de vue du juste, c.à.d. de l'homme surnaturel, du vrai chrétien," Weijenborg, p. 620 (no source reference).

[31] "Biel se montre indéniablement optimiste lorsqu'il parle des forces morales du juste [!!] auquel il reconnaît la faculté d'observer toute la loi divine; mais il n'accepte pas que le non-justifié puisse être honnête à l'égard de Dieu," Weijenborg, p. 629.

[32] *Prologi* q 1 A: "Circa primum articulum notandum primo quod viator est ille qui non est in termino ad quem tendit. Sunt autem duo termini rationalis creature scil. beatitudo finalis et miseria finalis. Viator ergo est quisquis qui neque beatus est neque finaliter damnatus."

39

grasps the meaning of these events and accepts them as meaningful. This explicit faith has as its object the order *de potentia ordinata* and can therefore be qualified as an historic-positive faith in the sense in which we speak of positive theology in contrast to speculative theology.

Though faith in the nominalistic vocabulary is exclusively related to the *events* of revelation, it is erroneous to conclude that this implies an existential interpretation of faith which would deviate from the main medieval tradition. Faith is basically *fides quae*, the content of the Christian creed, rather than *fides qua*, the act of faith in response to the revealing event.

It is important to note that the nominalistic emphasis on the truly historical nature of God's dealings with his creation postulates the unpredictability but *not* the arbitrariness of God's actions. The best illustration is perhaps to point out that in the *tempus legis naturalis*, the premosaic period, God's actions in the *tempus legis moysis* could not have been predicted by human reason, nor in this latter period the events of the *tempus legis gratiae*. Under the revealed and stable conditions of this last era, the *viatores* will live until the end of the world.

1. Natural knowledge of God

There are insights regarding God which are not restricted to the *corpus christianum*. The human reason knows a few things about God: that he exists, that he is a living God, and a wise God.[34] This knowledge is originally acquired by experience or abstraction, however, and is not *per se nota*. It belongs so much to human existence itself that one can say that God is not the object but the cause of our knowledge of him.[35] But since a truth *per se nota* cannot be doubted, while a fool — the fool of Anselm's ontological proof — indeed may doubt whether God exists, this part of

---

[33] I *Sent.* d 41 q 1 art. 3 concl. 5.

[34] *Prologi* q 1 art. 1 nota 3 D. In *S* II 39 B, a list is given of divine attributes: *summa essentia, summa veritas, summa unitas*, etc. "Hec sunt que gentiles philosophi de deo rationis naturalis ductu cognoverunt que utinam non a multis ignorarentur christianis cuius ignorantia destructio est totius religionis. . .," *S* II 39 C. In I *Sent.* d 2 q 10 art. 2 concls. 2–3, Biel follows Occam in asserting that the oneness of God is probable but not demonstrable. Cf. Occam, *Quodl.* 1 q 1. For Robert Holcot's position see Chapter Seven, section III.

[35] I *Sent.* d 3 q 1 art. 2 C.

man's natural knowledge of God has to be demonstrated by rational argumentation.[36]

The nominalistic "epistemology of the *viator*" is not intended to restrict the knowledge of the world in which the *viator* lives; of this world he can have experimental, intuitive and indirect, abstract knowledge. The purpose of this epistemology is rather to show the deficiencies in man's natural knowledge of *God*. Since the intuitive knowledge of God is only possible for the beatified and not for the *viator*, the resulting restriction of metaphysics highlights the importance of God's revelation, the chosen order.

2. Faith seeking understanding: *ratio de congruo*

For apologetics this means that the Anselmian *necessitas* is eliminated; even those who possess the habit of infused faith are not able to construct an argument which leads unbelievers necessarily to acknowledge the existence of one God.[37]

The *fides quaerens intellectum* is by no means sacrificed; this would mean the end of the theological enterprise. But to the unbeliever who lives in the circle of the *potentia absoluta*, under the law of non-contradiction, explanations can only be given in the form of probable opinions.

There is no sufficient reason to prefer one probable opinion above another unless one runs counter to the authority of the Church, to an unambiguous conclusion of natural reason or to experience. Parallel to Bonaventura's *rationes congruentes*, one can speak in Biel's case of a *ratio fidei* which is a *ratio de congruo*. It is in this area — and not in that of secular knowledge — that the authority of Aristotle's metaphysics is seriously questioned by Biel.

In so far as faith is *implicit faith*, on the authority of a priest or of the Church, the light of natural reason is darkened and extinguished by the light of revelation.[38] Only after faith has accepted the order chosen by God can the theologian start to point out the *ratio de congruo*.

---

[36] I *Sent.* d 3 q 4 art. 2 concl. 1.

[37] I *Sent.* d 2 q 10 art. 2 concl. 3.

[38] *S* I 4 E: "Sed et in adventu maioris luminis fidei, quo sol christus illuminat venientes in hunc mundum, sol intelligentie naturalis contenebrescat, nihil continetur, nec possibilitatem aut causas requirat aut prevaleat in suo lumine adversus divina instituta que per fidem innotescunt, scientes quia quod stultum est dei sapientius est hominibus."

3. Double truth excluded

Though the relation of natural reason and revelation which we have discussed indicates a *diastasis* between reason and faith which the creature can not eliminate, it certainly does not imply a *divorce* between the realms of reason and faith. Far from postulating a double truth, it rather excludes it. Faith is not irrational or contrary to natural reason but rather ungraspable by natural reason. This very conception allows for the reconciliation and harmonization of seemingly contrasting conclusions in science and theology by way of a "peaceful coexistence."[39]

III. The Theological Significance of the Dialectics of God's Power
Its Significance for Man's Moral Powers

The conditioning of the human reason by the distinction of the *potentia absoluta* and *potentia ordinata* affects the prolegomena and very first step toward the *fides acquisita*, that is, the faith man can acquire without supernatural aid. Man's intellectual power enables him to perceive the objects to which he reaches out in a voluntary act. Without this rational guidance the will is blind.[40]

With the resulting conditioning of the human will we enter the field of theology proper as a practical, nonspeculative science. Even when one thinks in terms of the *potentia absoluta* and therefore takes a hypothetical position outside the realm of God's revelation, one is nevertheless dealing with theological and not only philosophical or metaphysical problems.

[39] One of the hidden motives of the distinction under consideration may well have been the promotion and protection of the immunity of the Christian tradition vis-a-vis the contemporary rapid development of the natural sciences. Buridan and his school, so closely related to nominalistic theology, were laying the foundations of modern physics with its revolutionary understanding of cosmology and consequently with its new understanding of miracles. Cf. Anneliese Maier, *Studien zur Naturphilosophie der Spätscholastik*, I (1949), 19 ff., 145 ff., for an analysis of this development. Therefore it is not acceptable without qualification when Hägglund says after having pointed to a similar attitude of Luther, characterized as a "durchgreifender Gegensatz zwischen dem Bereich der Glaubenswahrheiten und der Vernunft": "Eine Tendenz, den Inhalt des christlichen Glaubens mit der zeitgenössischen wissenschaftlichen Bildung zu harmonisieren, liegt einer solchen Anschauung fern" (p. 13). Biel writes on miracles: II *Sent.* d 8 q 2 art. 4 dub. 1 G. Cf. the elaborate entry by Altenstaig, fol. 150ʳ f., sv.

[40] *S* IV 18 H: ". . . voluntas in nullum actum potest nisi fecundetur ab intellectu, neque enim aliquid amatur nisi cognitum."

This point of view has, of course, its impact on the assessment of man's moral capacities.

Thus, just as we first asked how man's reason is related to God's revelation, we must now ask how man's power to perform morally good acts is related to his reaching out for the highest good, again in the light of the basic distinction between the "two powers." Whatever the relation between God and his creatures may be *de potentia ordinata*, the mere possibility of another order shows that God was not compelled to develop that relation. With this thesis in mind Biel tries to solve the most basic question of theology: the tension between God's love and God's justice. Ideally this tension has been resolved in the work of redemption of the God-man Jesus Christ. But the fruits of his works are only applicable to those who participate in the moral order meritoriously; and therefore the tension between love and justice reasserts itself even more urgently.

In the established order God rewards human *bonitas moralis*, provided that it is produced in a state of grace, according to remunerative justice with the gift of *meritum de condigno*.[41] This order, however, is bracketed, "eingeklammert," by the order *de potentia absoluta*. The contrast indicates that this strict justice is not *ex natura rei debita*, an ontological or automatic necessity, but a free commitment.

1. God's love and the order *de potentia ordinata*

God's gratuitous, self-giving love, expressed in the very fact that he chose to commit himself at all, is not operative *actualiter* but *historice*; not existing *within* the order chosen, but *in the fact that* he chose this particular order in eternity.[42] Therefore to say that the inherent value of certain acts and the relation of these acts to their reward can be considered apart from God's acceptation is to treat these issues *de potentia absoluta*.

As a consequence Biel says that three elements constitute the *meritum*

[41] Cf. I *Sent.* d 17 q 3 art. 3 dub 1; and II *Sent.* d 27 q 1 art. 1 nota 3. See for a discussion of the distinctions between the *meritum de condigno* and the *meritum de congruo* below Chapter Six, section II, 3.

[42] "Ex quo sequitur quod non requiritur ad premium de condigno quod actus meriti secundum intrinsecam suam bonitatem sit condignus seu proportionatus tali premio; alioquin nullus actus temporalis esset eterno condignus premio. Sed illa condignitas attenditur in proposito ex divina acceptatione qua ab eterno voluit actum sic ex gratia elicitum esse dignum tali premio; incomparabiliter excedente actus bonitatem secundum se sine acceptatione divina consideratam." II *Sent.* d 27 q 1 art. 1 nota 3 C.

43

de condigno, that is, three conditions are required to relate the morally good deed to its eternal reward: (1) "*in operante* quod sit amicus"; (2) "*in opere* requiritur quod sit ordinabile ad utilitatem vel honorem premiantis"; (3) "*in premiante* requiritur acceptatio sive ordinatio actus sic eliciti vel imperati ad tale premium." [43]

This last requirement of acceptation or endowment with uncreated love, some scholars are convinced, expresses clearly the gratuitous gift of the grace of God and is therefore to be regarded as genuinely anti-Pelagian.[44] But again, this conclusion can be drawn only if we overlook the fact that within the established order, God is obliged to accept a deed as meritorious once the former two requirements *in operante* and *in opere* are met. The free character of God's acceptation is safeguarded only insofar as this order is bracketed by the order *de potentia absoluta*.

2. Reinterpretation of the *misericordia dei*

Biel's use of the distinction between *potentia absoluta* and *ordinata* results in a shift in the meaning of the term *misericordia*. *Misericordia dei* has now become a synonym for the liberty and contingence with which God chose in eternity to make himself debtor and to reward acts which, in themselves, that is, *de potentia absoluta*, have only *bonitas* but not *dignitas*. Outside the established order, that is, before that moment in eternity when God set the present order, his *misericordia* is unconditioned. Inside that order, however, there is the double condition of justice. Thus we find the equation: *libertas* = *liberalitas* = *misericordia*.

The tension between God's love and justice is relaxed insofar as the set order is governed by a mitigated form of justice. For its existential significance to Biel we shall have to probe his sermon literature especially.

3. Non-arbitrary character of the ordained order

Dealing with the decisive gift of the grace of eternal salvation as granted in the divine acceptation, Erich Hochstetter feels that it is clear that this is a free gift according to God's omnipotence and not a payment due for services rendered. Though we may not understand God's deci-

---

[43] II *Sent.* d 27 q 1 art. 1 nota 3 C. Cf. *Lect.* 59 N and *S* II 14 E ff.
[44] Vignaux, *Luther Commentateur des Sentences*, p. 52 ff. Weijenborg, p. 629.

sion, it is not therefore an arbitrary one; it comes forth out of his *misericordia*.[45]

Granted that God's eternal decision to choose one particular order was not considered arbitrary either by the Scotists or by the Occamists, we have to admit that God's decision is indeed mysterious; but man's uncertainty in respect to this does not originate in his ignorance of God's contingent will — *misericordia* — but in not knowing whether he is in a state of grace, that is whether he has fulfilled his obligations to God and thus attained *iustitia* to which God in eternity has linked his acceptation.

4. The relation of *misericordia* and *iustitia*

That this relation of *misericordia* and *iustitia* should be seen against the background of the eternal procession from *potentia absoluta* to *potentia ordinata* can be corroborated in yet another way.

The realm of the *potentia absoluta* is not merely hypothetical and the sum of all noncontradictory possibilities. It is also [46] founded on conclusions drawn from a few deeds which God in fact performed, according to biblical authority, where he deviated from the laws now in force, the *potentia ordinata*. The three examples Biel gives of actions of God by which the realm of the *potentia absoluta* breaks into that of the *potentia ordinata* are as many examples of the invasion of a greater degree of liberality and *misericordia* than usual in the realm of justice.

[45] In view of the identity of Occam's and Biel's doctrine of acceptation, the following judgment on Occam should be transferable to Biel: "Daraus [potentia absoluta dei] schliesst Ockham, dass die eigentliche und entscheidende Gnade Gottes in der acceptatio divina zu sehen ist, von der das "meritum" erst seinen eigentlichen Sinn erhält, und die über das jenseitige Schicksal allein entscheidet als ein freies Geschenk seiner Allmacht, nicht als ein Entgelt für diesseitige Leistung. . . Was verdienstlich ist oder nicht, ist für uns geheimnisvoll, kann aber nicht als Ausfluss blosser Willkür angesehen werden . . . seine Entscheidungen fällt er zwar "contingenter et libere," aber auch "misericorditer," Erich Hochstetter, "Viator mundi: Einige Bemerkungen zur Situation des Menschen bei Wilhelm von Ockham," *FS* 32 (1950), 19. Hochstetter refers here to Occam, *Quodl.* VI q 1; I *Sent.* d 17 q 1 Z; and III *Sent.* q 5 G.

[46] Hochstetter has well noted this non-hypothetical character of the order *de potentia absoluta*. He goes too far, however, when he says: "Die Bestimmung dessen, was de potentia dei absoluta möglich ist, geht also primär von dem aus, was Gott gemäss der Offenbarung schon getan hat, und weiterhin von dem, was seine Grundlage im Wesen Gottes hat" (p. 18). This would more nearly define the order *de potentia ordinata*.

In the first place there is the example Biel gives to clarify the meaning of the term *potentia absoluta*. As indicated above, under the New Covenant it is impossible to enter heaven without being baptized. In the Old Testament, however, it was sufficient to be circumcised: this shows that it is possible *de potentia absoluta*.[47]

A more radical example, insofar as it is not a comparison of two different actions under two different laws but an action running directly counter to the laws now valid, is provided by St. Paul. Though *de potentia ordinata* a certain disposition is required before grace can be given, St. Paul was lifted to the seventh heaven and thus granted the *visio beatifica* at the very time that he was persecuting the Church of Christ.[48]

The Immaculate Conception of Mary, the Mother of Christ, is a third example. In this case grace is not only given before a proper disposition is provided but is "concreated" with her soul before original sin can have its impact on her.[49]

5. The two eternal decrees of God

In view of these considerations we should like to suggest that we distinguish two decrees of God, coeternal with God's [50] being and of course not to be understood as successive in time.[51] In the first decree the *eternal* procession from *misericordia* to *iustitia* is established. Out of innumerable possibilities God has chosen one particular course of action; the contingent will of God has subjected itself to equally contingent laws. In the second

[47] ". . . aliquando introierunt in regnum dei sine omni baptismo, sicut patet de pueris circumcisis tempore legis defunctis antequam habuerunt usum rationis; ergo et nunc est possibile. Sed illud quod tunc erat possibile secundum leges tunc institutas nunc non est possibile secundum legem nunc institutam, licet absolute sit possibile." I *Sent.* d 17 q 1 art. 3 H.

[48] "Et in Paulo fuit malus usus liberi arbitrii, quia seviens in discipulos domini percussus est," I *Sent.* d 41 q 1 art. 2 concl. 3. Cf. the resulting qualification in the definition of "viator," *Prologi* q 1 art. 1 nota 1 A.

[49] "Sic potest dominus anime concreare gratiam et ita ab originali ne contrahat preservare," S III 1 G. Cf. also I *Sent.* d 41 q 1 art. 2 concl. 3.

[50] Cf. Scotus's use of "ex destinatione eterna," *Ox.* III d 20 q 1 nota 10.

[51] Too hasty comparisons with John Calvin are forbidden by some sharp statements of the Genevan reformer. *CR Op. Cal.* 9:288: ". . . quod de absoluta potestate nugantur scholastici, non solum repudio, sed etiam detestor, quia justitiam eius ab imperio separant." *CR Op. Cal.* 9:167: ". . . coniungi debet eius potentia cum beneplacito." Cf. *CR Op. Cal.* 23:354. Quoted by Simon van der Linde, *De Leer van den Heiligen Geest bij Calvijn* (Wageningen, 1943), p. 107.

decree, as a parallel to the first, a *temporal* procession from *misericordia* to *iustitia* is established. Parallel to the movement from *potentia absoluta* to *potentia ordinata*, God moves in time from the Incarnation to the last judgment.

With slight changes we can say the same about the incarnation of the Word as we said in (2) about the order *de potentia ordinata*: God's gratuitous, self-giving love in Christ is not operative *actualiter* but *historice*, not within the second decree but in the fact that this second decree was established.

Within the second decree the movement is again from *misericordia* to *iustitia*, this time, however, obliging not God but man: God's act of love in subjecting himself to the laws of the flesh obliges man to respond and bring forth the acts of love which will be tested on the last day.[52] The terminal point of God's *misericordia* is eternally the order *de potentia ordinata*; temporarily, the Incarnation in Jesus Christ. The content of these decrees is defined by *iustitia*.

Whether this interpretation succeeds in bringing together all the disparate elements of Biel's understanding of God and his revelation is a question which can be answered only in a more detailed analysis, especially of his Christology and of the doctrines of justification and predestination.

IV. The Meaning of the Expression *ex puris naturalibus*

1. The status of the *viator*

Biel himself indicates how he wants the term *ex puris naturalibus* to be understood.[53] The most fundamental aspect of this status is that its "purity" means that it is free from infused grace. The term is applicable

---

[52] "Infinita est misericordia que expectat sed nec minor iusticia si misericordiam negligentes contemnamus: neque solum pro peccatis nostris sed pro neglecta misericordia sumus rationem reddituri," *S* IV 24 G.

[53] II *Sent.* d 28 q 1 art. 1 nota 2: "Secundo notandum quod cum loquimur de puris naturalibus non excluditur generalis dei influentia que ut causa prima concurrit cum agente secundo, i.e., agente creato ad omnem actum positivum. Siquidem nullus actus positivus (immo nec peccatum quantum ad id quod in eo positivum est puta actum licet deformem) perfici potest deo tanquam causa prima non coagente: plus enim influit causa prima in effectum quam quecunque causa secunda. . . Sed per pura naturalia intelligitur anime natura seu substantia cum qualitatibus et actionibus consequentibus naturam, exclusis habitibus ac donis supernaturaliter a solo deo infusis."

47

therefore to the status of Adam before reception of the stabilizing original justice in paradise.

But it describes also — and in this sense we find it generally used by Biel [54] — the imaginary stage between *in culpa* and *in gratia*, the extremes that mark the life of the *viator*. This stage is imaginary because *de potentia ordinata*, man is always either *in culpa* or *in gratia*, not as an ontological necessity, but as the result of a particular decision of God. *De potentia absoluta*, for example, it would be possible to be declared guiltless without the accompaniment of infused grace.

2. God's preservation of creation

Not excluded, however, is the *influentia generalis* or *concursus* of God. According to this general influence God sustains his creatures by participation in all their acts, even deformed acts.

3. The state of pure nature

What are man's intellectual and moral powers in this state of "pure" nature? The intellect knows by nature the difference between good and bad, and what is more, judges that good deeds have to be performed out of an innate love of virtue.[55] Similarly, the will is able to conform to this judgment and elicit a morally good act, thus providing by doing what it is able to do a proper disposition for the reception of grace. By the same token man in this pure state is able to avoid falling into another mortal sin. Though man in this state can perform the acts God requires *quoad substantiam actus*, he cannot properly obey the will of God *quoad intentionem legislatoris*, as in that case they have to be performed in the state of grace, which by definition is impossible for those *in puris naturalibus*.

[54] Biel, III *Sent.* d 14 q 1 art. 1 nota 3: "[De potentia absoluta] potest dari status medicus inter damnatum et gratum, scilicet status in puris naturalibus." Hochstetter restricts the state *in puris naturalibus* to Adam before the reception of divine grace in paradise, "Viator mundi," p. 11.

[55] II *Sent.* d 28 q 1 art. 2 J: ". . . intellectus ex suis naturalibus potest cognoscere et iudicare bonum iustum et honestum esse faciendum ac malum fugiendum propter finem naturalem scil. virtutis amorem et honestatis. Et huic iudicio potest se voluntas conformare eliciendo actum bonum propter naturalem honestatem aut iustitiam; et actus sic elicitus est bonus moraliter."

5. The necessity of revelation

Indeed metaphysics and theology partly overlap; but only insofar as some aspects of the truth necessary for salvation are within reach of human reason, are *scientia*. Between these and the inner core of faith there is no harmony, in the sense used by Hägglund; [70] between them there is a gap unbridgeable by human reason.

Once the consequences of sin are primarily seen in ignorance or a loss of knowledge, it is a tautology to say that natural and revealed knowledge of God are similar, "gleichartig." In view of the different realms of faith and knowledge, however, metaphysics and theology are certainly not "prinzipiell gleichartig." [71]

Illuminating is the example Biel gives of the boy who as an infant was imprisoned by the Saracens. Does this boy sin by not knowing anything about evangelical faith and law? No — he could not possibly know these things: "Non enim potest habere instruentem [i.e., fidem adquisitam] *nec per semetipsum potest habere horum cognitionem.*" [72]

Not man but only God or the Church can bridge the gap between natural theology and revealed theology. Under the law of grace, however, God will not desert him who does what is in him, "facit quod in se est," and this means "uti ratione per quam potest comprehendere deum esse et invocare adiutorium deo." [73] This law of grace does not diminish but accentuates the disharmony between metaphysics and theology from the point of view of human reason.

Thus we meet in Biel's opus two kinds of *opiniones probabiles*: (1) those which show the rationality of the established order; here *authority* is the final standard; (2) those which can be called metaphysical speculations; here *ratio* — or more precisely, what is *rationabilior* — is the final standard. To complete the picture we could add that in "physics" the *ratio* is the final standard.

6. "Als/ob" theology

Against this background we must understand Biel's warning "quia revelatum non est, non est temere diffiniendum." He deals with this issue

---

[70] *Ibid.*, p. 40.
[71] *Ibid.*, p. 27.

[72] II *Sent.* d 22 q 2 art. 3 dub. 1 N.
[73] *Ibid.*

when attacking the foundation of Scotus' doctrine of predestination, which provides Biel with an occasion to describe again God's *potentia absoluta*.[74]

Biel refers here to the second kind of *rationes probabiles* in the context of a problem arising out of conceivable sacred history: "What would have happened if the fall had not taken place?" This problem falls outside the *potentia ordinata*: no revealed data can decide the issue. At the same time it falls outside the realm of *scientia* since no *notitia intuitiva* or *experimentalis* is possible here: neither authority nor *ratio per se* can provide the answer here; the cooperation of reason, experience, and authority is required to reach the relatively most reasonable solution. Though reason should be followed, it is still *credere* and not *scire*: "credi quod magis videtur consentaneum rationi."

This should not, however, be done "temere," with unrestrained imagination, and without proper respect for that which is known in an authoritative way through revelation. It is difficult to ascertain to whom Biel, apart from Scotus, directs this warning. Most likely it was to the Parisian school, which, in a similar way and for precisely the same reason, was criticized by Gerson:[75] this school would include, apart from anonymous *magistri* whose *questiones* we possess, Autrecourt, Mirecourt, and Jean de Ripa.[76]

It is not impossible that Occam's dealing with conceivable sacred history in the case of the incarnation and his defense of some extreme statements are also in the mind of Biel. Though he holds Occam in the highest possible regard as, for example, *profundissimus veritatis indagator*,[77]

---

[74] ". . . falsum est quod prius vult finem et post ordinata in finem, quia non est nisi unus actus divine voluntatis. . . Nec est ibi actus et actus sed unus tamen eternus actus . . . neque ordo effectuum temporalium infert actuum divinorum ordinem. Nam in effectibus est conversus ordo ad ordinem in notabili designatum [scil. Scoti opinionem] quia in effectibus primum est esse nature, deinde esse gratie, ultimo esse glorie. Nec tamen aliquid horum deus prius vult altero; sed quecunque vult similiter et ab eterno vult. Licet que vult, possit non velle, quia quecunque vult ad extra contingenter vult. . . Eo ipso enim quod vult recte et iuste et ordinate vult. Posset ergo dici quod si homo non fuisset lapsus, dubium nobis esset: utrum modo electi vel alii plures vel pauciores fuissent geniti. Quodlibet enim horum fuisset deo possibile. Quod autem fecisset, quia revelatum non est non est temere diffiniendum. Licet posset sine temeritate cum fidei pietate credi, quod magis videtur consentaneum rationi." II *Sent.* d 20 q 1 art. 1 nota 3.

[75] See André Combes, *Jean Gerson: commentateur dionysien* (Paris, 1940), p. 611.

[76] Cf. Oberman, "Some Notes on the Theology of Nominalism," p. 63 ff.

[77] ". . . sequor nunc opinionem magistri, quam etiam sequitur profundissimus

he emphasizes far more the fittingness of God's revelation and thus differs from Occam in respect to the first group of *rationes probabiles*. It is not surprising, therefore, that he sometimes criticizes Occam in his metaphysical speculations for being too "subtle."

7. Conclusion

It is worthwhile to note that Biel saw the danger lurking in nominalistic thought which has been described by Iserloh as an extreme "Als/ob" theology, typical of Occam *and his school*. Yet apparently Biel does not think that this extremism belongs to the essence of nominalism, and he makes this clear in more than just his *Collectorium*.

His Sermons are the best test for the religious quality of his theology proper; since in that setting there is no other educational responsibility, merely the *theological* significance of the *potentia absoluta* is reflected. And even so, it is used only to indicate that the explanations offered for God's decisions can never be more than acceptable possibilities.[78]

In conclusion we can say that the distinction between *potentia absoluta* and *potentia ordinata,* apart from its theological implications for the

---

veritatis indagator Guilhelmus occam cuius doctrinam tanquam clariorem frequentius imitor." IV *Sent.* d 14 q 2 art 2 N. The word "frequentius" used here is more to the point than the traditional presentation of Biel as the obedient commentator of Occam. This view is confirmed by a point of information which Peter Schott provides: "In practicis resolutissimum [Biel] dicit esse Scotus, in speculabilibus Ockam ponere veritates claras palpabiles," in "Questiuncule Petri Schotti, quas magistro Gabrieli Byhel, preposito uracensi, theologie doctissimo licentiato, obtulit," *Lucubratiunculae Petri Schotti,* ed. J. Wimpheling (Strassburg, 1498), fol. 145ʳ. Luther, too, noted the connection between Biel and Scotus: "Scio quid Gabriel dicat . . . ubi cum *suo* Scoto quantum pelagizet. . ." Quoted by Otto Scheel, *Dokumente zu Luthers Entwicklung (bis 1519),* 2 ed. (Tübingen, 1929), p. 293. To complete the picture one should add that Aquinas' "Secunda secundae" is highly esteemed while his work as a biblical commentator — together with that of Nicholas of Lyra — forms the basis of many of Biel's sermons. It is striking that Biel in his *Expositio* repeatedly uses the work of such a "young" Dominican doctor as Antoninus of Florence, whose *opera* were for the first time published, 1474–1479, in Venice.

[78] Cf. *S* I 2 F: "Sed forte diceret aliquis: Quare opus incarnationis in finem seculi est dilatum et non a principio casus humani consummatum. Responsio: licet rationes temporum que pater in sua potestate posuit, non est nostrum cognoscere. . . , tamen dubium non est quin sapientissimus dispositor temporum deus omnibus suis operibus congruentissimum tempus eligit. Licet hec congruitas a nobis plene in via sciri non possit, ponunt tamen doctores varias rationes. . ."

fides quaerens intellectum, has a philosophical implication. It delineates a field of knowledge between the world known by experience and the world known by faith: philosophical theology, not to be confused with the field of theology proper. The data of faith serve here only to complete experience and reason. From his side the metaphysician should be aware that his conclusions are never absolute, never scientifically certain, only more "reasonable." At the same time he should be diligent in handling his data so as not to undermine piety.

These thesis-like points of the prolegomena indicate something of the structure and atmosphere of Biel's thought. In the following chapters we shall find these points more systematically elaborated and analyzed.

Chapter Three

FAITH AND UNDERSTANDING

ॐ⊶

I. Anthropology

In this chapter we want to sketch the interrelation of faith and reason, their separate functions in the sphere of knowledge, and the results of their joint activity. At first we shall look into Biel's anthropology; later we shall be able to assess its impact on the relation of natural to revealed law and the question of ethical positivism.

1. Philosophical and theological anthropology

Notwithstanding Biel's assumption of the simplicity of the soul and thus the essential unity of the soul with intellect and will, an operational distinction of these powers plays an important part in his understanding of man and his existence.

The Thomistic real distinction and the Scotistic formal distinction — the latter being for Biel merely a different word for the same error underlying the *distinctio realis* — are denied. This applies not only to the distinction in God between his essence and his attributes but also to the distinction in man between his soul and the powers of his soul; the soul of man cannot be a direct object of knowledge and thus does not fall under the *notitia intuitiva*.[1]

Biel goes one step further than Occam had in emphasizing the unity and simplicity of man. Occam had defended — against Alexander of

[1] Occam, II *Sent.* q 24 B ff.; *Quodl.* 2 q 10–11; Gregory of Rimini, II *Sent.* d 16–17 q 3 art. 1 [fol. 87 F ff.]; Biel, II *Sent.* d 16 q 1 art. 2 concl. 3: ". . . potentie anime rationalis intellectus et voluntas eedem realiter non distinguuntur ex natura rei aut formaliter."

Hales and Thomas — a real distinction between the sensitive soul, the bodily form, and the intellective soul. Though difficult to prove, he felt that these anthropological presuppositions were more in accordance with the Christian faith.[2] At this point Biel follows Gregory of Rimini and attacks his highly esteemed master with an argument Occam himself had used so often, the principle of economy known as "Occam's razor": "non est ponenda pluralitas sine necessitate."[3] That means, in this case, that the plurality of forms in the soul is rejected: the sensitive soul is indivisible exactly because it is the same as the intellective soul.[4]

The traditional, biblical, and Augustinian distinction between the old and the new man, or between the inner and outer man, appears time and again in Biel's analyses of man's peculiar position between God and the animals. The ineradicable tension between the lower and the higher part in man, subdued by the stabilizing gift of original justice, belongs essentially to the species *Homo sapiens* and is not a consequence of the fall of mankind. This distinction, however, does not always refer to the difference between the sensual and the rational aspect of man; it equally well applies to the higher and the lower part of man's intellective soul.[5] The "outer man" can, therefore, refer to man's body or to the lower part of man's intellective soul. The distinction between old and new man, on the contrary, necessarily refers to man's state, either in guilt or in grace; in other words, it indicates two ways of life: living in sin and "self-finalization" or in obedience and longing for God as the highest good.[6]

The first distinction between inner and outer comes from Biel's philo-

---

[2] "Magis concordat cum fide ecclesie ponere distinctionem inter istas formas quam unitatem," Occam, *Quodl.* 2 q 11.

[3] Biel, II *Sent.* d 16 q 1 art. 1 nota 1 C. We find exactly the same argument in Gregory of Rimini (II *Sent.* d 16–17 q 3 art. 1 [fol. 86 E/F]). Biel concludes: ". . . opinio nona Gregorii sit principalis tam Philosophi quam aliorum communiter conformior et ideo probabilior," II *Sent.* d 16 q 1 art. 1 nota 1 C.

[4] ". . . anima sensitiva in homine est simpliciter indivisibilis quia est realiter anima intellectiva," *ibid.* art. 2 H.

[5] "Ex quibus colligi potest quid interest inter hominem exteriorem, hominem veterem et portionem inferiorem. Similiter inter hominem interiorem, hominem novum, et portionem superiorem. Nam homo exterior dupliciter accipitur. Aut pro parte sensitiva hominis. . . 'Deponite veterem hominem': corpus exterior homo est anima interior. Corpus accipitur pro anima sensitiva, anima pro parte intellectiva. Secundo accipitur homo exterior pro homine finem suum in exterioribus creaturis ponente. Homo interior per oppositum est homo finem suum in deo creatore constituens. . ." II *Sent.* d 24 q 1 art. 3 dub. 1.

[6] " 'Expoliate vos veterem hominem' — homo vetus vita vetus in peccatis secundum

sophical anthropology. These terms describe man *per se*: they are equally relevant for Adam before the fall and for the *viator* of history. The terms of the second distinction, between the old and the new man, belong to Biel's theological anthropology: they refer only to the *viator* after the fall of Adam.

It is important to note that within the context of this theological anthropology, the neo-Platonic-Manichean understanding of man becomes marginal because of the explicit assertion that the battle between the two ways of life does not take place at the frontier between body and soul, but *within the rational soul* at the frontier of its higher and lower part. Biel's expressions are nevertheless quite clearly colored by the traditional Augustinian traces of neo-Platonism. The terms are there, and at least part of his conception of the causes of the fall of Adam goes back to this root. For example, the relation of the temporal to the eternal ruler, of the State to the Church, is applied to the relation between the devil and Christ. Between these two, one as ruler over our perishable bodies, the other as ruler over our immortal spirits, an eternal battle goes on. While we owe to the devil the "sensual coin" imprinted with his image and inscribed with his name, how much more do we owe to Christ our soul impressed with his image, cleansed by his blood, and inscribed with virtues and sacramental gifts.[7]

The "sensual coin" is not the body as such but a way of life, inordinately related to the sensual world which, being only a shadow of the real world, is not meant to be enjoyed but to be used.[8] Though the terminology is definitely dualistic, Biel makes an effort to reinterpret man's double obligation and the eternal battle between soul and body in such a way that when man fulfills his obligations to the world, he is already

---

adam. . . . In interiore homine agitur hec vetustas et novitas; patet ergo quod homo vetus et novus pertinet ad interiorem hominem acceptum pro parte intellectiva et non ad exteriorem acceptum pro parte sensitiva." *Ibid.*

[7] "Cum itaque terreno cesari debetur sensualis denarius sua imagine signatus et nomine circumscriptus . . . quanto magis reddendum est quod debemus deo animam scil., nostram sua imagine signatam, sanguine mundatam, virtutibus donis et sacramentorum characteribus circumscriptam," *S* I 102 A. According to the spiritual meaning of this literal interpretation — "Ideo dimissa iam literali intellectu aliquid spirituale hauriamus. . ." — the earthly Caesar becomes the devil: ". . . nomen regis quantum in nobis est delevimus et adversarii sui nomen inscripsimus quem nobis peccando dominum fecimus. . . ," *S* I 102 B. Cf. D.

[8] "Reddenda itaque sunt cesari que sunt eius scil., vicia cum suis occasionibus, mundi scil., oblectationibus et sic demum que sunt dei deo," *S* I 102 B.

giving God his due. The struggle against the sensual world is spiritual-ized and subsumed under the call to obedience; obedience becomes the pacifier of the intellective soul and the unifier of its higher and lower part. We have to become wholly what we are already in part, in order to live well-ordered lives, directed toward God.

2. Nominalistic epistemology

When we scrutinize further the distinction between higher and lower part of the intellective soul we find that the higher part is concerned with incomprehensible eternal objects, the lower part with temporal objects, about which judgments have to be made.[9]

When we understand the higher part in the strict sense, its field of operation is indeed limited to eternal objects. Understood in a larger sense, it refers to all considerations and judgments regarding temporal objects made according to eternal law; the lower part deals with created objects according to natural law.[10] The intellective soul of man is, there-fore, the meeting-ground of eternal law and of natural law, which are to be distinguished, not as is usually suggested as two different, unrelated, arbitrary sets of law, but according to their different fields of operation.

[9] "Circa hanc distinctionem queritur: Utrum portio anime superior et portio inferior sint potentie aliquo modo ab invicem distincte. . . Quantum ad primum notandum quod portio inferior et superior ponuntur tamen in parte anime rationali et non in parte sensitiva. De portione superiore manifestum est quia illa est dumtaxat respectu eternorum que sensu non sunt comprehensibilia. Sed de inferiori similiter patet (Aug. de Trinitate XII.2.3 et in principio libri) . . . Portionis inferioris est circa exteriora sive temporalia ex his que in memoria sunt verisimilia a veris dis-cernere ac de illis disponere et iudicare quod ad rationem pertinet. Unde non id quod commune habemus cum pecoribus sed rationale nostrum in sui operis dis-pertitur officium." II *Sent.* d 24 q 1 art. 1 nota 1.

[10] "Accipitur autem portio superior dupliciter. Uno modo large, alio modo stricte. Large accipitur ut non tamen extendit se ad obiecta eterna sed etiam ad temporalia in ordine ad eterna sive secundum regulam legis eterne. . . Sic portionis superioris est actiones circa creaturas per regulas eterne legis moderari et in deum ordinare. Dum in agendis temporalibus consulit divinam voluntatem. Et sic portio inferior est que obiectis creatis adheret secundum regulas morales et naturalis honestatis tamen sine relatione ad divinas. Sed accipiendo portionem superiorem stricte sic est ea vis rationis que circa eterna versatur tanquam circa obiecta et non circa temporalia. . . Portio inferior est que ad temporalia gubernanda deflectitur id est ratio versata circa temporalia tanquam circa obiecta. Unde cognitio qua cognosco deum trinum et unum et cetera ad deum pertinentia pertinet ad portionem supe-riorem. Cognitio vero qua cognosco creaturam pertinet ad portionem inferiorem." II *Sent.* d 24 q 1 art. 1 nota 1.

Boehner's discovery of what he terms Occam's *realistic conceptualism* vindicates Occam from the traditional charge of an identification of conceptualism and idealism; indeed, Boehner's argument applies equally well to Biel.[11] Biel shares with Occam a confidence in the undisturbed connection between objects and thought and thus between thought and reality.[12] Similarly, the concept that universals coincide with individual things or with common nature is rejected.[13]

But the rejection of the universals in no sense implies a dissimilarity between thought and object. The intellect forms a concept of the experienced object; if the act of cognition has been perfect, this concept will correspond perfectly to the object. This perfect act of cognition is the *notitia intuitiva*, which is experiential knowledge of an individual object; [14] far from severing thought and reality, Biel claims "consubstantiality" between these two.[15]

[11] Boehner, p. 156 ff. Furthermore Léon Baudry calls attention to a text which seems to underscore the precision of intuitive knowledge: "Intuitiva est propria cognitio singularis non propter maiorem assimilationem uni quam alteri, sed quia naturaliter causatur ab uno et non ab alio, nec potest ab alio causari." Occam, *Quodl.* 1 q 13, in *Lexique philosophique de Guillaume d'Ockam: Etude des notions fondamentales* (Paris, 1958), p. 284. Cf. Biel, I *Sent.* d 3 q 5–6 art. 2 E.

[12] "Noticia intuitiva est noticia incomplexa termini vel terminorum rei vel rerum virtute cuius potest evidenter cognosci aliqua veritas contingens, maxime de presenti ut quod res est vel non est, quod est hic vel ibi. . . . Nam visio intuitiva dependet causaliter ab obiecto in fieri et esse. Hec noticia non est tantum sensibilium sed etiam intelligibilium. . ." Biel I *Sent.* Prol q 1 F. See also q 1 M. Cf. Occam, I *Sent.* Prol q 1 HH. On Occam's discussion of induction, see Erich Hochstetter, *Studien zur Metaphysik und Erkenntnislehre Wilhelms von Ockham* (Berlin and Leipzig 1927), p. 160 ff. and Ernest A. Moody, *The Logic of William of Ockham* (New York, 1935), p. 291 f.

[13] "Nulla res extra animam nec per se nec per aliquod additum reale vel rationis nec qualitercunque consideretur vel intelligatur, est universalis nisi forte signa ad placitum instituta que sunt res singulares et dicuntur universalia significatione vel predicatione; probatur quia propter considerationem intellectus res non mutatur . . . unde universale non est in re, nec realiter nec subiective nec est pars singularis respectu cuius est universale, non plus quam vox est pars sui signati." I *Sent.* d 2 q 7 art. 1 B. Cf. Occam, I *Sent.* d 2 q 7 art. 1 S and Gregory, I *Sent.* d 3 q 3 art. 2 [fol. 47 F/G].

[14] "Experimur in nostro intellectu quandam vim fictivam rei cognite per quam in seipso format imaginem, tanto rei cognite similiorem quanto ipsam perfectius cognoscit. Unde si intuitive et perfecte cognosceret imaginem simillimam fingeret que imago manet in intellectu," S II 34 C. Cf. S II 39 D; 41 B and F; *Lect.* 31 H and P.

[15] "Etsi haberet [intellectus] vim productivam produceret rem simillimam imo consubstantialem rei cognite ab ea in nullo differentem nisi quod hec ab illa esset producta," S II 34 C.

3. The theology of the *viator*

The relevance of this theory of knowledge for theology becomes apparent when we realize that it is impossible for the *viator* to have a perfect knowledge of God since it is clearly impossible to have intuitive knowledge of God.

Not even in paradise was it possible for man to have immediate knowledge of God; man in the state of innocence knew God only as in a mirror. For the *viator* this mirror has been obscured by sin so that he can only see God "per speculum in enigmate." [16] Immediate and perfect knowledge of God is possible only for the beatified and for those who have been given the grace of beatific vision or another form of direct revelation.

The image that man can form of God is therefore far from perfect. How, then, can man come to an adequate knowledge of God, apart from beatific vision or special revelation? For the average *viator* there are two answers to this question: by faith and by contemplation. These two avenues of knowledge correspond to two forms of God's presence. The first, to God's presence in others: God has made himself known by revelation and inspiration to some, on whose authority we believe. The second, to the presence of God in the effects of his own acts of creation. This second avenue excels insofar as one senses more clearly the presence of God's grace and insofar as one learns better how to perceive God through his creatures.[17]

[16] ". . . Cognitio status innocentie media est inter cognitionem status glorie et status presentis miserie. Sicut et locus paradisi medius est inter hanc miserie vallem et patriam celestem. . . Unde in solo statu glorie videbitur deus immediate et in sua substantia sicuti est . . . ita quod ibi nulla sit obscuritas. In statu innocentie et nature lapse videtur deus mediante speculo sed differenter quia in statu innocentie videbatur deus per speculum clarum. Nulla enim erat in anima peccati nebula. In statu vero miserie videtur per speculum obscuratum per peccatum primi hominis et ideo nunc videtur per speculum in enigmate. . ." II *Sent.* d 23 q 1 art. 3 dub. 2.

[17] "Unde quadruplex ponitur modus cognoscendi deum scl. per fidem, per contemplationem, per apparitionem et per apertam visionem. . . Primum est gratie communis. Secundum gratie excellentis. Tertium gratie spiritualis. Quartum glorie consummantis et illi modi distinguuntur secundum diversum modum divine presentie. Presentie dico secundum quod presens est in ratione obiecti. . . Nam in primo presens est deus aliis quibus se revelavit quorum auctoritati credimus. Quod enim credo deum esse trinum et unum, hoc credo dei filio qui hoc enarravit et predicavit et spiritus sanctus [sic] qui hoc patribus inspiravit. . . In secundo modo est presens in effectu proprio. Qui modus tanto est eminentior quanto effectum divine gratie

Before we ask why it is so vital to know God and what exactly man can know by the contemplation of God's creation, we have to remind ourselves that whatever opportunities there may be to know something of God, he escapes our intuitive cognition and can therefore not be comprehended, nor can what is understood be adequately formulated.[18] The beatified themselves do not know God in his inner being, in the complete way in which God knows himself. The saints are beatified by participation in God's beatitude, not by a comprehension of his beatitude. Even in heaven the infinite distance between creator and creature is not bridged.[19]

4. Voluntarism and rationalism

The question of the adequate or at least sufficient knowledge of God is one of the main themes of Biel's theology. Time and again, in the *Sentences* commentary, in his lectures on the Mass, and in his sermons, he returns to what must have been for him an extremely vital issue. We must ask, what is the reason for this particular emphasis? Why this stress on cognition when he is known to adhere to the primacy of the will and traditionally has been classified as a voluntarist? [20]

If terms such as voluntarism or rationalism were at all helpful, we should not hesitate to answer that Biel is evidently a rationalist for whom cognition and not volition is the first activity of the soul.[21] But at the same

---

magis sentit in se homo; vel etiam quanto melius scit considerare deum in exterioribus creaturis. In tertio est presens in signo proprio, sicut apparuit abrae. . . In quarto est presens in seipso . . . que visio merces est omnium meritorum." II *Sent.* d 23 q 1 art. 3 dub. 2 G.

[18] "Quamvis autem de deo nihil digne dici nec intellectu comprehendi nec sicut est videri possit, imperfecte tamen et ex parte de illo cogitamus et loquimur secundum nostram intelligentie ac vocis paupertatem," *S* II 6 G.

[19] ". . . solus deus seipso essentialiter est beatus, seque totum et infinitum visione et fruitione eque infinita plenissime ac integre comprehendit. Reliqui autem in solo deo beatificantur: participando non comprehendendo quoniam creatorem infinitum creatura finita comprehendere nequit." *S* I 31 D.

[20] See Nikolaus Espenberger, *Grund und Gewissheit des übernatürlichen Glaubens in der Hoch- und Spätscholastik* (Paderborn, 1915), p. 160 ff.; Hermelink, *Geschichte der Theologischen Fakultät*, p. 113; Feckes, *Die Rechtfertigungslehre des Gabriel Biel*, p. 11.

[21] Reinhold Seeberg has taken note of this problem: "Der Glaube ist bei diesen Theologen wie schon bei Duns Scotus immer mehr als eine intellektuelle Funktion erklärt worden . . . ," Seeberg *DG*, III, 783.

time, while stressing that the will is blind without the guidance of the intellect, he describes the intellect itself as absolutely inadequate to comprehend God and his actions.[22]

We are confronted here with a double limitation of man. First, in isolation the will as such is powerless and mutable; it needs the counsel of proper cognition. Yet in the second place, proper cognition is impossible, as God transcends man's intelligence. The most vivid example of this limitation comes from Biel's typological interpretation of the events surrounding Zacharias and Elizabeth in connection with the birth of John the Baptist. He interprets Zacharias as reason and Elizabeth as will, leading to a series of conclusions: the will must be fertilized by the intellect and is unable without the intellect to produce any act. But even when will and reason cooperate, man is unable to transcend the limits of nature. Because his intellect is limited to the world of the flesh, his acts can never be deserving of life eternal.[23]

Those who contend that Biel is a voluntarist may have in mind that according to him the human will is as free as — *mutatis mutandis* — the will of God. And indeed the relation of man's and God's will is constructed in a way similar to the relation of the *potentia absoluta* and *ordinata*: God has *freely decided* — *misericordia* — to endow the human will with freedom and has for this reason freely *committed* — *iustitia* — himself to cooperate with any movement of the created will.[24] But while the will is free over against God and undetermined, it is not free in the sense that it is independent from the intellect which has to provide the

---

[22] "Hec fidei confessio quia humanam transcendit intelligentiam dominus ipse ostendit cum dixit Petro: 'Caro et sanguis non revelavit tibi, sed pater meus qui in celis est' [Matt. 16:17]," *S* IV 21 C.

[23] ". . . voluntas in nullum actum potest nisi fecundetur ab intellectu neque enim aliquid amatur, nisi cognitum. . . Hec mulier sterilis est ex se quoniam nullum vitale opus, id est meritorium ex suis naturalibus parturire potest. . . Et licet frequenter coniungantur intellectus et voluntas non tamen sequitur fructus; quoniam intellectus curiosis, ista voluptuosis intendit, ex quibus nullus fructus vite sed corruptionis nascitur, quoniam qui seminat in carne sua, de carne metet corruptionem." *S* IV 18 H.

[24] ". . . utraque voluntas et divina et creata libere determinat seipsam et neutra necessario aliam ita quod ad alterius determinationem necessitaretur ad agendum; sed voluntas creata libere producit actum suum et divina libere coagit. Libere enim deus se determinat producendo voluntatem liberam sibi coagere ad producendum quemcunque actum interiorem elicitum." II *Sent.* d 37 q 1 art. 1 F.

will with an object.[25] The primacy of the intellect is as unquestionable as the freedom of the will in choosing what the intellect presents.[26]

5. *Synderesis* and conscience

In this context we have to deal with Biel's concept of the *synderesis* as the *scintilla conscientie*, which as a natural consequence of what has been said is an inherent quality of the intellect and not of the will. This *synderesis* is, of course, an important aspect of Biel's anthropology and stands for man's natural inclination to do good and refrain from evil.

Bonaventura [27] taught that the *synderesis* was located in the will and the conscience in the intellect, and that therefore the conscience was moved by the *synderesis*.[28] According to Thomas, however, the *synderesis* was a *habitus* belonging only to the intellect.[29] Duns Scotus followed Thomas in this respect and identified the *synderesis* with the practical reason; the conscience then applied the innate practical principles to particular situations.[30]

Biel feels that the *synderesis* cannot be a habit, as it is an inalienable possession of man, whereas neither an act nor a habit has to be always present in man. He agrees with Thomas and Scotus in that the *synderesis* cannot refer to a disposition of the will. The *synderesis* inclines necessarily to the right action and thus would interfere with the freedom of the will.[31]

Conscience is the herald of the laws contained in Scripture, and the

[25] "Requirit enim cognitionem obiecti volibilis sine quo non potest velle . . . ," *ibid.*

[26] "In processu autem nostro ad operandum concurrit potentia intellectiva et voluntas: intellectus ut ostendens operandum et dictans scil. illud quo fieri ostensum est ad operandum voluntas ut imperans et eligens," II *Sent.* d 39 q 1 art. 1 nota 3 D.

[27] Bernhard Rosenmöller, *Religiöse Erkenntnis nach Bonaventura* (Münster i. W., 1925), p. 45 ff. For a discussion of the medieval history of the meaning of *conscientia* see Emanuel Hirsch, *Lutherstudien* (Gütersloh, 1954), I, 11 ff.

[28] II *Sent.* d 39 art. 1 q 2.

[29] Aquinas, *De veritate* q 17 art. 1; *ST* I q 79 art. 13.

[30] Minges, *Ioannes Duns Scoti* I, 332 f.; Duns Scotus, *Par.* II d 39 q 2 nota 5.

[31] "Sinderesis que est scintilla conscientie non est actus vel habitus in voluntate; probatur quia sinderesis est aliquid necessario dirigens saltem in universali ad operationem iustam et rectam, sed nihil tale pertinet ad voluntatem," II *Sent.* d 39 q 1 art. 2 concl. 1. For the relation of Scotus and Biel it is noteworthy that Biel rejects implicitly such a formulation since "illud dictamen rationis imponit onus voluntati," Biel, II *Sent.* d 39 q 2 nota 3.

voice of conscience binds, therefore, with the authority of those laws.[32] Through this close interrelation of natural and written law, man should be able to achieve by "doing what is in him" a virtuous life. His free will is presented with advice derived from innate, indestructible moral principles. Against this background we can understand what proves to be the final result of Biel's anthropological considerations: *cognitio est radix et fundamentum omnium virtutum.*[33]

6. The image of God

There are two more aspects to the natural knowledge of God. While the *synderesis* as a vestige of man's pure nature enables him to obey natural law and thus to execute the will of God within the limits of his nature, creation in general and man as the crown of creation in particular point to a dimension beyond themselves. The whole creation surrounding man, in its double aspect of gift and punishment, witnesses to the existence of a source of all good and a punisher of all sins. Though less clearly than in Scripture, God has definitely revealed himself in his creation.[34] But man himself is a far more rewarding object of analysis, as the image of God is imprinted in the soul of man. We must investigate our souls to find the image of the Trinity in order to come to knowledge of God.[35]

Biel offers two different interpretations of the *imago dei.* According to the first, the three aspects of the human soul, intellect, will, and memory reflect the three Persons of the Trinity. They are, however, a highly im-

---

[32] "Continet autem lex in scripturis nobis tradita precepta, prohibitiones, consilia . . . conscientia vero est quasi preco legis. Ostendit enim nobis legis dictamina dictans assentive hec vel illa esse legis precepta, prohibitiones vel consilia. . ." II *Sent.* d 39 q 1 art. 3 dub. 2.

[33] *S* II 39 C. Cf. the traditional medieval and tridentine formulation: "fides radix et fundamentum omnis iustificationis," Cap. 8, Sessio VI, Trent (Denz. 801).

[34] "Revelavit siquidem seipsum nobis in creatura sed obscurius. Revelavit etiam se nobis clarius in scriptura." *S* II 43 F. "Omnes enim circa nos creature pro quanto in eis relucet divinum vestigium: beneficia quoque et flagella — nos ad deum dirigunt sicut ad principium omnis boni et iustum peccatorum ultorem." *S* III 17 G (pars secunda).

[35] "Inter ea autem que facta sunt nihil ita ducit in cognitionem dei sicut homo. Quippe cum in ceteris apparet vestigium trinitatis, in homine etiam imago eius impressa est. . . Ideo in spiritu seu anima nostra querenda est imago trinitatis ut per eam venire possimus in noticiam eius." *S* II 34 B. For the distinction between *vestigium* and *imago,* cf. I *Sent.* d 3 q 9 art. 1 nota 4.

perfect reflection. God knows, but he knows everything at once; God wills, but with an undisturbable immutability. Most basic is the epistemological difference: while God grasps immediately and without deliberation the essence of things, man does not go further than forming *phantasmata*, images of the objects under consideration.[36]

Another interpretation is that the image of God is not to be found in the acts of cognition, volition, and memory themselves; but through these acts we are capable of communicating with God before we participate in his being. The *imago dei* conceived in this way shows a closer resemblance to and becomes a broader form of that other vestige of God, the *synderesis*, which is limited to just one of the three aspects of man.[37]

Man can prove the existence of God more convincingly as the sustainer than as the creator of this world; to this can be added the natural knowledge of such attributes of God as goodness, wisdom, and intelligence.[38] But all this natural knowledge does not add up to more than the knowledge that there is a God.[39] All this natural knowledge is limited and confused and insufficient for man's salvation. To attain life eternal, one has to love God; to love God, one has to know God. Though the vestiges of God in creation and the image of God in man point beyond themselves, they are far from offering adequate knowledge.[40]

To summarize thus far: our investigation of Biel's anthropology indicates that he views *the tragedy of man as centered in a lack of knowledge which is not primarily explained as a result of his fall and loss of*

---

[36] *S* II 39 D and G, 40 C, 41 C and E; I *Sent.* d 3 q 9–10.

[37] ". . . non tamen per hoc quod anima meminit et vult est imago dei; sed quia per hec capax est dei, numismatis dei, intelligere deum, amare deum. Alias in brutis esset imago dei. Et quia secundum naturam capax est in natura est imago etiam antequam particeps est dei. . . Et illa deleri non potest." *S* I 95 E; *S* II 39 G.

[38] I *Sent.* d 2 q 10 art. 2 concl. 1; I *Sent.* d 3 q 2 art. 2 concl. 2–3; III *Sent.* d 24 q 1 art. 1 nota 3; *S* II 43 D–E.

[39] ". . . quid aliud scimus nisi quod nobis unus est deus," *S* II 43 E. This seems to be one of the few examples where a sermon quotation does contradict a — more subtle — statement in the *Sententiae*. Cf. I *Sent.* d 2 q 10 art. 2 concl. 2: "Tantum unum ens est simpliciter primum. Probatur. . ." Also concl. 3: "Tantum unum esse deum est creditum et non demonstratum ratione naturali nobis in via possibili. . ." Cf. *Lect.* 71 H.

[40] "Amor autem et desiderium presupponit cognitionem . . . ," *S* I 31 B. "Hec autem cognitio confusa quam ex creaturis per naturalem cognoscendi virtutem assequi valemus ad salutem nostram non sufficit . . . ," *S* II 41 D.

67

original justice, but as a natural consequence of his status as creature. By not excluding but by coordinating philosophical with theological anthropology, Biel's anti-Manichean trend is emphasized. All the distinguishable parts in man, the stratification of the higher and lower intellect plus the sensitive soul, form one man and are not more than names for different actions: "in homine realiter non distinguuntur licet actus differant." [41] In mortal sin the whole man, the higher level included, is averted from God and by the same token in the state of grace the whole man is called *homo novus.*[42]

Nevertheless we meet in Biel's anthropology a dangerous approximation of fall and creation. Though the unbridgeable gulf between creator and creation is not symbolized in a neo-Platonic sense by a sinful, sensual body which hinders the mind in its efforts to reach God, *it is nevertheless man's created condition as revealed in his epistemological limitations that frustrates his efforts to know God.*

The only way out of the tragic situation in which man thus finds himself is faith: ". . . quod investigari non potest nec investigatum eloqui, credi potest et creditum predicari." [43] Since the total (!) cause of the irreligiosity of Christians is lack of knowledge, faith promises not only to lead man out of his tragic epistemological situation, but also out of his impious moral situation.[44]

II. Faith: Acquired and Infused

1. Ecclesiastical positivism?

It has often been said that ecclesiastical positivism is the hallmark of late medieval nominalism.[45] Where the theory of knowledge is constructed in such a way that only the direct experience of individual objects

[41] II *Sent.* d 23 q 1 art. 1 nota 1.

[42] *Ibid.*, art. 3 dub. 2. "Innovat ergo ut simus filii regni, heredes testamenti, homines novi," *S* IV 36 C.

[43] *S* II 41 A.

[44] "Tota causa irreligiositatis christiani populi hec est: quia deum quem ore fatentur aut ignorant aut non cogitant. Et e diverso totius religionis causa est dei fidelis cognitio et frequens meditatio." *S* II 39 G.

[45] See Seeberg *DG*, III, 724: "Die Nominalisten haben der Reformation durch die alleinige Autorität der Schrift vorgearbeitet, aber sie haben zugleich durch ihren kirchlichen Positivismus ein gewaltiges Bollwerk wider sie aufgebaut. . ."

can lead to certain, evident knowledge of contingent things, faith by necessity must become a reliance on some form of authority, ecclesiastical, biblical or otherwise. In the religious realm neither experimental, intuitive knowledge nor syllogistic abstraction — the only possibilities of acquiring natural knowledge — are applicable. The intellect, it is alleged, must to some extent be sacrificed and replaced by a self-effacing confidence in the reliability of data which escape the critical test of experience and abstraction.

This is by no means a sudden development in the history of Christian thought; in fact, one of the main themes in this history is the constant tension between *ratio* and *auctoritas*. The drama around Bernard of Clairvaux and Abelard may serve as an example of the fact that a critical attitude toward a rationalistic emphasis can very well go hand in hand with a stress on the authority of the Church. This phenomenon, whether caused by mystical or epistemological motives — or both at once — became especially prominent in the old and new Franciscan school — from Alexander of Hales to William of Occam.[46] Though Biel was never a mendicant friar, in many respects he can be regarded as belonging to the Franciscan sphere of influence. Positivism, however, is a rather vague term easily confused or identified with blind faith, so Biel's concept of faith must be analyzed carefully before we can establish which of the many possible positions between the two extremes, *ratio* and *auctoritas*, is his.

As is usual in medieval theology, Biel understands faith in a twofold way: *fides quae* refers to the object of faith; *fides qua* refers either to the act or habit of faith. As act, it is the *assensus* or agreement with a particular revealed truth; as habit, it is either the result of repetition of these acts or of direct infusion by God.[47] If we now ask further how this act of faith comes about, we note two things: (1) the double character of faith as movement of intellect and will; (2) a new law in the realm of faith: to the rule *nihil amatur nisi cognitum* is added *nullus credit nisi volens*.

[46] Scheel points this out, *Martin Luther: Vom Katholizismus zur Reformation* vol. II, 3 & 4 ed. (Tübingen, 1930), p. 173.
[47] ". . . nam fides aliquando accipitur pro actu, quandoque pro habitu, quandoque pro obiecto. Pro actu est assensus veritatis revelate. Pro habitu est habitus ex huiusmodi assensibus frequentatis acquisitus, vel immediate a deo infusus inclinans intellectum ad assentiendum veritatibus revelatis. Pro obiecto est veritas credita aut res per ipsum significata." III *Sent.* d 23 q 2 art. 1 nota 1 A.

Divine authority instead of natural experiential evidence provides the basis for religious cognition. And in as far as the object of faith is truth, by whatever means its validity may have been established, so far faith is an act of the intellect. But the object of faith is not only the truth but also the good, and this belongs to the realm of the will, which always by nature chooses the best thing offered to it.

It is still true that nothing can be loved unless it be known; but in the case of religious knowledge this intellectual act is initiated by the will, which drives the intellect to a new field of knowledge and thus provides the intellect with a new basis for cognition.[48] In view of this understanding of faith, therefore, we can note already that the Gabrielistic concept of faith can hardly be qualified as blind faith.

2. Revelation as information and exhortation

With this double aspect of faith corresponds a double aspect of God's revelation: information and exhortation can be alternately emphasized. On the one hand God provides man throughout the course of the history of salvation, in the Old and the New Testament, with sufficient information to overcome the difficulties arising out of the fact that the Christian creed in principle exceeds the capacities of the intellect.[49] On the other hand, God's self-humiliation in his Son excites our will to all good and fills us with love; where the intellect still hesitates, the will grasps what it acknowledges as its highest good. But again, this highest good has to be presented by the intellect.[50]

[48] "Actus autem fidei est credere qui est actus intellectus vero assentientis producens ex voluntatis imperio quia nullus credit nisi volens. . . Et ideo actus qui est credere non solum habet pro obiecto verum quod est obiectum intellectus sed etiam finem vel bonum quod est obiectum voluntatis. . . Obiectum enim fidei est veritas non visa id est non evidens cui firmiter adheret fides non ex rei evidentia sed ex auctoritate divina. Obiectum voluntatis in verbo 'rerum sperandarum'. . . Per hoc quod dicitur 'non apparentium' distinguitur a scientia et intellectu et generaliter a non evidenti per quam fit aliquid apparens et quodammodo visibile intellectui." III *Sent.* d 23 q 2 art. 1 nota 1 C.

[49] "Credenda autem acumen nostre intelligentie naturalis excedunt propter quod cum difficultate intellectus eis assentit; ideo credendorum figuras obumbratas in factis et in verbis prorogavit quatinus per hec intellectus suaviter assuesceret et manuduceretur ad fidem firmam mirabilium operum dei suam facultatem excellentium," *S* I 76 A.

[50] "Cum autem voluntas sit de se potentia ceca, bonitatem obiecti vel maliciam

But we must note that the relation of reason and authority is not constant; some aspects of the Christian creed require more action from the will than others. In the case of the doctrine of transubstantiation, Biel confesses that the officially approved understanding of the consecration of the bread and wine is — as far as natural reason is concerned — one of the most improbable interpretations.[51] Obedience, and thus action of will, is the only possible reaction to a presentation of this doctrine.

Faith is a much more reliable form of knowledge than so-called scientific knowledge can be since it has as its object God, who is more infallible than any human object or inquiry ever could be.[52]

3. Fides ex auditu

Acquired faith, that is faith on the authority of the Scripture, Church, tradition, or preacher, is necessary to believe the articles of the Christian creed. This faith is not a product of man's own mind but comes from the outside, *ex auditu.* This outside authority is nevertheless not absolutely heteronomous, as it finds a natural disposition in man to confide in it. The proposition "God is true" is naturally known by man and can therefore be applied to any lower authority derived from God.[53]

---

non apprehendit nisi ostendatur per intellectum qui est tanquam consiliarius voluntatis. . . Unde patet quod actionis meritorie et peccati principium est in intellectu et consummatio in voluntate" (S I 101 D). "Huius autem amoris ex sola essentiali et intrinseca dei bonitate procedentis diligens meditatio excitat in nobis dilectionem amicicie qua eum propter seipsum-quia bonum est-diligimus . . . ," S II 36 G. Cf. S I 102 D and F.

[51] ". . . debetque ad eum [transsubstantiationem] suscipiendum captivari cuiuslibet intellectus fidelis in obsequium fidei christi" (*Lect.* 41 M). "Oportet igitur ab apparentiis naturalibus animum revocare et veritati matris ecclesie fideliter adherere et a fide non adulterari sequendo nostram intelligentiam quam experimur in multis deficere et errare. . . Fides enim tunc proficit nobis ad salutem quando innititur veritati in christo fundate non vanitati et naturalis cognitionis infirmitati." *Lect.* 41 N.

[52] "Non ergo vincitur certitudo fidei certitudine scientie humanitus acquisite; immo eam vincit pro quanto veritas prima, que deus est, cui fides innititur, infallibilior est quacunque inquisitione humana," III *Sent.* d 23 q 2 art. 1 D.

[53] "Fides acquisita ad credendum fidei articulos est necessaria; probatur . . . 'fides ex auditu est'. . . [Rom. 10:17] . . . que non possunt intelligi de fide infusa que non est ex auditu predicationis sed immediate creata a deo. . . Preterea homo non dubitat de veritate dei quia illud naturaliter cuilibet insertum est 'deum esse veracem.' Nec dubitavit de approbatione ecclesie que approbat dicta et scripta virorum

This acquired faith seems to be Biel's real and main concept of faith; out of the mere space allocated to it one would be inclined to read Biel's predilection. As always when there is an option between a naturally acquired or an infused habit, one senses his suspicion of all heteronomy, of all that may imperil the freedom of the will. Besides acquired faith, there is indeed another form, infused faith, but this does not in any way qualify anything that has been said. It cannot be proved to be necessary in any respect;[54] it is nevertheless believed to be necessary, because the Scriptures are quite unambiguous in their testimony that faith is a gift of God. Probably with these considerations in mind Wilhelm Link stated that the *fides acquisita* for Biel is the higher and genuine form of faith.[55]

In response to this common interpretation, we must first take into account the important point that while infused faith is one and undivided, inclining man to believe all articles at once, acquired faith refers to every single article separately: *"quot articula tot fides acquisite."*[56] There is therefore not one structure of faith but many parts which can only be grasped as a whole through supernatural enlightenment.

Biel himself, when raising the issue, gives what may seem to be a rather half-hearted answer that infused faith is not a necessity, but it is helpful to strengthen and perfect that act of faith. Hägglund rightly concluded that this forms an exact parallel to Biel's understanding of the relation between grace and nature; grace is only granted if man does what is in him.[57]

---

veracium, ergo eis fide acquisita ex auditu firmiter adheret." III *Sent.* d 23 q 2 art. 2 concl. 1.

[54] "Non potest naturali ratione probari fidem infusam ad credendum fidei articulos esse necessariam; probatur conclusio quia ad credendum omnia credibilia sufficit fides acquisita ergo preter illam alia non est necessaria." The unbaptised heathen brought up under Christians can believe anything Christians believe "quia crederet suos instructores esse veraces. . . Preterea per solam fidem acquisitam potest credi singulus articulorum, ergo omnes; tenet consequentia quia sibi non repugnat: Omne enim verum vero consonat." III *Sent.* d 23 q 2 art. 2 concl. 2.

[55] "Diese Weise des Begegnens (audire) ist das Gegenteil von infusio. So erscheint nun plötzlich die fides acquisita als die höhere, eigentliche Glaubensweise, nicht die fides infusa," Wilhelm Link, *Das Ringen Luthers um die Freiheit der Theologie von der Philosophie* (Munich, 1955), p. 302.

[56] III *Sent.* d 23 q 2 art. 2 concl. 5.

[57] ". . . non tamen posset [fides acquisita] producere actum ita perfectum et intensum ac firmum sine infusa sicut cum infusa," III *Sent.* d 23 q 2 art. 1 H *in fine.* Cf. Hägglund, p. 74 f.

We would underestimate Biel's concept of faith, however — and construct a too easy contrast with its Thomistic or Lutheran parallel concept — if we were to terminate our considerations at this point. Acquired faith is objective and not existential. The interpretations presented by Link, Feckes, and Hägglund, according to which acquired faith is more highly valued by Biel than infused faith, do not take into account that Biel states explicitly: acquired faith "etiam in demonibus esse potest." [58] Primarily due to their familiarity (!) with Holy Scripture, the demons have acquired an historical faith to which St. Paul could not possibly have been referring when he wrote, *iustus ex fide vivit* [Rom. 1:17]. Acquired faith refers only to the objective factuality of God's revealing acts in history and does not connote its redeeming impact on mankind. To be fair to Biel we must add that right and proper faith goes far beyond this "demon's faith." Real faith holds not only the factuality of God's historical deeds but implies at the same time that God's acts are saving acts for him who believes, are *pro nobis*. In another context we will probe into the extent to which this existential understanding of faith is really operative in Biel's theology; at this point it is important to note that the emphasis on this "for us" is marked and all-pervasive.[59] This "for us" excludes the demons, for they are aware of their state of damnation. Right faith does, therefore, presuppose infused faith, which is by no means as accidental as can be assumed from the *Collectorium* treatment.

Indeed, the infusion of faith is "only" necessary on grounds of God's *potentia ordinata*. But as we saw before, this is by no means an arbitrary decision.[60] God's will is only a title for a particular operation which is as much based in God's wisdom as in God's will. God must have had an inner reason for requiring infused faith.[61]

[58] III *Sent.* d 23 q 2 art. 1 concl. 3.

[59] "Recta itaque fides est credere christum pro nobis incarnatum esse, verum deum, patris verbum et simpliciter ac summe ac infinite perfectum, ac per hoc in sua incarnatione summam misericordiam nobis exhibuisse," *S* I 8 B; *Lect.* 11 D, 20 L, and 71 L. See also Chapter Seven.

[60] Cf. Feckes, *Die Rechtfertigungslehre des Gabriel Biel*, p. 12: "Kein Regulativ findet der göttliche Wille am Intellekte . . ." and "Sie [die Freiheit Gottes] artet zur Willkür aus."

[61] ". . . quia fides infusa a deo anime donatur dubium nullum esse poterit quin fructuose et ad perfectionem et utilitatem hominis infundatur. Non enim potest a divina bonitate procedere aliquod vanum et inutile, sicut nec a divina essentia aliquod inordinatum." III *Sent.* d 23 q 2 art. 3 dub. 1.

73

The fact that it is impossible to prove this necessity with natural reason is more revealing for the capacities of human reason than for the relevance of the infusion of faith. Though Biel's *fides acquisita* is an *assensus* to historic facts, equally available to demons, we are now sufficiently warned that his concept of faith is richer than the flat objectivity of his definition of acquired faith would suggest. Not acquired faith, but faith as a gift of God, usually sacramentally infused, transforms intellectual faith into living faith. It does this for Biel *concomitanter* since the infusion of sanctifying grace strengthens the *fides acquisita*. Its main purpose is to provide the sinner who does his very best with the supernatural habits of hope and love.

4. Biblical theology

The statement that there are as many forms of acquired faith, that is, as many acts of assent, as there are articles of belief [62] leads to an important rule for Biel's biblical theology.[63] Within the circle of faith where the infallible authority of Scripture is accepted as derived from God, one assents immediately to all and everything contained therein, but in such a way that every single point has to be believed with a new act of faith. There is no such thing as an inherent rational structure which can enable the systematic theologian to jump from one *locus*, accepted by faith, to another *locus* by way of sheer logical demonstration, without faith being involved.

As the authority of the Bible does not arise from its own content but is derived from a higher authority, there is no incentive for biblical criticism, nor any possibility to be selective in one's acceptance of the biblical record. The beginning of faith is, therefore, assent to the veracity of the Christian faith, that is, assent to the Bible in its entirety.

The dogmatic structure that is to be erected from this biblical foundation simply cannot take its point of departure in one point of revealed truth as expressed in a certain passage to prove another point syllogistically: the structure of biblical theology is never higher than the single step

[62] III *Sent.* d 23 q 2 art. 2 concl. 5: "Diversorum articulorum diverse sunt fides acquisite. . ."

[63] ". . . legens bibliam — si est fidelis — immediate assentit omnibus et singulis ibi traditis quia credit omnia revelata a deo, nec uni plus quam alteri, nec uni propter alterum," III *Sent.* d 24 q 1 art. 2 concl. 5.

from the particular passage to its doctrinal meaning. This does not exclude, of course, the laudable procedure of comparing Scripture with Scripture in order to clarify an obscure passage — but this should be restricted to one and the same doctrinal issue.[64]

5. The inner core of faith

Biel is extremely careful in defining the possibility of apologetics. In correspondence with the three levels of "theological density" in Scripture, there are three levels of apologetics. (1) The natural-philosophical and moral elements in the Bible make it possible for those who study the Scriptures to account for the faith that is in them (I Peter 3:15), and these scientific elements can be understood and accepted by non-Christians who do not believe in the infallibility of the Bible. (2) The study of the Bible can also produce some results which do not come forth from other fields of research; these results enable the *maiores*, in this case the doctors of Scripture, to defend the articles of faith to which they refer.[65] (3) The top level, however, is formed by *pure credibilia*, the inner core of faith; here even the faithful are unable to acquire evident knowledge. To explain these articles of faith, one has always to fall back on other articles of faith; for example, the proposition *deus est incarnabilis* can only be known if one knows in fact that God was incarnated in Jesus Christ. These points of pure faith fall, therefore, under the rule that a conclusion can never be more evident than its premise.[66]

We have here introduced distinctions which are not made explicit anywhere in Biel's *oeuvre*. As the sources obviously warrant this tripartition of the realm of faith, we shall find that these hitherto unnoted distinctions deeply affect the discussion of the *ratio fidei*, apologetics, and positivism in late medieval nominalism.

---

[64] III *Sent.* d 24 q 1 art. 2 concl. 6. For the joint rejection by Occam, Gregory of Rimini, and d'Ailly of the defense of theology as a science by Pierre d'Auriole see Chapter Seven, note 35; for the position of Holcot see Chapter Seven, section III.

[65] ". . . etiam quasdam que ad nullas naturales scientias pertinent. Per quas etiam credita possunt ab impugnatoribus defendere et contraria dissolvere." III *Sent.* d 24 q 1 art. 2 concl. 6.

[66] ". . . respectu pure credibilium etiam fideles scientiam acquirere non possunt quia quantumcunque illa probare nituntur semper assumunt aliqua credita . . . ," III *Sent.* d 24 q 1 art. 2 concl. 6 H.

When one complains [67] that there is a rationalistic aspect to nominalism which can lead to a transgression of St. Augustine's rule that faith has to precede a rational clarification, we should be clear about the fact that this objection is only applicable to the nominalist treatment of the first two levels. On the first level of scientific data, which is in some sense verifiable, the believer and unbeliever are in exactly the same, position. Here, indeed there is no requirement of faith; both can come to the same conclusions — apart from faith — on strictly secular grounds. This first level guarantees the scientific character of the theological prolegomena. Here, surely, *credo ut intelligam* does not apply.[68]

On the second level, theological conclusions are drawn which enable the apologists to defend the Christian faith. Here Biel has in mind such statements as "God exists." They still belong to the theological prolegomena in a broader sense. And again, faith is not required, for this statement can be defended by reason against the unbeliever. On the third level, however, the Augustinian-Anselmian rule of *credo ut intelligam* is applicable in its full force. If the revealed facts could convince the intellect, knowledge and not faith would be the result.[69] At the same time it is important to realize that Biel excludes from the inner core of faith only evident knowledge; this leaves still open the possibility of a *ratio fidei*, be it rigorous or not.[70]

If we wish to establish the exact character of the *ratio fidei* on this third level, we must look for additional evidence. Fortunately Biel offers elsewhere another tripartition of theology, this time in the context not

[67] See Hägglund, p. 79.

[68] ". . . quecunque per theologicum studium acquirere potest fidelis etiam potest hereticus aut infidelis preter fidem eiusque augmentum . . . ," III *Sent.* d 24 q 1 art. 2 concl. 6 H.

[69] "Neque enim ex intellectu credibilium fidem nanscisci oportet, sed ex fide intellectum," *Lect.* 41 N.

[70] It may well be that Luther is referring to this inner core of theology when he writes from Wittenberg, March 17, 1509, to his friend Braun: "Quod si statum meum nosse desideres, bene habeo Dei gratia nisi quod violentum est studium maxime philosophiae quam ego ab initio libentissime mutarim theologia, ea inquam theologia quae nucleum nucis et medullam tritici et medullam ossium scrutatur," (*WA B* I, 17, 40 ff.). Karl Holl suggested that this *medulla* refers to the doctrine of justification, *Gesammelte Aufsätze zur Kirchengeschichte*, vol. I; *Luther*, 6 ed. (Tübingen, 1948), p. 192. Vignaux suggests more general "science du salut," *Luther Commentateur des Sentences*, p. 5.

of apologetics but of systematics.[71] While what we have found to be the first level is not mentioned here, inasmuch as strictly natural knowledge does not belong to theology proper, the first level of systematic theology coincides with the second level of apologetics. This first category thus encompasses propositions like "God exists" and propositions concerning certain divine attributes. Though the simple man believes these propositions because they are revealed, Aristotle has demonstrated their truth, and doctors of theology know them scientifically.

This parallel tripartition becomes important and revealing in the fact that it introduces a distinction in the *pure credibilia*, the third level of apologetics. Within this inner core of faith two groups of articles are discerned: those that are evident for the *beati* who have intuitive knowledge of the divine reality, while not evident for the *viatores* who have to rely on faith and revelation as far as these articles are concerned; and those that are neither evident for the *viatores* nor for those who enjoy the beatific vision.[72]

The first of these two groups is exemplified by the proposition, "God is three and one." The *viator* has to believe this; the beatified have a *notitia intuitiva*, evident experimental knowledge, of this proposition. St. Paul after his rapture had such intuitive knowledge and could thus have evident knowledge of the Trinity, but this is exceptional; a real *viator* would not be capable of knowing this proposition.

The third group refers to articles regarding eschatology, the future acts of God, since these are unknown even to the beatified. The final resurrection and the last judgment, therefore, are placed in the darkest corner of the realm of faith.[73]

---

[71] "Quorundam credibilium potest esse scientia et apud viatores et apud beatos, quorundam tamen apud beatos, quorundam nec apud illos nec istos," III *Sent.* d 24 q 1 art. 2 concl. 1.

[72] ". . . sub fide non solum cadunt propositiones contingentes sed etiam veritates necessarie demonstrabiles. . . Unde omnes articuli fidei aliquid enunciantes de deo intrinsecum deo . . . sunt necessarie quarum multe sunt demonstrabiles . . . quedam tantum supernaturaliter cognoscibiles et dumtaxat in theologia beatorum demonstrabiles. Articuli vero qui aliquid enunciant de deo per respectum ad extra ad creaturam . . . contingentes sunt et per consequens indemonstrabiles et per consequens non sunt scibiles." III *Sent.* d 24 q 1 art. 1 nota 3.

[73] ". . . patet de veritatibus credibilibus contingentibus quarum non potest esse scientia secundum acceptationem scientie suppositam, licet possint evidenter cognosci ab habentibus noticias intuitivas extremorum," III *Sent.* d 24 q 1 art. 1 concl. 1 D.

From a comparison of these two possible classifications of the contents of theology, it appears that even within the circle of "pure faith" there is graduation in the relation of faith and reason, depending on the difference between the future and the past acts of God.

It is clear that what is not disclosed even to the beatified is utterly obscure and beyond the grasp of understanding for the *viator*. The other articles, however, which are known by the beatified, leave a possibility, even within the inner core of faith, for a *ratio fidei*, which stems out of the acceptation of the authority of those who have received a direct revelation, comparable with the beatific vision itself.

Apologetic Theology [*fideles — infideles*]	Systematic Theology [*viatores — beati*]
I. Scientific knowledge: *notitia evidens* for all *viatores*	
II. Metaphysics: accessible for believers and unbelievers, as e.g., the existence of God	I. Metaphysics: accessible for *viatores* and beatified, as e.g., the existence of God
III. *Pure credibilia*:	II. Trinity: past acts and aspects of God — evident for the beatified, non-evident for the *viator* III. Future acts of God: resurrection, last judgment — evident neither for the *viator* nor for the beatified

We may conclude, therefore, that for Biel there is a *deus absconditus* and a *deus revelatus*: God hidden and God revealed within the one circle of pure faith. This God, however, does not hide himself *in* his revelation. These two aspects of God refer to two different kinds of action: those in the past are revealed, those in the future are hidden.

6. The possibility of apologetics

Acquired faith is, as we saw on its third level, an act of reliance on a higher authority. As such it is *fiducia*, trust, which comes about by listening to a sermon and can be intensified by attending Mass.[74] To establish

[74] Bible study strengthens and deepens the *fides ex auditu*: ". . . inquirendo et exponendo scripturas nunc unam per aliam fidem prius acquisitam augmentant,

the exact character of the *ratio fidei* and to come to a proper assessment of the positivistic elements necessarily implied in this faith on authority, we have to analyze further the relation of faith and reason with regard to the inner core of faith.

On the one hand, it is clear that evident knowledge is ruled out; apart from other considerations, this kind of acquired faith would not answer the simplest definition of faith — it would be knowledge. On the other hand, faith is produced by a virtuous command of the will to the intellect, which by obeying this command accepts a particular article of faith. The will, however, in order to be virtuous, has in its turn to obey the dictates of reason. And so we seem to have gone full circle.[75]

Again, this dictate cannot be evident without changing faith into knowledge. If this dictate is not evident, the will then obeys its non-evident command because it spontaneously wants to do so. But, in that case, it would be virtuous, as it gives a just command to the intellect and thus still presupposes — by definition — a dictate of the right reason. This would lead to an infinite procession of cause and effect.

The solution Biel suggests for this dilemma is that the virtuous command of the will indeed presupposes a dictate of right reason but not an evident dictate of right reason. There is sufficient ground for the virtuousness of the will, if it obeys a probable dictate of right reason.[76]

It is possible, therefore, to say that this dictate, then, is the first step toward faith, awakened by semi-arguments. In this sense there is even for the inner core of faith a bridge between knowledge and faith. The usual judgment that late medieval nominalism represents a divorce between faith and reason must in view of this connection be qualified and reformulated in more careful phraseology.[77]

One can also say that the very first step is an illogical movement of the

dum quod in una parte scripture obscurius in alia parte clarius vel multiplicius affirmatum inveniunt." III *Sent.* d 24 q 1 art. 2 concl. 6.

[75] ". . . voluntas imperat virtuose intellectui quod assentiat articulis fidei, ergo virtuose imperando presupponit rationem rectam dictantem quod sic est imperandum. Alias non esset virtuosa." III *Sent.* d 24 q 1 art. 3 dub. 1 L.

[76] "Et quod illa volitio imperans presupponit rationem rectam dictantem quod sic est imperandum licet non presupponit dictamen evidens rationis sed dictamen probabile cui conformiter imperat. Sufficit enim quod ratio ita dictet assentiendo sic esse volendum." *Ibid.*

[77] See Robert Guelluy, *Philosophie et Théologie chez Guillaume d'Ockham* (Paris, 1947), p. 364: "Notons, d'autre part, qu'Ockham refuse de séparer le

will which does not conform to the dictate of reason and is therefore not virtuous, neither in the philosophical nor in the theological sense of the word.[78]

This very important point is not further elucidated. Biel may have had in mind, when suggesting an illogical movement of the will, that when faith is infused — which can take place at the same moment that faith is acquired — the will is to some extent forced to command the intellect to accept the Christian faith, according to his often-repeated statement that whereas a habit can hardly be laudable, an infused habit is even less compatible with the spontaneity of voluntary acts.[79]

However, this perhaps illogical movement of the will hardly fits Biel's assertion that he who will do what is in him, that is, use his right reason, may count on God's grace. Furthermore, there is no other evidence that Biel in general wanted to stress this illogical aspect of the acquisition of faith. On the contrary, in every other context when dealing with this issue, the initiative of the cognitive faculty is presupposed. In the description of the order of generation of the acquired virtues, faith is given priority with the argument that the will cannot love an unknown object: the act of cognition has to precede.[80]

At this point we should remind ourselves of the double character of the *pure credibilia*, and if we take this into consideration, the indicated inconsistencies seem to evaporate. Both possibilities are applicable: the first step of the dictate of reason on probable, non-evident considerations takes place with regard to that part of pure faith which is evident to the beatified. The illogical movement of the will, however, is the first step of faith with regard to those articles of faith which are absolutely obscure and even beyond the grasp of the *beatus*.

---

domaine de la théologie de celui de la métaphysique. . . Le venerabilis Inceptor ne semble . . . se donner pour but d'opposer la foi et la raison. . ." See further the clear and reliable survey of the bases of Occam's thought by F. van Steenberghen, "Ockham et la 'Via Moderna'," *Le mouvement doctrinal du IXe au XIVe siècle* in *Histoire de l'Église depuis les origines jusqu'à nos jours*, XIII (Paris, 1956), 449–465.

[78] Cf. Occam, III *Sent.* q 10 Q; and Holcot, I *Sent.* q 1 art. 3.

[79] "Secundo quia nullus habitus est de se laudabilis. Non acquisitus ergo nec infusus qui minus est in potestate voluntatis quam acquisitus." I *Sent.* d 17 q 2 A.

[80] "Unde manifestum est quod actus fidei prior est actu spei et charitatis quia non potest voluntas per actum suum tendere in obiectum nisi cognitum per intellectum," III *Sent.* d 26 q 1 art. 3 dub. 2.

Before we continue our pursuit of the grounds for the probability of articles belonging to the inner core of faith, however, we must stress again that except for the articles dealing with the last things we do *not* find *a sign of anything so extreme as the divorce of faith and reason.* Indeed, Biel is interested in safeguarding the peculiar character of faith and is keen not to have it subsumed under some form of higher reason. He thus makes every effort to distinguish between philosophy and theology by marking as clearly as possible where the one ends and the other begins. But there is no indication that this distinction is carried so far as to become a divorce between faith and reason. Such a divorce would upset his whole anthropology and understanding of God's cooperation with man. On the contrary, we have to ask ourselves whether Biel has not gone too far in stressing the part cognition plays in the act of faith. It seems to be true that, instead of being a voluntarist, Biel is a rationalist insofar as he holds that the distance between creator and creature as expressed in the distinction of the *potentia absoluta* and *potentia ordinata* can at least be partly bridged by reason.

7. The middle road between rationalism and positivism

Biel tries to find the middle ground between a rationalistic confusion and a positivistic divorce of faith and understanding. Parallel to, or better, as a consequence of his conception of the distinction between the two orders, *the rationality of faith is defended on grounds that God has disposed everything with wisdom; the difficulty of reaching this understanding, however, is based on the limitations of the human mind,* which is incapable of measuring the heights and depths, and especially the future course of God's decisions.

The truths of the inner core of faith can be attained either supernaturally through infusion of faith or naturally by trusting the teacher. Once within the circle of faith, it is possible for at least part of the articles of faith to offer certain probable considerations, *rationes probabiles,* which are enlisted in the service of an essentially negative apologetics; with the help of these opinions faith can be protected against false counter-arguments. In this way it can clear the ground for the right reason which can at least be convinced that there is no valid argument to withhold its dictate to the will.

This bridge formed by the probable right reason is therefore by no means a two-way but definitely a one-way connection between faith and reason. As far as the top level of the realm of faith is concerned, there is no way leading from human reason to faith, but only from faith by way of undemonstrable opinions to reason. Therefore an *infidelis* does not believe in a given aspect of revelation directly because he has gained understanding, but because he sees fit to trust the representative of authority exactly on grounds of semi-arguments; thus, he indirectly enters the circle of faith. This is, of course, even more true for those articles which refer to the contingent future acts of God, hidden even from those who enjoy the beatific vision.

For the believer, these probable reasons are not the ultimate and conclusive reason for accepting certain articles of faith. To give an example: in the case of a repetition of the sacrament of baptism, one has to accept the fact that this has no efficaciousness whatsoever for the remission of sins, simply because this would go counter to the way God has decided to act. Once such a decision of God is accepted, one is in a position to offer probable reasons or explanations for this state of affairs.[81]

For the unbeliever these probable semi-arguments may be the reason for his reaching the point that he can accept the authority which presents these arguments. Therefore, these probable reasons have a different function, depending on the question whether they are brought up before or after the decision to accept this authority.

The middle term here is a form of implicit faith which is most useful when it is an implicit faith in the Church, according to which one believes everything that the Church believes.[82] The search for the *ratio fidei* of a particular article is then to make this faith explicit. So long as one holds on to this implicit faith, one can err in the search for the *ratio fidei*, and even earn merit, so long as one does not defend one's error after it becomes clear that his position is contrary to the faith of the Church.[83]

[81] "Denique baptismus secundo datus nullam penitus habet efficaciam respectu remissionis peccati sicut iterata penitentia. Cuius radicalis ratio est institutio divina licet concurrant etiam alie congruencie . . ." IV *Sent.* d 14 q 3 art. 2 H.

[82] "Fides explicita est actualis assensus catholice veritatis sive universalis sive particularis . . . ," III *Sent.* d 25 q 1 art. 1 nota 2 E. "Fides implicita est fides habitualis aut actualis assensus alicuius propositionis generalis, multas particulares veritates in se includentis. . . Hec fides implicita qua fidelis credit quicquid ecclesia credit utilissima est fideli." *Ibid.*, corr. 4.

[83] On heresy: ". . . nec peccat dummodo hunc errorem pertinaciter non de-

8. Implicit and explicit faith

The use of these probable reasons is not to strengthen one's faith, for in such a case one would again rely more on human reason than on revelation or authority. But it helps one — and this is its main purpose — to understand his own faith better and so enables one to witness to those who stand outside the circle of faith who may be helped by these semi-arguments in confiding in the authority of the Church or of Scripture. It may also help to make one's faith more detailed, conscious and explicit.[84]

Probability does not exclude or limit certitude but is only the form under which certitude appears. These are not vital concepts inasmuch as certitude refers here to the infallibility of God and thus encompasses the whole realm of faith. Part of this realm presents itself to the human reason as probable.[85] And as probability is the rational aspect of certitude, it cannot in any sense endanger the meritoriousness of the act of faith. Inductive reason preceding the acquisition of faith, however, not only diminishes but abolishes the meritoriousness of such an act.[86]

---

fendit . . . immo quod amplius est nedum hec fides implicita ab heresi et peccato defendit sed etiam meritum facit et conservat in eo quod errans falsum opinatur. . . Non enim omnis credens secundum conscientiam erroneam peccat." III *Sent.* d 25 q 1 art. 1 nota 2 F.

[84] ". . . dum quis paratus est credere et credit tamen pro maiori credendorum intellectu querit et investigat latius non ut firmius credat, quia sic crederet humane rationi plus quam revelationi. Sed ut clarius intelligat et possit petenti rationem reddere de fide vel ut particularius intelligat credenda et cognoscat. Et talis ratio fidei meritum auget, non diminuit." *S* IV 5 D.

[85] Anneliese Maier gives an acceptable formulation of this point, which can, however, be misunderstood as constructing a contrast between *probabilitas* and *certitudo*. In fact, the rival concepts are *evidentia* and *certitudo*. ". . . neben die unbedingte und absolute Gewissheit der offenbarten Wahrheit und neben die — nicht übermässig hoch eingeschätzte — Autorität des Aristoteles tritt der Wahrheitsanspruch der eigenen Vernunft und der eigenen Erfahrung, wobei diese letztere aber immer als eine letzten Endes nur induktiv gesicherte probabilitas angesehen wird, die gegenüber der 'eigentlichen,' durch göttliche Autorität gesicherten Wahrheit etwas Untergeordnetes und Relatives bleibt." *Zwischen Philosophie und Mechanik* (Rome, 1958), p. 397 f. Cf. P. Raymond, O. M. C., "La théorie de l'induction: Duns Scot précurseur de Bacon," in *Etudes franciscaines* 21 (1909), 113 ff.

[86] Quoting Thomas (*ST* II.II q 2 art. 10), Biel rigorizes Thomas' statement by adding the italicized words: ". . . ratio humana inducta ad ea que fidei sunt dupliciter se habere potest. Uno modo ut precedens. Puta cum aliquis assentit veritati fidei propter rationem convincentem alias non credituram. Et sic ratio inducta

Children who are not yet able to use their reason in making their faith, infused by baptism, explicit, are saved not because of their own merits but through the merits of Christ alone. These merits are not sufficient to save those who have already the capacity to think; they have to add their own merits as well. The requirement of cooperation in the process of salvation is therefore founded on the intellect and its rational activities.[87]

Adults have to believe that everything revealed by God is true and thus that the Scriptures, revealed by God, are true. Finally they have to believe explicitly in a mediator. This may be very vague in the sense that God ordained some means of redemption by a mediator, either by the Word, an angel or in some other way.[88] Such a lax requirement of explicit faith in Christ seems, however, to be meant more for the mission fields than for the catechumen of a baptized nation; once the mediation of the Word of God has been revealed to a man, he is held to believe this explicitly.[89] We shall, of course, return to the issue of the meritoriousness of faith in the context of the doctrine of justification.

To summarize this nominalistic view of the contrast of faith to reason and theology to philosophy, it can be said that, whereas the method of reason, philosophy, and the sciences is inductive, the method of theology proper is deductive.

9. The mystery of the Trinity

Biel's treatment of the doctrine of the Trinity offers us a good example of the search for probable reasons within a doctrine that has to be accepted on authority. The creed of the triune God does not belong to the articles dealing with future acts of God; it does not exclude a *ratio fidei*.

---

diminuit meritum fidei *immo totum tollit ita quod sic assentiendo non meretur."* III *Sent.* d 25 q 1 art. 3 dub. 4. Cf. *S* IV 5 D.

[87] ". . . licet in non habentibus rationis usum non requiritur actus fidei eo quod non salvantur merito proprio sed in solo merito redemptoris, cum habentibus usum rationis non sufficit meritum christi sed necesse est etiam addere meritum proprium," III *Sent.* d 25 q 1 art. 2 concl. 1 H. Cf. *S* III 19 E.

[88] ". . . quod deus ordinaret aliquam viam redemptionis per aliquem mediatorem; etiam ignorando per quem. An per verbum dei vel per angelum aut alium modum." III *Sent.* d 25 q 1 art. 2 concl. 3 L.

[89] "Illis tamen quibus hoc revelatum fuerat magis particulariter tenebantur credere secundum revelationem eis factam," *ibid.*

Gerhard Ritter analyzed Marsilius of Inghen's application of his understanding of the relation of faith and reason to the doctrine of the Trinity and came to the conclusion that according to Marsilius, there is no disparity between the laws of logic and this doctrine.[90] William of Occam, also, did not sacrifice the universal validity of logic to this seemingly self-contradictory article of faith. A strict syllogism, however, yields a heretical result: "Omnis essentia divina est pater, filius est essentia divina; ergo filius est pater." [91] This forces him [92] to accept Duns Scotus' formal distinction which *per se* he does not hold in high regard. Paternity and sonship refer to distinct realities and are therefore predicated of the divine essence in a formally distinct way.

In a lengthy exposition Biel follows Occam almost *verbatim* to conclude with the concise formula: the divine essence is formally distinct from the person and its property.[93] This is, however, not the same as to say that the doctrine of the Trinity is a logical conclusion from evident premises. Gregory of Rimini, Pierre d'Ailly, Adam Woodham, Henry Totting of Oyta, and Robert Holcot are criticized with words that sound rather sharp coming from Biel's pen for their announced intentions of further research on this point.[94] Verification of this construction is im-

[90] Gerhard Ritter, *Studien zur Spätscholastik* I, (Heidelberg, 1921), p. 141, quotes Marsilius I *Sent.* d 1 q 8 [fol. 46 c]. Cf. Carl Prantl, *Geschichte der Logik im Abendlande*, IV (Leipzig, 1810), p. 99, no. 394 f; p. 94, no. 308.

[91] *Summa Logicae* III.1.5; *Pars Secunda et Tertiae Prima*, ed. Philotheus Boehner (St. Bonaventure, 1954), pp. 346, 96 f.

[92] Cf. the clear exposition by Boehner, *Collected Articles on Ockham*, p. 365 f.

[93] "Essentia divina distinguitur formaliter a persona et proprietate personali et econverso," I *Sent.* d 2 q 11 art. 2 concl. 2.

[94] "Sed quicquid sit stante semper fidei catholice firmitate non videtur quomodo illa verificatio contradictoriorum locum habeat nisi sit aliqua non idemptitas ex natura rei quam cum idemptitate essentiali capere sufficienter per intellectum non possumus in via; ideo tam Gregorius quam Petrus, Adam, Oyta et Holchot inutile dicunt se velle in illis plurimum occupare." I *Sent.* d 2 q 11 art. 3 dub. 3 O. For a discussion of the trinitarian doctrines of Occam, Holcot, Gregory, and d'Ailly see Roland H. Bainton, "Michael Servetus and the Trinitarian Speculation of the Middle Ages," in *Autour de Michel Servet et de Sebastien Castellion*, ed. B. Becker (Haarlem, 1953), p. 29 ff. Bainton builds his conclusion that Servetus "was the bridge from scholastic scepticism" to anti-Trinitarianism (p. 46) partly on the evaluation of Occam's position as "obviously indistinguishable from tritheism" (p. 39). Bainton's quotation from Occam (I *Sent.* d 30 q 4 F: "Sed secundum istam viam oportet ponere quod in deo essent tria absoluta realiter distincta") is not Occam's position but the point of view rejected by him. The argument of those who defend a real distinction is here carried *ad absurdum*. It is not Occam's concern

possible in any case; it is the best possible solution, which is not offered with certainty but as a suggestion. The point is that the proposition "three equals one" does not necessarily imply a negation of the laws of logic. Notwithstanding Biel's criticism of the "curiosity" of some leading *doctores moderni*, this may be said to be the typical nominalistic attitude.[95]

There are variations with regard to the extent of probability; Gregory of Rimini is somewhat more inclined to stress the fact that the *viator's* understanding is limited; d'Ailly feels that it is the task of the theologian to explore these probabilities as far as possible.[96] Biel seems to hold a middle position. He is more inclined than d'Ailly to assert that the doctrine of the Trinity belongs to the realm of pure faith and is therefore beyond the grasp of human reason. On the other hand, notwithstanding his inclusion of Gregory in his warning against rational pride, he tries to penetrate the mystery of the Trinity as far as human reason permits.

His main interest throughout this whole treatment is to stress the unity of the properties of God: intellect, will, power, wisdom, etc. These belong to God's essence and are therefore to be equally attributed to the three Persons. These differ only in their mutual relations. It is the unity of God's essence that guarantees the oneness of God's *opera ad extra*.[97]

---

to attack the doctrine of the Trinity but to prevent his opponents from using this theological doctrine to prove a philosophical point, *i.e.* the reality of universals, or the distinction between the soul and its powers.

[95] See on d'Ailly, Bernhard Meller, *Studien zur Erkenntnislehre des Peter von Ailly*; Freiburger theologische Studien 67 (Freiburg i.Br., 1954.) "Das Trinitätsdogma kann von uns als in sich warscheinlich aufrecht erhalten werden, da es uns glaubwürdig und vorstellbar ist, für seine Wahrheit probabele Gründe sprechen und es ohne Widerspruch behauptet werden kann," Meller, p. 212 f.

[96] See d'Ailly, I *Sent.* q 8 art. 3 C, criticizing Gregory: ". . . absurdissimum et scandalosum videtur esse in fide dicere, quod aliqua propositio sit credenda a catholicis et tamen nullus catholicus sciat assignare definitionem quid nominis sive descriptionem et differentiam significationis terminorum illius," as quoted by Meller, p. 212. D'Ailly may refer here to Gregory's assertion: "Quamvis autem intelligere ista [differentia generationis et processionis] non possumus, veraciter tamen sic esse confitemur et credimus." Gregory of Rimini I *Sent.* d 13 q 1 art. 1 [fol. 83 O]. For Biel's position see note 98 below.

[97] "Quia una essentia in tribus ergo quicquid respicit essentiam equaliter convenit tribus. Que vero respiciunt relativas proprietates originis conveniunt singulis personis et non omnibus. . ." (*S* II 40 D). "In deo omnia sunt idem in quibus non obviat relationis oppositio. Hinc intellectus, voluntas . . . et universalis omnis perfectio quia primo et principaliter respiciunt essentiam sicut ipsa essentia ita et illa unum et

Consideration of the image of God reflected in the triplicity of man can help us to gain a certain knowledge of God, but it does not enable us to analyze the inner life of God itself.[98] The traditional images of the Father as the Lover, the Son as the Beloved, and the Holy Spirit as their mutual bond of love are used to explain the inner-trinitarian relations. Love belongs equally to all three Persons, insofar as it is an aspect of God's essence, but it can also be used to signify especially the third Person of the Trinity.[99] It is, therefore, not correct to say that Occamism rejected Augustine's psychological interpretation of the inner-trinitarian relations.[100]

While his main interest may be the unity of the divine essence, Biel is strictly orthodox in asserting the three Persons without even the slightest indication of a tendency towards tritheism. The theologian is groping for images and examples to clarify this mystery.[101] He is confident that the *distinctio formalis* as applied to the inner-trinitarian life of God can

---

idem sunt cum essentia et inter se et communia tribus personis." *S* II 40 D. Compare I *Sent.* d 3 q 9 art. 1 nota 4 and *Lect.* 29 N.

[98] *S* II 34 C and E; also *Lect.* 20 E. "Hec de processione eterna spiritus sancti ad intra balbutiendo dicta sufficiant, que etsi non intelligimus non minus credamus," *S* II 34 H.

[99] "Amor increatus ipse spiritus sanctus est; non solum essentialiter quomodo et pater est amor et filius est amor sed notionaliter, i.e., amor spiratus. Cui etiam amor essentialiter appropriatur eo quod a patre et filio procedit per modum voluntatis sive amoris. Denique pater et filius diligere se dicuntur spiritu sancto." *S* II 37 E. Cf. III *Sent.* d 32 q 1 art. 1 nota 2.

[100] Paul Vignaux, "Nominalisme" and "Occam" in *DThC* vol. XI, cols. 783 and 881. Cf. Reynold Weijenborg, p. 631: "En accentuant la simplicité radicale de Dieu, l'Ockhamisme refusait d'admettre entre les personnes divines les rapports psychologiques qui, depuis S. Augustin, avaient servi à expliquer d'une certaine manière la vie de la Trinité." Weijenborg gives a wrong reference, III *Sent.* d 32 q 1 art. 2 dub. 3 H. "Sicut pater non sapit sapientia genita, ita nec diligit dilectione spirata." This is, of course, only meant with regard to God's essence and directed against an ontological interpretation. *Notionaliter*, however, Biel assigns love to the Holy Spirit and wisdom to the Word. The correct reference is III *Sent.* d 32 q 1 art. 3 dub. 2 G. Weijenborg's quote should be completed with the words: "Appropriantur tamen omnia que ad voluntatem pertinent spiritui sancto, sicut ea que ad intellectum pertinent verbo." In this way the psychological relations within the Trinity are preserved. See, on Augustine, the clear exposition by Irénée Chevalier, *La Théorie Augustinienne des relations Trinitaires* (Fribourg, 1940), p. 68 ff.

[101] "... filium in divinis non personam aliquam a patre separatam ... sed cogitare debitis quandam pulchram patris imaginem in ipso patre tanquam in speculo clarissimo manentem in qua pater et divina essentia et omne cognoscibile declaratur et relucet," *S* II 39 F.

guarantee the universal validity of logic. There is no indication whatsoever that Biel would be willing to say *"credo quia absurdum."* Nevertheless, what is offered is not evidence, but a probable opinion [102] which helps to clarify what is believed with certitude.

III. Conclusion

The most important conclusion of this chapter is perhaps a negative one: the traditional assertion that the thirteenth-century synthesis of faith and reason disintegrated in the later middle ages and was replaced by a radical emphasis on the divorce of faith and reason does not apply to the nominalism of Gabriel Biel. And passages parallel to those of other influential nominalist schoolmen indicate that Gabriel Biel does not stand alone in this respect. It is indeed quite clearly their intention to indicate the demarcation line between the operational spheres of the natural knowledge of God and of the revealed knowledge of God.

The *fides acquisita* on the one hand and the *rationes probabiles* on the other hand show that these two circles do not merely touch tangentially but also overlap in the realm of philosophical theology. Though the semi-arguments offered by the doctors of theology are never compelling, they are sufficient to refute the accusation of the absurdity of the basic tenets of the Christian faith. Parallel to the concept of semimerits, *merita de congruo* which we shall discuss shortly, one can therefore speak about the nominalistic defense of the *ratio de congruo* of faith.

This *ratio de congruo*, which applies even to such a mystery as the Trinity, does not run counter to the universal validity of the rules of logic. At the same time it may be said that the *pure credibilia* which constitute the inner core of faith are beyond the reach of natural reason and also in part beyond the grasp even of those who enjoy the beatific vision. But while natural man, limited as he is to theoretical reason, cannot pass over the demarcation line to the side of faith, the *ratio de congruo* enables the theologian to advance probable considerations appealing to practical reason to clarify even the most mysterious aspects of revelation.

The nominalistic view of theological apologetics can therefore be said

[102] "Hec que de distinctione formali posui humili cum submissione sine assertione temeraria et cuiuscunque sanius sentientis preiudicio recitavi . . . ," I *Sent.* d 2 q 11 art. 3 R.

to be unilateral or one-way apologetics. The inductive argumentation characteristic of human knowledge can never by sheer extension penetrate the inner core of faith and thus become the methodological tool for theological exploration.

The theologian is indeed committed to the deductive method, but he is nevertheless able to reach into the realm of natural knowledge to clear away the obstacles which otherwise would be reasons to reject the claims of the Christian faith. By this process man may have acquired a form of faith; it is, however, a merely historical faith, which he holds in common with the demons. Only after acquired faith has become infused faith does the Christian transcend the knowledge of the demons in that he knows that the Christian message is not only true in general, but also true for him.

After having probed the relation of faith and reason, we can now turn our attention from the question of creedal positivism to that of ethical positivism.

Chapter Four

NATURAL LAW AS DIVINE ORDER

ᔰ●

I. The Question *de odio dei*

1. The medieval tradition

The foundation of the moral order and the relation of natural law to eternal law is one of the most debated aspects of nominalistic thought. Parallel to the traditional statement that nominalism destroyed the medieval synthesis of faith and reason, and proclaimed a doctrine of double truth, there is a striking consensus that nominalism stood for a doctrine of double ethics, and broke asunder the unity between the law of God and the law of man. Since we do not believe that this is an adequate interpretation of the nominalistic position we would do well first to investigate the positions of Aquinas and of Scotus. These constitute the natural context for the nominalistic discussion of ethics.

In view of the "intellectualism" of Thomas Aquinas, it is not surprising that for him God's will is only a partner in the operation of the intellect in establishing the hierarchy of eternal law, natural law, and positive law. In his eyes it would be blasphemous to assert that justice would ultimately depend on the will of God, as this would imply that his will would not operate according to the order of wisdom.[1] Justice in its deepest essence as form and norm is a product of God's wisdom, and its standard is therefore right reason.[2]

---

[1] "Dicere autem quod ex simplici voluntate dependeat iustitia est dicere quod divina voluntas non procedat secundum ordinem sapientiae quod est blasphemum," *De Veritate* 23.6.

[2] See Odon Lottin, O.S.B., *L'ordre morale et l'ordre logique d'après St. Thomas* (Louvain, 1924); "L'intellectualisme de la morale thomiste," *Xenia Thomistica* I

Duns Scotus stresses the direct dependence of all law on God's will without, however, endangering the hierarchy of eternal, natural, and positive law. Nevertheless, his divergence from Thomas appears in his answer to the question whether the ten commandments are to be viewed as the direct expression of natural law. Thomas had answered this in the affirmative; Scotus felt that the acts forbidden in the second table of the law may not necessarily deflect the *viator* from his final destination. They are not therefore in the strict sense of the word an application of natural law.[3]

Yet despite this evidence of Duns Scotus' thoughtful and responsible use of the doctrine of the primacy of the will, his Franciscan type of theology is still generally held to have led to the disintegration of scholastic theology. As regards the issue of revealed and natural law, this appears again in the accusation that Duns Scotus divorced "at least potentially" the realms of natural and divine law, and that he therefore can be described as a legal positivist.[4] According to this prevailing school of thought, Occam is usually said to have actualized the disruptive potentialities of Scotus' thought. The *Venerabilis Inceptor* is then accused of relativism, fideism, actualism, and legal positivism.[5]

(1925), 411–427; Gallus M. Manser, *Das Wesen des Thomismus*, 3 ed., Thomistische Studien V (Fribourg, 1949), p. 202.

[3] *Ox.* III d 37 q 1 n 5. Cf. Reinhold Seeberg, *Die Theologie des Johannes Duns Scotus: Eine dogmengeschichtliche Untersuchung* (Leipzig, 1900), p. 488 f. See also Minges, I, 403 ff., who feels that this is no indication of legal positivism; "Scotus declarans praecepta secundae tabulae non esse stricte vel strictissime de lege naturae, *nonnisi exprimere vult ea non esse ita absoluta et necessaria quam praecepta tabulae primae*" (p. 407).

[4] G. de Lagarde, *La naissance de l'esprit laïque au déclin du Moyen Age*, III (Paris, 1946), 316 ff.; 2 ed., II (Paris, 1958), 238 ff. On d'Auriole, II, 292. Cf. Günter Stratenwerth, *Die Naturrechtslehre des Johannes Duns Scotus* (Göttingen, 1951), p. 112.

[5] Wilhelm Stockums, *Die Unveränderlichkeit des natürlichen Sittengesetzes in der scholastischen Ethik* (Freiburg i. Br., 1911), p. 161 f; Carl Feckes, "Die religionsphilosophischen Bestrebungen des spätmittelalterlichen Nominalismus," *Römische Quartalschrift* 35 (1927), 197; Maurice de Wulf, *Histoire de la philosophie médiévale* III, (Paris, 1936), p. 150; Sytse Ulbe Zuidema, *De philosophie van Occam* (Hilversum 1936), I, 104 f; Anita Garvens, "Die Grundlagen der Ethik Wilhelms von Ockham," *FS* 21 (1934), 243–273; 360–408; Elzarius Bonke, O.F.M. "Doctrina nominalistica de fundamento ordinis moralis apud Gulielmum de Ockham et Gabrielem Biel," *Collectanea Franciscana* 14 (1944), 57–83; Iserloh, *Gnade und Eucharistie in der philosophischen Theologie des Wilhelm von Ockham* (Wiesbaden, 1956), pp. 44–67.

A most interesting protest has been voiced against this already generally accepted judgment by Philotheus Boehner, whose conclusions drawn from the works of Occam were later applied to the thoughts of Biel by Leif Grane.[6] The two main arguments that are employed to defend Occam are: first, that undoubtedly he admits an absolute rule of ethics, namely, the obligation to obey God; and second, that the critics are inclined to forget that in nominalistic thought God's will is another word for God's essence, in the same way that intellect stands for essence. Essence, will, and intellect are thus in no sense mutually exclusive, let alone divorceable.

The famous question whether God can command someone to hate him forms the test-case here. Occam answers this in the affirmative: this act as such can be done by God himself; and if it were according to established law, a *viator* could even perform such an act with merit.[7] For Boehner this is nothing more than the expression of the theological truth that God is the primary cause of every effect. As a creature is able to command somebody to hate God, it is clear on "purely logical grounds"[8] that God can give the same command. However, a man so commanded would be thoroughly perplexed, for by obeying the will of God he would at the same time love God and not love God.[9] While this might be logically possible, psychologically it would be impossible. In a careful analysis of the relevant passages, Iserloh indicates rightly that while this is a psychological impossibility for men, the real issue is whether God would not

Francis Oakley, "Medieval Theories of Natural Law: William of Ockham and the Significance of the Voluntarist Tradition," *Natural Law Forum* 6 (1961), 65 ff.

[6] Boehner, p. 22 f, 151 ff. Cf. also his posthumously published studies, *Ockham: Philosophical Writings* (Edinburgh, 1957), p. xlviii ff. and Leif Grane, "Gabriel Biels Lehre von der Allmacht Gottes," *ZThK* 53 (1956), 53–75.

[7] ". . . dico quod licet odium dei, furari, adulterari habeant malam circumstantiam annexam et similia de communi lege quatenus fiunt ab aliquo qui ex precepto divino obligatur ad contrarium, sed quantum ad esse absolutum in illis actibus possunt fieri a deo sine omni circumstantia mala annexa, et etiam meritorie possunt fieri a viatore si caderent sub precepto divino. . ." II *Sent.* q 19 art. 1 ad 30. Bonke (p. 60), adds the following comment to this passage: "Clarius certe et magis concrete positivismus moralis exprimi non potuisset." G. de Lagarde reaches the same conclusion. *La naissance de l'esprit laïque au déclin du Moyen Age*, vol. VI: *L'Individualisme Ockhamiste. La morale et le droit* (Paris, 1946), pp. 55, 59 f.

[8] Boehner, p. 153.

[9] "Et ex hoc ipso quod sic diligeret, non faceret preceptum divinum per casum et per consequens sic diligendo deum diligeret et non diligeret," Occam, *Quodl.* III q 13.

contradict himself if he were so to command.[10] Iserloh's principal criticism of Occam is directed against the extreme voluntarism, the actualism, and above all, against the formalism that goes with this understanding of ethics. The ontological foundation of objective values is exchanged for a subjective consensus of man's will with God's law.[11] Similarly Bonke concludes that the danger implied in some of the extreme statements of Occam is that the natural order is not any longer the foundation of the moral order.[12]

2. The position of Biel

Keeping in mind this judgment by Bonke who, as a Franciscan, cannot be suspected of being biased against the religious quality of Franciscan theology, we now turn to Biel with the question of whether we find in him traces of ethical formalism. But contrary to Occam, the question of God's command to hate him is not treated as a major problem by Biel. He deals with it to some extent in the context of the question of whether God's omnipotence implies that he immediately concurs with second causes. This can be understood in two ways.

[10] Iserloh, *Gnade und Eucharistie . . . Ockham*, p. 50. Hochstetter, *Studien zur Metaphysik und Erkenntnislehre Wilhelms von Ockham*, p. 16, interprets the *Quodlibet* passage so as to imply the negation of the possibility for God to command somebody to hate him. It is possible that this passage does not exclude this *de potentia absoluta*. So W. Kölmel, "Das Naturrecht bei Wilhelm Ockham," *FS* 35 (1953), p. 58, n. 84. This would agree with Biel's point of view in I *Sent*. d 43 q 1 art. 4 concl. responsalis, where he refers the reader to Gregory and d'Ailly.

Robert Holcot holds: ". . . respiciendo ad virtutem voluntatis concedo, quod deus potest fallere et decipere, id est voluntarie causare errorem in mente hominis et facere eum credere aliter quam res se habuit." I *Sent*. q 1 art. 7 R. Alois Meissner points to *Determinationes quarundam aliarum questionum* (Lyons, 1497), q 1 art. 2 ZZ: ". . . potest deus precipere alicui, quod odiat deum," and concludes: "Der Moralpositivismus [Holcots] ist eindeutig erkennbar." *Gotteserkenntnis und Gotteslehre nach dem Englischen Dominikanertheologen Robert Holcot* (Limburg a.d. Lahn, 1953), p. 86. Cf. Gordon Leff: "God, as Holcot sees Him, is capable of anything," *Bradwardine and the Pelagians* (Cambridge, 1957), p. 221. For a balanced view of Holcot, one should however take into consideration *Sap*. Lect. 18 A, quoted below, note 41. See further Chapter Seven, section III.

[11] "Es geht nicht so sehr darum, Werte zu verwirklichen, als viel mehr, Gebote zu erfüllen, nach deren Sinn nicht weiter gefragt wird und zu fragen auch nicht sinnvoll ist. Von hier aus können wir vom Formalismus in Ockhams Ethik sprechen." Iserloh, *Gnade und Eucharistie. . . Ockham*, p. 66.

[12] "Tunc ordo naturalis non est amplius fundamentum ordinis moralis, neque intellectus norma agendi, sed exclusive voluntas divina," Bonke, p. 68.

In one sense God's omnipotence means that he is the direct or remote cause of everything that happens. It can be proved with natural reason that God is in this sense omnipotent.[13] In another sense the omnipotence of God implies that he can do everything without second causes. This cannot be proved with natural reason.[14] That God is omnipotent in this sense can only be believed *sola fide* on the authority of biblical texts and quotations from the Fathers. As a counter-argument comes now the objection that God cannot sin or cause someone to hate him. If God were to cause such a hate in someone, such a person not only would not sin in hating God, but would even act meritoriously.[15] Biel's answer is harmless and not unexpected: God would not create the *intention* of such an act, but he would certainly be able to produce the *act* as such.[16]

In Book III in which he deals with the relation of the Decalogue to natural law, he even explicitly denies what Occam, if not in his *Quodlibeta* then certainly in his commentary on Lombard, declares to be possible. Biel agrees here with Scotus over against Thomas that the second table of the old law is not in the strict sense of the word a necessary application of the natural law.[17] Though God could allow a greater laxity in obedience to this second table, he does not in fact do this because of its intimate relation with natural law.[18]

[13] ". . . potentia activa primi efficientis extendit se ad omnem effectum mediatum vel immediatum in ratione cause proxime vel remote," I *Sent.* d 42 q 1 art. 2 concl. 1.

[14] "Cum ergo non potest probari ratione naturali quod deus sit causa contingenter causans, non potest probari quod sit causa sufficiens se solo producere omnem effectum producibilem," I *Sent.* d 42 q 1 art. 2 concl. 2.

[15] "Item non potest producere odium dei, alioquin aliquis posset sine peccato — immo cum merito — odire deum si in aliquo produceret odium," I *Sent.* d 42 q 1 art. 3 dub. 1.

[16] "Id quod est peccare, hoc est actum positivum, qui dicitur peccatum, potest producere" (*ibid.*) ". . . de odio dei, non videtur quin entitatem absolutam quam importat odium dei deus potest producere, sicut eam in damnatis conservare" (*ibid.*). There are clear marks here of the influence on Biel of Gregory's argumentation against Occam. See Gregory, I *Sent.* d 42–44 q 1 art. 2 [fol. 165 B ff.]. Biel read Gregory on the question of God's omnipotence and refers to him — and d'Ailly — for a more elaborate discussion: ". . . de hoc latius vide Petrum de aliaco q 13 art. 1 et Gregorium articulo presenti." I *Sent.* d 42 q 1 art. 2, sub V. Cf. "de odio diaboli," Biel, II *Sent.* d 7 q 1 art. 1 concl. 3.

[17] ". . . Secunde tabule precepta tam affirmativa quam negativa sunt de lege nature non stricte sed large accepta," III *Sent.* d 37 q 1 art. 2 concl. 3. Cf. concl. 2: ". . . duo precepta negativa prime tabule sunt de lege nature accipiendo legem nature proprie." Biel here follows Duns "sententialiter": *Ox.* III d 37 q 1 n 6.

[18] ". . . quamvis legislator deus circa observantiam preceptorum secunde tabule simpliciter dispensare posset per precepti relaxationem non tamen sic dispensat

We must note here especially Biel's explanation as to why in this special case a relaxation *de potentia absoluta* would be possible. A dispensation, that is, a temporary relaxation,[19] of the commandments that are logically necessary conclusions of the natural law would even *de potentia absoluta* be impossible, because that would involve God in a *malum culpae*, which is of course inconceivable. Biel's understanding of the irrevocability — even *de potentia absoluta* — of the first two commandments of the Decalogue excludes, though not explicitly nevertheless implicitly, the possibility that God would be able to command somebody to hate him.[20] Thus we may conclude that in the famous question *de odio dei*, Biel prefers to follow Duns and Gregory of Rimini; he does not mention the *Venerabilis Inceptor*, and his position on this issue can be characterized as a more or less open departure from Occam.[21]

---

de facto propter magnam eorum cum lege nature proprie proximationem," III *Sent.* d 37 q 1 art. 2 concl. 5.

[19] III *Sent.* d 37 q 1 art. 1 nota 3.

[20] "Fidelitas ad deum in eo consistit ut principatus ad alium non deferatur, et de hoc datur primum preceptum de non habendo deos alienos. Reverentia requirit ut nihil iniuriosum in eum committatur et quantum ad hoc datur secundum preceptum de non sumendo nomen domini in vanum." III *Sent.* d 37 q 1 art. 1 nota 5 K. Cf. art. 2 concl. 2: "Summe reverendo non est irreverentia facienda, deus est summe reverendus quia summe bonus, ideo ei non est irreverentia facienda." See also the parallel passage in Scotus (*ibid.*, nota 6): "si est deus, est amandus ut deus, et quod nihil aliud est colendum tamquam deus, nec deo est facienda irreverentia." Cf. nota 10: "non odire enim est simpliciter de lege nature." See further, Biel, III *Sent.* d 23 q 2 art. 3 dub. 1.

[21] Kölmel comes to this same conclusion albeit with insufficient arguments. Kölmel refers to I *Sent.* d 17 q 7 art. 3 dub. 3, to draw the conclusion: "Die Stellung Ockhams in seinem Sentenzenkommentar ist hier sicher überwunden . . . ," in "Von Ockham zu Gabriel Biel: Zur Naturrechtslehre des 14. und 15. Jahrhunderts," *FS* 37 (1955), 218 ff., 251. The indicated passage, however, stands in the context of the typical nominalistic attack on Pierre d'Auriole's thesis that God is obliged to accept one adorned with sanctifying grace: ". . . non potest non diligere diligentes se aliqua dilectione seu complacentia generali . . . non tamen sequitur quod ea dilectione qua ordinatur ad vitam eternam, que dicitur complacentia specialissima." *Complacentia generalis* is, however, according to Biel's own definition not an act of God's will in the strict sense of the word and, as such, strictly to be distinguished from the act of love (I *Sent.* d 1 q 3 art. 3 dub. 2). The *complacentia generalis* is understood by Biel to connote the general good will of the creator "qua vult posse esse bona quecunque esse possunt," I *Sent.* d 17 q 1 art. 1 nota 2 B. Biel deals here therefore merely with that neutral will of God from which springs that neutral activity which is called the *concursus generalis, influxus dei, or influentia generalis.*

Also Otto von Gierke has noted, albeit without documentation, the difference between Occam and Biel on this point in his invaluable *Das Deutsche Genossenschaftsrecht*, vol. III. *Die Staats- und Korporationslehre des Altertums und des*

We must now look at Biel's understanding of the will of God, clearly the basis of his ethical system, in order to grasp his positive teaching. This preceding discussion has been mainly a negative approach to his ethical system, in that we have stressed what he did not believe.

II. God and Justice

1. God's freedom from the law

In two places Biel gives an almost programmatic statement of his deepest ethical convictions. The first and most elaborate one we find in his lectures on the Mass. Here he defines the priority of God's will over any moral structure by saying that God does not will something because it is good or right. If this were the case, God's will would be subject to created principles of morality, whereas Biel is convinced that nothing can be called good unless it be accepted as such by the "uncreated principle," God.[22] This seems to express the same absolute voluntarism and ethical positivism which even more moderate critics have noted in Occam's works.

The second passage in which Biel discusses this question is the negative counterpart to the first and corroborates our first impression: God can do something which he himself has declared unjust; however, if he does it, it then becomes right; therefore the will of God is the first rule of all justice.[23] It is not surprising that these extreme statements have led some scholars to extreme judgments.[24]

Mittelalters und ihre Aufnahme in Deutschland, 2 ed. (Darmstadt, 1954), 610, n. 256. Louis Vereecke's analysis of Gerson's *De Vita Spirituali* shows that the Parisian Chancellor describes the relation of the eternal and the natural law in the same way as Biel. See his "Droit et morale chez Jean Gerson," *Revue historique de droit français et étranger* 32 (1954), 420 f. Georges de Lagarde notes in Gerson even ". . . un recul sur la pensée de Saint Thomas," *Recherches sur l'esprit politique de la Réforme* (Douai, 1926), p. 30. For the relation of natural and positive law in Gerson, see J. Schneider, "Die Verpflichtung des menschlichen Gesetzes nach Johannes Gerson," *ZKT* 75 (1953), 1 ff.

[22] ". . . neque enim quia bonum aut iustum est aliquid ipsum deus vult sed quia deus vult ideo bonum est et iustum. Voluntas namque divina non ex nostra bonitate sed ex divina voluntate bonitas nostra pendet nec aliquid bonum nisi quia a deo sic acceptum." *Lect.* 23 E.

[23] "Deus potest aliquid facere quod non est iustum fieri a deo; si tamen faceret iustum esset fieri. Unde sola voluntas divina est prima regula omnis iustitie." I *Sent.* d 43 q 1 art. 4 cor.

[24] E.g., Erich Seeberg, *Luthers Theologie: Motive und Ideen,* vol. I: *Die Gottes-*

If we analyze the first of these statements, however, we find that the indicated relation between the goodness of God and man is set against the background of the doctrine of justification. A parallel passage is to be found in distinction seventeen of Book I in an argument against the Pelagian heresy: God's election is without cause; without any injustice on his part he can reject the *viator*.[25]

This concept of the absolute freedom of God with respect to man's moral standards and the human understanding of the distinction between good and evil reappears as an introductory statement to Biel's analysis of the doctrine of divine predestination: the Creator of the universe and Ruler of the world can do whatever he wants to do without injustice to his creatures.[26]

It is clear that in view of the context of election and acceptation, the confession of God's absolute rights is not meant as a systematic statement to express the relativity of ethical standards. As we saw before when we discussed the two powers of God — and anticipating our later scrutiny of the doctrines of justification and predestination — the concept of *misericordia* is central in both doctrines. It is the realm of absolute freedom in which God establishes the order *de potentia ordinata*. Because of the eternal procession from *misericordia* to *iusticia*, the order in which the *viator*

---

anschauung (Göttingen, 1929), p. 22: "Biel hat sich auch nicht gescheut, die Konsequenz aus diesem Gedanken zu ziehen; Gottes absoluter Wille ist auch nicht an die Logik oder an die Moral gebunden: sola voluntas divina est prima regula omnis iustitiae." Johannes Heckel, "Recht und Gesetz, Kirche und Obrigkeit in Luthers Lehre vor dem Thesenanschlag von 1517: Eine juristische Untersuchung," *Zeitschrift der Savigny-Stiftung für Rechtsgeschichte* 57 (1937), Kanonistische Abteilung 26, p. 286 f.: ". . . die schrankenlose Entscheidungsgewalt Gottes, der frei bestimme, was Recht sei." See also Heckel's "Initia iuris ecclesiastici Protestantium" (Munich, 1950), *Sitzungsberichte der Bayerischen Akademie der Wissenschaften.* Phil. Hist. Klasse (1949), pt. 15, p. 21. Georg Ott, "Recht und Gesetz bei Gabriel Biel: Ein Beitrag zur spätmittelalterlichen Rechtslehre," *Zeitschrift der Savigny-Stiftung für Rechtsgeschichte* 69 (1952), Kanonistische Abteilung 38, p. 256: "Mit diesen Feststellungen steigert Biel wie sein unmittelbares Vorbild Ockham die Freiheit und Allmacht Gottes ins Unbegrenzte. . ."

[25] "Et hoc dictum maxime recedit ab errore pelagii . . . libere et misericorditer de sua gratia dat vitam sempiternam et semper — sine sui iniusticia — posset non conferre, ipse enim est cui nullus dicere potest, 'cur ita facis,' et quecunque facere potest, faciendo iusta sunt et iuste sic ea facit." I *Sent.* d 17 q 1 art. 2 concl. 3.

[26] "Deus tanquam universitatis creator et dominus de creatura potest facere quicquid vult sine iniuria creature. . . Cui nemo dicere potest 'cur ita facis'," I *Sent.* d 41 q 1 art. 3 dub. 3.

97

finds himself is far from lawless; legal obligation is even one of its most characteristic aspects.[27]

In the thesis that God is the first rule of all justice, it is not the lawlessness of the set order which is expressed, but man's inability to discover the motives and causes of God's actions. This is the reason why without fail St. Paul's words are quoted at this point: "but who are you, a man, to answer back to God? Will what is molded say to its molder, 'Why have you made me thus?' Has the potter no right over the clay. . . ?[28] Since the time of Duns Scotus this text has been the traditional culmination of all analyses of the mystery of election and reprobation;[29] whenever used, it has stood not for the lawlessness of God but for the inscrutability of his ways and the absolute freedom with which he, indebted to no one, made himself a debtor to those who would fulfill certain set requirements. With the metamorphosis of *misericordia* to *iusticia* the set order shows forth a legal structure to which God freely committed himself. In this sense we must understand that God is the first rule of all justice.

2. The lawfulness of God's action

Still this does not answer the charge of those who claim that this legal structure of the set order is not an expression of God's holiness and inner being but the result of an arbitrary and changeable decision of God's unguided will.[30] This continues to leave room for a threat to the harmony

[27] The best treatment to date of Biel's concept of natural law is given by W. Kölmel. By accepting the traditional understanding of Biel's doctrine of justification, however, he was not in a position to see the unbroken continuity in Biel's treatment of natural law. "Bemerkenswert ist der Wechsel vom Primat des Willens in verschiedenen der Naturrechtslehre vorausliegenden Traktaten . . . zum Hervortreten der ratio in der Gründung der sittlichen Ordnung." "Von Ockham zu Gabriel Biel . . . ," *FS* 37 (1955), 256.

[28] Rom. 9: 20–21: "O homo, tu quis es, qui respondeas Deo? Numquid dicit figmentum ei qui se finxit: Quid me fecisti sic? Annon habet potestatem figulus luti. . ." (*Vulgate*).

[29] Cf. e.g., Gregory of Rimini, I *Sent.* d 41–42 q 1 art. 2 [fol. 159 M].

[30] Cf. Carl Feckes, *Die Rechtfertigungslehre*, p. 12: "Auch die höchsten Normen der Sittlichkeit sind nicht Ausstrahlungen der Heiligkeit und Vollkommenheit Gottes und daher unveränderlich und ewig, sondern reine Willkürlichkeiten." *Ibid.*, p. 13, n. 60; ". . . die wirkliche Weltordnung [ist] rein willkürlich festgesetzt . . . wodurch ihre Vernünftigkeit, ihre Abbildlichkeit Gottes, ihre Harmonie preis-

of the universe since the law *in* man and *for* man — natural law and positive law as formulated in the Decalogue and the golden rule — are contingent, mutually unrelated products of God's will, not subject to the eternal law.[31]

At this point, however, we must remember Boehner's defense of Occam mentioned earlier: the set order is for the *Venerabilis Inceptor* by no means a product solely of God's will; will and intellect are two different names for God's essence. This defense appears to be applicable also to Biel.[32] Against the Thomistic emphasis on the priority of God's intellect, the priority of God's will is not stressed as much as the simplicity of God's being and the resulting unity of his intellect and essence.[33] As the simplicity of God's being also implies a unity of essence and will, God's very essence guarantees the unbreakable relation and cooperation of intellect and will in God's *opera ad extra*.[34] There may be reason to doubt whether Occam has honoured this interdependence of intellect and will;[35] yet Biel constantly tries to make clear that, whereas the will of God is the immediate cause of every act, these acts are certainly not arbitrary products of God's will alone. On the contrary, God's will operates according to God's essential wisdom, though this may be hidden from man. One of many possible quotations in support of this interpretation is the continuation of the same *Lectura* passage, quoted above, which has led many scholars to accuse Biel of ethical relativism.[36]

---

gegeben ist." See, however, Biel's statement: "Non enim potest a divina bonitate procedere aliquod vanum et inutile sicut nec ex divina sapientia aliquod inordinatum. Dei enim sunt perfecta opera, etiam si nobis lateat utilitas doni." III *Sent.* d 23 q 2 art. 3 dub. 1. "Solus ergo deus bonus est et essentialiter bonus." *S* IV 36 D. Cf. *Lect.* 23 E.

[31] "Etwas ist also gut und gerecht, weil es Gott will, nicht weil es dem Wesen Gottes oder der sittlichen Wesensnatur des Menschen entspricht . . . als freie, gesetzlose Bestimmung Gottes relativ und zufällig," Georg Ott, p. 257.

[32] I *Sent.* d 7 q 1 art. 2 concl. 3 and 5.

[33] ". . . intellectio divina mediate per essentiam divinam feratur in res ad extra; hoc enim falsum est. Cum intellectus divinus et essentia divina sint penitus indistincta et omnibus modis intellectus divinus est essentia divina. . ." I *Sent.* d 38 q 1 art. 3 dub. 2; cf. Leif Grane, p. 55.

[34] "Voluntas divina sive essentia quod omnino idem est est causa immediata omnium que fiunt. . . ," I *Sent.* d 45 q 1 art. 2 concl. 1.

[35] Elzarius Bonke notes: ". . . concedit quidem Gulielmus de Ockham mutuam relationem inter voluntatem et intellectum, illam autem negligit et proinde negat in suis consequentiis. . ." p. 82.

[36] "Nam sicut voluntas divina est causa omnium ut sint ita etiam causa electorum

3. The reliability of the moral order

There remain still two points in the usual series of charges against Biel to be dealt with: the alleged unreliability of the set order which can change with every whim of God's will and the disintegration of the bond between eternal, natural, and positive law.

The set moral order is not only structured by law and a product of all God's properties; it is also immutable. Here again we approach an area where we can see one of the dangerous consequences of misunderstanding the dialectics between the two orders of God with which we began Chapter Two. Often enough Biel confesses the immutability of the set order. He restricts this statement, however, to the established order, *de facto* or *stante lege*, all synonyms for the more usual term *de potentia ordinata*.[37] If it is said that natural law as we know it now is immutable but could have been changed, then this statement is only a variation on the theme that God acts contingently in his *opera ad extra*. The content of this contingent will, however, has been defined before the foundation of the world and is strictly immutable.[38] Insofar as the wisdom of God which is involved in the establishment of the natural law is beyond human intellectual capacities, it would have been possible for God to have decided in favor of a natural law different from the present one. But *de facto*, this natural law is the direct extension of the eternal law and is as immutable in character.

The same is true for the first two commandments of the Decalogue which we discussed earlier. The other commandments have been granted

---

ut suis donis digni sint, ut ita nihil sit quod non de interiori atque intelligibili aula summi imperatoris egrediatur secundum ineffabilem iusticiam, non nostram sed suam," *Lect.* 23 E. Cf. *Lect.* 49 M; *S* II 34 E; 39 F; 40 D: "Et propter hoc operatio ad extra que exigit potentiam, sapientiam et bonitatem et per consequens intellectum et voluntatem una est . . ."

[37] "Naturale ius ab exordio rationalis creature incipiens manet immobile. Immobile de facto licet non de possibili accipiendo naturale ius ut extendit se ad omnia moralia," III *Sent.* d 37 q 1 art. 2 concl. 5. See Georg Ott, p. 285: ". . . die Unveränderlichkeit besteht nur [!] 'de facto,' nicht aber auch 'de possibili' . ." Cf. Occam, *Dialogus*, III.II 1, 10, ed. M. Goldast, in *Monarchiae S. Romani Imperii sive Tractatum de iurisdictione imperiali, regia, et pontificia seu sacerdotali*, II (Frankfurt, 1668), p. 878.

[38] "Deus licet contingenter vult quicquid ad extra vult tamen immutabilis est volendo, nec succedit velle nolle vel econverso, sed quod vult ab eterno vult, licet posset ipsum ab eterno non velle." I *Sent.* d 41 q 1 art. 3. dub. 3, summarium 3.

practically the same immutability on grounds of their close relation with immutable natural law. Because they are not a direct extension of natural law in the strictest sense of the word, God has reserved the right to dispense with them in some special cases as, for example, his commandment to Abraham to sacrifice Isaac and his commandment to Hosea to marry a whore. These are, however, isolated exceptions from the general rule which holds — in strict parallel with the canon-law concept of special dispensation — that these commandments as such are by no means abolished; rather they retain the same validity as the first two commandments.[39] If God wants in such a particular case to overrule a commandment, his decision can never be regarded as a dark fate caused by an arbitrary whimsical tyrant; such overruling would have to be explicitly revealed to the person concerned, since unawareness of a commandment of God is sufficient exoneration and does not even interfere with the meritorious character of such an act of "disobedience."[40]

The set moral order is guaranteed by an immutable natural law and the equally immutable first two commandments of the Decalogue. *De potentia ordinata*, in fact, God has reserved the right to change the other commandments exactly as he has changed the law of the Old Testament into the law of the New Testament, which means that the *viatores* are now under a new dependable dispensation of God's *potentia ordinata*. We cannot, thus, agree with Johannes Heckel and Georg Ott when they find here "despotic justice" and "unlimited decisionism" which the *via*-

---

[39] "Deus non potest facere malum nec precipere malum. . . Sed diceres deus posset precipere quod contra preceptum ageretur, sicut dixit 'Accipe fornicariam' et ita precipere male agere. Solutio: in casu tollit preceptum quantum ad illum. Sed manente precepto, non potest oppositum precipere, quia hoc implicat precipere et non precipere." I *Sent.* d 47 q 1 art. 2. concl. C. Compare Scotus, *Ox.* III d 37 nota 3.

For the contrary position see Aquinas *ST* I.II q 100 art. 8, resp. Aquinas sees in the cases of Abraham and Hosea only mutable applications of immutable laws (*ibid.* ad 3). Hochstetter notes that the discussion of the possibility of such exceptions is not restricted to the *via moderna*: "Viator Mundi," *FS* 32 (1950), 14. Roland Bainton has pointed out that the understanding that the Patriarch (Abraham, etc.) received a unique command from God is the most common solution of the problem. See "Immoralities of the Patriarchs according to the Exegesis of the Late Middle Ages and of the Reformation," *HTR* 23 (1930), 40 f.

[40] ". . . ignorantia invincibilis simpliciter excusat. . . ," *Lect.* 7 D. "Voluntas viatoris tenetur se conformare voluntati divine beneplaciti in particulari cognite nisi revelatio aut preceptum dei ipsam ad oppositum obligaret," *Lect.* 68 N.

tor would have to experience as threatening arbitrariness. On the contrary, the *viator* can build his ethics on a stable, immutable substructure of natural law and of Holy Scripture as a product of God's inscrutable wisdom.[41]

Georg Ott has claimed further that along with this *principle* of the unreliability of the legal order, Biel holds *in practice* that the Mosaic formulation of the natural law was in its totality absolutely immutable and eternal — a thesis not materially different from what Thomas Aquinas held on this point.[42] According to Ott, Biel thus would be highly incon-sistent, as he abandons his extreme voluntaristic principles, "positivistische Gebotsethik," for a rationalistic doctrine of natural law.[43]

The difficulty seems to be found not so much in the inconsistent thought of Biel as in Ott's misinterpretation of the meaning of the difference between the *potentia absoluta* and the *potentia ordinata*. For Ott this difference has only theoretical value and is seen as an unsuccessful effort to ward off the absurd consequences of the principle of God's omnipotence.[44] When it is not strictly necessary, it seems preferable to avoid

---

[41] ". . . Omnia cetera precepta ad decalogum reducuntur tam divina quam humana vel ut principia vel ut conclusiones vel ut eis rationabiliter consona," III *Sent.* d 37 q 1 art. 2 concl. 6 O. Cf., however, Heckel, "Recht und Gesetz," p. 286 f.; Georg Ott, p. 258: "So ist der Mensch in Wahrheit doch dem hemmungslosen Dezisionismus Gottes ausgeliefert." ". . . talem etiam certitudinem habemus et nos de articulorum fidei veritate et omnibus in canone biblie contentis in eo sensu in quo a sancto spiritu revelata. His namque assentiendo falli aut decipi non possumus quia deus qui summa et infallibilis est veritas non potest falsum tanquam verum revelare," *Lect.* 8 B. Gregory makes the same point when he criticises those extremists who claim that God is not committed to what is revealed through Scripture and Church: I *Sent.* d 42–44 q 2 art. 2 [fol. 167 D]. Cf. II *Sent.* d 30–33 q 1 art. 2 [fol. 111 L]. But Gregory's criticism does not apply to the Holcot of the *Sapientia*-commentary: "Et ideo tenendum est quod sic [resurrectio omnium sit futura], quia hoc sonat scriptura sacra expresse. Hoc etiam est sanctis patribus revelatum . . ." *Sap.* Lect. 18 A.

[42] Georg Ott, p. 286: "In Wirklichkeit ist auch für Biel wie für Thomas das ganze im Dekalog formulierte Naturgesetz schlechthin immutabel und ewig."

[43] *Ibid.*, p. 259. Ott in this way succeeds in making Biel at one and the same time responsible for rationalism and naturalism in the legal thought of the Enlightenment *and* for relativism and positivism in modern times (p. 296).

[44] ". . . eine Unterscheidung freilich, die kaum mehr als theoretischen Wert hat und die teilweise paradoxen und absurden Konsequenzen, die sich aus dem "Omnipotenz-Prinzip" ergeben, keineswegs abzuwehren vermag," *ibid.*, p. 258. It is an interesting variation on the usual interpretations that Ott characterizes the order *de potentia ordinata* as the hypothetical one: "Sie ist ja nur eine hypothetische

trying to resolve seemingly contradictory statements by an appeal to inconsistency. This necessity in fact does not arise here, since the proposition that God's will is the first rule of all justice does not imply a despotic voluntarism; it clearly does not exclude, but includes a dependable moral order in the realm of the *potentia ordinata*.

III. Eternal Law and Natural Law

1. Natural law as manifestation of eternal law

Finally we have to ask how man can know the will of God. Until now we have been discussing the objective aspect of Biel's ethics insofar as this concerns the laws established by God. Now we turn to the subjective aspect: how can man actually know the will of God with respect to particular issues so that he is able to fulfill his moral obligations?

Biel distinguishes here between several modes of God's will. On the one hand there is the *voluntas beneplaciti*, which may be either *antecedens* or *consequens*. On the other hand there is the *voluntas signi*, which may take the form of prohibition, precept, counsel, actual deed, or permission.

As antecedent, the *voluntas beneplaciti* is the divine will which enables a person to accomplish something or to execute a command or counsel given to him.[45] According to this will, for example, God wants Peter to earn merits, provides him with grace and free will, and finally adds the precepts and counsels to help him earn these merits.

The *voluntas beneplaciti consequens* is the direct will of God which is always executed.[46] Therefore we know with certainty that what was or is, God has willed to be. In the realm of ethics it is, of course, more vital for man to know the *voluntas signi* since the antecedent *voluntas beneplaciti*, invariably implemented by the *voluntas beneplaciti consequens*, is God's

---

Ordnung d.h. sie kann jederzeit von der absoluten Macht durchbrochen werden," *ibid*. Cf. the more usual interpretation of Elzarius Bonke, who locates the nominalistic "escape" in the hypothetical order *de potentia absoluta*, which he calls the "refugium nominalistarum" (p. 77).

[45] "Voluntas beneplaciti antecedens est voluntas divina dans alicui antecedentia unde potest consequi aliquid vel operari parata coagere si ille velit cum precepto vel consilio exequendi." *Lect.* 68. C, *Lect.* 69 D. Cf. Occam, I *Sent.* d 47 q 1 B.

[46] "Voluntas beneplaciti consequens est voluntas divina sibi efficaciter in esse alicuius complacens, ipsum diligendo esse aut producendo seu conservando," *Lect.* 69 D. Cf. *S* II 4 C.

eternal counsel which — as we will see in dealing with the question of pre-destination — is hidden.

The *voluntas signi* is the declaration of God's will for his creation which enables man to know the will of God, but which is certainly not always executed.[47] All human justice consists in conformity to the will of God as known through his *voluntas signi*. This is the ultimate norm and basic rule for man's moral behavior.[48] For this norm Biel uses the term eternal law; because of its conformity with this eternal law, natural law is right, and all other righteousness in man's laws is derived from this eternal law.[49] There is nothing unusual or original in this construction; Biel could have found these thoughts in Duns Scotus' works and actually did find them in Gregory of Rimini.[50]

In this context the question arises whether one can wish one's own damnation out of love for God. Biel here follows Gregory of Rimini's solution that if God should reveal that he wants to reject someone — which is highly improbable — such a person should conform himself to the will of God as the highest moral norm.[51] This is seemingly a close parallel to Occam's question *de odio dei*; Biel with his pastoral formula-

---

[47] "Voluntas signi est creatura aliqua sive effectus divine voluntatis. . . ," *Lect.* 68 E.

[48] "Omnis ergo iusticia et rectitudo rationalis creature consistit in conformitate ipsius ad dei voluntatem. . . Iusticia ergo nostra in hoc consistit ut nostra voluntas infirma de se non recta, conformetur divine voluntati tanquam sue regule cui convenit essentialiter esse rectam." *Lect.* 68 H.

[49] "Volens contra divinam voluntatem vult contra legem eternam et ita repugnat divine iusticie *que est secundum legem eternam*," *Lect.* 68 U. Cf. II *Sent.* d 35 q I art. I nota I. There is no reason why one should agree with Georg Ott that the term eternal law has lost its meaning for Biel, and has become an empty inheritance of the past, and a mere synonym for natural law. The suggestion is that Luther brings this Gabrielistic development to full completion by now also giving up the term itself. See Ott, p. 262: "Diese Formulierungen laufen praktisch alle auf eine Gleichsetzung der *lex aeterna* mit der *lex naturalis* hinaus." As we will see, the eternal law is far richer in meaning than the natural law, which is basic but nevertheless only one of several manifestations.

[50] *Ox.* IV d 15 q 2 n 6; *Ox.* IV d 33 q 3 n 7. Cf. Gregory I *Sent.* d 48 q I a I [fol. 181 H]: ". . . quilibet tenetur nihil velle contra eternam legem, ergo quilibet tenetur in nullo difformare suam voluntatem divine voluntati."

[51] ". . . ipse sciens dei voluntatem deberet contentari et velle quod eum deus damnaret, ex quo sic esset placitum deo et hic actus procederet ex maxima dilectione dei; nec esset culpabilis sed laudabilis," *Lect.* 68 S. In the parallel passage, I *Sent.* d 48 art. 3 dub 3., Biel raises the same issue but refers to *Lect.* 68 for the solution. Cf. Gregory, I *Sent.* d 48 q I art. I ad 3 [fol. 181 N] whom Biel follows *verbatim*.

tion escapes, however, the awkward consequences of Occam's syllogisms by transferring this issue from the logical into the theological sphere, as Gregory had done before him.

We know the will of God through such signs as precepts, prohibitions, and counsels. Man's most immediate guide is the innate dictate of right reason which is the natural law for man's will. As we saw before, this inborn law is immutable; no positive law that deviates from this can be right. Similarly, no human act can be right if it does not conform with this law, since the dictate of right reason is a manifestation of the eternal law of God.[52] A second manifestation of the eternal law of God is Scripture; a third, the institutions and traditions of the universal Church and positive canon law. The last manifestation consists of the events of past and present which we have come to know already under the term *voluntas beneplaciti consequens*.[53]

From the foregoing we may draw the conclusion that the *voluntas signi* and the *lex aeterna* are interchangeable concepts. Natural law is one of four possible manifestations. That natural law is not even its primary manifestation appears in another context, where Biel says that the divine law in a strict sense precedes natural law and positive law, since these are not as directly revealed by God as the other three manifestations.[54]

2. The significance of the natural law for ethics

Natural law is the direct and immutable extension of the eternal law. Biel has expressed this in his *Collectorium* in words that have caused some misunderstanding. He asserts here that law in the definition of sin should

---

[52] "Unde nobis innotescunt dei precepta, prohibitiones et consilia? . . . Primo per naturalis rationis dictamen et iudicium. Hec enim est lex naturalis et regula nostre voluntatis, nunquam discordans a regula divine rationis. . . Hanc enim deus contulit homini ut semper ad optima deprecetur. . . Huius enim legis naturalis principia sunt immutabilis rectitudinis a deo ut contra ipsa nulla alia lex statuta ab homine recta esse potest. Quod utique verum non esset nisi esset conformis rectitudini divine voluntatis. . . Eterna enim lex naturalem ordinem servare iubet. . . Dictamen igitur recte rationis manifestatio est legis divine." *Lect.* 69 A. Cf. III *Sent.* d 37 q 1 art. 1 nota 1.

[53] III *Sent.* d 37 q 1 art. 1 nota 1; *Lect.* 69 B.

[54] "Lex divina est signum verum creature rationali revelatum. . . Dicitur revelatum ad excludendam legem naturalem et humanam, que non habentur per revelationem immediate a deo sed aliter. . ." III *Sent.* d 37 q 1 art. 1 nota 1 C.

be understood as at once indicative and imperative law which indicates the differences between good and bad, commands the first and prohibits the second.[55] With this in mind it can be said that actual sin is a voluntary commission or omission contrary to right reason.[56] Then follows the startling explanation as to why sin is defined as contrary to right reason and not as contrary to the eternal law or divine reason: If God should not exist — which is impossible — and thus there were no divine reason, or if divine reason should err, one would still sin if one acted contrary to the right reason of an angel, of a man, or contrary to any kind of right reason one can conceive. This would be the case even if there were no right reason at all, but only its dictate.[57]

Georg Ott has interpreted this seemingly unorthodox thesis to be the proclamation of human reason as the autonomous source for natural law which has lost its ontological relation to eternal law. According to Ott, in Biel's thought natural law has lost its theological basis and derives its validity from its immanent rationality.[58]

[55] "Lex ergo et preceptum in diffinitione peccati debet accipi large ut legem tam indicativam quam imperativam contineat," II *Sent.* d 35 q 1 art. 1 D/E. In this sense Georg Ott's conclusion "die *lex naturalis* [ist] für Biel auch keine *"lex imperativa,"* sondern blosse [!] *"lex indicativa"* (p. 278), has to be amended.

[56] "Peccatum actuale est voluntaria commissio vel omissio contra rectam rationem," II *Sent.* d 35 q 1 art. 1 D/E.

[57] "Dicitur autem contra rectam rationem et non contra divinam rationem, ne putetur peccatum esse precise contra rationem divinam, et non contra quamlibet rationem rectam de eodem. Aut ne estimetur aliquid esse peccatum, non quia est contra rationem divinam inquantum rectam, sed quia est contra eam inquantum est divina. Nam si per impossibile deus non esset qui est ratio divina, aut ratio illa divina esset errans, adhuc si quis ageret contra rectam rationem angelicam vel humanam aut aliam aliquam si qua esset peccaret. Et si nulla penitus esset recta ratio, adhuc si quis ageret contra id quod agendum dictaret ratio recta si aliqua esset peccaret." II *Sent.* d 35 q 1 art. 1 D/E. Just like the definition of actual sin indicated above, this passage is with minor changes a *verbatim* quote beginning with the words "ne putetur" from Gregory of Rimini, II *Sent.* d 34–35 q 1 art. 2 [fol. 118 H/J]. Ott may have been influenced by Otto von Gierke, who first pointed to Biel's passage in *Johannes Althusius und die Entwicklung der naturrechtlichen Staatstheorien,* 3 ed. (Breslau, 1913), p. 74, n. 45.

[58] "Aber man erkennt unschwer, dass hier das Naturrecht rational konstruiert und die nach augustinisch — thomistischer Lehre bestehende ontische Beziehung zur lex aeterna ganz aufgegeben ist. Die menschliche ratio erscheint als autonome Quelle des Naturrechts." Ott finds here an "Einbruch der Renaissance" (p. 279). Bonke, too, seems on one occasion to identify Biel's concepts of natural and eternal law: "Propterea quoque docet Biel legem naturalem — quam etiam aeternam vocat — sese extendere non tantum ad praeceptum vel prohibitionem, sed simpliciter ad omnem rectam rationem" (p. 74).

As a matter of fact, this definition of *the* moral standard solely with regard to the dictate of right reason betrays an interest in the reliability of the order *de potentia ordinata* which is characteristic for nominalism. Its main epistemological thrust, based on the *notitia intuitiva*, can best be understood as a hunger for reality and unmediated, dependable experience. Certainly in its emphasis on the autonomy of man, late medieval nominalism is a parallel phenomenon to the early stirrings of the Renaissance.[59]

Without hesitation one can conclude that Biel finds this reliability of the moral order guaranteed in the immutability of natural law, and this implies an immanent validity. *This immanent validity, however, is reliable solely for the reason that its justice is derived from the eternal law or divine reason.* This eternal law in its turn is dependable because it is not subject to arbitrary decisions of God's will, or reason, but to a final standard of justice that would even endure if there were no divine reason at all; its steadfastness would not be shaken even if the divine reason would deviate from this norm.

If one sins, Biel says, against right reason, one sins *ipso facto* also against God's reason. It is nevertheless more precise to include in the definition of sin that it is an act against right reason than against God's reason, as there might be people who would think that something is a sin because it is contrary to *God's* right reason while in fact it is a sin because it goes against God's *right* reason. Biel wards off here the dangers of a heteronomous understanding of the moral order based on the arbitrary insights of a tyrant! This explains the other advantage of the definition chosen. If one were to define sin in its relation to *divine* reason and not to *right* reason, some would be misled into thinking that something would be a sin if measured according to divine reason and not a sin if measured according to some other right reason.[60]

From the foregoing it is clear that only when we take the bold statement quoted above out of its context can we interpret it as the abolition

---

[59] Cf. Oberman, "Some Notes on the Theology of Nominalism with Reference to the Italian Renaissance," *HTR* 53 (1960), 70–74.

[60] Gregory is somewhat more explicit on this point: ". . . cum igitur divina ratio utique rectissima semper sit omne quod est contra eternam legem est contra rectam rationem. Et quicquid est contra aliquam rectam rationem est et contra quamlibet rectam rationem de eodem; nam circa idem quelibet ratio recta cuilibet rationi recte consonat et nulla alicui adversatur. . ." II *Sent.* d 34–35 q 1 art. 2 [fol. 118 H].

of the meaning of the eternal law. The reliability of natural law and its universal, not individual validity is, however, secured by and derived from the eternal law with which it is in undisturbable harmony.[61]

This harmony between God and man assures man of the reliability of his knowledge of the objective standards for good and evil as concerns the temporal felicity of man. In this sense man has a direct insight into God's mind. As regards his eternal felicity, however, God's mind is beyond the reach of human understanding, and at this level man is dependent on revelation, which takes one of three forms: Scripture, Church, and history. At this level, natural law is not abolished but transcended. But whatever God may reveal through one of these three channels, man knows that it is the common product of all God's properties, his goodness, power, and wisdom.

Further precepts above and beyond natural law are a natural necessity in order to live a good life both in relation to God and to one's fellow human beings. This became even more necessary after the fall, for man through the influence of concupiscence often errs in the conclusions he draws from natural law.[62] Nevertheless, the impact of the loss of original justice, as we have seen with regard to the *synderesis*, does not imply the loss of man's inborn knowledge of the distinction between good and evil.

3. The Old Testament character of nominalistic ethics

In sum, we may say that according to Biel the moral hierarchy manifests two structures: first, the traditional three layers: (1) *voluntas dei* or *lex aeterna*; (2) in conformity with this and just as immutable: natural law; and finally, (3) positive human law. Parallel to the first stands a second structure: (1) *voluntas beneplaciti antecedens* and *consequens*; (2) *voluntas signi*; (3) natural law as its natural manifestation; Scripture, positive divine law (Church), and history as its revealed forms. The *voluntas signi* and the eternal law coincide as to their content, whereas the eternal law is the uncreated, the *voluntas signi* the created will of God. While natural law guides man in his search for temporal happiness, the

---

[61] ". . . lex naturalis ex hoc recta est quia conformat se divine voluntati. . . , *Lect.* 68 M. "Volens contra divinam voluntatem vult contra legem eternam et ita repugnat divine iusticie que est secundum legem eternam," *Lect.* 68 U.

[62] "Maxime post lapsum quia adeo vulnerata sunt hominis naturalia et damnate concupiscentia obfuscata ut in conclusionibus legis naturalis sepe erret et iudicet iusta que sunt iniqua. . . ," III *Sent.* d 37 q 1 art. 1 nota 5.

revealed forms of the eternal law guide man in his search for eternal happiness.[63]

On the lowest layer (3) both positive human law and positive divine law (Church) are binding on the conscience only insofar as they are just,[64] that is, conforming with the dictates of right reason and in accordance with the eternal law of God. In no sense, therefore, can it be said that the *viator* is caught in a lawless world without any set standard of judgment. Not only do there exist several exterior norms or manifestations of the one norm, but further these norms are in accordance and harmony with the innate moral norm, right reason, which by way of the *synderesis* and the conscience advises man with regard to his temporal and eternal good.[65]

The *lex naturalis* and its human appearance as the dictate of right reason is the nexus which binds man to God and his creation. At times Biel almost reaches a Thomistic position, so convinced is he of the immutability of natural law and its foundation in the eternal law.[66] However, while the eternal law is for Thomas the plan of divine world government preexistent in the mind of God,[67] Biel feels that this construction would undercut the simplicity of God. Therefore he identifies this eternal law with all the properties of God to such an extent that he can use the terms "will of God" and "eternal law" interchangeably. But as with Thomas, these terms stand for the eternal, that is, preexistent and immutable plan for world government both on the objective historical and on the subjective moral level.

On the basis of this we might expect to find a decisive difference be-

---

[63] Cf. III *Sent.* d 37 q 1 art. 1 nota 1.

[64] IV *Sent.* d 16 q 3 art. 1 nota 6.

[65] Therefore, Bonke's conclusion is correct (p. 75): ". . . concludi debet in theoria Gabrielis Biel fundamentum ordinis moralis esse ordinem naturalem et inseitatem boni et mali moralis sitam esse in relatione actus ad finem ultimum," and p. 78: "Quamdiu enim non excluditur mutua relatio inter voluntatem et intellectum, omnis positivismus in illius auctoris doctrina excludendus est. . . ," p. 75. The qualification of this statement, however, by the words "in theoria" and "quamdiu" is unwarranted.

[66] See Aquinas, *ST* I.II q 91 art. 2 [resp.]: "Lex naturalis nihil aliud est quam participatio legis aeternae in rationali creatura"; this is quoted by Ott, p. 278, to indicate the difference between Thomas and Biel! "Bei Thomas ist die *lex naturalis* metaphysisch begründet in der *lex aeterna*. . . Anders bei Biel. Die *lex aeterna* wird von ihm im Zusammenhang mit der *lex naturalis* mit keinem Wort erwähnt[!]."

[67] *ST* I.II q 19 art. 4; q 93 art. 1.

109

tween Biel and Aquinas at least in the different estimation of man's capacity to know the norms derived from the eternal law. This is indeed the case, though the chasm is far less striking than one might have expected. Aquinas distinguishes also between the *voluntas beneplaciti* and the *voluntas signi* and knows that this *voluntas* is not always known to man, insofar as it is related to future acts of God in history.[68]

For both Biel and Thomas natural law known by the dictate of right reason is dependable and immutable. The difference appears in that the sovereign God has, according to Biel, the freedom to dispense momentarily and in particular cases with some of the commandments derived through direct revelation. This is impossible for Aquinas since all the commandments of the Decalogue are, as norms in the strictest sense of the word, a direct extension of the natural law and share therefore its indispensability.[69]

Finally, it should be said that natural law, according to Biel, has an immanent rationality which enables man in principle to reach the right conclusions as to his temporal felicity. This may lead to the doctrine of the human conscience as the highest court of appeal. The fact that this individual decision can stand up to the scrutiny of any man is due to the universality and superindividual validity of the dictates of right reason, which in the last resort it owes to the eternal law of God.

It is quite evident, therefore, that the often-repeated charges — despotism, decisionism, positivism, and ethical relativism — made against the ethics of nominalism, here represented in Biel's ethics, are absolutely without foundation.

No lines can be drawn easily from Biel to the Age of Reason, Deism, and Enlightenment; Biel's God is not a *deus otiosus*, nor is natural law for him merely the harmony of a mechanized cosmos. Furthermore, all efforts to show in this connection that Gabrielistic nominalism is responsible for the "disintegration of the Middle Ages" must collapse in the face of the indisputable evidence of Biel's basic adherence to the general medieval concept of the divine basis of natural law.[70]

[68] *ST* I q 19 art. 11; I *Sent.* d 45 q 1 4 C; d 47 q 1 2 C; *de Veritate* 23.3 C.

[69] ". . . praecepti Decalogi sunt omnino indispensabilia," *ST* I.II q 100 art. 8 [resp.].

[70] We do not want to deny that the nominalistic emphasis on the fact that nothing and no one but God himself is the standard of good and evil is an important variant as compared with the pre-Occamistic position. It is regrettable, how-

We may well end this section by pointing out that in view of contemporary Old Testament scholarship, a more appropriate evaluation of the nominalistic position suggests itself.

4. An appropriate evaluation of the nominalistic position

In the nominalistic qualification of the Thomistic understanding of the relation of God and justice, there is a phenomenon parallel to what appears to be the special characteristic of Yahweh as compared with the deities in the polytheisms surrounding Israel. *The God of Israel does not act according to established justice, but establishes justice in his very acts.*

Without occupying ourselves with what in this context would be mere speculation as regards the ethics of Israelite religion *versus* the ethics of Aristotelian religion, the possibility of the comparison with the earliest Old Testament structures may warn us against a too hasty condemnation of the nominalistic position.[71] Our discussion of the nominalistic understanding of the eternal decrees and divine justice will show that this parallelism with the Old Testament not only originates in but is limited by the dialectics of the *potentia absoluta* and the *potentia ordinata*.

---

ever, that the discussion has hitherto exclusively centered on the question of positivism. Harry A. Wolfson in his important analyses of the history of the two major schools of interpretation of the Platonic ideas has provided a more pertinent and therefore more fruitful context for a further investigation. See "Extradeical and Intradeical Interpretations of Platonic Ideas," *Journal of the History of Ideas* 22 (1961), 3–32.

[71] "In the early strata of the Old Testament, Yahweh's historical judgments and acts constitute justice and righteousness for the community created by him. Yahweh's acts or judgments may in one sense be called arbitrary; they do not conform to objective norms of the right or true; they are not measurable against a cosmic principle or an eternal order as are the acts and judgments of the lords and powers in Near Eastern mythopoeic systems. Yahweh delivered the poor from human lords and oppressors. This defines and gives content to 'justice in Israel.' For what Yahweh does and says in Israel is, for Israel, justice and righteousness. The law in the early stages of Israel's faith is not positive law or a set of ethical principles. Torah consists of the stipulations of a historical covenant reflecting only the demand and pleasure of Yahweh." Frank Moore Cross, in a forthcoming study entitled "Yahweh as Judge." Cf. Walther Eichrodt, *Theologie des Alten Testaments*, vol. I: *Gott und Volk*, 3 ed. (Berlin, 1948), p. 6 ff., and his *Das Menschenverständnis des Alten Testaments* (Basel, 1944), pp. 13–27. See also the literature noted by Gerhard von Rad, *Theologie des Alten Testaments*, vol. I: *Die Theologie der geschichtlichen Überlieferungen Israels*, (Munich, 1957), p. 192 ff.

IV. Moses and Christ: Law and Gospel

1. The fulfillment of the Old Law

The unity of Holy Scripture is expressed by Biel with the image of two breasts which represent the Old and the New Testament. Their common characteristic is that both hold out rewards for those who labour.[72]

In a variety of ways, however, Biel shows what has to be regarded as their essential difference, which really is a difference in degree: the Old Law lacks the perfection of the New Law. The most concise formulation is perhaps the one where Biel points to the difference between *quo* and *qua*. The Jews knew the end of the journey, since the Lord had revealed himself to them just as to the Christians. But they did not know the path that led to this goal.[73]

In a more elaborate description he points to the fact that in two respects the imperfection of the righteousness of the law of Moses can be established. On the one hand it proved to lead not to the glory of God but to that of the Scribes and Pharisees. On the other hand — and more important — Moses' law required exterior acts and ceremonies, whereas Christ calls for interior acts which are not forced but voluntary.[74] In both instances righteousness is intended, but the righteousness of Christians has to be more ample and sincere and therefore more perfect than the righteousness of the Jews.

This imperfection of the Old Law — and, we add, by no means the imperfection of the law as such — is intended by St. Paul when he writes in his letter to the Galatians: ". . . by works of the law shall no one be

[72] "Duo ubera duo sunt testamenta, mercedem laborantibus promittentia. Testamentum vetus retributionem temporalem et abundantiam vini et olei et longevitatem super terram promittit populo rudi. Novum vero felicitatem eternam." *S* I 32 E. Cf. another interpretation: "Ubera hec due sunt partes iusticie, declinare scilicet a malo et facere bonum," *S* I 32 D.

[73] "Prima miseria erroris ex defectu verorum pastorum ac ducum contingit, paucissimi in illa profunda noctis ignorantia noverunt quo et qua eundum erat. Soli iudeorum genti revelatus erat dominus. . . Sed et iudei noverunt quo eundum, viam tamen quam ignorabant." *S* I 57 D.

[74] It is interesting to see how Biel applies the terms referring to the school differences in the universities of his day to late Judaism: "Inter iudeorum secta phariseorum probabilior fuit. Ideo Paulus eam nominat certissimam sectam iudeice religionis." *S* I 83 B.

justified" [2:16]. In short, the Law of Christ is the fulfillment of the Law of Moses inasmuch as it implies the interiorization of righteousness.[75] The righteousness of the New Law is in the full sense of the word legal righteousness.[76]

2. The medieval tradition

While this exposition has been drawn from sermon materials, we find that Biel takes exactly the same position in his academic works. Here, however, the treatment of the relation of the two laws is explicitly seen from the standpoint of the great schoolmen and in this way affords us the opportunity to compare Biel's interpretation with the legacy of the preceding medieval tradition. His main conclusion in accordance with the medieval tradition is indeed that the ceremonial and judicial laws — such as "an eye for an eye" — of the Old Testament have been abrogated; the moral law, with its core, the Decalogue, however, remains and stands approved by Christ.[77] This in itself would suggest that the yoke of the

[75] "Necesse est iusticiam christianorum quibus apertum est regnum celorum esse maiorem iusticia scribarum et phariseorum. Justicia phariseorum et scribarum quam simulabant se tenere, fuit iusticia legis moysaice et ideo [!] imperfecta. Nam imperfectionem veteris legis apostolus frequenter testatur. Gal. 1 [2:17]: " 'Ex operibus legis non iustificabitur omnis caro'; fuit enim figura et umbra legis evangelice. Figura autem deficit a veritate et umbra a luce. . . Potest tamen in genere legis veteris imperfectio ostendi ex obiecto et ex fine. Ex obiecto quia tantum versabatur circa exteriora . . . opera legis at cerimonias . . . [C]. Nobis itaque si salvari volumus necesse est nostram iusticiam esse abundantiorem, id est, non solum in exterioribus apparere sed multo magis in interioribus . . . nullum opus extrinsecum est de se liberum. Potest enim agens quantum ad illud cogi et violentari. . . Ex quo sequitur quod verus dei cultus non consistit in exterioribus, sed in interioribus piis affectionibus voluntatis . . . [D]. Ex fine ostendi potest imperfectio iusticie apparentis eorundem, quia scribe et pharisei non quesierunt gloriam et laudem dei, sed suam . . . [F]. "Ego autem qui veni non solvere legem sed adimplere dico vobis prohibendo non solum manum sed animum." S I 60 B ff.
[76] "Hanc [iusticiam perfectam] autem isti soli habent qui vere iusti sunt iusticia legali quo ad se, quo ad proximum, quo ad deum . . . ," S I 61 C.
[77] ". . . licet sint eadem precepta moralia in utraque lege scilicet precepta decalogi ad que omnia moralia reducuntur que etiam a christo approbantur in evangelio . . . precepta tamen ceremonialia et iudicialia in lege nova sunt revocata . . . ," III Sent. d 40 q 1 art 2. concl. responsalis. ". . . in omnibus moralibus preceptis non solum manus, id est operatio exterior, comprimitur sed et animus . . . ; secus de ceremonialibus que fuere figuralia ex facto, non ex animi motu, similiter et de iudicialibus que non puniebant intentionem animi, sed factum. . ."

New Law is lighter than the yoke of the Old Law, and it is obvious that Biel wants to defend this traditional point of view. His argumentation, derived largely from Scotus, is so laborious, however, that when he finally reaches this conclusion, it is surrounded by enough important qualifications to make the statement itself meaningless.

His argument in a few words is that the New Law is heavier as regards the moral law, since Christ not only affirmed it but also made it more explicit. The scales are tipped, however, by the fact that the ceremonial and judicial laws are lighter.[78] Especially this third category of judicial law is completely abrogated since it does not belong in the *lex mititatis et humilitatis* of Christ.[79] Biel's statement that the New Law is lighter than that of Moses is qualified by the assertion that this applies only to the Law as given by Christ himself. Insofar as priests and princes have the right and obligation to interpret the Law of Christ, Biel is willing to grant that it can be regarded as more burdensome than the Law of Moses.[80]

Quoting Scotus, Biel documents further the quantitative character of the difference between the old and the new. The sacraments of the New Testament are efficacious, not merely *ex opere operantis* but also *ex opere operato* and confer therefore more grace than the sacraments of the Old Testament. Christians have a more explicit body of doctrine and more and more efficacious examples of saints to follow; they have also more merits from the saints who help them through their intercession; and there is much to be gained from the fact that although the Jews seldom or never hoped for more than temporal rewards, Christians know about

---

III *Sent.* d 40 q 1 art. 3 dub. 1. See also Aquinas, *ST* I.II q 107 art. 2 ad 1 and q 104 art. 3 resp., where he makes a distinction between *mortua* as regards the judicial laws and *mortifera* as regards the ceremonial laws.

[78] ". . . [unless one accepts the rabbinic interpretations of the Decalogue] lex nostra gravior est quantum ad moralia, sed hec gravitas non equiparatur illi de qua statim dicetur. Quantum ad ceremonialia dico quod lex illa vetus fuit multo gravior. . . Quantum ad iudicialia lex nova est levissima quia nulla iudicialia Christus imponit. . ." III *Sent.* d 40 q 1 art. 1 G. Cf. *Lect.* 21 H; 34 O and P; 42 P; 53 G, K and L.

[79] "Iudicialia autem non sunt per christum imposita sed magis lex mititatis et humilitatis in qua non oportet habere iudicialia. . .," III *Sent.* d 40 q 2 art. 1 F.

[80] ". . . sic ergo breviter: pauciora sunt onera legis christiane inquantum est tradita a christo, sed forte plura inquantum addita sunt alia per eos qui habent regere populum christianum," III *Sent.* d 40 q 2 art. 1 G. See Chapter Ten, note 105.

the promise of life eternal, truly a great stimulant.[81] Indeed, whereas Christ himself is legislator, Moses is only a herald and a promulgator of the law of God. But, again, this is merely a difference of degree, between mediate and immediate, since through Moses God himself gave his law, as clearly appears from the form of the Decalogue.[82]

In the last two *dubia* of Book III Biel answers the question in what sense the distinctions between *lex occidens* (littera) and *lex vivificans* (spiritus); and between *lex timoris* and *lex amoris* are to be understood. It is clear that we are here confronted with far more radical categories, not only quantitative but also qualitative in character.

In answering the first question Biel conscientiously follows Bonaventura largely *verbatim*. We encounter here again the distinctions between eternal and temporal as regards the promises, between interior and exterior as regards the precepts, and between *ex opere operato* and *ex opere operantis*[83] as regards the sacraments. Whereas the literal sense of the Law — that is the Law without grace — kills, the spiritual sense of the Law conforms to the Gospel, which is the same Law — except for the ceremonial and judicial laws — but now with grace.[84]

In his answer to the second question Biel chooses Aquinas as his guide; and just as he proved to be borrowing words from Bonaventura, again he does not come forward with an independent solution. In the words of Aquinas he states that the cradle of the New Law is the revelation of God's love, since through the effusion of the blood of Christ the

[81] III *Sent.* d 40 q 2 art. 1 G *in fine* and *S* II 46 C. Cf. Scotus, *Ox.* III d 40 q 1 nota 8. Occam does not deal with this issue except in passing (IV *Sent.* q 1). Cf. Aquinas *ST* I.II q 107 art. 3 ad 1; art. 4 resp. For a discussion of the difference between *ex opere operato* and *ex opere operantis* see *Lect.* 87 N; cf. IV *Sent.* d 1 q 3 art. 1 nota 2, 3; *Lect.* 21 B; *S* II 46 C.

[82] ". . . Moyses non fuit legislator proprie sed preco, nuncius et promulgator legis divine; neque in persona sua sed dei legem proposuit, ut patet ex forma littere," IV *Sent.* d 1 q 2 art. 3 dub. 2 H.

[83] See the more elaborate discussion in IV *Sent.* d 2 q 1 art. 2 concl. 1 E and *S* II 13 N.

[84] ". . . ideo lex illa secundum sensum litteralem erat occidens, non secundum spiritualem; secundum hunc enim corcordabat cum evangelio. . ." IV *Sent.* d 1 q 2 art. 3 dub. 2 E. Bonaventura: ". . . non de observantia litterali, sed de observantia spirituali secundum quam Lex conformis erat Evangelio. Nos autem dicimus Legem occidentem esse secundum observantiam litteralem. . ." III *Sent.* d 40 art. 1 q 2 ad ob 5. The first part of Biel's statement is *verbatim* Bonaventura, III *Sent.* d 40 art. 1 q 2 resp. Cf. *Lect.* 34 P. Cf. Alexander, *Summa* IV n. 274; Aquinas, III *Sent.* q 1 art. 3.

New Testament is validated. The cradle of the Old Testament, however, is the revelation of God's power, which induces fear. Since, now, fear is the path to love, just so is the relation of the Old to the New Law.[85]

We have emphasized the fact that Biel's treatment is a *florilegium* of statements from a rich medieval tradition of which he readily reaped the fruits. There are only two peculiar aspects of his treatment of the problem of the Old Law and the New. First is the brevity of his discussion as compared with the average length of his *distinctiones*, and with the parallel passages in Alexander, Bonaventura, Aquinas, and Scotus. The second striking point is the complete absence of any of the usual references to post-Scotistic *doctores moderni*.[86]

---

[85] ". . . lex nova ex ostensione divine charitatis initium sumpsit quia in effusione sanguinis iesu christi, que fuit perfectissime charitatis signum, in eo etiam novum testamentum confirmatum est; lex autem vetus in ostensione divine potestatis (que timorem incutit) et initium sumpsit. . . Sicut enim timor est via ad amorem ita lex vetus ad novam." IV *Sent.* d 1 q 2 art. 3 dub. 3 F. *Verbatim* quote from Aquinas except for *confirmatum* (Biel) = *consumatum* (Aquinas). Aquinas, III *Sent.* d 40 q 1 art. 4 quaestiunc. 2; *ST* I.II q 107 art. 1 ad 2. Alexander, *Summa* IV n. 276 f. Though Bonaventura sees the contrast between power (fear) and love more indicated by the different circumstances under which the two Laws were given than by a difference in origin, he can say: "Lex Vetus principaliter habet oculum ad timorem, Lex vero Nova principaliter ad amorem. . ." III *Sent.* d 40 art. 1 q 1 ad ob 4. All authors refer to the Augustinian saying, "brevis est differentia Legis et Evangelii: timor et amor" (*Contra Adimanum*, c 17 nota 2 in *PL* XLII, 159), which Thomas is more ready to qualify than Bonaventura. On the relation of the death of Christ, the validation of the New Testament and the Eucharist, see more at length, *Lect.* 29 G; *Lect.* 52 L; *Lect.* 53 N and O. On the difference between the two laws see also the fifteenth-century commentary on Aquinas by Antoninus of Florence, *Summa* I.xv.1 [fol. 763 C ff.].

[86] For d'Ailly, see *Utrum Petri ecclesia lege reguletur*: ". . . lex divina sumitur pro lege divinitus inspirata, qualis est lex moysis vel Christi. . ." Gerson's *Opera omnia*, ed. L. E. DuPin (Antwerpen, 1706), vol. I col. 663 C. ". . . Lex divina moysayca viatori non est lex perfectissima creata" (col. 664 B). ". . . si [lex Christi] non sit ex fide infusa, non est viatori perfectissima lex creata" (664 C). The *signum* of the new law is seen by d'Ailly as a directive, a teaching, and is therefore not primarily connected with *charitas*, as with Biel, but with *fides* as the knowledge of this teaching: ". . . nullus viator per aliud signum, seu directivum creatum, nisi per huiusmodi fidem, vel eius actum, omnia ad quae tenetur perfecte cognoscit . . . et per huiusmodi signum illa perfecte cognoscit. . ." (664 C). See further the excellent articles by Altenstaig under the headings "Lex divina," "Lex evangelica," "Lex charitatis," "Cessatio legalium" and the excursus "De legibus veteris testamenti," in his *Vocabularius Theologie*, fol. 36ᵛ f and fol. 130ᵛ ff. Altenstaig refers here — next to Biel, d'Ailly, and Gerson — to Jacob Perez of Valencia, and especially — fol. 132ᵛ — to the prologue of Jacob's *Commentary on the Psalms*. A summary statement of this prologue is printed and discussed by Wilfrid Werbeck,

There is, however, one final passage in the third Book of his *Sentences* commentary which is not verbally dependent on any of the quoted authorities. It states that Christ, *legislator noster*, enjoined perfect love as *the* sign of his law.[87] Appended to it is a prayer which emphasizes the gratuity of this love as the gift of God. "May he who first loved us and gave himself for us deign to infuse this love in us and preserve this infused love. . ."[88] This, of course, raises the question of how the New Law can demand love, while at the same time this love cannot be obtained by man except as a gift of God.

The answer given in one of the sermons underscores the strictly legal character of the New Law. Biel points to the saying of Christ: "Come to me, all who labor and are heavy-laden, and I will give you rest" [Matt. 11:28]. This rest — that is, the infusion and preservation of grace — is indeed a free gift, but those who want to receive it are commanded to come to Christ, that is, to prepare themselves, taking into consideration the necessary conditions attached to this promise.[89]

There is, therefore, no basis for the view which has been advanced by Ott that Biel's position marks a break with the medieval tradition. This claim is based on the argument that for Biel Law and Gospel are essentially different since with respect to content, the new Law has shed to a high degree its legal character.[90] We conclude rather that Biel was

---

Jacobus Perez von Valencia: Untersuchungen zu seinem Psalmenkommentar (Tübingen, 1959), pp. 75 ff, 76, n. 1.

[87] "Siquidem perfecta charitas foras mittit timorem: hanc charitatem precipit christus legislator noster et tanquam signum sue legis ac discipulatus prestituit. . . ," III *Sent.* d 40 q 1 art. 3 dub. 3; *S* IV 36 C.

[88] "Quam nobis infundere et infusam conservare dignetur qui prior dilexit nos et dedit semetipsum pro nobis oblationem et hostiam deo patri in odorem suavitatis; cum quo regnat et vivit in unitate spiritus sancti deus gloriosus, in secula seculorum benedictus. Amen." III *Sent.* d 40 q 1 art. 3 dub. 3 F *in fine.*

[89] "Si infunditur per spiritum sanctum, non est a nobis; si precipitur, est a nobis. Non enim aliquid precipitur quod non est in nostra facultate. . . 'Venite ad me,' inquit, 'omnes qui laboratis et onerati estis et ego reficiam vos.' Hec refectio est charitatis infusio per quam iugum domini suave redditur. . . Et hec aliquo modo est nobis in preceptis, aliquo modo non. Non est in precepto quantum ad eius infusionem, nam solius dei est eius infusio. Est enim in precepto quantum ad nostram preparationem et eius conservationem, ad scil. faciendum quod in nobis est ut infundatur et infusa in nobis a deo conservetur . . . [D] immediatissima ac ultimata dispositio ad eam est . . . statim immo simul cum ea infundit charitas." *S* I 85 C.

[90] "Obschon Biel Gesetz und Evangelium noch unter ein und denselben Begriff 'lex' fallen lässt, liegt doch die lex nova in einer ganz anderen Seinsebene. . . Der

not particularly concerned with the problem of the two Laws. His report on the contributions of some of the major medieval authorities gives no indication that he has a special thesis to advance. Biel's choice of selections from Bonaventura, Aquinas, and Scotus does not indicate that he was searching for documentation of a thesis, consciously or unconsciously. If one wanted to point out any trend at all, it would be a certain interest in the continuity of the line: Old Law — New Law — Canon Law. From an analysis of Biel's concept of Tradition it is apparent that this interpretation can be well documented.[91]

Bartholomaeus von Usingen, disciple of Biel, teacher of Luther, and one of the first pamphleteers against early Lutheranism, is a good Gabrielist when he insists that Christ has redeemed the faithful from the servitude of sin and the power of the devil, but not from the Law. Though Christ abrogated the judicial and ceremonial laws of the Old Testament, he has given his Holy Spirit to the Church to establish new ceremonial and judicial laws, and he has retained the moral law. Christ has fulfilled and perfected the law of Moses in order that He be imitated.[92] The New Law is the *Lex imitationis*, necessary for salvation.

This survey of the material before us brings us to the conclusion that

---

'rechtliche Gegensatz' zwischen beiden (Heckel) von dem Luther spricht, ist somit bei Biel bereits vorgezeichnet. Terminologisch und auch formal durch die Hereinnahme in die Gesetzeslehre, ist der Gesetzescharakter der lex nova zwar noch bewahrt, aber inhaltlich doch bereits . . . weitgehend ihres rechtlichen Charakters entkleidet. . ." Georg Ott, p. 271, n. 86. On this "rechtlichen Gegensatz" see Heckel, "Recht und Gesetz," p. 317. Though he refers to Ott's article, Heckel does not pursue this point in his *Lex Charitatis: Eine juristische Untersuchung über das Recht in der Theologie Martin Luthers* (Munich, 1953). Biel is placed alongside Thomas over against Luther as regards the concept of divine law: "In den gleichen Worten lebt ein sehr verschiedener Geist" (p. 55).

[91] See Chapter Nine, section III.

[92] "Quoniam christus dedit se sub legem ut redimeret non a lege sed a servitute peccati et potestate diaboli. . . Et quamvis christus a iudicialibus et ceremonialibus legis veteris nos liberavit non tamen a moralibus. . . Nec voluit nos sine iudicialibus et ceremonialibus esse sed dedit spiritum sanctum ecclesie sue ex quo sibi consuleret instituendo nova pro qualitate nove legis ad regendum pacifice populum christianum et ad serviendum deo honesto modo . . ." *Libellus . . . contra Lutheranos* (Erphurdie, 1524), J 4r. ". . . non venit tollere et destruere legem sed eam magis perficere et implere. Non ergo redemit nos christus a lege, ut tu fabularis, sed exemplum nobis dedit ut sequimur vestigia eius; qui sicut vicit mundum in se sic etiam vult vincere illum in nobis." *Ibid.*, J 4v.

whether Old or New, both Testaments fall in the same category: Lex. With the medieval tradition Biel asserts that due to interiorization, origin, and effect, the two Laws differ. The Law of Christ remains the narrow gate that has to be passed through on the road to the fulfillment of the promises of the Gospel. Though the quantitative difference between the laws is clearly acknowledged, both their dispensors fall in the category of *Legislator.* It is, however, in the combination of the two aspects of the New Law, command and gift, that we find a prelude to the nominalistic doctrine of justification and predestination.[93]

[93] See Chapter Six, section II and Chapter Seven, section I.

Chapter Five

MAN FALLEN AND REDEEMED

ᕼ᚛

I. Doctrine of Sin

1. The ecclesiological setting of the doctrine of justification

As we begin to analyze the doctrine of justification, it is important to note immediately that we shall be considering a doctrine that Biel perceives as only a small part of the much more complex question of the justification of the godless. However, we shall use justification in its generally accepted sense — that is, the transition from the status of the sinner to that of the righteous. Biel gives this term a wider sense which we must not overlook and which can be seen clearly in the way he analyzes the Apostles' Creed.

He does not distinguish in traditional fashion the three articles by the different operations assigned to the three Persons of the Trinity, but he indicates as three central parts of the Creed the acts of creation, justification, and glorification. The first part is especially related to God the Father, the second and the third to the Holy Spirit. Christology, and especially the work of the incarnate Word, is of course presupposed, but Biel does not feel the need to emphasize the role of Christ in this context. This historical work of Christ is the necessary, but nevertheless the introductory prologue of the work of the Spirit.[1] Through Christ, indeed, new possibilities have been offered to mankind, but the realization of these possibilities is the work of the Spirit and the individual Christian.

Biel sets his interpretation of the creed in an anthropocentric context, but he tries to deemphasize the individual nature of the process of justi-

[1] "Hanc [i.e., spem] tanquam galeam salutis induamur, scientes quia non posuit nos deus in iram, sed in adquisitionem salutis, per dominum nostrum iesum christum, qui mortuus est pro nobis. . . ," *S* II 12 E.

fication by stressing the ecclesiological context of this event. The operation of the Spirit is not first of all directed toward bringing about an individual encounter with Jesus Christ or a personal union with God; rather the Spirit is primarily seen as the sanctifier of the community of the Church. In the *Collectorium* the context of the treatment of justification does not make sufficiently clear what the sermons make apparent immediately: the doctrine of justification, connected intimately with the sacrament of penance, gravitates not toward Christology but toward ecclesiology; the Spirit is primarily the *ecclesie rector et sanctificator*.[2]

We shall have an opportunity later on to note some individualistic counterforces; but if one wants to enter into Biel's understanding of this central doctrine, it is important to see at the outset that for Biel there are three aspects to the divine act of justification: (1) justification in its traditional sense, especially the infusion of grace, (2) incorporation into the Church, since there is no remission of sins possible outside the institution of the Church, and (3) participation in the *communio sanctorum* — here understood both as the communion of holy things and the communion of saints. These three together form the one act of justification of the godless, a necessary unity since each presupposes the other.[3]

2. Original sin in the medieval tradition

The infusion of grace is the first and doubtlessly decisive part of the operation of the Holy Spirit; however, this also must be seen in a wider context — Biel's concept of original sin and its universal consequences.

[2] "Deinde articuli exprimentes duas operationes trinitatis que appropriantur spiritui sancto scilicet impii iustificatio et glorificatio. Quorum principium est divina bonitas que spiritui sancto appropriatur. Unde ipse est ecclesie rector et sanctificator." III *Sent.* d 25 q 1 art. 1 nota 1 B. D'Ailly divides the "articulos in simbolo contentos" into two parts according to their christological content: ". . . septem circa deitatem et septem circa humanitatem christi . . . ," *Sacramentale seu Tractatus Theologicus de Sacramentis*, cap. 26 O.

[3] "Tria enim hec concurrunt in iustificatione impii scilicet infusio gratie et charitatis per quam peccatori peccata remittuntur. Ipseque gratificatur deo et per hoc iustificatur et ecclesie incorporatur ut membrum vivens. Non tantum numero sed et merito. Neque extra ecclesiam potest fieri remissio peccatorum. Hanc autem iustificationem per infusam charitatem sequitur communio sanctorum qua peccator iustificatus participat omnia bona sanctorum omnium. . . Charitas enim que non querit que sua sunt facit omnia communia. Et ita tria hec in uno articulo comprehenduntur quia pertinent ad unam operationem divinam scilicet peccatoris iustificationem." III *Sent.* d 25 q 1 art. 1 nota 1 A.

Biel defines his own position by presenting a short history of the understanding of original sin. He distinguishes three different schools. The first is the strict Augustinian school represented by Peter Lombard, for whom original sin is a *qualitas morbida anime, vitium scilicet concupiscentie*.[4] The second school rejected this identification of original sin and concupiscence: Anselm of Canterbury, followed by Duns Scotus, William of Occam, and Gregory of Rimini, saw as the main characteristic of original sin the absence of original righteousness, resulting in concupiscence as God's punishment of man.[5] A third school — Alexander of Hales, Bonaventura, and Thomas Aquinas — mediated these extreme positions by defending the thesis that absence of original righteousness would be the form and concupiscence the matter of original sin.[6]

Biel feels that it is not difficult to establish the proper intention of the tradition, though the exact formulation must be held in abeyance. Formally, the essence of original sin is indeed the absence of original justice, which appears from the fact that though after baptism the child is freed from original sin, concupiscence is still present.[7] In fact, however, original sin is always accompanied by concupiscence, that is, the law of the flesh, which inclines man to disobey the dictate of right reason. There is no decisive difference between the two alternatives of including concupiscence

[4] II *Sent.* d 30 q 2 art. 1 nota 1 A. See Johannes N. Espenberger, *Die Elemente der Erbsünde nach Augustin und der Frühscholastik* (Mainz, 1905).

[5] II *Sent.* d 30 q 2 art. 1 nota 1 B. Cf. the relevant texts in Raymond M. Martin, *La controverse sur le péché originel au début du XIVe siècle* (Louvain, 1930). And for general treatments see A. M. Landgraf, *Dogmengeschichte der Frühscholastik*, 3 vols. (Regensburg, 1952–1954); Johann Auer, *Die Entwicklung der Gnadenlehre in der Hochscholastik*, pt. I: *Das Wesen der Gnade* (Freiburg i. Br., 1942), pt. II: *Das Wirken der Gnade* (Freiburg i. Br., 1951), p. 7 ff.; Seeberg *DG*, III, 218 ff., 657 ff. For specific treatments see Seeberg, *Die Theologie des Scotus*, pp. 218 ff.; and Minges, *Ioannes Duns Scoti*, II, 318 ff. There is a clear exposition of Augustine's position in Seeberg *DG*, II, 509 ff., 554 f. The positions of Durand and Pierre d'Auriole are described by Cyril O. Vollert, *The Doctrine of Hervaeus Natalis on Primitive Justice and Original Sin* (Rome, 1947), pp. 129 ff., 236 ff., 316 ff.

[6] II *Sent.* d 30 q 2 art. 1 opinio III. See also Richard Bruch, "Die Urgerechtigkeit als Rechtheit des Willens nach der Lehre des Bonaventura," *FS* 33 (1951), p. 180 ff; Julian Kaup, O.F.M., "Zum Begriff der iustitia originalis in der älteren Franziskanerschule," *FS* 29 (1942), p. 44 ff.; J. B. Kors, *La justice primitive et le péché originel d'après S. Thomas* (Kain, 1932). Cf. the clear definition of Thomas in *ST* I.II q 82 art. 1: ". . . peccatum originale materialiter quidem est concupiscentia, formaliter vero est defectus originalis iustitiae."

[7] ". . . peccatum originale non dicit rem positivam quantum ad suum formale, sed originalis iusticie privationem debite inesse," II *Sent.* d 30 q 2 art. 2 concl. 3.

in the essence of original sin as its material aspect or as its automatic accompaniment.[8] Besides, Lombard certainly had not excluded the aspect Anselm stressed, nor had Anselm denied that Adam's children inherited concupiscence.

We must conclude that Biel sees his position as closest to the mediating position of the third school. Biel agrees with Anselm's definition of the formal aspect of original sin, but at the same time he definitely does not want to give up the Augustinian stress on the power and presence of concupiscence, as the matter of original sin.

3. Biel as an historian of Christian thought

One of the attractive aspects of Biel's *Collectorium* is that he does not merely report the opinions of others before adding his own dogmatic analyses — as, for example, is the case with the commentaries on Peter Lombard by Gregory of Rimini and Pierre d'Ailly. Biel tries to order these opinions systematically and thus to write what one may call a compendium of medieval theology.[9] From a modern point of view one may well complain that description and evaluation are not always sufficiently separated, but Biel does make a consistent effort to discern schools and movements. This systematic presentation better explains the popularity of the *Collectorium* in the late medieval theological faculty, evidenced by its many editions, than the often alleged neutrality of Biel.

In the modern period two charges have been made against Biel's historical and systematic presentation of the relation of original sin and concupiscence; these are too important to permit us to continue without a closer investigation. The first charge is made by Heinrich Denifle and by Carl Feckes, who judge Biel to have been correct in his presentation of Lombard and Anselm. In their opinion, however, Gregory of Rimini does not belong in the second but in the first school. Feckes also points out that Duns Scotus is erroneously assigned to the school of Anselm. In Feckes' opinion, Duns Scotus belongs to the mediating third school

[8] ". . . peccatum originale de facto non est sine fomite que est lex carnis," II *Sent.* d 30 q 2 art. 2 concl. 4. ". . . utrumque et fomitem includi in ratione peccati originalis tanquam materiale et ipsum non includi, sed esse annexum de facto, est probabile," II *Sent.* d 30 q 2 art. 2 concl. 5.
[9] "Quas pro tanto recitare volui sub compendio ut de materia tam necessaria aliorum sententie non laterent," II *Sent.* d 28 q 1 art. 1 C *in fine*.

since he agrees with Thomas that concupiscence forms the material aspect of original sin. For Denifle and Feckes this is one more proof that Biel's knowledge of medieval theology is haphazard and that therefore the *Collectorium* is unreliable as a late medieval textbook for the history of Christian thought.[10]

If we turn now to Gregory's *Sentences*, it is indeed surprising that Biel assigned the *Doctor Authenticus* to the school of Anselm. Gregory makes it quite clear that the absence of original justice is by no means to be equated with original sin itself. He does not, of course, deny this absence as such, but sees it as a consequence of original sin which was essentially concupiscence.[11] For Gregory to understand original sin in this way is another example of his independent position within the nominalistic tradition of theology.[12] This slip of Biel characterizing Gregory's view of original sin as Anselmian surprises us even more if, contrary to the thesis of Denifle, we note that Biel on two other occasions shows himself to be very well acquainted with Gregory's concept of original sin.[13]

A possible explanation is perhaps suggested by Gregory himself. After a description of the Anselmian and of the stricter Augustinian position, Gregory declares that many *doctores*, ancient and modern, have followed Lombard, that he himself has joined their ranks now, but that before in related matters he had supported the Anselmian school. Though this need not imply that Gregory himself underwent a change in his basic understanding of the problem, his avowed shift from the one school to the other may explain Biel's interpretation on this point.[14] But whatever may have

---

[10] "Dass Gott erbarm! Der Nominalist bezw. Occamist Biel als Vertreter der gesamten Scholastik! . . . Es blieb ihm [Dieckhoff] . . . ganz unbekannt, dass Biel selbst die Theologen der Blütezeit, und zwar von ihnen nur einige, bloss flüchtig durchgesehen, sie häufig bloss aus zweiter und dritter Hand zitierte, irrig auffasste und ihre Lehre falsch wiedergab. . ." Heinrich Denifle, *Luther und Luthertum*, vol. I, pt. 2, 2 ed. (Mainz, 1906), pp. 535 f., 870 ff. See also Feckes, *Die Rechtfertigungslehre des Gabriel Biel*, p. 25.

[11] "Nec tamen nego quin etiam homo careat originali iustitia. . . Sed huius carentiam non dico esse originale peccatum sed potius effectum originalis peccati. . ." Gregory of Rimini, II *Sent.* d 30–33 q 1 art. 2 [fol. 112 M]. Cf. ad 3 ff. [fol. 113 F f].

[12] Cf. Occam's definition of original sin: "Nam de facto est sola carentia iustitie originalis cum debito habendi eam. . ." II *Sent.* q 26 U; *Quodlib.* III q 8.

[13] II *Sent.* d 30 q 2 art. 3 dub 2 and dub 4.

[14] "Hanc eius [Augustini] sententiam secutus est Magister . . . et multi etiam antiqui ac moderni sequuntur doctores: ego licet aliquando ubi hec materia non

been the reason, it is clear that Biel indeed made a disputable decision in counting Rimini with the Anselmian school.

With respect to the position of Duns Scotus, there is not so much a misunderstanding on the part of Biel as on the part of his critic, Feckes. Scotus certainly can, legitimately, be called more Anselmian than Thomistic in his analyses of the problem of original sin. Whereas for Aquinas the material aspect of original sin is concupiscence, for Scotus it is not concupiscence but the unfulfilled obligation to possess original justice. Scotus to be sure allows for concupiscence, and in a way it can be understood as a factor in the unfulfilled obligation to possess original justice; for him, however, concupiscence has no place in a proper definition of original sin in a strict sense.[15] One might be justified in saying that Scotus stands on the other side of Anselm from Thomas, since he seems to go beyond the position taken by the Archbishop of Canterbury. He stresses that concupiscence belongs to man's very nature and that even in paradise it needed to be neutralized by the gift of original justice;[16] on the other hand and related to this, he also says that original sin destroyed the supernatural gifts but left man's nature intact.[17] Thus, while Anselm indeed helped Scotus understand better the spiritual nature of original sin, Anselm himself clearly taught the disrupting consequences of the loss of the original righteousness, even in the natural realm. We conclude, therefore, that in Biel's historical sketch it was absolutely justifiable, once a tripartition is accepted, to assign Scotus to the school of St. Anselm. Even

---

directe discutiebatur dixerim aliqua supponendo oppositam opinionem que satis etiam communis est; sequor tamen eandem sententiam." II *Sent.* d 30–33 q 1 art. 2 [fol. 112 K].

[15] ". . . ad istud peccatum concurrunt duo, carentia iustitiae, ut formale, et debitum habendi eam, ut materiale, sicut in aliis privationibus concurrit privatio et aptitudo ad habitum," *Ox.* II d 32 q 1 nota 15. "Carentia huius iustitie cum debito habendi eam, *complet* rationem peccati illius originalis," *Ox.* IV d 1 q 6 nota 7. See also Seeberg's conclusion: ". . . jeder positive und konkrete Sinn der Erbsünde oder auch der Erbschuld ist bei Duns ausgeschlossen. . . Es bleibt bei der farblosen Formel einer objectiven Karenz d. h. eines historischen Verhängnisses," in *Die Theologie des Scotus,* p. 220 and Seeberg *DG,* 5 ed., III, 657.

[16] *Ox.* II d 29 q 1 nota 4.

[17] ". . . si in peccando vulneratur in naturalibus . . . tunc si iterum peccaret, corrumperet substantiam voluntatis . . . posset tandem tota consumi per peccata atque gravia finita," *Par.* II d 33 q 2 nota 3. Minges concludes: "Per contractionem peccati originalis non videtur esse vulnerata ipsa natura," *Ioannes Duns Scoti doctrina,* p. 332.

after four hundred years of accumulative scholarship it proves still to be justifiable to do so.

4. Indomitable concupiscence

In a second historical theological charge, made by F. X. Linsenmann and Carl Feckes against Biel, it is alleged that he falls silent after his historical survey without declaring where he himself stands.[18] According to them, Biel was groping for as profound an understanding of original sin as that of Thomas, but was not able to transcend the position of Anselm, probably because of his interest in defending the doctrine of the Immaculate Conception of the Virgin Mary.[19] Notwithstanding the accusation of neutrality, the conclusion is drawn that original sin seems to imply for Biel rather guilt and punishment than sin in the strict sense of the word.[20]

The presentation of Biel's doctrine of justification by Feckes, in some central points an elaboration of Linsenmann's 1865 article, is correct in its main features. However, his interpretation repeatedly suffers from what seem to be two weaknesses. In the first place Feckes asserts that Biel's real intention is to be found in what is said *de potentia absoluta*. Feckes does not take account sufficiently of the dialectics of the two orders which we discussed in Chapter Two. In the second place Feckes refuses to evaluate Biel's theology according to its own merits; he constantly judges him by the theology of Thomas Aquinas, who was for Biel, of course, however highly esteemed, no more than *unus modernus doctor*. This leads Feckes to a more aesthetic than systematic critique — Biel has destroyed the beautiful, harmonious, theological system of high scholasticism.[21]

[18] Linsenmann, F. X., "Gabriel Biel, der letzte Scholastiker, und der Nominalismus," *Theologische Quartalschrift* 47 (1865), 662.

[19] Linsenmann, p. 665. Feckes, *Die Rechtfertigungslehre des Gabriel Biel*, p. 26.

[20] "Fasst man alles zusammen, so scheint nach Biel die Erbsünde mehr eine reine Schuld — und Strafverhaftung als eine eigentliche Sünde zu sein," Feckes, p. 26. In this chapter we shall have to refer more often to Feckes' valuable contribution to the understanding of late medieval theology, not only because his study was for nine years, until the publication in 1934 of Vignaux's comparison of the doctrine of justification and predestination in some major representatives of late medieval theology, the sole monograph in this field, but also because this study is more responsible than any other for the modern understanding and image of Gabriel Biel.

[21] Cf. Feckes, *Die Rechtfertigungslehre des Gabriel Biel*, p. 86.

Yet we have seen already that Biel's position with regard to the doctrine of original sin is unambiguous. His analysis of the respective positions of Lombard and Anselm lead him to the conclusion that they were not mutually exclusive, which by itself indirectly praises Thomas' mediating formulation. The rather vague conclusion that he stressed guilt and punishment more than sin itself applies to all post-Anselmian theologians except to the stricter Augustinian school to which Biel obviously does not belong. It must be noted that Biel explicitly denies that original sin is merely *poena* and not *culpa*.[22]

As Biel's critics have misunderstood both his and Anselm's actual position, we must come to the peculiar conclusion that, although the quoted interpretation is far from accurate, we agree with Feckes that Biel's position has to be defined as Anselmian. The Gabrielistic variant of Anselm's position, however, is characterized by an emphasis on the material aspect of original sin. Like Lombard, Biel speaks about the *fomes peccati* as the *pondus lapilli*. The infusion of grace strengthens man's powers but does not extinguish this *fomes*, the tinder of sin.[23]

At the same time, we should note that the concupiscence or *fomes* is said to be inextinguishable because it is seen as a natural aspect of man's life itself, an inherent condition which had to develop at the moment that the stabilizing original justice was lost.[24] It is therefore only "natural" that, after original sin is forgiven in the sacrament of baptism, the *lex carnis* or rebellion still remains a part of man's inherent weakness.[25]

Throughout the three stages that together constitute the history of mankind — the periods before the fall, after the fall, and after Calvary — this inner revolt is the constant factor which marks man as *homo creatus*.

[22] ". . . originale peccatum non tantum est pena sed est iniusticia, iniquitas sive culpa," II *Sent.* d 30 q 2 art. 2 concl. 2.

[23] "Et ita fomitem debilitat, non quod remittat aut extinguat secundum multos sed quia potentiam fortificat. Sicut si avi cui alligatus est lapillus propter quem minus expedite possit tendere sursum, potentia volitiva in alis fortificaretur; iam impedimentum diceretur minui licet lapilli pondus non esset alleviatum." *S* II 14 G. Cf. Peter Lombard, II *Sent.* d 30 cap. 6 ff., in *PL* CXCII, 721–724.

[24] ". . . causatur a causis naturalibus dum relinquuntur sue nature a deo propter peccatum hominis," II *Sent.* d 30 q 2 art. 3 dub. 2. Cf. Occam, *Quodlib.* III q 10. ". . . Si extinguitur fomes vita simul extinguitur. Non enim extinguitur nisi totus calor naturalis extinguatur." Biel, II *Sent.* d 30 q 2 art. 3 dub. 4. Cf. Biel II *Sent.* d 30 q 1 art. 2 concl. 1: ". . . rebellio virium inferiorum voluntati recte est naturalis i.e. sequitur principia nature."

[25] ". . . non restituitur originalis iusticia, cum etiam post baptismum manet virium rebellio," II *Sent.* d 32 q 1 art. 1 concl. 2.

Between the first and the second stage, however, a change takes place, through which the revolt from then onward can also become the mark of the *homo peccator*. Biel does not reject the opinion of Gregory of Rimini, according to whom the infection of the flesh is a new element introduced by the poisonous inflation of the devil; [26] but for Biel this diabolic attack merely actualizes a potentially present rebellion.

More than Duns Scotus and Occam, Biel stresses that man's original nature has been corrupted by original sin; man is not only *spoliatus a gratuitis* but also *vulneratus in naturalibus*.[27] Man's miserable condition after the fall is not only due to a vertical imputation by God, but also to a horizontal continuation of infirmity, through an infection in which all mankind partakes and through which the will is wounded, so that it is more inclined to evil than to good deeds.[28] However, Biel does not elucidate the exact relation of the potential disorder of man's created nature before the fall to the corruption of that nature — the law of the flesh reigning over man — after the fall.

5. Before and after the fall

For a proper understanding of Biel's term "facere quod in se est" and a further discussion of his doctrine of justification in general, it is important to establish that a mere acceptation or non-imputation is not sufficient for man's beatification. Man's wounded nature also has to be healed so that man's will, which in principle never lost its freedom of choice, can elicit the meritorious acts required for his acceptation by God.

The difference between the deficiencies of Adam's nature before and after the possession of original justice is certainly not a qualitative but a quantitative one: the difficulties have increased, the struggle has intensified.[29] For that reason we must not underestimate the difference between

[26] II *Sent.* d 30 q 2 art. 3 dub. 2. Gregory, II *Sent.* d 30–33 q 1 art. 2 and 3 [fol. 113 K].

[27] "Sed, heu, per peccatum omnibus his privatus. Nam gratuitis spoliatus et in naturalibus gravissime vulneratus. . ." *S* I 19 B. Cf. *S* II 21 E.

[28] ". . . fomes peccati originalis in anima contrahitur a carne morbida qualitate infecta." II *Sent.* d 31 q 1 concl. 1. "Huc accedit quod peccato originali vulnerata est voluntas in sua naturali potentia ita quod licet simpliciter sit libera tamen prona est ad malum ab adolescentia." II *Sent.* d 28 q 1 art. 3 dub. 2. Cf. for the *libidinosa propagatio*, II *Sent.* d 30 q 1 art. 2 concl. 1.

[29] ". . . [homo] nunc in statu nature corrupte magis impugnatur. . . Item propter difficultatem *magis* indiget homo adiutorio post lapsum quam ante." II *Sent.* d 29 q 1 art. 2 concl. 2.

homo peccator and *homo creatus,* between man depressed and corrupted by sin and man *in puris naturalibus.*[30] And yet we would go too far to the other extreme if we interpreted Biel's deviation on this point from Scotus and Occam, whose authority he usually values, to mean that in his doctrine of original sin Biel has become Thomistic or even Augustinian.[31]

Though man may be said to be in a miserable position, enslaved by the law of the flesh which requires that there be a healing aspect to the process of justification, his will is nevertheless free, original sin being a certain outgrowth of natural difficulties which can therefore be healed with natural medicines. Original sin has primarily a psychological, not an ontological impact on the free will of man; it destroys the pleasure of eliciting a good act and causes unhappiness and fear, thus changing the direction of the will.[32] This does not, however, interfere with the freedom of the will as such.[33] This presentation prepares us for Biel's psychological prescription for those who would like to reach the level of the *facere quod in se est* and thus dispose themselves for the infusion of grace.

One further point, however, demands our attention, that is, the indicated claim of Linsenmann that Biel had to be Anselmian in his analysis

[30] "Voco pure naturalia que nec peccato sunt depressa. . ." *S* III 2 B.

[31] Wilhelm Braun claimed that Biel was Occamist in his *meritum* doctrine, Thomist in his doctrine of sin and justification. See *Die Bedeutung der Konkupiszenz in Luthers Leben und Lehre* (Berlin, 1908), pp. 177, 198 f., 260. Cf. the justified criticism of Feckes, *Die Rechtfertigungslehre des Gabriel Biel,* p. 26; Otto Scheel, *Martin Luther . . .* II, p. 162.

[32] "Difficultas [peccatum originale] itaque non opponitur libertati in eliciendo sed facilitati. . . Et ideo quantumcunque crescit difficultas nunquam aufert libertatem, sed bene tollit delectationem et promptitudinem et per hoc frequenter mutat voluntatem ut desinat velle quod voluit, sublata delectatione, aut incipiat velle quod noluit, accedente metu vel tristicia; semper tamen manet libertas in volendo et nolendo." II *Sent.* d 28 q 1 art. 3 dub. 3 P. Modern systematic theologians are more sensitive to the advantages of such a nonphysical interpretation than Feckes could be from his Thomistic point of view. See Bernhard Stöckel's criticism of Aquinas: *Die Lehre von der erbsündlichen Konkupiszenz in ihrer Bedeutung für das christliche Leibeethos* (Ettal, 1954), p. 88 ff. Seeberg has underrated the importance of a psychological interpretation of original sin; see his evaluation of Duns Scotus' doctrine of sin: "Er hat mit scharfer Kritik das physische Element in Augustins Hamartiologie bekämpft, aber er hat keine positive Sündenlehre zu geben vermocht," *Die Theologie des Scotus,* p. 221.

[33] For Thomas this aspect of original justice is only restored through the sacrament of baptism. See William A. van Roo, S. J., *Grace and Original Justice according to St. Thomas* (Rome, 1955), p. 132 ff.

of original sin to be in a position to defend the Immaculate Conception of the Virgin Mary. Biel's doctrine of original sin is, as is to be expected, so intimately connected with his understanding of justification, grace, acceptation, predestination, and Christology that, if that claim were true, practically his whole theology would be a corollary of his Mariology. It is more likely that the order has to be reversed: on major theological and philosophical issues Biel thinks along the lines drawn by Scotus and Occam; it would be most remarkable if he did not also share their Mariology. His Mariology is important, not as a basis for his theology, but, so to speak, as a concave mirror which focuses the major christological and pneumatological rays.

When dealing with the problem of original sin in the second sermon on the conception of the Virgin Mary, Biel does not mention the third mediating opinion of Aquinas, nor does he exclude the possibility of a material aspect of original sin. He merely states that if one compares the opinions of Lombard and Anselm, the latter's position offers an easier and more intelligible explanation of the Immaculate Conception.[34] Neither this sermon nor any one of the others adds to the information the *Collectorium* gives.

As a conclusion to this section on Biel's doctrine of original sin, we can summarize by saying that Biel feels himself to stand in close affinity to the position of Thomas Aquinas, since this has the advantage of at once defining the formal aspect of original sin as the absence of the required original justice without at the same time contradicting the irrefutable experience of the power of the law of the flesh, concupiscence. Though Biel leaves unanswered the question whether this concupiscence forms the material complement of the absence of righteousness owed to God and would therefore be *culpa* and not *poena*, he goes beyond the position of Duns Scotus in teaching that Adam's sin not only deprived man of the gifts of grace but also corrupted his nature. Because this corruption differs

[34] "Et licet diversi diversimode loquantur de originali peccato. Aliter enim loquitur magister . . . aliter Anselmus. . . Quia tamen modus loquendi beati Anselmi facilior est et magis intelligibilis ideo hunc imitando dico quod peccatum originale non est *formaliter* aliquid positivum sive in anima sive in carne." *S* III 2 B. Cf. *S* I 26 E where, as in Scotus, the *macula* is seen as *ordinatio ad penam* whereas in *Lect.* 72 M, Augustine is quoted to emphasize the physical nature of the *macula*: ". . . sic vitiata est natura ut omnes qui ab eo per rationem seminalem processerunt de communi lege accipiunt et vitium et peccatum."

quantitatively from the rebellion stemming from man's status as creature and produces primarily psychological difficulties in an immutably free will, the assertion that Biel is Thomistic or Augustinian is groundless.

II. The Proper Disposition for Justification

1. Inalienable freedom of the will

The impact of original sin and its consequences leaves the freedom of the will intact. As we have seen before, the same is true for the *synderesis*, its rational principle. In so far as the *fomes peccati* darkens man's rational capacities, the will is misguided and not responsible for what are in themselves evil deeds: invincible ignorance is a complete excuse for any sin.[35]

For this reason Biel has to stress that Adam and Eve knew the commandments of God, and that Adam through an immoderate love for his wife and Eve through her striving for glory knowingly transgressed God's law.[36] Since therefore the knowledge of God's will is decisive for the ethical quality of an act, it is not surprising that the central term with regard to the proper disposition for the reception of grace, *facere quod in se est*, has to be variously defined. Christians know more about the will of God than heathens and therefore have to do more in order to do their very best. The infidel can fulfill this requirement at the moment when his will obeys the advice of his reason, and when he tries with all his heart to receive further light in order to know what is true and right.[37] The Christian, however, who has lost saving grace by committing a mortal sin has been brought up with and has been taught the Christian religion. He has lost the infused faith, the *fides formata*, but he has still at his disposal the truth he had acquired himself, the *fides acquisita*, in this case coinciding with the *fides informis*. His will has to conform not only to reason but

---

[35] "Ignorantia invincibilis precedens voluntatis actum sive positiva sive negativa sive iuris sive facti simpliciter excusat a peccato non solum in tanto sed in toto," II *Sent.* d 22 q 2 art. 2 concl. 1. Also for Holcot original sin could not be due to invincible ignorance: "Si invincibilis excusatur quia deus non exigit ab homine nisi quod homo potest benefacere." *Sap.* Lect. 28 A.

[36] ". . . primum peccatum ade fuit immoderatus amor amicitie uxoris et primum eve fuit immoderatus appetitus excellentie et neutrum horum precessit ignorantia pertinentium ad salutem," II *Sent.* d 22 q 2 art. 2 concl. 4.

[37] ". . . infidelis facit quod in se est dum arbitrium suum conformat rationi ac toto corde petit ac querit illuminari ad cognoscendum veritatem, iusticiam et bonum," II *Sent.* d 27 q 1 art. 2 concl. 4. Cf. *Lect.* 23 F; *S* I 85 C.

to reason illuminated by faith, that is, the *regula fidei*. He has to unlock the doors of his heart — *removere obicem* — by detesting his past sins and by resolving to avoid them further for God's sake.[38]

Biel's explanation of the possibility of this *facere quod in se est* makes it clear that, though the *facere quod in se est* means different things for different people, everyone is by nature in a position to discharge this first duty. For God, however, the *facere quod in se est* means only one thing: He is obliged, because he has placed the obligation on himself, to infuse his grace in everyone who has done his very best.[39]

2. The doctrine of the *facere quod in se est*

As far as we can see, the origins of the doctrine of the *facere quod in se est* go back to the *Ambrosiaster*, which interprets the justice of God as the merciful acceptance of those who seek their refuge with him: He would be unjust if he ignored them.[40] This concept especially influenced the old Franciscan school, whose representative, Alexander of Hales, was Biel's teacher on this point.[41] Following Alexander, Biel proves man's inborn concept of God by pointing to the fact that everyone knows that he has not always existed; he knows that he has been created by a first cause to whom he has to look for everything he needs. For this reason there has never been a nation which has wanted to be without a God on whom it could depend for aid. Though many have erred and deceived themselves in worshipping the wrong God, all men by nature know their first cause and ask from it enlightenment and faith.[42]

[38] "Fidelis vero facit quod in se est si secundum regulam fidei detestatur peccatum proponens in omnibus obedire deo et eius precepta servare; peccatum detestando removet obicem, volendo deo tanquam summo bono obedire propter deum habet bonum motum in deum," *ibid.*

[39] ". . . actum facientis quod in se est deus acceptat ad tribuendum gratiam primam. . . ," *ibid.* See also Chapter Seven, section III.

[40] ". . . Cum suscipit confugientes ad se, iustitia dicitur: quia non suscipere confugientem iniquitas est," *Ambrosiaster*, in *PL* XVII, 79. Cf. *Glossa ordin. super Rom.* 3:22, in *PL* CXIV, 480.

[41] Alexander feels that every adult man has the capacity to believe in God: ". . . habet in se unde se disponat ad fidei receptionem si facit quod in se est. . . Sicut enim natura non deficit in necessariis ad esse naturale, ita nec deus. Numquam deest facienti quod in se est ad esse gratuitum et spirituale. Facere quod in se est est uti ratione per quam potest comprehendere deum esse et invocare adiutorium dei." *Sum.* II q 129 me 8. Cf. *Sum.* III q 69 art. 2. Cf. II *Sent.* d 22 q 2 art. 3 dub. 1.

[42] ". . . scit suum principium et petit ab eo lumen cognitionis fidei et boni. . . ," II *Sent.* d 27 q 1 art. 2 concl. 4.

The Christian in mortal sin still has the *fides acquisita* which teaches him two things: the punishing righteousness of God with regard to the damned, and the divine mercy with respect to the elect.[43] We are not dealing here with secondary issues: the dialectic between fear and love is the general theme of Biel's sermons. Usually he does not dehistoricize these two aspects of God's action; he points to God's mercy in the incarnation and his punishing righteousness in the last judgment. The baptized *viator* who moves from one point in history to another, not knowing whether he is damned or elect, knows by way of the *fides acquisita* that God punishes sin and assists those who call on him for help. To desire God's help is doing one's very best, and those fallen Christians who in this way detest sin and adhere to God their creator may be certain that God will grant them grace, thus freeing them from the bonds of sin.[44]

But although a sinner may be certain of God's mercy in granting his grace to those who do their very best, he has no certainty that he has in fact done his very best. The standard required is a love of God for God's sake, that is, an undefiled love: *super omnia*. It is this last condition in particular which makes it practically impossible to know with certainty that one has really reached the stage of the *facere quod in se est*.[45]

We will have occasion later to return to the whole question of the certitude of salvation; but here we observe at least a sign of Biel's awareness that the requirement of a love of God for God's sake or above everything else is not easy to meet. Nevertheless, Biel feels that this absolute love is within the reach of natural man *without the assistance of grace*. In a natural culmination man ascends from self-love — *amor amicitie sui* —

[43] ". . . fides illa ad duo radiat scl. ad divinam iusticiam damnantem reprobos et ad divinam misericordiam salvantem electos," *ibid.*

[44] ". . . iste facit quod in se est qui illuminatus lumine rationis naturalis *aut* fidei vel utroque cognoscit peccati turpitudinem et proponens ab ipso resurgere desiderat divinum adiutorium quo possit a peccato mundari et deo suo creatori adherere. Hec facienti deus gratiam suam tribuit necessario, necessitate non coactionis sed immutabilitatis." *Lect.* 59 P. In the sermons, of course, Biel speaks strictly within the context of the Christian community to those who are baptized: "Sed est alia dilectio dei quam libere elicimus, presupposita cognitione dei per fidem secundum dictamen rationis recte, fidei lumine illustrate. . ." *S* II 18 J.

[45] ". . . homo non potest evidenter scire se facere quod in se est, quia hoc facere includit in se obedire deo propter deum tanquam ultimum et principalem finem quod exigit dilectionem dei super omnia quam ex naturalibus suis homo potest elicere. . . Et forte naturaliter impossibile quia etsi scire possumus nos diligere deum, non tamen evidenter scire possumus illam circumstantiam 'super omnia.'" II *Sent.* d 27 q 1 art. 3 dub. 5.

133

to a love of everything that is to his advantage — *amor concupiscentie* — which includes God as the highest good. From the fact that God is good *for him*, man concludes that God is good *as such*, and man thus ascends from possessive love, *amor concupiscentie*, to pure love, *amor amicitie*, for God.[46]

This formulation permits both the two possible points of departure for penance that we have already indicated: fear of God's punishment, attrition; or love responding to his goodness, contrition. The *amor concupiscentie* or self-love connotes the self-interest that is the prime stimulant for beginners in the Christian faith. Those who have already reached a higher stage of perfection — and even they can fall into mortal sin — respond to the love of God and his justice.[47]

We note in this description of a progression from love of self to the pure love of God *per se* a radical contrast with Biel's view of the relation between acquired and infused faith described in Chapter Three. Whereas the highest stage of *faith* is the transformation of a belief in certain acts of God *per se* into a faith that these acts are aimed at the believer, the highest stage of *love* is not God's love in its meaning for man but God's love as such, not as an aspect of his *opera ad extra* but as an intrinsic part of the inner-Trinitarian life of God.

3. First and second justification of the sinner

As may be expected, the major part of Biel's doctrine of justification in the strict sense of the word is to be found in the context of his analyses of the sacrament of penance. Since the first justification takes place by baptism, however, the problem of proper disposition for the infusion of grace includes also the adult catechumen, who, of course, belongs to the

[46] ". . . naturaliter homo seipsum diligit amore amicitie. Diligit etiam omne quod sibi bonum est amore concupiscentie et ita deum suum summum bonum. Et quoniam ex eo quod cognoscit deum esse bonum suum, cognoscit eum in se bonum; ideo ex amore concupiscentie assurgit ad amorem dei amicitie." III *Sent.* d 26 q 1 art. 3 dub. 2.

[47] "Posset etiam dubitari de origine penitentie an semper concipiatur ex timore. Illud dubium solum locum habet de penitentia acquisita. . . Et dicitur quod in incipientibus nondum perfectis (nam et perfecti quandoque labuntur iuxta illud 'septies in die cadit iustus') frequenter oritur ex timore pene qui oritur ex amore sui. Sed in perfectis oritur, ex amore dei et iusticie. . ." IV *Sent.* d 14 q 1 art. 3 dub. 7.

less experienced. In baptism sanctifying grace is infused; this implies *de potentia ordinata* the remission of guilt and of punishment for eternal and actual sins.[48] The *fomes peccati* is not extinguished, as we have seen, but diminished and forgiven.[49] In principle, all answers to theological questions arising from the preparation for the recuperation of sanctifying grace through penance are applicable to the preparation for adult baptism.

Infant baptism would seem to exclude the issue of proper preparation. Nevertheless, Biel feels that in a vicarious way the godparents are responsible for the disposition of the child. True, the child is baptized on the basis of the faith of the whole Church and not on that of the godparents alone. But as the quantity of grace granted in the sacrament of penance depends on the intensity of attrition or contrition, so the quantity of baptismal grace depends on the disposition of the godparents and even of the administering priest himself.[50]

To condense this now in a short formula: in the sacraments of baptism and penance an effect *ex opere operantis* is added to the basic effect *ex opere operato*. Because of this close parallelism there is no reason for us to distinguish further between first justification and its later renewal.

4. Extra- and pre-sacramental grace

Before we are in a position to establish the exact relation of attrition and contrition, we first must ask how the *facere quod in se est* is related to the *gratia gratis data*. We have seen that the abhorrence of sin and the love of God for God's sake is a sufficient preparation for the infusion of sanctifying grace, the *gratia gratum faciens*.

The question arises whether Biel excludes any special aid or preparatory grace from God's side; does he indeed reject the *auxilium speciale*

[48] IV *Sent.* d 4 q 1 art. 2 concl. 1, 2.
[49] ". . . quamvis baptismus fomitem peccati in rite baptisato non penitus extinguat ipsum tamen minuit et remittit," *ibid.*, concl. 3.
[50] ". . . fides aliena sine qua parvulis non datur remissio non est fides offerentium parvulum ad baptismum. . ." IV *Sent.* d 4 q 2 art. 2 concl. 4. ". . . si comparetur parvulus ad parvulum nulla erit ex hac parte inequalitas quia nullum habent motum libere voluntatis proprium propter quem in uno esset maior dispositio quam in alio. Potest tamen esse inequalitas in parentibus, patrinis et ceteris assistentibus, etiam in baptisante. . . Et propter horum merita deus potest uni parvulo conferre maiorem gratiam quam alteri in eius baptismo. . . Hec autem inequalitas gratie non est ex virtute baptismi sed meritorum." *Ibid.*, concl. 7.

as Gregory of Rimini had taught, or the *gratia gratis data* as taught in the old Franciscan school? Are there prevenient stirrings of God's grace which enable man to do his very best?

Uncreated grace as such is the Holy Spirit, which is never given without simultaneous infusion of the *gratia gratum faciens*,[51] after the sinner has succeeded in *facere quod in se est*. Created grace, however, is a key term which has to be more closely analyzed. It is of course vital to ascertain whether the first contact with grace takes place before or after the sinner has fulfilled all the requirements for the infusion of the *gratia gratum faciens*.

Of the three meanings Biel introduces for the term grace, the first and the third do not result in any special difficulties. In the broad sense of the word, grace means such various gifts as physical strength and capacity of speech. And in this form grace is undistinguishable from the natural gifts of creation. But, in a more strict sense, grace is a supernatural gift of God either for the benefit of others, such as the gift of prophecy and tongues, or for oneself, such as the infusion of virtues.[52] In the strictest possible sense, grace means the infusion by which man is made a friend of God and acceptable for final beatification.

The lack of clarity in Biel's concept of grace begins to show up at the point where he first states that grace in the strict sense of the word — the second meaning — can be understood as either *gratia gratis data* or *gratia gratum faciens*. A moment later, though, he announces that he will use the term grace in the strictest possible sense — according to its third meaning — as *gratia gratum faciens*.[53] From the use Biel makes of the term *gratia gratum faciens*, however, it is clear that he wants it to be understood in the traditional sense as the grace by which man is made a friend of God.[54] His distinction, therefore, between grace in the strict

---

[51] "Cum autem spiritus sanctus sic sese homini dat veluti donum increatum, semper infundit etiam gratiam gratum facientem, donum creatum quo anima ornatur et in dei sponsam adoptatur," *S* II 35 M. Cf. *S* II 14 D and F.

[52] "Proprie et stricte gratia est donum supernaturale a solo deo superadditum nature ut est donum prophetie, donum linguarum et virtutes infuse," II *Sent.* d 26 q 1 art. 1 nota 1.

[53] ". . . gratia proprie sive stricte pro dono supernaturali accepta dividitur in gratiam gratum facientem et gratiam gratis datam. . . In hac tamen distinctione et tribus sequentibus gratia accipitur propriissime pro gratia gratum faciente." II *Sent.* d 26 q 1 art. 1 nota 1 B.

[54] "Gratia gratum faciens est . . . quam habens amicus dei constituitur et dignus

sense and grace in the strictest sense does not function with regard to sanctifying grace.

Of more consequence is the ambiguity of the term *gratia gratis data*, grace not in the strictest but in the strict sense of the word. In the *Collectorium* Biel follows Alexander of Hales in defining it as the preparatory grace that can coexist with sin and does not make one acceptable to God; *or* as grace given for others, such as the power of the keys executed by the priest who may personally be living in sin.[55]

In the *Sermones* Biel follows Thomas by defining *gratia gratis data*, not in reference to a man's own justification, but solely in terms of the second part of the *Collectorium* definition, that is, as the kind of grace given for the use of others.[56] It is in this sense that Biel uses the term when he deals with the question whether the epithet "full of grace" used for the Virgin Mary does not apply equally to the twelve Apostles. In his reply he states that indeed Mary and the Apostles were all full of grace. But the Mother of God was full as well of the *gratia gratum faciens*, that is, holy, in the sense of personal sanctity. The Apostles, however, were full of the *gratia gratis data*, that is, the status of grace conferred upon them to execute properly their apostolic office, without necessarily implying a set degree of personal piety.[57]

We have to be aware of this oscillation in terminology to be prepared for some seemingly contradictory statements. Sometimes the *gratia gratis data* functions as the middle term between man in sin and man accepted

---

vita eterna," II *Sent.* d 26 q 1 art. 1 nota 1 B. Cf. *Lect.* 59 T; *S* I 29 D and 38 F; *S* II 14 E.

[55] "Gratia gratis data est donum supernaturale datum alicui ad utilitatem sui vel aliorum quod habens non est formaliter gratus deo. Potest enim tale donum stare in peccatore qui non est gratus deo." II *Sent.* d 26 q 1 art. 1 nota 1 B. Alexander of Hales, III *Sent.* q 64 m 5 art. 2; Bonaventura, II *Sent.* d 28 art. 2 q 3; Thomas, *ST* I.II q 109 art. 2; *De Veritate* q 24 art. 14.

[56] ". . . dupliciter datur alicui spiritus sanctus. Uno modo ad propriam et personalem sanctificationem et ita non datur nisi cum gratia gratum faciente. . . Alio modo datur spiritus sanctus alicui non tam ad sui ipsius quantum ad utilitatem ecclesie. Et sic datur in gratiis gratis datis. . . *S* I 38 F. Cf. Thomas: ". . . duplex est gratia. Una quidem per quam ipse homo deo coniungitur quae vocatur gratia gratum faciens. Alia vero per quam unus homo cooperatur alteri ad hoc quod ad Deum reducatur. Huiusmodi autem donum vocatur gratia gratis data. . ." *ST* I.II q 111 art. 1 resp.

[57] *S* III 12 C ff. Holcot follows Aquinas's usage of the term *gratia gratis data*, *Sap.* Lect. 102 B.

and is included in the *facere quod in se est*. In that case it forms a disposition *de congruo* for the infusion of the first grace which is understood as the *gratia gratum faciens*.[58] More often the *gratia gratis data* is not mentioned at all and the *facere quod in se est* is seen as a purely human performance, albeit under the general influence of God — the *concursus dei* which can be defined as grace only in its large sense since it is a gift of creation and not a gift of restoration. It is noteworthy that Biel can identify this general concursus with the first grace and call the *gratia gratum faciens* the second grace.[59] One thing is clear: when the term *gratia gratis data* is used, it is thoroughly naturalized and barely distinguishable from man's natural endowments.[60]

A simple comparison of some of the places where Biel says that the *status ex puris naturalibus* includes only the general *concursus* or influence of God with other places where this same state is described as only excluding the *gratia gratum faciens* allows for but one conclusion: the *gratia gratis data* is identified with man's natural capacities, and Biel

---

[58] ". . . faciendo quod in se est non meretur primam gratiam que est gratia iustificans peccatorem de condigno, licet mereatur de congruo. . . Nullum enim donum gratie gratis date commensurabile est gratie gratum facienti." *Lect.* 59 T.

[59] ". . . dicendum quod duplex est gratia creatoris quedam est gratuita sua voluntas qua omnia condidit ac condita gubernat, per quam naturam omnibus dedit. Est et gratia donum creature datum sine meritis. Sic vel quodlibet donum gratia dicitur . . . specialiter hoc donum quo hominem reddit sibi gratum, que communiter nominatur gratia gratum faciens. Omnis ergo actio humana et cuiuslibet creature prerequirit generalem dei influxum quoniam deo non cooperante nullum creatum agens agere potest. Verumtamen presto est per hanc homini cooperari ad omnem actum suum tam bonum quam malum. . . Et sine hac gratia [!!] omnino nec cogitare nec vivere nec esse valemus. Sed gratia gratum faciens prerequiritur operi meritorio et coexigit voluntatem peccato non infectam; non enim simul stant gratia et peccatum verum non prius tempore voluntas a peccato liberatur quam gratia infundatur. Sed per gratiam iustificatur, oportet tamen quod non insit voluntati obex sive propositum peccandi. Et hanc paratus est deus infundere cuicumque desideranti et quod in se est facienti. Per hoc dicitur quod sine prima gratia generali sive [!] dei influentia voluntas se non potest ad quodcunque convertere, nec aliquid agere. Sine secunda nihil meritorie. Potest tamen se ex naturalibus suis seclusa gratia gratum faciente habita peccati consideratione avertere se a peccato, concurrente prima gratia et convertere se ad deum licet non meritorie. Sic autem faciendo disponit se de congruo ad gratiam." *S* I 29 D.

[60] In the revealing survey of the different kinds of grace granted to man in comparison with God's gift of sanctifying grace to the angels, the *gratia gratis data* is no longer just barely but altogether indistinguishable from man's natural capacities; II *Sent.* d 4 q 1 art. 1 nota 2 E.

apparently does not feel that this link between nature and sanctifying grace is vital enough to be explicitly indicated.[61]

5. Nature and grace

This observation is corroborated by Biel's answer to the question whether the intercession of the Church is necessary at all when one assumes that man alone and unaided can prepare himself sufficiently for the infusion of grace.

Biel suggests two possible answers to the criticism of his position which this question implies. In the first place, the intercession of the Church is to be understood as related to man's final acceptance and admission to life eternal. And this, according to his own admission, can never occur without God's infusion of sanctifying grace. Thus, the necessity of intercession is not at all negated by a defense of man's natural capacities to dispose himself properly for the infusion of grace.

In the second place we must realize that often God performs supernaturally what he could have done naturally.[62] In other words, the intercession of the Church, however helpful it may be to the sinner seeking God, does not necessarily mean that he could not have reached the same level of perfection without it.[63]

When we apply this answer to the relation of the unshakable free will and the indomitable impact of the *fomes peccati*, we see again that the disruption of man's nature is not understood in an ontological but in a psychological sense. Man indeed needs medicine to regain the status of pure nature. While the elevation from this pure nature to life eternal presupposes a supernatural act of God, he can reach this first preparatory status on his own power, healed by natural medicine. Usually however, God does supernaturally what he could have done naturally, that is, what man through the gifts of creation could have done himself.

[61] Cf. note 59 above with the following passage in *S* I 87 E: "Ex puris naturalibus seclusa gratia gratum faciente: stante generali influentia dei potest homo sese ad gratiam disponere. . . Potest enim homo ex puris naturalibus stante adiutorio dei generali seu gratia dei generali facere quod in se est." Cf. *S* I 89 G, H, I and *S* I 91 D.

[62] ". . . multa operatur deus supernaturaliter que limites nature non excedunt," II *Sent.* d 28 q 1 art. 3 dub. 2 M.

[63] ". . . nonnullos sanavit ab infirmitatibus quibus naturaliter mederi potuissent. . . ," *ibid.*

Thus Biel allows for the gift of the *gratia gratis data*, so closely identified with the gifts of creation that it in this manner performs functions which man, not only in principle but as a matter of fact, can perform himself. And however strongly Biel speaks about man's misery resulting from original sin,[64] the preparatory grace of God is not understood as man's last and only hope, but as a divine intervention in the natural order which points to the freedom of God to relieve man in particular cases from the *arduous but possible* task of preparing himself. Here Biel criticizes Gregory of Rimini, who felt that man not only is sometimes assisted by grace, but in principle needs the *gratia gratis data* — or *auxilium speciale*, as Gregory calls it — for every good act.[65]

The most important point to be kept in mind for the further presentation of Biel's doctrine of justification is the conclusion that when Biel discusses the necessity of grace in the process of justification, its relation to man's free will, and its relation to the *ex opere operato* efficacy of the sacraments, he has always the *gratia gratum faciens* in mind — by which the sinner is made acceptable to God — and is not thinking of another kind of grace, traditionally often called *gratia gratis data*, the grace of divine vocation, by which the sinner is provided with the proper disposition for the reception of the *gratia gratum faciens*. Biel denies that the sinner would be incapable of providing such a disposition with his own power by doing good works. He can therefore quite boldly say that

---

[64] ". . . si non necessitatur nonnunquam tamen non nisi cum magna difficultate resistit. Licet enim naturaliter inclinatur ad bonum tamen frequenter seducitur. . ." II *Sent.* d 28 q 1 art. 3 dub. 2 N.

[65] "Nam est opinio Gregorii de arimini, qui parum attribuens liberi arbitrio . . . tenet quod nullus homo in statu presenti stante etiam generali influentia dei, potest absque speciali dei auxilio agere aliquem actum moraliter bonum." Biel II *Sent.* d 28 q 1 A. Thomas' judgment is according to Biel more balanced but somewhat obscure on one vital point: "Beatus Thomas . . . videtur temperantius loqui. . . Sed an illud auxilium art. 9 [*ST* I.II q 109] speciali ratione homini impensum, sit aliud ab influentia et cooperatione dei generali qua assistit omni agenti ipsum movendo, an sit idem, non determinat." II *Sent.* d 28 q 1 B. Gregory's stand is also taken by Hugolin of Orvieto and Jacob Perez of Valencia. Cf. Adolar Zumkeller, "Hugolin von Orvieto († 1373) über Urstand und Erbsünde," *Augustiniana* 4 (1954), 26 ff. Wilfrid Werbeck, *Jacobus Perez von Valencia: Untersuchungen zu seinem Psalmenkommentar* (Tübingen, 1959), p. 231 ff. See also the general comments by Carl Feckes, "Die Stellung der nominalistischen Schule zur aktuellen Gnade," *Römische Quartalschrift* 32 (1924), 157 ff.

grace does not prepare the sinner for the reception of this justifying grace since *grace is not the root but the fruit of the preparatory good works.*[66]

6. The late medieval tradition

In conclusion we must emphasize that by no conceivable standard can Biel be termed — as Denifle did — a "Halbwisser," someone ignorant of the medieval tradition. Biel was very well acquainted, and, as appears time and time again, at first hand, with not only a score of late medieval authorities but also with the works of the four leading "Old Doctors," Alexander, Bonaventura, Thomas, and Scotus, as well as with a number of others. And as his sermons indicate, he also knew the more practical works of Gregory the Great and Bernard of Clairvaux.

Denifle tried to document his low esteem for Biel's reliability as a teacher of medieval Christian thought by referring to two issues on which he held Biel to have been misinformed — Rimini's understanding of original sin and Aquinas's alleged oscillation between positing the necessity of special grace and merely requiring the *concursus generalis* for the philosophical virtues as sufficient disposition for justification. They are, however, not examples of a general lack of information on the part of Biel but rather of two interpretations which differ from those current in contemporary scholarship.

As regards Gregory of Rimini, we have referred above to a series of passages which prove that Biel was well acquainted with Rimini's thought in general and especially with his doctrine of sin.[67] As regards Biel's interpretation of Aquinas on the indicated point, first of all we must grant that Biel's main thesis according to which Aquinas speaks more moderately ("temperantius") than Gregory in trusting more man's natural capacities is correct, even from the point of view of contemporary scholarship. The choice of the word "temperantius" implies of course a value

---

[66] "Nam deus paratus est cuilibet disponenti se ad gratiam dare eam; ergo peccator disponens se recipit gratiam. Et quomodo disponet se ad recipiendum gratiam quam non habet nisi operando bona opera, licet nondum iustificatus? Neque enim potest se disponere ad gratiam per gratiam, alias haberet gratiam priusquam haberet et hic est maximus huiuscemodi operum fructus. Has et multas alias utilitates bonas ferunt bona opera extra charitatem facta. . ." *S* I 99 F. Cf. *Lect.* 59 P.

[67] See above note 13; below Chapter Seven, section I.

judgment which we want to leave to the responsibility of Biel. It merely indicates that understandably enough the standard and point of reference is Biel's own position. Few scholars today would deny that Thomas has "toned down" the strict Augustinianism Gregory came to represent insofar as the *concursus* or *influentia generalis* is assigned a more important role by him than by Gregory; and again, Thomas' thesis that works performed in state of sin are not necessarily to be regarded as sins, is rejected by Gregory as favoring Pelagianism. Denifle himself feels that Rimini went too far in his rejection of the Occamistic claim that man can love God above all *ex puris naturalibus*.[68]

But secondly, it must be noted that Biel, who is not usually given to a guarded and carefully qualified use of tradition, makes quite clear that his understanding of Aquinas is open to discussion and therefore a matter of interpretation.[69] Biel's unusual hesitation about the proper interpretation of Aquinas's position on this point may, of course, be due to the fact that he found in Gregory an interpretation of Aquinas exactly the opposite of his own view.[70] More likely, however, Biel noticed that Aquinas in his Commentary on the *Sentences* defended a positive ultimate disposition for grace on a purely natural basis.[71] In the light of this, Biel's hesitation is a good deal more understandable. It should also be noted that Henry Totting of Oyta with less reluctance than Biel had referred to the authority of Thomas to show that the sinner can perform morally good acts without grace.[72]

The fifteenth-century Thomists point to Thomas' mature position in

[68] *Luther und Luthertum*, vol. I, abt. 2 (Mainz, 1906), p. 549; cf. Denifle's reference to Gregory's "Überspanntheiten," *ibid.*, pp. 557, 574.

[69] See above note 65.

[70] Gregory, II *Sent.* d 29 q 1 art. 2 [fol. 110 F/G].

[71] Aquinas, II *Sent.* d 28 q 1 art. 4 O. See Johannes Stufler, *Divi Thomae Aquinatis doctrina de Deo operante* (Innsbruck, 1923) and H. Bouillard, *Conversion et grâce chez S. Thomas d'Aquin* (Paris, 1944). Bouillard rejects Stufler's conclusion that the young Thomas taught semi-Pelagian ideas (p. 223).

[72] See Albert Lang, *Heinrich Totting von Oyta: Ein Beitrag zur Entstehungsgeschichte der ersten deutschen Universitäten und zur Problemgeschichte der Spätscholastik* (Münster i. W., 1937), p. 225. Lang concludes that Henry's mature theology is fundamentally Thomistic (p. 223). Biel's "videatur" is echoed by Geiler von Kaysersberg: "Et potestne homo hoc facere ex naturalibus sine speciali dei motione? Dicit scotus quod sic. Vide Gabrielem d 28 secundi art. 2 quamvis beato tho. et Greg. contrarium videatur. . ." *Sermones fructuosissimi* (Strasbourg, 1519), fol. 57ᵛ 1.

the *Summa Theologica* and the *Summa Contra Gentiles* as *the* opinion of the authoritative teacher of their order. Antoninus of Florence can perhaps still be interpreted both ways.[73] Johannes Capreolus, the first to regard the *Summa* as the final determination and retraction of earlier statements of Aquinas,[74] leaves no room for doubt as regards Aquinas' position on the preparation for sanctifying grace.

Capreolus is particularly important for our purposes because in his discussion of the very question in the *Summa* to which Biel refers (I.II q 109), he explicitly rejects Durand's thesis that the *influentia generalis* is sufficient for good works — *merita de congruo* accepted by God as proper disposition for infusion.[75] He feels that Thomas and Gregory fully agree on this point. Both hold ambiguously that fallen man needs in addition to the *influentia generalis* also the *auxilium speciale* to be properly disposed for the infusion of grace.[76]

Denifle regards any effort to drive a wedge on this point between the positions of Gregory and Thomas as evidence that one is an *ignoramus* in scholastic theology; this criticism then is directed against both Biel and Luther. Therefore it is in order to point to one more episode of the medieval debate described. Luther claims in the often-quoted passage from his *Resolutiones super propositionibus Lipsiae disputatis* (1519) that

[73] "Non enim est impossibile observare hoc praeceptum quod est de actu caritatis ["Diliges Dominum Deum tuum"] quia potest se homo disponere ad caritatem habendum. . ." *Summa Theologica* (Graz, 1959), I.xiv.3 [fol. 686 D]. Works uninformed by grace are not sins. I.xiv.3 [fol. 686 C]. Cf. IV.vi.1 [fol. 300 ff.]. But also: the preparation for grace is due to grace. *Summa Theologica* IV.ix.4 [fol. 476 ff.].

[74] Martin Grabmann regards this as the marked contribution of the "Princeps Thomistarum." See his *Mittelalterliches Geistesleben: Abhandlungen zur Geschichte der Scholastik und Mystik* (Munich, 1936), II, 475 ff.

[75] Durand: ". . . in homine absque gratia sunt sufficientia principia bonae operationis moralis . . . meritum vero de congruo innititur libertati divinae quae etiam gratia dicitur . . . quamvis per se sufficiat ad eliciendum opus morale bonum ex genere, fine et circumstantiis. Per hoc autem quod dicitur 'per se' non excluditur generalis influentia. . . Et sic intelligitur illud Ioan 15 [:5] : 'sine me nihil potestis facere. . .'" II *Sent.* d 28 q 2 (Lugduni, 1562). See also his statement that the *meritum de congruo* is to be regarded as a *meritum ante gratiam*, II *Sent.* d 27 q 2.

[76] ". . . illa motio ad bene cogitandum non est sola generalis dei influentia immo est specialis dei directio ad recte cogitandum. Ex quibus sequitur quod mens sancti thome non discordat a gregorio quoad hoc quod uterque intendit quod nullus in statu presenti constitutus potest sine speciali dei auxilio. . ." Capreolus, II *Sent.* d 28 q 1 (ed. Venetiis, 1483).

Gregory, together with Karlstadt, stands alone as anti-Pelagian over against the *communis opinio* of the scholastic tradition in rejecting man's purely natural capacity to prepare himself for the reception of grace.[77] The reference to Karlstadt suggests that Luther is not — necessarily — here relying on Biel, as is now generally assumed,[78] but is referring to arguments employed in the bitter exchange of pamphlets between Karlstadt and Eck the year before.

What is remarkable here is that it was not Karlstadt[79] but the learned professor of Ingolstadt who was the first to isolate Gregory of Rimini as someone who stood against the common scholastic tradition. To Karlstadt's contention that the thesis *nulla sit ratio praedestinationis* is the *communis theologorum sententia* represented by Rimini, Eck answered that the contrary is true since many good and holy doctors have posited such a *ratio praedestinationis*, among them Bonaventura, Thomas (in his *Sentences* [!]), Alexander, Henry of Ghent, Thomas of Strasbourg, Gabriel Biel, etc.[80]

To conclude now this excursus on the late medieval discussion of Thomas' teaching in regard to the preparation for grace, we want to

---

[77] "Certum est enim Modernos (quos vocant) cum Scotistis et Thomistis in hac re (id est libero arbitrio et gratia) consentire, excepto uno Gregorio Ariminensi quem omnes damnant, qui et ipse eos Pelagianis deteriores esse et recte et efficaciter convincit. Is enim solus inter Scholasticos contra omnes Scholasticos recentiores cum Carolostadio, id est Augustino et Apostolo Paulo consentit. Nam Pelagiani, etsi sine gratia opus bonum, sed non meritorium fieri docent. Deinde super Pelagianos addunt, hominem habere dictamen naturale rectae rationis, cui se possit naturaliter conformare voluntas, ubi Pelagiani hominem adiuvari per legem Dei dixerunt . . ." *WA* II, 394 f.; cf. II, 308. "Wer nur einigermassen mit Thomas und der Geschichte der Scholastik vertraut ist, muss über die in diesen wenigen Sätzen niedergelegte Ignoranz und Konfusion Luthers staunen," *Luther und Luthertum*, II, 566.

[78] Cf. Seeberg *DG* vol. IV, part 1, p. 77, n. 1.

[79] Denifle suggests that Luther discovered the unique position of Gregory "durch Carlstadt, der wohl durch Gabriel Biel auf Gregor aufmerksam gemacht wurde," *Luther und Luthertum*, II, 566.

[80] "Plures tamen boni et sancti theologi rationum praedestinationis suo modo admisere, ut seraphicus doctor Bonaventura, S. Thomas in Scripto [= commentary on Lombard; cf. Grabmann, *Mittelalterliches Geistesleben*, II, 476], Alexander de Ales, Henricus de Gandavo, Thomas Argentinus, Gabriel Biel, Silvester de Prierio et alii. . . ," Johann Eck, *Defensio contra amarulentas D. Andreae Bodenstein carolstatini invectiones* (1518), II.17 [ed. Joseph Greving, *CC* I, (Münster i. W. 1919), 66]. In the *Chrysopassus* the same group is mentioned again as holding the doctrine "dass sowohl die Prädestination wie die Reprobation irgendwie durch das Geschöpf veranlasst sei," Greving, I, 66 n.

emphasize that the difference between the positions of the mature Thomas and Biel should not be glossed over. But before Biel is accused of ignorance in this matter, it must be pointed out that along with Biel, a significant group of late medieval theologians not only regarded Gregory's position as too extreme, but also felt that they had Thomas on their side. Capreolus' thesis that the authority of the *Summa* was to be more highly esteemed than that of the *Sentences* had to gain general acceptance before their claim could be rejected.

The seventeenth-century debate *De auxiliis* and its intensive discussion of the proper interpretation of Aquinas should warn contemporary scholars not to take late medieval theologians too rashly to task for their difficulty in establishing with clarity and precision the exact function of the *influentia generalis* and its relation to the *auxilium speciale* in the theology of Thomas Aquinas.[81]

[81] Johannes Brinktrine, who gives due weight to the seventeenth century in his discussion of the doctrine of grace, is able to see lines of continuation and to describe the nominalistic position with more detachment than Denifle: "Andere, wie Durandus O.P. († 1334), knüpften an die Lehre des jüngeren Thomas an. Der letztere verteidigte eine positive nächste Disposition auf die Gnade auf rein natürlicher Basis. Ähnlich wie Durandus lehrten Wilhelm Ockham O.F.M. († 1349) und Gabriel Biel († 1495) desgleichen Duns Skotus († 1308)." *Die Lehre von der Gnade* (Paderborn, 1957), p. 111.

Chapter Six

THE PROCESS OF JUSTIFICATION

ᔐᐁ

I. Attrition and Contrition

1. The glory and misery of fallen man

As we have seen, Biel's assessment of the extent of man's spiritual powers varies considerably. On the one hand he describes man's situation after the fall as one of utter depravity and misery; man's lost innocence is compared to a ship, wrecked beyond repair, even sacramental repair.[1] On the other hand, he describes the weight and impact of the *fomes peccati* or tinder of sin as matched by another natural instinct, a witness to man's original dignity so indomitable that even hell itself would not suffice to extinguish it.[2]

In line with these contrasting emphases is Biel's description of man's power to resist evil: this varies from an elaborate exposition of the natural capacities of the *homo peccator* to love God above everything else, to the statement that God *frequently* assists the sinner in such an act or that he

[1] "Navis est status innocentie in quo per gratiam facile satis secure homo creatus poterat pervenire ad portum salutis quia nondum erat illa scopulosa rebellio et periculosissima pugna sensualitatis et rationis . . . non tamen status innocentie restituitur quia manet peccati fomes, manet bellum intestinum, manent scopuli et arene multiplicium impedimentorum que in statu innocentie non fuissent." IV *Sent.* d 14 q 2 art. 3 dub. 2 P.

[2] "Est siquidem aliquid in anima quod omnino errare nequit, nec aliquando deviare, semper rectum, semper lucidum, quod etiam in inferno obumbrari non potest. Et hoc quicquid sit dicimus apicem rationis, scintillam vel naturalem instinctum ad bonum sive synderesim." *S* I 30 D. Feckes has not noted the nature of this ambiguity and therefore could say: "Der gefallene Mensch kann ja alle Gebote beobachten, selbst die schwersten; nur selten weist Biel darauf hin, es sei das mit grossen Schwierigkeiten verbunden," *Die Rechtfertigungslehre*, p. 23, n. 2.

146

assists *most* people with his gracious help, or even that man actually *seldom or never* is left without the help of preparatory grace.[3]

The same contrast appears also in Biel's discussion of the kind of love required for justification. In his main line of argumentation he speaks strongly in favor of contrition, filial love for God, and rejects attrition, servile love for God that is not based on God's essential goodness but on fear of God's punishing righteousness. In his sermons, however, Biel seems at times [4] to take a more positive attitude toward the teaching of Duns Scotus, according to whom the man who is attrite, who experiences out of fear of punishment a rather egoistic regret for sin which he has committed, is sufficiently prepared for sacramental restoration to his former state of grace.[5]

2. The medieval tradition

Exactly as in his treatment of the problem of original sin, Biel surveys traditional opinions regarding attrition and contrition and then discerns three major positions. According to the first "school," only genuine contrition can delete the guilt and punishment of sin, and in the sacrament of penance the priest has merely a declarative function: he merely indicates that justification has already taken place. Lombard is mentioned

---

[3] ". . . vix enim aut nunquam liberum arbitrium destituitur omni gratia gratis data," II *Sent.* d 28 q I art. 3 dub. 2. This is a *verbatim* quotation from Bonaventura, II *Sent.* d 28 art. 2 q I resp. This "vix" of course leaves the door of Bonaventura's doctrine of grace ajar for Pelagian intruders. It is still to be investigated whether in Bonaventura's theology the term *gratia gratis data* itself is not often indistinguishable from the creational endowment of man. Where the *gratia gratis data* is preserved as vocation, this is man's encounter with the law of God. See II *Sent.* d 28 q 3 resp. and compare Biel, *S* I 21 A, F, H. Mitzka, comparing Bonaventura with Alexander, feels rather "dass der Schüler mehr als der Lehrer in den Bahnen des hl. Augustinus wandelt," "Die Lehre des hl. Bonaventura von der Vorbereitung auf die heiligmachende Gnade," *ZKT* 50 (1926), 252. On the one hand, we must agree: "Sie [*gratia gratis data*] ist nach ihm notwendig, weil der Sünder aus eigener Kraft die heiligmachende Gnade nicht richtig erkennen [!] daher auch weder anstreben noch darum beten könne" (p. 71). But on the other hand, the *gratia gratis data* seems a part of the '*facere quod in se est*,' as when Bonaventura says: ". . . et sine hac [gratia gratis data] nullus sufficienter facit quod in se est, ut se praeparat ad salutem." *Breviloquium* 5.2.

[4] *S* I 38 B; *S* II 13 H.

[5] For Scotus, see N. Krautwig, *Die Grundlagen der Busslehre des Joh. Duns Scotus* (Freiburg i. Br., 1938).

as representing this point of view,[6] and Biel indicates that this contrition-
ist position cannot be termed extra-sacramental. The link between justification by contrition and the sacrament of penance is established by the
propositum confitendi.[7]

Biel betrays his preference for this opinion by, contrary to his usual
procedure, omitting any reference to the weaknesses of this theory. He
merely adds: "et illam opinionem communiter sequuntur doctores antiqui." Biel never classifies Duns Scotus or Thomas Aquinas as "doctores
antiqui." When he uses the expression he is usually referring to theologians writing in the period before the first part of the thirteenth century, a period which seems for the nominalist to have been the golden
age of a united theological vision and vocabulary, abruptly broken off
by the Babylonian disintegration of theological language caused by the
philosophical bias of Thomists and Scotists.

The two other schools of thought with which Biel cannot agree are
represented by Thomas Aquinas and Duns Scotus. Duns Scotus rejects
the opinion of Lombard primarily because he feels that by emphasizing
the declarative function of the priest, the *ex opere operato* character of
the sacraments of the New Testament is not duly acknowledged. If
contrition is required as a necessary disposition for reception of sacramental grace, the sacrament of penance has only an effect *ex opere operantis* like the sacraments of the Old Testament.[8] In his great goodness God
has established a double way leading to justification. (1) The sinner may
have attrition of such an intrinsic quality that it is *de congruo* a sufficient
disposition for the reception of sanctifying grace. This way we can term
extra-sacramental justification. (2) The sinner may be barely attrite
(*parum attritus*), having a minimal attrition which is not vigorous enough
to be a *meritum de congruo* but merely implies the voluntary reception
of the sacrament. In this second case justification takes place through the
sacrament, not *ex merito* but *ex pacto divino.*

[6] IV *Sent.* d 14 q 2 art. 1 nota 2 D.

[7] ". . . per sacramentum penitentie non remittitur culpa sed a deo per contritionem previam est remissa prius quam suscipiatur sacramentum in effectu, licet
non prius quam suscipiatur in voto et proposito," *ibid.*

[8] "Hec est, inquit, excellentia sacramentorum nove legis quod eorum susceptio
est dispositio sufficiens ad gratiam. . . ," *ibid.* E. Scotus, *Ox* IV. d 1 q 6 nota 10,
nota 11. Important material for this whole section is to be found in Minges, *Ioannes
Duns Scoti* II, 632 ff. Biel is again elaborate and accurate in his excerpts.

Since for Scotus contrition is attrition informed by grace, one can say that in his view God changes attrition into contrition in the first case directly through acceptation, in the second case indirectly through the sacrament.[9] Biel concedes that this second possibility would be most attractive if only it were supported by the authority of Scripture and the Fathers.[10] Its main attraction for Biel is that the *parum attritus*, who may trust the *ex opere operato* efficacy of the sacrament of penance, can be certain that he is in a state of grace.[11]

In view of the frequent charge of laxity levelled against Scotus' doctrine of the *parum attritus*,[12] — especially since Feckes names Biel as one of the first critics of the Doctor Subtilis on this point,[13] — it is important to note that the minimal attrition which merely required — to put it negatively — *non ponere obicem*, that is, avoiding *de facto* mortal sin, is what Biel sees as the strong point in Scotus' position. Such a position allows more than the usual conjectural certainty, and smooths the way toward certainty. Here he goes even further than Scotus, who feels that he who chooses the easier road to justification through the sacrament of penance can be *relatively* more certain than the person who chooses the exacting road of extra-sacramental justification.[14] Biel, however, finds Scotus' solu-

[9] "Idem motus qui prius fuit attritio in illo instanti fit contritio quia in illo instanti fit concomitans gratiae. . ." *Ox.* IV d 14 q 2 n 14. Compare the more psychological distinction made by Biel: ". . . imperfecta non sufficiens ex parte penitentis ad remissionem peccati vel propter obiectum quia non est de omnibus peccatis vel quia ordinatur in finem inhonestum . . . tunc vocatur attritio . . . Perfecta vero displicentia dicitur contritio. . ." IV *Sent.* d 16 q 1 art. 1 nota 4.

[10] Ista opinio esset valde acceptanda, si haberet firmamentum scripture et sanctorum patrum. . . ," IV *Sent.* d 14 q 2 art. 1 nota 2 E.

[11] Biel has in mind the frequently discussed statement of Scotus: "Nulla alia [via] est ita facilis et ita certa. Hic enim non oportet, nisi non ponere obicem ad gratiam, quod multo minus est quam habere aliquam attritionem, quae per modum meriti de congruo sufficiat ad iustificationem. . ." *Ox.* IV d 14 q 4 nota 14. Cf. *S* I 38 B.

[12] Minges rejects this criticism as invalid; so-called laxist statements are according to him directed against the rigorism of Lombard, *Ioannes Duns Scoti*, II, 648. For contrary interpretations, see Krautwig, pp. 148 ff. Cf. the articles by J. Klein, "Zur Busslehre des seligen Joh. Duns Skotus," *FS* 27 (1940), 108; and Valens Heynck, O.F.M., "Die Reuelehre des Skotusschülers Johannes de Bassolis," *FS* 28 (1941), 9 ff. Klein and Heynck both agree with Minges.

[13] Feckes, *Die Rechtfertigungslehre*, p. 66, n. 189.

[14] ". . . probabilior potest scire se tunc non peccare actualiter peccato interiori vel exteriori. . . ," *Ox.* IV d 14 q 4 nota 14.

tion to be attractive exactly because it would be not a relatively more certain, but an absolutely certain guarantee of justification.[15]

Nevertheless, Biel complains that what Scotus gives with the one hand he takes away with the other.[16] The first possibility mentioned by Scotus, the extra-sacramental road to justification, has indeed high requirements; but its stringency is not Biel's interest or worry. Biel is concerned with the resulting lack of certainty which Scotus here offers. Two points cause this uncertainty: neither the degree of intensity of the act of sufficient attrition nor the length of time this act must last are known to anyone nor are they specified by Holy Scripture.[17]

3. Biel's critique of Scotus

We have been so explicit in the analysis of this hitherto overlooked part of Biel's discussion with Scotus, not only because it is a prelude to Biel's own solution, but especially because it reveals that Biel, far from criticizing Scotus' lax attritionism, praises its underlying pastoral intention. Now he sets out to find a solution that avoids the ambiguity and the extremes of the two Scotistic paths to justification. For Biel, the possibility of presacramental justification is not ruled out; but in contrast to Scotus, Biel refuses to recognize this as extra-sacramental justification, as a second path apart from the one which leads to justification by way of the sacrament of penance. Only in exceptional cases is the total *culpa* and *poena* forgiven on the strength of the most perfect possible act of contrition. The general principle is that the sacrament of penance is the sign of the presence of grace, partly due to contrition, partly to sacramental infusion;

---

[15] "Certus etiam esse potest quod non ponit obicem, quia certus esse potest quod actu non peccat mortaliter et quod non habet voluntatem seu propositum peccandi mortaliter in futuro, quibus stantibus si suscipit sacramentum certus est se consequi gratiam et peccatorum remissionem. . ." IV *Sent.* d 14 q 2 art. 1 nota 2 E.

[16] Scotus' position would be most acceptable ". . . si sicut ex hac parte facilitat et relaxat viam ad consequendam gratiam et peccatorum deletionem non ex alia parte artaret et difficultaret," *ibid.*

[17] Not only certitude but also probable conjecture is impossible, ". . . cum omnino coniecturari non possit an gradum intensionis necessarium attingerit et terminum temporis quo deus ordinavit contingi deberi per motum bonum detestationis ut esse possit dispositio sufficiens ad gratiam, cum gradus ille ac temporis terminus nulli notus sit nec alicui per scripturam specivocatus [specificatus]," *ibid.* Cf. the — for Biel — violent criticism of Scotus in IV *Sent.* d 14 q 1 art. 2. U.

and this implies the remission of the *culpa* and the change of the *poena* from eternal into temporal punishment.[18] Justification by perfect contrition always implies the intention of confession and therefore has a sacramental anchorage.[19]

Emphasis on the necessity of contrition, of course, lays Biel open to the self-same criticism as that levelled by Scotus against Lombard: the sacrament would thus not work *ex opere operato* but *ex opere operantis*. Biel feels, however, that the *ex opere operato* efficacy of the sacrament of penance is sufficiently expressed by the condition *in voto* without which the deletion of sin cannot take place. He points to the parallel in the efficacy of the passion of Christ, which, before it actually took place in time, had already secured the salvation of the Old Testament fathers. In addition, there is here an *ex opere operato* growth in grace that the sacraments of the Old Testament did not confer.[20]

Like later Scotus scholars, Biel has noted the difficulties in interpreting Scotus' various statements on the nature of attrition required for sacramental justification. Sometimes they seem to imply merely that the exterior act of confession is accompanied by the *non ponere obicem* that is, the condition that there be no interference by mortal sin and that there be the wish to receive absolution.[21] At other points, however, Scotus speaks clearly enough about the necessity of a certain displeasure with sin as well as the intention not to sin in the future; Biel feels that Scotus' statements are better understood when interpreted in the light of the

[18] ". . . sacramentum verum et certum signum est inexistentis gratie partim per contritionem, partim per sacramentum infuse et per consequens remissionis culpe," IV *Sent.* d 14 q 2 art. 2 concl. 4. "Dicitur autem regulariter quia quandoque per contritionem previam tota pena dimittitur si fuerit perfectissima. . . ," *ibid.*, concl. 6.

[19] ". . . quandoque per contritionem previam tota pena dimittitur si fuerit perfectissima . . . non tamen [sacramentum] frustra suscipitur quia augmentat gratiam et liberat ab obligatione precepti et confessione," *ibid*. This is not the notorious empty nominalistic anti-ontological legalism. Compare Thomas Aquinas ". . . quamvis tota poena possit per contritionem dimitti tamen adhoc necessaria est confessio et satisfactio tum quia homo non potest esse certus de sua contritione quod fuerit ad totum tollendum sufficiens, tum quia confessio et satisfactio sunt in precepto unde transgressor constitueretur, si non confiteretur et satisfaceret." IV *Sent.* d 17 q 2 art. 1 ad 8.

[20] IV *Sent.* d 14 q 2 art. 1 E col. 4. Biel rightly claims that he quotes Thomas "sententialiter" in IV *Sent.* d 17 q 3 art. 5 ad prim. As appears from *S* II 13 N Biel is aware that he is using an argument against Scotus which he owes to Scotus.

[21] Biel refers to Scotus, *Ox.* IV d 14 q 4 [nota 7] and d 17 q 7 [nota 13].

latter explanation.[22] Nevertheless, Biel wants to make it very clear that fear is not the same as conversion nor a sufficient basis for justification. Along with the exterior acts of confession and absolution, the interior act of contrition is required. Thus he obviously excludes the *parum attritus*.

Biel also rejects the possibility of the Scotistic distinction between the two roads of sacramental and extrasacramental penance. Whether justification, the reception of the *gratia prima*, takes place before or at the moment of confession, in both cases man has "to do his very best" with the intention to confess at his earliest convenience. This *facere quod in se est* is the necessary disposition for the infusion of grace and implies a movement of the free will, which is at once aversion to sin and love for God according to Eph. 5:14: "Awake, O sleeper, and arise from the dead, and Christ shall give you light."[23] Conversion is the transition of the *amor sui* to the *amor dei*. This genuine love for God is not the same act as self-centered love, but as Augustine rightly taught, a radically opposed, new act of the will.[24]

As we will see, this does not mean that in a psychological analysis the *timor servilis* or the self-centered fear of hell cannot be a first step on the road to contrition. What Biel rejects here is Scotus' thesis that attrition and contrition are intrinsically, in *esse naturae*, the same.[25]

While Biel's insistence on love "for God's sake" — *amor amicitie, super omnia, propter deum* — definitely forms a stricter requirement than Scotus specifies, he rejects the necessity of the set duration and intensity of the penitential act as sheer imagination on Scotus' part.[26] At the very moment that this act of love for God's sake is reached, infusion of the first grace takes place. For this reason there is no ultimate and sufficient disposition which temporally precedes the infusion; genuine love for

---

[22] ". . . huic videtur suffragari quod in diffinitione qua diffinit penitentiam dicit absolutio hominis penitentis." IV *Sent.* d 14 q 2 art. 1 E, col. 2.

[23] "Hec resurrectio est per displicentiam mortalium peccatorum post somnum marcescentis corporis in eisdem." IV *Sent.* d 14 q 2 art. 1 E, col. 3.

[24] ". . . convertenda sunt ad deum in conversione a peccato. Hec autem aversio [contemptum dei] fit et conversio contrariis actibus intellectus et voluntatis." IV *Sent.* d 14 q 2 art. 1 E, col. 4.

[25] *Ox.* IV d 14 q 2 n 14.

[26] ". . . si fuerit elicita propter deum . . . sufficiens dispositio et meritum de congruo (quantumcunque fuerit remissa aut momentanea) ad gratie infusionem. . ." IV *Sent.* d 14 q 2 art. 1 H, col. 2.

God is not a previous but a concomitant disposition for the infusion of grace.[27]

4. Love of God for God's sake

When we analyze in somewhat greater detail the decisive moment at which man's moral ascent meets God's gracious descent, it appears that Biel has two principal interests. First, he wishes to emphasize that God's gracious gift is not given in order to help man produce the act of love *propter deum, super omnia*; this is within the realm of man's natural capacities. Infused grace does not create but is added to the act of genuine love of God.[28]

It is true that Biel in his *Exposition* can use the term *aliqualiter bene* to describe a sufficient disposition for infusion. We must not conclude, however, that Biel — at this point contradicting himself — abandons the requirement of contrition. The context makes it clear that Biel understands *bene* as referring to the proper motivation — *propter deum* — while *aliqualiter* indicates that this act is not necessarily of the highest possible intensity.

Second, Biel wants to stress that there is no time interval between

---

[27] ". . . omnis talis displicentia peccati sufficit ut ultimata dispositio ad gratie infusionem, imo non potest esse sine gratia et ideo non est dispositio previa sed concomitans. . . ," IV *Sent.* d 14 q 2 art. 1 corol. 2. ". . . omnis talis detestatio dicitur et est vera contritio," *ibid.*, corol. 3. ". . . attritio prout distinguitur contra contritionem non est sufficiens dispositio ad gratie infusionem," *ibid.*, corol. 4. For Holcot, attrition is the penance of the damned: ". . . dicendum quod velle non peccasse amore iusticie est bonum, non autem velle se non peccasse propter solam penam evitandum," *Sap.* Lect. 67 C.

[28] "Hoc tamen non est propter impotentiam liberi arbitrii absolute; posset enim actum dilectionis dei super omnia elicere ex suis naturalibus etiam si gratia non infunderetur. Sed est ex liberalitate dei gratiam liberaliter infundentis libero arbitrio aliqualiter bene disposito; etiam actus ille tanquam dispositio precedit gratie infusionem, natura et si non tempore. Et ideo non requiritur gratia ad eliciendum actum illum quo disponitur ad suscipiendum gratiam simpliciter, sed superadditur actui tanquam previe dispositioni qua subiectum disponitur ad susceptionem gratie." II *Sent.* d 28 q 1 art. 3 dub. 1 L. Biel confesses that he derives this argument from Scotus. In III *Sent.* d 19 q 1 art. 2 concl. 5 the *parum attritus* position is mentioned as one of the possible contributions to complement the work of Christ which is not *causa totalis meritoria.* Here Biel obviously wants to strengthen his thesis by using the opinions of all schools without committing himself to any one of them.

contrition and the reception of the first grace; in principle it is not necessary for justification and sacramental absolution to coincide temporally. Biel brings this argument to bear on the third school of thought regarding the relation of attrition and contrition. Thomas, Bonaventura, Richard of Mediavilla, Durand de Saint-Pourçain, and Peter de Palude, according to Biel, have steered a middle course between the contritionism of the Magister and the attritionism of Scotus.[29] On the one hand they emphasize, as does Lombard, the importance of interior acts as necessary disposition; and on the other hand they emphasize, as does Scotus with his *parum attritus* possibility, that the infusion of the first grace is linked to the sacrament of penance. The *ex opere operato* efficacy of the sacrament appears in that insufficient contrition (attrition) is changed into sufficient contrition by the reception of the sacrament. Biel is now in a position to make short shrift of this third school of thought, after his elaborate discussion of the Scotistic view. Preparation for the infusion of the first grace, he replies, is either insufficient or sufficient. If the preparatory penitential act is not *propter deum*, the sinner will not be justified. If, however, this act is one of genuine love for God, grace will be immediately infused. In that case the sacrament of penance has still the important function of providing an increase in grace and of absolving the sinner from canonical punishment, *in foro ecclesie*.[30]

5. An evaluation of attrition

In view of erroneous presentations of Biel's understanding of the sacrament of penance which have been due to a wrong understanding of the relation between the *potentia ordinata* and *absoluta*,[31] it is important

[29] Thomas, IV *Sent.* d 17 q 2 art. 1; Cf. *De Veritate* 28.8 ad 3; Bonaventura, IV *Sent.* d 17 p 2 a 2 q 3 resp., does not seem to differ from Scotus; Richard, IV *Sent.* d 23 a 1 q 5 ad 1. Cf. Josef Lechner, *Die Sakramentenlehre des Richard von Mediavilla* (Munich, 1925), p. 274 ff; Durand de Saint Pourçain, IV *Sent.* d 18 q 2; Paludanus, IV *Sent.* d 17 q 8.

[30] ". . . sacerdos ut arbiter virtute clavium aliquod pene remittit; pene scil. temporalis satisfactorie pena eterna per contritionem iam in temporalem commutata," IV *Sent.* d 14 q 2 art. 2 concl. 4.

[31] "The *potentia ordinata* is really born of theological embarrassment. . . At this point [necessity of sacramental absolution] Biel appeals to the *potentia ordinata* and thus makes his peace with the Church." Gordon J. Spykman, *Attrition and Contrition at the Council of Trent* (Kampen, 1955), pp. 84, 86. Although otherwise helpful in his treatment of Trent, Spykman depends, as far as Biel is concerned,

to point here to an argument by Biel that is very revealing. Far from really thinking in terms of the *potentia absoluta* — and using the *potentia ordinata* merely as a subterfuge — Biel defends the heart of his doctrine of contrition against those who judge this issue from the point of view of the *potentia absoluta*, the unconditioned freedom of God. The contingent character of God's act in the infusion of grace, Biel states, is by no means threatened by linking this to the human act of full contrition. *De potentia absoluta* God is indeed not forced to grant his grace, but he has freely decided *de potentia ordinata* always to infuse his grace concomitant with the act of love for God's sake.[32]

As we survey Biel's position on this vital issue of attrition and contrition, we can see that Biel inclines more toward the early medieval emphasis on contrition, penance as virtue, than toward the later and especially Scotistic emphasis on absolution, penance as sacrament.[33] But as we shall see presently, these two, virtue and sacrament, are for Biel certainly not alternatives.

It is fair to interpret Biel as holding that in moral self-fertilization man can and should produce, even if it is only for one moment and without a prescribed intensity, an act of pure love. This is at once more and less than Scotus had asked for in his doctrine of the *attritio sufficiens*; therefore, we should refrain from repeating the traditional verdict that in the contritionistic position of nominalism, Scotus' attritionism is rejected. Indeed the concept of the *parum attritus* is severely criticized: but Biel does not hold this to be Scotus' intended opinion.

If this minimal attrition is interpreted — as contemporary Scotus scholars tend to do — as a form of attrition that is insufficient to earn extra-sacramental grace but yet sufficient to serve as a disposition for sacramental infusion by which it is changed into contrition, Scotus would fulfill Biel's requirement of the presence of an interior act of penance.

---

on Feckes, *Die Rechtfertigungslehre*, p. 61 ff. See also B. Poschmann, *Handbuch der Dogmengeschichte*, IV, 3 (Freiburg i. Br., 1951), 102.

[32] "Nec valet si diceretur: quia deus qui solus gratiam infundit, contingenter agit et ideo non necessitatur per quamcunque dispositionem subiecti ad gratie infusionem; quoniam licet ita possit non infundere gratiam de potentia sua absoluta tamen secundum ordinatam qua statuit non de esse facienti quod in se est. . ." IV *Sent.* d 14 q 2 art. 1 opinio 3 H.

[33] Cf. Ludwig Hödl, *Die Geschichte der Scholastischen Literatur und der Theologie der Schlüsselgewalt*, vol. I: . . . *bis zur Summa Aurea*, in *BB*, vol. XXXVIII, pt. 4 (Münster i. W., 1960), p. 376 ff.

However, this would still not satisfy Biel's second requirement: namely that this interior act be one of genuine love *propter deum*. On the force of this requirement, Biel has to reject both the "Scotistic position" and the third school of opinion and must opt with Occam for the contritionism of Lombard.[34]

It should not surprise us that Biel takes this particular position, given the total context of his opus. First and most important, Biel is convinced that man can, without the aid of grace, *ex puris naturalibus*, love God above all else, for his own sake. The restriction that man can execute the will of God only *quoad substantiam actus* but not *quoad intentionem precipientis* in no sense qualifies this statement. It is the intention of the legislator that his laws be obeyed in the state of grace, and this is of course not within the reach of man's natural capacities.[35] But the substance of the act, in this case sincere repentance, falls within man's power.

[34] "Et quoniam ut recitatum est in priori articulo diverse sunt opiniones quarum quelibet habet graves viros defensores sequor nunc opinionem magistri quam etiam sequitur profundissimus veritatis indagator guilhelmus occam cuius doctrinam tanquam clariorem frequentius imitor. . ." IV *Sent.* d 14 q 2 art. 2 N. Cf. Lombard IV *Sent.* d 18 cap. 5 f.

[35] II *Sent.* d 28 q 1 art. 2 concl. 3. The distinction between the fulfillment of the commandment *quoad substantiam actus* and *quoad intentionem precipientis* is certainly not typically nominalistic. We find the same distinction with slightly different terms — *quantum ad genus operis* and *quantum ad intentionem mandatoris* — in Bonaventura II *Sent.* d 28 art. 1 q 3 resp. The difference is that whereas the nominalists agree with Bonaventura that the intention of the lawgiver requires *gratia gratum faciens*, Bonaventura stands over against the nominalistic tradition in requiring for the fulfillment of the law *quantum ad genus operis* the *gratia gratis data*. See, however, note 3 above. And for a further discussion of the positions of Occam, Holcot, and Woodham on this point, see Oberman, *Bradwardine*, pp. 35 ff., 46 ff. See also note 53 below.

In his *Sapientia*-commentary Holcot denies the meritoriousness but not the possibility of loving God *super omnia ex naturalibus*. For the question, "Utrum preter virtutes morales acquisitas necesse sit ponere theologicas," Holcot assembles the following arguments: at first sight the negative answer seems appropriate, because man can *ex naturalibus suis* assent to the preached faith. Similarly he can love God, once He is thus known, *super omnia*. The contrary argument is based on St. Paul's words on faith, hope, and charity in I Cor. 13:13. Holcot's solution is: "Primum est quod sicut revelatum est sanctis patribus sic scola catholica tenet et ecclesia tradit . . . homini superadduntur virtutes theologice, que ideo theologice dicuntur quia a solo deo infunduntur et sola divina revelatione in sacra scriptura nobis traduntur. . . Ad secundum patet quod hoc non potest homo facere meritorie ex naturalibus. Ad tertium non simpliciter latent sed credimus nos tales habitus habere." *Sap.* Lect. 3 B. Cf. Holcot, I *Sent.* q 4 art. 4 D. The denial of meritoriousness of acts uninformed by grace does not imply the rejection of the *merita de congruo*; see Chapter Seven, section III.

Second, there is Biel's over-all interest in moral integrity.[36] Sacramental efficacy cannot balance moral deficiencies, and exterior acts of penance must correspond with interior penitential sincerity. Like many other fifteenth-century preachers, therefore, Biel warns his congregation not to think that they can remove their sins by all kinds of good works without inner contrition.[37]

If we compare this position with Scotus' *attritio sufficiens* as a rigorous extra-sacramental way — possible only for the great saints — it is clear that Biel's concern is to provide a way to justification within reach of the average Christian. The requirements of time and intensity are omitted. Biel's pastoral interest goes so deep that at one place Biel reintroduces what had traditionally been termed attrition; he considers the *timor servilis*, an act of penance out of self-love, a preparation for that disposition which is *de congruo* worthy of the infusion of grace.[38]

Nevertheless Biel makes it clear that self-centered fear as such is not a sufficient condition, but merely a first step toward the necessary pure love for God. The meditation on God's punishing righteousness should therefore be followed by meditation on God's goodness and love. And as we have noted before, this is exactly what Biel understands to be the task of the sermon. This observation should not tempt us to conclude that Biel shifts the medium of justification from the sacrament of penance to the preaching of the Word. It belongs to the very essence of contrition that it is *in voto* connected with the sacrament of penance.[39]

6. Penance as virtue and as sacrament

Twice in Biel's sermons such sacramental anchorage is stressed to the point that the *aliqualiter bene* condition of the *Collectorium* becomes indeed the *attritio* of Duns Scotus. To this we referred earlier when we

---

[36] "Nemo ex aliena sanctitate se sanctum presumat, sed quilibet apud se solicitus vigilet ut emendatis defectibus proprias virtutes colligat et iustitie operibus sedulo insistat," *S* IV 13 C.

[37] ". . . nonnulli errantes elemosynis peccata a quibus recedere noluerunt redimere nitebantur," IV *Sent.* d 14 q 1 art. 2 concl. 5 O.

[38] "Potest enim homo seipsum diligere sine peccato et incommoda propter seipsum nolle. . . Non meretur gratiam et peccatorum remissionem. . . Potest tamen esse aliqua dispositio remota ad dispositionem de congruo. . . Sic timor servilis introducit charitatem." IV *Sent.* d 14 q 2 art. 3 dub. 3 S.

[39] ". . . sine voto suscipiendi sacramentum penitentie displicentia peccati non dicitur contritio," IV *Sent.* d 14 q 2 art. 2 concl. 2.

noted that Biel's ideal theological anthropology does not always coincide with what he as a pastor knows the average Christian to be. Linsenmann was the first to note a passage in the *Sermones dominicales* where Biel seems to abandon altogether his criticism of Scotus' *parum attritus* concept.[40] Feckes, intent on showing Biel's lack of understanding of the *ex opere operato* efficacy of the sacrament of penance, discounts this passage as a mere quotation from Scotus.[41] However, not only does the passage itself indicate that Scotus' opinion is more than a footnote unrelated to the text proper; a second passage makes it even more explicit that Biel finds great merit in the opinion of Scotus.[42]

In view of our understanding of Biel's academic treatment of the relation of contrition and the sacrament, there is no reason to ignore these passages as mere quotations. In our previous analysis of the *Collectorium* statements, we concluded that Biel was intent on combining the advantages of each of the two ways of Duns Scotus: the sacramental anchorage of the *parum attritus* and the high moral requirements of the extra-sacramental road to justification.

There can be no doubt that whatever name Biel may give to the disposition necessary for the sacramental justification, in the sermons he presupposes also the proper motivation of pure love for God's sake.[43] At the

[40] Linsenmann, "Gabriel Biel, der letzte Scholastiker. . . ," p. 671. "Nec excusat a confessione alia via recuperandi gratiam, que est per sufficientem contritionem de peccato qua stante immediate per seipsum, non ministerio sacerdotis, deus et peccatum remittit et gratiam infundit. Quoniam ubi est via facilior id est magis in potestate hominis et certior ad gratiam recipiendam tenetur quilibet ad illam viam, ita quod non (omissa sic illa) attentet aliam difficiliorem et incertiorem, quia tunc exponeret se periculo salutis sue et videretur esse proprie contemptor salutis. Sed via ista suscipiendi sacramentum penitentie est magis possibilis homini et certior ad primam gratiam recuperandam, quia ad hanc requiritur et sufficit non ponere obicem: secundum Scotum et secundum aliquos alios attritio aliqualis commissorum cum proposito non peccandi pro futuro. Sed longe certius potest se scire quis hec habere, quam scire se habere attritionem [!] sufficientem de congruo ad peccati remissionem sine penitentie sacramento." *S* I 38 B.

[41] "Tatsächlich spricht Biel an der angezogenen Stelle so, aber er gibt alles nur unter der Verantwortlichkeit des Duns Skotus wieder," *Die Rechtfertigungslehre*, p. 76.

[42] "Quorum [sacramenti fructum] principalis hoc est quia per ea consequimur gratiam non solum ex opere operante sed ex opere operato, quod nullis aliis operibus est concessum neque ceremoniis veteris legis ut eliciunt doctores ex verbis Augustini que ponit magister d 1. quarti. Sic autem conferunt gratiam ex opere operato quia ad consequendum gratiam per ea non requiritur secundum Scotum . . . patet in parvulis baptizatis et penitentibus solum attritis." *S* II 13 H.

[43] See the often-repeated warning against postponing confession until the death-

same time he tries to break through the traditional wall of separation between *poenitentia interior* and *exterior*, penance as virtue and as sacrament.

We can illuminate this discussion with a reference to the sermon which is especially and entirely dedicated to the sacrament of penance.[44] In an exposition of Luke 17:14, "Go and show yourselves to the priests," traditionally the favorite text of all contritionists, Biel stresses most convincingly the interdependence of interior and exterior penance. He sees in the cleansing of the ten lepers, of course, a prefiguration of the sacrament of penance. From this story then, he draws two major doctrinal conclusions: (1) the sacrament of penance is absolutely necessary, to be undertaken actually or at least *in voto*, since only *after the lepers left Christ* to go and show themselves to the priests were they cleansed;[45] (2) the priest's absolution itself does not grant the forgiveness of sins. The ministerial and subordinate position of the priest with respect to Jesus Christ appears from the fact that forgiveness may occur before the priest's pronouncement of absolution, possibly as late as the moment when the sinner undergoes the experience of confession, or long before in the moment at which contrition took place. This is expressed in the fact that the lepers were healed *before they reached the priests*.[46]

7. The psychological impact of the sacrament of penance

The foregoing analysis makes it clear that Biel's pastoral presentation in no sense contradicts his academic discussion of the problem of attrition and contrition. Whenever the attritionism of Scotus is referred to, it serves

---

bed: ". . . si aliquam penitentiam homo tunc extorqueret aut ore confiteretur raro tamen vera est et ad salutem sufficiens quoniam oportet huiuscemodi penitentiam procedere ex libertate arbitrii . . . et propter deum super omnia dilectum . . . querit [deus] charitatem, non tantum timorem." *S* I 102 E. Cf. *S* I 89 D.

[44] *S* I 76.

[45] "Ad mundationem a spirituali lepra mortalis peccati necessaria est vocalis confessio in actu vel ad minus in voto seu proposito . . . non prius quam irent se sacerdotibus ostensuri ad preceptum domini mundati sunt." *S* I 76 D.

[46] "Non a sacerdote absolvente, sed a christo autore principaliter et immediate peccatum remittitur, quandoque sola previa contritione, quandoque sacramenti penitentie exhibitione [!]," *ibid.* ". . . mundantur prius quam ad sacerdotum iudicium venirent," *ibid.*, E. Biel finds here his *Collectorium* treatment corroborated and refers to it for a more elaborate discussion.

the purpose of stressing the vital necessity of the sacrament of penance. Biel does not take responsibility for the *parum attritus* opinion. What seems surprising in the sermons is that he grants the sacrament of penance the power to change attrition into a sufficient disposition for the infusion of grace.

Biel does not merely mention this power as an opinion of Duns Scotus, but he accepts the validity of his thesis and merely adds as a point of information that this is the teaching of Duns Scotus.[47] This may seem an unexpected concession to Scotus; in reality, however, Biel does not say that *sacramental grace*, but that the *psychological impact* due to confrontation with the sacrament transforms attrition into contrition. This experience provides, therefore, at the very last moment the proper disposition, contrition, which the *Collectorium* and all the other passages in the sermons proved to require. In accordance with his contention that man without the aid of grace is able to love God above everything else but that concupiscence tries to sway the will away from God, the exterior rite of the sacrament of penance serves as the means to strengthen man's natural powers. Under all conditions love *propter deum* is the unalterable requirement.

We conclude: the strictness of Biel's contritionism necessarily would enhance scrupulousness and despair. Biel is aware of this problem and would have liked in view of this to accept Scotus' *parum attritus* solution. But Biel's doctrine of the *facere quod in se est* and a high estimate of the natural capacities and dignity of man forced him to reject this solution.

II. *Habitus* and *Acceptatio*

1. The Augustinian simile of horse and rider

Here we approach not only a vital point in Biel's theology but also one of the moot points in contemporary late medieval scholarship. For Biel the main question was: what are the respective roles that God and man play in man's justification and final glorification? In contemporary scholarship the most discussed issue is the question whether the *habitus*

[47] ". . . quandoque sola previa contritione, quandoque sacramenti penitentie exhibitione. Patet primum pars per Magistrum. . . Secundum est doctrina Scoti." *S* I 76 D.

of grace still played a role in nominalistic theology or whether it had functionally disappeared, the term alone surviving as a reminder of a dead tradition.[48] Behind this looms large the question of whether or not the gratuitous character of grace is sufficiently protected and effective in Biel's theological system.

The fundamental distinction to be observed in discussing the habit of grace is that of the *bonitas* and the *dignitas* of every human act. The *dignitas* of an act is its *bonitas* with respect to its eternal reward; in other words *sub specie aeternitatis*. To summarize Biel's doctrine of justification in one sentence: the habit of grace is the necessary bridge between *bonitas* and the *dignitas* which gives the *viator* a *de condigno* claim on his eternal salvation.

We have seen previously that Biel has a high regard for man's natural capacities even outside the state of grace. If man really does his very best, he can love God more than anything else. He defines the freedom of the will as inalienable spontaneity. This is the basis of both goodness and meritoriousness since only spontaneous acts are acts for which man can be held responsible.[49]

While the freedom of the *will* is spelled out in terms of spontaneity, that is, psychological freedom, the freedom of *man* is understood to be metaphysical freedom, that is, the freedom to choose between good and evil. The will is blind and has to be guided by the reason which presents alternatives to the will and advises the will by the *dictamen rationis* to produce spontaneously a morally good act.[50] Biel by no means denies

---

[48] On this point see Vignaux, *Luther Commentateur des Sentences*, p. 79, n. 3: ". . . le Nominalisme demeure dans la perspective de l'habitus", and Iserloh, *Gnade und Eucharistie . . . Ockham*, p. 132: "Weil gratia creata nur noch ein Begriff war nach dessen Seinsinhalt nicht mehr gefragt wurde. . ." Cf. Iserloh, p. 77 ff. See also the parallel discussion: "Le Nominalisme ne nie point la causalité créée, il l'estime indémonstrable et la tient pour un *probabile* — du point de vue de la raison," in Vignaux, p. 84. He contrasts this with the Reformation position: ". . . on a justement lié l'avènement de la Réforme à une dévaluation des causes secondes." Cf. Etienne Gilson, *L'Esprit de la philosophie médiévale*, II, 118 and Iserloh, *Gnade und Eucharistie . . . Ockham*, p. 281: "Die starke und einseitige Betonung der souveränen Allmacht Gottes führt bei Ockham zu einer Unterbewertung, ja Verflüchtigung der causae secundae."

[49] "Hec dicitur libertas contingentie. Sic accipitur quoniam est principium meriti et demeriti. Nam per hec que vitare non possumus nec meremur nec demeremur." II *Sent.* d 25 q 1 art. 1 D. Cf Augustine, *De lib. arb.*, III.18.50 in *PL* XXXII, 1295.

[50] "Voluntas non est causa sufficiens suorum actuum. Probatur quia si esset suffi-

that habitual grace assists man's natural capacities in establishing the *bonitas* of an act once he is in state of grace. At one place he even applies the Augustinian image of the free will as the horse that is driven by grace as a rider.[51] Biel's introductory words to this particular section, however, suggest that the driver is more like a second horse running side by side with the first (*concurrit*) than a rider guiding the blind instincts of the horse as in Augustine's description.[52]

The well-known nominalistic distinction between the two aspects of the one act: *quoad substantiam actus* and *quoad intentionem precipientis* has to be interpreted according to the indicated distinction of *bonitas* and *dignitas*. A meritorious act presupposes a basic goodness, *bonitas*, to which the habit of grace contributes as an additional impetus and ornamentation. The requirements of the eternal lawgiver cannot be fulfilled, however good such an act as such may be, unless the act be informed by grace. For the acceptability of an act, *dignitas*, the habit of grace is the basic requirement.[53]

---

ciens posset producere volitionem nullo actu concurrente, stante generali influentia que hic semper supponitur. Consequens falsum quia tunc posset velle nullo obiecto cognito. . ." II *Sent.* d 25 q 1 art. 3 dub. 3 N. Our works can be considered as "a nobis operata virtute nostra activa naturali quam accepimus in prima nostra constitutione. In qua facultatem accepimus libere operandi sive opera bona sive mala secundum quod dixit propheta 'Anima mea in manibus meis semper.' In manibus meis, i.e., in potestate mea semper. . ." *Lect.* 59 L. Cf. *S* I 101 D.

[51] "Et beatus Augustinus in de libero arbitrio: Gratia se habet ad liberum arbitrium sicut sessor ad equum. Sessor autem active regit et movet equum. Ita et gratia movet voluntatem ad aliquem actum eliciendum vel operandum." *Lect.* 59 L. Cf. *Lect.* 29 K.

[52] ". . . ad eorum [opera nostra] productionem concurrit cum nostra voluntate singulare donum dei quod gratiam appellamus," *Lect.* 59 L. Cf. Pseudo-Augustine, *Hypognosticon* III.11.20 in *PL* XLV, 1632: "Quia sicut jumentum animal vivacissimum, ut dometur ad opus homini necessarium, de armento vagum apprehenditur et incipit per curam domantis se ad eius proficere voluntatem, ita et liberum arbitrium quod vulneratum vivit in homine gratia dei apprehenditur. . ." Biel writes: "Alio modo considerari possunt opera nostra ut non solum sunt a nostra virtute active. Sed ad eorum productionem concurrit cum nostra voluntate singulare donum dei quod gratiam appellamus." *Lect.* 59 L. He quotes the passage from Augustine a second time in his sermons to prove that meritorious acts require grace: "Sessor equum regit et quorsum tendit dirigit," *S* II 14 F. Grace is here more like the *concursus* or *influentia generalis.*

[53] "opus meritorium . . . requirit terram bonam et cultam: hoc est voluntatem mandatorum dei obedientia exercitatam et gratiam dei . . . desuper incrementum dantem. . . Sed in bonis merendis causa principalis gratie attribuitur et acceptationi divine. . . ," *S* IV 27 C.

If for the sake of clarity and by way of interpretation we may mix Biel's metaphors, we can say that grace, the seed of acceptability, has to be planted in fertile earth, that is, the *bonitas* of the act. As regards making the earth fertile (*bonus*), free will is the horseman, grace the horse. As regards making the act acceptable to God (*dignus*), grace is the horseman and free will the horse.[54]

Biel is obviously more convincing in his application of Augustine's driver-horse image to the *dignitas* than to the *bonitas* aspect of the act performed in the state of grace. One wonders how he could distort Augustine's intention to the point that he could compare free will with the horse while nevertheless defining it as the *causa principalior?*

The partly exculpating and certainly convincing explanation is that on this point Biel must have read Augustine with Scotistic spectacles, since Duns Scotus, in a way very similar to Biel, reverses the Augustinian argument.[55] Occam, on the other hand, makes Augustine's image apply only to the acceptability of an act by stating explicitly that as regards eternal reward, the relation of grace to free will is that of driver to horse.[56]

[54] "Pro cuius intellectu advertendum quod in actu meritorio duo est considerare. Primum est ipsa substantia sive realitas actus. Secundum acceptabilitas actus. Substantia actus est a libero arbitrio seu voluntate simul et a gratia, quia gratia et voluntas sunt due cause partiales et una causa totalis actus illius. Voluntas tamen est causa principalior quia voluntas habet rationem potentie. Gratia rationem habitus. Potentia autem utitur habitu et non econverso. . . Acceptabilitas autem ipsius actus meritorii similiter est a voluntate et etiam a charitate. Non enim actus quicunque a deo acceptatur in ordine ad beatitudinem conferendam nisi sit libere a voluntate elicitus. Neque tamen hoc sufficit sed oportet quod hoc sit secundum inclinationem charitatis. Que quia ratio ponitur merendi ipsa est causa principalior quoad acceptabilitatem. . . Et pro illo facit dictum beati Augustini in de libero arbitrio: Gratia se habet ad liberum arbitrium sicut sessor ad equum." *Lect.* 29 L. Cf. Occam, III *Sent.* q 5 J.

[55] ". . . ponatur quod ascensor intenderet aliquam rem naturaliter et quod equus liber iret ad illum terminum, tunc ascensor determinat equum inquantum ex parte sui naturaliter est ad illum terminum. Sed ponatur quod sufficienter ipsum determinat, tamen equus ex libertate et fortitudine sua libera potest sequi vel contrariare." *Lectura prima* I d 17 (Wien Nat. Bibl. 1449, f 53 a), as quoted by Auer, II, 200. Cf. *Ox.* I d 17 q 3 nota 23. Auer's observation is applicable to Biel's treatment of the *bonitas* of an act: "Das augustinische Bild von Ross und Reiter wird hier ebenfalls ganz neu gedeutet indem das Pferd frei und der Reiter naturnotwendig wirkt in dem Gnaden- und Willen-Verhältnis . . . eben das Gegenteil des Bildes," II, 200.

[56] ". . . quia sicut sessor regit et gubernat equum ita caritas voluntatem quantum ad acceptationem divinam et vitam eternam. . . ," IV *Sent.* dub. ad F.

It is revealing that Biel, like Scotus and Occam before him, quotes the passage under discussion with a reference to Augustine's *De libero arbitrio*. In this treatise, however, the image of horse and driver is nowhere used nor applied to the relation of free will and grace. The only time the word "horse" is mentioned, it represents the spontaneity of the will which marks the dignity of man even after the fall, as compared with the world of dead matter. The activity of the horse is praised, not as it would later be interpreted in comparison with grace, but in comparison with the inertness of stone.[57]

The quotation itself is correct and of Augustinian origin. Biel's un-Augustinian interpretation cannot be explained as due to this erroneous reference to a passage where Augustine discusses not the metaphysical but the psychological freedom of the will. Nevertheless its use in this context is indicative of a striking lack of sensitivity for the important distinction between metaphysical and psychological freedom of the will.

While, as we saw, the *gratia gratis data* does not seriously enter the discussion on justification and when mentioned either connotes a special charisma for the use of the Church at large or more generally a gift of God — in the same sense in which the natural powers of man are gifts of God — the *gratia gratum faciens*, habitual sanctifying grace, is seen as a power that directs the will to produce meritorious acts. At the same time it is obvious that Biel does not show the intrinsic necessity of the habit of grace. Even his use of the strong Augustinian image of the driver and the horse to describe the relation of grace and free will proves on closer investigation to be far from convincing. Grace certainly exerts influence; but parallel to the relation of infused faith and acquired faith, it has an auxiliary function of facilitating and perfecting the acts of man's free will. Here again the maxim applies: God does often in a supernatural way things that are within the power of nature.[58]

Doubtless for Biel sin has not made it impossible for man to act rightly without the aid of grace. That is to say, the will is still able to obey the *dictamen rationis*. Not absence of grace, but improper cognition prevents

[57] Augustine rejects the Stoic necessity: "Sicut enim melior est vel aberrans equus quam lapis propterea non aberrans quia proprio motu et sensu caret. . ." *De lib. arb.*, III.5.15 in *PL* XXXII, 1278. Cf. *De gratia et lib. arb.*, I.14.29 in *PL* XLIV–XLV, 898.

[58] ". . . multa operatur deus supernaturaliter que limites nature non excedunt," II *Sent.* d 28 q 1 art. 3 dub. 2. Cf. Occam, I *Sent.* d 17 q 3 F.

man from acting rightly.[59] While the will can spontaneously choose the best offered to it, it is dependent on the reason for finding the proper objects for volition.[60]

At this point the much discussed nominalistic voluntarism finds its limitation: reason or knowledge, not good will, is the root and foundation of all virtues.[61] The primary task of the Church is therefore not to provide grace, but to provide the Christian people with the proper information about God which necessarily leads to moral improvement.[62]

This knowledge is partly natural knowledge of God, partly preternatural knowledge of him, accepted on the authority of the Church in general or of a particular preacher. These two components form together the *fides acquisita*;[63] it is this kind of faith, therefore, that is the source of all virtue. Nevertheless, the moral goodness due to the philosophical virtues does not fulfill the requirements set by God, not only because the *fides acquisita* encompasses the kind of knowledge which is also within reach of the demons, but more fundamentally because of the basic difference between good deeds and meritorious deeds, philosophical and theological virtues.

[59] "Cum autem voluntas sit de se potentia ceca, bonitatem obiecti vel maliciam non apprehendit nisi ostendatur per intellectum. . . Unde patet quod actionis meritorie et peccati principium est in intellectu et consummatio in voluntate." *S* I 101 D.

[60] "Voluntas non est causa sufficiens suorum actuum. Probatur quia si esset sufficiens posset producere volitionem nullo actu concurrente, stante generali influentia que hic semper supponitur. Consequens falsum quia tunc posset velle nullo obiecto cognito. . ." II *Sent.* d 25 q 1 art. 3 dub. 3 N.

[61] ". . . cognitio radix et fundamentum omnium virtutum. . ." *S* II 39 C. The voluntaristic character of nominalism is strongly stressed by Paul Vignaux in his articles on "Nominalism," in *DThC*, XI, col. 762; and "Occam" in *DThC*, XI, col. 879. When the enlightenment of the congregation is said to take place through the preaching of the Word, it should be noted that the result is not the healing of the will but the restoration of the knowledge of good and evil, which enables man to take the initiative in the process of conversion: ". . . verbum dei, quo eruditur mens humana ad dei cognitionem bonorum malorumque discretionum, per que homo initium sumit sue conversionis ad deum. . ," *S* I 21 A. "Ad eos qui nec initium faciunt converti ad dominum, omnino nec venit." *Ibid.* Cf. note 90 below.

[62] "Hec omnia obtinere possumus si deum secundum predicta cognoscimus . . . tota causa irreligiositatis christiani populi hec est quia deum quem ore fatentur aut ignorant aut non cogitant. Et e diverso totius religionis causa est dei fidelis cognitio et frequens meditatio." *S* II 39 G.

[63] For this reason the *dictamen fidei* is always added in the definition of *bonitas*. E.g., ". . . bonitatem que est rectitudo seu conformitas actus ad rationem rectam secundum dictamen prudentie vel fidei," II *Sent.* d 27 q 1 art. 1 nota 1 A.

2. The necessity of the habit of grace

All that has been said about the significance of the habit of grace with respect to the *bonitas* is actually merely preliminary to a discussion of the real function of this habit: the *dignitas* or acceptability of an act by God. Biel can speak in what appears to be such bold Pelagian language about the respective contributions of free will and grace as regards the moral quality of an act because he feels that he brings the full biblical doctrine of grace to bear on the relation of good deeds and meritorious deeds.[64]

As he shows in I *Sent.* d 17, the habit of grace is not a necessary requirement for a meritorious act *de potentia absoluta*. In II *Sent.* d 27, however, he deals with this question *de potentia ordinata*, and it is here that we have to look for Biel's actual theological teaching.[65]

[64] "Siquidem ex operibus nostris gratia adquiri non potest sicut cetere virtutes morales que ex operibus moraliter bonis frequentatis in nobis naturaliter generantur . . . [gratia] a solo deo est cum natura de nihilo nihil facere possit. Si denique ex creatura esse possit gratia, cum gratia illa sufficit ad salutem, posset aliqua creatura ex suis naturalibus salvari, illa scil. que gratiam producere posset, quod est error Pelagii." *S* II 14 C. Cf. Holcot, ". . . opera nostra ex sua naturali bonitate non merentur vitam eternam de condigno sed de congruo tantum quia congruum est quod homini facienti secundum potentiam suam finitam, deus retribuat secundum potentiam suam infinitam," *Sap.* Lect. 35 B; also Holcot, IV *Sent.* q 1 art. 3. The *meritum de congruo* can nevertheless very well be connected with the concept of prevenient grace: "Hic autem loquitur spiritus sanctus de actu meritorio: in quo ipse nos prevenit gratia preveniente sine qua nullum opus meritorium exercere valemus," *Sap.* Lect. 81 A.

[65] ". . . loquimur secundum potentiam dei ordinatam secundum quam ultra substantiam actus et omnes conditiones actus quas experimur, scl. ultra delectationem et facultatem in agendo, bonitatem que est rectitudo seu conformitas actus ad rationem rectam secundum dictamen prudentie vel fidei. Ultra hec omnia creditur esse una conditio in actu . . . quod est acceptabilis deo . . . acceptatione speciali que est ordinatio divina huius actus ad vitam eternam tanquam meriti condigni ad premium." II *Sent.* d 27 q 1 art. 1 nota 1 A. The fact that Occam elaborately comments on I *Sent.* d 17, while omitting II *Sent.* 27, on the one hand indicates his interest in the philosophical theology of the *potentia absoluta*, but reminds us, on the other hand, that his *Sentences* commentary is truncated, which at least justifies the speculation that if he had written on II *Sent.* 27 he might well have stressed more, like Biel, the *de facto* requirement. Though Occam himself carries some of the responsibility for later misinterpretations — see Iserloh's careful analyses of the relation of habit and acceptation in Occam, *Gnade und Eucharistie* . . . , p. 77 ff. — Iserloh's conclusions lose some of their radicality when seen in this light (p. 279 ff.). See Occam, I *Sent.* d 17 q 1 H ff.; III *Sent.* d 13 C. On the parallel passage, III *Sent.* d 27 q 1, see Paul Vignaux, "Luther: lecteur de Gabriel Biel," *Eglise et Théologie* 22 (1959), 33 .

The habit of grace is required as disposition for man's ultimate acceptation, that is, beatification by God, and Biel makes clear the principal reason why such a habit should not be denied. It is interesting to note one of these reasons, not only because we observe once again an effort to stress the *ratio fidei*; but also because, in the perspective of the history of theology, it shows what may happen once the *habitus*-doctrine is rejected, or vice-versa, what may lead up to the rejection of the *habitus*.

The proof that grace cannot be limited to *gratia actualis* is the fact that if our disposition would depend on just that, any contrary, yea even indifferent act would destroy the disposition and thus prevent acceptation.[66] Such actualization of grace would require an absolute dedication to God since God cannot possibly accept indifferent or sinful — albeit venial — acts. Habitual grace, on the other hand, allows for a certain form of sinfulness and indifference to coexist with acceptability: partly *iustus*, partly *peccator*.[67]

But where now does this habit of grace fit in? According to Biel there are only two conditions that have to be met for an act to be worthy of reward. The first is that it should be a laudable act and thus a free act in the above-indicated sense — *bonitas* — since merits and free acts have in common that they are laudable acts. But the basic goodness of an act is not sufficient. A second condition has to be met: the acceptation by God of the act for its reward.[68]

The second condition for the reward by agreement and according to strict justice, that is, the *meritum de condigno*, is in turn spelled out in a threefold way: (1) the actor should be a friend of God since an enemy of God earns punishment and not reward; (2) the *act* should be "directable" to God. Thus even if one is a friend of God, that is, in a state of

---

[66] "Hoc autem [gratia actualis] non sufficit ad hoc quod actus elicitus acceptetur. Alioquin enim habens gratiam non posset habere aliquem actum indifferentem nec peccare venialiter." II *Sent.* d 27 q 1 art. 1 nota 1 A.

[67] Since "partly *iustus* and partly *peccator*" is the exact opposite of "simul iustus simul peccator," we have to disagree with van de Pol's statement that this latter concept is Occamistic. Willem H. van de Pol, *Het Wereldprotestantisme* (Roermond, 1956), p. 36 f.

[68] "Secundo notandum quod ad rationem meriti in actu duo requiruntur in genere. Primum libera eius elicitio. Secundum ad premii retributionem acceptatio. . . Actui enim extra charitatem facto quantumcunque sit bonus moraliter, tamen nullus gradus beatitudinis sibi correspondet in premio." II *Sent.* d 27 q 1 art. 1 nota 2 B. Cf. Occam, I *Sent.* d 17 q 1 E.

grace, indifferent acts or venial sins cannot be considered for reward; (3) as concerns the *rewarder* an acceptation or agreement is required, by which he commits himself to reward certain actors and acts. The condignity or equality of deed and reward is not based on any natural or intrinsic goodness of the act, but on this agreement to which God in eternity freely committed himself. This is the only way in which condignity can be established between a temporal act and an eternal reward.[69]

There is no doubt that *de facto* the habit of grace is required for acceptation and that it is only this habit which raises the free act to equality, to meet the conditions of the agreement.[70] We should not be confused by the fact that Biel takes pains to remind his auditors and readers that this is only the case within the context of the eternal decree and not a metaphysical necessity. It is the freedom of God Biel has in mind when he adds: "Sed ratio formalis precise, unde actus dicitur meritorius aut agens deo carus, est gratuita dei voluntas que est spiritus sanctus."[71]

It is indeed true that this eternal decree itself is a free commitment; but within the context of this agreement — and this means *de potentia ordinata* — God would act illegally if he did not grant the reward once the conditions in actor and act have been met. The whole dispensation of grace, that is, the incarnation and salvation by Jesus Christ, is contingent on this eternal decree; in itself it is not necessary, for only the *bonitas* of the act and its acceptance are required; yet "per gratiam domini nostri Jesu Christi credimus salvari."[72]

[69] ". . . non requiritur ad premium de condigno quod actus meriti secundum intrinsecam suam bonitatem sit condignus seu proportionatus tali premio. Alioquin nullus actus temporalis esset eterno condignus premio. Sed illa condignitas attenditur in proposito ex divina acceptatione qua ab eterno voluit actum sic ex gratia elicitum esse dignum tali premio. Incomparabiliter excedente actus bonitatem secundum se sine acceptatione divina consideratam. Et secundum hec verum est quod deus semper premiat ultra condignum. . . Sic ergo patet quod debitum iusticie in premiando. . . [innititur] divine ordinationi que est quedam promissio, sive conventio et pactum." II *Sent.* d 27 q 1 art. 1 nota 3 C. Cf. *Lect.* 59 N and *S* II 35 K.

[70] ". . . de facto deus neminem acceptat ad vitam nisi cui infundit habitum charitatis," I *Sent.* d 17 q 3 art. 2 concl. 1 B *in fine.*

[71] *Ibid.*, concl. 2 C.

[72] I *Sent.* d 17 q 3 art. 2 concl. 1 B. See Holcot: "Necessitas coactionis nullo modo cadit in deo, necessitas vero infallibilitatis cadit in deo ex promisso suo et pacto sive lege statuta et hec non est necessitas absoluta sed necessitas consequentie . . . concedendo quod ex misericordia et gratia sua pro tanto quia talem legem misericorditer statuit et observat; sed statuta lege necessario dat gratiam necessitate consequentie." *Sap.* Lect. 145 B. These two kinds of necessity reflect the distinction be-

3. A classification of merits

Thus it has become clear to us that the habit of grace is the middle term between the freely elicited good act and God's acceptation. In the prolegomena and in what has been said above, the relation between the habit of grace — *gratia creata* — and God's acceptation — *gratia increata* — has been analyzed. The deepest and ultimate reason for acceptation proves to be God's free decision to do so. The emphasis here is clearly on the *gratia increata*: something created can never in itself be a moving cause of God's action.[73]

De potentia ordinata the infusion of grace, the inhabitation of the Holy Spirit and the acceptation by God coincide.[74] Now we proceed to inquire into the relation — within the set acceptation structure — between the habit of grace and the freely elicited good act: in other words, how are the two conditions which we have mentioned related? We have seen in what manner grace and free will cooperate and constitute together the *bonitas* of an act. But within the context of God's eternal decrees arises the question: are not the requirements in actor and act mutually exclusive? How can the act be directable to God, that is, laudable, spontaneously performed, while the actor possesses the habit of grace which

---

tween the "two powers." The *statuta lege* makes clear that for Holcot also God is committed to the order *de potentia ordinata*, which is therefore dependable. Cf., however, G. Leff, who assigns to Holcot an "extreme scepticism, which allows anything to be possible," *Bradwardine and the Pelagians* (Cambridge, Eng., 1957), p. 223.

Alois Meissner has also concluded: "Zumindest sind alle Grundgedanken, die wir in den Werken Holkots finden, bereits bei Ockham festzustellen. Holkot hat wohl noch klarer und konsequenter die von Ockham festgelegten Prinzipien, besonders nach der ethischen Seite, durchgeführt." *Gotteserkenntnis und Gotteslehre nach dem Englischen Dominikanertheologen Robert Holkot* (Limburg an der Lahn, 1953), p. 123. This implies, "Die bisherigen Forschungsergebnisse über den Nominalismus . . . scheinen mir jedoch die gut begründete Meinung zu rechtfertigen, dass das Kernstück des Nominalismus wohl in seinem Skeptizismus und Kritizismus zu suchen sei. . ." (p. 132). See, however, Chapter Seven, section III.

[73] ". . . nihil creatum potest esse ratio actus divini. Nec in se nec ut tendit in tale obiectu. Quia actus divinus est eternus et immutabilis. . . Sed mutabile non potest esse ratio immutabilis. . ." I *Sent.* d 17 q 3 art. 3 dub. 2 G. Cf. Occam, I *Sent.* d 17 q 1 K.

[74] "Cum autem spiritus sanctus sic sese homini dat, veluti donum increatum, semper infundit etiam gratiam gratum facientem, donum creatum, quo anima ornatur et in dei sponsam adoptatur," *S* II 35 M.

made him a friend of God? Is not a habit coercive, is one not "enslaved" by habits?

It is here that we find the motive behind Biel's transformation of the rider-horse image into an image of grace and free will in which two free-running horses together carry the act toward virtue; the free and — in an absolute sense — unnecessary "symbiosis" of the supernatural and the natural can in no way threaten the moral integrity of the natural act. While Biel affirms in no uncertain terms that at least an important part of merit is the good disposition, the natural understructure, he can find the gratuity of God's gifts expressed in the fact that man's salvation is primarily due to God's acceptation.[75] The gratuitous character of God's remuneration is therefore not based on the *activity* of the habit of grace nor on the *presence* of the habit of grace, but on God's eternal decree according to which he has decided to accept every act which is performed in a state of grace as a *meritum de condigno*.

While God in eternity freely decided to establish this pact, in time he is committed, *ex debito iusticie*, to the announced rules. In time, that is, in the present reality, acceptation is connected with the habit of grace through the iron link of justice: where the one is present the other follows.[76] It is obvious that with this state of affairs, it is of overriding importance for the sinner to acquire the habit of grace since its possession at the moment of death guarantees acceptation and beatification. We must agree therefore with Paul Vignaux that the doctrine of acceptation does not make the habit of grace superfluous: *de facto* the infusion of grace is necessary for salvation.

We turn now to the *meritum de congruo*, since this forms the link between the supreme achievement of natural man — *facere quod in se est* — and the infusion of the habit of grace, parallel thus to the *meritum de condigno* which in the second stage links the habit of grace to the divine acceptation.

Biel defines this semi-merit in contrast with the full merit *de con-*

---

[75] "Magis ergo meritum est quia est a deo ad reddendum operanti magis acceptum quam quia est in potestate nostra aut libere elicitum," I *Sent.* d 17 q 3 art. 3 dub. 1 F. Cf. *S* II 14 F.

[76] "Meritum condigni super rationem meriti addit debitum reddendi premium secundum iusticiam," *Lect.* 59 N. "Ita etiam quod stante sua promissione qua pollicitus est dare vitam eternam," servantibus sua mandata non posset sine iniusticia subtrahere eis premia repromissa," *ibid.*, S.

digno; this semi-merit also has to be a spontaneous act and also has to be accepted as worthy of its reward. But it does not presuppose condignity between reward and act, neither in the act nor in the actor nor in the remunerator. That such an act is accepted at all is due not to justice but to generosity on God's part.[77]

The sharpest formulation of this contrast between the two kinds of merit appears in Biel's commentary on the Mass: the infusion of grace is granted to the sinner when he does his very best, not on grounds of a previous pact, but on grounds of God's generosity.[78] Biel invites his auditors and readers to find God's overriding love and sovereignty expressed in the most articulate way, not in the full merit of justice, but in the semi-merit of generosity.

With what impresses the reader as honest pathos Biel rejects the idea that a sinner is able to earn the first grace *de condigno*: neither with an act that precedes nor with an act caused by this first grace can he do so. Not preceding, as condignity requires the status of a friend of God; not caused, as the cause cannot follow its effect. Similarly, God does not grant the first grace merely because he foresees the resultant meritorious deeds. In that case he would never grant grace to those who would abuse it. This, however, would violate the rule that he infuses grace into all who do not resist this infusion, regardless of later behavior, as can be shown in the case of baptized children who as adolescents may turn their backs on God.[79]

[77] "Meritum de congruo est actus libere elicitus, acceptatus ad aliquid retribuendum, non ex debito iusticie sed ex sola acceptantis liberalitate. Et hoc meritum non coexigit equalitatem dignitatis cum retributo, neque in operante, nec in opere, nec in retribuente. Potest enim premians aliquid retribuere operanti intuitu alicuius actus alias non daturus, non tamen tanquam digno in se, nec ratione operis condigni, sed ex sua liberalitate etiam ei qui inimicus est." II *Sent.* d 27 q 1 art. 1 nota 3. Cf. art. 2 concl. 4 and Altenstaig, s.v., "Facere quod in se est," fol. 84ʳ.

[78] "Sic etiam si quis bonum excedens actum operantis non ex debito precedentis pacti sed nuda liberalitate donet; non daturus illud nisi operatio illa precessisset in premiando talis operatio esset meritum de congruo non de condigno," *Lect.* 59 N.

[79] "Anima non potest actu a voluntate libere elicito mereri primam gratiam de condigno. Probatur quia neque actu precedente gratiam neque sequente. . . Deus autem dans primam gratiam non dat illam intuitu meritorum sequentium." II *Sent.* d 27 q 1 art. 2 concl. 2. See also Holcot: "Anima enim non est perfecte bona nisi per gratiam et charitatem qua debito modo ordinatur in deum . . . primam gratiam nullus potest promereri. Nam cum omne meritum sit ex gratia, si prima gratia caderet sub merito, primam gratiam precederet gratia. Et ideo deus sponte dat homini primam gratiam, homini, inquam, se ad gratiam disponenti dis-

That one cannot earn the first grace *de condigno* does not preclude earning an increase of grace *de condigno*. The reward of beatification even presupposes a proportional increase of grace — a thesis which shows again how much Biel is interested in finding an inner logic in the requirement of created grace. The negation of the possibility of earning the first infused grace with full condignity leaves room for the semi-merit with which one indeed can earn the infusion of grace.[80]

This contrast between a pact of justice and an act of generosity, however, is extremely misleading. The gift of the habit of grace is by no means an *ad hoc*, arbitrary, or contingent act which God in some cases may decide to do and in others not. If the infusion of grace in those who do their very best may not be called an eternal pact, as Biel insists, it definitely is an eternal commitment to which God is as irrevocably tied as to the acceptance of acts performed in a state of grace.[81]

4. The two stages of justification and the two eternal decrees

There is a striking similarity *and* disparity between God's granting of the acceptation and his granting of the infusion of grace. These two acts of God, corresponding to the *meritum de condigno* and *de congruo*, are similar in respect to the 'necessity' with which they take place and in the origin of this 'necessity.' They differ in respect to the conditions under which they are given.

After what has been said, there is no need for proof that in neither case can this be a *necessitas coactionis*: God's *opera ad extra* are contingent.[82] But just as God's acceptation occurs with necessity within the

---

positione naturali et non prebenti obicem gratie per malum usum liberi arbitrii. Licet autem ante primam gratiam requiratur dispositio conveniens. Illa tamen non meretur gratiam merito condigni sed congrui tantum." *Sap.* Lect. 116 A/B. Cf. Holcot, I *Sent.* q 1 art. 3 F.

[80] "Anima obicis remotione ac bono motu in deum ex arbitrii libertate elicito primam gratiam mereri potest de congruo. Probatur quia actum facientis quod in se est deus acceptat ad tribuendum gratiam primam, non ex debito iusticie, sed ex sua liberalitate, sed anima removendo obicem, cessando ab actu et consensu peccati et eliciendo bonum motum in deum tanquam in suum principium et finem facit quod in se est. Ergo actum remotionis obicis et bonum motum in deum acceptat deus de sua liberalitate ad infundendum gratiam." II *Sent.* d 27 q 1 art. 2 concl. 4 K.

[81] "Hec facienti deus gratiam suam tribuit necessario . . . ," *Lect.* 59 P.

[82] I *Sent.* d 41 q 1 art. 3 dub. 3 G.

context of his eternal decree, so of necessity God rewards with the robe of infused grace those who do their very best.[83]

This second commitment is formulated in a "second eternal decree" and is anchored in the necessity of his own being, the only kind of necessity in God acknowledged by Biel.[84] But in this latter case there is no strict justice. It seems that in his second eternal decree God has decided to bridge a wider cleavage. His is not a disproportionate love for a *friend*, but, still more disproportionate, love for one who only *tries hard* to be a friend. Still Biel stresses the reliability of this second decree in very strong words, and biblical evidence is brought to bear on this question: Zach. 1:3: "Return to me, says the Lord of hosts, and I will return to you"; James 4:8: "Draw near to God and He will draw near to you"; Rev. 3:20: "Behold, I stand at the door and knock; if anyone hears my voice and opens the door, I will come in to him and eat with him and he with me." [85]

Here we may well be touching on what is for Biel the heart of the Christian religion, the essence of the biblical message: this reward *de congruo* is unwarranted and rests solely on God's goodness and mercy. But because of his immutability we can take this unmerited benevolence for a rule, an eternal decree, a law of grace, in an exact parallel to God's free decision to reward those who possess the habit of grace with eternal bliss.

Indeed Biel tries hard to contrast God's rewards *de condigno* and *de congruo* as one of legal commitment and one of free initiative: *non ex debito iusticie sed ex sua libertate.*[86] God's freedom, *libertas*, allows him to express his generosity, *liberalitas*, in ignoring the lack of proportion between deed and reward, so that his mercy, *misericordia*, is revealed.

---

[83] ". . . deus dat gratiam facienti quod in se est necessitate immutabilitatis et ex suppositione quia disposuit dare immutabiliter gratiam facienti quod in se est. . . Illa ergo ordinatione stante et suppositione, non potest non dare gratiam facienti quod in se est, quia tunc esset mutabilis." II *Sent.* d 27 q 1 art. 3 dub. 4 O.

[84] "Deus est immutabilis . . . probatur quia est necesse esse." I *Sent.* d 8 q 7 art. 2 concl. 1 B. The simplicity of God does not of course permit a real succession of first and second decrees.

[85] "Converti ad deum — Appropinquare deo — Aperiri illi est facere quod in se est. Convertitur autem deus ad hominem. Appropinquat ei et intrat habitando in eo et cenando cum illo, per gratiam quam infundit." II *Sent.* d 27 q 1 art. 2 concl. 4 K.

[86] II *Sent.* d 27 q 1 art. 2 concl. 4 K.

Nevertheless, it should be noted that this distinction, which really functions in the theology of the old Franciscan school,[87] loses its edge with the nominalist Biel because he emphasizes again and again that the reward *de condigno* shows up a disproportion similar to that illustrated by the reward *de congruo*: the soul, albeit dressed up in the robe of grace, is created and remains created and as such can never claim the uncreated reward of beatification and vision of the Holy Trinity.

If one wants to argue that this lack of proportion is abolished by eternal decree and that thus a relation of justice is established, this point should be granted. But God is as much committed to his second decree of generosity as to his first immutable decree of justice. To show that this interpretation is justified it is worthwhile to give a full-length quotation: "Thus Augustine comments on 2 Tim. 2, 'God cannot deny himself.' Because he is just, he cannot deny his justice. Therefore, because he is compassionate, he cannot negate his own goodness and mercy, since he is more prone to give out of mercy and goodness than to punish out of justice. Now, if he is not able to deny his justice to malefactors, much less is he able to deny his goodness and compassion to those who beg for it. But he who does his very best begs for goodness and compassion. Therefore, God grants this to him. This gift is the infusion of grace. In this sense Augustine comments on Rom. 5: 1: 'Since we are justified by faith we have peace with God': God takes notice of those who seek their refuge with him. Otherwise there would be iniquity in him. But it is impossible that there be iniquity in him. Therefore, it is impossible that he would not receive those who take refuge with him. But if one does his very best, one does take refuge with him. Therefore, it is *necessary* that God receive him. This reception, now, is the infusion of grace."[88]

---

[87] See Alexander of Hales, *Quaestiones disputatae* q 33 d 4 m 1; pseudo-Alexander, *Summa* I.II q 91 m art. 1; Bonaventura, II *Sent.* d 28 art. 2 q 3 resp; rejected by Thomas, *ST* I.II q 109 art. 6; Cf. II *Sent.* d 28 art. 4; *Summa c. Gent.* III.C.149; *De verit.* q 24 art. 15; Duns Scotus, *Par.* II d 28 n 9.

[88] "Item Augustinus super illud 2 ad Thimo. 2: negare seipsum non potest. Cum sit iustus non potest negare suam iusticiam. Ergo cum sit misericors non potest negare suam bonitatem et misericordiam, quia pronior est ad largiendum de sua misericordia et bonitate quam ad puniendum de sua iusticia. Si ergo non potest suam iusticiam negare facientibus malum, multo magis non potest suam bonitatem et misericordiam negare illis qui requirunt eam. Sed qui facit quod in se est requirit bonitatem et misericordiam. Ergo dat ei. Hoc autem est infundere gratiam. Item Augustinus super illud Rom. 5 'Justificati ex fide, pacem habeamus ad deum'

5. The profile of Biel's doctrine of justification

After this detailed analysis several conclusions can be drawn:

(1) God owes it to his own immutable decision, based on his compassion, to reward those who do their very best: "qui faciunt quod in se est."

(2) This is an eternal law of mercy. It does not overthrow the structure of justice of the present order, but establishes it.

(3) The sinner cannot promote himself from a state of sin to a state of grace since the state of grace presupposes the infusion of grace; and this is a gift of God. But the sinner can reach the demarcation line where sin and grace meet because when he removes the lock on the closed door of his heart, that is, assent to sin, and loves God for his sake, he does what he is able to do. This demarcation line is the *status in puris naturalibus*.

(4) After the fall man is still able to detest sin and seek refuge with God with his own powers, without the help of any form of grace. This, of course, does not exclude God's general *concursus* in every deed, good, bad or indifferent, since without this 'natural' energy man would not be able to act at all.[89]

(5) Every man possesses a natural knowledge of God as his creator. He knows that all he possesses comes from him and that he should turn to God to supply what he lacks. This is what every *heathen* knows and therefore has to do. It includes to some degree the *fides acquisita* — a typical example of "turning towards God," — but it stops short of the *fides infusa*.[90]

(6) As his sermons show, Biel's real interest is in the problem of what a *Christian* in the stage equivalent to that of a heathen is able to do and

---

dicit: Deus respicit confugientes ad se. Aliter in eo esset iniquitas. Sed impossibile est quod in eo sit iniquitas. Ergo impossibile est quod non recipiat confugientes ad se. Sed faciens quod in se est confugit ad ipsum. Ergo necesse est quod ipsum recipiat. Recipit autem infundendo gratiam." II *Sent.* d 27 q 1 art. 2 concl. 4 K.

[89] ". . . quia removendo obicem qui est consensus in peccatum, et eliciendo per liberum arbitrium motum in deum bonum facit quod in se est. Ultra enim ex se non potest, supposita semper generali influentia dei, sine qua omnino nihil potest." *Ibid.*

[90] "Cum ergo . . . per liberum arbitrium operatur homo, recurrendo ad illum quem scit suum principium et petit ab eo lumen cognitionis fidei et boni facit quod in se est. Et hoc generaliter in quolibet homine." *Ibid.*

thus has to do. This equivalent stage in the life of a Christian exists when he has fallen into mortal sin and thus has lost the *fides infusa* (or *fides formata*), so that only the *fides acquisita* (or *fides informis*) remains. This is a somewhat sharper knowledge of God than the natural knowledge of the heathen: it knows God's righteousness and compassion. A Christian in this state does his best when he ceases to give in to sin by considering God's punishing righteousness and begins to love God by considering the compassion with which he saves the elect.[91]

(7) This "doing one's very best" is not limited to the first step toward faith operative in works. It marks the whole life of the *viator*. When natural man has reached a certain level of perfection, grace will be infused. Though this infusion may stabilize and perfect the will, it does not change anything in the requirement that man should do his very best. The human will continues to be responsible for the goodness of its acts; God's grace is responsible for the meritoriousness of its acts. Only in this sense can Biel take over Augustine's "driver and horse image" for the relation of grace and free will.[92]

(8) Finally, it is clear that Biel has a remarkable doctrine of justification: seen from different vantage points, justification is at once *sola gratia* and *solis operibus*!

By grace alone — because if God had not decided to adorn man's good works with created and uncreated grace, man would never be saved. *By works alone* — because not only does man have to produce the framework or substance for this adornment, but God by the two laws of grace is committed, even obliged to add to this framework infused grace and final acceptation. Once man has done his very best, the other two parts follow automatically.

[91] "Potest brevius dici quod . . . fidelis vero facit quod in se est si secundum regulam fidei detestatur peccatum, proponens in omnibus obedire deo et eius precepta servare. . ." *Ibid.*

[92] In this connection it is of interest to note one of the ways in which Weijenborg contrasts Luther and Biel: "Ici Luther nous paraît s'écarter considérablement des sentiers battus de l'ockhamisme. D'abord il sépare fortement le libre arbitre de la charité infuse. Pour Biel, la charité n'est qu'une qualité surnaturelle du libre arbitre procurant à celui-ci l'habitude et la facilité d'accomplir des actes meritoires; chez Luther, au contraire, elle est devenue une entité nouvelle, existant à côté du libre arbitre qu'elle n'influence plus que de l'extérieur. De cette manière Luther embrouille la structure bien calculée [!] de l'anthropologie gabriéliste." Weijenborg, p. 636. Since according to Luther grace transforms the human will while for Biel grace exists alongside the free will, merely assisting it, Weijenborg has misunderstood both to such an extent that he has had them reverse positions.

It is clear that the emphasis falls on "justification by works alone"; the concept of "justification by grace alone" is a rational outer structure dependent on the distinction between *potentia absoluta* and *potentia ordinata*. The outer structure is, of course, discernible by one who in pious meditation retraces God's revelation to its very sources, to that point where God could *de potentia absoluta* have decided otherwise. But the message preached and taught by the Church is the inner structure itself. An analysis of Biel's sermons proves that this is indeed the case. *It is therefore evident that Biel's doctrine of justification is essentially Pelagian.* This conclusion runs counter to the suggestions of Vignaux [93] and Weijenborg,[94] who limited their discussion to the outer structure of Biel's doctrine of justification.

Previously we had occasion to agree with Vignaux as concerns the necessity of the habit of grace. However, he goes too far, when he concludes from Occam's dialectical use of the *potentia absoluta* that this is how Occam warded off the danger of Pelagianism. Since Biel's presentation of the doctrine of justification is structurally identical with that of Occam, we are able to indicate at what point Vignaux failed to draw the right conclusion.[95]

The *potentia absoluta* indeed represents the order of God's mercy, but this mercy functions in a radically restricted way within the *potentia ordinata*. Vignaux does not distinguish between the *fact* of the *proclamation* of the eternal decrees and the *content* of these decrees. At the same time it should be noted that Lortz's general observation that the Occamistic system "as a matter of fact makes of grace a superfluous appendix" [96] does reflect the inner structure but takes it out of its systematic context.

However, in one respect the *sola gratia* message does enter the inner religious content itself. That is, it enters at that point where parallel to the act of fear of the day of judgment — the second advent — the act of love for God's goodness and loving-kindness is evoked by the consideration of the incarnation — the first advent — but even so, it appears as

[93] Vignaux, *Luther Commentateur des Sentences*, p. 89 ff. As regards Occam, see Vignaux, *Justification et Prédestination*, pp. 137, n. 2, 185 ff.

[94] Weijenborg, p. 629 f.

[95] "Contre Pierre d'Auriole, pour Duns Scot, la dialectique d'Occam semble aller à l'essentiel: l'âme justifiée se tient à l'ombre de l'amour divin, sans un acte gratuit, et non pas un acte juste; *ipse nullius debitor est* en donnant la charité, Dieu ne contracte aucune dette." Vignaux, *Justification et prédestination*, p. 127. Cf. p. 139 f. and "Nominalisme" in *DThC*, vol. XI, col. 774 f.

[96] Lortz, *Die Reformation in Deutschland*, I, 173.

only one of the two psychological stimulants to evoke the "facere quod in se est." In this limited way the *sola gratia* message not only functions as the outer structure, but also finds itself a place within the message of justification by works alone. Even so, this token of God's mercy places the *viator* under an extra obligation.[97]

Not only the Christian layman in Biel's audience, but also the professional theologian would have found here an extraordinary emphasis on man's contribution to his salvation. Although the theologian would be able to follow Biel's analysis of God's revelation to its foundation, to that point in eternity where God's liberty, generosity, and compassion meet, he would be able to see as clearly as the modern investigator that this understanding of God's self-giving love actually merely accentuates the character of the *iustitia dei* as the punishing righteousness of God.

6. Bartholomaeus Arnoldi von Usingen on justification

At this point we shall turn to one of Biel's disciples and one of Luther's teachers, Bartholomaeus Arnoldi von Usingen, to see where this Augustinian friar stands with respect to justification. According to the present state of scholarship, we ought to expect Usingen to be implicitly or explicitly a critic of Biel. Heinrich Denifle, who terms Biel an "ungesunde" theologian, a "Halbwisser," and the source of Luther's "ignorance," refers repeatedly to Usingen as a fine representative of medieval piety and as Luther's "ernsten Lehrer." [98] Nicolaus Paulus comes to the conclusion that this Erfurt professor should be viewed as a protagonist of justification by grace alone.[99] If this is true, either Biel's influence was

[97] "Infinita est misericordia que expectat, sed nec minor iusticia si misericordiam negligentes contemnamus; *neque solum pro peccatis nostris sed pro neglecta misericordia sumus rationem reddituri*," S IV 24 G. Cf. II *Sent.* d 27 q 1 art. 2 concl. 4 K.

[98] Usingen took his M.A. at Erfurt in 1491 and died in 1532. See Denifle on Usingen, *Luther und Luthertum*, I, abt. 1 (Mainz 1904), 5, 129. On Biel, I, abt. 2 (Mainz 1906), 574, 587, 870 ff.

[99] Nicolaus Paulus, *Der Augustiner Bartholomäus Arnoldi von Usingen: Luthers Lehrer und Gegner* (Strasbourg, 1893), p. 63 f. According to Otfried Müller, Usingen posits the necessity of the special aid of God: "Um zu dem heilsnotwendigen Glauben zu gelangen, ist eine besondere übernatürliche Hilfe Gottes notwendig, die am Anfang jedes Heilswerkes steht. . ." *Die Rechtfertigungslehre nominalistischer Reformationsgegner, Bartholomäus Arnoldi von Usingen O.E.S.A. und Kaspar Schatzgeyer O.F.M., über Erbsünde, erste Rechtfertigung und Taufe*, Breslauer Studien, VIII (Breslau, 1940), 72 ff. Nikolaus Häring is more precise in noting the

extremely limited, even on a theologian who is obviously proud of belonging to the nominalistic school of thought,[100] or we may have to reconsider our conclusion about the Pelagian quality of Biel's doctrine of
justification.[101] For Usingen presents an interpretation of someone standing close to Biel in time and thought.

Indeed, there is a series of passages which clearly supports a non- or
even anti-Pelagian interpretation. Thus, Usingen can say: "righteousness
and salvation are from God alone and are due to his grace alone and
not to merit. Otherwise as St. Paul says, grace would not be grace. Salvation which is the attainment of glory in the heavenly Fatherland is
equally solely a gift of God." [102]

On closer consideration it becomes clear, however, that such passages
refer only to what we have called the outer structure. Usingen distinguishes, as does Biel, between *bonitas* and *dignitas*. As far as the *dignitas*
is concerned, salvation is unmerited; but God has obliged himself to
accept man's virtuous acts.[103] Man provides the substructure, the substance of the act; its meritoriousness is a gift of God.[104]

At one place Usingen also uses the Augustinian driver-horse image,
this time not to indicate the relation of grace and free will, but interest-

---

distinction between an indirect preparation for justification through *bona opera
in genere* and a direct preparation through living faith. Häring concludes that
Usingen "die Notwendigkeit des göttlichen Beistandes wenigstens für irgend ein
Stadium ausspricht, nämlich für die Vorbereitung durch den lebendigen Glauben,"
*Die Theologie des Erfurter Augustiner-Eremiten Bartholomäus Arnoldi von Usin-
gen* (Limburg an der Lahn, 1939), p. 140. For a discussion of Kaspar Schatzgeyer, see Valens Heynck, O.F.M., "Zur Rechtfertigungslehre des Kontroverstheolo-
gen Kaspar Schatzgeyer, O.F.M.," *FS* 28 (1941), 129 ff.

[100] Paulus, *Der Augustiner Bartholomäus Arnoldi von Usingen*, p. 13.

[101] Paulus suggests the latter; *Der Augustiner Bartholomäus Arnoldi von Usingen*, p. 67.

[102] "Concedo iusticiam et salutem a solo deo provenire et ex sola gratia eius.
Quia gratia qua iustificamur est a solo deo et non ex merito; alias, ut Apostolus
habet, gratia non esset gratia. Salus autem que est gloria celestis patrie pariter a
solo deo est. . ." *Libellus . . . contra Lutheranos* (Erphurdie, 1524), fol. D. 1ᵛ.

[103] "Respondeo hec procedere de nostris operibus secundum se consideratis ac
naturalem bonitatem eorum et quam habent a voluntate eliciente conformiter recte
rationi, sed non secundum dignitatem quam habent a gratia cooperante et divina
acceptatione qua ordinantur ad meritum vite eterne . . . ; quamvis ex natura rei
neminis sit debitor deus potest tamen ex sua liberalitate se debitorem constituere
promittendo premium pro opere." *Ibid.*, D 4ʳ. Cf. H 2ʳ.

[104] "Quamvis enim nos opus faciamus quoad substantiam actus tamen illud
facere meritorium glorie solius dei est et non nostrum . . . ," *ibid.*, fol. D 1ᵛ.

ingly enough to defend his use of Aristotelian philosophy. The light of grace uses the light of nature — in this case the fruits of Usingen's earlier intensive study of Aristotle — as the driver uses the horse.[105] At another place Usingen seems to stress more than Biel does the necessity of prevenient grace. But the way the relation between this initial help of God is related to man's free will makes clear that the sinner first has to take the initiative to open the door of his heart for God's gracious assistance by an act of penitence.[106]

It is exactly because of this emphasis on man's natural capacities to act virtuously without the aid of grace that Usingen's Lutheran opponent confronts him with the words of confession: "I know that there is no good in me." Usingen answers that this statement does not refer to the basic goodness of acts but to the meritoriousness of acts, which is indeed not in our power.[107] If grace were absolutely necessary, how then would the Gentiles who have not the assistance of grace but only of the law be able to act virtuously? While there is indeed concupiscence which arouses the flesh against the spirit of man, this spirit in turn rebels against the flesh since it is allied with the law of Christ through the dictate of natural reason.[108] This passage makes it clear that Usingen is a true disciple of Biel with respect to the doctrine of justification: seen from different van-

[105] "Nondum obschurati sunt seni usingo oculi fidei qui hisce videt limpide te in fide hallucinari. Nec obest illi lumen nature in quo olim ex aristotele profecit, quod nunc habet in rudimentum gratie que lumen nature non extinguit sed eo utitur ut sessor equo. . ." *Ibid.*, fol. H 3ᵛ.

[106] "Deus hec omnia facit per spirituale adjutorium quo prevenit hominem et juvat eum se disponere ad suam gratiam. Dominus stat ad ostium et pulsat, scil. per spirituale adjutorium et monitorium cui si quis aperuerit per poenitentiam intrat per gratiam; quoniam liber est homo an pulsanti aperire velit necne. . ." *Libellus . . . Contra Lutheranos*, fol. C 4ᵛ, quoted by Paulus, p. 66. "Non ergo sinet nos perire christus si penitentiam egerimus quoniam sic retribuet nobis gratiam quam peccando amisimus. . ." *Libellus . . . Contra Lutheranos*, fol. F. 4ʳ.

[107] "Postremo subdis sicut sonant sequentia verba: 'scio quod in me non habitat bonum; hoc est in carne mea ex quo defectu necessario sequi oportet etc.' Respondeo: Non necessario sequi nisi intellexeris quoad intentionem precipientis quod est meritorie qualiter implemus ea ex gratia dei." *Ibid.*, fol. J 2ʳ.

[108] "Si ergo gentes ex natura que legis sunt faciunt quomodo vos dicitis illa impossibilia his qui auxilium legis habent . . . ," *Ibid.*, J 2ᵛ; cf. K 1ʳ. 'Spiritui autem hominis lex christi semper amicabilis est quia consona rationi naturali eo quod sicut caro semper concupiscit adversus spiritum, idinverso spiritus concupiscit adversus carnem. Hec etenim sibi adinvicem adversantur ad Gal. 5. . ." *Ibid.*, J 3ʳ.

tage points, his doctrine is at once *sola gratia* and *solis operibus*. Its core and inner structure, however, is clearly Pelagian.

7. Oscillation between "mercy" and "justice"

Now when we survey Biel's doctrine of justification, we see that the eternal decrees arise out of God's freedom, generosity, and mercy. *De potentia absoluta* he could very well have established requirements which no creature would ever be able to meet. In his great *mercy*, however, God established an order of *justice* to which he and his creatures are subject until judgment day. To this eternal procession from mercy to justice corresponds the temporal procession from the incarnation and the passion to the day of judgment.

This understanding of the justification of the sinner explains not only why the relation of *misericordia* and *iusticia* is the main theme of Biel's sermons, but also the remarkable oscillation[109] in Biel's thought between these two attributes of God. While the academic works stress relatively more God's eternal mercy, which resulted in the establishment of eternal decrees, the sermons emphasize God's mercy in the historical past: without any merits at our part, solely through the mercy of God, have the incarnation and the redemption by Jesus Christ taken place.[110]

When Biel speaks on this theme he calls human righteousness *quasi pannus menstruate*[111] and preaches on the Gospel for the Eleventh Sunday after Pentecost — Luke 18:10 ff, the Pharisee and the Tax Collector — as if his doctrine of justification were clearly *sola gratia*.[112]

---

[109] For the meaning of this for the spiritual life of the individual Christian see the discussion in Chapter Ten, section III.

[110] "Neque hoc opus nostre redemptionis (cuius initium fuit missio precursoris) ascribi poterat veritati et iusticie sicut bonitati et misericordie, quia, nullis nostris meritis sed sola sua bonitate et misericordia actum est . . . ," *S* II 20 C. "Sed quid mereri potuimus deum creati rebellantes inimici et totius misericordie et bonitatis indigni penas solvere debuimus. Sola ergo causa tantorum beneficiorum intrinseca et essentialis bonitas est dei qui nullis nostris meritis prior dilexit nos," *S* II 36 G.

[111] II *Sent.* d 27 q 1 art. 2 concl. 1 F.

[112] ". . . humilitatem publicani imitantes, nihil de nobis sed solum in divino adiutorio presumentes, dicentes humiliato corde: 'Deus propitius esto mihi peccatori. . ." *S* I 70 F. Cf. *S* I 89 K. We must be extremely cautious with the conclusions to which Adolar Zumkeller comes in his article "Das Ungenügen der

181

But hand in hand with God's mercy goes God's righteousness, which is clearly understood as punishing righteousness.[113] Thus, while his mercy appears in the invitation extended to all to attend the messianic banquet, his justice brings judgment on all who are unwilling to come.[114] The

menschlichen Werke bei den deutschen Predigern des Spätmittelalters," *ZKT* 81 (1959), 265–305. He wants to prove that the insufficiency of human works is clearly held by many late medieval preachers, especially those of the Augustinian Order, and that therefore Luther's similar emphasis is not an unexpected phenomenon: ". . . als wichtiges Ergebnis unserer Untersuchung [bleibt] die Feststellung, dass der junge Augustiner seine religiös-monastische Bildung in einem Milieu empfing, dem der Gedanke an die Mängel der guten Werke und aller menschlichen Gerechtigkeit offensichtlich nicht so fern lag, als man bis jetzt anzunehmen geneigt war" (p. 305). His sources, however, are mostly sermons that were preached on the Eleventh Sunday after Pentecost. The Gospel for that day is Luke 18:10 ff. — the Pharisee and the Publican — which is the traditional place to stress the importance of humility and God's grace. Even Biel can appear "Lutheran" or proto-Lutheran if one isolates this particular sermon. Several arguments of Thomas Ebendorfer for the insufficiency of human works — Ebendorfer, *Sermo* 36 T, cited in Zumkeller, "Das Ungenügen," p. 291 — appear with Biel *S* I 70 D. Cf. ". . . omnis nostra sufficientia a deo est[!!]" *S* I 1 F; *Lect.* 8 D.

[113] "Patet ergo misericordie et iusticie concordia ex scriptura canonica que misericordiam extollit et iusticiam commendat. Misericordiam in eos qui a peccato cessante penitendo bene vivunt. Iusticiam in eos qui gratiam deserentes vitam peccando concludunt," *S* I 64 F. ". . . thesaurizas tibi iram in die ire et revelationis iusti iudicii dei qui reddit unicuique secundum opera eius," *S* I 20 G. Cf. *Lect.* 56 U. It is hard to understand how such a specialist as Heinrich Denifle could have held that *iustitia* in its main meaning was "Gottes unverdiente rechtfertigende Gnade, eine durch den Glauben zuteil werdende wahre und wirkliche Rechtfertigung des Menschen," and that none of the sixty leading medieval doctors nor any of Luther's medieval sources "unter Gerechtigkeit Gottes die strafende Gerechtigkeit, den Zorn Gottes verstanden hat." *Luther und Luthertum*, I, abt. 1 (Mainz, 1904), p. 395. For the Franciscan tradition see Bonaventura, II *Sent.* d 32. art. 3 q 2 resp. ad 3 and Duns Scotus, IV *Sent.* d 46 q 1 n 4, which show again that Biel is not an innovator. See also Altenstaig, sv. "Ira Dei," fol. 121ᵛ; sv. "Iusticia," fol. 127ᵛ. And for the definition of *justificatio* by an older contemporary of Biel see the Dominican Bishop Antoninus of Florence: "Nam *justificationes* de quibus sit mentio frequens in psalmis, possunt dici omnia praecepta legis, in quantum sunt quaedam executiones legalis justitiae. Vel etiam ipsae poenae vel praemiae . . . possunt dici justificationes secundum quod Deus aliquos juste punit vel praemiat . . . praeceptum est de his quae sunt de necessitate salutis servanda. . ." *Summa Theologica* (ed. Veronae 1740 ff.), I.xiv.2 [fol. 680 B/C]. On his life and works, see R. Morcay, *Saint Antonin: Fondateur du Convent de Saint Marc, Archevêque de Florence* (Tours, 1914). Since Biel quotes Antoninus of Florence in the first part of his *Expositio*, he must have started reading this protagonist of Aquinas remarkably soon after publication of his works.

[114] "Nec cessavit per se suosque vocare convivas. . . Prerogatam misericordiam secuta est non minor iusticia qua perdidit infideles venire nolentes." *S* I 90 B. Cf. "Horruimus iusticiam . . . ," *ibid.*, G. Cf. *S* I 96 A and B.

viator is driven simultaneously by hope and fear. The constant refrain is: *Nescit autem homo an odio vel amore dignus sit.*[115] The last judgment therefore is stressed as often as God's self-sacrificing love in Jesus Christ.[116]

Biel explicitly rejects the position which later was to be characterized as "Protestant": the *sola fide* understanding of justification is an error of carnal and idle men. They may quote the text: "He who believes and is baptized will be saved," but they overlook the teaching of Scripture that faith without works is dead.[117] As appears from a parallel passage where Biel obviously attacks the same error, for him justification *sola fide* and justification *sola gratia* are formulations of the same position: to believe that one can be saved *sola gratia* is to scorn God's justice.[118]

The modern interpreter must not confuse this justification by divine acceptation with justification by imputation of righteousness. The sinner is justified by meeting the requirements of God, a part of which is the habit of grace, another part his own righteousness, the legal righteousness of observing the commandments. When a distinction is made between *iusticia coram deo* and *iusticia coram mundo*, nothing more is intended than to emphasize that the world may be fooled by good appearances while God knows the sinner better than he knows himself.[119]

---

[115] E.g. *S* I 70 F.

[116] "Timeamus tandem, dilectissimi, iudicium finale certissime futurum, ubi secundum opera sua quilibet iudicabitur. Nullum ibi fuge presidium, nulla excusatio, nullum de alienis meritis auxilium, nulla omnino personarum acceptio." *S* I 5 F. "Unusquisque accipiet secundum opera sua retributionem. Ibi non suffragabuntur aliena merita. Ibi prudentes virgines oleum negabunt fatuis. Ibi vix iustus salvabitur et peccator ubi parebit . . . non ibi tempus merendi, sed mercedem precedentium meritorum recipiendi." *S* I 66 E. Cf. *S* I 55 H.

[117] "Non aliter nisi operando secundum fidem rectam, in vinea domini, id est unitate ecclesiastica, ad regni premia possumus pervenire. . . Per hanc doctrinam tollitur error et presumptio quorundam carnalium et ociosorum hominum qui in sola fide salvari se putantes; allegant pro se illud Matt. 40 [Mark 16:16] 'Qui crediderit et baptizatus fuerit salvus erit.' Non attendentes quod fides sine operibus mortua est. Hebr. 11 [6:1]." *S* I 19 C.

[118] "Includit autem presumptio deordinationem dupliciter vel ex parte hominis presumentis, ut quia presumens de suis meritis se sine gratia salvari putat. Aut quia totum attribuit misericordie dei, iusticiam dei parvipendit putans se sine meritis sola gratia salvari, utrumque malum est. Primum sapit errorem pelagianum, secundum est contra illud Rom. 2 [:4]: 'An divitias bonitatis eius et patientie contemnis' . . . Certissimum itaque est fidem informem non sufficere cum baptismo ad vitam sine mandatorum observantia." *S* I 64 D, E. Cf. *S* I 65 F.

[119] "Ad cenam magnam non nisi magni veniunt. Magni non mole corporis sed virtute. Regnum celorum vim patitur et violenti rapiunt illud. Matt. 11 [:12] et Luc. 16 [:16]. . . Et autem magnus coram deo qui vere magnus est; deus enim in

8. Conclusion

We are able to understand now that, for Biel, the primary task of preacher and teacher is to provide his readers and his congregation with the data of revelation and so with the *fides acquisita* which in turn stimulates the sinner to love God above everything else. In the first place the sinner is to be provided with the knowledge of the mercy of God in its eternal and temporal aspects, displayed in the incarnation and passion of Jesus Christ. In the second place the sinner is to be provided with the knowledge of the justice of God, established by the eternal decrees, conclusively promulgated by Christ as the legislator, to be feared as the coming test for acceptation to eternal life.

A genuine love for God, above everything else, is within the reach of man, not only in paradise, but also after the fall. Indeed, the material aftermath of original sin, concupiscence, has made for serious difficulties, but the psychological counterforces of the past mercy and future justice of God are extremely powerful. Under these circumstances, it is doubtless possible for the sinner to come to a genuine act of contrition.[120] Once this genuine love for God's sake is reached, the last obstacle is removed and the road to acceptation is paved by the eternal decrees of God according to which this *facere quod in se est* is first *de congruo* rewarded with the infusion of grace, while then, secondly, acts performed in state of grace are rewarded *de condigno* with acceptation by God.

This makes it clear that the task of the preacher is to concentrate on the removal of the first obstacle by evoking pure love for God: from that point onward man is in the hands of God, who, after his requirements have been met, shows himself again as the God of mercy. The requirement to do one's very best applies to the *viator* until the end of his life, but the infused habit of grace will facilitate and perfect his love for God, from now onward assisted by the sacraments. Yet since the *viator* never knows whether he is actually in a state of grace, or perhaps has unconsciously committed a mortal sin, the preacher must address himself to the total congregation in his call for conversion and contrition.

iudicio non fallitur." *S* I 52 C. ". . . vocati sunt et venerunt ceci terrena, nescientes contra deum: hi sunt iusti, iusticia legali," *S* I 52 G.

[120] ". . . contritio secundum totum illud quod ex parte nostra requiritur ad peccati remissionem est in facultate voluntatis," *S* IV 24 E. ". . . patet quod nullus potest pretendere excusationem de non posse sequi penitentem mariam, aut non conteri pro peccatis: illa enim sunt in potestate nostra . . . ," *S* IV 24 F.

Chapter Seven

BETWEEN FEAR AND HOPE:
THE RIDDLE OF PREDESTINATION

ᘑᘏ

I. Election and Reprobation

1. The systematic interrelation of predestination and justification

It is a reliable rule of interpretation for the historian of Christian thought that the position taken with respect to the doctrine of predestination is a most revealing indicator of the understanding of the doctrine of justification. It is not surprising therefore to discover in the theology of Gabriel Biel how closely his treatments of these two major doctrines correspond.

In the medieval tradition of the commentaries on Lombard's *Sentences*, the relation of created and uncreated grace is analyzed in I *Sent.* d 17 and II *Sent.* d 26–27. In the context of the sacraments of baptism and penance, the actual *process* of justification is discussed in Book III. It is I *Sent.* d 40 and d 41 which provide the opportunity, however, to discuss God's plan for justification under the aspect of the election of the saints and the rejection of the reprobate. The fact that Biel follows Magister Lombard in locating his discussion at this traditional place between the treatment of God's omniscience and God's omnipotence is, of course, no indication whatsoever whether he will stress relatively more a predestination *ante* or *post praevisa merita*, God's free will or God's foreknowledge.[1]

---

[1] However, Erich Seeberg states: "Auch hier erlebt man den Intellektualismus als Überraschung; schon die Stelle, an der die Prädestination behandelt wird, gibt einen Fingerzeig in dieser Richtung; sie steht nämlich zwischen den von der Allwissenheit und von der Allmacht handelnden Distinktionen; aber die Beziehungen

The analysis of Biel's doctrine of justification has shown that it would not be appropriate to distinguish his discussion of the doctrine of predestination as God's *plan* too sharply from that of the doctrine of justification as the historical *execution* of this plan for salvation. We have seen that Biel could teach simultaneously a justification by grace alone and a justification by works alone due to the eternal procession from compassion and mercy to justice, temporally reflected in the procession from Incarnation to judgment. God's compassion finds its eternal expression in the proclamation of two eternal decrees by which an order of justice was established.

The order *de potentia absoluta* signifies, as we have seen, God's mercy according to which He chose, absolutely free from exterior interference, undetermined by any cause whatever apart from Himself, to accept man's moral virtue as meritorious for his salvation. The order *de potentia ordinata*, on the other hand, proves to be the "dome" within which the actual life of the *viator* unfolds, where justice reigns and judgment day looms large as the day on which it will be disclosed whether the *viator* has indeed done his very best.

One cannot but admire the unity and consistency of this structure of thought.[2] As the history of theology can well be written in terms of a constant effort to reconcile or relate God's love and God's wrath, it is impressive to see how Biel tries to give both their due by joining them organically. Nevertheless, God's gratuitous self-giving love, expressed in his willingness to commit Himself, the uncreated, to deficient creatures is not operative existentially *within* the order chosen, but *in the fact that* He chose this particular order in eternity.

---

zur Allwissenheit dürften die engeren sein. So wird denn auch die Prädestination als eine *species providentiae* gefasst. . ." *Luthers Theologie: Motive und Ideen,* vol. I: *Die Gottesanschauung* (Göttingen, 1929), p. 26. Note that Gregory of Rimini has a doctrine of predestination which, similarly seen as *species providentiae,* is anything but intellectualistic, since even for the reprobate foreknowledge is eliminated: ". . . nullus est eternaliter reprobatus quia previsus finaliter fore cum obice gratie sive originali sive actuali." I *Sent.* d 40, 41 q 1 art. 2 [fol. 159 Q]. Cf. his definition of election as *preacceptatio* [fol. 160 E] on reprobation: ". . . deus proposuit se aliquorum non misereri . . . non est dare causam preter sui beneplacitum" [fol. 161F].

[2] We are unable to discover any evidence which would support Joseph Lortz's judgment that late medieval theology in general, and Occamism, in particular, are marred with "Unklarheit." Cf. Lortz, I, 139 f, 205 ff.

Now we must investigate how God's plan of predestination is related to the described plan of salvation formulated in the two eternal decrees, and to the order of justice thereby established. An understanding of the organically joined but dual form of justification — at once by grace alone and by works alone — paves the way for a proper evaluation of Biel's doctrine of predestination.

2. Two doctrines of predestination in Biel?

Viewed in isolation there *seem to be* two mutually exclusive doctrines of predestination in Biel's theology. On the one hand there is what appears to be a doctrine of absolute predestination *ante praevisa merita*, in the form thus in which Augustine, Thomas Bradwardine, and Gregory of Rimini understood predestination — God's unprecedented and uncaused eternal decision with respect to the salvation of his creation. On the other hand predestination seems oftentimes to be understood as foreknowledge.

We must note immediately that the problem of reprobation does not trouble Biel. The solution is so clear for him that he usually calls the reprobate the foreknown, *presciti*, according to the maxim *deus non prius sit ultor quam aliquis sit peccator* which constituted for Scotus and Occam sufficient grounds to reject a doctrine of double predestination.[3] Biel does not labor the point that the foreordination of the reprobate cannot be admitted without making God a tyrant. Reprobation is foreknowledge of guilt and preparation of the corresponding punishment.[4]

Apart from the issue of reprobation, therefore, Biel can speak in terms of an absolute predestination: all the elect are predestined from eternity and entered in the books of life and death from which they cannot, once entered, be stricken. No change in the elect or reprobate could ever affect

[3] *Ox.* I *Sent.* d 41 q 1 n 11; I *Sent.* d 41 q 1 D. For Scotus's position see the excellent study of Wolfhart Pannenberg, *Die Prädestinationslehre des Duns Skotus* (Göttingen, 1954); for Occam, Paul Vignaux, *Justification et prédestination*, pp. 127–140; for Bradwardine and Gregory of Rimini, Oberman, *Bradwardine*, pp. 95–122, 211–223.

[4] ". . . capitur magis stricte [presciencia dei] pro precognitione sola quam habet deus de damnatione reproborum. Et hoc modo respectu eiusdem est presciencia et reprobatio, licet reprobatio aliquid addit scil. preparationem pene eterne. . . Eo quod culpe (deus reprobans) non est actor sed solum precognitor." I *Sent.* d 40 q 1 art. 1 nota 2 B.

187

or influence God since there is no cause for predestination outside God.[5] God's eternal decision to predestine a man is due to the contingent will of God who has the power to accept and to reject.[6]

The immutability of God guarantees the set number of the elect which is liturgically expressed by the priest when he prays, not that we be added to the elect, but that we may be counted with the number of the elect.[7] At the end of the presentation of his own theses, Biel warns that they should be understood as stressing the independence of God's will since the eternal will of God is unmotivated.[8]

When one ponders whether there is any cause for predestination, he should realize that two kinds of causes can be distinguished. A cause in the strict sense of the word implies that when it exists, something else follows as its effect. In the larger sense of the word one can say that "cause" refers to an order of priority between two situations which are nevertheless not related by an efficient, material, formal or final cause. This is, for instance, the case where the fact that a fire does not warm is said to be "caused" by the fact that one does not stand close enough to it.[9]

---

[5] "Omnes electi ab eterno sunt predestinati sicut et reprobi ab eterno presciti. Neque ascriptus deletur propter dei immutabilitatem que salvari non posset ponendo novitatem in predestinatione et reprobatione finali. Requirit enim successiva contradictoriorum verificatio de eodem mutationem aut in altero extremo aut motu vel temporis lapsu. Sed ad eternitatem nihil facit tempus vel motus nec sufficit mutatio in predestinato vel prescito, quia nihil in re extra deum ponitur causa predestinationis. . ." Lect. 33 F.

[6] ". . . quicumque est predestinatus contingenter est predestinatus et ita potuit non predestinari et per consequens potest damnari et potest non salvari. Tum quia salvatio eius dependet a voluntate divina contingenter causante in cuius potestate est cuicumque vitam eternam conferre vel non conferre. Tum quia nulli adulto confertur vita eterna nisi propter aliquid eius meritum. Omne autem meritum est in potestate merentis. . ." I Sent. d 40 q 1 art. 2 concl. 2 C.

[7] "Deus tanquam universitatis creator et dominus de creatura potest facere quicquid vult sine iniuria creature; hinc potest salvare quem vult et damnare, sicut habens plenum dominium in re sua. . ." I Sent. d 41 q 1 art. 3 dub. 3. "Deus licet contingenter vult quicquid ad extra vult tamen immutabilis est volendo, nec succedit velle nolle vel econverso sed quod vult ab eterno vult. . ." I Sent. d 41 q 1 art. 3 dub. 3. Summa III; Lect. 33 F.

[8] "Et nota quod conclusiones non debent intelligi, quod aliquid sit ratio illius quod predestinatio importat ex parte dei, quia nihil esse potest ratio eterne et divine voluntatis. . ." I Sent. d 41 q 1 art. 2 concl. 3. Cf. Occam, I Sent. d 41 q 1 art. 2 H.

[9] ". . . per causam quandoque intelligitur res aliqua ad cuius esse sequitur aliud tanquam effectus. Illo modo manifestum est quod cum predestinatio et reprobatio

When "cause" is understood in the strict sense of the word, one has to say that a creature can never cause his own election or reprobation since this is a free decision of God which stands from eternity. Only in the second sense, when "cause" is understood to mean the order of priority, can one say that God's decisions are "caused" by merit or guilt. The distinction between the two kinds of causes not only functions within the context of the doctrine of justification but — as is to be expected — also underlies the doctrine of the sacraments, the natural setting of justification. The sacraments also are causes in the second sense of the word; they derive their effectiveness not "ex natura rei" but "ex voluntate dei." [10] Since this revealed will of God is to be understood *de potentia ordinata* and constitutes therefore a commitment on God's part, there is no reason to subscribe to the traditional verdict of occasionalism as applied to the nominalistic concept of causality.

3. Predestination and foreknowledge

The application of the distinction between the two kinds of causes takes us already into what seems to be a second doctrine of predestina-

---

sit divina voluntas qua illi vult dare vitam eternam, isti penam perpetuam que voluntas nihil aliud est quam deus ipse nulla est causa ex parte creature, ipsius predestinationis neque reprobationis cum ipsa sit eterna et incausata. Et hoc est quod alii dicunt quod predestinationis effective sive ut actus divinus nulla est causa. Alio modo capitur causa ut dicit quandam prioritatem unius propositionis ad aliam secundum consequentiam sicut si queritur causa quare ignis non calefacit quia non est approximatus passo et sic frequenter dicitur quod antecedens est causa consequentis et tamen non est proprie causa quia nec causa efficiens, materialis, formalis vel finalis. Quando enim ab una propositione ad aliam est consequentia naturalis et non econverso potest aliquo modo antecedens dici causa consequentis et non econverso." I *Sent.* d 41 q 1 art. 1 nota 2. Cf. I *Sent* d 40 q 1 art. 1 A: ". . . communiter dicitur quod [predestinatio] etiam connotat gratie collationem in presenti, licet forte hoc non sit de per se ratione predestinationis." Occam, I *Sent.* d 40 q 1 art. 1 G.

[10] IV *Sent.* d 1 q 1 art. 1 concl. 1; cf. d'Ailly, IV *Sent.* q 7 art 7. For a discussion of Occam's position, cf. Hochstetter, *Studien zur Metaphysik und Erkenntnislehre von Ockham*, p. 153.

Some of the parallel passages quoted from Occam led Pannenberg to conclude: "Occams Prädestinationslehre hat also nicht eigentlich semipelagianische Tendenz. Vielmehr ist ihr Leitmotiv Gottes absolut freie Willkür" (p. 143). This interpretation leads him then a step further to conclude that Gregory of Rimini has learned from Occam on this point: "Von diesem voluntaristischen Gottesgedanken aus hat Gregor von Rimini den Rückweg zu der deterministischen Prädestinationslehre Augustins und des Lombarden gefunden." See below note 17.

tion which stresses that predestination is really not more than God's foreknowledge of man's future behavior. The indicated maxim, *Deus non prius sit ultor quam aliquis sit peccator*, is not merely applied to reprobation but encompasses now also the predestination of the elect. Just as God foresees that the stubborn sinner will persevere in sin and will be, "therefore," condemned, thus God also foresees that the righteous man will persevere in love and "therefore" he predestines him.[11]

In some exceptional cases there is indeed no reason whatsoever — not even in the second sense of the word "cause" — for predestination: St. Paul and the Virgin Mary had no chance to do their very best and thus to earn *de congruo* the infusion of grace. In both cases special prevenient grace was given, to the Virgin at the time of the infusion of her soul into her body, to St. Paul even at the time that he was persecuting Christians.[12]

Usually — *regulariter!* — however, God does not grant salvation without merits. God created man with a free will which enables him to choose between good and evil. God, now, has decreed that no one will be damned unless for personal guilt, and that acceptation will require personal merits. To enable man to acquire merits, God has committed himself to assist all those who do their very best with the infusion of grace which is necessary for salvation.[13]

[11] "Dare est aliquam causam reprobationis accipiendo causam secundo modo quia sequitur iste peccabit finaliter ergo damnabitur. Non enim est deus prius ultor quam sit aliquis peccator . . . Alicuius predestinationis est aliqua causa vel ratio secundo modo capiendo causam. Patet quia aliqui propter meritum salvantur ita quod si non voluntarie mererentur non salvarentur; horum predestinationis est aliqua ratio sicut reprobationis. Nam sicut damnandi reprobantur quia previdentur finaliter peccaturi, ita tales predestinantur quia previdentur finaliter perseveraturi in charitate." I *Sent.* d 41 q 1 art. 2 concl. 1, 2.

[12] "Alicuius predestinationis nulla est causa vel ratio totalis. Patet quia aliqui ex gratia speciali ordinati sunt ad vitam, ita quod sibiipsis non sunt derelicti sed preventi ne ponere possent obicem et ne possent peccare vel in peccatis permanere: sicut beata virgo maria et paulus a domino percussus et illuminatus. In illis enim nulla videtur ratio quare deus illos predestinet sic gratia preveniendo, nisi sola dei voluntas. Non enim potest poni ratio bonus usus liberi arbitrii quoniam gratia prevenit. . ." I *Sent.* d 41 q 1 art. 2 concl. 3. Occam, I *Sent.* d 41 q 1 art. 2 G.

[13] "Deus contingenter operatur ad extra . . . Deus creavit hominem arbitrio liberum, ideo contingenter vult homo quecumque vult. . . In potestate hominis est bene vel male uti suo arbitrio . . . Statuit deus nullum damnare pena sensus nisi pro culpa personali. Nec adultum salvare regulariter [cf. BV Maria, S. Paulus] sine merito personali . . . Deus adest omnibus obicem non ponentibus offerens gratiam. Nec alicui adulto (rationis usum habenti et quod in se est facienti) subtrahit neces-

4. Occam and Biel

In the foregoing Biel has followed Occam. As usual he leaves out large parts of Occam's philosophical considerations. This is particularly obvious in I *Sent.* d 40 which he divides into two parts as Occam did. The first part serves to show that predestination is not an act separate from God but indistinguishable from his being. This lays the foundation for the important attack on Scotus' "three instances theory" which will be discussed below. It further shows that predestination is contingent insofar as God was free in all eternity not to commit himself to a plan of predestination. The second and more formal part, which in Occam's commentary makes up the main body of d 40, is reduced by Biel to a few lines in which the traditional distinction between the *sensus divisus* and the *sensus compositus* of a proposition is described.[14]

On one point only does Biel deviate in content from Occam's presentation. After the discussion of the two kinds of causes and the reference to St. Paul and the Virgin Mary, Occam concludes that God predestines some with and some without cause,[15] a conclusion which suggests two equally possible ways that God may choose to follow. In contrast, while Biel does not say that St. Paul and the Virgin Mary are the only exceptions,[16] he makes it clear, nevertheless, that *usually* God requires

---

saria ad salutem; vult enim omnes homines salvos fieri. . ." I *Sent.* d 41 q 1 art. 3 dub. 3. Occam, I *Sent.* d 41 q 1 art. 2 G. The identification of predestination and foreknowledge is most explicit in *Lect.* 31 C: ". . . ab eterno deus vidit petitionem hominis futuram . . . determinavit se ab eterno remissurum peccatum. . ." See also Erich Seeberg, *Luthers Theologie in ihren Grundzügen*, 2 ed. (Stuttgart, 1950), p. 37.

[14] We fail to see how one can justify Feckes' statement: "Das 'contingenter' Predestiniertsein Biels hat keine andere Bedeutung als die Kontingenz alles Geschaffen. Seine Erörterungen in der 40. Distinktion sind eben nichts als akademische Erörterungen und logische Spielereien." *Die Rechtfertigungslehre*, p. 88, n. 270. See also Hermelink, *Geschichte der theologischen Fakultät*, p. 110. Distinction 40 lays the foundation for the conclusions of d 41 and apart from a significant attack on Scotus' penetration into the divine psyche, it stresses the contingence of predestination; this is the parallel passage to II *Sent.* d 27 and *Lect.* 59 in which the contingence of the two eternal decrees for justification is discussed.

[15] ". . . alicuius predestinationis est aliqua causa et ratio et alicuius non est talis causa vel ratio"; in the same section reformulated as "aliqui . . . aliqui," I *Sent.* d 41 q 1 G.

[16] Biel undoubtedly has John the Baptist in mind (*S* III 15 E) as well as children dying after baptism.

that one must do his very best. This is certainly not a difference in principle: even if Occam would allow for relatively more cases in which God justifies without any preceding merits, it is merely a quantitative and not a qualitative difference.[17] In view of our experience in the constant comparison of Occam and Biel, we are inclined to explain this difference as due to Occam's relatively greater predilection for exceptions to the established rules *de potentia ordinata*.

5. Biel's single doctrine of predestination

When we now survey the two series of considerations which stressed respectively predestination *ante* and *post praevisa merita*, we can see that Biel, far from leaving us with two unrelated doctrines of predestination, presents us again with the same organic construction as we discovered in his doctrine of justification.

The first line of thought stresses again God's freedom to predestine or not to predestine: the omnipotent ruler is not committed to his subjects. The discussion of the tension between mercy and justice so prominent in the context of justification recedes. That means at this point that the concept of freedom is not linked with those of generosity and mercy. With this variation corresponds the fact that what God establishes in all freedom is not so much the justice of the eternal decrees as the freedom of the human free will, the condition for fulfilling the requirements of justice.[18]

The discussion of the two kinds of causes must be seen against the

---

[17] In this sense Pannenberg's conclusion should be qualified: "Im Ausgang des 15. Jahrhunderts hat Gabriel Biel die Lehre Occams synergistisch interpretiert" (p. 148). It is impossible not to interpret Occam's doctrine of predestination synergistically!

[18] "In his omnibus manet libertas arbitrii in homine qui se ad deum convertere poterit et donec in via constitutus fuerit gratia cooperante salvari. Unde patet quod non inanes sunt preces et merita nec frustra fiunt virtutum opera." I *Sent.* d 41 q 1 art. 3 concl. 6. Wilhelm Link has been stimulating but too speculative in his effort to subsume nominalistic theology under the general title of the "tension between theology and philosophy." The methodological weakness in his presentation of nominalism is his indiscriminate and simultaneous quoting of Biel and Luther. "Über Prädestination ist alles gesagt, wenn gesagt ist, dass Gottes Allmacht keine Grenzen hat." *Das Ringen Luthers um die Freiheit der Theologie von der Philosophie*, p. 273. See also pp. 257, 277. Accordingly Link finds a schism between the doctrines of predestination and justification (p. 283).

background of Biel's discussion of the *meritum de condigno*. Strictly speaking, even virtuous works performed in a state of grace do not cause acceptation; but God has graciously committed himself to accept good deeds that are only in order of priority related to acceptation as "causes" of his acceptation. All that has been said about the freedom of God's will as the only cause of predestination refers to this decision of God which he could equally well not have made.

We see, thus, that there is a direct parallel between "the two kinds" of justification and "the two kinds" of predestination. Justification by grace alone and its protective complement, predestination *ante previsa merita*, are stressed insofar as God in all eternity ruled as a full sovereign with unlimited power. He freely decided to delegate some of this power to his creatures: *de facto*, therefore, the *viatores* live an existence conditioned by justification by works and by predestination *post previsa merita*.

The organic unity of the doctrine of justification reappears in the doctrine of predestination: there is no trace of the often-claimed ambiguity and lack of clarity in this understanding of the movement from eternity to history as a movement from freedom to commitment.[19] This commitment implies that man on his part has to rely on his resources; he has to do his very best in order to acquire the habit of grace. St. Paul and the Virgin Mary are exceptions very clearly stated in Holy Scripture, and the privilege granted the Virgin becomes a vital point in the context of Mariology; in the case of *the normal viator, however, predestination is foreknowledge*.[20]

---

[19] In this sense Feckes' conclusion has to be revised: "Gottes Allwerksamkeit und menschliche Verdienste sind nicht miteinander in Einklang gebracht, so dass man nicht weiss, ob man Biel für die zweite Art [Biel's *regulariter*] der Prädestination zu den Vertretern einer Prädestinationslehre *ante* oder *post praevisa merita* rechnen soll." "Biel scheint sich in der Prädestinationslehre ebenso unwohl zu fühlen wie in der Erbsündenlehre. Darum wohl seine Kürze und Unklarheit." *Die Rechtfertigungslehre*, pp. 88, n. 268; 87, n. 259. Feckes could have referred for the same opinion to Ferdinand Kattenbusch, *Luthers Lehre vom unfreien Willen und von der Prädestination nach ihrem Entstehungsgründe untersucht* (Göttingen, 1875), p. 83, and to Albrecht Ritschl, "Geschichtliche Studien zur christlichen Lehre von Gott," *Jahrbücher für deutsche Theologie* 10 (1865), 317 f.

[20] Therefore even the careful conclusion of Ernst Wolf is not precise enough: "Der Widerstreit zwischen der Kontingenz göttlichen und menschlichen (natürlichen wie übernatürlich geförderten) Handelns wird deutlich: man könnte fast sagen, alles liege an Gottes Entscheid aber ebenso auch an dem des Menschen. Praktisch genommen kann bald der eine, bald der andere Gesichtspunkt jeweils für

Schema I.   A Chart of the Interrelation of Justification and Predestination

GOD'S TWO ETERNAL DECREES OF COMMITMENT [misericordia dei]	FALL	SACRAMENT OF BAPTISM	THE SINNER'S DISPOSITION	THE SACRAMENT OF PENANCE	ETERNAL REWARD
			He Does His Very Best	The Decisive Transition	Acceptation
THE ELECT [predestinati] Those foreknown to fulfill the requirements set in God's eternal decrees [iustitia dei]	Original Sin [spoliatus a gratuitis, vulneratus in naturalibus] State of mortal sin The Virgin Mary exempted	Habit of Grace Infused and substituted for original righteousness → Usually a relapse into state of mortal sin	[facit quod in se est] Not necessarily aided by prevenient grace [gratia gratis data] Ordinarily [regulariter] facere quod in se est is the basis [causa] for infusion The Virgin Mary, the Apostle Paul, and some others are exceptions to this rule God's general assistance [influentia generalis] is necessary for all acts, both good and evil	Confrontation with the preached Word [lex nova] Acquired faith [fides acquisita] → Supreme love for God [amor dei super omnia] → God has committed himself — first decree — to reward those who are doing their very best Semi-merit [meritum de congruo] → Restoration of the state of grace in anticipation of [in proposito] or at time of absolution [gratia gratum faciens] by infusion of faith, hope and love	Good works produced in state of grace are necessarily by God's commitment — second decree — accepted as full merits [merita de condigno] They determine man's status in purgatory or heaven [N.B. The status in purgatory can also be influenced by indulgences acquired from the treasure of the Church and applied to members of the Church Militant which encompasses not only the living but also the dead who are not beati.] Immediately or eventually → gloria

	Original Sin [spoliatus a gratuitis, vulneratus in naturalibus]	Habit of Grace	He Does Not Do His Very Best [non facit quod in se est]	Persisting in Sin	Rejection
THE REPROBATE [presciti] Those foreknown not to fulfill the requirements set in God's eternal decrees [iustitia dei]	State of mortal sin	Infused and substituted for original righteousness → Usually a relapse into state of mortal sin	Remains in a state of mortal sin; or if temporarily in a state of grace, he is in a state of sin at the time of his death Guilt [culpa] God's general assistance [influentia generalis] is necessary for all acts, both good and evil	demerita	Guilt is punished by eternal damnation. [culpa → pena damnationis]

As we can gather from the absence of any discussion of predestination in his sermons, this doctrine does not really function in Biel's theology. This should not surprise us. It is the traditional task of the doctrine of predestination proper to form a protective wall around the doctrine of justification by grace alone — a doctrine which does not necessarily imply justification by faith alone. Since we have found that Biel teaches an essentially Pelagian doctrine of justification, absolute predestination is not only superfluous but would even be obstructive. And seen against the background of his doctrine of justification, we can well understand that foreordination would in Biel's hands have to be transformed into foreknowledge.[21] For a graphic presentation, we refer to Schema I.

6. Nominalistic diversity: the position of Gregory of Rimini

The fourteenth- and fifteenth-century nominalists were by no means of one mind as regards justification and predestination. It is clear that at least Gregory of Rimini and Marsilius of Inghen defended the authority of Augustine just as passionately as Thomas Bradwardine had done half a century before, albeit with different weapons. The impact of the English left-wing nominalists on both the philosophical and theological faculties of the University of Paris[22] can be documented from a large

---

den einzelnen massgebend werden. . ." *Staupitz und Luther: Ein Beitrag zur Theologie des Johannes von Staupitz und deren Bedeutung für Luthers theologischen Werdegang* (Leipzig, 1927), p. 175.

[21] Though Erich Seeberg did not see the forceful unity of Biel's thought and therefore his argumentation is not flawless, we have to agree with his main conclusion: "Das Gesagte wird es deutlich gemacht haben, dass die Prädestination letzten Endes auf die Präszienz reduziert und damit aufgehoben wird. . ." *Luthers Theologie*, I, 28. Cf. p. 30 f. See also Otto Scheel whose section on the theology of Biel is the most reliable interpretation to date: "Auch die Vorherbestimmung der Seligen wurde darum nicht nur tatsächlich, sondern auch in der theologischen Theorie zu einem Vorherwissen ihrer Verdienste . . . mit der paulinischen Erwählungslehre hatte dies nichts mehr zu tun." *Martin Luther: Vom Katholizismus zur Reformation*, II: *Im Kloster* 3rd and 4th printing (Tübingen, 1930), p. 181. The same reference, 1st and 2nd printing (Tübingen, 1917), p. 103.

[22] Gerhard Ritter, *Studien zur Spätscholastik*, I, 84 ff. Herman Schwamm, *Magistri Ioannis de Ripa O.F.M.: Doctrina de praescientia divina, Inquisitio historica* (Rome 1930), p. 204 ff; *Das göttliche Vorherwissen bei Duns Scotus und seinen ersten Anhängern* (Innsbruck, 1934), p. 329 ff. Louis Saint-Blancat, "Recherches sur les sources de la théologie lutherienne primitive (1509–1510)," *Verbum Caro* 8 (1954), p. 81 ff. "La théologie de Luther et un nouveau plagiat de Pierre d'Ailly",

number of sources, among which is the important *Sentences* commentary of Gregory of Rimini.

This is the point to raise the question of whether it is at all proper to call Gregory of Rimini a nominalist. Gregory's independence of the nominalistic schools of his day on such a central point as the *merita de congruo* and his defense of an Augustinian doctrine of double predestination are indeed incontestable. He may be more moderate in his attacks on the Pelagian tendencies of his day than Thomas Bradwardine in his crusade against the *Pelagiani Moderni*, but Rimini does not leave room for doubt as to his own position.[23]

There is, however, a long scholarly tradition which claims Gregory as a nominalist[24] on the basis of equally solid documentation drawn primarily from his epistemology, including his rejection of the Thomistic *distinctio realis* and the Scotistic *distinctio formalis*. Yet it has generally been acknowledged that also within this more philosophical context Gregory preserves his independence from Occam on two related points: (1)

Positions Luthériennes 4 (1956) p. 61 ff; cf. the report by Horst Beintker, "Neues Material über die Beziehungen Luthers zum mittelalterlichen Augustinismus," *ZKG* 76 (1957), 144 ff. Damasus Trapp, O.E.S.A. "Augustinian Theology of the Fourteenth Century," *Augustiniana* 6 (1956), 146 ff.

[23] Whereas Bradwardine speaks about the "Pelagiani pestiferi" — *De causa dei* III.1.637C — Gregory states: "Quia de proposita questione multi modernorum tenent partem affirmativam in quo ut mihi videtur salva eorum debita reverentia ac iudicio meliori plurimum dissonant a doctrina sanctorum et ab ecclesiasticis diffinitionibus, faventque cuidam errori Pelagii condemnato. . ." II *Sent.* d 26, 27, 28, q 1 art. 1 [fol. 92Q/93A]. The best study on this point to date is Martin Schüler's *Prädestination, Sünde und Freiheit bei Gregor von Rimini* (Stuttgart, 1934), esp. pp. 61 ff., 151 ff. Its English counterpart is G. Leff, *Gregory of Rimini: Tradition and Innovation in Fourteenth Century Thought* (Manchester, 1961), p. 196 ff.; this section does not replace Schüler. The innumerable errors in the Latin footnotes — the better part obviously not due to variant readings from the extant manuscripts but to misreadings of the abbreviated Latin text — qualify the usefulness of Mr. Leff's study. Cf. my review in *Speculum* 37 (1962), 456 ff.

[24] Pierre Bayle, *Dictionnaire historique et critique*, IV (Basel, 1739), 56; Prantl, *Geschichte der Logik*, IV, 9; Ueberweg and Baumgartner, *Grundriss der Geschichte der Philosophie*, 10 ed. (Berlin, 1915), II, 614, as quoted by Joseph Würsdörfer, *Erkennen und Wissen nach Gregor von Rimini* in BB, vol. XX, pt. 1, p. 99; Würsdörfer supports this contention on pp. 56, 60, 96, 99, and 120 ff. The English counterpart to Würsdörfer is Leff, *Gregory of Rimini*, p. 31 ff. Leff's assertion that Schüler has overlooked the nominalistic aspects of Gregory's "outlook" — *Gregory of Rimini* (p. 236) — is unfounded; cf. Schüler, p. 22. Schüler shows that Gregory employed nominalistic tools to reach his Augustinian position (p. 31).

his acceptance of the *species intelligibiles* which allow for an alternative mode of knowing besides the *notitia intuitiva* which supplies empirical sense knowledge;[25] (2) his rejection of Occam's thesis that the object of our knowledge is the conclusion of a syllogism; for Gregory this object is rather the *significatum totale conclusionis*, that is, the meaning and truth, the *sic esse*, of this conclusion. But these two points are rather to be viewed as interesting remnants of thirteenth-century Augustinian epistemological theories, than as centers of Gregory's thought.[26]

In a first report on his important investigation of manuscripts from the hand of Peter Ceffons of Clairvaux, Damasus Trapp has indicated further evidence bearing on the question at hand.[27] Peter, writing shortly after the middle of the fourteenth century, regards the masterminds behind the condemnations of John of Mirecourt and Nicolaus of Autrecourt as his personal enemies: "three foreign old witches." [28] Trapp builds a strong case for the identification of Gregory of Rimini as one of these. The interesting conclusion is that Gregory, instead of being the *antesignanus nominalistarum*, might rather have to be viewed as the standard bearer *against* the nominalists.[29]

Important as this finding is, we should like to point out that even if Gregory shares responsibility for the condemnations of 1347, this does

[25] Leff finds the divergence of Gregory from Occam — without quoting the latter — crystallized in the fact that the former with "uncompromising Augustinianism" accepts the self-awareness of the soul, and a division between sensory and intellectual knowledge, whereas ". . . Ockham gave no recognition to what Gregory has treated as intelligible knowledge. . ." (*Gregory of Rimini*, p. 50). See, however, Occam: "Patet etiam quod intellectus noster pro statu isto non tantum cognoscit sensibilia sed etiam in particulari et intuitive cognoscit aliqua intelligibilia que nullo modo cadunt sub sensu "(*Prologi*, q 1 HH). Occam defends intelligible knowledge as the realm of inner experience: ". . . dico quod non est de intentione philosophi quod nihil intelligitur ab intellectu nisi prefuit prius in sensu, sed quod nullum *sensible* extrinsecum intelligitur ab intellectu nisi prefuit prius in sensu "(*Ibid.* UU). The obvious differences between Gregory and Occam, acknowledged by all Rimini scholars, require a more detailed investigation.

[26] I *Sent.* d 3 q 1 art. 1 [fol. 38 B; 39 A; 42 A]. Occam on the object of knowledge: I *Sent.* Prol. q 9. Gregory, I *Sent.* Prol. q 1 art. 1 concl. 1 [fol. 2 B]. "Aber bezüglich der Objectivität oder Subjectivität dieser Erkenntnisbilder hat sich Gregor, soweit wir feststellen konnten, für keine der beiden Auffassungen endgültig entschieden" (Würsdörfer, p. 122). On the object of knowledge: ". . . ein klares Erfassen des Problems finden wir bei ihm nicht" (p. 123).

[27] Damasus Trapp, O.E.S.A., "Peter Ceffons of Clairvaux," *RTAM* 24 (1957), p. 101 ff.

[28] *Ibid.*, p. 148.

[29] *Ibid.*, p. 154.

not conclusively stamp him as a campaigner against nominalism in general; he may rather be understood as a *doctor modernus* who combats the unorthodox excesses of nominalism.

Elsewhere we have tried to show that we should look to Robert Holcot and Adam Woodham as the spiritual fathers of the Parisian "determinists." [30] Ceffons' exceptionally high praise of Holcot as *vir notabilis litteraturae et in doctrinis theologicis plurimum eruditus* [31] suggests a very considerable amount of respect, not surprising in view of the suggested relation between Holcot and Peter's Cistercian brother, Mirecourt.

One more important recent discussion of Rimini's position has to be considered. Within the larger context of the problem of Luther's knowledge of Gregory of Rimini — which does not concern us in this volume — Louis Saint-Blancat brings out Gregory's anti-Occamism. [32] He points to a striking plagiarism by Pierre d'Ailly who copied large sections of Gregory's *Prologue*. This seems therefore to imply that according to Saint-Blancat, not only Gregory but also d'Ailly should be seen as an opponent of Occam, at least on the point covered by this plagiarized passage.

A first glance in the parallel texts as presented by Saint-Blancat [33] shows that though d'Ailly acknowledges his indebtedness to Gregory at one place, [34] the passages are sufficiently identical — often *verbatim* — to warrant the verdict of plagiarism, though of course the medieval understanding of copyright is to be taken into consideration. A closer investigation of the plagiarized texts, however, makes clear that whereas d'Ailly at places in his formulation is dependent on Gregory, in content and *ad sententiam* he follows obediently his master Occam.

The texts concerned fall in two main groups. The first one deals with

---

[30] Oberman, *Bradwardine*, p. 204 ff.

[31] Quoted by Trapp, "Peter Ceffons of Clairvaux," p. 113, from MS Troyes 930. *Tractatus trium libellorum*, fol. 98ʳ. The first part of this encomium is a contemporary witness to Holcot's place among "the friars in the classicizing group"; Beryl Smalley, *English Friars and Antiquity in the Early Fourteenth Century* (Cambridge, 1960), p. 133. Trapp rightly opposes the terms "scepticism" and "despair" as an appropriate description of the general intellectual climate of the fourteenth century: "The many among the Moderni [in the fourteenth century] never despaired of reaching eventually universal truth, at least such a general despair has never been proved." "CLM 27034. Unchristened Nominalism and Wycliffite Realism at Prague in 1381," *RTAM* 24 (1957), p. 321. Cf. below, Chapter Seven, section III.

[32] Louis Saint-Blancat, "La théologie de Luther," p. 67 ff.

[33] *Ibid.*, p. 77 ff.

[34] Pierre d'Ailly, *Questiones magistri Petri de Aylliaco* (Lyon, 1500), q 1 art. 3. JJ.

the contention of Pierre d'Auriole in the first question of his *Prologue* that a proper theological argumentation can be built on merely probable conclusions which are not necessarily theological but possibly metaphysical in nature.[35]

Gregory and d'Ailly reject this and call upon the authority of St. Augustine to prove that theological truths are to be drawn from revelation — Holy Scripture — and not from always essentially unreliable human knowledge.[36] Though Occam does not mention d'Auriole by name in this connection, in the first question of his Prologue he makes the same point, also by referring to the authority of Augustine. In question three he then proceeds to describe d'Auriole's position at length and refutes it by stressing the radical contrast between *fides* and *opinio* (R).[37]

Related to this understanding of theological truths is the statement

[35] The Gregory edition used by Saint-Blancat (Venice, 1503), deviates at places from the Venice 1522 edition reprinted by the Franciscan Institute. My references are to this more readily accessible text. Gregory takes issue with Pierre d'Auriole, I [I *Sent.* Prol. q 1 art. 2], fol. 2 H ff. D'Ailly, I *Sent.* Prol. q 1 art. 3 EE = Gregory I, fol. 2 Q.

[36] D'Ailly, I *Sent.* Prol. q 1 art. 3 EE *in fine* = Gregory I fol. 3 B/C. Cf. Gerson, *Opera* I, 457 C. Gerson's insistence on the fact that Holy Scripture has "suam logicam propriam" militates against Pierre d'Auriole's position. *Opera* I, 3 A. The criticized passage is *Prooemium*, sect. 1, A [q 1] 11: ". . . [though relying on probabilities] moralis et naturalis scientia possunt proprie scientiae appellari . . . Ergo theologia, cum ex multis probabilibus ac verisimilibus inductivis probet ea quae sunt fidei et alia quae concludit, dici potest scientia sicut et physica vel moralis." Pierre d'Auriole, *Scriptum super primum sententiarum*, ed. E. M. Buytaert, I (St. Bonaventure, N.Y., 1952), 135.

[37] ". . . omnes veritates necessarie viatori ad eternam beatitudinem habenda sunt veritates theologice, hoc patet per beatum Augustinum. . . " Gregory, *Prol.* q 1. F. Explicit rejection of d'Auriole's position, *Prol.* q 3 N.P.Z. Cf. *Ibid.* O: ". . . sine fide nullus potest assentire veritatibus credibilibus, ergo respectu illarum non est scientia proprie dicta." Cf. Biel, *Prol.* q 1 nota 3 D. D'Ailly, who independently of Gregory contended that theological truths in the larger sense of the word were not necessarily related to Holy Scripture, is taken to task for this by Biel. D'Ailly in q 1 art. 2 and art. 3 EE. Biel, *Prol.* q 1 nota 3 D. On this vital point the line does not run from d'Ailly to Gregory but from Biel to Gregory! Cf. Gregory ". . . non sequentium ex dictis sacre scripture nullam dico esse conclusionem theologicam," *ibid.*, fol. 3 C. We have to disagree therefore with Saint-Blancat's conclusion: "Gregoire veut que la théologie ne soit qu'une argumentation biblique . . . Toute théologie rigoureusement biblique est absente de fait et de droit de ce long débat [i.e., absent from the Prologues of Occam and Biel]." "La théologie de Luther," p. 73 f. The author's observation that Occam and Biel quote Holy Scripture only once in their Prologues loses some of its power in view of the fact that Gregory does not seem to quote Scripture even once.

of Gregory and d'Ailly that Augustine's famous "Ego evangelio non crederem nisi me ecclesie catholice commoveret auctoritas" [38] is not to be employed against their insistence on the axiomatic character of scriptural truths. The Church does not establish scriptural truth, but is a motivating cause for the acceptance of its claims. A theological truth exists prior to its official formulation by the Church and is in no way dependent upon it.[39] As we will show in Chapter Eleven, this is exactly the position taken by Occam.[40]

Here we want to emphasize that there is no reason to construct an antithesis between a so-called biblical position of Gregory [41] and a philosophical or non-biblical position of Occam and Biel. All three hold that it is the task of the doctor of theology to interpret and develop biblical and not other truths; and none of the three feels that this excludes the authority of the tradition of the Church. Gregory's rejection in his *Prologue* of the thesis that scriptural truths cannot be axiomatic since they are derived from the authority of the Church has been too readily interpreted as an indication of biblicism. Within the context of the discussion of the task of the *doctor ecclesiae*, the *sola scriptura* principle envisages and militates against *philosophy* and not against interpreted scripture, that is *Tradition*. In an important passage which has not yet been taken into consideration, Gregory states as clearly as one might wish that he will not allow any encroachment on the reliability of the authority of the Church, since she is like Holy Scripture a medium through which God speaks.[42]

---

[38] For a discussion of this passage and its late medieval interpretations, see below, Chapter Ten.

[39] D'Ailly, I *Sent.*, Prol. q 1. art. 3. FF = Gregory, I fol. 3 G/H.

[40] As an elaboration of Occam's quoted statement from *Prol.* q. 1 F, we can point to Occam, I *Sent.* d 1 q 5 Q: ". . . si sit expressum in scriptura sacra vel ex determinatione ecclesie vel formaliter sequitur ex illis." Cf. "Dico quod unum est notum per scripturam et aliud non et ideo [!] debet unum concedi et non reliquum," *ibid.* T.

[41] Saint-Blancat's view is also expressed by Paul de Vooght, *Les Sources de la doctrine chrétienne d'après les théologiens du XIVe siècle et du début du XVe* (Paris, 1954), p. 106, "La position biblique de Grégoire de Rimini. . ." This is a central point in Saint-Blancat's proof that: ". . . Luther s'éloignait d'Ockham pour subir l'influence de Grégoire de Rimini grâce aux plagiats d'Ailly"; "La théologie de Luther," p. 76.

[42] ". . . si deus potest dicere falsum potuit etiam per prophetas et apostolos et maiores ecclesie et adhuc potest per maiores ecclesie ad quos spectat determinare

The second group of texts plagiarized by d'Ailly is concerned with the rejection of Thomas' definition of theology as a strict science. Aquinas employs the term "subalternated science" to show that theology is as much a science as music, since it accepts its principles — or axioms as we called them — from a higher science, revelation, even as the axioms of music are accepted from arithmetic. This time d'Ailly not only follows Occam contentwise, but he reports faithfully and often word-by-word the argumentation which he found with both Gregory and Occam.[43]

As we have seen, Luther — or any other reader of d'Ailly — would not have been led via these plagiarisms *away from Occam to Gregory of Rimini* but *via Gregory of Rimini to Occam, to the Inceptor himself.*

Though the foregoing may clear up some questions surrounding Gregory of Rimini, we are still faced with the underlying problem of Gregory's relation to nominalism. We believe that in view of the present state of scholarship we must say — however strange this may appear — that from the point of view of Gregory's own writings *per se*, that is, taken in isolation, no further clarification should be expected. There is a general consensus that Gregory preserves an essentially Augustinian independence of the nominalistic tradition both on philosophical and theological points. The margins of his *Sentences* commentary are a clear testimony to his free criticisms of leading nominalists like Occam and Woodham; and though Holcot's name is never mentioned, one suspects strongly that he is envisaged time and again when Gregory attacks *unus doctor* or addresses himself to *aliqui viventes doctores universitatis anglicane.*[44] At the same time it is incontestable that Gregory wears the garb of the *via moderna* with zest and conviction. The same margins witness to the fact that at important junctures, Occam's opponents are also Gregory's opponents, for example, Thomas, Scotus, and Pierre d'Auriole. The question therefore is whether Gregory merely used the tools of nominalism to find an audience for himself and for his greatest authority, Augustine,

---

que spectant ad fidem, dicere falsum . . . Et eodem modo si inter dei dicta vel ecclesie aliqua falsa admissa fuerint, nihil penitus remanebit auctoritas." I *Sent.* d 42–44 q 2 art. 2 [fol 167 D]. Cf. II *Sent.* d 30–33, q 1 art. 2 [fol. 111 L].

[43] D'Ailly, I *Sent.* Prol. q 1 art. 3 JJ = Gregory, I fol. 6 K = Occam, *Prol.* q 7 O = Biel, *Prol.* q 7 art. 1 nota 1. Elaborated by d'Ailly, *ib.* f. = Gregory, I fol. 3. N f. = Occam, *Prol.* q 3. Q. Theology as *scientia subalternata*: cf. Aquinas, *ST* I q 1 art. 2 resp.

[44] I *Sent.* d 42–44 q 1 art. 2 [fol. 163 D].

or whether Gregory's involvement in nominalism is of a more substantial nature.

There are no reliable categories available for the historian of ideas to use for distinguishing sharply and definitely between vehicle and content; there is no way to determine at what point the language Gregory employed started to shape his very thought and his basic presuppositions. A comparison between Gregory and Bradwardine, elsewhere pursued,[45] lends weight to this consideration. Gregory's use of the *potentia absoluta* principle to deny the ontological necessity of the habit of grace, and even more his proposition that according to God's absolute power man can love God meritoriously without this habit, is a marked departure from pre-Gregorian Augustinianism.[46] Whereas Bradwardine had focussed his campaign against the *Pelagiani moderni* in the absolute indispensability of the infused habit of grace, Gregory of Rimini relied not solely, but primarily on the more dynamic concept of the *auxilium speciale* at a time when the self-evident necessity of the habit of grace seemed outdated.

Whereas the debate on the relation of vehicle and content is necessarily inconclusive, we suggest that it is important to pay close attention to the fact that d'Ailly and Biel, whose nominalism has never been doubted, are eager to quote Gregory, to copy him and to come to terms with him; all the post-Scotistic theologians treated by Biel in a similar fashion are today regarded as standing in the nominalistic tradition. A perusal of Biel's *Sentences* commentary will show that Gregory is as often quoted by Biel as d'Ailly, very often in the same breath. Wendelin Steinbach is justified when he states in his introductory letter that next to the *veteres theologi*, Biel esteems a second group as highly: Occam, Holcot, Gregory, Adam, Oyta, and d'Ailly. Biel sees very well that Gregory does not agree with Occam on certain points such as his defense of the *complex significabilia*.[47] But there is the constant effort to show that Occam and Gregory basically agree. At one point, it is true, Biel airs more than usual his personal feeling, in this case, disapproval of Gregory's daring to attack the Inceptor: ". . . in hoc minus bene Gregorius impugnat Occam," but

---

[45] Oberman, *Bradwardine*, p. 217 ff.

[46] ". . . possibile est de potentia absoluta aliquem esse deo carum et acceptum non habendo charitatem infusam . . . ; possibile est aliquem non habendo charitatem diligere deum meritorie." I *Sent.* d 17 q 1 art. 2 [fol 86 F]. Cf. II *Sent.* d 26–28 q 1 art. 3 [fol. 99 D ff.].

[47] I *Sent.* d 3 q 4 art. 1 nota 1.

adds then: "quia in ea parte penitus idem sentiunt." [48] On another point, however, Biel has noticed that Gregory stands together with the leading nominalists over against the *Inceptor Venerabilis*.[49]

A survey of Biel's references to Gregory indicates that in most cases Biel hands the reader over to Gregory as a reliable guide for a more extensive discussion than would be suitable to his *Collectorium*; in a number of cases Biel goes out of his way to reconcile Gregory with Occam or one of the other nominalistic authorities; on only a few points Biel flatly disagrees with Gregory. Finally, we should take into consideration that not only as regards the invincibility of concupiscence does Biel side with Gregory, but also that on the issue of the relation of the eternal and the established law, Biel goes as far as copying Gregory at length to prove the essential goodness of God which informs even the possibilities *de potentia absoluta*.

When we at this point look back at this section on Gregory of Rimini, it appears that the Doctor Authenticus is (1) openly critical of Occam as interpreted by some leading English nominalists; (2) probably responsible for the condemnations of 1347. In view of these two points he may be seen as a standard-bearer against these varieties of nominalism. (3) The School of Occam as interpreted by d'Ailly and Biel, however, holds Gregory in high regard and certainly does not regard Rimini as the archenemy of progress, as Peter of Ceffons had done. (4) The basic difference in the doctrine of justification and predestination between this latter school and Gregory of Rimini, however, marks a barrier which the historian cannot possibly ignore.

These considerations lead us to view Gregory of Rimini as a right-wing nominalist who is one of the most impressive representatives of a school of late medieval Augustinianism which is still to be explored in more detail.[50] His right-wing position is marked by his outspoken defense

[48] I *Sent.* d 1 q 1 art. 3 dub. 2. Cf. q 3 art. 3 dub. 2 G: ". . . facile possent concordari Gregorius et Occam, ut potest colligi ex Henrico de Oyta, q 2. art 2, qui bene loquitur in hac materia." Cf. also q 4 art. 3 dub. 1: "Plura ad hanc questionem valentia vide in Gregorio . . . in Petro . . . in Oyta . . . in Holchot. . ."

[49] The point concerned is the *distinctio formalis* between God's essence and the three Persons of the Trinity. I *Sent.* d 2 q 11 art. 3 dub. 3.

[50] Henry of Oyta presents us with a problem in many respects similar to the one posed by Gregory. Albert Lang came to the conclusion that ". . . Heinrich sich den radikalen und verderblichen Auswirkungen der nominalistischen Theorie entge-

of a predestination *ante praevisa merita* which we found to be the position of Scotus. He goes beyond Scotus, however, in also holding to reprobation *ante praevisa demerita*.[51] From the point of view of the main current of late medieval nominalism, this seems an unnecessary deviation from the school tradition since they believe they have done full justice to the basic Augustinian insights. Though indeed men like d'Ailly, Gerson, and Biel share with Gregory a continuous and significant employment of the dialectics of God's "two powers," they prove to be unable to absorb the remarkably tenacious late medieval Augustinian tradition.

Jean Gerson expresses his serious concern about the philosophical turn of the debates on these points, but this does not move him to join arms

---

gengesetzt und sie durch den Anschluss an das theologische Erbe der Vergangenheit zu überwinden versucht hat," *Heinrich Totting von Oyta*, p. 243.

Feckes did not regard Henry as a nominalist, *Die Rechtfertigungslehre*, p. 115, n. 84. On the strength especially of the *Quaestiones Sententiarum*, which stem from Henry's Parisian period (1377–1381), Lang characterizes Oyta's position as "eklektisch-nominalistische Vermittlungstheologie," p. 161. According to Lang the works of Henry's Viennese period show a return to Thomism and the medieval tradition, which is said to imply also a departure from his earlier adherence to the Augustinianism of Gregory, p. 225. Oyta is highly esteemed not only by Biel but also by Gerson (*Opera* I.100 B/C) as quoted by Lang, p. 177. Lang's documentation even as regards this last period concerning the doctrine of penance, the Immaculate Conception, the concept of tradition, and justification presents as many examples of the close relation between Oyta's and Biel's positions.

For the Augustinianism of Hugolin of Orvieto see the articles by Adolar Zumkeller: "Hugolin von Orvieto [† 1373] über Urstand und Erbsünde," *Augustiniana* 3 (1953), 35 ff. 165 ff.; 4 (1954), 25 ff. and "Hugolin von Orvieto [† 1373] über Prädestination, Rechtfertigung und Verdienst," *Augustiniana* 4 (1954), 109 ff.; 5 (1955), 5 ff.

[51] Rimini teaches a doctrine of double foreordination, reprobation being implemented by an act of *praeterire*. ". . . sicut deus quos voluit ab eterno predestinavit et non propter merita aliqua futura, ita quos voluit ab eterno reprobavit, non propter demerita futura." I *Sent.* d. 40–41 q 1 art. 2 [fol. 160 B]. Cf. ". . . [deus reprobat] nec quemquam ad peccandum impellendo sed eum ad bene agendum per suam gratiam non trahendo," *ibid.* [fol. 160 K]. The *adiutorium gratie* is *predestinationis effectus, ibid.* [fol. 158 M].

A late testimony provides circumstantial evidence to confirm our view that Gregory should be assigned to a third school alongside the Thomist and Scotist schools — in conjunction with but distinguished from Occam. Ambrosius Catharinus Politus, O.P., paraphrases St. Paul's words "Ego Apollo, ego Pauli, ego vero Cephae" [I Cor. 1:12] with "ego Thomae, ego Scoti, ego Ocham vel Gregorii." *Apologia pro veritate catholicae et apostolicae fidei ac doctrinae adversus impia ac valde pestifera Martini Lutheri dogmata* [1520], ed. Josef Schweizer in *CC* vol. XXVII (Münster i.W., 1956), p. 63.

with the defenders of Augustine's understanding of predestination. His main theme is the call for repentance and genuine love for God with the encouragement that God has committed himself to infuse his grace in those who do their very best.[52]

Biel can be termed a disciple of Gerson with respect to the mystical elements in his theology and also with respect to his primary interest in the theological aspect of the problems implied in the doctrines of justification and predestination. The impact and influence of nominalism outside the faculties of arts and sciences on the theology taught and preached in the fifteenth century may well have been due to the mediating alliance of Gerson and Biel.[53]

Biel's marked theological interest along with his *regulariter* thesis constitute here the only two points on which he deviates from Occam. Essentially, therefore, we may say that Biel in his understanding of predestination — and as we also found with respect to justification — follows faithfully his master Occam in understanding predestination as foreknowledge.

7. The view of Reinhold Seeberg

In view of this conclusion, we must take into account the opposite opinion of two properly highly regarded students of late medieval theology: Reinhold Seeberg and Paul Vignaux.

Seeberg finds a strict concept of predestination in Occam's theology. The free will of God is not only the sole cause of election but also of rejection.[54] From the adduced references it appears that Seeberg has understood Occam's insistence on God's *eternal* freedom *before* and *in* the act of commitment as an *historical* freedom *from* commitment. Seeberg finds the conclusive proof of the correctness of his interpretation in the statement: "whatever guides the *viator* toward salvation is to be taken as

[52] *Opera* III.7.D; III.86.C; III.123.C.

[53] In a second volume this point will be buttressed with a presentation of the most important sermons of Biel together with a selection of sermons of influential contemporaries.

[54] "Also ist nach Ockham lediglich das freie Wollen Gottes die Ursache der Erwählung wie auch der Verwerfung," Seeberg *DG* III, 769 f. In the note added: "Auch hier folgt die Erörterung wesentlich dem Duns Skotus, der aber [!] für die Verwerfung nach einem Grunde sucht. . ." p. 770, n. 1.

the fruits of predestination; this applies also to the very first preparation for glory since this is only possible with the *auxilium divinum*."[55] As a result of this interpretation, Seeberg comes to the paradoxical conclusion that the theologians of the *via moderna* were Pelagians in their doctrine of sin and predestinarians in their doctrine of grace.[56]

In view of the far-reaching consequences of this over-all evaluation of nominalism, it is of considerable import to point out that Seeberg's conclusion is based on a misreading of the text. The opinion quoted is *not* the opinion of Occam but rather that of Scotus.[57] Occam *rejects* the Scotistic argumentation with a twofold objection.

He directs his first attack against the Augustinian-Scotistic position according to which God is the sole cause of the fruits of predestination such as grace and eternal life. He begins by reminding his readers that *de potentia ordinata*, nothing in the sinner can be designated as such a fruit of predestination. According to the Fathers and the Doctors, however, good works performed in a state of sin are meritorious *de congruo*, not earning eternal life but providing a disposition which God is graciously willing to reward with infusion. Thus Occam argues that the sinner can work his way into the operational sphere of predestination where he becomes a recipient of grace. In the context of the decrees of God, there-

---

[55] "Danach ist bloss der Wille Gottes Ursache des Heils eines Menschen. Das gilt sogar von der ersten Vorbereitung zum Heil: quicquid est in ordine ordinans ipsum in salutem totum comprehenditur sub effectu praedestinationis, etiam ipsa prima praeparatio ad gloriam, neque est enim haec nisi per auxilium divinum, Ock. B." *Ibid.*

[56] "Das paradoxe Resultat unserer Untersuchung ist also, dass die Modernen in der Sündenlehre Pelagianer und in der Gnadenlehre Prädestinianer gewesen sind," *ibid.*, p. 771.

[57] ". . . deus non previdet istum bene usurum libero arbitrio nisi quia vult vel preordinat istum bene usurum eo. . ." *Ox.* I *Sent.* d 41 n. 10. ". . . gratia, fides, merita et bonus usus liberi arbitrii omnia ad istum finem sunt ordinata. . . igitur propter nullum istorum praevisum vult ei beatitudinem," *ibid.*, n. 11. Cf. Aquinas, *ST* I q 23 art. 5: "Divina enim providentia producit effectus per operationes causarum secundarum, ut supra dictum est. Unde et id quod est per liberum arbitrium est ex praedestinatione" ". . . quidquid est in homine ordinans ipsum ad salutem, comprehenditur sub effectu praedestinationis etiam ipsa praeparatio ad gratiam." See also *Summa c. Gent.* III.q 163; *De Veritate* q 6 art. 2; I *Sent.* d 41 q 1 art. 3. See further C. Friethoff, *Die Prädestinationslehre bei Thomas von Aquin und Calvin* (Fribourg., 1962), p. 10 ff. and the clear review by A. H. Maltha of A.D.R. Polman's *De Praedestinatieleer van Augustinus, Thomas van Aquino en Calvijn*, . . . in *Bulletin Thomiste* 5 (1938–1939), 570 ff.

fore, it can be shown that God is not the sole cause of all fruits of pre-destination.[58]

The disposition that Scotus had classified along with grace and merits as one of the fruits of predestination can never, according to Occam, be regarded as such. It is acquired before the infusion of grace and there-fore belongs to the sphere common to the elect and the reprobate; and since it is common to both, it cannot be designated as a fruit of predestina-tion.[59]

Occam's second attack is directed against the Scotistic interpretation of the *auxilium divinum*. Since nothing whatsoever can be done without divine aid, one cannot assert that acts performed with this aid spring from predestination. Occam does not include but excludes the disposition for the infusion of grace from the operational sphere of predestination. It is exactly on grounds of the *meritum de congruo* that Occam rejects

[58] "Contra istam opinionem, primo quod dicit quod totus effectus predestina-tionis non habet aliquam causam, non videtur verum quia totus effectus predestina-tionis repugnat secundum leges ordinatas existenti in peccato mortali; ergo nihil quod est in existente in peccato mortali est effectus predestinationis. Sed opera bona ex genere facta in peccato mortali sunt aliquo modo causa quare dat alicui gratiam. Unde secundum sanctos et doctores quamvis opera facta in peccato mortali nihil faciant ad vitam eternam nec remunerabuntur in vita eterna, tamen remunerantur temporaliter et sunt facienda ut citius deus det alicui gratiam qua mereatur vitam eternam. Ergo aliquo modo quamvis non sufficienter nec simplici-ter meritorie, talia opera bona disponunt ad gratiam et per consequens ad effectum predestinationis. Nec sua ratio valet. Nam licet quicquid in homine ordinans ipsum ad salutem tanquam quo posito est dignus vita eterna comprehendatur sub effectu predestinationis, non tamen omne quocunque modo ordinans scl. disponendo vel impedimentum amovendo comprehenditur sub effectu predestinationis. Et huius-modi est ipsa preparatio ad gratiam qua non sub effectu predestinationis cadit quia quicquid precedit gratiam est commune existenti in peccato mortali et digno pena eterna et digno vita eterna; sed preparatio ad gratiam precedit gratiam ergo est communis utrique, ergo non est effectus predestinationis. Nec valet quod dicitur quod non potest fieri nisi per auxilium divinum quia non omne quod non potest fieri nisi per auxilium divinum est effectus predestinationis quia nihil positivum potest fieri nisi per auxilium divinum et tamen non quodlibet tale est effectus pre-destinationis." Occam, I *Sent.* d 41 C. Cf. Biel, I *Sent.* d 40 q 1 art. 1 nota 1 A, where he follows Occam closely.

[59] Luther's famous observation (1518?) that except for Gregory of Rimini the whole medieval tradition — Occamists, Scotists, and Thomists — agree on this point (*WA* II, 394) was reason for Denifle to declare Luther a "Halbwisser." *Luther und Luthertum* I, abt. 2, p. 536. Scheel defended Luther on grounds that this understanding was due to the "Geschichtsbild seiner Erfurter Lehrer," *Martin Luther*, II (1921), p. 163. We can go one step further by pointing out that Luther, Usingen, and Biel could refer here to Occam who in turn could point to Alexander and Bonaventura. See above, Chapter Six, note 3.

Scotus' absolute doctrine of predestation, while still leaving ample room for God's absolute sovereignty insofar as the *meritum de congruo* is only a cause in the second sense of the word, that is, a particular human condition which God in all eternity freely decided to reward with acceptation. This means, of course, existentially and actually for the *viator* living in the "dome," that his salvation depends on himself, insofar as he has to do his very best. Thus we can conclude that with Occam and Biel, rather than speaking about the *doctrines* of predestination and justification, we should preferably speak of *one doctrine* of predestination and justification. These two form one consistent structure of thought where the arguments for the one doctrine are equally applicable to the other.[60]

8. The view of Paul Vignaux

Paul Vignaux, we note first of all, in contrast to Seeberg, sees Occam's doctrine of predestination as a deviation from and a critique of the position taken by Scotus. To be sure he comes to the conclusion that Occam, with regard to justification, has rediscovered Scotus' original intention which was obscured by Pierre d'Auriole.[61] But Vignaux grants that Occam in his doctrine of predestination plots a more independent course. This difference does not, however, imply that Occam would have rejected Scotus' concept of absolute predestination. It is, according to Vignaux, more a matter of differing techniques due to different intellectual tools: Occam's rejection of the formal distinction forces him to reject Scotus' analyses of the divine psyche leading to the assumption of an interior order of decisions. For Occam, God is absolutely simple, and any order posited in him is the result of the limitations of the human mind: the posterior order of Occam replaces the interior order of Scotus.[62]

---

[60] Biel: "Nec tamen propter hoc gratia non est gratia quia non datur propter bonum usum liberi arbitrii tanquam propter meritum condignum sed tanquam dispositionem de congruo, qua non existente gratia non infunderetur, de hoc in secundo libro [II *Sent.* d 27]. Hic autem bonus motus seu usus liberi arbitrii non est effectus predestinationis licet sit a deo, quia communis est etiam non predestinatis." I *Sent.* d 41 q 1 art. 3 dub. 1. The *licet sit a deo* is Biel's parallel to Occam's requirement of the *auxilium dei* for every act.

[61] "Occam semble retrouver l'intention même de Scot: magnifier l'Amour créateur, tout puissant sur les choses créées," *Justification et Prédestination*, p. 138.

[62] "Avec le problème de la prédestination, la "technique" vient au premier plan. Scot et Occam n'usent pas du même outil intellectuel. . . ," p. 139. See also his article, "Occam," in *DThC*, vol. XI, col. 881 f.

But as far as the cause of predestination is concerned, Vignaux does not hesitate: with Occam as with Scotus this is based on the absolute and loving will of God.[63]

It is remarkable that Vignaux has so well noted that God's gracious decision indeed disappears in the abyss of his being while he fails to see that this gracious decision equally disappears — in the realm of the *potentia ordinata* — in the rule of justice. One wonders of course how he interprets the passages which speak so unambiguously about man's self-produced disposition for the infusion of grace and therefore as disposition for predestination. Vignaux does not grant this point. On the one hand he sees in the infusion of grace in those who do their very best an act of God's love. On the other hand, he points to the *auxilium divinum* necessary for this disposition which would make it hard to accuse Occam of Pelagianism.[64]

As we saw, Occam does indeed require this divine assistance for every *actus positivus*. But does this mean that the human virtue of doing one's very best is due to the impact of divine grace? Though Occam nowhere, so far as we know, defines the *positive* act, it is clear from the way he employs the term that it should not be understood as positive in the sense of moral goodness, but rather as the actuality of the act; "positive" thus in contrast with mere potentiality.[65] The positivity of an act is therefore the same as the substance of an act from which the goodness, the intention of the act, has to be discerned as an additional element.[66]

Occam's *auxilium* is therefore nothing else than the *concursus dei* or *influentia generalis*, needed for every act, whether good or bad; an act therefore of preservation and not of redemption.[67] If this assistance im-

---

[63] "Par cette contingence, par cette liberté, nous découvrons au principe de la grâce comme de la nature, un acte absolument gratuit, qui se fond et se perd, pour ainsi dire, dans l'essence divine, abîme de simplicité: tout analyse devenant impossible, notre pensée n'a plus où se prendre. . . ," p. 139.

[64] "Noter l'appel à l'*auxilium divinum* dans la préparation à la grâce á considérer si l'on veut traiter du 'pélagianisme' d'Occam," p. 139.

[65] "Omne positivum quod est in peccato potest poni per deum . . . Et ideo peccatum nihil dicitur quia omne positivum in eo potest causari sine omni peccato." Occam, IV *Sent.* q 8, 9 S *in fine*. "Capitur prout distinguitur contra esse in potentia, id est contra illud quod non est in rerum natura, sed potest esse." *Summulae* I.c.16, p. 19 as quoted by Baudry, *Lexique*, p. 13.

[66] See the clear discussion in III *Sent.* q 10 Q: "Si autem queras quid addit bonitas actus vel malicia super substantiam actus. . ."

[67] Biel: ". . . generalis dei influentia que ut causa prima concurrit cum agente

plied more than this general influence of God, Occam would not have been in a position to hold that man *in puris naturalibus* — a state which by definition excludes supernatural influences — can love God with a genuine love.[68] Gregory of Rimini would later attack Occam's position by requiring not merely the general assistance of God necessary for every act, but also a special assistance for proper disposition for grace.[69] Indeed, Occam, like Biel, teaches that there are those like St. Paul and the Virgin Mary who are from the very beginning led to their salvation by grace. But this aid of grace does not *help* them to provide a proper disposition but *prevents* them from providing such a disposition. Besides, this grace is *gratia specialis*, granted in special cases, and is therefore not to be identified with the *auxilium divinum* with which God cooperates in every act.

In conclusion, therefore, it is clear that since the arguments brought forth by Seeberg and Vignaux in favor of an absolute doctrine of predestination are not convincing, we have to say that *Occam and Biel teach a predestination "post praevisa merita."* Not merely on a technical point but on one of the most central theological issues, predestination and justification, Occam and Biel reject the Scotistic position. The usual description of the development of late medieval thought according to which Occam would merely have radicalized the principles of Scotus' theology must be revised. Albeit with more of a theological emphasis, Biel follows Occam in the central doctrine of predestination and justification.

In view of this state of affairs it is not surprising that the fourteenth-century syncretistic Parisian school, where the positions of the Scotists and nominalists were often fused to the point where their boundaries are difficult to discern, occupied itself primarily with a discussion of the relation of foreordination and foreknowledge.

secundo, id est agente creato ad omnem actum positivum." II *Sent.* d 28 q 1 art. 1 nota 2.

[68] ". . . ex puris naturalibus potest [voluntas] habere actum ordinatum quamvis non meritorium. . ." I *Sent.* d 1 q 2 D.

[69] ". . . Adam post suum lapsum non potuit per suas vires naturales absque speciali auxilio dei facere aliquem actum moraliter bonum." II *Sent.* d 29 q 1 art. 2 [fol. 105 M]. ". . . nec posse virtuose agere nisi adiutam ab illo cui quotidie dicimus: 'adiuvas nos deus salutaris noster' — et hoc contra pelagium," *ibid.*, resp. 3 [fol. 110 Q].

9. Scotus, d'Auriole, Occam: Biel's contribution

Before we can take up the question of the significance of the doctrine of justification and predestination for the *viator's* certitude of salvation, we have to note one more point where Biel does not contradict, but nevertheless goes beyond the position of Occam. Biel's general understanding of the operation of the will is that the will is directed first to the end and only after that to the means to this end, though in actual execution this order is reversed.[70] Biel however rejects Scotus' application of this principle to the relation of the behavior of man and his predestination.[71] Scotus had concluded that God wants first the salvation of the elect, and only on the basis of this, "afterward" — *quasi posterius* — the means to this end. This understanding enabled him to hold an absolute doctrine of predestination, undetermined by foreknowledge.[72] The famous formal distinction made it possible for Scotus, therefore, to view the order of decisions in the divine counsel as fourfold, applied to Peter and Judas as the traditional examples of the elect and of the reprobate. In the first two moments Judas does not enter God's considerations, which are therefore solely concerned with Peter. In the first moment God predestines Peter to eternal glory. In the second moment he wants to give Peter the means to this end, grace. In the third moment Judas appears for the first time as an object for God's will: God permits Peter and Judas to belong to the mass of perdition. Finally Peter is saved and Judas rejected, according to justice since Judas perseveres in sin.[73]

As had already become the established tradition within nominalism, Biel rejects the formal distinction, posits the absolute unity of the essence of God and his attributes, and therefore rejects any order of decisions in the divine counsel. The Scotistic inequality is replaced by the nomi-

---

[70] ". . . Finis vero . . . est obiectum primarium et principalissimum cum magis vult voluntas finem quam media." III *Sent.* d 23 q 1 art. 1 cor. 5 L *in fine*. Cf. the analysis in III *Sent.* d 32 art. 1 nota 3. Occam, *Quodl.* IV q 6.

[71] *Ox.* I d 41 q 1 n 11; Cf. *Par.* I d 41 q 1 n 3.

[72] "Ergo primo isti vult deus beatitudinem quam aliquod istorum [gratia, bonus usus liberi arbitrii] et prius vult ei quodcunque istorum quam prevideat ipsum habiturum quodcunque istorum, igitur propter nullum istorum previsam vult ei beatitudinem." *Ox.* I d 41 q 1 n 11.

[73] *Ox.* I d 41 q 1 n 11.

nalistic equality between the responsibility of Peter and Judas for their respective destinies.[74]

We should note that this discussion is not one of merely technical importance. Scotus' thesis of God's primordial decision as regards the final acceptation of the *viator* to glory is the insuperable wall of defense against the inroads of Pelagianism. It is on grounds of this position that Scotus can afford to stress the priority of guilt as a cause of damnation and more generally the freedom of the human will to a point where scholars who have overlooked this doctrine of predestination can accuse him of full-fledged Pelagianism.[75]

The nominalistic attitude toward Scotus was by no means purely negative. But what happened was that while retaining Scotus' teaching with regard to the dignity of man and the sinner's responsibility for his own damnation, final acceptation as a primordial decision of God, which was Scotus' safeguard against Pelagianism, was rejected by the nominalistic theologians. This rejection of an intrinsic order of decisions in God is the philosophical complement of the theological thesis of a predestination *post praevisa merita.*

The obvious question now arises, how can the nominalists escape self-contradiction when they do not seem to apply their general rule of operation of the human will to the operation of the will of God? They understand the human will to be first of all directed toward its ultimate goal and only then to the means to reach this goal. Why should they not follow Scotus in holding the same as regards God's will, first predestining the elect and then providing the means to this end? Pierre d'Auriole solves the problem by granting that the operation of both the human and the divine will is governed by the same principle: both are teleologically

---

[74] ". . . falsum est quod prius vult finem et post ordinata in finem quia non est nisi unus actus divine voluntatis . . . quia ordo presupponit distinctionem ordinatorum . . . Nec tamen aliquod horum deus prius vult altero, sed quecumque vult similiter et ab eterno vult." II *Sent.* d 20 q 1 art. 1 nota 3. Cf. I *Sent.* d 41 q 1 art. 3 dub. 2. Occam: ". . . non videtur bene dictum quod deus velit prius finem quam illud quod est ad finem; quia non est ibi talis prioritas actum nec sunt ibi talia instantia. . ." I *Sent.* d 41 q 1 F.

[75] E.g., Harnack *DG* IV, 4 ed., 565 ff., 650 f.; A. W. Hunzinger, *Lutherstudien, II: Das Furchtproblem in der katholischen Lehre von Augustin bis Luther* (Leipzig, 1906), p. 84 ff.; A.D.R. Polman, *De praedestinatieleer van Augustinus, Thomas van Aquino en Calvijn* (Franeker, 1936), p. 291.

oriented. This by no means necessarily implies that God's *telos* and man's *telos* coincide.[76] Occam repeats d'Auriole's argumentation in its simplest form without any further elaboration or clarification.[77]

While traditionally in medieval thought goodness had been seen as the common motivation of God and the elect, the nominalistic emphasis on the simplicity of God forbade the assumption of any such inner motivation as predicable of God. Particularly in the shortened form in which Occam presents this argument, one is left with the impression that though eternal bliss is the goal of the elect, God himself has some other ulterior and unknown motive.

Viewed against this background, it is interesting to note that Biel was not satisfied with Occam's short and not very illuminating statement. Since there are no corroborating parallel passages, we cannot labor the point; but it is noteworthy nevertheless that Biel clarifies the relation of the respective motives of God and the elect with a reference to the relation of employer and employee: whereas the employee works for his wages, the employer is not motivated by the wages of the employee, but rather by the work performed.[78] This seems at least to allow for the interpretation that Biel was interested in emphasizing, more than had been usual in prenominalistic theology, the intrinsic importance of the life of the *viator* on earth, the value of which was now less exclusively defined in terms of the eternal Jerusalem, the final destination of the *viator*, and more in terms of the journey itself.

This agrees very well with a more general characteristic of nominalistic theology: the dignity of man is as important a theme here as in its parallel movement, the early Italian Renaissance. The "dome," the sphere established by the *potentia ordinata*, excluding all God's nonrealized possibilities, provides the *viator* with a realm within which he comes into his own, free to realize his innate endowment of dignity.[79] The intensive

[76] For a clear discussion of Pierre d'Auriole's position and his critique of Scotus, see Vignaux, *Justification et Prédestination*, p. 70 ff. Pierre d'Auriole, I *Sent.* d. 42 II a 1 E.F.

[77] ". . . beatitudo respectu cuius est predestinatio non est finis dei predestinantis sed est finis predestinati." I *Sent.* d 41 q 1 J. Cf. I *Sent.* d 42 q 1 C.

[78] ". . . licet vita eterna sit finis predestinati tamen non est finis dei predestinantis sicut premium licet sit finis laboris apud laborantem, non tamen apud premiantem sed magis econverso." I *Sent.* d 41 q 1 art. 3 dub. 2.

[79] See my "Notes on the Theology of Nominalism," p. 63 ff. Note also that Biel is well acquainted with Pico's *Apologia*. Cf. above Chapter One, note 46.

interest, not only in the moral capacities of the *viator*, but increasingly also in the structural composition of the world alongside the road to the eternal Jerusalem as appears in the contributions by nominalistic school-men to mathematics, mechanics, and the sciences in general, bears out this general observation.

10. Supralapsarianism rejected

The rejection of Scotus' psychology implied for Biel finally also a rejection of Scotus' supralapsarianism. Like many a theologian before him,[80] Scotus found it hard to see in the supreme moment of the history of salvation, the Incarnation, merely an *ad hoc* decision of God to neu-tralize the horrid consequences of Adam's fall. The originality of Scotus' position in this respect can be explained as due to the fact that his psy-chology of God gave him the tools to formulate as a well-reasoned thesis what before had been merely a certain theological uneasiness.

Since the number of the elect had been decided upon before the fall of Adam was foreseen, the election of Jesus Christ was decided irrespective of the fall. The Incarnation permitted Christ to acquire the glory for which he had been eternally elected. Since the glory of Christ is a greater good than the glory of Adam, it would be absurd to make the Incarna-tion accidental to the fall and redemption of Adam.[81]

For Biel this is sheer speculation which can be abused to prove that the elect owe their salvation rather to the fact of predestination than to the passion of Christ. Once one grants that predestination takes place before the fall, thus separating the passion of Christ from the salvation of the elect, the work of Christ becomes necessarily meaningless.[82] In answer

---

[80] Bonaventura, III *Sent.* d 1 q 2; Thomas, *ST* III q 1 art. 3; Thomas, III *Sent.* d 1 q 1 art. 3. The discussion of what we termed "conceivable sacred history" is by no means a nominalistic innovation! For an interesting comparison with patristic thought on this point, see Georges Florovsky, "Cur Deus Homo? The Motive of the Incarnation," in *Festival Volume Hamilcar Alivisatos DD* (Athens, 1957), pp. 3–12.

[81] "Non propter solam istam causam [redemptionem generis humani] videtur deus predestinavisse illam animam ad tantam gloriam . . . Imo ulterius sequeretur absurdius, scil. quod deus predestinando adam ad gloriam prius previdisset ipsum casurum in peccatum quam predestinasset christum ad gloriam si predestinatio illius anime tantum esset pro redemptione aliorum. . ." *Ox.*. III d 1 q 3 n 3.

[82] "Nec unum prius, aliud posterius et ideo non est ille ordo in divinis. Et si dicis, saltem ibi est secundum nostram considerationem. Dicitur autem nostra con-

to the challenge of Scotus, Biel subordinates the passion of Christ to the redemption of the elect. God had foreseen that the glory of the elect would be acquired by means of the passion of Christ which was ordained for this particular purpose.[83]

We may conclude that Biel — independently from Occam who, surprisingly, as far as we can see, did not discuss this question — reverts to the infralapsarian position of pre-Scotistic medieval theology.[84] Severing the connection between the Incarnation and redemption would indeed undercut Biel's main christological interest, so clearly expressed in his sermons: to stress along with the coming judgment the condescension of God in order to stimulate love in the sinner through the psychological impact of the proclamation of the past acts of God, who through Incarnation and passion of his son offered himself for the redemption of mankind.[85] Though Incarnation and passion are not seen by Biel as the total cause of redemption, it is precisely to help man complement the merits of

---

[83] sideratio imaginatur talem ordinem vere esse in divinis et sic nostra consideratio est speculatio falsa: aliter rem esse intelligens quam sit. Aut nostra consideratio prius considerat christi predestinationem secundum hominem et post predestinationem aliorum electorum, deinde eorum casum etc.: sic erit ordo nostre considerationis per diversos actus cognitionis in nostro intellectu; sed hec ordinata consideratio nullum ordinem ponit in divinis, alioquin si primo considerarem deum ut creatorem, deinde tres personas, ex hinc essentiam divinam talem, oporteret ponere ordinem in divinis ut potentia creandi esset prior essentia et personis et persone priores essentia. Item si sequitur quod si christus passus non fuisset, electi nihilominus essent salvati, quia prius previdit deus electos salvandos quam Christi passionem." III *Sent.* d 19 q 1 art. 2 concl 4 *in fine.*

[83] After extensive and precise quotations from Scotus — *Ox.* III d 7 q 3 n 3 and d 19 q 1 n 6 — Biel answers: ". . . sicut predestinavit deus electos ad gloriam ita et previdit media quibus perveniendum fuit ad gloriam. Unde non simpliciter previdit eis gloriam sed previdit eis gloriam per christi passionem tanquam per meritum ad hoc preordinatum assequendam." III *Sent.* d 19 q 1 art. 2 concl. 4.

[84] The conclusion of A. Michel that Biel followed Duns Scotus on this point is therefore unjustified. "Incarnation," in *DThC*, vol. VII, col. 1495. Since Biel rejects all forms of necessity in God's *opera ad extra*, his pre-Scotistic infralapsarianism does not imply that he accepts the thesis typical of that period according to which redemption required incarnation: ". . . non fuit simpliciter necesse hominem reparari, sicut non fuit necesse hominem creari," III *Sent.* d 20 q 1 art. 1 nota 1 B.

[85] "Ignis utique liquefaciens animos ad divinas influentias recipiendas per amorem quem excitat divinus amor meditatus, consumens, resolvens et comminuens peccata per excitatam verecundiam et contritionem." The preaching of the word makes such a meditation possible: ". . . quecumque in scriptura continentur et in predicationibus sonant: vel misericordiam dei vel iusticiam que sunt universe vie domini commendant." *S* I 101 G. Cf. *S* 1 F.

Christ that the connection between Incarnation and redemption has to be preserved.[86]

II. *Spes* and *Fiducia*

1. Certainty of grace and certainty of salvation

Now we are in a position to undertake the analysis of Biel's teaching with regard to the certainty of salvation. As we saw in our analysis of the relation of faith and knowledge, Biel distinguishes between three basic types of knowledge: (1) supernatural or certain knowledge, which is the knowledge of faith acquired through revelation: (2) natural or evident knowledge, which is the reliable knowledge of this world through self-evident principles and intuition, and their corollaries: (3) moral or conjectural knowledge, which has to depend on signs which are not always reliable.[87] The first form of knowledge is the only knowledge that leads to certainty, indeed not certainty of final salvation, but of being in a state of grace, that is of the presence of the habit of grace.

One can never ascertain with experiential knowledge typical of this world whether grace is present. And though the soul by intuitive self-knowledge understands its own emotions, all that results from the habit of grace can also be experienced by a heretic and infidel; the heretic pur-

---

[86] ". . . licet christi passio sit principale meritum propter quod confertur gratia, apertio regni et gloria nunquam tamen est sola et totalis causa meritoria. Patet quia semper cum merito christi concurrit aliqua operatio tanquam meritum de congruo vel de condigno recipientis gratiam vel gloriam. . ." III *Sent.* d 19 q 1 art. 2 concl. 5. Cf. the "pro nobis" in *S* II 9 J: "An adhuc dubitamus quid faciat nos filios dei qui pro nobis nasci voluit filius hominis." And again "Recta itaque fides est credere christum pro nobis incarnatum esse verum deum, patris verbum, et simpliciter ac summe ac infinite perfectum, ac per hoc in sua incarnatione summam misericordiam nobis exhibuisse," *S* I 8 B. Cf. *S* II 10 K; *S* II 12 E; *Lect.* 11 D; *Lect.* 20 L; *Lect.* 79 I.

The sharpest formulation of the "pro nobis" theme is perhaps in its application to the preaching of the Word, *S* IV 8 E: ". . . que in sermonibus . . . audire contingit suscipiantur a te tanquam verbum non hominis sed dei ad te et propter te solum prolatum; etiamsi cum decemmilibus audire contingat non aliter suscipe quam si solus audisses . . . quam si ad te solum deus tuus verbum salutis transmisisset." As we have seen, this *verbum salutis* is not the Gospel but rather the New Law. See Chapter One, notes 60, 61, and 63; Chapter Four, notes 75 ff.

[87] For Occam's discussion of certainty, see *Prol.* q 7 Q.

sues his error with as much alacrity as Biel's Christian. The experience of such enthusiasm is therefore no guarantee at all.[88]

It is possible, however, to have conjectural knowledge of the presence of the habit of grace: the light of truth, the joy in doing good works, and peace of conscience; but all this may be due to tricks of the devil. Biel characterized this satanic certainty as "sophistic." Gerson in his commentary on the *Magnificat* had already connected the concepts of sophism and the devil.[89] The devil is more interested in seeming wise than in being wise,[90] and thus undermines Christian piety.[91] It is already clear therefore at this point that for Biel certitude of salvation is not a virtue but a liability.

In view of the fact that God has committed himself to infuse grace in those who do their very best, it would be sufficient to know whether one indeed had produced this ultimate act to be certain of the possession

[88] "Licet enim anima intuitive cognoscat actus suos ut intellectiones et volitiones non tamen habitus sibi inexistentes. Item quicquid in se experitur habens gratiam simile potest experiri carens ea ut hereticus et infidelis ut dulcedinem, delectationem, leticiam, firmitatem, promptitudinem sequendi suum errorem." II *Sent.* d 27 q 1 art. 3 dub. 5 P. Cf. *Lect.* 8 B. Biel follows here the common medieval teaching: Alexander, III *Sent.* q 61 m 7 a 3; Bonaventura, IV *Sent.* d 20 p 1 dub 1; Thomas, *ST* II.I q 112 art. 5; *de Ver.* q 10 art. 10. Gerson: ". . . nisi prout in moralibus sumenda est certitudo ex his que ut in pluribus secundum verisimiles et probabiles conjecturas, eveniunt," "De Concilio," *Opera omnia*, II.31.D. For the different emphases of Augustine and Gregory, the Franciscan School, and Thomas, see G. Ljunggren, *Zur Geschichte der christlichen Heilsgewissheit von Augustin bis zur Hochscholastik* (Göttingen, 1920), esp. pp. 174 ff.; 292 f.; 324 ff. Also, Karl Heim, *Das Gewissheitsproblem in der systematischen Theologie bis zu Schleiermacher* (Leipzig, 1911), pp. 41 ff.: 162 ff. According to Seeberg, Biel is more sceptical as regards the possibility of subjective certainty than is Alexander, Seeburg *DG* III, 782. Such a contrast exists rather between Biel and Scotus. See below notes 96 and 99.

[89] Gerson sees in the devil the prototype of the sophist: "Constitue satanam quasi sophistam cuius hoc totum studium est fallere; non querit sapiens esse, sed videri," *Super Magnificat* VIII in *Opera Omnia* IV. 374 A.

[90] Cf. Occam's more philosophical definition of a sophist: "Sophista est ille qui vult videri sapiens magis quam esse . . . qui vult videri facere opus sapientis quamvis non faciat, maxime utendo syllogismo sophistico." *Tractatus super libros elenchorum* (Paris BN. lat. 14721 fol. 97 a.b.) as quoted by Baudry, *Lexique d'Ockham*, p. 253. Cf. Holcot: ". . . arguit diabolus per sophisticas obligationes. Obligat enim hominem ad sustinendum falsam," *Sap.* Lect. 79 B.

[91] Thomas Bradwardine is included in the indictment of this type of scholasticism: "Omnis absque dubitatione ratio que militat contra pietatem, sophistica est. . . Itaque dum subsummit Doctor iste Anglicanus, quem profundum cognominant, quod. . ." Gerson, *Super Magnificat* VIII in *Opera* IV. 377 C.

of grace. But one only does his very best when motivated by genuine love for God above everything else. Since it is nearly impossible to be absolutely certain of this heroic motivation, it is indeed not more than conjecture if one feels on these grounds that he is in a state of grace.[92]

This uncertainty of being in a state of grace is only part of the problem. The Christian is really interested in knowing whether he belongs to the elect, that is, knowing whether he will *die* in a state of grace and thus be accepted as worthy to enter eternal bliss. Even if one could be certain of possessing grace in the present, it would not necessarily follow that this would be true tomorrow or on the decisive last day of life: to be in a state of grace is not the same as belonging to the elect. There is a vital difference between reprobation *according to present justice* and *according to the eternal foreknowledge of God*. The reprobate according to present justice are the elect who have temporarily fallen from grace but who will eventually enter heaven. The reprobate according to God's foreknowledge are, on the contrary, those who may seem to be elect since they live for some time in a state of grace: but eventually they will be rejected by God on grounds of their foreknown sins. The same argumentation applies then of course to predestination.[93]

[92] ". . . homo non potest evidenter scire se facere quod in se est quia hoc facere includit in se obedire deo propter deum tanquam ultimum et principalem finem quod exigit dilectionem dei super omnia quam ex naturalibus suis homo potest elicere. Hec enim est proxima dispositio ad gratie infusionem, qua existente certissime infunditur gratia. Difficillimum autem est scire se habere illam dilectionem. Et forte naturaliter impossibile quia etsi scire possumus nos diligere deum non tamen evidenter scire possumus illam circumstantiam 'super omnia.' " Biel, II *Sent.* d 27 q 1 art. 3 dub. 5 Q. As we have noted in our discussion of Biel's contritionism, his rejection of Scotus' *parum attritus* implies a rejection of Scotus' "certitude of grace."

[93] ". . . dupliciter quis dici potest prescitus. Similiter et predestinatus scil. vel secundum presentem iusticiam vel secundum eternam dei previdentiam seu prenotionem. Prescitus secundum presentem iusticiam dicitur ille qui est in tali statu in quo si decederet eterne pene deputaretur. Talis est quilibet viator existens in peccato mortali. . . Et hoc modo multi ad eternam beatitudinem predestinati secundum presentem iusticiam sunt presciti. Cadunt enim nonnunquam electi a gratia habituali per mortale peccatum. . . Prescitus secundum eternam dei scientiam est ille qui secundum preordinationem et determinationem divine voluntatis propter peccata sua similiter previsa eterne subiacebit damnationi. Talis est quilibet et solus ille qui in peccato finaliter moritur. . . Isto modo multi presciti pro certo tempore sunt predestinati secundum presentem iusticiam." If one discerns between the two groups then one can also pray for those who are rejected, i.e., "secundum presentem iusticiam," *Lect.* 79 M.

For two reasons therefore certitude of salvation is beyond the reach of the *viator*: there is no way in which he can ascertain that he possesses the habit of grace; and furthermore, even if everything points to his being in a state of grace, this may very well be only according to present justice which by no means implies his perseverence to the end. The Augustinian divorce of grace and predestination by means of the added requirement of the *donum perseverantiae* is effective even in a theology where this gift does not play a part.

2. The rising tide of Donatism: the problem of the wicked priest

Biel gives careful consideration to the question whether this lack of certainty would not also undermine the reliability of the sacraments of penance and the Eucharist. Most elaborately he takes up this problem with respect to the sacrament of penance, the relatively more crucial sacrament since it can provide the first grace of justification while the Eucharist provides only a growth in grace. Since one cannot have certainty about one's own status in the sight of God, this is of course even less true with respect to someone else, in this case the priest to whom one wants to confess. It would then follow that sinners must always doubt whether they are truly absolved, especially when they have reason to be suspicious. This would apply also to the priests themselves; though they may have fulfilled all canonical requirements, they nevertheless cannot be certain of being in a state of grace. That the proper intention is present one may assume, but the personal sanctity of the priest cannot be taken for granted.[94]

This is a most interesting point because we know that here Biel is not

---

[94] "Cum enim nemo sciat an amore vel odio dignus sit; et hoc de seipso multominus de alio nunquam securi esse possent subditi, sed nec presidentes. Quippe semper dubitare haberent peccatores an fuerint rite, vere et sacramentaliter absoluti cum semper dubitarent de mundicia sacerdotis ex multis contra eos conceptis suspitionibus. Sed et ipsi sacerdotes si potestatem in ordinatione rite susceperint si etiam recepta potestate vere consecrent, si absolvant etc. cum se tunc vel nunc charitatem habuisse aut habere ignorent. Et licet in his non posset haberi certitudo evidentie absque divina revelatione propter intentionem ordinantis, consecrantis, absolventis que aliis ignota est. . . Credibilius tamen est et veresimilius intentionem debitam fuisse consecrandi, conferendi ordines recipiendi et generaliter exequendi quam oppositum. Secus de ministrorum sanctitate." *Lect.* 2 F.

dealing with a merely academic question. In Southern Germany and Bohemia, a disintegrating Utraquist Church witnessed the rapid rise of the *Unitas Fratrum*, part of a larger pan-European Donatist upsurge. The most important constitutive factor in the formation of this movement was precisely the fear of the "wicked priest." [95] But outside Bohemia also the problem of "the wicked priest" is pondered and thus presents one of the most important pre-Reformation theological challenges to the medieval Church. We listen therefore with added interest to Biel's answer which is surprising because of its lack of conviction. He merely states as a probable opinion that it would not seem to be in accord with the goodness of God to punish one man for the iniquity of another, especially not when salvation is at stake.

In view of the fall of mankind in Adam and the reconciliation in Christ, such a reference to individual versus corporate responsibility is not a particularly convincing argument for a theologian! For Biel, however, this is reasonable enough grounds for believing that God will guarantee the reliability of the fruits of absolution.[96]

Biel is far more positive in his discussion of the problem of the worthy celebration and reception of the Eucharist. Conjectural certainty is sufficient to avoid unworthy celebration as well as reception. Provided one has searched one's own heart, to be in a state of grace is not an absolute requirement, though only then an additional gift of grace can be acquired.[97]

It is clear that Biel generally rejects the Donatist fear of the "wicked

[95] "They created their religious brotherhood for fear of forfeiting their salvation if they remained in the morally lax church." Marianka S. Fousek, "Church Discipline in the Early Unitas Fratrum" (unpublished doctoral diss., Harvard, 1960), p. ix. Cf. ". . . in a treatise from the same year or next (1468–9), it is stated that it is mortal sin which voids a person's priestly office," p. 96, n. 40. This helpful study emphasizes the contritionism of the *Unitas*. See also her "The Perfectionism of the Early *Unitas Fratrum*," *CH* 30 (1961), p. 396 ff.

[96] ". . . non videtur divine bonitati consentaneum alterum pro alterius iniquitate puniri in his presertim [!] que ad salutem pertinent . . . rationabile est ut deus assistat sacramento penitentie ad peccatorum remissionem quam significat. Assistat dico certitudinaliter respectu significati in fieri ne propter signi incertitudinem negligat quis sacramentum suscipere." *Lect.* 2 G. Cf. *S* I 66 D.

[97] ". . . diligentia eiusque coniecturalis certudo sufficit ad digne celebrandum . . . [E] . . . dicendum quod ad cavendum indignam celebrationem non requiritur quod sacerdos sit in gratia et charitate et ideo sine mortali, quoniam si sic ut dictum est dispositus accedat, non indigne accedit." *Lect.* 8 D.

priest." [98] This rejection is less decisive, however, where he deals with the sacrament of penance than in his treatment of the same problem with regard to the Eucharist. This discrepancy can be understood perhaps against the background of his adamant insistence on the necessity of full contrition and his rejection of anything that might tend to encourage the *parum attritus*.[99]

3. Christ's work of hope and justice

Biel employs conjectural certitude as contrasted with absolute certitude to the full extent against the presumptuous thought of the Pharisee who in his self-righteousness rejects the most basic Christian virtue: humility. Humility can be acquired when we consider our insufficiencies and the abyss of God's judgment which does not allow us to know our present state or future destiny.[100]

At the same time and often even in the same context, Biel's line of argumentation takes a radically different turn. The two aspects of his doctrine of justification — by grace alone, by works alone — and of his doctrine of predestination — foreordination and foreknowledge — reappear in his teaching with regard to the possibilities of certainty for the *viator*. The same organic unity and integrity of structure typical of his understanding of justification and predestination characterizes Biel's doctrine of certainty. This parallelism can again be reduced to what we found to be the two central concepts: the mercy and the justice of God.

These eternal attributes of God, respectively motive and content of the eternal decrees, take historical form in the Incarnation and the self-oblation of Christ on the one hand and in the last judgment on the other hand. At one place Biel discerns these two aspects of the work of Christ to the point that he can speak of two different works of Christ: the *opus*

[98] *S* II 17 G. Cf. the explicit rejection of the Donatistic *ex opere operantis* in *Lect.* 27 A ff. This does not only apply to the priest but also to the preacher, *S* I 22 B.

[99] Biel rejects Scotus' reasoning from a mere "obicem removere" to the certitude of receiving grace. See II *Sent.* d 27 q 1 art. 3 dub. 5 Q.

[100] ". . . oculus considerationis dirigi debet ad sua infirma ac defectus . . . ad profunditatem abyssus divinorum iudiciorum. Propter quam ignoramus an opera nostra de quibus extollimur sint apud deum placentia vel reproba. Ad incertitudinem evenientium futurorum, propter quam homo nescit an odio an amore dei dignus sit, eoque omnia in futurum reservantur incerta." *S* I 8 D.

spei and the *opus iusticie*.[101] These two separate christological themes have a joint psychological impact on the *viator* and establish at the moment that they are combined in the heart of the sinner a subtly balanced fiducial certainty which is at once safeguarded against despair and against presumptuousness.[102]

There are two groups — those who despair because they stress too much the *opus iusticie* and those who are presumptuous [103] because they isolate the *opus spei* — to whom Biel in his sermons constantly directs himself in an effort to show them the proper middle way. As a pastor Biel must have been aware of the extreme precariousness of this balance. Once he makes one of his listeners put to him a question — exactly the same question that was to preoccupy Luther — which expresses the perplexity resulting from the divorce of "the two works of Christ": "How can I flee to him whose judgment I fear greatly?" The parable with which Biel answers is an illuminating summary of the above: a young boy is caught by his father while taking something that had been forbidden him; and when he sees that there is no escape possible, he throws away what he has stolen, goes to his father, gets hold of his rod, embraces his irate father, promises to mend his ways — and finally manages to placate the father. "Do the same yourselves."

---

[101] "Et attendite quam pulcre opus iusticie sequitur opus spei ne fiat vana presumptio si non conversi nec penitentes vitam speremus," *S* II 12 E. "Proponit vero ecclesia timorem post amorem ut si quem advenientis amor non trahit qui est in carne, in benignitate et humanitate, trahat saltem adventuri timor qui est in iusticia et equitate inflexibili et in maiestate tremenda, sicut primus fuit in benignitate ineffanda," *S* I 4 A. It is noteworthy that in Gregory there are not any such traces of an oscillation between two *opera dei*. At one place he emphasizes explicitly the perichoresis of the mercy and justice of God: ". . . omnis res subiecta misericordie est subiecta iusticie et econverso; et opus omne misericordie est opus iusticie et econverso." Gregory, I *Sent.* d 8 q 2 art. 2 [fol 71 E.] Though this is an expression of the general theological principle that God's *opera ad extra sunt una* and of the special nominalistic insistence on the simplicity of God, the application is Gregory's.

[102] ". . . contingit excessive sperare bona futura sicut patet in presumptuosis et diminute sicut in desperantibus. . ." III *Sent.* d 26 q 1 art. 1 nota 2 C. Cf. *ibid.*, art. 3 dub. 5. ". . . spes tendit in deum desiderio ei fiducialiter adherendo tanquam infinite largitati." *Ib.* art. 1 nota 2 C col. 2. Cf. Occam: ". . . hoc complexum sit subiectum spei: visio et fruitio divina est homini conferenda propter merita." III *Sent.* q 8 G.

[103] This group is the *iactantes* condemned by the Council of Trent: ". . . nemini tamen fiduciam et in ea sola quiescenti peccata dimitti vel dimissa esse dicendum est. . ." Sessio VI. cap. 9; Denz 802.

It is revealing to note that the parable of the prodigal son, which Biel must have had in mind, has the father take initiative on points where the boy of Biel's parable has to act himself. But the decisive difference is that the father of Luke 15:11 ff. does not have to be moved from justice to mercy, but runs out to meet his son, moved by sheer love.[104]

4 Fiducial certainty

For a proper understanding of the kerygma of Biel implicit in his academic works and explicit in his sermons, the oscillation between the fear and love of God in the heart of the sinner cannot be sufficiently stressed. The effort to find the exact balance by weighing the one against the other is the theme which returns in various forms but is most often expressed by a three-stage argument.

(1) By fear we do not honor God but detest him as a tyrant. In that case our respect for God is not true but fictitious. It has to be because we do not know him as the one who in the Incarnation comes to this world in love; and one cannot love — and thus not properly prepare for the encounter with — a person who is an unknown entity. We may conclude that faith must first provide proper knowledge of God. Apart from faith God is the unknown entity, the God of the countless possibilities of the *potentia absoluta*. It seems that it is at this point that we come closest to understanding Biel's motive for rejecting Scotus' *parum attritus* concept: the *parum attritus* does not know the God of the *potentia ordinata*, God, as he has revealed himself and as he can be known in faith.[105]

(2) We have to know the ineffable love of God to acquire in response love for him. This love appears in the examination of Christ who took

---

[104] "Dicis: Quomodo fugiam ad eum cuius iudicium pertimesco. Disce a puerulo parabolam: deprehensus a patre in aliquo sibi vetito, nullum videns fuge presidium, proiicit que male tenuit, currit ad patrem, preoccupat virgam, amplectitur iratum, spondet emendam, ut tandem habeat placatum; tu quoque fac similiter. Proiice que male contra illum tenuisti, occurre, paterna implora viscera, misericordiam appellato, propone emendam et mutabit vindicte sententiam, si tu mutaveris vitam. . ." *S* I 7 F.

[105] "Incognitum amari non potest nec digne suscipi qui non amatur; quoniam etsi per timorem nonnunquam reveremur quorum tyrannidem formidamus. Non est ista reverentia interior cordialis et vera sed exterior verbalis et ficta quam dominus qui tanquam sponsus plenus amore venit, non acceptat sed detestatur." *S* I 7 A.

the form of a servant in order to save inveterate sinners. This makes clear that he did not come in punishing righteousness but in gentle mercy. As the kenosis brings forth the response of love, so the fact that he did not empty himself for his own sake, but *pro nobis*, evokes in us the security of faith, *fiducia*. In summary we may say that *the witness of the Church concerning the opus spei of Christ provides the certainty of faith which leads to the security of hope and the perfection of love*.[106]

(3) While the love of God is the psychological impact of the past on the present, the resulting response of love is matched by the fear of God, based on the coming judgment. Christ has indeed opened the doors of salvation, but now we have to enter through them by subjugating our *asinus*, the exterior man, to the rule of Christ, the law. Otherwise we would reap damnation from grace.[107]

The coming of Christ is not a mere fact that belongs to past history: Christ is still present but now first of all as judge. Though he is at the right hand of God, he is still present among us by keeping a close watch

---

[106] ". . . sponte nos avertimus, eum magis magisque offendendo contempsimus et corda nostra penitus induravimus, ita ut servos vocantis nos contumeliis et morte afficeremus. Et is qui offensus est qui se vindicare potuit quia omnipotens, inimicos suos dilexit, ipse omnium summus pro nihilo in peccatore se exinanivit, formam servi accepit, ovem perditam quesivit, vocavit verbis, allexit beneficiis, portavit in humeris, debitum mortis ipse moriens solvit ut nihil sibi sed nobis inimicis suis et contemptoribus vitam eternam, nostra sponte perditam, recuperaret et non iuxta merita nostra per iusticiam damnaret. . . [C] Ex quibus patet veniendi modus qui fuit in misericordia et mansuetudine, non iusticia et severitate. . . [D]. Quia vero non sibi sed nobis venit cum magna gratiarum actione totam spem nostram et fiduciam in eum proiiciamus. . . [E]. Necesse est ut ei fide recta, spe secura, charitateque perfecta adhereamus. . . Ex his in nobis oritur charitas et dilectio qua eum diligimus, nedum amore concupiscentie sed et amicicie." *S* I 1 C ff. "Sacrarum scripturarum ac verbi dei consolationem qua spem excitat futurorum promissione. Fidem fundant factorum narratione. Charitatem accendunt beneficiorum dei multiplici narratione." *S* I 2 G.

[107] "Sed nunc charissimi, nos qui plenitudine temporis quo gratia et veritas per christum facta sunt, in esse prodivimus de somno torporis et inertie evigilemus, nostram salutem operaturi. . . Nunc enim propior est nostra salus, tempore scil. isto gratie quo per christum ianua salutis est aperta quam cum credidimus scil. tempore legis, quo salutis adhuc ianua erat clausa. . . Solvamus asinum nostrum educentes ex stabulo fetenti nostre carnalitatis. . . Ne etiamsi iam venientem audire contemnimus: de gratie exhibita plenitudine nostram damnationem exageremus . . . [H] . . . ad consequendum fructum dominice incarnationis necesse est exteriorem hominem nostrum a vinculis mundane conversationis solvere et sessioni christi i.e. divino regimini subiugare. Divinum regimen est regimen secundum leges et precepta." *S* I 2 E.

on our response to his coming and our preparation for the encounter with him.[108] We should serve the Lord as one who is with us and can see us.[109] The same attitude of respect, diligence, and fear as characterizes the relation of the serf to his master, the underling to the judge and the pauper to the prince, should mark our attitude to Christ.[110]

In this context also, the concept "by the merits and grace of Christ alone" is operative; but whereas under (2) it expresses the spontaneous love and mercy of God shown in Jesus Christ, here it functions as a weapon against idle presumption: the merits of Christ are the gifts of God and not ours! This fear results in humility, the basic virtue necessary for the inhabitation of Christ. Humility is therefore not "Abgeschiedenheit" or passivity but an intensely active hope of acquiring what is not ours.[111]

Summarizing, we may conclude that though under (1) the anxiety of servile fear is rejected as dishonest, in (3) the *opus iusticie* is stressed to the point that the joyful trust and confidence in God, so clearly stated in (2), assumes almost the same characteristics as those of servile fear. Nevertheless, there is an important difference between (1) and (3): In the first case God is viewed as the tyrant; God is seen as the unknown entity apart from revelation, the arbitrary God of the *potentia absoluta*. The knowledge of faith is the reliable information of Scripture and Church which does away with this distorted concept of God. The true knowledge of God, the God of revelation and thus of the *potentia*

---

[108] "Nec quem moveat quod omnia illa iam transierunt et christus mortuus est ac resurrexit etc. Iam enim in celo ad dexteram patris collocatus diligenter attendit et considerat qualiter se unusquisque servorum eius ad digne commemorandum et celebrandum eius nativitatem preparat." *S* I 1 F. On the mystical quality of this encounter, see Chapter Ten, section III.

[109] ". . . quia deus sine mutabilitate cuncta simul respicit et bona que ad vitam remunerat et mala que iudicans damnat. Nihil eius cognitionem preterit, nihil in oblivionem transit." *S* I 7 E.

[110] "Hi, si dominum presentem et videntem crederent, saltem hunc honorem, diligentiam et timorem servarent ad eum quos ad terrenum dominum custodit servus subditus ad iudicem, ad principem quoque pauper." *S* I 7 H. Cf. G.

[111] "Cum solo merito christi ac gratia christi dona dei recipimus que non nostra sed dei sunt bona. Propter quod dominus ait: 'Nemo bonus nisi solus deus' [Luc 18:19] . . . Ecce humilitatem preparantis viam domini. Hunc imitemur si dominum habitatorem nostrum desideramus. . . Studeamus ergo, charissimi, corde humiliari quia sine humilitate virtus nulla est. . ." *S* I 8 C. For a discussion of humility and inhabitation, see Chapter Ten, section III.

226

ordinata, is expressed in (2) and (3). In (3) God is the judge who will pass judgment according to well-known and established rules, the law of the Old and New Testament, not arbitrarily but justly. The meaning of the considerations under (2) is that God has provided in his first advent a reliable object for the hope of the *viator*.

The mercy of the Incarnation is indeed "pro nobis." But this mercy of God expresses only God's motive for establishing the present order of justice; his mercy is shown and offered in Jesus Christ. One can only profit from it by acquiring merits through fulfilling the law in its totality according to the example of Christ in his earthly life.

5. The *pro nobis* theme: *sola fide* and *sola gratia* rejected

As we have noted before, the Gabrielistic kerygma of the Incarnation has the psychological function of stimulating responsive love in the heart of the sinner. The kerygma of the last judgment has the psychological function of stimulating fear. The decisive question which now arises from our discussion of Biel's teaching with regard to certainty of salvation is: what does it mean existentially for the *viator* living between past and future? In answer we can say: the Christian can have and has to have an objective *certitude of faith*, that is, he can rely on the veracity of the articles of faith since God is truth, and therefore all that God has revealed is true.[112]

The *viator* cannot have a subjective certitude of salvation. He can be certain of the object of his hope, but not of the final satisfaction of his hope. He can have and has to have what Biel terms the *security of hope* or the *certitude of hope*. This may be clarified by a comparison of the status of the *viator* with that of the angels and the demons. Since the fall both these last groups are certain of their eternal destiny.[113] The *viator*, now, holds a middle position between the angel and the demon: the angel has certitude of salvation, the demon of damnation. The security or certitude of the *viator* differs from the situation of the demon in that to the

---

[112] ". . . habens fidem non credit articulum verum esse ex evidentia obiecti, sed ex hoc quia assentit veracitati dei asserentis. . . Omne revelatum a deo est verum in sensu quo revelatur esse verum. . ." III *Sent.* d 23 q 2 art. 1 G H, col. 2; ". . . certitudo fidei (que est quedam infallibilitas) non innititur necessitati veritatis credite, sed divine revelationi que fallere non potest. . ." *Ibid.* E.

[113] II *Sent.* d 4 q 1 art. 1 E *in fine*.

objective knowledge of faith, the qualification "pro nobis" is attached. In comparison with the angel who never fell, however, the *viator* lacks the gift of stability.[114]

Since Christ is present as judge since the Ascension, the psychological impact of the future judgment weighs heavier than the psychological impact of the past. The certitude of faith and the security of hope do not add up to certitude of salvation due to the emphasis on the *opus iusticie* of Christ.

Two points have to be mentioned here. First, in anticipation of our discussion of mystical elements in the theology of Biel, we must add that Christ is present not only as the judge but also as the bridegroom: he wants to live in the soul of every Christian; this inhabitation is necessary for salvation. But he can only come in the present after the requirements of the judge have been fulfilled.[115] Second, even within the order of justice there is a certain flexibility due to the mercy of God. On this ground God will not punish the commission of venial sins by withdrawing the habit of grace. Here we meet again the understanding of the sinner on the road to justification as partly *iustus*, partly *peccator*. Biel's comment that one is thus not obliged to punctilious justice makes clear that this latitude is more a form of permissiveness than of compassion.[116]

While it had been Biel's point of departure to say that no certitude of salvation is possible, we find him at many places stressing the importance and the possibility of the conjectural certainty. This can be stressed to the

---

[114] ". . . propinquiores fuerunt ad gloriam quam nos viatores variis miseriis subiecti et nos habemus certitudinem spei." II *Sent.* d 4 q 1 art. 3 dub. 2. Biel feels that before the fall the good angels did not yet have *certitudo salutis* but *certitudo probabilis*: "supposito quod conditi essent ornati gratuitis habuerunt confidentiam non solum ex naturalibus sed etiam ex gratia quod perventuri essent ad gloriam," *ibid.*

[115] "Felix enim et superfelix domus que meretur habitatorem christum. Non enim illum domus sed ille domum suam conservat et beatificat in eternum. Ad huius domus preparationem tota vigilemus diligentia ut complaceat domino habitare in ea et nos in eternum beatificare. Consistit hec preparatio in fide recta quoad intellectum, in humilitate profunda quoad affectum, in obedientia perfecta quoad executivam." *S* I 8 A.

[116] ". . . voluntatis rectitudo admittit aliquam obliquitatem et hoc ex divina misericordia que superexaltat iudicium qua noluit obligare hominem ad punctualem iusticiam. . . Condescendit siquidem nostre infirmitati et iugum leve onusque suave imposuit, conformitatem nostre voluntatis que est nostra iusticia ponens non in indivisibili sed in certa latitudine que est inter precepta." *S* II 4 J. Cf. K.

point that he seems to promise real certainty of being in a state of grace.[117] On closer investigation it is clear, however, that this certainty is not more than conjecture, exposed to exactly the same tension as described above. Biel's disciple Bartholomaeus von Usingen stresses the same point.[118]

Usually three signs of conjectural certainty are indicated: genuine love for Christ through which one is incorporated into him; the firm determination to conform to the will of God in imitation of Christ who showed us that we also have to fulfill the law in its totality; and finally fear of the coming judgment.[119] The seventeen points of advice with which Biel ends his special lecture on the manifold temptations that accompany the *viator* can be reduced to the same three basic points.[120]

In line with the constant warning in his sermons about the presump-

---

[117] "Sed quia non sufficit ad salutem expulsio nisi in digito dei eiiciatur, laborandum nobis est ut sciamus si sic eiectus sit a nobis. . . His signis in nobis compertis possumus scire nos eiicere vel eiecisse demonia in digito dei." *S* I 30 C and F.

[118] "Permixta sunt ergo in evangelio iucunditas et metus ut unum temperet alterum ne vel desperemus vel ne presumamus: sic enim ambulat vita fidelium in hac valle lacrimarum inter spem et metum. Tu autem totus iucundaris ex evangelio tuo. . ." Usingen, *Libellus . . . Contra Lutheranos*, fol. J 3ᵛ. A more perceptive description of the difference between the theology of late medieval nominalism and that of the Reformation on this point would be hard to find.

[119] "Qui ergo credit in christum ei amore inherendo hic habet testimonium. Refert autem credere deum et in deum. Credere in deum non est sine spe et charitate. Credit ergo in eum qui ei charitate unitur et incorporatur. . . Secundum signum est propositum de recuperando iusticiam neglectam. Hoc est propositum firmum conformandi se voluntati divine. Iusticia enim de qua spiritus sanctus mundum arguit est iusticia legalis non particularis, scilicet efficax impletio omnis paterne voluntatis et obediens subiectio toti legi. . . Misericordie fuit quod causam nostram agendo peccata nostra portavit in corpore suo super lignum. Iusticie fuit quod post gloriosum mortis triumphum ad patrem rediit. Hec enim iusta quedam merces fuit obedientie illius. . . 'Si vis ad vitam ingredi, serva mandata.' Mat. 19[:17] Tota vero iusticia est legis observatio. Hanc vero christum tenuisse probat patens ascensus eius ad patrem; si enim iniustus et non ex deo fuisset. . . ad patrem non ascendisset. Tertium signum est. Si timemus iudicium finale futurum. . . Si enim nos hic iudicaverimus concipientes propositum salubre vivendi deo non iudicabimur a domino. Ideo hoc attendamus arguentem spiritum et reformemur ad eius correptionem: ut ibi eum habeamus eundem nos salvantem et omnia remittentem . . . imitemur iusticiam eius qui ascendit ad patrem, non patiamur frustrari exemplar nobis ostensum. . . Timeamus iudicium quia si princeps mundi huius iudicatus est. . . quid de nobis fiet? Hec cogitantes et opere perficientes testimonium habemus spiritus sancti presentie." *S* I 44 G. Cf. *S* I 45 B. *S* I 66 D.

[120] *Lect.* 77 T; II *Sent.* d 21 q 1 does not suggest remedies.

tuous who think that they can be saved *sola fide* and *sola gratia*,[121] Biel declares the peace of the absence of temptations to be the most dangerous of all the tricks of the devil. This kind of peace leads to an empty security which lays the Christian wide open to unexpected attacks of the devil.[122] This idle security is the exact opposite of the security of hope which is marked, as was mentioned before, by the intensive activity of humility and fear.[123] This definition of the greatest temptation is, of course, by inversion the most effective consolation for those who are heavily tempted.[124]

It is here, we would suggest, that we find the explanation as to why Biel can at once stress the combination of fear and love and the necessity of ascertaining whether one is in a state of grace: *the constant oscillation between love and fear is in itself a sign for the viator that he is still on the road to the heavenly Jerusalem and that he is sufficiently prepared for the inhabitation of Christ.*[125]

[121] ". . . damnatur eorum error qui putant ad salutem sibi sufficere fidem informem cum baptismo." *S* I 9 E. Cf. *S* I 19 C. Gerson says the same, e.g., in *Contra heresim de communione laicorum sub utraque specie*, in *Opera* I.458 A. It is therefore remarkable that Biel can admonish to "return to one's baptism" as the eleventh advice for Christians in temptation: ". . . consideratio quod consecrati sumus in baptismo et quod caracterem christi et imaginem vivam sancte trinitatis gerimus." *Lect.* 77 T. Another aspect of presumptuousness, like faith without good works, is faith without Bible study: ". . . sunt et presumptuosi qui sine scripture studio sibi sufficere putant." *Lect.* 71 I. D'Ailly mentions another form of "return to one's baptism." In case the wish to be baptised was fictitious, the effect is indeed the ablution of sins but grace is granted only at the moment of contrition: ". . . conteri debet de fictione et tunc suscipit gratiam et virtutem suam obtineret sacramentum." *Sacramentale seu Tractatus Theologicus de Sacramentis*, cap. 7 E.

[122] "Septima diaboli astutia et omnium periculosissima est ipsa pax, id est cessatio a perceptibilibus tentationibus . . . est fatua securitas qua negligitur dei timor qui est electorum vigilantissimus simul et fidelissimus custos. . . Hec enim securitas facit nos seorsum a cura et sollicitudine custodienda et per hoc exponit nos hostibus totos incautos." *Lect.* 77 N.

[123] "Si hec feceritis . . . possitis securi coram homine rege comparere, rationem de actibus vestris singulis reddituri," *S* I 101 D.

[124] Ernst Wolf has shown, Staupitz was able to help Luther in his despair in relation to the uncertainty of predestination. *Staupitz und Luther*, p. 217. Still it may be important to note that Staupitz could have drawn on suggestions of Biel. The difference is that Biel would not point to the wounds, but rather to the cradle and the Ascension of Christ as the centre of the *opus spei*.

[125] "Sicut infirmus cui predixit medicus quod operante medicina salutem tales inducet viscerum torsiones et puncturas . . . gaudet, sperans quia appropinquit sanitas corporalis. Ita et his in nobis incipientibus dum contenebratur sol naturalis

6. *Theologia crucis* in Gerson and Biel

Finally, at the end of this analysis of Biel's doctrine of the security of hope, we are prepared to ask in what exactly the fiducial character of the relation of the *viator* to Jesus Christ consists. For a wider perspective, we have to call on Jean Gerson who, far more than Biel's other authorities, shares with him a deep pastoral interest in the spiritual life of the individual Christian. We have noted above that both reject full certainty of salvation as a sophistic inspiration of the devil. In accordance with the most common medieval opinion, both make an exception to this rule for special revelation.[126]

Gerson, like Biel, sees in the Christian hope the middle road between despair and presumptuousness.[127] Again as with Biel, Gerson sees the Christian charged with the task of constantly ascertaining whether he is in a state of grace, and whether he may count himself among the elect.[128] And Gerson is aware also of the precariously narrow road between despair and presumption and the constant effort of the devil to unbalance the *viator* one way or the other.[129] But an important difference between Gerson and Biel comes to the fore in their discussion of possible remedies against these temptations.

---

intelligentie, dans locum lumini gratie etc. gaudendum nobis est spiritualiter in tribulatione. . . Scientes quod non aliter spei nostre caput levare possumus hic et in futuro. . ." *S* I 4 E.

[126] "Vitalis presentia spiritus sancti in nobis, quibus signis agnoscitur et si certitudo in se possit haberi. Respondetur quod certitudo moralis bene habetur, non simplex et absoluta; nisi per revelationem." Gerson, "Sermo de Sancto Spiritu," Consideratio 3 in *Opera* II. 42 C.

[127] ". . . circumcidentes omnem errorem et superstitionem per fidem, omnem desperationem et presumptionem per spem. . ." Gerson, "Sermo habitus Tarascone in die Circumcisionis;" *Opera* II. 58 A. Cf. Holcot: "Superior et inferior mola spes et timor. Spes ad alta subvenit. Timor ad inferius premit. Una mola sine altera inutiliter habetur. In peccatoris ergo pectore semper debent spes et formido coniungi quia incassum misericordiam sperat si iusticiam non timeat. Et incassum metuit qui non confidit." *Sap.* Lect. 150 D. Cf. *Sap.* Lect. 153 B.

[128] "Faciat igitur quilibet per bona opera vocationem suam certam, ne ab expectatione nostra nos confundat Deus." Gerson, *De Absolutione Sacramentali* in *Opera* II. 410 C.

[129] *Sermo de tentatione*, in *Opera* III. 1062 ff.; Cf. III. 582 ff.; III. 1495 ff.; IV. 359 ff.; IV. 370 ff. A special study on Gerson's understanding of temptations and their remedies would be most welcome. In the following, we have to limit ourselves to the more central points.

We should like to call attention to an autobiographical passage hitherto overlooked in which Gerson relates how a certain Agnes, a relative of Pope Urban V, asked him once what the most powerful antidote against temptations would be. Before he could answer, Agnes herself said: "the cross." Gerson continues by describing this event as though it were a real *Turmerlebnis*. This answer came to him as a revelation from heaven; thus the cross of Christ became for him the most concentrated and effective weapon against the devil and the most helpful consolation in despair.[130]

However, while this *theologia crucis* may have been essential for Gerson personally, this is not always apparent in other passages in his writings: dealing with the problem of despair and fear of damnation, he points time and again merely to conjectural certainty and to the great value of temptation since it leads "per desperationem ad spem." [131] Like Biel he encourages those who despair by pointing to God's mercy,[132] and

[130] "Interrogavit me pridem virgo . . . nomine Agnes, propinqua quondam Urbani Papae V: 'Quod est potissimum contra diaboli tentationes subsidium?' Dum suspenderem ego cogitabundus responsionem: ipsa subintulit mox: *crux.* Suscepi protinus hanc vocem quasi de coelo sonuisset et ita sonuerat . . . non invenio compendiosius, non efficacius antidotum. . . *O crux ave spes unica*"; *Super Magnificat* VIII in *Opera* IV. 360 A. It belongs to the small ironies of history that the same author has written: "Omnis doctrina mulierum maxime solemnis verbo vel scripto reputanda est suspecta. . ." *De examinatione doctrinarum*, cons. 2 in *Opera* I. 15 A. An isolated parallel to the *Super Magnificat* passage cited above appears in Biel *S* IV 29 D.

More noteworthy is that this *Turmerlebnis* has escaped the attention of Gerson biographers and Luther scholars alike. The usual discussion of Gerson's wrestling with scruples in his younger years is limited to relatively unrevealing passages as *Opera* IV. 727 ff., and the passages dealing with the *nocturna pollutio*. Cf. Henry Strohl, *L'évolution réligieuse de Luther jusqu'en 1515* (Strasbourg, 1922), p. 108; Otto Scheel (1917), II, 127; Alphons V. Müller, *Luthers Werdegang bis zum Turmerlebnis neu untersucht*, (Gotha, 1920), p. 76 ff; James L. Connolly, *John Gerson: Reformer and Mystic* (Louvain, 1928), p. 358; Helmut Appel, *Anfechtung und Trost im Spätmittelalter und bei Luther* (Leipzig, 1938), p. 35; Wilhelm Link, *Das Ringen Luthers*, p. 296 ff. That Luther did not note this line in Gerson's thought can be explained as due to the fact that he — as far as we can ascertain — was not familiar with the *Super Magnificat*. Luther noted the main line of argumentation: "Gersonis tres veritates: poenitere, emendare vitam, confiteri." *WA TR* I. nr. 104; quoted by Scheel, *Dokumente zu Luthers Entwicklung*, nr. 188, p. 73.

[131] *De Consolatione Theologiae*, IV. 2 in *Opera* I. 173 D. This whole treatise is especially dedicated to the problem of predestination and despair.

[132] " . . . damnandus in curia Iusticie habeat aditum cum fiducia ad Thronum gratie eius que [sic] salvat damnantes se . . . ," *Opera* I. 173 A. Müller, who

those who relax in vain security by referring them to the judgment of God.[133]

Taking everything into account, it does not appear that the Doctor Consolatorius differs from Biel in his method of using the mercy and justice of God in order to keep the *viator* well balanced, and to refer him to the conjectural certainty based on self-analysis. The object of analysis is the *facere quod in se est*, which in its turn assures one of the absolution of sins in the sacrament of penance.[134]

This survey of Gerson's position enables us, however, to note an important difference between Biel and Gerson. Where the *opus spei* of Christ for Gerson is concentrated in the kerygma of the cross, we found that Biel primarily stresses the Incarnation. Thus, the fiducial hope of the *viator* is not so much evoked by the crucified Christ as by the Christ of the exinanition. There is with Biel also a theology of the cross, but this is limited to a discussion of the objective work of Christ through his self-sacrifice and his victory over the devil. As far as the kerygma of the cross is concerned, it is clear that the relevance of the cross as consolation for the *viator* in despair is negligible. Seldom does Biel speak about the consolation of the cross. In his discussion of the word from the cross: "it is finished," he makes the point that Jesus said this with much sorrow since he knew that only a few would benefit from his sacrifice. The consolation of the cross is therefore limited.[135] This is the high point of what Biel calls the *conditio testamenti*.

---

regards this passage as crucial and extraordinary, has failed to see that the context is that of a real dialogue, p. 81; Gerson judges the weight of this argument more soberly than Müller when he lets Monicus answer: "Talia frequenter [!] audivi, Volucer," *Opera* I. 173 A.

[133] "Neque enim est alia veritas efficacius generativa timoris domini . . . ," *Opera* I. 133 C.

[134] Notwithstanding the limitations of Gerson's theology of the cross, its appearance as such indicates its compatibility with mysticism. See, however, Walther von Loewenich: "Von ihrem Zentrum aus gesehen bilden Mystik und theologia crucis die schroffste Antithese," *Luthers Theologia Crucis*, 4 ed. (Munich, 1954), p. 209. Given his concept of mysticism, von Loewenich is right. For another interpretation of mysticism see Chapter Ten, sections I and II.

[135] "Consummatus est labor et pena pro redemptione hominis usque ad expirationem proximam. Videri posset hoc verbum esse consolationis pro durissimorum laborum expletione. Sed non sine dolore nimio hoc dixit quia noverat hunc paucis prodesse, ingratis obesse. Hinc dominus ipse, misericordiarum pater, qui vult omnes homines salvos fieri, satis et supra pro omnibus laboravit, offerens passionem suam efficaciter pro electis tantum; horum paucitatem, prescitorum multitudinem videns

If we can characterize this in any sense as a "theology of the cross," it can hardly be characterized as a *kerygma* of the cross.[136] At some points it would even seem that the Incarnation itself would have been sufficient for the redemption of mankind.[137] Biel goes very far indeed in stressing the life of Christ at the expense of the death of Christ. It is not only the Incarnation itself which for Biel forms the *opus spei*. Christ took the form of a slave to fulfill in all humility the law in its totality. Thus he earned for himself eternal glory.[138] By fulfilling the law Christ set the example, escaped the clutches of the devil, and showed the possibility of man's elevation to the ranks of the blessed: this is the significance of the Ascension.

The *fiducia* of the *viator*, in the theology of Gabriel Biel, rests on the

---

abundantes lachrimas fudit." *S* II 24 pars 4 art. 3.6. Cf. *S* I 64 F; *Lect.* 54 B. Bruno Dreher has pointed to the equally striking absence in Biel of a kerygma of the resurrection in *Die Osterpredigt von der Reformation bis zur Gegenwart* (Freiburg i.Br., 1951), p. 31 ff. His statement, "dass in der breiten Masse der Predigten keine wesentliche Heilsfrage mehr gestellt wurde" (p. 26), certainly does not apply either to Biel or to late medieval preaching in general. Furthermore, it must be noted that for Biel the resurrection is the beginning of the Ascension which — as we saw — is a central part of Biel's kerygma. Gerson's emphasis is also echoed once by Biel, *S* IV 29 D. See also Chapter Eight, note 79.

[136] This is the only point, insofar as I can see, where Usingen deviates from Biel; see his *Sermo de sancta cruce predicatus erphurdie* (Erphurdie, 1524): ". . . non minus in cruce christi gloriantur cum opera illa aliunde meritoria non sint, quam ex gratia, quam nobis christus meruit in cruce." *Libellus . . . contra Lutheranos*, fol. 4ᵛ. Cf. fol. G 3ᵛ, K 2ᵛ. We must take into consideration the fact that Usingen answers the Lutheran challenge: "Paulus nescit gloriationem quam in cruce," *ibid.* fol. 4ᵛ.

[137] "Ecce quanta perfectio doctrine initialis christi que etiam sola videtur sufficere ad salutem," *S* I 10 F.

[138] "Non debet quemquam deterrere laboris magnitudo si delectat resurrectionis gloria et premii celsitudo. Ad magna enim premia non pervenitur nisi per magnos labores. Et cum beatitudo sit premium pro meritis reddendum, ex divina tamen misericordia potissimum donandum preexigit meritum. Christi denique actio nostra est instructio. Et non est discipulus super magistrum. Ideo necesse est ea via consequi beatitudinem qua et christus ingressus est in gloriam suam. Luce ultimo. Hec doctrina ex evangelio colligitur cum dominus ait: 'Mulier cum parit tristiciam habet, cum autem natus est. . .'" *S* I 43 D, E. "Iusticie fuit quod post gloriosum mortis triumphum ad patrem rediit. Hec enim iusta quedam merces fuit obedientie illius. . . Merito ergo mundus de iusticia christi qua ad patrem vadit arguitur: qui que sua sunt querit: non que iesu christi, per inobedientiam et non impletionem legis. . ." *S* I 44 G. ". . . imitemur iusticiam eius qui ascendit ad patrem non patiamur frustrari exemplar nobis ostensum. . ." *S* I 44 G.

kerygma of the Incarnation and Ascension of Jesus Christ.[139] Since this fiducial hope would stand or fall with the true humanity of Christ, one can well understand that Biel must try to be extremely careful in his application of the *communicatio idiomatum* and his interpretation of the hypostatic union.

The tension between fiducial hope and the divine nature of Christ is not resolved within the realm of Christology. As we will see, it proves to be this tension which forms the matrix of a central point in Biel's mariological teaching.

We may conclude that between this kind of *fiducia* and the certitude of salvation stands the categorical imperative of the law of the Old and the New Testament. It is the same movement from mercy to justice that we observed in the doctrine of predestination and justification which stimulates the *viator* to earn his salvation in fear and trembling in a constant oscillation between despair and presumption.[140]

II. *Sola Fide* and *Sola Gratia* in the Theology of Holcot

1. *Sola fide tenetur*: Holcot's scepticism

When the English nominalist and Dominican friar Robert Holcot reaches the sixteenth verse of the seventh chapter in his *Wisdom* commentary, he seizes the opportunity to underscore his main theme

[139] "Immensitas misericordie et charitas qua salvare vult patet . . . hec est mira dei exinanitio et condescensio:

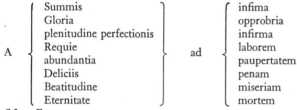

S I 55 E.

[140] Though no sermons of Occam are preserved, the indicated doctrinal parallels between Occam and Biel force us to disagree with Hochstetter's conclusion: ". . . das Wesen Gottes ist amor und dilectio absoluta. . . Ausgeschlossen ist damit jedoch das, wogegen sich Ockham, stärker noch als Duns, mit seinem immer wiederkehrenden Aufweis der zwar durch das Prinzip des Nichtwiderspruchs, aber nicht durch irgendwelche Verbindlichkeiten begrenzten Allmacht Gottes zu wehren sucht: das Eindringen des Rechtsdenkens in die christliche Theologie." "Viator Mundi," pp. 19–20.

which he had so passionately presented on the preceding pages as well as in his *Sentences* commentary: Wisdom is a gift of God: therefore man's claim that he can have a natural knowledge of God is false.

We should not be tempted to regard this statement as the solution of a Christian obscurantist who, bewildered by the challenging claims of philosophy, *scientia*, withdraws into the safe citadel of theology, *sapientia*. The riddle of Holcot's place in the medieval history of the relation of faith and reason forces itself upon the reader. In this one lecture both the inaccessibility of true knowledge of God and the accuracy of the natural knowledge of God on the part of the great philosophers is brought out.

It is first emphasized that the wisdom of God stands over against the wisdom of man since "we preach Christ crucified, a stumbling-block to Jews and folly to Gentiles." [141] Nevertheless at the climax of this same discussion, Holcot introduces an extensive quotation from the source of all pagan philosophy, Hermes Trismegistos! He gives as his reference the eleventh book of the *De natura deorum*, and cites a passage which forms the last part of *Asclepius* in the *Corpus Hermeticum*.[142] Holcot's purpose is to show that Hermes knows that God is self-sufficient. For Hermes, God has no need to receive anything from man, and so it makes no sense to burn incense for him. On the contrary, man depends on God for everything, including his wisdom; thanksgiving is therefore the best incense man can offer God.[143] Notwithstanding the fact that Hermes is a pagan, Holcot observes, he returns his thanks to God in everything.[144]

It is not the choice of Hermes Trismegistos which is the surprising element here. Holcot's contemporary Thomas Bradwardine, who had a career remarkably similar to that of Holcot, also likes to quote Hermes and regards him as "Father of the philosophers." [145] Both Bradwardine

[141] I Cor. 1:23; *Super Libros Sapientie* (Hagenau, 1494) *Sap.* Lect. 97 A.

[142] *Sap.* Lect. 97 B = *Asclepius* 41; *Corpus Hermeticum*, II, Texte établi par A. D. Nock et traduit par A. J. Festugière (Paris, 1946), pp. 352–355.

[143] "Melius hominum naribus apponere, asclepi. Hoc enim sacrilegi simile est cum deum roges thus ceteraque incendere. Nihil enim deest ei. Et quia ipse est omnia et in eo sunt omnia, sed nos agentes gratias adoremus. Hee sunt enim summe incentiones cum gratie deo aguntur a mortalibus. . . In hora enim ista adorantes te bone voluntatis tue. Hoc tantum deprecamur ut nos observare digneris perseverantes in amore cognitionis tue et numquam ab hoc gratie vite genere separari." *Sap.* Lect. 97 B. The most radically different reading in the critical edition is that of the first sentence: "Melius, melius ominare, Asclepi," *ibid.*, II, 352.

[144] ". . . sic deo regratiatur quamvis gentilis," *ibid.*

[145] "Pater philosophorum," *De causa dei contra Pelagium et de virtute causarum*.

and Holcot in the thirties of the fourteenth century were part of the household of Richard de Bury, Bishop of Durham.[146] Arthur Darby Nock, in his introduction to the critical edition of *Asclepius*, has called attention to the familiarity with the *Corpus Hermeticum* which de Bury's important *Philobiblon* reveals.[147] In view of the fact that Holcot and Bradwardine had access to the same library, it does not surprise us that a part of Hermes' prayer at the end of *Asclepius* appears not only in Holcot's *Super libros Sapientie*, but also in Bradwardine's *De causa dei*.[148]

But here then arises the problem: it is by no means extraordinary that Thomas Bradwardine, whose first axiom is Anselm's ontological proof of God's existence, draws on the wisdom of pagan philosophers.[149] The consistent theme of the first book of *De causa dei* is the concordance of philosophy and theology,[150] and quotations from Hermes serve to show that philosophy provides a reliable natural theology.[151] Holcot, however, does not share Bradwardine's confidence in the capacities of natural reason, and he does not tire of showing that it is impossible to prove that God exists: "hec propositio est mere credita" [152] or "sola fide tenetur." [153]

Opera et studio Henrici Savilii (Londini, 1618), I.1.141 C; I.2.149 D. Cf. Oberman, *Bradwardine*, p. 24.

[146] Oberman, *Bradwardine*, p. 43.

[147] *Corpus Hermeticum*, II, 273. On the connection between Holcot and de Bury, see J. de Ghellinck, "Un évêque bibliophile au xive siècle," *Revue d'historie ecclésiastique* 18 (1922), p. 495. On the long debated possibility of Holcot's authorship of the *Philobiblon* see *Philobiblon: Richard de Bury*, ed. Michael Maclagan (Oxford, 1960), p. xxxv ff. Since no clear evidence is available Maclagan makes the plea: "It seems simpler to suppose that Richard de Bury was in fact himself the author of the work which has so long borne his name; and it is certainly more agreeable to do so," *Philobiblon*, p. lxxvi. On Holcot's life and works see Beryl Smalley, "Robert Holcot O.P.," *Archivum Fratrum Praedicatorum* 26 (1956), 7–28. Cf. also "Some Latin Commentaries on the Sapiential Books in the Late Thirteenth and Early Fourteenth Centuries," *AHDL* 18 (1950–1951), 117–121.

[148] "Hoc, inquit [Hermes], loquens Deo deprecamur, ut nos velit servare perseverantes in amore cognitionis tuae et nunquam ab hoc vitae genere separari." *De causa dei*, I.6.182 A.

[149] *De causa dei*, I.1.2 E: "Nam necesse esse perfectius est et melius, quam possibile esse, praesertim in bono perfecto et summe perfecto."

[150] ". . . sicut tam philosophis quam theologis satis constat," I.12.200 E. Cf. I.4.172 B; I.9.194 C.

[151] I.2.154 C/D; I.2.155 B; I.2.157 B; I.10.195 E / 196 A; I.12.201 C; I.19.226 D.

[152] I *Sent.* q 4 art. 3 M.

[153] I *Sent.* q 4 art. 3 M; cf. *ibid.* R: "Ad argumenta probantia deum esse non esse mere creditum, sed naturali ratione scibile, dicitur, quod non."

This denial of the possibility of a natural knowledge of God has earned Holcot the reputation of a sceptic.[154] Gordon Leff, limiting his investigation to the *Sentences* commentary, concluded that "Robert Holcot well illustrates how fruitfully Ockham provided for his followers along the path to scepticism."[155] Beryl Smalley broadens the basis of judgment when she concludes that "Holcot admitted as an exegete to the scepticism that he professed as a theologian."[156] The implications of this charge of scepticism may appear from Miss Smalley's general conclusion: "Consistency was not Holcot's outstanding virtue as a thinker, unless it may be that he was true to his scepticism in his being inconsistent. Scepticism makes it difficult to hold a clear-cut theory in politics as in theology, witness William of Ockham."[157] Alois Meissner goes merely one step farther when he suggests that Holcot stands for a stark agnosticism as regards the possibility of a natural knowledge of God.[158] Though we cannot discuss the problem in all its dimensions, we should at least note that the issue before us transcends the importance of the individual case of Robert Holcot. The scepticism of Holcot has been seen as representative of nominalism as such and even as characteristic of the climate of the whole fourteenth century.[159]

If Holcot is indeed such a thoroughgoing sceptic and agnostic as

[154] C. Michalsky, "Les courants philosophiques à Oxford et à Paris pendant le xive siècle," Présenté 19 Jan. 1920, *Bulletin de l'Académie Polonaise des Sciences et des Lettres* (Cracow, 1920), p. 70; David Knowles, *The Religious Orders in England*, II (Cambridge, 1955), 80 ff.

[155] Leff, *Bradwardine and the Pelagians* (Cambridge, 1957), p. 216. Leff seems to qualify his judgment when he observes: "The human intellect can, by its own powers, believe that God is the highest good . . . ," p. 218. Leff has however misunderstood I *Sent.* q. 4 art. 3 M where Holcot categorically denies this possibility. Only when *assuming* that God exists one can show that He is to be loved above everything else: ". . . an deum esse super omnia diligendum possit naturali ratione demonstrari? Ubi dico duas conclusiones. Prima est hec cathegorica non potest naturali ratione probari: deus est diligendus ab homine super omnia. Secunda est hec hypothetica sive conditionalis potest naturali ratione probari: si deus est, deus est super omnia diligendus ab homine."

[156] "Robert Holcot," p. 82; *English Friars and Antiquity in the Early Fourteenth Century* (Oxford, 1960), pp. 183, 185 f.

[157] "Robert Holcot," p. 93; *English Friars*, p. 198.

[158] "Holkot vertritt in der behandelten Frage einen schroffen Agnostizismus, Fideismus und Traditionalismus," *Gotteserkenntnis und Gotteslehre nach dem Englischen Dominikanertheologen Robert Holkot* (Limburg a.d. Lahn, 1953), p. 30.

[159] Gordon Leff, *Gregory of Rimini: Tradition and Innovation in Fourteenth Century Thought* (Manchester, 1961), p. 19.

hitherto has been claimed, one wonders, of course, why he values so highly the authority of Hermes — or for that matter the authority of Socrates, Plato, and Aristotle.[160] If there is such a radical cleavage between the realm of reason and the realm of faith, what then can philosophers, and especially pagan philosophers offer to the field of natural theology? It is possible to answer this question by pointing out that Holcot holds the Augustinian [161] doctrine of an aboriginal revelation to Adam, his children and the holy prophets who handed this knowledge of God down in oral and written form. This revelation finally reached the Greek and pagan philosophers, who thus *received* but did not *produce* the knowledge of God.

Though this doctrine of 'the splendid pagans' or of the philosophical cloud of witnesses is not exclusively Augustinian — we find it, for example, also with Pelagius [162] — the fact that this revelation is a gift administered to the elect is a characteristic emphasis of Augustine.[163] In greater detail but true to Augustine's intention, Thomas Bradwardine shows that behind the natural theology of Hermes and Aristotle stands

---

[160] "Quarto dico quod de istis philosophis aut mundi sapientibus quidam in divino cultu secundum aliquos ritus et protestationes perstiterunt et salvati sunt, sicut constat de Iob, de Socrate, de Platone, Aristotele et plurima turba stoicorum presumi potest." III *Sent.* q 1 TT. Beryl Smalley quotes the parallel passage *Sap.* Lect. 156 A (in her numbering 157 A), "Robert Holcot," p. 84 f; *English Friars*, appendix I, p. 327 f.

[161] Holcot refers to *De Civitate Dei* 18.28; his inclusion of Job makes it likely that he rather has in mind *De Civitate Dei* 18.47: "An ante tempora christiana fuerint extra Israeliticum genus, qui ad coelestis civitatis consortium pertinerent . . . homines autem quosdam non terrena, sed coelesti societate ad veros Israelitas supernae cives patriae pertinentes etiam in aliis gentibus fuisse, negare non possunt, quia si negant facillime convincuntur de sancto et mirabili viro Job. . ."; *PL* XLI, 609. Cf. *Epistula* 102.2, 12: "Itaque ab exordio generis humani, quicumque in eum crediderunt . . ."; *PL* XXXIII, 374. *Epistula* 102.2, 15: ". . . nec qui in eum crederent defuerunt ab Adam usque ad Mosen . . . cur non credamus etiam in caeteris hac atque illac gentibus alias alios fuisse . . . nulli unquam defuit qui dignus fuit et cui defuit, dignus non fuit"; *PL* XXXIII, 376.

[162] *Epistula Pelagii ad Demetriadem* 3; *PL* XXX, 19.

[163] "Divinitus autem provisum fuisse non dubito, et ex hoc uno sciremus etiam per alias gentes esse potuisse qui secundum Deum vixerunt eique placuerunt, pertinentes ad spiritualem Jerusalem. Quod nemini concessum fuisse credendum est, nisi cui divinitus revelatus est unus mediator Dei et hominum homo Christus Jesus . . . ut una eademque per ipsum fides omnes in Dei civitatem, Dei domum, Dei templum praedestinatos perducat ad Deum." *De Civitate Dei* 18.47; *PL* XLI, 610.

ultimately the gift of revelation given to Seth, Enoch, Noah, Abraham, and Solomon.[164]

Holcot remains within this Augustinian tradition when he points out that all those who had knowledge of God without contact with Old Testament revelation were instructed by God rather than by their own rational argumentations. We are however forewarned that Holcot's position cannot simply be identified with that of Augustine by the fact that this gift of knowledge of God is not bestowed on the elect, but on those who live according to the principles of natural law.[165] Unlike Augustine and Bradwardine, Holcot is not interested in an aboriginal revelation to explain the great insights of Hermes and Aristotle. He is more interested in the general ethical corollary that such knowledge of God is available to all who live according to the principles of natural law. It is this peculiar emphasis which throws a very different light on Holcot's understanding of the relation of faith and reason than the traditional charge of scepticism has led us to believe.

In *Lectio* 28 of his *Wisdom* commentary, Holcot explicitly asks the crucial question whether there are Christian doctrines which transcend the power of reason, and yet still have to be revealed and believed since they are necessary for salvation.[166] Holcot first advances two arguments for the opposition: there are no such articles of faith which simultaneously transcend reason and are necessary for salvation since (1) nature does not fail in necessary things and therefore does not fail in establishing articles necessary for salvation; (2) certain doctrines such as those concerning Incarnation and transubstantiation are contrary to reason; since this implies a negation of the powers of reason, which is blameworthy, it is immoral to believe these articles of faith.[167]

---

[164] *De Causa Dei*, I.1.74 E–76 D.

[165] "Dico quod gentes que legem Moysi non habent, viventes secundum principia iuris naturalis, perceperunt fidem et gratiam a deo sine lege moysi et faciebant legem . . . instructi a deo, non per demonstrationes naturales. . ." I *Sent.* q 4 art. 3 Q ad 7.

[166] ". . . Utrum aliqua credenda supranaturalia fuerunt homini revelanda necessario ad salutem." *Sap.* Lect. 28 B.

[167] "Et videtur quod non, quia natura non deficit in necessariis . . . ergo per rationem naturalem potest homo acquirere omnem noticiam necessariam ad salutem. . . Preterea negare rationem est vituperabile; sed qui credit ea que rationi non consonat, negat rationem; ergo credere talia est vituperabile. Sed fides suadet credere talia que rationi repugnant sicut videtur de sacramento altaris et incarnatione filii dei et de multis talibus ergo, etc." *Sap.* Lect. 28 B.

It is not surprising that Holcot, along with the whole medieval tradition, rejects this concept of Christianity as a rational-natural religion.[168] What is important is the way in which he replies to the two arguments advanced.

In contrast to what one might expect of a radical sceptic, Holcot answers to the first point that God has so disposed nature that if man does what is in him, *facit quod in se est*, that is uses his natural powers, he can acquire sufficient information about the articles of faith which are necessary for salvation.[169]

In his answer to the second argument, Holcot points out that the supernatural articles of faith are *not contrary to reason* but go *beyond reason*. To deny reason is indeed blameworthy, but one does not deny reason if one grants that reason cannot reach beyond itself into the realm of supernatural faith which transcends the realm of the senses. The *facere quod in se est* means for Holcot that the act of faith is not merely the exercise of the theoretical reason but an exercise of the whole man: *sine discursu rationis et perceptione voluntaria veritatis, fides non habetur*.[170] The knowledge philosophers like Hermes and Aristotle possess is therefore not necessarily due to their acquaintance with the aboriginal revelation. They "have done what is in them" by using their natural powers and have thus reached enlightenment, though this does not exclude the possibility that they made use of the available tradition of truth.[171]

[168] "Ad oppositum est apostolus ad Heb. 2 [11:1]: *Fides est sperandarum rerum substantia, argumentum non apparentium* scl. naturaliter, sed sine fide impossibile est placere deo; necessarium est ergo habere fidem de non apparentibus per rationem. Ad questionem dicendum quod sic. Et ratio est quia finis sive beatitudo humana est felicitas supernaturalis . . . ideo necesse fuit ut homo haberet media supernaturalia ad illum finem et huiusmodi sunt fides, spes et charitas et sacramenta ecclesie nobis revelata; et ideo omnia talia sunt necessaria ad salutem." *Sap.* Lect. 28 B.

[169] "Ad primum dicendum quod in ista propositione natura supponit pro deo. Ille enim est qui omnia naturalia ordinat secundum beneplacitum sue voluntatis et concedendum est quod non deficit in necessariis. Nam si homo facit quod in se est satis informabitur de illis que sunt necessaria ad salutem suam." *Sap.* Lect. 28 B.

[170] "Ad secundum quando arguitur quod negare rationem est vituperabile: concedo. . . Dicendum ergo ad formam: negando probationem minoris videlicet illam quod fides suadet credere illa que rationi repugnant, sic videlicet quod nulli rationi consentit, sed tantum credulitati. Quia sine discursu rationis et perceptione voluntaria veritatis, fides non habetur." *Sap.* Lect. 28 B.

[171] ". . . bene utentibus ingenio Deus seipsum aliquo modo revelat vel per extrinsecam informationem vel per intrinsecam inspirationem." *Sap.* Lect. 156 A.

Actually it is only the latter possibility in which Holcot, the moralising exegete, is interested. The philosophical pre-Christian tradition is not a live option anymore; it has been absorbed by the Church, and only there is the true tradition to be found. One should not turn therefore to the philosophers but to Christ and his Church, since compared with Christ, the philosophers' wisdom is stupidity.[172] Holcot does not refer here explicitly to Augustine, but the parallel with Augustine's letter to Dioscorus, *Epistula* 108, is obvious and striking: the true members of the *Plotini schola* recognized in Christ the personification of truth and went over to the Church. So it came about that only within the Church truth is to be found.[173]

Holcot proclaims indeed on every page of his *Wisdom* commentary the insufficiency of philosophy.[174] He holds with Augustine that only the authority of the Church can provide a solid basis for the understanding of supernatural truths.[175] Yet to embrace this authority does not mean a negation of reason or a blind jump. This indeed would substantiate the charge of scepticism. Holcot makes quite clear that the God to which the Church witnesses can to a degree be known from his creation.[176] Miracles are probable reasons which engender the act of faith.[177] The same kind of

[172] ". . . Plato, Pithagoras et Aristoteles absorpti sunt Petre iuncti, id est comparati Christo; per se videntur aliquid dicere sed iunge et compara eos Christo et nihil sunt, mortui iacent et stulta est sapientia eorum." Prol. *Sap.* E.

[173] "Tunc Plotini schola Romae floruit habuitque condiscipulos multos acutissimos et solertissimos viros. Sed aliqui eorum magicarum artium curiositate depravati sunt, aliqui Dominum Iesum Christum ipsius veritatis atque Sapientiae incommutabilis, quam conabantur attingere, cognoscentes gestare personam in eius militiam transierunt. Itaque totum culmen auctoritatis lumenque rationis in illo uno salutari nomine atque in una eius ecclesia recreando et reformando humano generi constitutum est." *CSEL* 34.2 (Vindobonae, 1898), p. 697.

[174] Cf. E. Gilson: ". . . la doctrine d'Augustin proclame à chaque page l'insuffisance de la philosophie," *Introduction à l'étude de Saint Augustin*, 3 ed. (Paris, 1949), p. 311.

[175] "Robor namque scientiarum secularium non excedit potestatem rationis humane, sed certe robor sacratissime theologie est prime veritatis auctoritas que cuiuslibet ingenii vim excedit," Prol. *Sap.* F.

[176] "Licet enim ex cognitione creaturarum assurgere possumus aliqualiter in dei noticiam quantum ad multa, videlicet quod potens, bonus, omnipotens et clemens est . . . tamen ad evidenter cognoscendum consilia sua et precepta que vult nos servare in hac vita pertingere non possumus sine ipsius revelatione." *Sap.* Lect. 122 A; cf. *Sap.* Lect. 82 B.

[177] ". . . ad hoc enim deserviunt miracula et rationes quedam probabiles, que sufficiunt ad causandum fidem," I *Sent.* q 1 art. 6 J.

reasonable consideration, which one may call commonsense argument or *ratio de congruo*, is admitted by Holcot when he tells the story of how a heretic who did not believe in the immortality of the soul is converted by a lay brother who argues that one cannot lose anything in believing this, but only gain eternal bliss if this proves to be true.[178]

The main reason however why one should be sceptical about such charges as agnosticism, fideism and scepticism is that whereas Holcot consistently enough emphasizes that all these semi-arguments as such are insufficient without revelation on the part of God, this revelation is granted only to those who use their rational capacities to the utmost to seek and understand God. To clarify Holcot's use of the *facere quod in se est* as regards the problems of faith and understanding, we turn to his doctrine of predestination and grace which provides us with an elucidating parallel.

2. *Sola gratia salvatur*: Holcot's predestinarianism

In the first part of this section, we have seen that Holcot does not believe that man through his own power can acquire a saving knowledge of God: *sapientia* is a free gift of God. The transcendence and sovereignty of God is preserved and posited beyond the reach of man's *scientia*.[179]

---

[178] *Sap.* Lect. 14 B; *Sap.* Lect. 18 A. Beryl Smalley concludes: "This is real scepticism. It goes with fideism." "Robert Holcot," p. 85; *English Friars*, p. 187. However, to the *facere quod in se est* belongs *prudentia*, and this plays a part in missionary efforts, not in the form of strict demonstrations but of persuasive arguments. Christ himself is the example: "Sic de Christo loquamur quod venit in mundum persuadere et predicare, non dicta sua scientifice demonstrare et ideo doctrina sua non scientia sed fides nominatur. Sunt tamen dicta sua nihilominus credibilia . . . quia in eo viguit prudentia. . ." *Sap.* Lect. 197 B.

[179] "Quia primo ostendit [Salomo] quod attingere cognitionem supernaturalium excedit limites humane facultatis. Secundo quod talium cognitio nullo modo haberi potest nisi ex dono divine liberalitatis. . . Ad primum arguitur sic. Si nos homines non possumus id quod minus est nec poterimus id quod maius est; sed minus est cognoscere creaturas dei et cognitiones naturales earum que sunt in terra nobiscum quam cognoscere divinam voluntatem que est in celo. . . Ergo ista quotidiana que fiunt in terris nescimus comprehendere. . . Facile est quantum ad principia. . . Sed difficilis est quantum ad conclusiones que ex principiis eliciuntur in quibus a multis erratur. . . Cum ergo ad illa insufficientes sumus constat quod sine dono et revelatione dei attingere non possumus ad ea ad que nullus sensus, nullum experimentum perducit. . . Sensum autem tuum, id est consilium prescientie tue et ordinationis future, quis sciet nisi per donum liberalitatis tue?" *Sap.* Lect. 123 A.

This "scepticism" is considerably mitigated, however, by the concept of the *facere quod in se est*. Man can not only acquire some knowledge of God from creation, but he can also acquire the gift of enlightenment if he makes the best possible use of his natural capacities. Since exactly the same structure of arguments reappears in Holcot's discussion of the relation of free will, grace, and predestination, we can now be more concise in our discussion.

Just as we found strong indications which seemed to support the claim that Holcot be regarded as a full-fledged sceptic, so we find explicit documentation for the claim that Holcot holds a seemingly Augustinian doctrine of unmerited grace and predestination without cause. Again God's transcendence and sovereignty is established and posited beyond the reach of man.[180]

Especially if one accepts the view that Holcot is one of the *Pelagiani moderni*, so bitterly attacked by Thomas Bradwardine, the *sola gratia* theme is striking. Though man's responsibility is not denied, all good works are clearly said to be effects of God's predestination.[181] The famous question whether God's predestination is based on foreknowledge of the future good works is answered in the negative.[182] Several times the prevenience of grace is clearly enunciated; the beginning of the process of justification is said to be due to the initiative of the Holy Spirit.[183] One

---

[180] Holcot makes the parallel between the problem areas of faith and reason on the one hand and will and grace on the other explicit: ". . . quantumcunque homo sit perfectus et sanctus in scientiis quas potest acquirere per naturam, sine tamen gratia nihil faciet meritorium vite eterne." *Sap.* Lect. 118 B.

[181] ". . . tota multitudo effectuum predestinationis non habet causam in predestinato; hoc patet quia bona operatio habet causam in homine et tamen est unus effectus predestinationis." II *Sent.* q 1 U.

[182] ". . . an deus ordinaverit se alicui daturum vitam eternam propter aliquid in predestinato vel propter hoc quod prescit aliquid futurum in predestinato. . . Et dicitur quod non . . . ," II *Sent.* q 1 X. "Et ideo in acceptione dei vel predestinatione non est acceptio persone quia deus non facit iniustum creature sue eam reprobando; sicut nec facit iustam .[sic] creaturam ipsam predestinando et ideo in mere gratiosis non peccat homo dando uni et non alteri cum neutri teneatur quicquam dare." *Sap.* Lect. 79 D. See the more elaborate treatment by Bradwardine in *De causa dei* I.35–I.46 and in *De Praedestinatione et Praescientia*, ed. Oberman, published in *NAK* 43 (1960), 195–220.

[183] "Si est iustus hoc non est nisi per graciam tuam quia nullus potest iustus fieri nisi te iniciante et incipiente bonum motum. . ." *Sap.* Lect. 149 A.; ". . . nisi gratia preveniat hominis voluntatem saltem natura vel causalitate homo iustus esse non potest." *Ibid.* Cf. *Sap.* Lect. 148 D: ". . . nisi spiritus sancti gratia per suam benignitatem hominem mollificat salubrem penitentiam non attemptat."

can therefore very well understand that it has been argued that Holcot does not deviate from the theology of Aquinas and the Dominican order in his doctrine of grace and predestination.[184]

But again, as was the case with Holcot's "scepticism," we are confronted with a series of statements which seem to contradict this emphasis on God's sovereignty as expressed in the uncaused nature of predestination and in the prevenience of grace. Holcot takes I Tim. 2:4 quite seriously: "[God] desires all men to be saved and to come to the knowledge of the Truth." [185] Yet with this general will for salvation goes the condition that God only wants those to be saved who live according to the laws established by him. This, then, man can and has to decide in all freedom.[186]

Now the question arises with a new urgency how man can be held responsible to live according to the established laws and thus lay claim to the promised salvation while the actualisation of his natural capacities depends on God's granting him the gift of prevenient grace. It is again the doctrine of the *facere quod in se est* which reverses the predestinarian trend and which forms the bridge between the transcendent sovereignty of God and man's responsibility for his own salvation.

Holcot solves the problem in the same way as his fellow nominalists, William of Occam [187] and Gabriel Biel.[188] God is committed to give his grace to all who do what is in them. This does not detract from his sovereignty, since in eternity God was free to establish totally different laws; he was free to act with absolute power, the *potentia absoluta*, sub-

---

[184] "Die Grund der Prädestination liegt nur in Gott, in seinem Willen, die Prädestination ist letztlich Gnade." Alois Meissner, *Gotteserkenntnis und Gotteslehre*, p. 102. "Holkot folgt also in seiner Prädestinationslehre der allgemeinen thomistischen Ansicht," *ibid.*, p. 104.

[185] *RSV*; *Sap.* Lect. 144 A.

[186] ". . . non est intentio sua simpliciter et absolute, quod omnes salventur, sed vult quod quicumque vixerit secundum leges statutas salvetur." II *Sent.* q 1 D. ". . . deus fecit homines capaces salutis et statuit precepta, que si omnes homines facerent, salvi forent." II *Sent.* q 1 CC.

[187] I *Sent.* d 41 q 1 G.

[188] "Deus adest omnibus obicem non ponentibus offerens gratiam. Nec alicui adulto rationis usum habenti et quod in se est facienti subtrahit necessaria ad salutem: vult enim omnes homines salvos fieri." Biel, I *Sent.* d 41 q 1 art. 3 dub 3. We note also that Biel and Occam exactly like Holcot insist that nevertheless God's predestination is to be regarded as uncaused: "Et nota quod conclusiones non debent intelligi, quod aliquid sit ratio illius quod predestinatio importat ex parte dei, quia nihil esse potest ratio eterne et divine voluntatis." I *Sent.* d 41 q 1 art. 2 concl. 3; Occam, I *Sent.* d. 41 q 1 H.

ject only to the law of non-contradiction or the law of consistency. Out of sheer mercy and grace, he freely decided in eternity to establish the law that he would convey grace to all who make full use of their natural capacities. Though the law as such is freely given, and therefore an expression of God's *potentia absoluta*, God is now committed to it, in the order chosen by him, the order of his *potentia ordinata*, and he therefore gives his grace "necessarily." [189]

The dialectics of the two powers of God permits Holcot, as it did Occam and Biel, to hold an extreme predestinarian position which centers around the idea that God does not owe anything to any man. While this is true *de potentia absoluta*, Holcot can now at the same time assert a doctrine which one cannot but term Pelagian, according to which man can earn first grace and ultimately — in cooperation with grace — earn his salvation, *de potentia ordinata*.[190] The fact that God *accepts* this *facere quod in se est* as meritorious, while this action as such has no intrinsic condignity or meritorius value, is expressed with the terminological differentiation between *meritum de congruo* and *meritum de condigno*.[191]

Holcot rejects the application of the potter and the clay simile of Rom. 9:21 — which was so important for Bradwardine in his defense of justifica-

[189] "Necessitas coactionis nullo modo cadit in deo, necessitas vero infallibilitatis cadit in deo ex promisso suo et pacto sive lege statuta et hec non est necessitas absoluta sed necessitas consequentie. . . Concedendo quod ex misericordia et gratia sua pro tanto quia talem legem misericorditer statuit et observat. Sed statuta lege necessario dat gratiam necessitate consequentie." *Sap.* Lect. 145 B. These two kinds of necessity reflect the distinction between the "two powers." The *statuta lege* makes clear that also for Holcot God is committed to the order *de potentia ordinata*, which is therefore dependable. Cf., however, Leff who assigns to Holcot an "extreme scepticism, which allows anything to be possible," *Bradwardine and the Pelagians*, p. 223. Though Leff has retracted some of his earlier statements he still regards the order *de potentia ordinata* as an unreliable whim of God, constantly threatened by God's *potentia absoluta*: ". . . its [the *potentia absoluta*] purpose was not the emancipation of man from limits *in statu isto* but of God from His obligation to abide by those limits . . . ," *Gregory of Rimini*, p. 22.

[190] ". . . talis [malus senex] penitens in articulo mortis habet propositum satisfaciendi sub conditione 'si posset' et hoc sufficit divine misericordie; quia si homo vellet facere quod in se est ad penitentiam, deus facit quod in se est ad misericordiam." *Sap.* Lect. 48 C.

[191] ". . . opera nostra ex sua naturali bonitate non merentur vitam eternam de condigno sed de congruo tantum quia congruum est quod homini facienti secundum potentiam suam finitam deus retribuat secundum potentiam suam infinitam." *Sap.* Lect. 25 B. Cf. *Sap.* Lect. 116 B; IV *Sent.* q 1 art. 3.

tion by grace alone [192] — on the grounds that there is no pact or commitment binding the potter over against the clay,[193] while to be so bound is exactly the mark of God's relation with his creatures.

We may conclude that the commitment by which God in eternity obligated himself conveys to man's action a dignity which it would not have in itself: if man goes halfway, God will meet him with the gift of grace. Without this gift of grace man is *helpless;* but it is just as true that without the full use of man's own natural powers, the offer of grace is *useless.*

If we now apply our findings with regard to the relation of free will and grace to the relation of reason and revelation, we are in a position to assess the validity of the charge of scepticism. There can be little doubt that Holcot denies that man unaided by grace can with his natural reason prove the existence of God, or grasp the mysteries of the Holy Trinity and of the Incarnation. In view of the foregoing, we may say that Holcot holds that man cannot reach the posture of faith *de condigno.* Only to this extent is Holcot a sceptic. It would perhaps be more appropriate to say that for Holcot, man without revelation is subject to philosophical uncertainty and that therefore man is freed from scepticism by faith.[194] This form of scepticism, however, is not without a precedent in medieval theology and can even be said to be rooted in the Augustinian tradition.[195] Holcot's emphasis on the intrinsic deficiencies of man's rational powers as compared with the confidence in natural reason on the part of Anselm, Aquinas, and Bradwardine tends to give his views an air of radicalism which places him on the left wing of the nominalistic tradition.[196]

[192] *De Praedestinatione et Praescientia* [69], ed. Oberman, *NAK* 43 (1960), 210.

[193] ". . . quamvis sumus sicut lutum per comparationem ad deum aliquo modo, non tamen similitudo tenet in omnibus: nec est pactum inter artificem et lutum. . ." *Sap.* Lect. 145 B.

[194] "Ex parte vero corporis duplex surgit difficultas acquirendi scientiam de deo et necessariis ad salutem. Primo quia corpus infectum fomite concupiscentie corrumpit affectum anime et facit animam ad surgendum ad spiritualia gravem. . . Secundo quia sollicitudo circa necessaria corporis et ista temporalia deprimit sensum hominis cogitantis multa et reddit eum distractum a studio et scientia acquirenda." *Sap.* Lect. 122 B. Cf. *Sap.* Lect. 118 A.

[195] "Il n'y a pas d'augustinisme sans cette présupposition fondamentale: la vraie philosophie présuppose un acte d'adhésion à l'ordre surnaturel, qui libère la volonté de la chair par la grâce et la pensée du scepticisme par la révélation." E. Gilson, *Introduction à l'étude de Saint Augustin,* p. 311.

[196] Cf. Occam: ". . . alique veritates naturaliter notae seu cognoscibiles sunt

Nevertheless Holcot does not reject the possibility of acquiring *de congruo* the knowledge of faith which is necessary for salvation. Man can and therefore has to do his very best in going halfway in his search for God; thus he will receive enlightenment. Man's natural reason is *helpless* when confronted with the task of solving the mysteries of faith, but at the same time man's natural reason is the very presupposition and precondition for this enlightenment. Without man's effort to search out God with all his might, the offer of enlightenment is *useless*.

We may conclude that for Holcot the way to faith does not bypass, but rather presupposes the full use of natural reason. The doctrine of the *facere quod in se est* is the key both to Holcot's "scepticism" and "predestinarianism." What first seemed to be the contradictions and the inconsistencies of one who despairs of reason proves to be the reflection of the dialectics of the two powers, and the "unnecessary" but dependable commitment of God to man's serious efforts in thought and action.

---

theologice, sicut quod deus est, deus est sapiens, bonus, etc. cum sint necessarie ad salutem," *Prol. Sent.* q 1 F. Philotheus Boehner calls attention to a revealing observation by Peter of Candia: "Alii doctores quos videre potui, tenent quod talis propositio non est per se nota, sed est bene demonstrabilis. Et huius opinionis fuerunt beatus Thomas, Doctor Subtilis, Ockham, Adam (Wodham), Johannes de Ripa . . . ," ms. Vat. lat. 1081, fol. 42 ᵛᵇ; *Collected Articles on Ockham*, ed. E. M. Buytaert (St. Bonaventure, N.Y. 1950), p. 413.

CHRIST AND THE EUCHARIST

ᔒᗝᗝ

I. Nominalism and Chalcedon

1. The state of scholarship on the question of nominalistic Christology

A detailed presentation of Biel's understanding of the incarnate and eucharistic Christ within the context of late medieval thought, which would include also secondary issues, would require a separate volume. Such a project would certainly be important. To establish precisely the relation of Scotus, Occam, Gerson, and Ailly on this point would be a significant contribution to late medieval and reformation scholarship.

Before such a project can be profitably undertaken, however, some major barriers to a fair evaluation of nominalistic Christology must first be removed. Therefore we shall restrict our inquiry to the hard lines of Occam's and Biel's Christology and to the question of the nature of the nominalistic interest and motivation in the effort to understand the person and work of Jesus Christ. It is not due to repetitiousness on our part that we have to begin again by pointing out that the thesis of the "disintegration of late medieval thought" has also affected the presentation of the Christology of that period. Though from the usual vantage point, this thesis has seemed to arise from an assessment of the fourteenth and fifteenth-century treatment of Christological issues,[1] it can be argued that

---

[1] J. A. Dorner, *Entwicklungsgeschichte der Lehre von der Person Christi*, vol. II: *Die Lehre von der Person Christi vom Ende des vierten Jahrhunderts bis zur Gegenwart*, 2 ed. (Berlin, 1853), 447 ff.; Karl Werner, *Die Scholastik des späteren Mittelalters*, vol. II: *Die nachscotistische Scholastik* (Vienna, 1883), p. 330 ff.; Robert S. Franks, *A History of the Doctrine of the Work of Christ in its Ecclesiastical Development*, 1 ed. (London, n.d. [1918]), 2 ed. (Edinburgh: Nelson, 1962), p. 258;

a predetermined judgment on the nature of nominalism has moulded the choice and evaluation of the sources.

We have here particularly in mind the alleged *asinus-Christology* of Occam and his school: in other words the statement that God could as well have chosen to be incarnate in an ass as in a human being. When one ignores the *function* of this proposition in Occam's argumentation, it is understandable enough that this statement seems to mark the end of the scholastic enterprise to clarify and unfold the Christian faith.

In the *Centiloquium* it is indeed clearly stated that God, without violating the rule of non-contradiction, that is, *de potentia absoluta*, could have assumed, if he had so wished, the nature of an ass in a hypostatic union, so that the divine Person would have become its carrier, *suppositum*.[2] In view of the fact that the authorship of the *Centiloquium* is debatable,[3] we will refrain from presenting the parallel passages in this work which hitherto has long formed an important part of documentation for a criticism of Occam's Christology.[4]

Ernst Borchert, *Der Einfluss des Nominalismus auf die Christologie der Spätscholastik nach dem Traktat de communicatione idiomatum des Nikolaus Oresme*, in *BB*, vol. XXV, pts. 4–5 (Münster i. W., 1940), p. 74 ff.; Ignaz Backes, "Die christologische Problematik der Hochscholastik und ihre Beziehung zu Chalkedon," in *Das Konzil von Chalkedon: Geschichte und Gegenwart*, vol. II: *Entscheidung um Chalkedon*, ed. Aloys Grillmeier, S.J. and Heinrich Bacht, S.J. (Würzburg, 1953), p. 938 f.; Erwin Iserloh, *Gnade und Eucharistie in der philosophischen Theologie des Wilhelm von Ockham* (Wiesbaden, 1956), pp. 27 ff., 75 f.

[2] "Sexta conclusio . . . probatur: Deus assumpsit aliquam naturam in unitatem suppositi, ergo Deus potest assumere omnem. Item: non includit contradictionem Deum assumere naturam asininam; igitur Deus illud potest facere." *Centiloquium theologicum*, concl. 7 A, ed. Ph. Boehner, *FStud* 17 (1941), pt. 2, p. 44. Cf. Calvin's bitter criticism, *Inst.* II.xii.5: "Eousque erupit quorundam vesania dum praepostere acuti videri appetunt, ut quaererent an naturam asini assumere potuerit Dei filius." *CR Op. Cal.* II, 344.

[3] E. Iserloh defends against Ph. Boehner the authenticity of Occam's authorship in "Um die Echtheit des 'Centiloquium': Ein Beitrag zur Wertung Ockhams und zur Chronologie seiner Werke," *Gregorianum* 30 (1949), 309 ff. In his answer "On a recent study of Ockham." *FStud* 10 (1950), 191 ff., Boehner adds to his impressive series of considerations an argument based on the startlingly different use of the term *moderni* here and in the "other" writings of Occam. Boehner acknowledges his indebtedness to Ernest Moody, *The Logic of William of Ockham* (London, 1935), p. 7. Again answered by Iserloh, *Gnade und Eucharistie . . . Ockham*, p. 35.

Biel took Occam to be the author of the *Centiloquium*. Cf., e.g., III *Sent.* d 6 q 1 art. 3 dub 1 and III *Sent.* d 22 q 1 art. 3 dub. 1.

[4] "Die conclusio 13 seines Centiloquium enthält dann die mit Recht als einen

A shift of the discussion from the *Centiloquium* to the *Sentences* and to the identical treatment in the *Quodlibeta* does not, however, seem to vindicate Occam from charges of "logical games" and "unreligious frivolity" because there also we meet with the use of the ass simile.

2. The development of medieval Christology: Lombard, Thomas, Henry of Ghent, Scotus

To understand Occam's purpose and the direction of his attack and defense, we have to look for a moment at the christological developments in pre-Occamistic scholasticism. Early and high scholastic Christology is informed by the discussion of three distinct interpretations of the mode of the union of God and man or of the bond between the two natures in Jesus Christ.[5]

The first of the three opinions reported by Peter Lombard [6] is now generally called the *assumptus* theory. Its characteristics are that the incarnation thus understood entails the assumption by the Word of a complete man. Here not human nature, *humanitas*, but a human person, *homo*, is taken into the divine Person. This assumption does not mean a fusion of the two natures; the two natures and their two carriers remain distinct.

The second opinion, the *subsistence* theory, stresses that while normally every nature or substantial form has its own carrier,[7] the mystery of the Incarnation would consist precisely in the fact that now two natures

---

Tiefpunkt der nominalistischen Christologie angesehenen Ausführungen Ockhams zur Idiomenkommunikation. . ." Borchert, *Der Einfluss*, p. 77 f.; cf. Dorner, *Entwicklungsgeschichte*, II, 447, n. 6; Werner, *Die Scholastik*, II, 356.

[5] ". . . drei Lehrmeinungen, die gleichsam den Grundstock der frühscholastischen Christologie ausmachen. . ." Bernhard Barth, O.S.B., "Ein neues Dokument zur Geschichte der frühscholastischen Christologie," *Theologische Quartalschrift* 100 (1919), 419. For the classification of the three positions as *assumptus, subsistence* and *habitus* theories, we are indebted to Barth's influential article, p. 423 ff. continued in *Theologische Quartalschrift* 101 (1920), p. 235 ff. The same terms used by Borchert, p. 28 f. Cf. Ludwig Ott, "Das Konzil von Chalkedon in der Frühscholastik," in *Das Konzil von Chalkedon: Geschichte und Gegenwart*, vol. II, *Entscheidung um Chalkedon*, ed. Aloys Grillmeier, S.J. and Heinrich Bacht, S.J. (Würzburg, 1953), p. 909 ff.; Ignaz Backes, "Die christologische Problematik," p. 921 ff.

[6] III *Sent.* d 6 cap. 2 and d 7 cap. 1.

[7] For Aquinas' use of the term *suppositum* see Ludwig Schütz, ed., *Thomas-Lexikon*, 2 ed. (Stuttgart, 1958), p. 793 ff.

are carried by one *hypostasis*, the Word. Christ would be composed of body and soul — the substantial form of man — and divinity, all three carried by the Person of the Word.[8]

The third position, the *habitus* theory, is characterized by the idea that the immutable God cannot change and did not change in the Incarnation but dressed himself in the human nature as in a mantle. Here the union between the two natures is indeed minimal since the bond between humanity and divinity in Christ, though indissoluble, is only external in character: body and soul are not part of the essence of Christ.[9] The Christology derived from this latter theory has been called "nihilianism" in view of the fact that the assumed humanity of Christ is only a mantle, not something essential or substantial. This concept is reflected also in the supposition that the body and soul of Christ are not united by nature but separately assumed by the divine Logos.[10] The importance of this last point will appear when we deal with the question as to the hypostatic union during the *triduum*, the period between Good Friday and Easter morning.

In 1177 this *habitus* theory was officially rejected by Pope Alexander III.[11] It is indeed in the spirit of Chalcedon that this Nestorian-like emphasis on the accidental relation of humanity and divinity should be viewed as unorthodox. And after this condemnation, the *assumptus* theory became for a period the more authoritative basis for christological discussion. After it had been unmasked as Nestorian by Thomas Aquinas, however, this view soon lost support.[12] It became increasingly clear that the object of assumption should not be seen as *homo* but as *humanitas*, and that the subsistence theory could best serve as the interpretation of the mystery of the one divine Person existing in two natures.

Thus medieval scholasticism, primarily due to the incompatibility of

---

[8] Lombard, III *Sent.* d 6 cap. 3 and d 7 cap. 1, 2.

[9] Lombard, III *Sent.* d 6 cap. 4, 5, 6; d 7 cap. 2 and d 10 cap. 1.

[10] Ludwig Ott, p. 910.

[11] "Cum Christus perfectus Deus perfectus sit homo, mirum est, qua temeritate quisquam audet dicere, quod 'Christus non sit aliquid secundum quod homo.'" Denz. 393.

[12] "Haec positio (duas hypostases vel dua supposita esse in una persona christi) de necessitate in errorem Nestorii dilabitur." *Summa contra gentiles*, IV, cap. 38, as quoted by Barth, p. 259; Cf. *ST* III q 2 art. 6 *in fine corp.* Cf. also Ignaz Backes, *Die Christologie des heiligen Thomas von Aquin und die griechischen Kirchenväter* (Paderborn, 1931), p. 194 ff.

Greek and Latin idiom, had to find its way through trial and effort back to the formulations of Chalcedon. Late medieval theologians could build further on the christological foundation given in the now uncontested subsistence theory. The road to Nestorianism seemed barred by the clear rejection of both the *habitus* and the *assumptus* theories.

But exactly this anti-Nestorian prehistory of the acceptance of the subsistence theory engendered fear of possible Eutychian deviations in the application of this subsistence theory. Whereas Aquinas stressed the instrumental function of the human nature of Christ as regards the divine Person,[13] it was the primary concern of Duns Scotus to safeguard the real humanity of Christ, maintaining a certain degree of independence of the human nature from the Logos.

Scotus argues for a special *esse actualis existentie* of the human nature beside that of the divine nature. The existence of the human nature is in the hypostatic union not annihilated, but added to the existence of the Word. Though the human nature subsists in and is carried by the Person, it must have had its own form of life since otherwise Christ could not have died on the cross. In the case that the human nature would have been separated from the Word, it would not have received a new existence but retained the *esse actualis existentie* it had before.[14] Scotus by no means falls back into the implications of the *assumptus* theory by arguing for a prior existence of the human personality before the assumption by the Word. But at the same time he wants to stress that the subsistence of the humanity of Christ in the Logos as the carrier is not to be defined as *unity* but as *union*. This interest of Scotus is expressed further in the thesis of the twofold sonship of Christ, with respect to God the Father and his mother, the Virgin Mary. Further, like any other man, Christ could have sinned if he had not actually been preserved from this by union with God. And again as regards the knowledge of Christ, the soul of Christ knows everything through the Logos, not actually however, but habit-

---

[13] *ST* III q 19 a 1; *Contra gentiles* IV. c. 36; Cf. Backes: ". . . die thomasische. . . Eigenlehre von der werkzeuglichen Wirksamkeit der menschlichen Natur Christi," "Die christologische Problematik," p. 939.

[14] "Si ista natura dimitteretur a verbo non oporteret sibi acquiri novum esse per generationem nec per creationem . . . haberet aliquod esse in actu et novum. . ." *Ox.* III. d 6 q 1 n 3. Cf. Karl Werner, *Die Scholastik des späteren Mittelalters*, vol. I: *Johannes Duns Scotus* (Vienna, 1881), p. 437; Seeberg, *Die Theologie des Duns Scotus*, p. 234 ff.

ually. As a real man he learns and develops by experience; thus is actualized what is habitually present in his memory.[15] Scotus claimed that he had to defend the concreteness of the human nature in Christ against Henry of Ghent,[16] but it is obvious that his arguments are also directed against Aquinas.[17]

This whole presentation may leave the impression that Scotus' Christology is Nestorian in its emphasis on the duality of the two natures and a regression to the *assumptus* theory characterized by the assumption of a real and complete man. Such a conclusion is certainly unwarranted. In his proof of the possibility of the hypostatic union, Scotus takes up the typical assumptionist argument that no nature can be assumed unless it has first a concrete independent and personal existence. In his answer he distinguishes between the individuality of the human nature and the person.[18] While Scotus is concerned with preserving the integrity of the former, there is for him no doubt that it is the Person of the Logos, and the Logos only, that carries the human nature.[19]

Still speaking against the assumptionist theory and still discussing possible forms of Incarnation — and therefore not describing the actual event of the Incarnation — Scotus makes clear that hypostatic union does not at all presuppose the assumption of a human person. God could very well have chosen to assume the nature of a stone or of fire. According to the rule of the *communicatio idiomatum*, one would then be able to conclude, parallel to the statement "God is man," that "God is stone," or "God is fire." [20]

---

[15] *Ox.* III d 8 q 1 n 2; *Ox.* III d 14 q 3 n 6; n 8.

[16] Pending a more detailed study of the Christology of Henry of Ghent, it is noteworthy that he without apparent inhibition still uses the Augustinian dress-simile for the humanity of Christ assumed by the Word, so characteristic of the *habitus-theory*. *Summae quaestionum ordinarium* (Parrhisiis, 1520; reprinted St. Bonaventure, N.Y., 1953), art. 30, q 4 [fol. 183 O.]

[17] ". . . oportet dicere, quod esse substantiale quod proprie attribuitur supposito in christo est unum tantum . . . si tamen ponatur humanitas a divinitate separari tunc humanitas suum esse habebit aliud ab esse divino." Thomas, *Quodlib.* 9 art. 3; quoted by Werner, *Die Scholastik* I, 437. Cf. on the matter of the two *filiationes*, *ST* III q 35 a 5; on the knowledge of Christ, *ST* III q 10 art. 2.

[18] *Ox.* III d 1 q 1 n 1; n 17.

[19] "Dico quod non praecessit tempore animatio incarnationem quia tunc natura ista fuisset aliquando in se personata et non in verbo quando scl. fuisset caro animata." *Ox.* III d 2 q 3 n 3.

[20] ". . . diceretur hypostasiari vel sustentificari non tamen personari. . . Cum

As Minges has pointed out, Scotus was not the first to consider the possibility of God's assumption of an irrational creature. Aquinas made exactly the same point with the same purpose in his *Sentences* without clarifying his observation with the examples of stone and fire,[21] but rather by referring in general to a *creatura irrationalis*.

3. The intention of Occam's *asinus-Christology*: rejection of the charge of Nestorianism

After this survey of pre-Occamistic christological developments, when we turn now to the issue of Occam's *asinus-Christology*, we can begin with the observation that Occam's thesis of the possibility of God's assumption of an irrational being in a hypostatic union is by no means as startling as it could seem if taken outside its historical context. In Occam we find the same hypothesis, but now illustrated with the examples of a stone and an ass.[22] As was the case with Thomas and Scotus, Occam does not deal with the actual event of the Incarnation — *de potentia ordinata* — but he wants to investigate the possibility of the Incarnation, that is, of the hypostatic union.[23]

---

ratio huius communicationis sit quod suppositum recipit praedicationem in concreto illius naturae, in qua subsistit, et subsisteret in natura lapidis, non videtur ratio quare lapis non praedicatur de eo dicendo: Deus est lapis, sicut modo dicitur quod Deus est homo, et aequaliter utraque est vera." *Ox.* III d 2 q 1 n 13. For the parallel passages with Durand and Pierre d'Auriole see Werner, *Die Scholastik*, II, 338, 347.

[21] "Dicendum quod deus de potentia absoluta creaturam irrationalem assumere potuit, non impedit quod creatura irrationalis personalitatem non habet. . . Quamvis in natura irrationali non inveniatur persona, invenitur tamen in ea hypostasis et suppositum. Unio autem non tantum facta est in persona, sed etiam in hypostasi et supposito," *Ox.* III d 2 q 1 art. 1.

[22] ". . . dico quod non videtur mihi inconveniens plus concedere quod lapis sit personalis a persona divina quam homo; quia personari a persona divina nihil aliud est quam sustentificari a persona divina. Nunc autem potest indifferenter sustentificari natura irrationalis sicut rationalis a persona divina, et ideo potest ita lapis vel asinus sic personari sicut homo." III *Sent.* d 1 q 1 U.

[23] On two scores we have to challenge Iserloh's conclusion: "Ockham dagegen [as compared with Aquinas] gibt im Sent . . . nicht nur die Möglichkeit der hypostatischen Union mit der unvernünftigen Kreatur zu, sondern betont, dass eine solche Vereinigung nicht weniger angemessen [!] sei als die mit der menschlichen Natur und er unterstreicht seine Ausführungen noch durch drastische [!] Beispiele. So spricht er von der Vereinigung der göttlichen Person mit einem Stein oder einem Esel." *Gnade und Eucharistie . . . Ockham*, p. 76. (1) Occam's examples do not seem "drastic" when seen in their historical context. (2) Occam does not plead

In a closer investigation of three related passages which bear directly on what we have called the *asinus-Christology*, we see that Occam's purpose is the same as that of Thomas and Scotus: not merely to investigate but actually to defend the possibility of the hypostatic union and at the same time to ward off the dangers of the assumptionist theory. The entire discussion is a sample of the *fides quaerens intellectum*, an enterprise supposedly abandoned by late medieval nominalism.[24] The first passage presents the basic thesis, the second an objection to it, while the third answers this objection.

According to Occam there are two ways to understand the assumption of the human nature into the unity of the divine Person. The first interpretation is false: the human nature becomes one person with the Person of Christ and thus becomes the Person of Christ. This would be even more absurd than if the human nature were to become an ass. The second interpretation is correct: the human nature is carried by the divine Person and not by its own "personality" or carrier.[25] This last point is consistently carried through in the whole first question of Book III and the two parallel questions of the *Quodlibeta*: the Logos assumed humanity and not a person or a man.[26]

---

for the "Angemessenheit" of this kind of hypostatic union. He discusses here not the issue *quod decet* but *quod potest*. As appears also from Rimini's discussion of the coexistence of categories, the words *asinus* and *lapis* had become common symbols "Sed quid de potentia absoluta . . . sic anima et forma lapidis simul informare possent unam materiam et anima hominis et anima asini et sic idem videretur simul posse asinum et hominem et lapidem." I *Sent.* d 17 q 3 art. 2 [fol. 101 I]. Cf. fol. 157 B.

[24] "Circa primum sciendum quod licet unio non potest demonstrari sed sola fide tenetur, tamen ad intelligendum istam unionem possumus manuduci per aliam unionem puta materie et forme, substantie et accidentis." Occam, III *Sent.* d 1 q 1 H. The rest of this question discusses the necessary qualifications of such a comparison.

[25] ". . . dico quod naturam humanam assumi in unitate persone divine potest intelligi dupliciter. Uno modo quod natura humana fiat una persona cum persona christi et fiat persona christi. Alio modo potest intelligi quod natura humana sustentificatur a persona divina. Et sic iste intellectus verus est, quia natura illa non subsistit in proprio supposito sed sustentificatur a verbo modo quo accidens sustentificatur a suo subiecto." III *Sent.* d 1 q 1 G.

[26] ". . . hoc est impossibilis: iste homo est assumptus, sed hoc humanitas potest esse assumpta est vera. . ." III *Sent.* d 1 q 1 ad primum principale. "Ad aliud dico quod natura assumpta non est aliqua persona quia nec divina nec humana; tamen dicitur personata a persona dei quia sustentificatur ab ea. Non quia est persona divina; immo hoc est ita impossibilis sicut hoc homo est asinus, quia sustentificatur ab ea, non quia persona divina." III *Sent.* d 1 q 1 ad tertium. Cf. *Quodlibeta* 5 q 10,

Before we turn to a second central passage, it is important to note that the first time Occam uses the term *asinus*, it is not to suggest a possible mode of the incarnation of the Logos, but to illustrate the utter absurdity of an unorthodox interpretation of this event.

It is in the objection raised by an opponent to Occam's defense of the possibility of the hypostatic union that for the first time the matter of God's incarnation in an irrational being is brought up. According to this objection the union of human nature and divine Person could not be "merely" a question of the nature being carried by the Person, since in that case God could as well have chosen to be incarnate in an irrational being.[27] In his answer to this objection Occam makes it clear that he is not impressed with the force of this argument. Like Thomas and Scotus before him, he can of course find few difficulties in the hypothesis that God *de potentia absoluta* could have chosen an irrational object of assumption.[28] In his closing remark he returns again to his initial statement: it is as absurd to hold that the human nature would be the uncreated Person as to say that the human nature would be a stone or an ass.[29] It is clear that the *asinus* illustration is not used for idle speculation on a series of possible modes of the Incarnation, but to establish by logical demonstration the strength of the subsistence theory.

Occam's final conclusion is worded in exactly the same way as we

---

11. Iserloh does not seem to acknowledge the decisive importance which the distinction between *homo* and *humanitas* had acquired for fourteenth-century theologians. At least he argues that the overly extensive — "lang und immer wieder" — treatment of this problem would be due to Occam's identification of existence and essence and also that it "seiner Vorliebe für logische Spielereien besonders entgegenkommt." *Gnade und Eucharistie . . . Ockham*, p. 29.

[27] "Item contra hoc quod dicitur quod naturam uniri ad personam non est nisi sustentari a persona verbi et personari non est nisi sustentari ab aliqua persona, quia tunc quelibet natura irrationalis tam animata quam inanimata posset assumi ad unitatem persone divine et personari a persona divina, quia quelibet natura creata potest sustentari ab ea." III *Sent.* d 1 q 1 ad nonum.

[28] ". . . potest ita lapis vel asinus sic personari sicut homo." III *Sent* d 1 q 1 ad nonum. Cf. ". . . potest hoc esse vera: lapis sustentificatur a persona divina si esset assumptus sicut nunc [de potentia ordinata] est natura humana." *Ibid.*

[29] "Et quando dicis quod sibi repugnat esse persona creata vel increata, dico quod ita repugnat nature humane esse persona increata sicut lapis vel asinus. Quia sicut hoc est impossibilis 'lapis est persona divina,' etiam si esset assumpta a persona divina ita hoc est impossibilis 'natura humana de facto est persona divina.' Sed solum hoc est vera; natura humana sustentificatur a persona divina quia subsistit in persona divina." III *Sent.* d 1 q 1 ad nonum.

noted with Scotus: for the proper understanding of what actually happened when the Word became flesh, it is important to realize that God could have assumed the nature of a stone: God did not assume a complete man but human nature.[30] Occam rejects the *assumptus* theory, which as we noted has a definite Nestorian bias, but he is as concerned as Scotus to show that the subsistence theory should not lead to monophysite misunderstandings. The adoption of Christ as the son of God, his peccability and growth in actual knowledge express the realistic and concrete character of Christ's humanity. Theologians should, however, be extremely careful with this kind of statement, since it may lead others into error.[31]

Though Occam, like Scotus, stresses a valid aspect of the Nestorian position, that is, the real humanity of Christ, he is so adamant in the rejection of the *homo assumptus* position and genuine in the defense of the hypostatic union that *there is reason to plead for a reconsideration of the usual allegation that nominalistic Christology manifests strong Nestorian tendencies.*[32]

Anticipating the results of our investigation of Biel's Christology to which we shall now turn, we are inclined to say that nominalism did not fully succeed in safeguarding the true and perfect humanity of Christ and can in this respect even be criticized for not having been sufficiently persistent in incorporating the valid elements in the Nestorian christological position.

[30] Werner observes: "Das Occam hiermit dem Begriffe der gottmenschlichen Persönlichkeit Christi nicht gerecht zu werden weiss, liegt wohl offen da; die menschlichen Natur Christi ist zwar an sich nicht persönlich, aber bloss deshalb nicht weil sie an der Personhaftigkeit der göttlichen Natur Christi Anteil hat." *Die Scholastik,* II, 353. Occam would heartily agree with the latter part of this statement; cf. III *Sent.* d 1 q 1 BB, ad secundum.

[31] ". . . dico quod potest concedi quod christus est filius adoptivus, sed propter hereticos negatur ne detur occasio errandi. Eodem modo dico deus potest peccare si assumeret naturam humanam sine aliquibus donis et natura esset sibi derelicta; nec hoc est maius inconveniens quam quod christus patitur, verberatur, moritur; quia tamen illud abhorret homo audire et male sonat, ideo negatur." III *Sent.* d 1 q 9 BB ad septimum.

[32] Werner mentions the ". . . unvermittelte Dualität, welche Occam's Auffassung der Person Christi durchherrscht. . ."; *Die Scholastik,* II. p. 354; Borchert sees in Oresme a defender of orthodoxy against nominalism, at one point identified as the ". . . im 14. Jahrhundert sich regenden Trennungstendenzen und häretischen Lehranschauungen eines abgewandelten Nestorianismus. . ," *Der Einfluss,* p. 151; cf. p. 120, 123; also Iserloh, *Gnade und Eucharistie . . . Ockham,* p. 32.

4. Biel evaluated in terms of the medieval christological tradition

Our presentation of Biel's understanding of the Person of Christ can be brief since the indicated positions of Scotus and Occam are as usual his primary frame of reference. Therefore our treatment can be limited to a comparison of Biel with Scotus and Occam and to an indication of some of the central christological passages in the *Sermones*.

Biel makes short shrift of the *habitus* theory. Since this implies separate assumptions of the body and the soul as a dress for the Logos, the real humanity of Christ is endangered.[33] His main interest, however, is clearly in the defense of the hypostatic union against the *assumptus* theory. If human nature had become a person before, in, or after the assumption by the Word, there would be two persons and two natures in Christ. This would defeat the reality of the union and therefore of the redemption of God in Christ.[34]

At the same time Biel shares the concern of Scotus and Occam that the subsistence theory, which proved to be such an excellent barricade against the inroads of Nestorian errors, should not itself become a matrix for the opposite danger: monophysitism. The two natures of Christ should be neither fused nor divorced, but clearly distinguished.[35] Thus, in his academic works and his sermons Biel is constantly searching for the right middle course between the two christological extremes.[36]

As regards the question of the possibility of God's incarnation in an irrational being, twice Biel cites the opinion of Occam that God could

[33] ". . . verbum in sui incarnatione carnem et animam non divisim assumpsit sed coniunctim substantiam humanam ex his vere et realiter compositam, non ut indumentum sed ut naturam in qua subsistere personaliter sibi univit. Probatur conclusio . . . non esset ibi vera humanitas sive natura humana. . ." III *Sent.* d 6 q 1 art. 2 concl. 3.

[34] III *Sent.* d 6 q 2 art. 3 dub. 2; ". . . Christus est unus id est una persona subsistens in duplici natura." *S* II 2 D; "Unde homo christus est suppositum verbi subsistentis in natura humana . . . Verbum non suscepit personam sed naturam" *Lect.* 50 F. Cf. I *Sent.* d 23 q 1 a 1 cor. B.

[35] "Non enim humana natura transit in divinam ita quod suum esse perderet, sed manet integra et quoad se invariata, habens suas naturales proprietates illesas, sed nunc per gloriam perfectas distincta realiter a divina." *S* II 2 C.

[36] "Ita propter hanc unionem qua verbum assumpsit humanitatem verbum vere est homo et homo verbum non alia persona hominis, alia verbi ut dicit heresis nestoriana; sed non est verbum humanitas, corpus scl. aut anima. Nec econverso sicut mentitus est appollinaris . . . Hec est fides catholica." *S* III 9 I.

259

have assumed another nature than that of a man. The first time he states that the opinion of Scotus and Occam as regards the definition of "person" and "to personify" is probable, and that the question whether God could have assumed the nature of a stone is a matter of defining one's terms.[37] The second time Biel merely describes the point of view of Occam [38] and declares that this is also the position of Scotus, commonly held by the *moderni*.

Biel identifies Henry of Ghent [39] as the opponent of Scotus and Occam and reports conscientiously Henry's arguments against the possibility of God's assuming the nature of an irrational being. Biel adds that Henry first held the position of his later opponents. We include this observation not because of its intrinsic interest, but because Biel reports that he found this information in Pico della Mirandola with whose *Apologia* he is apparently well acquainted.[40] This provides us with the first piece of internal evidence for our conjecture of an interrelation between early Italian humanism and nominalism.[41]

Though Biel states first that neither position can be demonstrated to be improbable, he grants in his *Puncta summaria*, intended as a christological introduction for the beginning theological student,[42] that *de*

[37] "Si tamen personari seu personaliter assumi nihil aliud dicit quam sustentari vel sustentificari a persona tunc quicquid assumitur a persona personatur et suppositaliter unitur. Sic dicit Occam . . . quod lapis sit personabilis a persona divina . . . Quamvis que dicta sunt de persona sint probabilia et opinioni Scoti et Occam consentanea. . ." III *Sent.* d 1 q 1 art. 1 cor. 2 E.

[38] "Ille sunt possibiles: deus est lapis, deus est asinus, deus est homo damnatus, deus est diabolus. . ." III *Sent.* d 1 q 2 art. 1 concl. resp.

[39] "Circa materiam huius questionis sunt due opiniones contrarie quarum neutra est demonstrative improbabilis. Una est Scoti et Occam et communiter modernorum . . . alia opinio est Henrici de gandavo . . ." III *Sent.* d 1 q 2 art. 1 A. Cf. Henry of Ghent, *Quodlibeta commentariis doctissimis illustrata* (Paris, 1518) art. 13 q 2. Neither Scotus, Durand nor Occam named his opponent. Durand has more than one theologian in mind: "Circa istam quaestionem est duplex opinio. Prima aliquorum dicentium quod persona divina non potest assumere aliquam naturam irrationalem." Durandus de sancto Portiano *Commentaria in IV libros Sententiarum* (Lugduni, 1562), III *Sent.* d 2 q 1 n 6.

[40] ". . . ut refert Joannes Picus in appologia [sic] sua q 4." Biel III *Sent.* d 1 q 2 art. I A; cf. *ibid.* art 2 ad 5. Pico, *Apologia* in *Opera Omnia*, vol. I (Basiliae, 1572), p. 160.

[41] Cf. above Chapter One, section III.

[42] "Hec breviter et humili cum submissione succinctim ex predictis elicere placuit pro qualicunque incipientium eruditione." This survey is printed between III *Sent.* d 22 and d 23.

potentia absoluta God could have chosen anything created as the object of assumption. Biel, however, prevents this form of *asinus-Christology* from becoming mere speculation by adding that *de facto* — that is, *de potentia ordinata* — God can probably only assume the nature of a human being or an angel.[43] Biel's intention is the same as that of Scotus and Occam: God did not assume a complete man but human nature. Biel's parallel interests appear finally also from the fact that he tries to stress the reality and concreteness of the humanity of Christ.[44]

After surveying the late medieval official ecclesiastical pronouncements, we have to conclude that measured by the doctrinal standards of his time, Biel is formally orthodox in his christological teachings.[45] It is only in the mariological corollaries that it becomes clear that his orthodox rejection of the statement *homo purus*, intended as a rejection of the assumptionist theory,[46] actually undermines the Chalcedonian confession: Christ is *homo verus*.

II. *Christus Victor*

1. Medieval understanding of the *communicatio idiomatum*

We have already mentioned once the term *communicatio idiomatum*. Though Biel discusses its role and meaning in the context of the analyses of the person of Christ, it is in the presentation of the work of Christ that we have to assess how the mutual communication or exchange of the properties of the two natures of Christ really functions.

This expression of long standing[47] has not been further developed in

[43] "Tametsi omnem entitatem absolutam, creatam suppositum divinum possit assumere; quia tamen solam naturam rationalem de facto assumpsit pro humani generis redemptione posset probabiliter et humili cum submissione teneri quod de facto sola illa natura assumi potest a verbo que est capax gratie unionis aut tali unita." *Ibid.*

[44] On twofold filiation, III *Sent.* d 8 q 1 art. 2; peccability, III *Sent.* d 12 q 1 art. 2; progressive knowledge, III *Sent.* d 14 q 1 art. 2 concl. 2; two wills, III *Sent.* d 17, q 1 art. 2 concl. 1.

[45] Bartholomaeus M. Xiberta, *Enchiridion de Verbo Incarnato: Fontes quos ad studia theologica collegit*, (Madrid, 1957) 44: 9–34.

[46] "Si enim natura humana ante assumptionem fuit persona, virgo maria concepit hominem purum quod est contra evangelium." III *Sent.* d 5 q 1 art. 3 dub. 2. Biel quotes here Bonaventura, III *Sent.* d 5 art. 2 q 2. resp.

[47] Cf. *Index doctrinarum XVI* drawn up by Xiberta, *Enchiridion*, p. 782 f. See also Altenstaig, fol. 44, fol. 104 f.

late medieval theology. In the nominalistic tradition, it is Gabriel Biel and Nicholas Oresme [48] who pay special attention to the exposition of the meaning of this term.[49] After Thomas Aquinas there was no material addition to the clear discussion of this problem by the Doctor Communis,[50] and neither Oresme nor Biel is an exception to this rule. Nor is the logical approach to the question which underlies the *communicatio idiomatum*, that is, whether one can say the same about Christ the Son of God as about Christ the man, a new development in late medieval theology.[51]

The one methodological difference is the frequent use of the distinction between God's *potentia absoluta* and God's *potentia ordinata*.[52] This emphasis, however, on the omnipotence of God, Biel asserts, is not meant to overrule logic but to strengthen the usefulness of this pagan auxiliary science, derived from observation of the natural order, by baptizing it

[48] Critical edition of Oresme's *De Communicatione idiomatum* by Borchert, *Der Einfluss*, p. 5*–41*.

[49] Biel is to a large degree dependent in his *Tractatus de potestate et utilitate monetarum* on Oresme's treatise *De origine, natura, iure et mutacionibus monetarum;* in the context of Christology he indeed quotes Oresme's work on the *communicatio idiomatum* with regard to the exact definition of the term but then structures his own discussion independently. III *Sent.* d 7 q 1 art. 1 nota 1. Cf. *Lect.* 20 E. Critical edition and translation of Oresme's *De origine . . . monetarum* by Charles Johnson, *The De Moneta of Nicholas Oresme*, (Edinburgh, 1956), p. 1–48. Cf. Albert D. Menut, "Maître Nicole Oresme, Le livre de Yconomique d'Aristote," in *Transactions of the American Philosophical Society*, new series, 47.5 (1957), p. 784 ff. For Biel see IV *Sent.* d 15 q 9 and the English translation of Biel's treatise *De Potestate . . . monetarum* by R. B. Burke, 1930.

More positive was the judgment of W. Roscher. He felt that as an economic thinker Biel stands in the same relation to the Saxon inventor of mercantilism as the "Reformatoren vor der Reformation" stand to the Reformation: "Ein ziemlicher Grad nationalökonomischer Einsicht im südwestlichen Deutschland . . . gipfelt in den Schriften Gabriel Biels . . ."; "Die Blüthe deutscher Nationalökonomik im Zeitalter der Reformation," Sitzung am 12. Dezember 1861 zur Feier des Geburtstages seiner Majestät des Königs, in *Berichte über die Verhandlungen der Königlich Sächsischen Gesellschaft der Wissenschaften*, Philol.-Hist. Klasse 13 (1861), p. 164 f.

[50] Backes, *Die Christologie des heiligen Thomas von Aquin und die griechischen Kirchenväter*, p. 287 ff. Borchert, *Der Einfluss*, p. 38 ff. Also with Nicholas of Cusa we find the usual unoriginal treatment of *communicatio idiomatum*. See Rudolf Haubst, *Die Christologie des Nikolaus von Kues* (Freiburg i. Br., 1950), p. 132 ff.

[51] Cf. Backes, *Die Christologie . . . Aquin*, p. 290; Borchert, *Der Einfluss*, p. 39.

[52] This point is stressed by Borchert, *Der Einfluss*, p. 74 ff.

in the knowledge of revealed truth in which the omnipotence of God is attested.[53]

Two questions have to be answered anew with respect to every individual theologian. First we must determine whether the principle of the *mutual* predication of the properties of the two natures of Christ is indeed honored or whether perhaps the concrete presence of one of the two natures is the pivot and point of departure while the other nature only appears in the form of predication. If the latter is true, the rule of the *communicatio idiomatum* serves to gloss over a basically monophysite deviation from the Chalcedonian formulation. In the second place, we must be on our guard against a mere verbal subservience to the subsistence theory: in this case the unity of the two natures is captured only in the *communicatio idiomatum*, with the result that the mutual predication camouflages an essentially Nestorian Christology.

An investigation of Biel's commentary on the *Sentences* does not help us to answer these questions. Here he repeats what since the time of Aquinas and Scotus had become the generally accepted interpretation and application of the mutual exchange of the properties of the two natures of Christ. To mention only the two most important points: first, the hypostatic union is viewed as the basis of this exchange; second, abstract predication is rejected. This latter point is necessary in view of the fact that the divine and the human nature are not to be identified, though they find their common carrier in the Person of Christ. The *communicatio idiomatum* does not therefore imply that one may say in the abstract, divinity is humanity. Concrete predication always presupposes the common carrier since it refers to *this* person Jesus Christ and is only as such valid.[54] In the *Puncta de incarnatione* and in his discus-

---

[53] "Et hoc dicere [deus est homo] non est logicam pervertere sed eam ad veritatis normam reducere ac eius veritatem declarare; quomodo si non cognoverunt perypathetici infideles, aristoteles scl. cum suis sequacibus, quid mirum si in his sicut in multis aliis erraverunt in quibus naturalem potentiam quam experientia docuit tantum attenderunt, divinam omnipotentiam que super naturam est ignorantes. Nec in hoc sunt immitandi a fidelibus quoniam fides orthodoxa et certissima multas veritates logicales naturalis et metaphisicalis revelavit ad quas gentiles philosophi minime pervenerunt." III *Sent.* d 7 q 1 art. 3 dub. 1.

[54] Dico primo quod abstracta nature humane non dicuntur de supposito divino. Hec enim est impossibilis: humanitas christi est christus, est verbum, est deus. . ." III *Sent.* d 7 q 1 art. 1 nota 1. Cf. Thomas, *ST* III q 16 art. 5; Scotus, *Ox.* III. d 7 q 1 n 4. On the different modes of proper concrete predication, see Biel, III *Sent.*

sion of "the mystery of the passion of Christ," under which title the work of Christ is presented, we find no further distinctive statements that help us to define Biel's position more sharply.

2. Biel's understanding of the Incarnation: *kenosis* and *extracalvinisticum*

When we turn to the christological statements in the *Sermones*, we still have to be extremely cautious not to reach too hasty conclusions. These passages usually are cast in a traditional garb which makes it hard to discern Biel's own mind behind the formulation. But judging on the grounds of his selection of traditional statements, we seem to find here a further elaboration of the accident-substance simile as applied to the relation of the human nature and the divine person, a simile suggested by Scotus and Occam and mentioned but not discussed at length in Biel's commentary on the *Sentences*.[55]

As in the *Sentences*, the reality of the personal union is repeatedly stressed.[56] Humanity and not man is assumed by the divine Person, and this humanity does not become the Word but is carried by it. Its relation now to the Word is that of the white color of the milk to the milk itself: the color is not the milk — but, as we would add — only an accident of the milk.[57] The accident-substance example excludes at the one hand the possibility of a confusion of the two natures. At the other hand it stresses the real relation between the two, whereas it does not admit of a Nestorian duality through parallelism.

On the one hand we may therefore say that the kerygma of the In-

---

d 7 q 1 art. 1 nota 2. Cf. III *Sent.* d 14 q 1 art. 3 dub. 3; III *Sent.* d 22 q 1 art. 3 *in fine.*

[55] "Unio illa inter ceteras uniones creaturarum magis assimilatur unioni forme sue accidentis ad subiectum suum. . .," III *Sent.* d 1 q 1 art. 1 cor. 7 K. Cf. *Lect.* 46 P.

[56] "Est enim facta unio duarum naturarum, humane et divine, non in natura aliqua, sed in persona," *S* III 9 F.

[57] ". . . hanc humanitatem filius patris sibi assumpsit personaliter ut humanitas illa in se non esset persona sed personaretur in verbo. Non tamen fieret verbum. Nec verbum fieret natura ista creata. Sed aliquomodo similiter subsisteret in verbo quomodo albedo est in lacte propter quam lac dicitur et est album; non tamen albedo est lac nec econverso." *S* III 9 I.

carnation is for Biel clearly based in the exinanition and condescension of God: God became man and sacrificed his glory to assume the miseries of the human condition.[58] On the other hand the accident-substance example functions at places in such a way that the Incarnation does not seem to entail a sacrifice on God's part, since the human nature is only the accident of the divine Person.

We see how this interpretation functions when Biel describes in one sermon what is for him the heart of the mystery of the Incarnation. This proves to be not the humanity, but the divinity of Christ; not the internal *kenosis*, but the fact that the immutable God became man without diminution or loss as regards any of his attributes. What would later be called the *extracalvinisticum* — the existence of the second *person* of the Trinity *et extra carnem*, and erroneously seen as an innovation on the part of John Calvin — tempers here the kenotic understanding of the Incarnation.[59]

In Chapter Seven, we noted how important it is for Biel in connection with the *fiducia* of the Christian that Christ can be shown to be a real man.[60] And in that context we noted a tension between fiducial hope and emphasis on the divine nature of Christ. In the present context we encounter this again in the unresolved tension between a decided concern, shared with Duns Scotus and Occam, to protect the concreteness of the human nature of Christ — and therefore a real exinanition of God precisely *in* the Incarnation — and the other pole of Biel's understanding of the human nature as merely external and accidental, expressed in his emphasis on the immutability of God, *notwithstanding* the Incarnation. The preponderance of this latter interpretation appears, as we shall see, from Biel's discussion of the *fiducia* of the Christian with respect to the Virgin Mary.

[58] *S* I 55 E.

[59] "Si autem extrema huius unionis consideramus quid mirabilius cogitari potest: deus immutabilis eternus sine sua mutatione fit homo novus in tempore. Deus infinitus, incomprehensibilis, ubique existens sine contradictione sui nihil perdens eorum que ipse est, unitur personaliter nature finite et loco circumscripte — ita ut nec minus in assumpta natura esset quia in se infinita, nec minor in se existeret quia in ista fuerat totum." *S* III 10 I. Cf. *S* II 30 E, F, and I. "Ita de celo descendisse dicitur non quia suam amitteret plenitudinem, sed quia in unitatem persone naturam terrenam suscepit." *S* II 30 D.

[60] See Chapter Seven, section II.

3. Biel's modification of Anselm: centrality of the life, not the death of Christ

The focal points of the work of Christ in Biel's theology can be best expressed with the titles "physician" and "instructor"; the decisive actions of Christ were his institution of the sacraments and his proclamation of the new law.[61] Thus the *viator* is provided with the energy and the knowledge to escape the prison broken open by the absolute obedience of Christ.[62] Therefore when we deal especially with the meaning which the passion of Christ has for Biel, it is not because Christ's role as mediator and victor is to be more emphasized than his role of physician or teacher, but because the victory of Christ is the precondition for the efficacy of his other roles.

Structurally Biel preserves the argument of Anselm's *Cur deus homo*. The *necessitas* motif is omitted, of course, in view of the other possibilities open to God *de potentia absoluta*, but the main structure of Anselm's argumentation looms up time and again.[63]

Apart from the rejection of the necessity of Christ's self-sacrifice, there are two more significant changes which are intimately related. The death of Christ does not seem to have the same centrality and significance for Biel as it has for Anselm. Expressed in terms current since late sixteenth-century orthodoxy, Biel stresses more the *obedientia activa* — Christ's fulfillment of the law throughout his life — than the *obedientia passiva* — his expiatory death for the sin of mankind.[64]

The passion of Christ is a continual suffering that began at the mo-

---

[61] "Universalis medicus christus universalia medicamenta attulit, quibus universa vulnera ac infirmitates sanavit," *S* I 81 A. "Omnis Christi actio nostra est instructio. Quia veritas, ideo nedum verba sua veritatem denunciant sed et facta, sive opera prolate veritati attestantur. . ." *S* I 82 A. Cf. *Lect.* 64 T and 70 T. ". . . non ut eadem agamus sed ut ex sua actione spiritualem doctrinam accipiamus," *Lect.* 78 F. See further the inventory of christological titles in *Lect.* 20 K.

[62] *S* II 11 G.

[63] III *Sent.* d 16 q 1 art. 2 concls. 1–4. *S* II 13 N. Cf. III *Sent.* d 20 q 1 art. 2 concl. 1. The chosen way of redemption is, however, *congruentissimus* and based on God's wisdom, *ibid.*, concl. 2. On the structure of Anselm's argumentation see the clear presentation by Krijn Strijd, *Structuur en inhoud van Anselmus' "Cur Deus Homo"* (Assen, 1958), esp. p. 70 ff. With a summary in English and extensive bibliography, p. 301 ff.

[64] Cf. Heinrich Heppe and Ernst Bizer, *Die Dogmatik der evangelisch-reformierten Kirche* 2 ed. (Neukirchen, 1958), pp. 358, 369 ff.

ment of his birth, the flight to Egypt, and the poverty of his youth.[65] Christ's death on the cross is only the culmination of a whole life dedicated to obedience and fulfillment of the law. Death was incidental; for what God required of his son was perseverance in righteousness and truth.[66]

This is more than a traditional declaration of the spontaneity of Christ's offer. Biel is primarily interested in the quality of Christ's life, tested and exemplified in his death.[67] And although the propitiation motif is by no means absent, one surmises that the imitation-of-Christ ideal shapes Biel's presentation of Christ's passion. The God-directed Anselmian interpretation of Calvary is markedly less characteristic of Biel's position than the man-directed Abelardian understanding of the work of Christ.

This observation leads us to another related point. The emphasis on the paradigmatic significance of the life and death of Christ determines also the evaluation of the fruits of Christ's obedience and sacrifice. According to what we have called the second eternal decree, the *viator* has to fulfill the law and meet certain set standards of justice. In the life of Christ, especially in the incarnation but also in the passion, a love of God is revealed that has a profound impact on the *viator*. Nevertheless, one cannot profit from the work of Christ without a spontaneous love for God above everything else. The sufficiency of the work of Christ is seen as a sufficient revelation of God's will;[68] in other words it is viewed as a testament.

[65] "Passio domini inter omnes vite huius passiones fuit maxima . . . propter temporis communitatem quia passus est in infantia angustias uteri, fetorem stabuli, indigentiam materni obsequii, persecutionem adversarii, fugam egypti, circumcisionem secundum legem moysi. In puericia et adolescentia labores . . . in iuventute paupertatem, famem . . . , diaboli tentationem. . ." *S* II 24 *in fine*. Largely *verbatim* in III *Sent*. d 15 q 1 art. 2 pars 2 concl. 2.

[66] "Tenendo igitur indeclinabiliter veritatem et iusticiam christus fecit id quod paterna exigit obedientia . . . mortem ergo non exigit pater a filio sed iusticie et veritatis perseverantiam, ad quam malicia iudeorum mors est subsecuta." *S* I 33 D.

[67] "Mors ergo non fuit principaliter intenta tanquam propter se eligibile bonum, sed perseverantia veritatis et iusticie," *ibid*.

[68] "Hac tractione [John 12:32] omnes traxit, quia per sui exaltationem in cruce super terram omnia sufficienter exhibuit quibus se ad se trahi volentes sibi iungantur et trahi non volentes inclinentur ut velint petentque ut trahantur. Quia enim redemptio et liberatio hominis quocumque modo fieret, ex divino tamen decreto nulli proficeret ad salutem qui libera voluntate per amorem dei non adheret." *S* IV 29 B. Cf. *S* I 39 F; *Lect*. 85 X.

The sacrifice of Christ is also sufficient with respect to the remission of sins of baptized children who are redeemed by the work of Christ *alone*.[69] With respect to adults, however, the work of Christ alone is not sufficient: "Though the passion of Christ is the principal merit on account of which grace is infused, the kingdom opened and glory granted, yet it is never the sole and complete meritorious cause." And again: "If we do not add our merits to those of Christ, the merits of Christ will not only be insufficient, but nonexistent." [70]

4. Imitation of the *Christus Victor*

The same imitation motif which we surmised behind Biel's primary interest in the *obedientia activa* seems here to lead him to statements that according to late medieval doctrinal standards can hardly be called orthodox.[71] What Biel actually wants to express is not that the work of Christ as such is insufficient,[72] but that the intention of his work can be frustrated by the disobedience of the *viator*. This possibility of frustration is the counterpart of the *pro nobis* theme which we discussed in the context of the doctrine of justification. Christ not only gained a victory over the devil and thus liberated mankind, but he also showed those who are freed from prison the way out and home.

In the first sense, Christ as *victor*, the work of Christ is complete and sufficient. In the second sense, Christ as example or as *dux*, the work of Christ awaits completion pending the decision of the freed *viator* to follow and imitate him.

The same sermon from which we quoted the bold statement that the

[69] ". . . sufficiens et valde sufficiens fuit pena christi innocentis ut propter eam pater dimitteret etiam sine alia pena peccata omnium christo coniunctorum que etiam sola operatur remissionem peccatorum in baptismate parvulum," *Lect.* 72 I.

[70] ". . . sequitur quod licet passio christi sit principale meritum propter quod confertur gratia, apertio regni et gloria nunquam tamen est sola et totalis causa meritoria," III *Sent.* d 19 q 1 art. 2 concl. 5. "Cui nisi nostrum meritum iungatur insufficiens, imo nullum erit," *S* II 11 G.

[71] "Ex quo sequitur: nisi christum imitemur beatitudinem non consequamur," *S* IV 15 E.

[72] "Sola christi passio in cruce consummata medium est quo regenerationis sacramento denuo nascimur et christo capiti tanquam membra incorporamur," *S* IV 16 E. "Hanc charitatem a nobis habere non possumus sed eam per meritum christi in assumpta humanitate recepimus — gratia enim per iesum christum facta est," *S* IV 15 D.

work of Christ is even less than insufficient unless complemented by human merits suggests that this is to be understood within the imitation context, and therefore indicates that the work of Christ will prove to be of no avail on judgment day for the unconverted sinner.[73] The passion of Christ, sufficient in itself, will be efficacious only for the elect who indeed imitate Christ and follow him as their leader.[74]

It is in the *Christus Victor* theme that Biel expresses the sufficiency of the work of Christ. His victory over devil and hell is complete: the power of the devil to incarcerate those who are informed by faith and love is broken once and for all. As *victor* he becomes the *dux* who leads (*eduxit*) the innocent children and the saints of the Old Covenant out of their prison.[75]

The *Christus Victor* concept, though not the dominant theme of Biel's kerygma, proves to be the systematic key to Biel's Christology since here the disparate lines we noted above suddenly converge. The first of these lines was the emphasis on the divinity of Christ. While the body of the Son of Man lies in its grave, it is the Son of God, in hypostatic union with the soul of Christ but no longer true man,[76] who descends to break open the gates of Hell.[77] Second, it is through Christ's complete fulfillment of the law, his *obedientia activa*, that the devil cannot hold Christ in his power, a reverberation of the early Christian image of the fish and the hook.[78] And third, we see how Christ's work can be suffi-

---

[73] "Venit dominus propter nos non solum redimendos sanguinis effusione, sed et docendos verbis et exemplis nihilominus instruendos . . . Sed, charissimi, attendite hunc ducem, toto animo sequamini, qui viam precedens ostendit," S II 11 G. Cf. S I 52 A.

[74] ". . . satis et supra pro omnibus laboravit, offerens passionem suam efficaciter pro electis tamen," S II 24 s.v. *consummatum*. Cf. S. I 9 E; S II 13 H.

[75] "Eduxit . . . omnes quos fide et charitate formatos repperit . . . Destruxit autem infernum illum: diaboli potestatem auferendo ut decetero diabolus nullum in ibi detinere possit nec per instans qui est deo charitate coniunctus, nisi fuerit debitor pene sensus. Et ideo infantes baptizati mox evolant ad vitam, si moriuntur in innocentia." S II 26 D. Cf. *Lect.* 56 C and Bartholomaeus von Usingen: ". . . christus dedit se sub legem ut redimeret non a lege sed a servituti peccati et potestate diaboli," *Libellus . . . contra Lutheranos*, fol I 4ʳ.

[76] "Christus in mortis triduo non fuit verus homo," III *Sent.* d 22 q 1 art. 2 concl. 1. Cf. concls. 2 and 3. "Mors ad tempus carnem et animam separavit sed neutrum a verbo dei," S II 26 C. "Corpus vero christi unitum deitati mansit in sepulchro," *ibid.* D. Cf. S II 28 D.

[77] "Invasor est iste, non debitor; effractor, non peccator," S II 25 C.

[78] "O, princeps noster, lucifer, ad quid illum adducere voluisti? Si eum aliqua

cient and complete for baptized children, while for the common *viator*, swayed between fear and hope, Christ is only a *dux* to be followed in trial and error.

Finally, Biel's pastoral advice, in light of the *Christus Victor* idea, speaks for itself: the most powerful weapon and strongest antidote against attacks of the devil is the cross.[79] To what we have noted in Chapter Seven "Between Fear and Hope," we need only add that resurrection and ascension follow the victory over hell and the devil as its result, reward, and evidence; and as such they are definitely more important than Calvary.[80]

It is clear that Biel's Christology exemplifies the compatibility of the imitation-of-Christ ideal with the *Christus Victor* motif. Nevertheless these two themes should be distinguished; they can be discerned as pointing respectively to the insufficiency and to the sufficiency of the work of Christ. Whereas passive obedience belongs in the context of an Anselmian interpretation of the work of Christ, Biel stresses active obedience together with an Abelardian interest in the impact on mankind of the work of Christ.

It is the active obedience of Christ that serves as an explanation of the victory over the devil. *The Christus Victor motif provides the systematic key to Biel's Christology.* The viator must first reap the fruits of the victory of the *Christus Victor*.[81] To the degree to which the *viator* imitates Christ's active obedience, to this degree he too will overcome the powers of devil and hell.

---

delicta sustentarent, nunquam nostras tenebras suo dissiparet fulgore," *Ibid.* "Sed venit redemptor et victus est deceptor," *S* I 34 C.

[79] "Nullum cruce christi contra diaboli insidias compendiosius et efficacius antidotum quia nullum humilius, nullum insuper arrogantie diaboli magis adversum, nullum quod ita impium prostraverit," *S* IV 29 D.

[80] "Ipse enim est fortior superveniens qui fortem armatum vicit, arma abstulit, spolia reduxit . . . Ecce in christi resurrectione hodierna nostra natura iam suam consecuta est beatitudinem." *S* II 28 A,C. "Christus autem ad honorem deitatis secundum naturam humanam ad beatitudinem patris . . . propinquius accedit. . ." *S* II 30 H.

[81] "Ad hoc autem quod nos in finem reduceret quattuor requirebantur. Primum quod pugnator noster institueretur, quod factum est in nativitate. Secundum quod pugnaret quod factum est in passione. Tertium quod vinceret quod factum est in resurrectione quoniam eternitatis aditum devicta morte reseravit. Quartum quod victorie sue omnes suos participes faceret, quod erit in iudicio quando bonis bona et malis mala reddet. . ." III *Sent.* d 25 q 1 art. 2 concl. 5 O.

III. The Two Offerings: The Cross and the Altar

1. The sacraments linking Christology and justification

At this point we begin to discern the connecting links between Christology and the doctrine of justification: the devil is overcome, the prison is opened; now the Christians have only to follow their leader.[82] What one may call the "subjective" link between Christology and justification we shall pursue in Chapter Nine on Mariology. In this chapter we shall be concerned with the "objective" link: the institution of the sacraments.

To provide the power actually to follow him, Christ instituted the sacraments.[83] The last passage of Book Three of the *Sentences* — very similar in tone to the *Sermones* — provides the transition from Christology, via the concept of Christ as the legislator, to the sacraments, the means provided to partake in Christ's merits.[84]

2. The cross as testament; the sacrifice of the Mass as representation

In the context of the doctrine of justification, two of the major sacraments, baptism and penance, were discussed. Here we shall confine our treatment to some aspects of the Eucharist. Whatever reservations one may have with respect to Iserloh's interpretation of Occam's doctrine of the Eucharist, or Anatriello's lack of interpretation in his study of Biel's doctrine of the Eucharist,[85] their studies have thrown light on the thought

[82] "Nec restat nisi viam arripere et cenam ingredi, seseque celestis mense convivam futurum facere. . . ," *S* I 52 A.

[83] "Salvavit populum suum iesus noster medicinam preparando," *S* II 13 D. ". . . usus necessarius magis . . . eucharistia, baptismus, penitentia," *S* I 76 A.

[84] "Siquidem perfecta charitas foras mittit timorem: hanc charitatem recipit christus legislator noster et tanquam signum sue legis ac discipulatus prestituit dicens Joh. 13 [:35]: 'In hoc cognoscent omnes quod mei discipuli estis, si dilectionem habueritis ad invicem.' Quam nobis infundere et infusam conservare dignetur qui prior dilexit nos et dedit semetipsum pro nobis ut nos redimeret ab omni iniquitate. Dedit autem se pro nobis oblationem et hostiam deo patri in odorem suavitatis. Cum quo regnat et vivit . . . Amen." III *Sent.* d 40 q 1 art. 3 dum 3 F. Cf. *S* II 9 I.

[85] Pasquale Anatriello, *La dottrina di Gabriele Biel sull'Eucaristia* (Milan, 1937). Biel's doctrine of transubstantiation is judged orthodox except for one secondary point where his teaching runs counter to a decision of the Council of Florence (p. 177). It is important to note that the extensive discussion of transubstantiation is not a mark of "philosophical theology" but rather an apologetic response to scepticism:

structure and especially on the philosophical problems underlying the doctrine of the Eucharist according to Occam and Biel.

Our aim is to show briefly what the Eucharist meant in terms of academic theology for Biel as well as the manner in which he discussed its significance outside the strictly academic setting. Although Biel in his *Sentences* commentary discusses philosophical aspects of eucharistic theology, in his sermons he warns repeatedly against curiosity about problems such as the quantity and ubiquity of the eucharistic Christ. The mystery of transubstantiation is to be accepted on grounds of God's omnipotence and trustworthiness.[86] It would be fallacious to interpret this as an oblique criticism of the approach of his revered teacher Occam in an academic work such as *De sacramento altaris*. It is rather an expression of the general nominalistic agitation against the impact of metaphysics on the realm of the *pure credibilia*, and a protest against the "vain curiosity" of theologians who deafen the ears of the simple, for whom the *fides implicita* is the most salutary form of faith. But this view does not prevent Biel from going into subtle details in *S* II 45.

The institution of the sacraments as such is already a token of God's love since it implies the condescension and adaptation of God to the fragility of carnal men. By these visible means, God disposes man for the knowledge and possession of invisible grace.[87] The institution of the Mass is similarly and in a very special sense a token of God's love. While Christ

---

"Ille obiectiones mote sunt propter infideles et philosophos, qui specialiter propter hunc articulum invehere solent contra fidem et eam deridere." *Lect.* 44 H.

[86] Biel is concerned that academic theology not undermine the faith. "Curiosas autem questiones quomodo magnus sub parvo, quomodo idem in diversis simul locis esse possit et similes, relinquant: totum deo committant, apud quem non est impossibile omne verbum, qui de nihilo mundum creavit et in nihilum cum placeret redigere potest." *S* II 19 C. Cf. "Nec curiositate allectus querat hincinde quomodo ista ita se habere possint, sed captivet intellectum suum in obsequium christi, innitens eius omnipotentie et veritati infallibili. . . ," *S* II 21 F. However, his criticism of curiosity does not imply that Biel refrains from pointing out in detail the "miraculous" aspects of transubstantiation. See *S* II 45 *in toto*.

The doctrine of the Eucharist is discussed in IV *Sent.* d 8–13, with constant referral to the parallel passages in the *Expositio*. See further the critical apparatus of the forthcoming edition of the *Expositio*, of which Part I will soon be published.

[87] "Ut ergo ex omni parte nostre infirmitati consuleret etiam sensibilia signa instituit quasi vasa gratie et medicinas efficaces quibus nos homines carnales sensuali cognitioni inherentes disponeremur ad gratie invisibilis cognitionem, appetitionem et consecutionem," *S* II 13 F. Man is more susceptible to the images which he can see than to the sermon which he hears: ". . . quoniam que oculis videntur fortius movent quam que ore proferentur et solo percipiuntur auditu," *Lect.* 19 K.

merited the efficacy of all the sacraments by the effusion of his blood,[88] his sacrifice on the cross is particularly connected with the Eucharist. The word "testament" used in the words of consecration, "Hoc est enim corpus meum. Hic est enim calix sanguinis mei, novi et eterni testamenti," signifies the distribution and promise of the fruits of the work of Christ on Calvary.

Even as a testament becomes unchangeable and valid through death, so Christ established and validated through his death the new testament which is the right faith and the new law. Thus Christ distributed and promised an eternal inheritance to his brethren.[89] We note here explicitly that this inheritance of Christ is not the remission of sins, but primarily the establishment of the New Law.

It is this element of the unchangeable testament that plays such an important part in Biel's discussion of the relation of the sacrifice on the cross and the sacrifice of the Mass. One conceivable relation of these two offerings is explicitly rejected: the offering of the Mass is not a reiteration of the offering on the cross. Positively, Biel expresses this relation with the same concept Aquinas had used before him and which was to be used by the Council of Trent after him: *representatio*.[90] Biel does not deny that the offering of the Mass is a true sacrifice: the same victim is daily offered up. But nevertheless Christ has offered himself on the cross once and for all and thus acquired the benefits of which the Church partakes in the representation of this offering.[91]

[88] "His efficaciam meruit sanguinis effusione. . . ," *ibid.*

[89] ". . . cum testamentum sit ultima distributio bonorum morte testatoris firmata seu constitutio vel traditio de ordinandis bonis attestatione legitima firmata: recte fides et lex christi est testamentum novum. In illa siquidem christus eternam hereditatem fratribus suis et fidelibus distribuit, ordinat et promittit. Hec autem lex confirmata est per mortem et passionem christi in qua sanguis eius effusus est que effusio est sui testamenti legitima attestatio et confirmatio. Testamentum enim nisi in morte testatoris roboretur non est immobile et stabilitum pro quanto semper a testatore poterit et revocari et immutari. . ." *Lect.* 53 N. "Ecce novus rex, nova lex, novum sacrificium, novum testamentum . . ." *S* II 44 G. Cf. Nicholas de Lyra, *Postilla* Ad Hebraeos 9: 16, 17; IV. 1303ᵛ. Iserloh has pointed to Lyra's comment on Ps. 110:5 in *Postilla* II. 526ᵛ, in his *Die Eucharistie in der Darstellung des Johannes Eck*, p. 171. On the testament-motif in Eck, see p. 70 ff., 168 ff.

[90] "Offertur idem Christus a nobis non in mortem, sed in mortis memoriam. Unde nostra oblatio, non est reiteratio suae oblationis in poenam, sed repraesentatio ad provocandam Dei misericordiam." *SCE* 77ᵛ; *Lect.* 19 I; *Lect.* 85 F. Cf. Thomas, *ST* III, q 83 a 1; Trent, Sessio 22 (Sept. 1562), cap. 1; Denz. 938.

[91] "Institutum est primo in verum sacrificium . . . sed ecce sicut verbum abbreviatum fecit dominus super terram (ait Gerson) ita et hostiam abbreviatam . . .

Biel does not use the Tridentine terms, "cruente" and "incruente," to distinguish the two offerings,[92] but states in a similar fashion that the same victim which was offered on Calvary to carry the punishment, who was wounded and died once and for all, is now daily offered under the form of bread without these marks of punishment.[93]

There are nevertheless two reasons why the same sacrifice is daily offered. The *whole* liturgy of the Mass, that is, its three chief elements: consecration, oblation, and communion, represent Calvary and are its continuous memorial. In the second place the results which Christ acquired through his offering on the cross in general, for all, are now applied to those who offer and eat him.[94]

The reiteration in the Mass is therefore not of an historical nature but is one of imitation and memory.[95] To clarify further the relation of the two offerings, Biel quotes the words of St. Augustine in "Ad Simplicianum," where it says that we call the original and its image with the same name: "Just as when we see a painting or a mural, we say, that is Cicero, that is Salustius." [96] Biel does not use this quotation from St. Augustine to express a Platonic *identity*, but to describe the *dissimilarity* of the two modes of offering.[97]

Hostiam semel oblatam in cruce . . . Eandem in sacramento quotidie offerendam in qua omnia illius oblationis in cruce facte beneficia et fructus participamus." *S* II. 22 B. *Lect.* 15 F; *Lect.* 21 E. Cf. Gerson *Tractatus nonus super Magnificat* in *Opera Omnia,* IV. 413 C. See for "verbum abbreviatum": *S* II 44 G. For the same term in Wessel Gansfort, see van Rhijn, *Wessel Gansfort,* p. 175.

[92] Denz. 94.

[93] "Quamvis autem semel oblatus est in cruce christus offertur, nihilominus quotidie idem ipse velatus tamen sub panis sacramentali specie. Non quidem quantum ad ea que penam important quasi iterum vulneraretur, pateretur et moreretur. Surrexit enim in corpore impassibili et glorioso: non iterum moriturus." *S* II 46 E. Cf. *Lect.* 27 K.

[94] "Sed ex aliis duabus causis: prima quia illius sacrificii uniti in cruce immolati huius panis in altari consecratio oblatio et sumptio representativa est et continuum memoriale. Secunda quia similium effectuum operativa in singulis offerentibus vel sumentibus quos unica illa generaliter in omnibus operata est in cruce." *S* II 46 E. Cf. *Prol.; Lect.* 27 L; *Lect.* 85 F. Aquinas, *ST* III q 79 art. 1.

[95] "Ibi in veritate passionis qua pro nobis occisus est, hic in figura et immitatione passionis eius qua christus non iterum vere patitur sed ipsius vere passionis memoria quotidie nobis iteratur." *S* II 46 E.

[96] "Solent autem . . . imagines illarum rerum nominibus appellari quarum sunt imagines; sicut cum intuentes tabulam aut parietem pictum, dicimus: Ille Cicero est, ille Salustius." *Lect.* 85 F. Augustine, *PL* XL, 143. Cf. *S* II 46 E.

[97] *S* II 46 E. "Est ergo oblatio altaris satis inferior quantum ad fructum ad illam in cruce. . . ," *ibid* H. Cf. *Lect.* 27 L.

It would be wrong to conclude at this point that the Eucharist is for Biel a "mere memorial," a psychological representation of a past historical event. The *representatio* of Calvary means participation in the inheritance disclosed in the testament signed by the blood of Christ on Calvary.

3. Transubstantiation and the real presence of Christ

Through transubstantiation Christ's real presence on the altar is effected not only so that the same victim can be offered but also so that communion with Christ can take place by which the communicant is incorporated in his mystical body.

In his discussion of the philosophical aspects of the problem of transubstantiation, Biel restricts himself mainly to a presentation of Scotus and Occam. On the understanding of the successive stages of transubstantiation, these two authorities do not agree. As usual, however, Biel shows that this disagreement is a matter of defining one's terms.[98] A more serious matter concerns the quantitative aspect of the presence of Christ in the Eucharist. It had been the special opinion of Occam that "quantity is only a connotative term which signifies either a substance or quality."[99] Christ's body, though definitely present, is not present as a quantity.[100] Since Scotus taught the common scholastic opinion that quantity is really distinct from substance and quality, Biel is forced to choose, and indeed opts for Occam's interpretation.[101] At the same time, however, it is in this context that Biel once notes a subtlety in Occam which does not satisfy him.[102] But along with Occam, Biel defines the real presence of Christ in the Eucharist in such a way that the historical

---

[98] ". . . ita doctores illi non dissident quantum ad rem, sed tantum quantum ad vocabuli rationem." *Lect.* 40 A. Cf. *Ib.* K. This is again an example of the general nominalistic effort to overcome the thirteenth-century party strife among theologians. Cf. Occam: "Difficultas est tantum in voce." III *Sent.* q 9 H, noted by Iserloh but interpreted as escapism; *Gnade und Eucharistie . . . Ockham*, p. 282.

[99] Gabriel Buescher, *The Eucharistic Teaching of William Ockham*, (Washington, D.C., 1950), p. 67 ff; p. 143.

[100] *De corpore christi*, c. 31; *The De sacramento altaris of William of Ockham*, ed. T. Bruce Birch (Burlington, 1930), p. 92 ff.

[101] ". . . corpus christi (ut in sacramento) non est quantum quia ut ibi non habet partem extra partem, sed omnes partes coexistunt similiter cuilibet puncto speciei sacramentalis. . ." *Lect.* 43 O; cf. IV *Sent.* d 10 q 1 art. 2 concl. 1, 2.

[102] *Lect.* 48 P. "Sed quamvis hec imaginatio sit subtilis, non tamen videtur satisfacere. . ." *Lect.* 47 P.

body of Christ, the issue of the Virgin Mary, becomes present on the altar.[103]

There are two forms of physical presence: *circumscriptive* and *definitive*. The first form is the usual mode of local presence of a thing. In this case the total thing is present in the whole space it occupies, and every single part of it is in every single part of this space. The second form is illustrated by the presence of the soul in the body and of an angel on a certain place. Here again the whole object is present in the whole space it occupies — and not outside of it — but this time not a part, but the whole is in every part of the space it occupies.[104]

While the body of Christ exists *circumscriptive* in heaven, it is present on the altar *definitive*; in heaven Christ leads a quantitative existence, on the altar not.[105]

From two directions Biel finds this position threatened; remarkably enough both enemies are represented by Berengar of Tours. The first group are the spiritualists, who hold that when Christ says "this is my body," this has the same figurative meaning as when it is said, "this rock is Christ." They feel that Christ is only eaten *in signo*, and that till the end of the world Christ is in heaven at one and the same place; only his truth is everywhere present.[106]

Biel assails this position with some of the sharpest words he ever uses. He describes it as most dangerous, pernicious, against the Christian faith, against the greatness of God's love and also against the dignity of the sacrament. His main argument is that this miraculous presence of Christ reveals the omnipotence of God and requires therefore true faith.[107]

While the spiritualistic position was Berengar's before his condemnation, Biel feels that — as usual with those who recant — after his con-

---

[103] ". . . imitans in hoc clarissimum doctorem Guilelmum Ockam . . . pono hanc conclusionem: corpus christi quod sumptum est de virgine maria . . . sub specie panis vere et realiter continetur." Cf. *De corpore christi*, c. 7; cf. ed. Birch, p. 6.

[104] *Lect.* 35 Z. In I *Sent.* d 37 q 1 a 1 nota 1 C. Biel mentions a third possibility, *repletive*, which differs from the *definitive* mode of presence in that the above cited qualification "and not outside of it" is omitted: This last form is the general ubiquity of God. For Occam, see Iserloh, *Gnade und Eucharistie . . . Ockham*, pp. 174, 197 ff; Buescher, p. 75 ff. See also *penetrative* in *Lect.* 46 E.

[105] IV *Sent.* d 10 q 1 art. 2 concl. 2.

[106] *Lect.* 39 A.

[107] *Ibid.*, B. Cf. *S* II 13 L.

demnation he went too far in the opposite direction. Unless one interprets the terms Berengar used, such as "to break" and "to rip to pieces," in relation to the accidents and not in relation to the indivisible substance, one falls into a worse error than the spiritualistic error of Berengar ever was.[108]

4. Communion as participation in the messianic meal: the problem of non-participation

We terminate our discussion with two final observations. The eschatological dimension is not absent. Biel sees the sacramental eating as the "earnest" of the messianic meal to come.[109] The Eucharist as participation in the inheritance of the fruits of Christ's work means also the communion with the Church triumphant.[110]

Though the sacrifice of the Mass is chiefly intended for those who participate in communion, its fruits can also be applied to those who are present and to all for whom the Mass is especially celebrated.[111] "I speak

[108] ". . . est vera manducatio corporis christi . . . sed non digeritur nec convertitur in substantiam sumentis . . . nec tamen est ibi masticatio corporis christi nec divisio . . . Sed ibi est masticatio, fractio et divisio specierum sive sacramenti, non contenti." *Lect.* 80 N.

[109] "Ego sum, inquit, panis vivus qui de celo descendi, qui maducat ex hoc pane vivet in eternum Joan. 6 [free version of John 6:51–52]. Propter hoc enim se dedit discipulis, datque quotidie christicolis se panem sub sacramenti velamine, quia daturus est se nobis panem fruendum in patria in clarissima visione. Hinc de pane sacramentali canit ecclesia: "O sacrum convivium in quo christus sumitur etc. future glorie nobis pignus datur." *S* I 31 D. Cf. *Lect.* 29 H; *Lect.* 39 A f.

[110] ". . . extra unitatem ecclesie non est locus offerendi sacrificium unitatis. Ideo sanctorum memoriam agimus in sacrificio quatinus in ipsorum oratione communionem habentes sacrificium offeramus . . . Ideo ut non rumpatur unitas offerimus laudis sacrificium cum sanctis communicantes. Communicantes scl. in usu et oblatione huius sacrificii cum sanctis qui hoc sacrificio medio salutem consecuti sunt quoniam ipsum est viaticum ad vitam eternam perducens . . . communicantes dixi in usu quia de sanctis dicitur quod erant perseverantes in doctrina apostolorum et in communicatione fractionis panis. Actus 2 [:42]. Communicamus igitur cum sanctis in hoc sacrificio per continuationem . . . communicamus cum sanctis in sacramento altaris quia quod illi percipiunt in rei veritate, nos frequentamus in sacramentali specie." *Lect.* 30 A. Cf. *Lect.* 57 C, E; 56 G; 74 O, Q.

[111] "Offertur autem principaliter pro participantibus sumendo ipsum atque manducando . . . etiam pro circumstantibus. . ." *S* II 46 K. This "principaliter" is not honored by C. W. Dugmore when he says: ". . . Biel remarked that it is not at all necessary to communicate in order to participate. . . ," *The Mass and the English Reformers* (London, 1958), p. 64. Cf. Trent, sessio 22, Denz. 950.

of those standing around, not those loafing around," Biel adds with a jibe.[112]

Though Biel accepted transubstantiation as the proper interpretation of the mystery of the Eucharist, because this had been the decision of the Church, on other grounds other interpretations would have been more feasible. This does not imply that for Biel the decision of the Church had been arbitrary; the Church guided by the Holy Spirit chose this interpretation, notwithstanding its difficulties, because it was the true one.[113]

In accordance with our earlier conclusion that Biel in his *Sermones* and *Expositio* adds a broader theological perspective to Occam's discussions, we note that the problem of transubstantiation is certainly not the only eucharistic issue as Anatriello's study would seem to suggest. Along with a clarification of the relation of the offerings of Calvary and the Mass, Biel is interested in preserving the unity of consecration, offering, and communion. Though he does not of course deny that it can be fruitful to be present and hear the Mass, it is communion, along with faith and baptism, which makes one a Christian.[114]

[112] "Unde notanter dicitur circumstantium, non circumgirantium. . ." *Lect.* 29 B. See his sharp criticism of selling and shopping in churches and churchyards at the time of the service, *Lect.* 29 C. For the same abuses in Strasbourg see L. Dacheux, *Un réformateur catholique à la fin du XVe siècle: Jean Geiler de Kaysersberg* (Paris, 1876), pp. 70 ff, 87 ff. On other abuses of the time, especially concerning the clergy, see Adolph Franz, *Die Messe im deutschen Mittelalter* (Freiburg i. Br., 1902), p. 292 ff. Here also the most explicit discussion available on Egeling of Braunschweig (p. 537 ff.).

[113] ". . . ideo intellectum hunc difficilem elegit quia verus est." *Lect.* 41 M. Cf. L. Seeberg's judgment is too radical to be applicable to Biel: "Die Transsubstantiation stand kirchenrechtlich fest, die Theologie des ausgehenden Mittelalters hat an ihr keine Freude gehabt." Seeberg *DG* III, p. 791. Cf. Occam, IV *Sent.* q 6 D. Whereas Hochstetter sympathizes with Occam's emphasis on God's omnipotence ("Nominalismus?" *F Stud* 9 (1949), 347 f.), Guelluy criticizes Occam's logical rigorism, p. 129. Fritz Hoffmann, discussing Lutterell's criticism, comes to the same conclusion as Iserloh: "Man zweifelt an der religiösen Zielsetzung der Allmachtslehre Ockhams." *Die Schriften des Oxforder Kanzlers Iohannes Lutterell: Texte zur Theologie des vierzehnten Jahrhunderts* (Leipzig, 1959), p. 153. We have seen, however, that Biel — in his *Sentences* Commentary in basic agreement with Occam — shows throughout the religious potential of the nominalistic system.

[114] ". . . tria sunt que faciunt nos christianos fides, baptismus et altaris participatio," *S* II 16 A. "Instituit . . . eucharistie sacramentum pro quotidiana nutritione interioris hominis," *S* II 21 E.

5. Critical evaluation of Biel's position

We need to know far more about the precise late medieval positions of the spiritualists and the material realists, between which Biel finds the orthodox, that is, his own position, before we can establish precisely to which side Biel and the late medieval majority opinion would be relatively more inclined. If one accepts the appealing thesis of Dugmore [115] that we can discern a realistic Ambrosian tradition and an Augustinian tradition of realist symbolism, we can conclude on the grounds of the respective characteristics enumerated by Dugmore that Biel indeed achieved what he intended: to steer the middle course.[116]

Though the historical body of Christ is present, the sacrifice of Calvary is not reiterated. At the same time the *representatio* is not a mere memorial or a psychological exercise, but indeed an offering in a new mode of the same victim in communion with the Church triumphant. The Occamistic rejection of the quantitative presence of Christ as distinct from his substantial presence helped Biel to ward off a hypermaterialistic interpretation of the real presence of Christ. At the same time the doctrine of transubstantiation stimulated him to reject a spiritualization of the presence of Christ.

In a final evaluation of Biel's position, we must conclude that with all due appreciation for his efforts to *distinguish* the two offerings, Biel does not succeed in showing their *unity*.[117] Though Hebrews 10:19 is mentioned,[118] the high-priestly function of Christ which would success-

---

[115] C. W. Dugmore, *The Mass and the English Reformers* (London, 1958), pp. 22, 29 ff., 130 f.

[116] B. J. Kidd's judgment does not seem to portray the balance of Biel's position: "In short we have in Biel's language all the elements of a merely mechanical theory of sacramental operation abundantly provided for." *The Later Mediaeval Doctrine of the Eucharistic Sacrifice* (London, 1898; repr. 1958), p. 50.

[117] "Quamvis autem semel oblatus est christus in aperta carnis effigie, offertur nihilominus quotidie in altari, velatus in panis vinique specie. Non quidem quantum ad ea que poenam important; non enim christus quotidie vulneratur, patitur et moritur; sed ex aliis duabus causis eucharistie consecratio et sumptio sacrificium dicitur et oblatio. Tum quia illius sacrificii veri et immolationis sancte facte in cruce representativa est et memoriale. Tum quia similium effectuum operativa et principium causale." *Lect.* 85 F. Father J.H. Crehan has called attention to the fact that Biel is perfectly orthodox except perhaps where he speaks of *similar* effects rather than of *same* effects, as Trent's decree implies ("ratione diversa . . . sola offerendi." Denz. 940). "Biel on the Mass," *Clergy Review* 43 (1958), 610. He

fully link the two offerings is not adduced to clarify the exact content of the term *representatio*. Biel indeed explains his introduction of the term *representatio* as an attempt to avoid reiteration, but the emphasis in his use of the Cicero-Salustius simile is placed so heavily on the *representatio* aspect that the unity implied in *presentatio* is obscured. Without trying to force Biel into the mold of contemporary theology, still it seems necessary to point out that for Biel the sacrifice of the Mass remains a second sacrifice, proffered *ad provocandam dei misericordiam* — only historically related to the sacrifice of Christ on the cross.

---

argues that Luther "could not accept the idea of the Mass effecting any result like unto that of Calvary, and so it was that the second part of Biel's comparison of Mass and Calvary must go, but the first part could remain, and therefore the Eucharist was now to be for Luther no more than a showing forth and memorial of the Lord's death." *Ibid*, p. 609. It is hard to recognize in this description anything other than the doctrine of the Eucharist *rejected* by Luther at the Marburg Colloquy (1529). Not only from the point of view of Trent but also from the point of view of Luther the "similar" is to be rejected. It implies an indefensible distinction between Calvary and the Mass. Unlike Luther, Biel's "similar" can be seen as symptomatic of a theory which undercuts a true representation by designating the Mass as the *principium causale* of its effects.

[118] *Lect.* 29 H. Cf. *S* II 44 E, F on Hebrews 9:7 ff. *Lect.* 30 F on Hebrews 7:24 f. *Lect.* 20 I stresses the uniqueness of the *cruentum* aspect of the sacrifice of Christ.

Chapter Nine

MARIOLOGY

꙳ꙮ꙳ꙮ꙳ꙮ꙳ꙮ꙳ꙮ꙳ꙮ꙳ꙮ꙳ꙮ꙳ꙮ꙳ꙮ꙳ꙮ꙳ꙮ꙳ꙮ꙳ꙮ꙳ꙮ꙳ꙮ꙳ꙮ꙳ꙮ꙳

THE VIRGIN MARY AND GOD

I. Introduction

1. Distinctive treatments in academic and homiletical works

THE Mariology of Biel reflects the structure which usually characterizes systematic discussions of the work of Christ. Parallel to the two successive stages in the life and work of Christ — as the Word incarnate and as the glorified Son sitting at the right hand of the Father — one can distinguish two aspects of Biel's Mariology. The first concerns the Immaculate Conception, her maternity, and in general, Mary's instrumental cooperation with the Incarnation and passion of her son Jesus Christ. The second is her assumption into heaven and elevation to a position surpassed only by the Trinity from which she participates and mediates in the salvation of mankind.

We should further observe that, contrary to what we have come to expect, there is in Biel's Mariology a marked difference between his teaching and his preaching, that is, between the relevant sections in the *Collectorium* and *Expositio* on the one hand, and his sermons, especially the volume *De festivitatibus virginis gloriose* on the other. The latter contains groups of four sermons on each of the main events in Mary's life: the conception, purification, annunciatory visitation, nativity of the Son, and assumption, plus a general sermon on mariological issues, totaling sixty-two folios in four closely printed columns. It is only natural that the sheer quantitative difference from the relatively short passages in the other two works partially accounts for the peculiar character of this particular collection of sermons.

It is remarkable that this difference cannot be reduced to what one might expect, that is, Biel's approach to different audiences, or a difference between the academic and the homiletical style of presentation. The sermons are as carefully worded, as precisely divided and subdivided, as learned in presentation as might be expected in any commentary on Lombard. There is no overflow of sentiment, no rhetorical questions, although the language is undoubtedly more flowery than that of Biel's academic works, since he uses many direct and indirect quotations from Bernard of Clairvaux and Jean Gerson. However, Biel defends several mariological positions in these sermons which are only touched upon or are completely absent in his *Collectorium* and *Expositio*. Apparently, Biel the preacher felt more free to witness to what is clearly his own Marian piety than Biel the teacher, who felt primarily responsible for the traditionally much debated points of Immaculate Conception and cooperation with the Incarnation. While with respect to other aspects of his theology we have been able to quote indiscriminately from either academic or homiletic works, the mariological sermons are so much more personal in presentation that in this case we must distinguish between these two sources. However, as popular Marian piety has been the basis for later important developments in mariological doctrines, it is important to draw on these sermons to complete the picture of Biel's Mariology. In addition the presentation of these matters serves, of course, as a further commentary on our findings concerning such problems as justification, *fomes peccati*, and merits, and indirectly also on the Incarnation and passion of Jesus Christ.

It appears from all the sources concerned that Biel had more than a technical interest in mariological issues.[1] To gain the perspective neces-

---

[1] "In ihnen [the *Sermones de festivitatibus Marie*] geht dem Prediger erst recht das Herz auf, aber nun überwuchert auch die Phantasie; die Zucht des Geistes schwindet and die christliche Wahrheit wird arg entstellt." Gustaf Plitt, *Gabriel Biel als Prediger* (Erlangen, 1879), p. 19. If judged in the light of late medieval thought, Biel would neither here nor elsewhere seem to suffer from a lack of mental discipline. Note Plitt's further judgment on Biel's presentation of Mary's assumption: "Das heisst doch, wenn man die Sache beim rechten Nahmen nennen will, bei aller guten Meinung den Gläubigen von der Kanzel her etwas vorgelogen," p. 22.

sary for comprehension of Biel's position and also to assign him his proper place in the history of Marian theology, we shall begin with a discussion of some of his more influential authorities. The traditional and the original elements in Biel's thought can be highlighted in this context. Moreover it presents an objective basis for further evaluation. While the interest of mariologists has often been drawn to less prominent individuals who supported a future development, it seems equally important to analyze what a preacher as renowned as Biel, with a wide audience in an influential archiepiscopal see, taught with regard to these matters.

The theological background against which Biel presents his Mariology is the thought of the men who were important authorities for him in other matters as well: Duns Scotus, William of Occam, Jean Gerson, and Gregory of Rimini. In view of the excellent studies that have already been devoted to the Marian thought of the first three,[2] we shall when necessary refer to these, but concentrate our attention on Gregory of Rimini. Little attention so far has been paid to this aspect of the thought of the celebrated and influential General of the Augustinian order. He is all the more important for our purposes since Biel presents his own ideas in discussion with and in contrast to Gregory's.

2. The Immaculate Conception in the medieval tradition

The usual judgments about religious thought in the later Middle Ages have been applied also to its Mariology. René Laurentin, for example, feels that except for a few theologians such as Jean Gerson, and except for the issue of the Immaculate Conception, this "decadent" period

---

[2] Karl Balić, *Duns Scoti Theologiae Marianae elementa* (Sibenici, 1933); E. M. Buytaert, "The Immaculate Conception in the Writings of Ockham," *FStud* 10 (1950), 149 ff.; André Combes, "La doctrine mariale du chancelier Jean Gerson," *Maria: Etudes sur la sainte Vierge* 2 (Paris, 1952), 865 ff.; Aquilin Emmen, "Heinrich von Langenstein und die Diskussion über die Empfängnis Mariens," in *Theologie in Geschichte und Gegenwart: Festschrift Michael Schmaus*, ed. Johann Auer and Hermann Volk (Munich, 1957), p. 625 ff.; we are especially indebted to this author's: "Einführung in die Mariologie der Oxforder Franziskanerschule," *FS* 39 (1957), 99 ff.; Hyacinthius Ameri, *Doctrina theologorum de Immaculata B.V.M. Conceptione tempore concilii Basiliensis*, (Rome, 1954); Ignatius Brady, O.F.M. "The Development of the Doctrine on the Immaculate Conception in the Fourteenth Century after Aureoli," *FStud* 15 (1955), 175 ff.

shows a lack of original Marian thought coinciding with the reign of nominalism and philosophical "disintegration."[3]

Indeed, the issue of the Immaculate Conception of the Virgin Mary did absorb much of the theological interest of the time. The battle of the maculists versus the immaculists had raged since the days of Scotus' critique of Aquinas.[4] Scotus' influence spread quickly through Franciscan mediation at Oxford and Paris. In the second half of the fourteenth century the doctrine of the Immaculate Conception was already generally accepted within the Franciscan order,[5] and many influential theologians of other orders joined the ranks. In the last decade of this same century the immaculists' battlecry reached Vienna, where such a leading theologian as Henry of Hesse, after initial resistance, was won over to this doctrine.[6] Jean Gerson was instrumental in establishing the official Parisian law requiring all doctors there to teach the Immaculate Conception.

Thus the definition of this doctrine by the Council of Basel could not

[3] ". . . en général, on répète plus qu'on ne repense. L'appareil philosophique se complique et se sclérose. Le nominalisme sévit. La théologie tombe en poussière. Fuyant un intellectualisme desséché, on cherche la vie au plan de l'imagination et du sentiment. Durant cette décadence. . ." René Laurentin, *Court traité de théologie Mariale* (Paris, 1953), p. 52. Cf., however, for a different point of view, Clement Dillenschneider, *Marie: au service de notre rédemption* (Hagenau, 1947), pp. 214–234, on the corredemptrix theme in the 15th century.

[4] M. Jugie and X. Le Bachelet, "Conception Immaculée," in *DThC*, vol. VII, cols. 845 ff.

[5] F. de Guimaraens, "La doctrine des théologiens sur l'Immaculée Conception de 1250 à 1350," *Etudes Franciscaines* 3 (1952), 181 ff.; 4 (1953), 23 ff.; 167 ff. Brady, p. 194. The Dominican Holcot, however, did not accept Scotus' defense of the Immaculate Conception: "Fuit enim sanctificata in utero ita quod mundata a peccato originali et in ea fomes ligatus . . ." The concluding passage suggests an effort to mediate: "Necnon ab omni qualitate inordinata quam contraxerat ratione propagationis seminalis purgatum et emundatum. Et sic patet quod isto modo capiendo nomen conceptionis stricte et proprie, beata virgo non fuit concepta in peccato originali." *Sap.* Lect. 160 C. His discussion goes beyond the position of contemporary Dominicans, such as Thomas Sutton and Nicholas Trivet as they are presented by F. de Guimaraens, p. 37 ff. De Guimaraens, however, holds that "Holcot nie ouvertement l'Immaculée Conception dans le commentaire au livre de la Sagesse," p. 39. Cf. the position of Thomas Aquinas: "Sanctificatio beatae Virginis non potuit esse decenter ante infusionem animae quia gratiae capax nondum fuit, sed nec etiam in ipso instanti infusionis," III *Sent.* d 3 q 1 ad 2. See also *Quodl.* VI q 7 and *ST* III q 27 art 2 ad 3.

[6] Emmen, "Heinrich von Langenstein," p. 646: "Es erscheint uns auch unzweifelhaft, dass die Epistola von Langenstein die Behandlung der Frage der Empfängnis Mariens auf dem Konzil von Basel mitveranlasst hat."

have come as a surprise, well prepared as it was. The decision was made on September 15, 1439, and the doctrine of the Immaculate Conception was officially proclaimed two days later in the thirty-sixth session.[7] But since only the first twenty-two sessions of the Council were officially acknowledged by the *curia*, the battle over the doctrine was not yet ended. In all places where the decisions of Basel were accepted as legitimate such as Aragon, Germany, France, Savoy and Switzerland, this Marian doctrine found immediately a warm and wide reception. Nevertheless, the uncertainty surrounding the question of the ecumenicity of this Council laid its decisions open for attack. The Dominicans especially criticized its decision and used such strong language that they did not refrain from calling it the synagogue of Satan, whose diabolic first-born was the definition of the Immaculate Conception.[8] It is clear that the decision of the Franciscan Pope Sixtus IV, on February 27, 1476, to grant special indulgences to all attending services on the Feast of the Immaculate Conception could not be received with equal enthusiasm by all parties concerned.[9] The ensuing discussion took on such bitter and irreverent forms that further debate was forbidden in 1482 on pain of excommunication, a command which had to be repeated in 1483 and 1503.[10]

This outline of the development of the discussion about the doctrine

---

[7] See Ludwig von Pastor, *Geschichte der Päpste, seit dem Ausgang des Mittelalters*, I, 335 f.; Hefele, C. J. and H. Leclercq, *Histoire des Conciles*, VII (Paris, 1916) 1141; *Monumenta conciliorum generalium seculi decimi quarti Concilium Basiliense* ed. E. Birck, III (Basel, 1932), 362.

[8] I. De Turrecremata, *Tractatus de veritate conceptionis*, p. xiii c 18, ed. B. Spina et (De) Cataro OP (Romae, 1547), 276 f. as quoted by Meinolf Mückshoff, "Die Mariologische Prädestination im Denken der franziskanischen Theologie," *FS* 39 (1957), 457.

[9] Cf. the text Bulla "Cum praecelsa" in CIC, p. 1285. List of indulgences published in *Sermo in festo corporis christi*, Biel, S II 46 [fol. 276].

[10] A very interesting description of a phase of this ongoing debate is given by Otto Stegmüller, "Der Immaculata — Traktat des Basler Franziskaners Franz Wiler († 1514)," *Basler Zeitschrift*, 60 (1960) 47–64. A sermon on Prov. 8:24 by Johannes Zierer, O. P., preached at Strasbourg in 1478, is discussed by Florenz Landmann.: "Die unbefleckte Empfängnis Mariae in der Predigt zweier Strassburger Dominikaner und Geilers von Kaysersberg," *Archiv für elsässische Kirchengeschichte* 6 (1931), 189 ff. "Der Prediger erwähnt mit keinem Worte die Erbsünde, von der Maria bewahrt worden wäre" (p. 191). Charles Schmidt in *Histoire littéraire de l'Alsace* I, 19, mentions Biel as a protagonist of the immaculate conception together with Jacobus Wimpheling, Trithemius, and Johannes Heynlin a Lapide. For Sebastian Brandt, see Schmidt, I, 258 f.

of the Immaculate Conception makes sufficiently clear in what sphere Biel had to preach and lecture. On the one hand the doctrine of the Immaculate Conception already was for Biel himself part of the infallible tradition and teaching of the Church so that it could form a dependable basis for further mariological considerations; but on the other hand it was still open to so much debate that Biel's treatment has the flavor characteristic of a chronicle of contemporary events. Yet Biel is keen on omitting, especially from his sermons, anything that smacks of party strife or that might add to the bitterness with which this battle was being fought, often to the detriment of pastoral care.[11]

Biel's presentation has a freshness that may well be due not only to the continuation of the forbidden debate but also to the fact that for him this was not a stale issue which had been settled once and for all by such a high authority as Duns Scotus. On this point Gregory of Rimini, the leading nominalist schoolman of his day, had withstood the wave of Scotistic pressure to accept the doctrine of the Immaculate Conception and declared himself in favor of the position of Augustine, Bernard of Clairvaux, and Aquinas. Since Gregory is so often and extensively quoted by Biel in the *Collectorium*, it does not surprise us that he figures so prominently in Biel's mariological presentation.

II. The Mariology of Gregory of Rimini

1. Gregory between Scripture and tradition

In the second book of his commentary on the *Sentences*, Gregory first of all introduces three arguments from tradition in favor of the Immaculate Conception. These arguments, which can be found previously in William of Ware [12] and Duns Scotus, are intended to prove that God indeed

[11] ". . . advertendum quod de materia huius questionis fuerunt opiniones due contrarie frequenter nedum in scholis sed nonnunquam in declamatoriis ad populum sermonibus non sine scandalo populi ventilate," III *Sent.* d 3 q 1 art. 1 nota 3. The influential Dominican Archbishop of Florence, Antoninus of Florence, an older contemporary of Biel and quoted already in earlier parts of the *Expositio*, generally follows Albertus Magnus in his Mariology. He belongs to the maculists, but he does not pursue the debate when he preaches "De conceptione beatae Mariae," *Summa Theologica* (Graz, 1959) [photo reprint of ed. Veronae 1740 ff.], IV.xv.4 [col. 928 ff.] Cf., however, his academic discussion in *Summa*, I.viii.2 [col. 547 ff.].
[12] Master of Duns Scotus at Paris.

de facto preserved the Virgin Mary from original sin.[13] The first argument is based upon Augustine's statement that when dealing with the doctrine of sin, one should leave the Mother of God out of consideration.[14] Augustine would never have used these words according to this argument, unless he had firmly believed that Mary was exempted from original sin. The second rests on the authority of Anselm's *De Conceptu Virginali*, in which he formulated his influential mariological rule, parallel to his most famous proof of God's existence: "It would be fitting that the Virgin should be adorned with so much purity that more than that one cannot possibly imagine except for God."[15] If she had existed in original sin, it would have been possible to imagine a higher form of purity. Therefore the contrary must be true. The third argument refers to the old tradition of the yearly celebration of the feast of Mary's conception. This would never have been instituted if Mary had been under the yoke of original sin. The *sed contra* argument in Gregory is derived from St. Paul's letter to the Romans, according to which all men have sinned in Adam, through whom death spread over the whole race of men.[16]

In taking up the discussion Gregory deviates somewhat from the traditional structure of the solution of this problem. Since the days of Duns Scotus,[17] the generally accepted procedure was to ask first whether the Immaculate Conception was possible, then whether it was suitable, and finally whether it had in fact happened in this way. Gregory cuts short any question about possibility or suitability: the main issue is whether it has *de facto* happened; as there is here no *notitia intuitiva* and therefore no unquestionable evidence so far as the human reason is concerned, we must

[13] *Par.* III d 3 q 1 n 3, 7; *Ox.* III d 3 q 1 contra 1.

[14] Gregory, II *Sent.* d 30–33 q 2 art. 1 [fol. 114 C]; Augustine, *De natura et gratia*, cap. 36.42 in *PL* XLIV, 267.

[15] "Decens erat, ut ea puritate, qua maior sub Deo nequit intelligi, *Virgo* illa niteret." Anselm, *De conceptu virginali*, cap. 18 in *PL* CLVIII, 451 A. Cf. Scotus, *Ox.* III d 3 q 1 contra 2; Gregory, II *Sent.* d 30–33 q 2 art. 1 secundum [fol. 114 D].

[16] *Vulg.* Rom. 5:12 "Propterea sicut per unum hominem peccatum in hunc mundum intravit, et per peccatum mors; et ita in omnes homines mors pertransiit, in quo omnes peccaverunt." Gregory II *Sent.* d 30–33 q 2 art. 1 [fol. 114 D].

[17] "Quod autem horum triumque ostensa sunt probabilia esse factum sit, Deus novit; si auctoritati ecclesiae vel auctoritati scripturae non repugnet, videtur probabile quod excellentius est attribuere Mariae." *Ox.* III d 3 q 1 art. 1. Ignatius Brady has pointed out that Francis de Mayronis is responsible for the trilogy: *potuit - decuit - fecit*, Brady, p. 192. Cf. however Eadmer, *Tractatus de conceptione*, PL CLIX, 301.

answer the question of fact according to the witness of Scripture and tradition. "Therefore without any prejudice against a better opinion and without any reflection on the reverence due the Mother of God, it seems to me that one should say that she has been conceived with original sin."[18]

Gregory in no sense contrasts Scripture and tradition. It is the Romans passage on the all-pervasiveness of sin, as understood by the Fathers throughout the centuries, which led him to reject the three arguments quoted for the opposite opinion. Primarily drawn from Augustine, his arguments are: 1) everyone needs the remission of sins; if the Virgin Mary had been conceived without original sin, she would be exempt from this rule; 2) Christ alone was exempt from the law of sin; 3) through the *commixtio corporum* man comes under the general curse of Adam. Mary was conceived in exactly that way.[19]

Had Gregory closed the discussion at this point, his presentation would have been the usual one within the tradition of the Augustinian order. Giles of Rome,[20] Albert of Padua,[21] Augustinus Triumphus,[22] had written along these lines. Many of Gregory's nominalistic fellow schoolmen, however, such as Pierre d'Auriole,[23] and William of Occam,[24] had started to cross the boundary and accepted Scotus's opinion. This situation must have forced him to take the arguments of the Doctor Subtilis more seriously. For two of the principal arguments of his opponents Gregory presents with his own counterarguments.

[18] ". . . non queritur an fuerit possibile eam concipi sine tali peccato. Sed an de facto fuerit sine illo concepta; cum de hoc per humanam rationem certitudo haberi non possit, in hac parte id potius tenendum mihi videtur quod magis consonum est sacre scripture et dictis sanctorum; et ideo absque preiudicio melioris sententie et salva semper reverentia matris dei dicendum mihi videtur eam fuisse cum originali peccato conceptam," II *Sent.* d 30–33 q 2 art. 1 [fol. 114 D/E].

[19] ". . . constat quod nec beata virgo nec aliquis homo alius preter christum conceptus est sine concubitu parentum. . ." II *Sent.* d. 30–33 q 2 art. 1 [fol. 114 H]

[20] X. Le Bachelet, "Immaculée Conception," *DThC*, vol. 7 (Paris, 1922), col. 1055.

[21] John of Basel, O.E.S.A., took the immaculist position. See Sophronius Clasen, O.F.M., *Henrici De Werla, O.F.M., Opera omnia. I. Tractatus de Immaculata Conceptione Beatae Mariae Virginis* (St. Bonaventure, 1955), pp. xxvi, 56 f.

[22] E. Dublanchy, "Marie: Les privilèges essentiels de la Vierge Marie," *DThC*, vol. 9 (Paris, 1927) col. 2385.

[23] A. di Lella, "The Immaculate Conception in the Writings of Peter Aureoli." *FStud* 15 (1955), 146–158.

[24] E.M. Buytaert, "The Immaculate Conception in the Writings of Ockham," *FStud* 10 (1950), 149–163.

2. Gregory's criticism of Scotus

The most telling objection against the doctrine of the Immaculate Conception for a long time had been the one Gregory himself used: this doctrine would limit the perfection of the work of Christ, who died for all mankind. The great invention of Scotus was to use this precise argument to *defend* the doctrine under discussion: the most perfect redeemer must be able to redeem at least one person in the most perfect way possible. For no one other than his mother would he use this most perfect manner of redemption. Since it is more perfect to *preserve* than to *liberate* someone from original sin, the Immaculate Conception is a necessary conclusion.[25]

The second argument of the immaculists was the Anselmian principle or rule, to which we have already referred, according to which one should ascribe to the Virgin Mary the highest possible honor that does not contradict Scripture or tradition.[26]

To the first argument of perfection, Gregory replies that it is just as probable that the perfect redeemer would be the most perfect redeemer to everyone. And if one were to apply the Scotistic manner of argumentation, this would mean that Christ would in fact have preserved everyone from original sin, and this is obviously not true.[27] The weight of his argument is therefore not first of all directed against the final conclusion of the Scotistic argument, but against the method of argumentation; it is therefore a prelude to Gregory's later statement that in the realm of revelation we should not spin a web of mere possibilities, since in that way theology is imprisoned within the limitations of the human reason.

We must note here immediately that the basic disagreement between Gregory and Duns Scotus is due to Gregory's nominalistic conception of the relation between faith and understanding. Since there is only a one-

---

[25] *Ox.* III d 3 q 1 n 4; Gregory, II *Sent.* d 30–33 q 2 art. 1 [fol. 114 M].

[26] *Ox.* III d 3 q 1 n 10; Gregory, II *Sent.* d 30–33 q 2 art. 1 [fol. 114 O].

[27] ". . . illud antecedens non habet maiorem evidentiam quam si diceretur perfectissimus mediator habet respectum cuiuslibet persone pro qua mediat perfectissimum actum mediandi, ut clarum est; et sic secundum illum modum arguendi probaretur quod etiam omnes alios christus preservat ab originali peccato quod non est dicendum." Gregory, II *Sent.* d 30–33 q 2 art. 1 [fol. 114 O]. To the argument of Scotus, Robert Cowton answered already: ". . . non magis concludunt de beata virgine quam de quacumque alia vetula." Cowton, III *Sent.* d 3 q 1. Oxford, Exeter College, cod. 43, f. 205b. Cf. Emmen, p. 126.

way bridge between *pure credibilia*, revealed truth, and rational explanation, human reason cannot establish the fact of the Immaculate Conception. For Gregory the argument of perfection *necessarily* has to be insufficient. Scotus and his followers are convinced that the Immaculate Conception is indeed *de facto* the way chosen by God; the argument of perfection functions therefore in their argumentation as one of the *rationes probabiles.* The discussion partners cannot come to grips with each other because they are speaking on different levels as soon as the one accepts this doctrine *de facto* and as consonant with Scripture and tradition, while the other denies it. From all appearances Gregory is willing to follow the Scotistic structure of possibility, congruence, actuality, only if the order is reversed: it makes sense to speak about possibility and congruence only after the actuality has been established. Thus, his answer to the second, Anselm's mariological rule, is very short — whatever the possibilities are, *in fact*, the Immaculate Conception is indefensible, as it is contrary to Scripture and tradition.[28]

3. Immaculate Conception rejected

Gregory then shifts his attack away from the method to the content of the Scotistic argumentation. He claims that the argument that Mary should have the highest possible purity "apart from God" should be more precisely formulated as "apart from Christ." In this sense he is willing to accept the Anselmian rule; but, if Mary had been conceived without original sin, she would have been equal with Chirst in purity, which would then violate this rule.[29] Furthermore, if the Virgin Mary had indeed been preserved from original sin, she would have been equally preserved from its consequences, of which death is one, and obviously, so Gregory argues, this is not the case.[30]

[28] "Ad secundam rationem quicquid sit de maiore, dico ad minorem quod oppositum habetur ex Scriptura in suo antecedenti et in dictis aliorum sanctorum, ut supra probatum est." Gregory, II *Sent.* d 30–33 q 2 art. 1 [fol. 115 C].

[29] ". . . deus pro christo ponitur ut sit sensus sub deo, id est sub christo. . . Et secundum hoc auctoritas Anselmi est pro consequente quam teneo, quia nisi habuisset originale, fuisset ut videtur puritatis equalis cum christo." Gregory, II *Sent.* d 30–33 q 2 [fol. 115 H].

[30] ". . . deduceretur quod beata virgo fuit etiam preservata ab omni pena temporali corporis et anime et ab ipsa etiam corporali morte quod utique est falsum et quod ita deduceretur clarum est." Gregory, II *Sent.* d 30–33 q 2 art. 1 [fol. 114 P].

Taking up next the argument of Scotus that Christ owes to his mother the highest possible obligation and would therefore have preserved her from sin, Gregory argues *ad absurdum*, it would follow that Christ should not merely have preserved her from original sin but should also have granted her immediately the beatitude which she actually, however, received only after her death.[31] Even better, Christ should have glorified his mother's body in her lifetime! [32]

Gregory's argumentation has, we may conclude, a double thrust. On the one hand, Gregory is willing to take up the argument of perfection but feels that this applies equally to all mankind without exception. Otherwise it would lead to gross contradictions. On the other hand, he cuts off this kind of argumentation by referring to the status *de facto*. While the basic difference with the immaculists on the question of fact has been indicated, there seem to be two principal reasons why Gregory cannot accept the Scotistic probable reasons as convincing either. One is that for him the maternity of Mary is strictly instrumental in the passive and not in the active sense of the word. This stand is clearly in harmony with his understanding of man's part in the process of justification.[33] The other reason is that the assumption of the Virgin is not particularly stressed by Gregory; he shies away from any privileged position for her as far as the temporal consequences of original sin are concerned. The doctrine of the Immaculate Conception seems to him to open the door for a further doctrine of bodily assumption.

History indeed proved Gregory to be right.[34] Though in the early Middle Ages assumption piety stimulated immaculation piety, in the official doctrinal development since the Council of Basel, the *immaculata* doctrine became in its turn the point of departure.

It completes the picture to add that Gregory does not, of course, deny

---

[31] ". . . probaretur quod beata virgo in primo instanti sue conceptionis fuit beata, quoniam et tale bonum potuit habere per christum mediatorem, et similiter quod fuit in corpore glorificata, que falsa sunt," *ibid.*

[32] ". . . ille tantum dicatur esse summe obligatus quem non est possibile esse magis obligatum et sic constat beatam virginem non fuisse summe obligatam, christo etiam dato quod fuerit preservata ab originali peccato, nam potuisset christus tunc ei contulisse beatitudinem quam nunc haberet; et multo etiam maiorem et simul gloriam perfectam corporis. . ." Gregory, II *Sent.* d 30–33 q 2 art. 1 [fol. 114 Q].

[33] See Oberman, *Bradwardine*, pp. 217–223.

[34] See M. D. Koster, O. P., "Die Himmelfahrt Mariens gleichsam die Vollendung ihrer unbefleckten Empfängnis," *Virgo Immaculata* 10 (1957), 92–114.

that, in the first moment of her conception, Mary was cleansed from original sin. This is the place where Gregory calls upon the argument that the institution of the Feast of the Conception of Mary is a celebration in honor of the only one who was conceived in sin and yet not born in sin.[35] Similarly, in the second sanctification of Mary, that is, at the moment that the Holy Spirit overshadowed her to make her the Mother of God, the *fomes peccati* is either extinguished or neutralized by such an abundance of grace that it could not possibly cause sin. The first of these alternatives seems to Gregory the more probable one.[36] But this is an issue which is generally considered to be of secondary importance. When now we turn to Biel, who takes up the cause of those who sympathize with Scotus, we are warned and informed where to look for the more basic points of disagreement.

III. Biel's defense of the Immaculate Conception

1. The question of fact

Biel starts his presentation as usual with a definition of the terms used. Following this he devotes a complete article to a fair and elaborate presentation of the position and the arguments which we have met in Gregory's discussion. Then in his reply, without taking up these arguments in too much detail, Biel, exactly like Gregory whom he quotes several times verbally and refers to three times explicitly, emphasizes the question of fact. This he introduces with the declaration that the most blessed Mother of God, the Virgin Mary, has been totally preserved from any contagion of original sin.[37]

This has first to be proved with authorities, then with probable opinions. The three authorities he quotes are the same three Gregory

[35] ". . . ecclesia universalis celebrat eius nativitatem quod non faceret si cum peccato nata fuisset," II *Sent.* d 30–33 q 2 art. 2 [fol. 115 C].

[36] ". . . puto satis probabiliter dici quod tunc iste qualitas morbida carnis ex qua causatur fomes in anima cum primo carni coniungitur totaliter fuerit consumpta et ab ipsa penitus tota virginis caro purgata," II *Sent.* d 30–33 q 2 art. 3 [fol. 115 F].

[37] "Sed questio est de facto utrum sit aliquo dictorum modorum preservata sic. . ." III *Sent.* d 3 q 1 art. 2 F. "Beatissima genetrix dei Virgo Maria ab omni originalis peccati contagio fuit penitus preservata," III *Sent.* d 3 q 1 art. 2 concl. 1 F. Cf. *S* III 1 E.

described as belonging to the usual defense of the immaculists. To the quotations from Augustine's *De natura et gratia* and from Anselm's *De Conceptu Virginali* is added again the reference to the institution of the feast of Mary's conception. Biel criticizes Gregory for distorting the evidence in such a way that it seems to support his view. There is only one way, Biel claims, to interpret the quotation from Augustine and that interpretation exempts Mary, also according to the *Doctor Gratiae*, not merely from actual but also from original sin.[38] Nor should Gregory feel that the rule of Anselm proves his point. Even if one understands "apart from God" as "apart from Christ," there is a form of purity that allows for her Immaculate Conception without making her the equal of Christ in purity. Adam and Eve in paradise, before the fall, were without original sin and yet were not equal with Christ in purity.[39] Finally, there is the authority of the Church universal, which is always more telling than that of individual *doctores*. The Church has instituted the Feast of the Conception, which refers therefore (!) to the *Immaculate* Conception.[40] The Council of Basel officially promulgated this doctrine before its dissolution, and — for those who dare to doubt the legitimacy of the Council at that time — Pope Sixtus IV has lent it authority by granting many and rich indulgences to all who attend services on this feast. Though there is now a command of silence and further debate is forbidden, to deny the Immaculate Conception would be a wild assertion.[41]

It is clear that the primary foundation laid by Biel is a careful and extensive argumentation designed to prove the fact of the Immaculate Conception. It is noteworthy that the Romans 5 text at the heart of Gregory's presentation is peripheral to Biel's. All his arguments are derived from tradition which, as Biel probably felt, sufficiently clarifies the meaning of St. Paul.

[38] "Et ita Maria Virgo vicit per gratiam originale peccatum per quam preservata est ne incideret," III *Sent.* d 3 q 1 art. 2 G.

[39] ". . . ita stat auctoritas etiam si intelligatur sub deo id est sub Christo, ut exponit Gregorius . . . quia minor christo Adam etiam in statu innocentie. Nec fuit propter hoc equalis puritas virginis et puritas Christi hominis." *Ibid.*

[40] ". . . ecclesia statuit festum conceptionis . . . celebrandum, ergo eius conceptio fuit sancta, et per consequens peccato immaculata, ergo sine [peccato] originali cum conceptio passiva non potuit peccato actuali maculari." *Ibid.*

[41] ". . . temerarium est premissis de puritate virginis oppositum asserere vel sentire. Licet idem Sixtus papa prefatus propter multa scandala exorta singulis partibus imposuerit silentium ne alterutrum de heresi inculpent. . ." *Ibid.*

2. The eternal predestination of Mary

The main argument based on reason is for Biel as for Gregory the argument of perfection. If one compares the *Collectorium* text with Gregory's *Sentences*, it is striking that Biel could almost have transcribed large portions of Gregory without any knowledge of other authorities; he would only have had to change Gregory's negative into his own positive conclusion. But note that Biel may well have been convinced by Gregory's biting criticism of the argument of obligation. Biel drops this one and inserts in its place the argument that Christ came to fulfill the law, of which one commandment says that one should honor one's mother. The most perfect way to do this is, of course, to defend Mary against the dishonor of original sin.

At this point we encounter for the first time in Biel's Mariology the concept of the eternal predestination of Mary. While it did not appear in the works of Scotus[42] and was not mentioned by Gregory, it is a highly important aspect of Biel's Mariology which he uses time and again to clarify Mary's privileged position and to emphasize her maternity. In the argument before us, the predestination of Mary helps to solve the problem that Christ would have honored Mary by preserving her from original sin before she had actually given birth to him. According to the argument of eternal predestination, she had always been the Mother of God.[43]

Finally, Biel adds an argument that is absent from Gregory's treatment but was repeatedly used by Pierre d'Auriole. It is based on the pseudo-Augustinian treatise *De Assumptione virginis*.[44] According to

[42] Scotus' extensive treatment of the absolute predestination of Christ can be understood as an implicit treatment of the predestination of Mary. See Mückshoff, "Die Marialogische Prädestination im Denken der franziskanischen Theologie," *FS* 39 (1957), especially on Scotus, pp. 347–356. "Christus ist der in absoluter Prädestination praeexistentente Heiland. Ewig ist er deshalb auch des Bösen Überwinder, bevor es geschah, und es geschah, weil es seiner Verherrlichung diente" (p. 356). Cf. *Ox.* III d 7 q 3.

[43] "Item ad benignitatem pertinet dei matris servare honorem qui legem solvere non venit sed implere. . . Cum ergo christus potuit matrem ab inhonoratione peccati que utique maxima est preservare, credendum est eum hoc omnimodis fecisse; nec impedit quod concepta nondum mater fuit quia quod nondum fuit inhibitione semper fuit in eterna predestinatione, nec enim temporaliter sed ab eterno in matrem dei electa est." III *Sent.* d 3 q 1 art. 2 G. Cf. *Ibid.* I.

[44] For Biel, of course, still from the hand of Augustine, *PL XL*, 1143 ff. Pierre d'Auriole, III *Sent.* d 3 q 1 resp.

this work, the body of the Virgin Mary was preserved from the shame of incineration, an argument which also could be applied in this case to the *fomes peccati*.[45] We will return to this point later since the authority of this pseudo-Augustinian treatise forms a nexus between the Immaculate Conception and the other elements of Biel's Mariology.

3. Mariology and the authority of the Church

Biel stresses that all these arguments as such can never be convincing, for they deal with one of God's *opera ad extra*, which are contingent and inscrutable. The foundation of his presentation of the Immaculate Conception is the tradition and decision of the Church.[46] In defense of Basel's decision, he wants to make clear that this doctrine in no sense implies a limitation of Christ's all-sufficient work nor leads to a separation of Mariology and Christology. The predestination of Mary links these two firmly together. As we have seen, Biel uses the Scotistic argument that the preservation of Mary from original sin is the most perfect application of Christ's work of redemption, insofar as it is more perfect to preserve than to liberate someone from the impact of original sin. As this privilege has been granted to Mary solely because of Christ, if the Virgin Mary had died before the death of Christ she would not have been admitted directly to heaven. In view of the anticipated work of the Son, the Father is willing to forgive sins and admit the faithful of the old covenant to the *limbus patrum*. Acceptation and admission to heaven, however, can only take place after the work of redemption has in fact taken place. Mary is no exception to *this* rule.[47]

---

[45] "Preterea omnes rationes quas beatus Augustinus facit in sermone de assumptione virginis ad probandum quod corpus virginis preservatum est ab opprobrio incinerationis, habent hic locum de opprobrio fomitis et culpe originalis ut patet facile applicanti." Biel, III *Sent.* d 3 q 1 art. 2 G. Cf. "Maria propter singularem dignitatem excipienda est a quibusdam regulis generalibus: exempta fuit a maledictione Evae." *De Assumptione Virginis*, cap. 4 in *PL XL*, 1144 as quoted by Emmen, p. 203.

[46] "Verum demonstratio haberi non potest cum ad omnia exteriora deus contingenter se habet et secundum beneplacitum sue voluntatis omnia gubernat et disponit. Nec est qui dicat 'cur ita facis.' Sufficiunt igitur auctoritas et ecclesie determinatio. . ." III *Sent.* d 3 q 1 art. 2 G. Cf. Chapter Eleven, section IV.

[47] ". . . ideo maxime redemptori indiguit et nobiliori modo mors christi previsa in ipsa redemptione operata est quam in quocumque alio homine. . . Nec sequitur quod si fuisset defuncta ante mortem Christi intrasset regnum celorum." III *Sent.* d 3 q 1 art. 2 I. Cf. *S* III, 2 F: "Quisquis ergo a peccato vel pena immunis

After this defense of the Immaculate Conception, it is clear that Biel does not need very many arguments to prove that Mary was equally free from all actual sin. The tradition is unanimous on this point; besides, it becomes her who is the *advocata peccatorum, corona iustorum, trinitatis triclinium, filii reclinatorium* to be not only immaculate of mind but also of body.[48] The question whether the *fomes peccati* is totally extinguished or rather neutralized by an abundance of grace, and a second question whether this cleansing took place at the moment of animation before the birth of Mary — that is, the first sanctification, or passive conception — or at the moment of conception by the Holy Spirit — that is, the second sanctification or active conception, Biel does not want to answer in the *Collectorium*.[49] In his sermons on the Feast of the Conception, however, Biel applies the Anselmian rule to this question and goes beyond the position of the *Collectorium*. Here he adds the further clarification that Mary's soul is created with sanctifying grace, not merely in the womb of Mother Ann but at the beginning of creation.[50]

4. Biel and Gregory

Before we can turn to such issues as cooperation, assumption, and mediation, we must evaluate Biel's discussion about the doctrine of Immaculate Conception in comparison with Gregory's point of view, since the General of the Austin Hermits did not commit himself on other mariological issues.

As far as their method is concerned, Gregory and Biel agree that the issue of fact is the decisive one. What God could have done is not worth discussing; the givenness of revelation does not allow for what has been called *Als/ob* theology.[51] In the second place both agree with the general

---

est, per gratiam dei mediatoris dumtaxat immunis est, sine qua etiam virgo maria peccatrix fuisset."

[48] ". . . beata virgo ab omni peccato actuali tam mortali quam veniali fuit immunis. . ." III *Sent.* d 3 q 1 art. 3 dub. 1 K; cf. III *Sent.* d 3 q 2 art. 3 E.

[49] ". . . ille novit qui eam eligit et sancto spiritu implevit. Sufficit nobis quod nunquam peccavit aut a meritorum profectu impedita fuit." III *Sent.* d 3 q 2 art. 1 concl. 1.

[50] "Fuit quoque anima eius nedum in utero sed in creationis principio sanctificata per gratiam sibi concreatam," *S* III 1 H.

[51] See the discussion of this in Iserloh, *Gnade und Eucharistie . . . Ockham*, pp. 77, 279.

consensus of the doctors that Mary was preserved from actual sin. Yet Gregory opts for an extinction of the *fomes peccati* at the moment of the first sanctification; while Biel — though indecisive in the *Collectorium* — in his Marian sermons states that this sanctification took place at an even earlier time, at the moment of creation.

Apart from these two points, however, Biel and Gregory go separate ways. Biel accepts the Immaculate Conception as a fact, testified to by Church and tradition. He is in a position to give probable reasons which are by definition not convincing for the *protervus* who can only be convinced by logically compelling syllogisms. As Gregory does not accept the fact of the Immaculate Conception, he is in Biel's eyes exactly in the position of such a *protervus*. From Gregory's point of view, however, the problem is not the absence of logically compelling syllogisms but the lack of evidence for this dogma in Scripture, Church or tradition.

Materially, the differences between Gregory and Biel coincide with those between Gregory and Scotus and his followers. For Biel the maternity of the Virgin Mary has more than a natural instrumental significance with, as we still have to see, an undertone of active cooperation. A still more basic difference is the absence in Gregory of any movement beyond the *immaculata* doctrine to further mariological conclusions such as the assumption. In contrast, Biel's emphasis on the privileged position of Mary because of her Immaculate Conception is the point of departure for his further mariological presentation. The Virgin Mary shares the state of innocence of Adam and Eve in paradise before the fall, and even surpasses them since she has never been able to sin. She is still subject to the law of death but seems to belong more to the order of re-creation than to the order of creation. The influence of a treatise which so strongly supports this, the pseudo-Augustinian *De assumptione virginis*, which was not quoted by Gregory, is obvious in the thought of Biel. The deepest cause for the noted disparities seems to be the fact that the eternal predestination of Mary does not appear at all in Gregory's treatment of mariological issues.[52] In Biel's presentation it plays an important part in

---

[52] Where nominalists in the question dealing with the *ratio predestinationis* usually mention St. Paul and the Virgin Mary, Gregory refers only to St. Paul. I *Sent.* d 40–41 q 1 art. 2 [fol. 158 E]. Cf. for the contrary: Occam, I *Sent.* d 41 q 1 G. In a fourteenth-century treatise, probably from the hand of Thomas Bradwardine, the predestination of Mary is one of the main arguments for a predestination *ante previsa merita*. ". . . si non esset personarum acceptio apud deum tunc

fusing her temporal and eternal relation to God. The earthly life of the Virgin Mary is continuously seen in the light of her eternal destiny as the Queen of Heaven and the *trinitatis triclinium*, the footstool of the Holy Trinity.

It is, of course, impossible to know with any degree of certainty where Biel would have stood on the question of the Immaculate Conception if he had lived before the Council of Basel. It is at least revealing that he exculpates the great dissenting theologians on grounds that they lived before 1439. We may further point to Biel's sudden shift of position in the matter of the efficacy of indulgences for the dead as soon as he became aware that his position had been authoritatively contradicted.[53]

Once the Immaculate Conception became a part of the deposit of faith and thus a presupposition of Biel's theology, it allowed and actually prepared the way for exactly those conclusions which Gregory had believed to be so absurd that he used them to prove the untenability of this doctrine.

IV. *Maria corredemptrix*

1. The maternity of Mary

The next point to be investigated in detail is the question of the extent to which the Virgin Mary actively cooperated with God in the Incarnation. On a more medical level, Biel declares himself to be in accord with Scotus, Occam, and Oyta that a mother has as active a part in the production of a child as a father. In this case the Virgin Mary can be called the Mother of Christ in a very real sense. She participated just as fully in the formation of her child as any other mother — and even more fully in that she alone provided the bodily substance and was in a supernatural

---

si alia filia de domo Iacob consimilis fuisset in merito cum domina mea, ipsa similiter filium dei genuisset, et tunc plures potuissent genuisse eundem filium dei, et sic etiam domina mea non per electionem nec divinam providentiam sed fortuitu et creaturaliter facta fuisset mater dei." Nat. Bibl. Vienna, Cod. 4306 fol. 102. Cf. Oberman, "*De Praedestinatione et Praescientia*: An anonymous fourteenth century treatise on predestination and justification," *NAK*, n.s. 43 (1960), 207.

[53] "Nec propter hoc culpandus est beatus Bernardus, sed nec sanctus Thomas, sanctus Bonaventura, ceterique doctores cum magno moderamine oppositum opinantes, quoniam eorum tempore hoc licuit." III *Sent.* d 3 q 1 art. 2 G. Cf. Chapter Eleven, section IV.

way assisted in her natural role.[54] Biel joins the ranks of the Scotists with this defense of Mary's active role in her maternity.[55] Yet the supernatural context of this natural activity is so stressed that her maternity, parallel to her conception, belongs more to the order of re-creation than of creation.

2. The Virgin's merits and the Incarnation according to the *Collectorium*

Does the Virgin's cooperation in the Incarnation imply that the Virgin Mary earned the Incarnation or earned the privilege of becoming the Mother of God? Biel denies the first of these questions, and in a passage which we find *verbatim* in Scotus, the very possibility of earning the Incarnation is flatly denied. The Incarnation stands alone among the works of God as the one which cannot be earned, as an act of sheer grace. Though some merits may have preceded the time of conception, they could never have earned more than perhaps an acceleration in the coming of God.[56]

This does not mean, however, that given God's decision to become flesh, his choice of the Virgin Mary as his instrument and his preparation of her through the first sanctification, Mary could not still have earned her status as the Mother of God. According to Bonaventura and Aquinas, Mary's merits could only be *merita de congruo*, since the conception of Christ surpasses all merits and this conception alone is the basis for all her other merits.[57] In contrast Biel feels that she could have earned this status

---

[54] "Nam in ceteris matribus etiam concurrit semen patris. . . Fuit ergo ex hac parte verius mater christi quam quecunque alia mater sui filii naturalis. Ipsa etiam quoad virtutem activam cooperata est productioni prolis plus ceteris matribus quia in ceteris est tantum virtus naturalis." III *Sent.* d 4 q 1 art. 2 E. Cf. also concls. 1 and 2 and Scotus in *Ox.* III d 4 q 1: "Utrum beata virgo fuerit vere mater dei et hominis."

[55] See Ephrem Longpré, "De B. Virginis maternitate et relatione ad Christum," *Antonianum* 7 (1932), 289–313.

[56] ". . . in operibus dei non fuit aliquod opus mere gratie nisi sola incarnatio filii dei. Et licet tempore conceptionis precesserunt aliqua merita bona Marie tamen non erant merita absolute respectu incarnationis, sed forte respectu accelerationis ut impleretur incarnatio preordinata." III *Sent.* d 4 q 1 art. 3 dub. 3. Scotus, *Ox.* III d 4 q 1; see also Karl Balić, "Die Corredemptrixfrage innerhalb der franziskanischen Theologie," *FS* 39 (1957) 234.

[57] Bonaventura, III *Sent.* d 4 q 4. See also L. Di Fonzo, *Doctrina Sancti Bonaventurae de universali mediatione Beatae Virginis Mariae* (Rome, 1938); Aquinas,

of Theotokos *de condigno*. It is probable, he argues, that God accepted her humility and purity after the first sanctification — which she could not earn — as full merits earning for her the privilege of the maternity of Christ. Biel is not following but shaping the theology of his school on this point.[58]

If we try to analyze the relation of grace and works in the case of the Virgin Mary, it appears that here the sovereignty of God is better safeguarded than proved to be the case generally in Biel's doctrine of justification. Not only the double requirement of temporal grace and divine acceptation, but the concept of the predestination of Mary constantly sets the tone of discussion. The Scotistic concept of the impossibility of earning the Incarnation structures also, of course, the question of merits with regard to the conception: *potuit christus de alia matre incarnari!* [59] It is not surprising that this is the case: the Virgin Mary is one of two exceptions to the nominalistic rule that God has a reason for accepting some and rejecting others. God's decision in this case could not have been influenced by Mary's good works because Mary's soul was at the moment of its creation equipped with grace that guarded her from original sin; this makes a claim to her own righteousness impossible.[60]

3. Pelagian Mariology in the sermons

The *Collectorium* doctrine of the Immaculate Conception therefore necessarily excludes any Pelagian misinterpretation of Mary's cooperation with the Incarnation. At the same time, however, we note that in the pastoral-homiletical application this aspect of the Immaculate Conception seems to be repeatedly forgotten. Either there is so much stress on the

---

ST III q 2 art. 11 ad 3; and George Kokša, *Die Lehre der Scholastiker des XVI. und XVII. Jahrhunderts von der Gnade und Verdienst der alttestamentlichen Gerechten* (Rome, 1955), p. 15.

[58] ". . . probabile est quod deus pater post virginis sanctificationem quam non meruit eius bona opera acceptaverit ad hoc ut de ipsa formaretur corpus assumendum a filio." Biel, III *Sent.* d 4 q 1 art. 3 ad 1. Kokša, appropriately dealing with this issue within the larger context of the merits of the Fathers of the Old Covenant, indicates that Jacob Almainus holds the same position as Biel, while Johannes Maior opts with the majority for the opinion of Bonaventura and Aquinas; pp. 24 f., 258.

[59] III *Sent.* d 4 q 1 art. 3 ad 2.

[60] "Non enim potest poni ratio bonus usus liberi arbitrii quoniam gratia prevenit usum liberi arbitrii in beata virgine, cui fuit gratia concreata," I *Sent.* d 41 q 1 art. 2. concl. 3.

fittingness of God's election of this pure and humble Virgin, or she serves as such an inspiring example that everyone who becomes as humble as she may count on God's grace: *facientibus quod in se est deus non denegat gratiam*! For example, one sermon dedicated to humility describes the four *results* of Mary's great humility: the fullness of grace, inhabitation of the Holy Spirit, special election, and the Incarnation of the Word. In the case of the election as *sponsa verbi*, humility is a partial cause; the love of the Father constitutes the other part.[61]

It would be possible to interpret the fullness of grace and the inhabitation of the Holy Spirit in such a sense that it would fall under the acceptation of merits on grounds of the Immaculate Conception, but the other two effects of humility clearly contradict statements in the *Collectorium*. The election even as only partially caused contradicts the passage quoted from I *Sent.* d 41, while the first sanctification as preparation for conception and incarnation cannot be caused by humility according to III *Sent.* d 4.[62]

While in Biel's academic theology the proper — that is, if one accepts the Immaculate Conception — conclusions are drawn from the intimate bond between Christ and the Virgin Mary, and Mariology is consequently closely connected with Christology, in his sermons popular Marian piety is stimulated and encouraged to isolate Mary as an individual from her son. In this presentation of the Virgin Mary we meet again the nominalistic emphasis on man's capacities before the reception of grace.[63]

[61] ". . . quattuor attendere possumus fructus et effectus in virgine quos mater humilitas generavit: hi sunt gratie plenitudo, spiritus sancti inhabitatio, singularis electio, verbi incarnati conceptio. . . Deus superbis resistit, humilibus autem dat gratiam. Hec virtus propria secundum cuius mensuram unicuique distribuit suarum dominus talenta gratiarum. . . Hinc ergo virgo maria super omnes gratia repleta fuit quia infra omnes se . . . humiliavit. [N]. Per eandem etiam humilitatem facta est habitatio spiritus sancti. . . Electionem denique singularem qua electa est ut esset sponsa et mater verbi humilitas operata est ex parte virginis et benignissima charitas patris. . . Causa electionis virginis fuerat humilis subiectio. [O] Per humilitatem etiam mater electa, mater verbi patris summi efficitur eius sacrosancta conceptione." *S* III 25 M.N.O.
[62] "Nam quia se humiliter, quod erat, ancillam cognovit, ideo quod non erat sublimiter mater dei esse promeruit," *ibid.*, O.
[63] See Oberman, "Some Notes on the Theology of Nominalism. . .", p. 67. See also Emmen, p. 157: "Bei einigen der besprochenen Autoren hat man zuweilen den Eindruck, die angeführten Kongruenzgründe fanden ihren eigentlichen Stütz-

The purpose of this isolation in Biel's homiletical Mariology is clear. The more she is seen as an individual preparing herself for a great task, the more emphasis can be given to her function as *cooperatrix*. These Mariological considerations seem to function primarily in the doctrine of justification. Mary's humility can be imitated; she received the Holy Spirit through her quiet humility. The same can be easily[!] obtained by imitation of the Virgin. Humility is the golden rule of the new law, since humility is the perfect justice according to which one gives and does not covet.[64]

4. Cooperation in the passion of Christ

This cooperation of the Virgin Mary with her Son is not restricted to her maternity or the incarnation in the limited sense of the word but extends itself equally to Christ's work on earth and especially to his passion. Her behavior at the marriage of Cana is an example of her cooperation in Christ's work on earth. When there appeared to be a shortage of wine, she did not command her Son to take action, but in all humility she called his attention to this situation, and trusting that He would answer her prayer, she made the necessary preparations in obedience and humility.[65]

Even more explicitly Biel speaks of her cooperation in Christ's passion.

---

punkt in Maria selbst und in ihrer Ehre." In Biel's sermons they are not even "Kongruenzgründe." This disparity between academic and homiletic Mariology should be taken into consideration when one uses collections of testimonies to mariological doctrines, such as Karl Balić, *Testimonia de assumptione B.V.M. ex omnibus saeculis*, vol. I (Rome, 1948); vol. II (Rome, 1950); Juniper B. Carol, O.F.M., *De Corredemptione B.V.M. Disquisitio positiva* (Vatican City, 1950).

[64] "Super quem requiescet spiritus meus nisi super humilem et quietum. Hanc facile obtinebimus si matrem domini imitabimur. Nihil illa sibi aut suis meritis attribuit: sed totum ad illius donum retulit qui solus essentialiter bonus est atque magnus. . . Sine modo: sic enim adimplere nos decet omnem iusticiam — Glossa — id est humilitatem que est omnis iusticia. Est autem perfecta iusticia alteri quod suum est dare et alienum non concupiscere. Hoc perfecte facit humilitas." *S* III 5 C.

[65] "Iterum dum in cana galilee filium alloquitur pro vino, ut nubentium confusionem preveniret rogatura, non ut mater filio imperavit nec importunas preces porrexit, sed velut humilis ancilla rogare non audens, tantum defectum insinuat dicens: vinum non habent; que tamen de sua exauditione certam se ostendit cum ministris ait: quecunque vobis dixerit, facite . . . quibus verbis eosdem ad humilitatem subiectionis et obedientie erudivit." *S* III 25 G.

As Christ came into the world to serve and not to be served, so Mary did not want to be served; she participated in his self-sacrifice by suffering under the cross, thus cooperating in the redemption of many. In this way the Virgin's *cooperatio* in Christ's *operatio* seems reverberated in the Virgin's *compassio* in Christ's *passio*.[66] Nevertheless, viewed in its proper perspective, that is, the general preoccupation of the time with this aspect of Mary's function as *corredemptrix*, Biel's stand on this point strikes one as restrained.[67]

This cooperation is not always seen as a result of her self-attained humility. Repeatedly we receive at least a glimpse of the doctrine of eternal predestination as the ultimate cause. In that case the *Collectorium* argument that God could equally well have chosen another woman as the instrument of the incarnation again takes the interest away from Mary's individual honor and qualities. A variation on this theme is the argument that Christ could have formed a body from any place he liked between heaven and earth; but he wanted to form this body out of a virgin, so that, while he would be the father of the redeemed, she, through cooperation, would become the mother of the redeemed.[68]

[66] ". . . facta est redemptionis mater non ut ei ministretur sed ut ministret et similiter animam suam per compassionem effundat sub cruce, redemptionem multorum cooperando." *S* III 13 B; ". . . singularis huius sacrificii ministra fuit [virgo] et liberalissima dispensatrix." *Lect.* 32 A. ". . . [ministra] sacrificii autem cruci qua velut in ara sacrificium oblatum est assistens et simul participato dolore patri offerens." *Ibid.* C. "Ex merito compassionis anime christo in cruce pendenti commorientis, semel enim mortua dolore anime sub cruce, non iterum sentire dolorem mortis debuit." *S* III 3 B.

[67] Biel never goes as far as the opinion which Michel Menot, a French preacher on the Eve of the Reformation, reports he heard in the Parisian convent of the Dominicans, "quod si non alius se obtulisset Virgo Maria tanto zelo amabat redemptionem generis humani quod propriis manibus filium crucifixisset." *Sermons choisis de Michel Menot,* ed. Joseph Nève, (Paris, 1924), p. 453. Antoninus of Florence emphasizes Mary's indirect cooperation in an elaborate discussion. See his *Summa Theologica,* IV.xv.20 [col. 1064 f.]. See also E. Brandt, *Die Mitwirkung der seligsten Jungfrau zur Erlösung nach dem heiligen Antonin von Florenz* (Rome, 1945), esp. p. 36 f.

[68] "Poterat filius patris sibi de celo aut terra, vel undecunque vellet, corpus formare et nostram redemptionem operari. Sed voluit de virgine assumere ut quorum ipse redemptionis iure esset pater, ipsa redemptioni cooperando fieret pia mater . . . ," *S* III 13 C.

V. Mariological Rules

1. The superlative rule

Biel applies in his sermons the rules or principles (*regulae*) which were widely used in late medieval, especially in Franciscan Mariology. While agreeing in his *Collectorium* with Gregory that the number of probable propositions should be kept to the bare minimum in order to concentrate the attention upon the question of fact, in his *Expositio*, and even more so in his sermons, these probable opinions become pious testimonies which are often asserted as if they were already officially taught by the Church universal.

As we have seen, these probable opinions, as for example, the Scotistic argument of perfection, in Biel's academic presentations were no more than a helpful commentary on a decision of the Church, directed to those of good will. In his sermons they become the very content of the kerygma. This is true for all aspects of theology in so far as they lend themselves as subject matter for sermons, but it is especially striking in the case of Mariology.

The guiding rules for these probable opinions by no means necessarily further the emphasis already noted on the honor of the Virgin Mary as an individual in her own right. On the contrary, they are the formal principles, of which the predestination of Mary is the material counterpart, which if properly applied can help to keep Mariology within christological boundaries.

In the first place, we have noted the influence of the *superlative rule*, or *regula convenientiae*, introduced under the name of Augustine, according to which the highest possible privileges are assigned to the Virgin on the sole condition that they should not contradict Scripture or tradition.[69] Scripture and tradition have in this rule only the negative function of

---

[69] See the pseudo-Augustinian *De Assumptione B.V.M.*, cap. 2–3 in *PL* XL, 1144. Pierre d'Auriole acknowledged this rule as valid: "Illud igitur secundum regulam, quam hic dat Augustinus, attribuendum est virgini gloriosae, quod congruit rationi ac tantae sanctitati ac tantae praerogativae sanctissimae aulae Dei." *Nondum*, cap. 4 as quoted by Aquilinus Emmen, p. 195. We are indebted to Emmen for his analyses of the late medieval use of what he calls the three secondary mariological rules (pp. 195–200). We fail, however, to see in what respect the second of these, the *regula comparationis*, differs from the Anselmian rule, which we described above and which is for Emmen a primary rule.

elimination. In Biel, however, we find an interesting variation on this rule. Everything may be said about Mary insofar as it is said "catholice," that is according to Scripture and tradition, because in that case it pertains *simultaneously* to the honor of Mary and Christ.[70] This last clause is an important further elaboration of the pseudo-Augustinian rule as understood by Pierre d'Auriole. Not only is the function of Scripture and tradition formulated in a positive way, but a further characteristic of such a statement concerning Mary is added: it should express the bond of honor between mother and son.

2. The comparative rule

The second guiding principle in establishing probable explanations is the comparative rule (*regula comparationis*). We have seen already how this principle functions in the *Collectorium* treatment of the Immaculate Conception. In Biel's sermons, also, either it lays the foundation for the claim of the highest possible purity for Mary, the Anselmian argument from *De conceptione virginis*, or it means that Christ, as the most perfect mediator, must redeem her in the most excellent manner, the Scotistic argument of perfection.[71]

A less well-known application is found in the question whether Mary, full of grace, could not have been granted grace for a complete union with God on earth. Biel's answer is that according to God's *potentia ordinata* more grace could not have been granted to her unless he made her God. This, however, transcends the possibilities of creation: *under God* she has the highest possible purity and honor.[72]

[70] " . . . Profecto desperationi succumberem, si (quod impossibile est) omnia dicenda forent. Sed animat ex adverso, quia quicquid catholice dici potest, ad utriusque laudem pertinet quoniam gloria filii honor parentis et parentis corona gloria filiorum." S III 12 B.

[71] "Congruum autem valde erat tum ex parte virginis tum ex parte christi . . . ; decuit enim . . . ut virgo ea puritate niteret qua maior sub deo intelligi non posset. . . Cum ergo passio christi perfectissime satisfecit ac liberavit . . . quare hanc perfectam liberationem respectu alicuius persone habuit et non alterius nisi matris." S III 1 G.

[72] "In via autem maiorem gratiam habere non posset nisi ipsa divinitati uniretur, hoc est nisi ipsa esset deus. Sed sic exiret genus creature . . . manens autem in hoc genere maior gratia intelligi non potest quam quod ipsa esset dei mater." S III 12 H. Biel refers here to Albertus Magnus, *De laude virginis* q 31. Albertus deals with this problem, however, in *Mariale* q 35; *Opera omnia*, ed. A. Borgnet (Paris,

Finally, the comparative rule is applied to the relation of *latria, dulia* and *hyperdulia*. While *latria* is due only to God, and *dulia* to all saints who are in some special way related to God, *hyperdulia* is due to the Virgin who has a position above the saints under God.[73]

In Biel's Mariology these first two rules are not always clearly distinguishable; both stress that Mary is the *apex creationis*. The first one, however, is especially concerned with clarifying the exceptionally high position of Mary with regard to mankind and the whole created order; the second with indicating that even this exalted position is only the highest possible under God.

If we remind ourselves of Gregory's suggestion that this "under God" should be understood as "under Christ," one must grant that for Biel this means merely "under Christ" as part of the Trinity, which does not necessarily imply "under Christ" as the incarnate Word.

3. The rule of similitude

The third late-medieval, mariological rule, the *rule of similitude with Christ*, the *regula similitudinis*, is handled with such consistency that this "under Christ" becomes "like Christ" and then "with Christ" as the incarnate Word.

We have noted already one example of this emphasis on "like Christ," where Mary is said to have come to serve, not to be served, and thus to cooperate in the redemption of mankind. In general, the humility of Mary is repeatedly seen as a parallel to the *kenosis* of Christ. In one case Biel goes as far as to apply to Mary the words of Philippians 2:8–9 in the following formulation: "And being found in human form she humbled herself . . . therefore God has highly exalted her." Nevertheless, he adds to the statement that Mary has been exalted above everyone, that she has humiliated herself on the example of Christ and received the highest name *after Christ*.[74]

1899), pp. 37, 74b. See also Robert J. Buschmiller, *The Maternity of Mary in the Mariology of St. Albert the Great.* (Carthagena, Ohio, 1959), p. 49.

[73] "Etsi excellentius ceteris ad deum pertinent ut humanitas christi et que ad eam pertinent: . . . arma passionis, virgo dei mater honor eis debitus dicitur hyperdulia. Aliis vero exhibetur dulia." *S* II 51 E. Cf. *Lect.* 49 F.

[74] ". . . semetipsum exinanivit formam servi accipiens. . . Propter quod et Deus exaltavit illum et donavit illi nomen quod est super omne nomen. . ." *Vulg.* Phil.

This third rule does not, therefore, necessarily contradict the "under God" requirement of the second rule, even if this be understood as "under Christ." Christ and Mary, and thus Christology and Mariology, are closely linked so as to exclude any possibilities which the first two rules still may leave of considering the Mother of God *apart from Christ.*

4. Merits and granted privileges

At this point the question must arise as to how it is possible, in view of Biel's use of these three rules and the apparent care he takes to present Mary's privileges as *granted* privileges — at the summit of creation but after Christ in order of perfection — that we concluded earlier: in the Mariology of his sermons we find a nominalistic emphasis of man's natural capacities. Are we justified in accusing Biel of a distortion of his academic Mariology in the kerygmatic application of his sermons?

The disparity between the *Collectorium* and the *Sermones de festivitatibus marie* is due to the fact that the scope of the Mariology of the first is almost entirely restricted to a treatment of the Immaculate Conception, the annunciation, and the purification. But the *Sermones* deal also with the assumption of Mary and her role as advocate of sinners. Thus we have restricted ourselves in the foregoing to a presentation of Biel's Mariology concerning Mary's earthly life.

It is when we come to deal with Mary's glorified status in heaven that we find a new concept which runs counter to the tendency already noted to keep Mariology within the boundaries of Christology. It is remarkable that this new concept is prepared by and is a direct result of the three rules and the doctrine of Mary's eternal predestination which, with regard to Mary's earthly status, formally and materially safeguarded her basically subordinate position to Christ. Applied to Mary's heavenly

---

2:7, 9. "Exinanivit enim se exemplo filii formam ancille accipiens propter quod et deus exaltavit illam et donavit illi nomen quod est super omne nomen post nomen filii." S III 25 O. Biel, thoroughly familiar with the works of Gerson, draws often on the *Super magnificat* of the Parisian Chancellor. Cf. Gerson, *Tractatus tertius* in *Opera*, IV, 264 B. "Unde palam intelligo beatam Mariam nedum pia devotione, sed altissima, metaphysicalique ratione suam pulchritudinis beatificae perfectionem plus insinuasse per humilitatem subjectionis, quam respexit in ea Dominus, quam si dominationis nomen aliquod posuisset," as quoted by André Combes, "La doctrine mariale du Chancelier Jean Gerson," *Maria: Etudes sur la sainte Vierge* 2 (Paris, 1952), 874.

status, they lead consecutively to *Maria Corredemptrix, Mediatrix,* almost *Concreatrix,* and as we will have to conclude finally — to *Maria Spes Omnium.* It is in this last function of Mary, though derived from her intimate bond with Christ, that at the borderline where Mariology and the doctrine of justification meet, she occupies a position of priority.

THE VIRGIN MARY AND MANKIND

I. Annunciation

1. The second sanctification

Here we have to investigate in what sense the indicated titles of Mary are to be understood. We must first take up the thread at a moment in Mary's earthly life: the second sanctification, the annunciation by the archangel Gabriel. This is the moment at which the Word becomes flesh in the womb of Mary; at this moment she becomes the Mother of God.[75]

The salutation of the archangel Gabriel, "Ave Maria," is philologically analyzed as a-ve, — the pain or "Weh" has disappeared.[76] In the first sanctification, her conception in the womb of Mother Ann, she is preserved from all imperfections normally resulting from original sin. In the second sanctification she is freed from the usual stain of body and soul otherwise the result of the act of conception.[77]

In the context of his exposition of Mary's eternal virginity, Biel responds to a Jewish argument later accepted by most biblical scholars according to which the prophecy of Isaiah 7:15 does not refer to a virgin but more generally to a young woman. Biel's answer is more pastoral than philological when he claims that this text has to refer to the *Virgin*

---

[75] "Hodie namque verbum caro factum est in Marie utero ac per hoc ipsa mater facta, manens virgo," *S* III 11 B.

[76] "Ave . . . quod interpretatur sine ve: evacuationem imperfectionum importat a quibus multipliciter virgo sanctissima singulari privilegio noscitur preservata." *S* III 11 C. See Jean Gerson, *Ave Maria,* ed. Louis Mourin, "Les sermons français inédits de Jean Gerson," in *Scriptorium* 2 (1948), 221–240.

[77] ". . . libera fuit virgo Maria quia nec sterilis permansit, nec per pudorem commixtionis aut sensum libidinis, puritatem utriusque amiserat virginitatis," *S* III 11 C.

Mary as otherwise the Incarnation would not be a token of God's omnipotence.[78]

2. The Virgin as token of restoration

In connection with the Feast of the Annunciation by the archangel Gabriel, we find the first traces of what in a more explicit formulation later becomes Biel's doctrine of Mary, the Hope of the World. The preservation of Mary's virginity [79] as a form of restoration provides mankind with a certain hope in its own future bodily freedom from corruption.[80] Here Mary's purity can still be understood in a purely instrumental sense as one of the mighty acts of God which give cause to all for wonder and hope: the effects of God's power and love. The fact of her eternal predestination can mean that Mary's ability to inspire hope is based here on her priority in the succession of time. Mary was the first saint; it is apparently possible for others to gain a victory over sin. Her very bond with Christ, however, makes her also the Mother of the Saints, and therefore of the Church, not merely temporally but causally.[81]

To apply the mariological terms now in use, though the Virgin Mary is in a strict sense only *fundamentum remotum*, she is from the point of view of the *viator* also *fundamentum proximum* of the redemption of mankind and as such may be called *corredemptrix*.[82] We saw above how

[78] "Nec audiendi sunt iudei qui dicunt quod verbum 'virgo' apud eos sonat 'iuvencula' sive sit virgo sive corrupta. . . Si puella hec ut iudei loquuntur quam concepturam dicit propheta esset de coniugii lege conceptura, quale signum fuisset divine potentie . . . ," *S* III 11 F.

[79] "Fuit itaque primo virgo a ve corruptionis intacta, quia ante partum, in partu et post partum virgo perpetua," *S* III 7 C.

[80] "Congruum autem fuit ita nasci christum de virgine. . . Propter restaurandum etiam hominem ut nobis esset certa spes future incorruptionis in nostra carne." *S* III 7 H.

[81] "Nec enim solum mater est benedicti fructus ventris sui primogeniti . . . sed et omnium fratrum suorum, omnium siquidem salvandorum, quos genuit per fidem, fovet per charitatem, defendit per continuam intercessionem. Vere itaque de se dicit: ab eterno ordinata sum. . ." *S* III 1 D.

[82] See L. Di Fonzo, *Doctrina Sancti Bonaventurae*, pp. 10–12; I. Keuppens, *Mariologiae Compendium* (Antwerp, 1938), pp. 101–115; J. Lebon, "Comment je conçois, j'établie et je défends la doctrine de la médiation mariale," *Ephemerides Theologicae Lovanienses*, 16 (1939), 655–744. It is remarkable that Biel is not mentioned in the historical survey of Juniper B. Carol, O.F.M., *De Corredemptione B.V.M.*

Biel defends not only a cooperation with the Incarnation through the maternity and humble disposition, but also a cooperation with the sacrifice of Christ through her offer of compassion.

Mary cooperated thus with that aspect of Christ's offering which, as understood by Anselm, is essentially God-directed. To an even higher degree, however, she cooperates with the offering of Christ as understood by Abelard: the man-directed expression of God's love in Christ. She is on the one hand the completion of the work of redemption and restoration; on the other hand she administers the sacrifice of Christ and thus applies the fruits of his work.[83]

II. Bodily Assumption: Mediation

1. The Queen of Heaven

Since Mary's assumption into heaven, she has been elevated to the right hand of Christ, where she, the Queen of heaven, through continual intercession softens the heart of her Son, the judge. As mediatrix to the mediator she completes the work of salvation, she pleads the case of mankind and balances by her *misericordia* the *iustitia* of her Son.[84] Her earthly and heavenly status seem to be fused when it is said that Mary has given life to mortals, has purified the world and opened the doors of paradise and hell; she herself is the door of heaven and the staircase over which Christ descended to the world.[85]

2. Mary's intercessory task

To this Bernardean concept of the Virgin Mary as the staircase of Christ is easily linked the concept that Mary is the staircase of salvation

[83] "Totius ergo reparationis nostre opus virginis existentia cernimus completum," *S* III 13 C. ". . . singularis huius sacrificii ministra fuit et liberalissima dispensatrix," *Lect.* 32 A.

[84] "Exultantes cum celi civibus de tanta benedicte virginis matris magnificatione que sine dubio nostre salutis magna est perfectio quoniam advocatam premisit peregrinatio nostra que tanquam iudicis mater et mater misericordie suppliciter et efficaciter salutis nostre negocia pertractabit. Precessit nos regina nostra," *S* III 19 G.

[85] "O vere Marie beata humilitas que deum hominibus peperit, vitam mortalibus edidit, celos innovavit, mundum purificavit, paradisum aperuit et omnium animas fidelium ab inferis liberavit. O vere gloriosa Marie humilitas que porta celi efficitur, scala dei constituitur. Facta est certe Maria scala celestis per quam christus descendit ad terras," *S* III 13 H.

as such, which means that no one can come to Christ except through his Mother.[86]

In one of his most fascinating Marian sermons Biel describes in detail and with great warmth Mary's arrival in heaven and reunion with her Son. In his welcoming speech Christ announces that he will share the kingdom of his father with her; of its two parts Christ will give his mother the responsibility for compassion. He himself will be responsible for justice and truth. In the usual pseudo-Dionysian terms her place at the right hand of the Son is called the first hierarchy, above the angels and creatures, directly under the Trinity, prepared for her from all eternity, from which she is to rule over the empire of heaven and earth.[87]

We should note here that Mary does not rule by power but by influence; not to command, *imperare*, but to implore, *impetrare*, is her task, and her special place has been granted to her as a gift from God.[88] Nevertheless, we find here the beginnings of a last stage of development in the application of the third rule of similitude. "Under Christ" became "like

[86] "Sicut per virginem matrem ad nos venit salvator, ita per eandem redeamus ad salvatorem. . ." *S* III 8 A. Cf. *Lect.* 32 B. The mariological references in the *Expositio* are almost all quotations from the sermons and the *Super Missus est* of Bernard of Clairvaux.

[87] "Sume igitur thronum regni . . . tibi ad dextram meam ab eterno preparatum. Partior tecum regnum patris mei. Huius regni via misericordia et veritas sive iusticia; mihi veritas, tibi misericordia, ut ego regnem per iusticiam, tu imperes per misericordiam. Et sicut ego constitutus sum iudex vivorum et mortuorum, tu sis mater misericordie, miseris subveniendo et omnibus ad te clamantibus misericordiam, gratiam, et gloriam impetrando. Tu itaque sub trinitatis imperio proximam et primam hierarchiam sola tenes super angelos et omnes creaturas . . . imperium celi et terre mecum tenes per secula." *S* III 20 F. ". . . matrem misericordie, reginam pietatis et clementie, imperatricem totius celestis curie," *S* IV 37 F. The interest of the following generation in what Biel had to say is attested to by the attack of Philip Melhofer von Eriszkilch, in *Offenbarung der allerheimlichisten heymlichkeit der ytzigen Baalspriester durch wölche die Welt langezyt geblendt unde das lyden Christi jhämerlich geschmecht worden ist, genannt Canon oder die Styllmess.* (Schachen, 1525), fol. O ii f. Melhofer refers several times to Biel's *Expositio*.

[88] The difference between these terms disappears, of course, when this *impetrare* is described as *efficaciter pertractare*. See *S* III 19 G and also note 84 above. Holcot describes the difference in accessibility between the Virgin Mary and Christ: "Sic omnino christus se habet ad reverentiam matris sue, quia ubi preces cuiuscunque creature repellentur, ibi preces marie continue et gratanter exaudiuntur efficaciter." *Sap.* Lect. 174 C. Cf. *Sap.* Lect. 40 B.; ". . . ipsa dignabitur nostram orationem portare et pro nobis filio suo presentare. Nam quicquid filio suo offert, necessario acceptum est." *Sap.* Lect. 202 B.

Christ" and "with Christ"; this "with Christ" is now further spelled out as *in contrast with Christ*. Christ becomes more and more the severe judge, almost identified with God the Father. The righteous God could not possibly hear the prayer of a sinner; what is needed is therefore a mediator with the mediator. From eternity God has provided one, thus erecting a new trinitarian hierarchy: the Virgin Mary hears the sinner, the Son hears his Mother, and the Father his Son.[89]

3. Death and assumption

The contrast between the Virgin Mary and Christ is developed in still another direction. According to the comparative and the superlative rule, the fact is stressed that Mary is the summit of creation and in every respect pure nature. Twice sanctified she is free from all the consequences of original sin. She is subject, however, to one inescapable law, the law of death; if this were not the case she would not be a creature, but God. Her assumption, therefore, took place on the day of her death.[90]

Probably because of the silence on this point of Bernard of Clairvaux, Biel's great authority on mariological issues,[91] Biel makes it clear that, though he himself firmly believes in the bodily assumption, this is still a matter of private theological opinion.

He argues for his own position that apart from the law of death Mary is free from every form of corruption. While other men are of dust and will return to dust, Mary is preserved from this humiliation. Besides,

---

[89] "Scimus quod peccatores deus non exaudit. . . Opus ergo erat mediatrice ad mediatorem. Dedit ergo et ab eterno ordinavit piam nobis matrem . . . quam semper filius audit et filium pater nunquam non exaudit; ut per illam omnes nostre preces et sacrificia porrigantur et ita nunquam repulsa patiantur. Hec est scala peccatorum per quam christus rex celorum ad se traxit omnia." *S* III 22 I. For the *officium mediationis* see *Lect.* 30 K and 32 B. Bernard, *Sermones*, in *PL* CLXXXIII, 429.

[90] "Hodierna quoque die per realem separationem anime a corpore vere mortua fuit," *S* III 18 B.

[91] Karl Balić notes: "Mirum forsan alicui videbitur nec apud maximum gloriae Marianae mediiaevi apostolum S. Bernardum . . . clarum testimonium de corporali Virginis in caelum translatione nos reperire potuisse. . ." *Testimonia de assumptione B.V.M. ex omnibus saeculis*, I, 198 f. The causal connection between the immaculate conception, denied by Bernard, and the bodily assumption clarifies Bernard's silence on this second doctrine.

the body of Christ was not subject to corruption, and as Mary's body is of the same kind, it cannot have been subject to corruption.[92]

III. *Fiducia* in the Virgin Mary

1. Greater *fiducia* in Mary than in Christ

The bodily assumption of Mary, which clearly belongs to Biel's personal creed,[93] is the premise for a last conclusion. Though we know that Christ was bodily resurrected from death, this fact is by no means as much a guarantee of our own future bodily resurrection as the bodily resurrection of Mary. For Christ was not pure nature. He was of course "pure" nature in the sense that he was not subject to original sin; but in Biel's sense, he was not pure nature because his humanity was united in a

---

[92] "Pulvis es et in pulverem reverteris. . . Ab hoc autem opprobrio credimus virginem omnino preservatam." She is with Christ ". . . non solum secundum animam quod et aliis concessum est sed etiam corpore. . . corpus filii quod non vidit corruptionem est eiusdem nature cuius est corpus maternum de quo sumptum est quare nec corpus matris vidit corruptionem. . ." *S* III 18 G. Cf. the argument based on Christ's love for his mother, *ibid.*, I.

[93] For this reason we cannot agree with Balić that Biel ". . . parum gradum certitudinis facto assumptionis B. Virginis ascribet." *Testimonia*, I, 338. In *S* III 18 L Biel states merely that to hold the doctrine of the bodily assumption is not *de salutis necessitate*; he does not even mention a counterargument. His final statement does not betray hesitation, but is the usual nominalistic gesture of submission after the defense of a doctrine not (yet) officially taught, while the warning against unproductive discussions should be understood in connection with such parallel passages as III *Sent.* d 3 q 1 art. 1 nota 3 and *S* III 1 D, where Biel warns against the evil of theological mock battles in connection with the doctrine of the immaculate conception. *S* III 18 L in fine: "In his vero sic pie tenendis cavere oportet curiositatem in inquisitione ne pretermissis salubrioribus studiis minus necessariis intendamus et dum affectum delectare cupimus, salutem negligamus; . . . sed semper pie credens, paratum habeat animum ad cedendum sententie saniori." See Wendelin Steinbach's assertion in *Gabrielis Biel supplementum in 28 distinctiones ultimas quarti magistri sententiarum* (Parisiis, 1521), d 43 q 1 art. 3 dub. 7, where he deals with the question "an in eodem instanti futura sit omnium hominum resurrectio generalis." All men will see corruption except Christ: "De virgine Maria Augustinus tenet eiusdem, quod sit corpore et anima translata in celum super choros angelorum." The same opinion was held by several influential Vienna theologians as, for example, Henry Totting of Oyta, with whose work Biel was familiar. See Carl J. Jellouschek, *Die ältesten Wiener Theologen und das Dogma vom Jahre 1950* (Vienna, 1956).

hypostatic union with the Godhead. In contrast with Mary, Christ did not therefore really and fully belong to mankind.[94]

Here we see that though the bodily assumption has been argued with the rule of *similitude with Christ*, the further theological-kerygmatic interpretation of this doctrine nevertheless tends to isolate the Virgin Mary as in herself the Hope of the World, in whom we can trust and have *fiducia* more than in Christ, *in contrast with Christ*.

2. Mary the hope of the world

This interpretation of Biel's understanding of the relation between Christ and the Virgin Mary is further corroborated in a parallel christological passage. Dealing in a Christmas sermon with the hypostatic union, Biel stresses that through Christ's assumption of human nature, this nature is not only restored to its original integrity but also exalted above its paradise status. Then he continues with an even stronger formulation of the same point: since the hypostatic union would abolish all hope for man's own resurrection, Christ preserved his mother from pain and shame.[95]

The ambiguity of the term "pure nature," which we have met already in the context of justification whenever the term *in puris naturalibus* was used, serves in this context as a basis for establishing a gulf between Christ and mankind which can only be bridged by the Virgin Mary.[96]

In a final sermon in the mariological collection not dedicated to any feast in particular but meant to be a summary of the foregoing ones,

[94] "Quamvis enim scimus corpus domini corruptionem videre non potuisse; quia unitum est deitati quod in nullo alio homine invenitur, idcirco nequaquam [!] tantam spei sumimus fiduciam nostre resurrectionis future, quantam ex resurrectione virginis que puram habuit humanam naturam i.e. deitati hypostatice non unitam." *S* III 18 J.

[95] "Et ut nobis fiduciam daret quia hec tolleret, id est auferret [!], a nobis, prius matrem suam immunem ab utroque [dolore et pudore] servavit." *S* II 2 E.

[96] ". . . licet factus sit homo mansit tamen deus. Advocatum habere vis et ad ipsum: ad mariam recurre. Pura siquidem humanitas in Maria, non modo pura ab omni contaminatione sed et pura singularitate nature." *Lect.* 32 B. Though Antoninus of Florence does not explicitly draw the same conclusion, he shares with Biel the basic argument: ". . . inter Deum et creaturam, medium est creatura unita Deo. Similiter inter esse creaturam puram et esse creaturam unitam medium est creatura, de qua sumitur quod nascitur et unitur. Et haec est ergo inter creaturas et filium medium, scilicet B. Maria. . ." *Summa Theologica*, IV.xv.20 [col. 1066 B].

Biel once again makes this point which is apparently an important one for him. As man's pure nature is represented in the Virgin Mary and has been elevated above the ranks of the angels, no doubt is left that human creatures at some time will join their ranks. True, in Christ our nature has preceded us in heaven, but this was not our pure nature. *Christ is not a pure man but a man-God*: how could man made from dust and earth, excluded from paradise, dare to aspire to heaven if he did not know that his own pure nature had preceded him? [97]

3. Mariology graphically presented

It is certainly not true that the theme of Mary the Hope of the World is accentuated by Biel only in contrast with Christ. Biel can equally well say in another context that Mary humiliated herself to the status of a married woman to give hope and trust to all so that no one in whatever status he might live should despair of his salvation.[98] A striking parallel!

But the contrast of Mary with Christ as a contrast between *homo purus* and *homo deus* points to the basic trend that permeates all of Biel's mariological considerations. In the transition from the doctrinal presentation to its kerygmatic application, parallel thus to the development indicated from the academic to the homiletic formulation, an important change of emphasis takes place. At the moment that the *locus de Maria*

[97] "Gaudeamus . . . quoniam in eius assumptione nostram exaltationem certissimam intuemur: nihil hesitationis relinquitur quin angelicis inserendi sumus choris, cum nostram naturam puram in virgine Maria super omnes angelorum ordines fideliter credimus elevatam. Et quidem precessit natura nostra in christo domino, sed non in se subsistens quinimo deitati in verbo hypostatice unita. Neque christus enim homo purus sed homo deus ad dexteram patris regnat omnipotentis. Quomodo enim homo terra et pulvis, de terrestri paradiso extrusus, ad celestem adspirare auderet si non in aliquo suam naturam puram precessisse cognosceret?" *S* III 25 A. Cf. *Lect.* 32 B and F. *Lect.* 32 X states that *fiducia* in the saints is based on the fact that they are real, mortal, human beings. Cf. Bernard of Clairvaux: ". . . nec cessare debet a laudibus humana mortalitas, cum hominis *sola* natura supra immortales spiritus exaltatur in virgine." *Sermo IV in Assumptione B.V. Mariae*, in *PL* CLXXXIII, 425. The theme of *fiducia* in the Virgin is also present in Holcot: "Et ideo non in armis nostrarum virtutum confidamus, sed in istius virginis gratia in qua est omnis spes vite et virtutis." *Sap.* Lect. 35 C.

[98] "Ideo non tantum esse virgo voluit sed usque ad statum coniugalem se humiliavit et vidualem, ut enim omnibus spem et fiduciam salutis daret, nullusque status salutem desperaret. . ." *S* III 25 L. ". . . tutissimum nostre calamitatis est asilium et misericordie sinus generalis. . ." *Lect.* 32 A.

Schema II.   Christology and Mariology

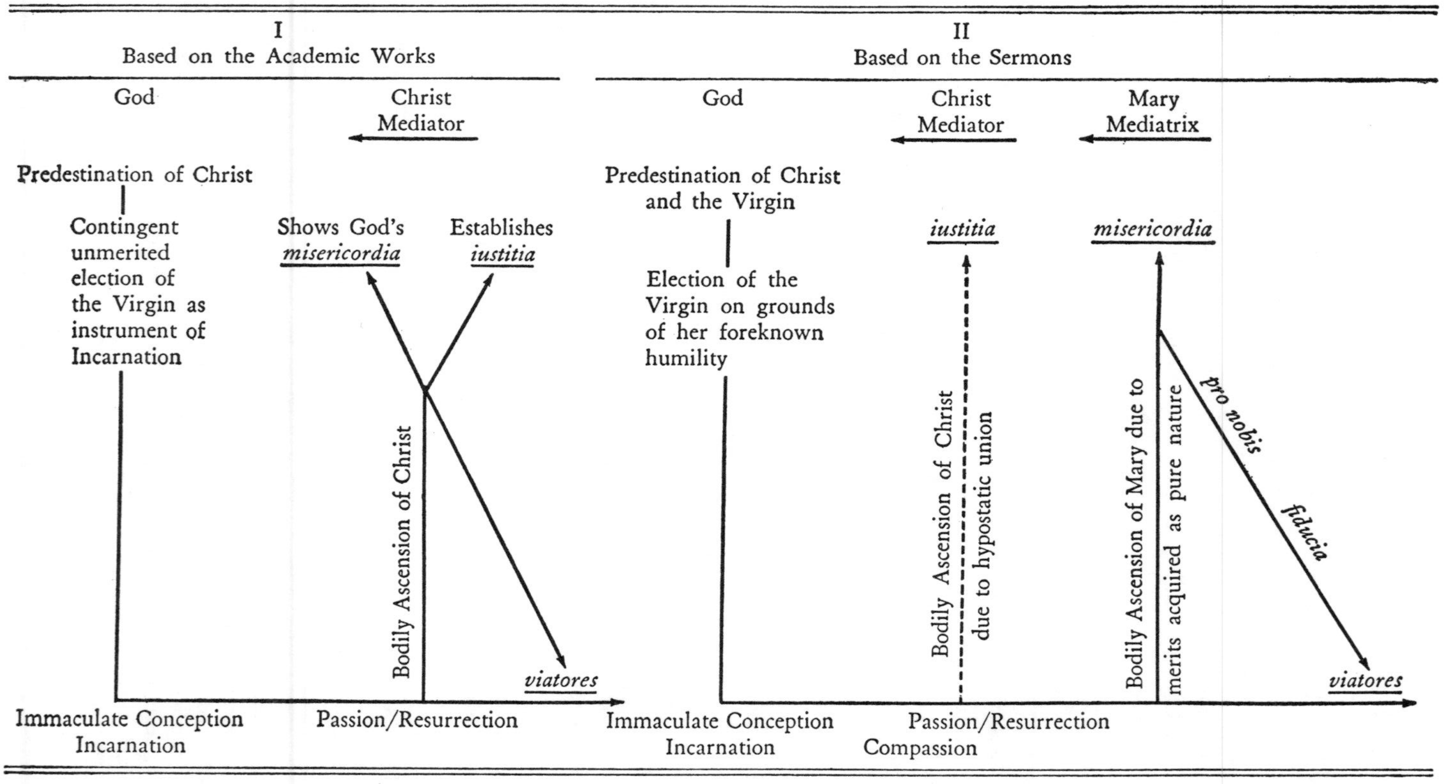

I
Based on the Academic Works

II
Based on the Sermons

I — Based on the Academic Works

God

Christ
Mediator →

Predestination of Christ

Contingent unmerited election of the Virgin as instrument of Incarnation

Shows God's *misericordia*

Establishes *iustitia*

Bodily Ascension of Christ

viatores

Immaculate Conception
Incarnation

Passion/Resurrection

II — Based on the Sermons

God

Christ
Mediator →

Mary
Mediatrix →

Predestination of Christ and the Virgin

Election of the Virgin on grounds of her foreknown humility

iustitia

Bodily Ascension of Christ due to hypostatic union

misericordia

Bodily Ascension of Mary due to merits acquired as pure nature

pro nobis   *fiducia*

viatores

Immaculate Conception
Incarnation

Passion/Resurrection
Compassion

starts to function in a wider theological or religious context, the original order: God — predestination → Mary — maternity → Christ — incarnation and passion — impact on Mankind [Column I], changes into the order: God — predestination → *Christ and Mary* — incarnation and passion through maternity and compassion — Mary — pure nature and mediatrix — impact on Mankind [Column II].

This outline is not to be regarded as a description of the originality of Biel's position. All the primary and secondary sources consulted suggest that Biel's views represent on most points an emerging late medieval piety which draws on a long medieval tradition and which transcends narrow school boundaries. Nor should the distinction between Parts I and II be taken in an absolute sense; elements of the two schemes can be found both in the academic and the homiletic sources. In the sermons Mary is at once the staircase by which Christ descended to earth and the staircase by which all the other gifts of God reach mankind. Nevertheless it should be noted that in the first instance nothing more is said than that she is the Mother of God, the *theotokos*; in the second instance she becomes more than the historic instrument of salvation, she is the permanent and most dependable means of salvation and the consummation of the salvation of mankind.[99]

4. *Sophia* speculations

The doctrine of predestination which at first seemed to qualify Mary's individual importance with the argument that God could have equally well elected another instrument for the incarnation loses this function as a result of the influence of extensive *sophia* speculations; this tradition reached Biel through Bernard of Clairvaux. The idea of the eternal wisdom seems to lift the Virgin Mary out of history and to make her so

---

[99] "Nihil nos deus habere voluit quod per marie manus non transiret. . . Ego quasi aqueductus exivi de paradiso per quam universa nobis influit gratia, omnis consummatur salus et redemptio per eam. . ." *S* III 15 F; cf. 13 H. *Vulg.* Eccl. 24:41 has only the words "sicut aquaeductus exivi de paradiso." For this interpretation see Bernard of Clairvaux, *Sermo in nat. B. V. Mariae*, in *PL* CLXXXIII, 439 f., as quoted by H. Lennerz, *De beata Virgine Tractatus dogmaticus* (Rome, 1957), p. 205. Pope Leo XIII used these same words in his "Octobri mense," *ASS* 24 (1891/92), 1961. See further Hermann Seiler, *Corredemptrix: Theologische Studie zur Lehre der letzten Päpste über die Miterlöserschaft Mariens* (Rome, 1939), esp. p. 54 ff.

nearly coeternal with the Father that she, though not fully *concreatrix* and thus still subordinate to the Father, becomes his assistant at creation.[100] On the one hand this concept becomes easily identified with the Genesis 1:2 reference to the Spirit of God; but on the other hand she cannot really become God without endangering her status as *homo purus*. Still another point where Mary cooperates in a task which is usually assigned solely to the Holy Spirit is an interesting variant on the Mary-Eve theme; the Mother of God is a guarantee of the veracity of the earliest Christian tradition; while the creation disintegrated through Eve, it regained its stability through Mary, the *doctrix apostolorum*.[101]

It is clear that the doctrine of predestination increases rather than balances the tendency of the superlative rule combined with the rule of similitude with Christ to transcend the limits of pure nature. In connection with the modern debate about the sacerdotal status of Mary, it is interesting to note that the only Marian limitation Biel accepts is that she, the Queen of Heaven and the ruler of the earth, was nevertheless not a priest since she lacked the authority to consecrate.[102]

[100] "Nec tamen ab eterno ordinata sed etiam cum eterno cuncta composuit. . . Non ita quod ipsa fuerit concreatrix cum fuerant disposita a creature principio; non enim tunc erat in rerum natura. Sed eo modo cunctis his aderat et cum eo creatore cuncta componebat. . . Que quia ad finem creationis cooperata est recte creatori astitisse dicitur. . ." *S* III 22 F. Cf. *Vulg.* Prov. 8: "Ab aeterno ordinata sum (23). . . Cum eo eram cuncta componens." (30).

[101] "Licet enim apostoli per eundem spiritum omnia cognoverint et in omnem edocti pervenerint veritatem, multum tamen ex illius relatione profecerunt . . . hec ipsa fidei doctrinam tradidit que nequaquam subverti poterit, domino mirabiliter ordinante ut sicut per feminam mundus ceciderat ita super feminam fundatus stabilimentum acciperet sempiternum." *S* III 19 D. The same tendency is implicit in modern mariological discussions. See Georg Söll: ". . . die mit Maria verbundene Urgemeinde [war] Keimzelle und Garant von Tradition und Glaubensbewusstsein . . ."; "Die Anfänge mariologischer Tradition: Beitrag zur Geschichte der Marienlehre," in *Kirche und Ueberlieferung* [Festschrift Geiselmann] (Freiburg i. Br., 1960), p. 51.

[102] ". . . et si in gratie plenitudine creaturas supergrediatur universas, gerarchis tamen cedit ecclesie in commissi mysterii executione." *Lect.* 4 B. If one accepts René Laurentin's definition, Biel's formulation would not exclude a *regale sacerdotium*. "Ainsi possède-t-elle à titre personnel comme Mère du Christ-Dieu ce sacerdoce universel que les autres chrétiens possèdent selon une mode collective. C'est en ce sens riche et limité qu'elle est le type de l'Eglise en son sacerdoce." *Marie: L'Église et Le Sacerdoce* (Paris, 1952), p. 668. Cf., however, A. Müller, *Ecclesia-Maria: Die Einheit Marias und der Kirche* (Fribourg, 1951), p. 231 f. See also *Lect.* 32 C.

From the fact that Mary executes the three tasks which are traditionally assigned to the third Person of the Trinity: that is, application of
the work of Christ,[103] assistance at the creation, and guaranteeing the
tradition, it is tempting to conclude that Biel presents here a new trinitarian doctrine: God the Father, God the Son, and God the Holy Spirit
have been changed into Father, Son, and Mother.

Such a presentation, however, would not do full justice to Biel's continual stress on Mary as pure nature, real man. The fact that Mary assumes some divine prerogatives is clearly the result of Biel's close identification of Mary with the second Person of the Trinity. It does not prevent
Biel from speaking of the Holy Spirit in traditional fashion as responsible
for the preservation of the tradition in the apostolic succession and for
the sanctification of the sinner through created and uncreated grace.

5. Evaluation: Maria *pro nobis*

Still there appears in Biel's Mariology a basic deviation from the early
Christian tradition at a related point: in the dialectics of Mary's contrast
and similarity with Christ. The high elevation of Mary as *corredemptrix*
and even more as *mediatrix* introduces unadulterated docetic elements
into Biel's conception of Christ. The Chalcedonian christological formulation: Christ, real God and real man, is implicitly negated in order to
give Mary a place of priority in the process of salvation and in the application of the work of Christ. There could hardly be a clearer instance of
docetism than the statement: Christ is not fully man, but [!] God-man.[104]

The fact that Mary is pure nature has a two-fold significance, both
aspects of which define her position as the object of *fiducia* and hope of
the world. In the first place, she is more closely allied with the created
order than Christ and has, therefore, a greater understanding of the weaknesses and general situation of mankind. She represents love and pity in
contrast to the severity of Christ the judge.

This is a parallel to the phenomenon noted previously that the first

---

[103] Cf. *S* III 1 D.
[104] *S* III 11 H — and especially Steinbach's summary in the Table of Contents
of this sermon [fol. 297ʳ] — show that the contrast *purus homo — deus-homo* as
such has an anti-Nestorian intention and can be regarded as orthodox. Our criticism concerns its application as the basis for greater *fiducia* in the Virgin Mary
than in Jesus Christ. Cf. III *Sent.* d 4 q 1 art. 2 concl. 1 D.

advent, the Incarnation, inspires love; the second advent, the return of Christ, will cause fear. The eternal procession from *misericordia* to *iustitia* with its temporal sequence is personalized in Mary and her Son. Mary is therefore more accessible; unlike her Son, she can answer the prayer of a sinner; she is the hope of sinners. In this sense, Mary holds a place of priority compared with Christ. There is *only fiducia in Christ insofar as one has fiducia in Mary and her merciful influence on her Son.*

The second significance of Mary's status as pure nature affects the kerygma of Biel's sermons in an even deeper way. Mary is not only contrasted with Christ; she is also highly exalted because of and toward a great similarity with Christ. She not only knows the created order in view of her natural existence, but she also is and represents this nature and gives unquestionable evidence that this nature is not necessarily bound to time and space but can transcend the consequences of fall and — one must add — creation. She is also the hope of the world in the sense that one can find in her the precedent for man's bodily resurrection. Christ proves that a bodily resurrection is possible; Mary proves that this *possibility can become reality "pro nobis."*

This possibility is not merely due to the acts of God in her life such as the Immaculate Conception, double sanctification, and bodily assumption, but also to her disposition which more or less directly brought these events about. We have already seen how according to the *Collectorium* Mary's predestination and Immaculate Conception were the results of God's decisions without any exterior cause. Biel felt, however, that in view of these two decisions of God, Mary earned her maternity with a full merit, *de condigno.* When Biel, however, starts to preach and to apply these mariological doctrines to the individual sinner, the Virgin Mary becomes the example of the rule that self-humiliation is the surest way to God. Thus, along with a *fiducia* in the position granted to Mary as advocate of sinners, there is a *fiducia* in the imitation of Mary, as the virgin who became through her humility the Queen of Heaven.[105]

Due to the same dialectics of contrast and similitude with Christ, there is an unresolved tension in this mariological kerygma. Through her close bond with Christ as expressed in Immaculate Conception and bodily assumption, Mary seems radically isolated from creation by her special

---

[105] ". . . ut placeret virginitas, humilitas proculdubio fecit." *S* III 11 D: "Profunditati igitur humiliationis respondet sublimitas hodierne exaltationis." *S* III 25 Q.

privileged position. Especially in what we can call doxological passages, her special position is stressed; in exhortative passages, however, Mary is primarily seen as the first-born of the saints, the first, but one of them. However this tension does not seem to have disturbed Biel for sometimes he presents these two ideas side by side.[106] As a matter of fact it is noteworthy that some of the saints fulfill the same functions as the Virgin. St. Martin is even said to be able to provide reconciliation with God, resurrection from the dead, and liberation from God's judgment.[107]

If he had been asked, Biel would undoubtedly have pointed to Adam and Eve before the fall as proof of the possibility that one can be sinless and yet pure nature.[108] As this would still not explain how a sinner, excluded from paradise, is able to imitate one adorned with the innocence of paradise, he would have pointed to the rule that God assists the humble, that is, those who do their very best.[109]

We have suggested already that it is vital for a truly catholic and biblical Mariology to be systematically subordinated to Christology. Such a Mariology is necessarily concentrated in the doctrine of Mary's maternity and her function as *theotokos*. Apart from the influence of postbiblical mariological speculation and piety, this largely applies to the Mariology of the *Collectorium*. In the sermons, however, Mariology is correlated with the doctrine of justification in such a way that the Virgin Mary becomes the prototype of man's way to salvation.

[106] "Sola siquidem hec virgo est que immunitate peccati cunctos etiam sanctos antecessit. Hec sola est quam nulla peccati macula denigravit. . . Sola virgo Maria ita ex utroque parente fuit concepta ut tamen ab originali prerogativa singulari sit preservata." *S* III 1 E.

[107] "Neque omnino diffidendum est de efficacia precum beati martini quoniam non solum potens est viatores domino reconciliare, sed etiam vitam hanc excedentes et ad pristinam revocare vitam et a sententia iudicis liberare." *S* IV 47 F. For the "sanctorum cultus *in*discretus," see *Lect.* 32 Y Z. Biel tends to be more cautious in attributing mediatorial powers to the Virgin than to St. Martin; perhaps because of her *proximity* to Christ! The quotation above (*S* IV 47 F) echoes the more restrained medieval hymn on St. Martinus, famous as the patron saint of the ancient and honored archiepiscopal see of Utrecht: "Martine par apostolis. . ." Published by Henricus Quentell with the additional comment: ". . . id est equalis in resuscitatione mortuorum trium, quia tres mortuos suscitavit ut apostoli." *Expositio himnorum . . . ex quibus possunt faciliter de eisdem sanctis colligi sermones peroptimi* (Colonia, 1494), fol. 43ʳ.

[108] See Biel's answer to Gregory of Rimini, III *Sent.* d 3 q 1 art. 2 G.

[109] "Ex omnibus his declaratur humilitatem Marie fuisse excellentissimam sub deo," *S* III 25 K. Cf. 13 G.

In every respect there is a strict parallel — though, of course, in different proportions — between the Virgin Mary and the sinner. By her humility Mary attracted and preserved the grace of God; the sinner attracts God's grace by doing his very best. Mary earned her eternal glory; still this reward exceeds her merits and is a gift of divine liberality. The sinner also must earn his salvation but is still subject to God's acceptation. Since even before the reception of the first grace Mary had more humility than any other creature, she has been elected above all other creatures. But her way to glory is essentially the same as that of any other creature.[110]

In not only an ontological but also a cognitive sense, the concept of the pure nature of Mary leads to the conclusion that Mary is the hope of the sinner. In life and word she reveals the will of God; she is at once the example to be imitated and the staircase to be climbed. With respect to the first part of this chapter that dealt with Mary's relation to God, the Virgin Mary — however closely identified with either the Son or the Spirit — occupies a position above all angels but under the Trinity, and thus under the eternal Word. With respect to the second part, insofar as Mary's relation with mankind is concerned, she has definitely a kerygmatic priority over Christ, the incarnate Word.

A valuable way of bringing together the varied strands of Biel's Marian piety and mariological thought is to recount some of the titles which he most frequently applies to the Virgin: *regina coeli, domina mundi, mediatrix ad mediatorem,* and *advocata peccatorum.* Yet there is still another title which Biel does not explicitly mention which best characterizes his understanding of the role of the Mother of God: *Maria Spes Omnium.*

---

[110] "Nemo ad hoc nos conari existimet ut vel fructuum patrie quos nunc possidet vel magnitudinem vel multitudinem eloqui presumamus. Tanti enim sunt et tam ineffabiles ut nec humano nec angelico intellectu poterint mensurari: Cuius denique humilitatis profunditatem — qua in via gratie plenitudinem *et attraxit* et conservavit ac tantam quam nunc possedit gloriam meruit — nec cogitare nec eloqui sufficimus quomodo premia huiuscemodi merita secundum ditissimam remuneratoris liberalitatem valde excedentia. . ." *S* III 25 P; cf. *Lect.* 32 D.

Chapter Ten

NOMINALISTIC MYSTICISM

꧁•꧂꧁•꧂꧁•꧂꧁•꧂꧁•꧂꧁•꧂꧁•꧂꧁•꧂꧁•꧂꧁•꧂꧁•꧂꧁•꧂꧁•꧂꧁•꧂꧁•꧂꧁•꧂꧁•꧂꧁•꧂

I. Nominalism and Mysticism

1. The Great Schism as turning point of the Middle Ages

THOUGH periodization is admittedly a matter of opinion, there is much to warrant the thesis that the later Middle Ages were born in Avignon and were shaped by the uncertainty and hierarchical confusion due to the Babylonian Captivity of the papacy (1309–1377) and the succeeding period of the Schism (1378–1415). The impact of this event can scarcely be overestimated, so much so that we are inclined to advocate the terms "preschismatic" and "schismatic" Middle Ages to replace the traditional terms "early" and "later" Middle Ages.

The condemnation by Etienne Tempier, Bishop of Paris, at the instigation of Pope John XXI, on January 18, 1277, of 219 propositions drawn primarily from Averroistic authors and partly also from Thomas Aquinas is certainly also of crucial importance. There is even good reason to agree with Gilson that this event should be regarded as a dividing line in the history of medieval philosophy, "both a point of arrival and a point of departure." [1] However, to regard this event as *the* decisive turning-point in the history of medieval thought, one must be willing to make the fallacious identification of the medieval history of ideas with the history of medieval philosophy.

Four major developments which would prove to have increasing influence on schismatic thought till the eve of the Reformation are all in-

[1] *History of Christian Philosophy in the Middle Ages*, p. 385.

timately connected with the fourteenth-century schism. In the realm of political theory, one has only to be reminded of the very cause of the Babylonian Captivity, the bull *Unam sanctam* (1302) [2] and the ensuing popularity with which Marsilius of Padua's *Defensor Pacis* (1326) was welcomed and immediately put to use by Louis the Bavarian in his struggle with Pope John XXII (1316–1334).

The influence of the anticlerical *Defensor Pacis* on such church-dedicated men as William of Occam and Jean Gerson is still largely over-rated.[3] However, it does indicate a different conception of the relation between Church and society and a new interpretation of the theocratic ideal, and it also came to stimulate the Church to concentrate on its primary spiritual task of inner reform.

Of equal but less obvious importance is the condemnation by Pope John XXII of the stricter interpretation of the last will of St. Francis. In 1317 he declared the *spirituales*, who rejected even communal possessions as contrary to the will and example of Christ, subject to the Inquisition. Six years later his *Cum inter nonnullos* caused as much division within the Franciscan order as Boniface VIII had done earlier in Christendom at large with his *Unam sanctam*. The ideal of poverty was so deeply engraved in the medieval mind that the rise of the Fraticelli movement and its identification of the papacy with Babylon should not be seen as an isolated and local Italian reaction. French and German fifteenth-century sermons and popular literature reveal the extent to which hierarchy, Pope, bishops, priests, and monks are understood to have exchanged poverty for greed. German preachers may have been moved to criticize the Avignon taxation by more national considerations, but also such an orthodox and devout preacher as the Frenchman Michel Menot liked to pit the poverty of Christ against the this-worldly interests of the Curia and could conclude by saying: "Never could less devotion be found in the Church." When somebody from the audience asked him why he did not do something about this horrible abuse, he simply an-

---

[2] Denz. 468–469.

[3] Cf. the otherwise useful survey of Marcel Pacaut, *La Théocratie, L'Église et le Pouvoir au Moyen Age* (Paris, 1957), pp. 200 ff. and Alexander Passerin d'Entrèves, *The Medieval Contribution to Political Thought*, 2 ed. (New York 1959), p. 86. For the opposite contention see J. G. Sykes, "A Possible Marsilian Source in Ockham," *English Historical Review* 51 (1936), 496 ff.

swered: "Friend, we do not have the man (who can bring this about)," and again: "I have no great hopes for the Church unless it be planted anew." [4]

The call for decision between "Christ or Mammon" was by no means a new one.[5] But while the preschismatic claims of the Waldenses could be rejected on the grounds of the successes of the Reform papacy, the bull of John XXII weakened the position of the Church precisely at a time when it had to face the transition to a money economy as well as the concomitant rise of the third estate.

The two other developments with which we are now more directly concerned are related to schismatic nominalism and mysticism. Both these aspects of late medieval thought have in fact a history that reaches back beyond the Avignon period. But while it is difficult to ascertain to what extent they are related to and reflect changes in the political and economic climate, it is a matter of record that at the time of the Babylonian Captivity, the Church felt that these two movements, insofar as they were represented by William of Occam and Meister Eckhart, should be investigated as to their orthodoxy.

The same Pope John XXII in 1326 set up a board to investigate the writings of William of Occam; and though three of the selected fifty-one theses were stigmatized as Pelagian, the Franciscan master of theology was never officially condemned.[6] In 1329, two years after Eckhart's death, twenty-eight propositions of this Dominican doctor of theology were

---

[4] "Nunquam in ecclesia fuit minor devotio," in *Sermons choisis de Michel Menot*, p. 16. "Sed, Frater, quare non ponitur remedium, cum abusus sit adeo magnus? Amice, non habeo hominem" (p. 343). "Nec de ea spem magnam habemus, nisi iterum de novo plantetur" (p. 374). The *restitutio* idea as expressed in this *iterum de novo* is according to modern scholars of the Radical Reformation *the* characteristic of this movement; this idea is then contrasted with the *reformatio* idea of the Magisterial Reformation. A survey of late medieval sermonic literature indicates, however, that the *restitutio* idea marks the rise of the Donatistic tide towards the end of the Middle Ages and is not restricted to such isolated groups as the Waldensians and Fraticelli to which the Radical Reformation is usually related. Cf. Biel on the fall of the Church: *S* IV 11 B.

[5] Cf. Ernst Werner, *Pauperes Christi: Studien zu sozial-religiösen Bewegungen im Zeitalter des Reformpapsttums* (Leipzig, 1956), pp. 165 ff.

[6] A. Pelzer, "Les 51 articles de Guillaume Occam, censurées en Avignon en 1326," *RHE* 18 (1922), 240 ff; J. Koch, "Neue Aktenstücke zu dem gegen Wilhelm von Ockham in Avignon geführten Prozess," *RTAM* 7 (1935), 353 f.; 8 (1936), 79 ff., 168 ff.

condemned by John XXII [7] for what can be summed up as a heretical doctrine of creation.

This condemnation is not only indicative of the fact that mysticism had entered a new phase in its history; it also would affect and caution the disciples of Eckhart. Tauler, Suso, and Ruysbroeck would later be extremely careful to avoid the alleged heresies of Meister Eckhart. If the censure of Occam had also received the official status of condemnation, its impact would have been equally apparent. As it was, of the two most central doctrines of Christian theology, the doctrines of redemption and creation, the former was not safeguarded in the same way as the latter against heretical interpretations. Nevertheless, it seems clear to us that the nominalists whom we have met in the preceding chapters can only be understood once one has noted their great zeal to be orthodox and obedient to the *magisterium* of the Church.

2. The common thesis: nominalism and mysticism mutually exclusive

The fact that both movements, nominalism and mysticism, drew the attention of Pope John XXII does not of course indicate any inner relationship. On the contrary it is striking that John XXII introduces his condemnation of Eckhart with the words: ". . . we regret to relate that a certain contemporary of ours, a native of Germany, Ekardus by name . . . *wanted to know more than he should.* . ." This is the extreme opposite of the usual charge against Occam which labels his thought as scepticism and open warfare of faith against reason.[8]

[7] Denz. 501 ff.; complete text, H. Denifle, *ALKM* 2 (1886), 636 ff.; M. H. Laurent, "Autour du procès de Maître Eckhardt: Les documents des Archives Vaticanes," *Divus Thomas* 13 (1936), 331 ff., 430 ff. Cf. the excellent contribution by Otto Karrer and Herma Piesch, *Meister Eckeharts Rechtfertigungsschrift* (Erfurt, 1927).

[8] "Faith was intact, but to follow Ockham was to give up any hope of achieving, in this life, a positive philosophical understanding of its intelligible meaning." Etienne Gilson, *History of Christian Philosophy in the Middle Ages,* p. 498. "Les données de la foi qu'il déclare inaccessibles à la raison ne tarderont pas a être jugées contraires à la raison." Maurice de Wulf, *Histoire de la philosophie médiévale,* III, 46. Cf. however the criticism of Philotheus Boehner, "A recent presentation of Ockham's philosophy," in *FStud* 9 (1949), pp. 443 ff. A. Renaudet: ". . . le nominalisme terministe était une doctrine trop sèche et trop formelle . . . pour ne pas provoquer une révolte de la sensibilité et ne pas rejeter les esprits vers le mysticisme." *Préréforme et Humanisme à Paris pendant les premières guerres d'Italie 1494–1517,*

Indeed it is fair to say that while generally the opposition of scholasticism and mysticism is rejected by scholars today as untenable, nominalism and mysticism are still supposed to be mutually exclusive. As great an historian of Christian thought as Reinhold Seeberg felt that though these two movements share a psychological interest and are both basically indifferent as regards ecclesiastical dogma [sic!] they form the sharpest possible contrast: empiricism versus idealism.[9] In Luther scholarship one finds without exception the same thesis: the mystical and nominalistic elements in Luther's theology are reduced to two absolutely independent sources. No one has formulated this more succinctly than Erich Seeberg who stated that the difference between Luther's theology and nominalism was to be found in Luther's mystical teaching: and vice versa, what differentiates his thought from mysticism would be his nominalism.[10]

3. The problem of defining mysticism

It seems to us that there is a ready explanation for the fact that the thesis which holds nominalism and mysticism to be mutually exclusive

---

2 ed. (Paris, 1953), p. 67 f. "Chez les élèves d'Ockham, la doctrine nouvelle ne créa qu'une soumission inerte à un dogme qui cessait de parler à l'esprit et au coeur," p. 66.

[9] "Zunächst ist es klar, dass Nominalismus und Mystik in scharfem Gegensatz zueinander stehen. . . . Das Erfahrungsprinzip, das die Nominalisten auf die natürlichen Dinge anwenden, wird von diesen mystischen Theologen in Bezug auf Gott und sein Wirken gebraucht. Darin ist die Differenz wie die Gemeinsamkeit des beiderseitigen Interesses enthalten, daraus begreift sich auch die beiderseitige Gleichgültigkeit dem kirchlichen Dogma gegenüber." Seeberg, DG III, p. 675. Adolf von Harnack employs the term "nominalistische Mystik" but follows Albrecht Ritschl in identifying this type of mysticism with quietism. Ritschl, Geschichte des Pietismus, I (Bonn, 1880), 467 ff. Harnack DG III, 443.

[10] "Man kann wohl die Frage: Worin unterscheidet sich Luther vom Nominalismus? durch den Hinweis auf seine Beziehung zur Mystik beantworten! wie man umgekehrt sagen kann, dass es gerade die positivistischen. . . Elemente der Ockhamistischen Theologie sind, die ihn letztlich von der Mystik unterscheiden." Erich Seeberg, Luthers Theologie in ihren Grundzügen, 2 ed. (Stuttgart, 1950), pp. 39 f. Though we are not concerned here with Luther and Reformation thought, an indirect and implicit conclusion will be that Luther's enthusiasm for such mystical authors as John Tauler and Gerard Zerbold of Zutphen can be adequately explained from his intimate knowledge of Biel's oeuvre and marks therefore the hypothesis of a second formative influence by so-called German Mysticism as redundant.

was advanced and has since gone unchallenged. The boundaries of mysticism are defined in such a way as to exclude the possibility of nominalistic mysticism from the outset. Mysticism is then supposed to deal with the intellectual intuition of transcendental reality.[11]

This definition represents very well the position of Thomas Aquinas. Thomas taught that the goal of mysticism or its equivalent, the contemplative life, is the vision of God understood as the ultimate truth: "contemplation pertains to the simple act of gazing on the truth." [12] Insofar as the union itself is not a comprehensive knowledge of God but a complete satisfaction of the longing for God, the will of course participates in this mystical experience; God as the highest truth is at the same time the highest good.[13]

With Eckhart and his school we meet with an even greater emphasis on the intellect in the contemplative life. This appears at two points. In the exposition of the doctrine of God, it is stated that God does not know because he is, but that he is because he knows. In the analyses of the nature of man, the *Fünklein* or *Grund* in man is seen as the spark of divine intelligence. As only the intellect is beyond multiformity, "it is the same thing to say that God is wholly Intellect and that God is one"; [14] in this sense there is a God beyond God: the godhead beyond the trinitarian God of the Christian faith.[15]

The Dionysian themes of the darkness of God and the need for the negative approach are spelled out in such a way that the three characteristics of the created order, time, pluriformity, and corporeality, are seen as *the* obstacles which hinder a union or reunion with God, the source

---

[11] "Contemplation," *Dictionnaire de spiritualité*, ed. Charles Baumgartner, S.J., II (Paris, 1953), col. 1643 ff. Cf. the excellent introduction by Ray C. Petry, *Late Medieval Mysticism* (Philadelphia, 1957), pp. 17 ff.; Evelyn Underhill, *Mysticism*, 12 ed. (London, 1930), p. 72; A. B. Sharp, *Mysticism: Its True Nature and Value* (London, 1910), pp. 74, 96.

[12] *ST* II.II q 180 art. 3 ad 1:". . . contemplatio pertinet ad simplicem intuitum veritatis." Cf. *Contra Gentiles* II q 83: "finis igitur hominis est pervenire ad veritatis contemplationem."

[13] "Ici-bas comme au ciel, imparfaite ou parfaite, la contemplation est formellement un acte d'intelligence. Non que la volonté n'y joue un grand rôle, mais l'intelligence est la faculté qui saisit la vérité." F. D. Joret, *La Contemplation mystique d'après S. Thomas d'Aquin* (Lille, 1923), p. 54.

[14] Etienne Gilson, *History of Christian Philosophy*, p. 440.

[15] *Die lateinischen Werke*, ed. Ernst Benz, Josef Koch, IV (Stuttgart, 1956), 40 ff.

of all being.[16] Escaped from this prison of creation, "the soul is unified with the godhead itself in such a way that it has lost its identity in the same way as a drop of wine disappears in the sea." [17]

Without attempting to settle the issue regarding the relation of the Eckhartian school to Dionysius the Areopagite or to Thomas Aquinas, it seems clear to us that the Christian doctrine of creation is threatened here through a close approximation of creation and fall. The distance between creator and creature is not abolished — and in this sense the vague charge of pantheism certainly does not apply — but the broken union between God and man is traced back, not to the fall of man, but to his creation. Of the traditional three stages, purgation, illumination, and union, the first stage refers to the effort to break down the wall or veil of creation to reach then the intellectual intuition of transcendental reality, the union with God in which the soul is absorbed.

If one defines mysticism in this way, it does indeed exclude the possibility of a nominalistic type of mysticism. The very mark of nominalism is its rejection of the Thomistic and Neoplatonic elements constitutive for the Eckhartian position. The first point made in a Prologue to Lombard's *Sentences* by a theologian of the nominalistic school of thought is that intuitive knowledge of God is strictly the prerogative of the *beati*, the members of the Church Triumphant. The only exceptions to this rule are Jesus Christ and St. Paul. The soul of Christ, however, was beatified in the first instant of his birth. The *raptus* of St. Paul indeed presents a difficulty, but is nevertheless an exception from the established rule: the terms *viator* and *comprehensor* or *beatus* are defined in contrast to each other.[18]

[16] J. Quint. ed., *Meister Eckhart: Die deutschen Werke*, I, *Predigten* (Stuttgart, 1958), pp. 178, line 4 ff.; p. 193, line 3 ff. Franz Pfeiffer, ed., *Meister Eckhart*, 4 ed. (Göttingen, 1924), p. 78, line 22 ff.

[17] Pfeiffer, p. 467, 6 ff.: "Dâ wirt die sêle vereinet in der blôzen gotheit, daz si nimmer mêr müge funden werden, als vil als ein tropfe wînes mittem in dem mer." Cf. Tauler, F. Vetter, *Die Predigten Taulers* (Berlin, 1910), p. 33; Suso, M. Diepenbrock, *Heinrich Suso's, genannt Amandus, Leben und Schriften*, 3 ed. (Augsburg, 1854), p. 266.

[18] ". . . Christus autem semper habuit noticiam intuitivam deitatis secundum humanitatem quia anima eius in instanti creationis fuit beata . . ."; "[From the life of the viator] excluditur intellectus beati deum clare videntis . . . viator et comprehensor ex opposito distinguuntur." Biel, Questio I. Prologi. Cf. III *Sent.* d 13, q 1, art. 3, dub. 1. Cf. Occam, Prologi I QQ.

The typical nominalistic use of the distinction between God's *potentia absoluta* and *potentia ordinata* provides a structure within which there is no place for a contemplative life understood as the ascent to a vision of the highest truth.

The established order is the product of a decision of God. The highest truth attainable by the *viator* is the knowledge of the decisions of God, that is, of his revelation. This is the knowledge of faith resting on the authority of the Church and Holy Scripture.[19] As the realm of the *potentia absoluta* refers to all the possible decisions of God, the nominalist as a theologian is concerned with what God actually decided. The summit of his reach is therefore not the intellect or being of God but the will of God. Purgation, the first stage, is not an effort to pierce the veil of crea-tion — this would run counter to man's ordained status as *viator* — but is the battle against sin to regain the perfection of the original righteous-ness of Adam before the fall.

At the point where human reason finds its limitations, the soul meets the divine will and is united with it in love, not through conformity of intellect, but *per voluntatis conformitatem*.[20] The divine abyss with which the nominalistic mystic is united in love can no longer be the abyss beyond God, which involves scrutiny of divine truth, but the mystery encountered in loving union with the inscrutable will of God. The application of the whole vocabulary of traditional mystical theology cannot obscure the fact that we find here an essentially different type of mysticism.

Before we trace in more detail the mystical elements in the theology of Gabriel Biel, we should like to point out that we are not reintroducing the long-debated distinction between speculative and practical mysticism. Cuthbert Butler and Ray Petry have shown convincingly enough that medieval mysticism was consistent in its effort to establish a proper bal-

[19] ". . . omnis cognitio dei viatoris est cognitio fidei." Biel, III *Sent.* d 34 q 1 art. 2 concl. 1; ". . . non sit alia patris cognitio quam ea que per fidem, aut nar-rantis ei ingeritur simpliciter aucthoritatem." Gerson, *De simplif. cordis*, XIII, *Opera* III 461 D.

[20] Gerson, *De mystica theologia Speculativa* Cons. 39 O; *Opera* III. 393 C: "Spiritus ergo noster cum deo adheret per intimum amorem, unus spiritus est cum eo per voluntatis conformitatem. . . Itaque qui sic [Jesus, praying in the Garden] unitur deo et adheret per amorosam voluntatis conformitatem utique stabilitur in eo!" Cf. *De Cons. theol. Opera* III; I. 157; *De Mystica theol. spec.* 39 O; *Opera* III. 393 C. *Ioannis carlerii de Gerson, De mystica theologia*, ed. André Combes (Lucani, s.a., [1958]), p. 104, line 22 ff. Biel: ". . . gaudium . . . ex conformitate sue voluntatis cum voluntate paterna." *Lect.* 64 F.

ance between contemplation and action.[21] On the condition that it is understood that in the Thomistic and Eckhartian type of mysticism the will, and in the Gabrielistic type knowledge, plays an important auxiliary part, the distinction between speculative and affective mysticism is perfectly acceptable.

To conclude this first section on the relation of nominalism and mysticism, we can say that if one defines mysticism as intellectual intuition of transcendental reality, there is no such phenomenon as nominalistic or affective mysticism. If, however, we find one of Gerson's descriptions of mysticism acceptable, according to which mysticism is the outreach of the soul to a union with God through the desire of love,[22] which resides not in the intellective but in the affective power of the soul and has not the *verum* but the *bonum* as its object,[23] we find that the sources themselves allow for an affective type of mysticism which in nominalistic circles replaced speculative mysticism.[24]

II. Jean Gerson: Nominalist and Mystic

1. Gerson's attitude toward Thomism and nominalism

Biel's authority par eminence for all problems concerning the contemplative life is Jean Gerson, the influential Chancellor of the University of Paris from 1395 throughout the turbulent beginnings of the con-

[21] Cuthbert Butler, *Western Mysticism*, 2 ed. (London, 1926); Petry, "Social Responsibility and the Late Medieval Mystics," *CH* 21 (1952), 3 ff. I do not see, however, how Maria Lücker could come to the conclusion that Eckhart teaches that the contemplative life merely forms the introductory stage for the active life. *Meister Eckhart und die Devotio Moderna* (Leiden, 1950), p. 9. Cf. Pfeiffer, p. 53, line 1 ff.: "Maria was ê Martha, ê si Maria wurde. . ."

[22] ". . . theologiam mysticam sic possumus describere: theologia mystica est extensio animi in deum per amoris desiderium. . . Aliter sic: theologia mystica est experimentalis cognitio habita de deo per amoris unitivi complexum. Aliter sic: theologia mystica est sapientia sapida noticia habita de deo dum ei supremus apex affective potentie rationalis per amorem coniungitur et unitur." *De mystica theologia spec.*, Cons. 28 E [*Opera* III, 384 B; Combes, ed., p. 72, line 34 ff.].

[23] ". . . speculativa theologia est in potentia intellectiva cuius obiectum est verum. Mysticam vero reponimus in potentia affectiva cui pro obiecto bonum assignamus." *Ibid.*, Cons. 29 F [*Opera* III, 384 C; Combes ed., p. 73, line 10 ff.].

[24] We have therefore to disagree with Ray Petry's conclusion: "Perhaps of more working validity than the speculative-affective character is the applicability of the threefold way to the mystic experience." *Late Medieval Mysticism*, p. 21. As we shall see, the interpretation of the threefold way depends on the prior question, in which of the two schools the mystic stands.

ciliar high tide of the fifteenth century. For Biel, Gerson was a great systematic and mystical authority whom he honored and quoted, not only from his university lectern in Tübingen, but also from his pulpit at the Cathedral of Mainz. There was no doubt in his mind nor in that of the other nominalistic schoolmen that Gerson belonged to the *via moderna*.[25]

A reference to the thought of Gerson could have sufficed to prove the compatibility of nominalism and mysticism if there were not less unanimity as regards Gerson's position in our time than in the fifteenth century. We are faced with the remarkable situation that those who stress the nominalistic aspects of his thought challenge his place in the mystical school of thought; [26] while at the same time, those who find in him primarily a mystic are not willing to count him with the nominalistic school of thought.[27] It cannot be far from the truth to explain these contra-

[25] Cf. Johannes Altenstaig, *Vocabularius theologie*. After Gabriel Biel, Jean Gerson is the second authority to whom Altenstaig turns for reference; with regard to such mystical terms as, e.g., "assimilatio," "abyssus," etc., Gerson becomes the main and in most cases the sole authority. In a section specially dedicated to the relation of Gerson and Occam André Combes points to the sermon *A Deo exivit* to establish an "opposition radicale." *Essai sur la Critique de Ruysbroeck par Gerson* III (Paris, 1959), p. 219 ff. For extensive bibliography on Gerson see Mgr. Glorieux, ed., *Jean Gerson. Oeuvres Complètes*, vol. I: *Introduction Générale* (Paris, 1960), p. 153 ff.

[26] "Auch sein Kampf gegen den von ihm falsch verstandenen Ruysbroeck bestätigt seine Distanz von der wirklichen Mystik." Walter Dress, *Die Theologie Gersons. Eine Untersuchung zur Verbindung von Nominalismus und Mystik im Spätmittelalter* (Gütersloh, 1931), p. 50. For Gerson's criticism on Ruysbroeck see André Combes, *Essai sur la critique de Ruysbroeck par Gerson*, vol. II: *La première critique gersonienne du "De ornatu spiritualium nuptiarum"* (Paris, 1948). According to Combes, Gerson's nominalism prevents him from admitting more than a moral union and forces him thus to do Ruysbroeck injustice: "Ne concevant pas de moyen terme entre la metaphysique et la morale, et ne pouvant réduire la troisième partie du De ornatu à une thèse d'union morale entre l'homme et Dieu, il a rétréci ses textes scripturaires aux limites d'une pure morale. . ."; *Ibid.*, p. 249.

[27] Fr. Ehrle characterizes Gerson's thought as "Reaktion gegen den Ockamismus," *Der Sentenzenkommentar Peters von Candia, des Pisaner Papstes Alexander V* (Münster i. W., 1925), p. 92. Cf. James Connolly, *John Gerson: Reformer and Mystic* (Louvain, 1928), p. 85; ". . . though his training and the whole tradition of his learning was Nominalistic, Gerson was a Realist in his Theology and in his mysticism," p. 236. Connolly refers here to B. Bess, "Gerson, Joh. Charlier," in *RE* VI, 613, J. B. Schwab, *Johann Gerson: Professor der Theologie und Kanzler der Universität Paris* (Würzburg, 1858), p. 311. Cf. Gilson, *History of Christian Philosophy*, p. 529: "In fact, Gerson had never adhered to nominalism except against a certain realism. . ." In his analyses of what he calls the "Journey's End" Gilson

dictory conclusions from the indicated presupposition that there exists no common ground between nominalism and mysticism.

It is not our purpose to present another analysis of Gerson's mysticism in all stages of development. In his meticulous and detailed research on Gerson, André Combes is in the process of going through the relevant sources exhaustively. It is obvious that his analyses centering around Gerson's critique of Ruysbroeck have at once dated the earlier studies on Gerson's mysticism and mark a monumental contribution to our understanding of the mystical theology of the Parisian Chancellor, a necessary point of departure for future investigations.

We want to focus on the mysticism of Gerson insofar as this proves to be an important source for Gabriel Biel. Combes has shown that Gerson's attitude toward mysticism is by no means static and that what we term penitential mysticism is replaced in the later stages of Gerson's life by an essentialistic type of mysticism hardly compatible with the philosophy of Occam.[28]

We are particularly concerned with those Gersonian passages which a later generation regarded as representative of his thought, and with those aspects that have led scholars to assume either that, driven by his mystical insights, Gerson broke away from the nominalism of his teacher

---

comes to the harsh judgment: "This doctrinal confusion finds its saddened and powerless (sic!) witness in the person of John Gerson . . ."; *Ibid.*, p. 528. Cf. Combes: "Ce que Gerson demande à Ockam, c'est un service défini. Il a besoin de lui contre des abus de réalisme." *Essai* . . . III [*L'Évolution spontanée de la critique gersonienne*] (Paris, 1959), p. 217. Note however Gilson's more restricted understanding of nominalism as merely a movement in the history of philosophy. Johann Stelzenberger regards nominalism and mysticism as two unrelated aspects of Gerson's thought: "Im Bestreben, Scholastik und Mystik zu einen, vergisst er seine philosophische Richtung. . . Er ist Ockhamist eigentlich bloss im theoretischen Teile, im praktischen aber nicht." *Die Mystik des Johannes Gerson* (Breslau, 1929), p. 54.

[28] For a summary of Gerson's development see André Combes, *Essai sur la critique de Ruysbroeck par Gerson* [= *Essai* . . .], III.1 (Paris, 1959), p. 316 f. On the "retour à dieu," *ibid.* p. 223 ff. Cf. the sermon "A Deo exivit," in *Essai* . . . I (Paris, 1945), p. 636 ff. In *Essai* . . . III, 98 f., Combes finds a greater contrast between *Epistola 1 ad Bartholomaeum* and *De Mystica Theologia* than in *Essai* . . . II (Paris, 1948), though the possibility of development is noted there, *ibid.*, 364. We are rather inclined to find Gerson's break with penitential mysticism in the period following *De Mystica Theologia*. Combes rejects the possibility of a true mysticism founded on the *conformitas voluntatis*, which is interpreted as "un accord purement extérieur de volontés." *Essai* . . . II, 249. Cf. note 26 above.

d'Ailly, or duped by his adherence to nominalistic concepts, he misunderstood and rejected mysticism as such.

His attack on the scholastic theology of his time, which indeed pervades most of his writings, should not be interpreted as an attack on nominalism. His two lectures "against vain curiosity in matters of faith" are as explicit as one might possibly wish. In these he complains about the lack of piety and unity in theological education; instead of being wiser than God, one should in all humility submit to the inscrutability of God's will.[29] This now is the main theme of nominalism: the *viator* cannot go beyond the revelation of God to enter the inner chamber of his wisdom — a clear reaction against essentialist theology. This implies that the reach of human reason is limited to the realm of revelation. Operating within this realm, it can succeed in proving that the articles of faith are not contrary to the results of the secular sciences.[30] His criticism of party strife and disunity certainly does not mean that nominalism stood under the same curse of vain curiosity; neither does his quoting of the opinions of Aquinas indicate that he would favor Thomism.[31]

It is the *formalisantes*, the followers of Duns Scotus, that Gerson has especially in mind when he is criticizing the Franciscans for deserting the great Bonaventura.[32] His claim to absolute impartiality [33] makes it

[29] ". . . pergere ultra volentes defecerunt scrutantes scrutinio. Quo pacto sic? Quia certe ea quae in liberrima potestate dei posita erant, dum attingere et ad quasdam necessitatis regulas adducere conati sunt, ipsi 'evanuerunt in cogitationibus suis et obscuratum est insipiens cor eorum.' Rom. 1:21. Philosophi igitur dum hoc secretum divinae voluntatis penetrare duce experientia, moliuntur, quidni deficiant? *Quoniam sicut divina voluntas huius ratio est, ita solis illis scire concessum est, quibus ipsa voluerit revelare.* Ita de incarnatione et de reliquis nostrae fidei articulis. . . " *Opera* I, 92 A. "Et vitium est velle plus quam oportet sapere. . ." *Opera* I, 93 C.

[30] ". . . articulos fidei nullo modo esse contra philosophiam naturalem, sed eidem potius consoni sunt, quamquam eos attingere et invenire suum non est; praesertim nisi praevia fidei revelatione quae tales veritates subministret." *Opera* I, 92 A. Cf. *Sermo Dominice* IV Adv.: "Deus enim facere potest de creatura sua ad eam secundum beneplacitum suum obligare; sufficit pro rationabili causa, ut dicat: sic mihi placet." *Opera* III, 928 B.

[31] For Gerson's references to Thomas see Connolly, p. 286, n. 1.

[32] ". . . nec admirari sufficio qualiter patres et fratres minores dimisso tanto doctore . . . converterunt se ad nescio quos novellos. . ." *Opera* I, 91 D; ". . . studeo eos quos scotistas appellamus ad concordiam cum aliis doctoribus adducere. . ." *Opera* I, 101 C.

[33] ". . . obtestor ne quis existimet me velle cuiquam doctori vel personae vel religioni detrahere." *Opera* I, 97 A.

all the more significant that the only modern doctor openly attacked is John of Ripa,[34] a fervent Scotist. Here Gerson is a true disciple of d'Ailly and Occam.[35]

In view of this clear witness of the sources we should beware lending too much weight to the fact that shortly after the two lectures 'against vain curiosity' were held, Gerson permitted the Dominicans to return to Paris (1403).[36] In a letter published on the occasion of the return of the Dominicans, Gerson makes clear that he did not for a moment wish to justify their aberrations, but that Christian love required him to give them an opportunity to prove themselves. Frankly enough he concedes that this act of Christian love happens to be the more expedient decision as regards the unity and honor of faith and university.

Again, Gerson is motivated by a nominalistic ideal: to restore unity within the realm of theology by humbly concentrating on the data of faith which alone would neutralize the rift-causing influence of philosophy.[37] In a striking parallel to the unity efforts of the Council of Pisa (1409), it was to be the tragic fate of nominalism that instead of reforming the existing schools of St. Thomas and Duns Scotus, it added to the confusion by becoming a third party in schismatic university life.

2. Penitential mysticism *versus* transformation mysticism

Turning now from the "formalisantes" to the second enemy against whom Gerson is taking up arms, heretical mysticism, we have to inves-

[34] "Concipere itaque quod in divinis sit aliquod esse formale . . . ut ripa posuit, istud parit in animo meo majorem difficultatem quam sit illa propter quam elucidandam ista talia reperiuntur, imo nequeo non videre ista palam esse erronea." I, 101 B. Cf. A. Combes, "Jean de Vippa, Jean de Rupa ou Jean de Ripa," *AHDL* 14 (1939), 235 ff. and *Jean Gerson: commentateur Dionysien* (Paris, 1940), p. 608 ff.

[35] A. Stöckl, *Geschichte der Philosophie des Mittelalters*, II, 960 f.; Meller, *Studien zur Erkenntnislehre des Peter von Ailly*, p. 187 ff.; p. 140.

[36] H. Denifle and E. Chatelain, *Chartularium universitatis Parisiensis* III (Paris, 1894), p. 506. Connolly, p. 85, stresses this point to show Gerson's "conversion" from nominalism to realism.

[37] "Nolo putet aliquis, me hoc loco justificationem seu defensionem partis illius quae depulsa vel avulsa est suscepisse, fratres praedicatores loquor. . ." *Opera* I, 111 D / 112 A. "Ergo non tam quod liceat ex juris rigore quam quod expediat exquiratur." *Opera* I, 112 B. André Combes terms the underlying concept "gersonisme," and adds: ". . . ce gersonisme ne doit rien à Ockham, sauf peut-être, une confirmation en sa sobriété instinctive: il est bonaventurien." *Essai . . .* III, 223.

tigate to what extent this polemic affects Gerson's attitude toward mysticism as such.

After what has been said, we are not surprised to find that humility is for Gerson the central value, not only in the first stage of purgation, but as the abiding context within which alone the mystical experience can be attained. Humility stands here for the submission of intellect and will to the spiritual authority of Scripture and Church.

In his treatise on mystical theology, Gerson casts his whole treatment within the structure of the question, "whether the knowledge of God can be better acquired by the penitent affect than by the intellect."[38] The answer is twofold. First, while it would be ideal to combine mystical and scholastic theology,[39] mystical theology is more perfect than scholastic theology because it cannot be abused except — to be certain — by those who lack humility. The most common abuse of scholastic theology is that one theologizes with the mouth and not with the heart.[40] This is now impossible in mystical theology which by definition is theology of the heart.[41]

In the second place mystical theology is not the special field of some learned men but can be acquired by a mere woman and simpleton. It is acquired through intensive exercise of moral virtues which prepare the soul for purgation, illumination, and perfection.[42] From this vantage point Gerson criticizes two kinds of heretical mysticism, both resulting

[38] III, 361.

[39] "Et quoniam nostrum hactenus studium fuit concordare theologiam hanc mysticam cum nostra scholastica. . ." *Opera* IV, 54 B.

[40] "Alioquin tales theologizant solis auribus corporis. . . Mystica vero theologia sicut non versatur in tali cognitione literatoria, sic non habet necessariam talem scholam que schola intellectus dici potest, sed adquiritur per scholam affectus. . ." *Cons.* 30 G; *Opera* III. 385 f.; ed. Combes p. 77, 11 f. "Quis autem appropinquaverit igni et vestimenta eius non ardeant vel calescant?" *Cons.* 8 P; *Opera* III. 369 A; ed. Combes, p. 19, 12 f.

[41] "Sic ergo de theologia speculativa dicimus quod non quelibet perversa est aut perversos inhabitat, nec in ea vitia esse ponimus. Sed in abutentibus ea qualiter nullus in theologia mystica abusus . . . , nisi forsan in modo pretacto per superbiam obiective." *Cons.* 32 I; *Opera* III. 387 D f.; ed. Combes, p. 85, 47 ff.

[42] ". . . per exercitium vehemens moralium virtutum disponentium animam ad purgationem et in theologicis illuminantibus eam in beatificis virtutibus eam perficientibus proportionaliter ad tres actus hierarchicos qui sunt purgare, illuminare, et perficere . . . licet sit suprema et perfectissima notitia ipsa tamen potest haberi a quolibet fideli etiam si sit muliercula vel idiota. . ." *Ibid.* Cf. *Opera* III. 406; ed. Combes, p. 77, 18 ff.: "Saepe enim ubi minus cognitionis ibi plus affectum."

from a lack of humility. In the first place he reproaches the sect of the Beghards with such words that he must have had in mind the propositions which were censured in 1311 by Pope Clement V.[43] He especially protests against the concept that the mystic in the third stage is freed from his obligations to ecclesiastical and divine law. This antinomianism of course runs counter to the nominalistic thesis that the creature, however high a level of perfection he attains, remains unable to escape the set limits of the established order, and that his understanding of God can never break through the boundaries of revelation. Within this dome of the established order, the Christian is intellectually and ethically dependent on the teaching of the Church, which he cannot possibly scorn, even while finding union with God.[44] In a treatise against the flagellants, written while attending the Council of Constance (July 1417), Gerson indicates that the greatest danger of this heresy is that it leads to a bypassing of the sacrament of penance, the very heart of man's disposition for union with God.[45] The affections of the heart have to be regulated by the law of Christ, and this law is sufficiently revealed in the Decalogue and authoritatively unfolded by the Apostles and Holy Doctors.[46]

While the antinomians threaten a proper understanding of the cen-

---

[43] ". . . itaque sequebantur (Beghardi) affectus suos sine regula et ordine postposita lege christi, presumptio nequissima precipitavit eos ut dicerent hominem postquam ad pacem tranquillam spiritus pervenisset, absolutum esse legibus divinorum preceptorum. . ." *Cons.* 8 P; *Opera* III. 369 A. Cf. Denz. 473: "Quod illi, qui sunt in praedicto gradu perfectionis et spiritu libertatis, non sunt humanae subiecti oboedientiae, nec ad aliqua praecepta ecclesiae obligantur. . ." Cf. A. Mens, *Oorsprong en betekenis van de nederlandse Begijnen en Begardenbeweging* (Antwerp, 1947), p. 147 ff.; 198 ff.; E. W. McDonnell, *The Beguines and Beghards in Medieval Culture* (New Brunswick, 1954). Extensive bibliography here.

[44] ". . . pronissimi sunt ad errores, etiam supra indevotos, si non regulaverint affectus suos ad normam legis christi. . ." *Cons.* 8 P; *Opera* III. 369 A.

[45] He quotes the opinion of the flagellants as ". . . haec flagellatio potior est ad delendum peccata, quam quaecunque confessio. . ." *Opera* II. 660 D. One side remark is the only passage known to us where Gerson contrasts the "once for all" character of Christ's work with the "imitation of Christ" theme, a contrast which would later shape the foundation of the Reformation understanding of justification and sanctification: — "Christus autem ex gratia sua (sicut notatur in dicto petri prius allegato [Acts 15:10]) voluit nos misericorditer salvare per sanguinem suum semel effusum. . ." *Ibid.*

[46] "Lex christi sufficienter data est in praeceptis decalogi. . ." *Opera* II, 661 C. "Lex christi sufficienter ab apostolis et sacris doctoribus explicata. . ." *Opera* II. 662 A. ". . . cupidius fertur in illa quae sunt adinventionis suae, quam quae sunt divinae jussionis et hic est unus superbiae gradus. . ." *Opera* II. 661 D/662 A.

tral function of the sacrament of penance, Gerson attacks a second mystical heresy which endangers the Christian understanding of the union
with God. This second heresy can be reduced to the same fundamental
lack of humility and insufficient understanding of the qualitative difference between the creature and the Creator. Once it is understood that the
mystical union should be interpreted in terms of perfection, that is, as
submission to the will of God, and through this conformity as an intimate
union of love,[47] the dangers of speculative mysticism are avoided.

The union of will, in contrast with the essential union as taught in
the condemned theses of Eckhart and in his school of speculative mysticism, bespeaks the nominalistic emphasis on the disproportion between
God and man.[48]

Gerson, in his presentation of this second heretical point of view, remains so close to the text of the condemned tenth proposition of Eckhart
that there can be little doubt that he had this German mystic in mind;
he goes on to say that this position is renewed by Ruysbroeck.[49] Gerson
finds two Eckhartian symbols of union especially misleading: first, the
image of the drop of water which falls in a wine jar and thus loses its
identity like food when it is digested; and secondly, the image of transubstantiation which encourages exactly the same error.[50]

[47] ". . . dum ita fuerit conformis et subdita quod ipsius et dei sit unum velle et
unum nolle, quod amicitiae proprium est. . ." *De consolatione theologiae* III, prosa
1 in *Opera* I, 157 A; ". . . unitur deo et adheret per amorosam voluntatis conformitatem. . ." *De Mystica Theologia, Cons.* 40 in *Opera* III. 393 D; ed. Combes,
p. 104, 12 ff.

[48] In the essentialist school ". . . anima perdit se et esse suum et accipit verum
esse divinum sic quod iam non est creatura nec per creaturam videt aut amat deum
sed est ipse deus qui videtur et amatur." *Cons.* 41 in *Opera* III. 394 A; ed. Combes,
p. 105, 12 ff. Cf. the tenth condemned Eckhartian proposition: "Nos transformamur
totaliter in deum et convertimur in eum; simili modo sicut in sacramento panis
convertitur in corpus christi; sic ego convertor in eum, quod ipse me operatur suum
esse unum, non simile; per viventem deum verum est, quod ibi nulla est distinctio."
Denz. 510.

[49] "Hanc etiam nisus est renovare auctor illius tractatus cuius titulus est 'de ornatu
spiritualium nuptiarum'. . ." On the contrary: ". . . anima talis semper remanet in
esse suo proprio quod habet in suo genere sed dicitur tantummodo similitudinarie
transformari sicut amatorum dicimus cor unum et animam unam quod utique
concedimus." Gerson, *ibid.* B; ed. Combes, pp. 106, 20 f.; 25 ff.

[50] "Dixerunt enim quod anima sic unitur deo et in ipsum transformatur quemad-
modum, si gutta aque mittatur in dolium fortis vini. Illa namque gutta tunc perdit
esse proprium, convertiturque totaliter in alienum velut etiam si cibus per nutri-

This survey of Gerson's thought enables us to define our earlier distinction between affective and speculative mysticism with somewhat greater precision. His emphasis on the abiding necessity for submission to God's revealed will expressed in sacramental confession on the one hand, and his rejection of the Eckhartian type of essentialist mysticism on the other hand, suggest the parallel distinction of *penitential versus transformation mysticism*.

The foregoing analyses have shown that nominalism and transformation mysticism are indeed mutually exclusive. The second kind, *penitential mysticism*, however, *cannot only be adjusted to nominalistic presuppositions, but forms a natural complement to this type of scholastic thought*. Gerson has proved — in the period under consideration — not to be a split person torn between two incompatible allegiances; his regard for the qualitative difference between God and man has been shown to provide the one basis from which he attacks both the vain curiosity of the systematic theologians and the presumptuousness of the Beghards and Eckhartians.[51]

Finally, we need to make one more point. Penitential mysticism is in no sense proleptic but implies a strong eschatological emphasis. The awareness of the contrast between the status of the *viator* now and the status of the *comprehensor* in the heavenly Jerusalem indicates this clearly.[52] The clear vision of God is an eschatological experience about which we

---

tionem convertatur in cibatum . . . Rursus propter eandem rationem similitudo transubstantiationis que fit in benedicto sacramento non satis est idonea ad explicandum transformationem . . . in deum amatum." *Cons.* 41 P; *Opera* III. 394 f. This transformation image of the drop of water falling into the wine is found in Bernard, *De diligendo Deo*, cap. 10.28 in *PL* CLXXXII, 991 as quoted by Stelzenberger, p. 84. André Combes discusses the parallel passage in the letter of the Parisian Chancellor to Bartholomew: "Addit quod perditur anima contemplantis in esse tali divino abyssali ita ut reperibilis non sit ab aliqua creatura." *Epistola I ad Bartholomaeum*; in Combes, *Essai* . . . II, 108 ff. He argues that Gerson in his attack on Ruysbroeck does not make an aside against Aquinas but against Jean Courtecuisse [Breviscoxa], a disciple of John of Ripa. *Ibid.* II, 229.

[51] "Sane tota vel praecipua causa difficultatis ad intelligentiam scholasticam in hac parte videtur esse *propter omnimodam finiti ad infinitum, creatura scilicet ad creatorem improportionem.* . . " *Super Cantica Canticorum* IV; *Opera* IV. 54. B.

[52] Louis Mourin points to the evidence in Gerson's sermons: ". . . dès les premières oeuvres, il [Gerson] souligne le caractère transcendental de la foi par rapport à la raison. . ." *Jean Gerson: Prédicateur Français* (Bruges, 1952), p. 254. Cf. Biel *Lect.* 18 K; *Lect.* 19 B.

can only speak on the authority of such a witness as St. Paul after his return from the seventh heaven. Because of this point of view Gerson was, even in his own time, accused of not being a genuine mystic.[53] These accusations have been repeated till the present day.

There are passages which are widely interpreted as containing a confession of Gerson that he has never experienced the highest stage of mystical vision. These interpreters, however, have misunderstood the nominalistic image of "color-blindness" which Gerson uses in this connection. This is merely another way of saying: *fides ex auditu*: I believe on the authority of the Church that these colors — the vision of God — exist, and only on this condition can I relive this experience insofar as the status of the *viator* permits.[54]

Union with the abyss of God's inscrutable will is Gerson's understanding of the mystical experience granted to privileged *viatores*. This union forms the highest stage and the goal of penitential mysticism. The union with the abyss, which is union with the Godhead beyond God for Eckhart — and union with the essence of God's being for Ruysbroeck — is for Gerson an eschatological event granted only to the *comprehensores*.

III. The Mystical Elements in the Theology of Gabriel Biel

1. Biel in the footsteps of Gerson

In view of our conclusions regarding Jean Gerson, it is not surprising to discover a similar marriage between nominalism and mysticism in the works of Gabriel Biel. Yet Biel did not write any treatise on mystical theology, nor is his type of mysticism in every respect identical with the one we encountered with Gerson. Often he disappoints us by merely

[53] E. Vansteenberghen, "Autour de la 'Docte Ignorance': Une controverse sur la théologie mystique au XVe siècle," in *BB*, vol. XIV, pts. 2–4 (Münster i W., 1915), in which the *Tractatus cuiusdam carthusiensis de mystica theologia* is published: "Ex hac elici potest quod venerandus doctor in hac dumtaxat materia fuit unus ex illis, de quibus scribit apostolus, semper discentes et numquam ad scientiam veritatis pervenientes." *Ibid.* p. 165.

[54] "Hic est nunc punctus difficultatis et mysterium absconditum quod nemo novit per experientiam nisi qui accipit" *De Cons. theol.* IV in *Opera* I. 177A. "Hoc autem est manna absconditum et nomen novum in calculo scriptum, quod nemo novit nisi qui acceperit." *De Probatione Spirituum, Cons.* 1 in *Opera* I. 38 A. See for the contrary opinion Dress, pp. 123 f. and Connolly, p. 271.

referring back to the mystical *opus* of Gerson with which he shows himself to be well acquainted. Furthermore, we have not found a trace of the Gersonian juxtaposition of speculative and mystical theology which would have led Biel to deal with mysticism *per se*.

Finally, there is no mention in the secondary literature of the mystical teaching of Biel. This is undoubtedly due in part to the common presupposition discussed above that nominalism and mysticism must be mutually exclusive. But this striking silence can also be explained from the fact that Biel scholars have till the present day relied almost exclusively on Biel's commentary on Lombard's *Sentences* and to a lesser degree on his *Exposition of the Mass*. These two writings constitute, however, only a part of the whole *corpus* of his writings. Biel's sermons are far more revealing in this respect than his more academic publications.

Though one is not justified in speaking of Biel's mystical theology as such — it is more appropriate to speak of the mystical elements in Biel's theology — an analysis taking all of his writings into consideration does not leave room for doubt that Biel took the mystical aspect of the life of the *viator* most seriously.

In the following presentation we will survey these mystical elements in more detail. As appears from Biel's frequent quotations from and references to Gerson, the mystical teaching of the Parisian Chancellor as sketched above provides us with the natural context within which Biel's presentations should be placed; at the same time this context enables us to note possible deviations, additions, or derivations.

2. Biel's distinctive contribution: democratization of mysticism

The most striking aspect of the mystical elements in Biel's theology is what one can characterize as a strong tendency towards (a) *democratization of mysticism*. This does not, however, prevent him from stressing (b) the *eschatological dimension* of the perfect union and (c) the special union granted in this life to the *spiritual aristocracy*.

The possibility of coexistence of the democratic and aristocratic emphases is due to a reinterpretation of the traditional tripartition of beginning, advanced, and perfect Christians.[55] While the term "hierarchy"

---

[55] As evidence that the tripartition into beginners, advanced and perfect is not abandoned, we point to a section which is also interesting from the point of view

is still understood as constituted by progressive stages of holiness,[56] this meaning is qualified by Biel's appreciation of the peculiar perfection and integrity of each of these three groups in themselves: the three *stages* are understood as three *statuses*.[57]

The nominalistic doctrine of the *facere quod in se est*, the obligation of each man to do his very best, and of the implied natural capacity of man to love God above everything else is necessarily accompanied by a relativization of the commands of God. Not only the beginners, but also the advanced and so-called perfect have to do their very best. Perfection is not an absolute static standard but is dynamically related to the circumstances of a particular individual. Gerson had already defended this thesis against the presumptuousness of those who had chosen the monastic life and thus were tempted to consider themselves as belonging to a higher

---

of Luther research. To the three groups are assigned three forms of penance: 1) contrition for mortal sins; 2) contrition for mortal *and* venial sins; 3) substitutionary contrition *i.e.* contrition by proxy for the sins of others as well as for one's own: ". . . (myrrha) opera penitentie et interiora et exteriora que amaritudinem habent ex peccatorum detestatione representat. Et hanc igitur offerunt in primo gradu qui peccatorum contritione, confessione et penali satisfactione peccata laborant extinguere et recidivam cavere. Et hoc omnium est ut ad minus semel de quolibet mortali commisso confiteantur. . . In secundo gradu offerunt qui nondum semel sed quoad vivunt peccata deflent. . . Sic Deut. 9 [:7] dicit Moyses: 'Memento et ne obliviscaris quomodo ad iracundiam provocas dominum deum tuum.' Nec solum de mortalibus sed et venialibus vehementer se affligunt et dolent, memores illius Eccl. 19 [:1 free rendering]: 'Qui minima negligit, paulatim decidit in maiora.' In tertio gradu perfectissime offerunt qui nedum sua sed et fratrum et totius populi peccata tanquam propria deflent, pro aliorum culpis se castigant." *S* II 18 M.

[56] "Notandum quod hierarchia dicitur a 'gera' quod est sacer, et 'archia' quod est principatus, quasi 'sacer principatus'." Biel, II *Sent.* d 9 q 1. art. 1 nota 1. "Vel clarius et aliter accipitur hec distinctio (hierarchie create) secundum tres status et officia qui sunt: status contemplativorum, prelatorum et activorum" *Ibid* C. Cf. *S* IV 32 I. For the medieval use of Dionysian terminology cf. F. Ruello, "Etude du terme 'Agathodotis' dans quelques commentaires médiévaux des Noms Divins," in *RTAM* 24 (1957), 225 ff.; 25 (1958), 5 ff. André Combes, *Jean Gerson: commentateur Dionysien*, esp. p. 180 ff.

[57] "Scimus quoniam in magna domo Dei multa sunt vasa diversis usibus apta. Et in corpore ecclesie mistico diversa sunt membra, omnia autem membra non eundem actum habent sed pro perfectione corporis huius facti sunt necessarii pedes quoad suum officium quam oculorum vel manuum." *De communi vita* [fol. 15ᵃ], p. 91; W. M. Landeen, "Gabriel Biel and the Brethren of the Common Life in Germany," pp. 23 ff. On p. 25 ff. Landeen reports the general content of this interesting treatise. It should be noted that its theme and structure are the same as *S* IV 11.

class.[58] Biel formulates this succinctly by stating that *every Christian in a state of grace is in a state of perfection.*[59] The contemplative life may be the purer one; the active life is often nevertheless more intense and fruitful.[60]

3. The spirit of the *devotio moderna* and of observantism

This democratic ideal forms the basis for Biel's rejection of excessive asceticism in general and the observantist reform movement in particular. Going beyond the position taken by Gerson in his treatise against the flagellants, Biel criticizes not so much antinomianism as the arrogance resulting from a pretentious legalism.[61]

In Gerson's treatise *Super Magnificat*, we find conclusive evidence that this contrast between Gerson and Biel is not a mere hypothesis. In one passage, Gerson describes how the devil travels through the world to confuse the children of God. In accordance with his approach to Eve, he tempts those who are on the point of entering an order with questions to make them reconsider their decision. He asks why they want to flee the world: isn't it man's nature to live in society; can't one work out one's salvation in worldly garb, under the one abbot Jesus Christ; shouldn't

---

[58] "Beati qui perfecte et totaliter deum diligunt non faciunt opus consilii sed magis praecepti quoniam maxime obligantur perfecte deum diligere. Ex quo apparet ultra, quod illud quod cadit sub praecepto potest diversimode impleri absque culpa vel transgressione. Aliter enim diligunt deum viatores aliter comprehensores; aliter perfecti viri, aliter incipientes et aliter proficientes. Et tamen minus peccant imperfecti si non aeque deum diligant velut perfecti iam in charitate firmati et radicati; nec imputatur viatoribus ad culpam si non eo amore unitivo deo haereant quo et ipsi beati. . ." *De consiliis evangelicis et de statu perfectionis; Opera* II. 672 C. This impatience appears again in the *Tractatus de Perfectione Cordis, Opera* III, 439, to which Gerson refers in one of the "Consultations" recently published by P. Glorieux: ". . . de perfectione statuum contencio qualiter fit a non-nullis, sapit fermentum pharisaicum."; "L'Activité littéraire de Gerson à Lyon: Correspondance inédite avec la Grande-Charteuse," *RTAM* 18 (1951), 257.

[59] "Omnis existens in gratia gratum faciente est in statu perfectionis religionis christiane," *S* IV 30 K.

[60] "Et licet vita contemplativa simpliciter sit melior et nobilior vita activa, videntur tamen se habere sepenumero ut excedens et excessum. . . ," *S* IV 7 C. ". . . contemplativa est deo familior et purior, tametsi alia sit sepenumero intensior et fructuosior," *S* IV 7 B.

[61] ". . . qui ex hoc se putant bone voluntatis quia singularibus quibusdam observantiis puta orationibus, ieiuniis, celebratitibus ceterisque spiritualibus exercitiis intendunt etiam laboriose multum," *S* II 5 F. Cf. *Lect.* 27 N.

one enjoy the law of freedom given by God and purchased by Christ; why observe all these extra rules when one has not even sufficient power to obey the basic commandments; do not all these obligations merely force one to abound in sin? [62]

The self-same arguments which according to Gerson are diabolical are used by Biel in his treatise on the communal life to defend the secular form of life in the *devotio moderna*. The life of the Brethren of the Common Life is for him characterized by a life in the freedom of the Christian law, under the one abbot Jesus Christ, without obligation to observances above and beyond the precepts. Thus in all humility, the apostolic admonition is obeyed that everyone should remain in the state in which he is called.[63] Though Biel even in this short treatise refers to Gerson to support his own position,[64] it is hard to construct a sharper contrast than between Gerson and Biel as concerns the monastic life.[65]

Although the *devotio moderna* is believed in our day to mark the beginning of the observantist movement,[66] Biel feels that the *devotio mod-*

---

[62] "Circumit iste Satan terram et perambulat eam, ut circumstantias omnium consideret . . . Itaque considerat dum circumit et observat volentes placere deo. Videt aptum aliquem ad religionis ingressum, impellit ad oppositum sic illudens: Cur civilem vis deserere conversationem; quoniam homo natura civile animal est. . . Cur non poteris sub habitu seculari salutem tuam operari sub uno Abbate suo Christo? Gaudeas lege libertatis, quam dedit tibi deus et emit christus. Quid pulchrius, quid eligibilius libertate? Cur tot et tales vis subire observationes et vota super te inducere, qui non sufficis ad precepta servanda? Quid sunt obligationes tot, nisi laquei totidem ad transgressores? Vide ne illaqueatus verbis oris tui cadas . . . Ecce quot quales in religionibus defecerunt; quot ceciderunt. . ." *Tractatus Octavus Super Magnificat; Opera* IV. 364 A. ff.

[63] ". . . nobis interim satis est ad omnem perfectionem stare et vivere in libertate legis christiane sub uno abbate christo Jhesu servando pro posse primo quidem regulam preceptorum suorum sine quibus non est salus . . . In his vero que non possumus satius non iudicamus non esse irretitos et obligatos voto vel professione strictiori . . . Sumus itaque contenti sorte nostra non alta sapientes sed humilibus consentientes et obedientes verbo apostolico quo suadet, ut unusquisque in qua vocatione vocatus est, permaneat." *De communi vita* [fol. 3/3ᵃ], p. 81.

[64] *Ibid.* [fol. 2], p. 80.

[65] For completeness sake, we should add that Biel does not want to reject "nonsecular" monastic life: "Quotquot igitur sunt qui ad ardua scandere multaque et magna profiteri, vovere ac reddere domino deo suo possunt, laudamus eos. . ." *Ibid.* [fol. 3], p. 81.

[66] "De *Devotio Moderna* verspreidde zich . . . Temidden van deze groei ontstond ook het begin van het observantisme. . ." R. R. Post, *Kerkgeschiedenis van Nederland in de Middeleeuwen*, 2 vols. (Utrecht, 1957), II, 355. "Haar mannen [de congregatie van Windesheim] kwamen op voor een strikte observantie. . ." II, p. 97.

erna stood for reform through an active life of simple piety. This ideal of reform stands for him *over against* the rigoristic ideal of the observantist "second generation," an ungrateful heir to the successes of the *devotio moderna.*[67] External evidence documents this attitude of Biel in an unexpected way. The famous ascetic protagonist of radical reform, Geiler von Kaysersberg, known as the German Savanorola, seems to have been in close contact with Biel. In an interesting passage, Jacob Otherus writes in the dedication of Geiler's posthumously published *Navicula Penitentie* to prior Gregor Reisch of the Carthusian monastery near Freiburg in Breisgau that Geiler would have become a hermit if Biel had not thwarted his wishes.[68]

In an eloquent indictment of observantism, Biel first defends explicitly the laxer ideal by referring to the basic goodness of creation, the dangers of self-destruction, and the decisive importance of inner piety; not exterior observances but a pure conscience marks the perfect monk.[69] Yet the deepest motivation for Biel's opposition to rigoristic asceticism is, as

[67] ". . . ex ista radice annuente gratis dei pullulaverit fructus tam universalis reformationis non solum illius ordinis [Windesheim] verum etiam plurimorum aliorum ordinum. . ."; "multi ex hiis qui noviter surrexerunt atque defunctis patribus successere etsi debita gratitudine non responderunt;" ". . . [assumimus etiam laborem manualem] pro devitando ocio quod malorum omnium seminarium est perniciosum." ". . . [mendicitati] qui peccata populi comedunt debitores se orationum et suffragium constituunt." "Cantica vero divina cantare etiam manibus operantes facile possunt." *De communi vita* [fol. 12ᵃ/13], pp. 88–89; [fol. 17], p. 92.

[68] *Navicula Penitentie,* (Augsburg, 1511). *Dedicatio:* "Adeoque vitam secretiorem amavit ut secum tacite deliberans eremum ipsum nisi a Gabriele Buehel et Eggelingo prohibitus intrasset." On what grounds Biel would have this authority is unclear. Eggelingus is Biel's predecessor as Cathedral preacher in Mainz; Biel confesses that he owes much to him for his *Expositio.* Cf. *Lectio 88 P.* For Geiler's observantism cf. the study by L. Dacheux, *Un réformateur catholique à la fin du XVe siècle: Jean Geiler de Kaysersberg,* (Paris, 1876), esp. p. 180 ff. It is difficult to assess whether perhaps also Biel's nominalistic loyalties played a part in his advice to Geiler. Gregor Reisch helped the realistic school to gain a position of pre-eminence at Freiburg in 1489. Cf. Adolf Vonlanthen, "Geilers Seelenparadies. . . ," p. 282 f. On the relation of Biel and Geiler see Chapter One, note 46.

[69] "Tertio ideo dominus duxit vitam laxiorem . . . ut per hoc doceret fideles suos quia non est standum in solis exterioribus, sed per ea tendere debemus ad interiora." *S IV* 19 G. "Non enim alba aut nigra cuculla, non alta tonsura, nec ampla corona, sed conscientia pura et mentis munditia, abiectio voluntatis proprie, et charitas perfecta monachum facit. Qui in mundo est, fugiat in claustrum; sed caveat ne ibi dormitet . . . vita enim confert meritum, locus non facit sanctum . . . nihil prodest esse observatorem in rebus minimis cum principalia negligantur." *Ibid.* H. Cf. *S IV* 30 K.

we have seen, not to be found primarily in his rejection of antinomianism or observantism, but in his own understanding of the indomitable and abiding power of sin, an important aspect of his democratization of the ideal of perfection: the law of the flesh may be mitigated by abstinence, but its fire cannot be extinguished in this life.[70] This Gabrielistic emphasis, so important for his understanding of justification, prevents his sometimes exuberant descriptions of union of the "perfect" with God from contradicting the law of relativity which proved to apply on the two lower levels, those of the beginners and the advanced: even the perfection of the "perfect" is subject to the law of sin; in their clearest possible vision of God and their most intimate union with God, they are bound to be severely attacked by temptations.[71]

The stubborn nature of sin prevents even the aristocrats of the spirit from transcending the set limitations that mark the existence of the *viator*. Thus an equilibrium is established between the theological virtues of love and hope. While in the Eckhartian school, Christian hope is fulfilled and thus absorbed by love, the perfect vision of God will, according to Biel, be granted only at the end of time when the *viator* has been transformed into the *comprehensor* and *beatus*.[72] We will have to keep the essential eschatological character of this future transformation in mind when we proceed to analyze Biel's understanding of the highest possible union with God in this life.

[70] II *Sent.* d 30 q 2 art. 2 concl. 4 G. "Lex enim membrorum sive fomes temperata abstinentia mitigari potest sed in hac vita extingui non valet." *S* II 3 H. This *fomes peccati* is — as already appears from Biel's optimistic doctrine of the *facere quod in se est* — of course not sin but inclines man to sin; it is indeed *pena* but not *culpa*. Cf. Gregory's insistence that after Baptism sin remains not *quoad reatum*, but *quoad essentiam*. II *Sent.* d 30.31 q 2 art. 4 [fol. 113 O]. Though Biel shares with Trent, Session V.5, the "ex peccato est et ad peccatum inclinat" [*Denz.* 792] of the *concupiscentia*, we find with him more of an emphasis on its insuperability in this life. See also *S* II 45 P, where due to communion — and by way of analogy with transubstantiation — the subject of sin is said to disappear, while its accidents remain.

[71] "Sed gradus ille tertius qui solum perfectorum est habet deum nedum pro fine sicut duo priores, sed etiam pro obiecto immediato, quia eorum opus est contemplari divinas perfectiones et ferventissimo amore soli deo inherere cum contemptu omnium temporalium et terrenorum. Nec tamen ita quiete possunt his inherere quin licet non a carne vel mundo omnino non temptentur vel modice. . ." III *Sent.* d 29 q 1 art. 3 dub. 2.

[72] "In presenti quidem pane verbi, pane sacramentali, pane devotionis et in futuro pane beatifice visionis et fruitionis . . . ingredientes per fidem, egredientes a fide ad speciem, a credulitate ad contemplationem. . ." *S* I 41 G. Cf. *Lect.* 64 O.

4. Mystical description of contrition

After this survey of the three characteristics of the mystical elements in Biel's theology, we will have to investigate them in greater detail. We will ask what now precisely is meant by the tendency towards democratization of mysticism on the one hand and the special union granted to the spiritual aristocracy on the other, and finally how these two are related.

In the history of asceticism from the Essenes and the Eastern desert fathers via John Cassian, Gregory the Great, and Hugh of St. Victor, a series of scales and methods had been elaborated which usually did not replace, but clarified the tripartite mystic route of purgation, illumination, and union taught by Dionysius.[73] The close relation of monasticism and asceticism indicates already that these scales are meant as descriptions of the growth from perfection to perfection, under the counsels and not only under the precepts. Though the terms are not always clearly defined and have different meanings for different authors, *lectio, meditatio*, and *oratio* are generally understood as exercises of Christians in state of grace who climb in this way to the highest stage of contemplation.[74]

These stages mark a growth in grace and are, therefore, an unfolding of the initial gift of sanctifying grace in baptism or its restoration in the sacrament of penance. Its point of departure is thus the sacramentally infused *gratia gratum faciens*. While this *gratia gratum faciens* is necessary for salvation, the indicated stages lead to a higher form of perfection; they lead beyond the point of the requirements of the evangelical precepts.

While there is no indication that Biel consciously breaks with this tradition, he brings the scales and methods of perfection to bear on the sinner *on his way to* repentance and thus *before* the infusion of the *gratia*

---

[73] U. Berlière, *L'ascèse bénédictine des origines à la fin du XIIe siècle*, (Paris, 1927); F. Vernet, *La spiritualité médiévale* (Paris, 1929). For Dionysius see M. de Gandillac, *Oeuvres complètes du Pseudo-Denys l'Aréopagite* (Paris, 1943), p. 295 f. Most helpful and seemingly forgotten, the general study by J. Heerinck, *Introductio in theologiam spiritualem, asceticam et mysticam* (Rome, 1931).

[74] Biel's authorities at this point are Hugh of St. Victor and John Gerson. Cf. Hugh, *Eruditio Didascalia*; "Quattuor sunt in quibus nunc exercetur vita iustorum et quasi per quosdam gradus ad futuram perfectionem sublevamur, videlicet lectio sive doctrina, meditatio, oratio, operatio. Quinta deinde sequitur contemplatio." PL CLXXII, 797. Cf. Gerson, *Opera*, III, 383.

gratum faciens. The most important consequence of this shift is that what was traditionally a freely chosen exercise of the just, with *contemplation* as its highest level, has now become an effort necessary on the part of the sinner for his salvation, under the precepts, with *contrition* as its highest level.[75]

This contrition is understood as the absolute love for God, unadulterated by egoism; and while the road leading to this act of deep and honest penitence is marked by the stages of *lectio, meditatio,* and *oratio,* which in other systems *follow* contrition, the act of contrition itself is described in terms closely resembling those traditionally used for the mystical union with God.

In this context Biel's most common form of argumentation runs as follows: to be saved, one has to fulfill the law, that is, to love God with all his heart. Man is able to produce this love before the infusion of grace, the *gratia gratum faciens.* In this way if he does his very best, he will receive immediately at the moment that he reaches the point of love for God above everything else this gift of sanctifying grace.[76]

How can man unaided by grace reach that high point of love? By reading and meditation. Reading informs our darkened minds and provides them with such data as the Incarnation and the coming judgment. Thus informed, meditation inflames the will with love for a God who gave himself for the sinful world, and chills the will with fear for a God who knows every thought and will return to judge the quick and the dead.[77]

---

[75] III *Sent.* d 26 q 1 art. 3 dub. 2 N. IV *Sent.* d 14 q 2 a 1 n 2, *in fine:* ". . . nunquam sacramentum penitentie delet peccatum sine contritione previa vel concomitante."

[76] "Et hec aliquo modo est nobis in precepto, aliquo modo non. Non est in precepto quantum ad eius infusionem, nam solius dei est eius infusio. Est autem in precepto quantum ad nostram preparationem et eius conservationem: ad scl. faciendum quod in nobis est ut infundatur . . . Sed quomodo illam charitatem tam necessariam adquirere possumus? Respondetur breviter quod immediatissima ac ultimata dispositio ad eam est . . . actualiter diligere dominum ex toto corde etc. Hac enim actuali dilectione stante in anima statim imo simul cum ea infunditur charitas. Sed quomodo ad hanc dilectionem perveniemus? Responsio: tribus gradibus quos ponit Hugo in de scala paradisi. Hi sunt lectio, meditatio, oratio, quam sequitur contemplatio. . ." *S* I 85 C/D.

[77] "Affectus autem preparatur lectione et meditatione . . . Neque enim est affectio aliqua bona et laudabilis quam meditatio non pariat. Siquidem meditatio attenta divine potentie, sapientie et bonitatis, proprie infirmitatis, ignorantie, malicie, affectus parit timorem, ammirationem, amorem ut late ostendit Joannes Gerson de

348

While meditation on the punishing righteousness of God restrains the will from disobedience, the self-sacrifice of God excites the will to such a point that the sinner is properly disposed for the inhabitation of the Holy Spirit. At this point Biel preaches a stern anti-Pelagian doctrine of unmerited love. As we noted before, however, the unmerited sacrifice of God proves to be an act of the past which has merely a psychological relevance in the present, and thus functions as an inspiring example for the sinner to break with his own power the bonds of sin and pride.[78]

5. The birth of Christ in the soul

The sinner is called upon to cleanse the house of his soul by a sincere love for God. The more mystical descriptions of the ensuing infusion are given when the gift of the *gratia gratum faciens* is understood as the birth of Christ in the soul.[79] Christ is called the sole and only dependable foundation, in whom the Christian lives through faith, moves through hope and with whom he is united through love. This Christ-birth in the soul is not an exalted stage of perfection for a small privileged group, but necessary for the salvation of every Christian.[80] The initiative that

---

mystica theologia practica c. 8. . . . Primum ergo est per prudentiam cognoscere petenda que confert lectio. Secundum vigilans et studiosa cognitorum masticatio, que est meditatio excitans fervorem et affectum. Demum sequitur desideratorum bonorum petitio." S I 47 C. Gerson, *De mystica theologia speculativa* Cons. 8 G; *Opera* III. 411 f.

[78] "Sola ergo causa tantorum beneficiorum intrinseca et essentialis bonitas est dei qui nullis nostris meritis prior dilexit nos . . . Huius autem amoris ex sola essentiali et intrinseca dei bonitate procedentis diligens meditatio excitat in nobis dilectionem amicicie qua eum propter seipsum (quia bonus est) diligimus, qua dilectione tanquam principalissima dispositione in nobis existente sine mora spiritus sanctus illabitur. Non enim potest hec dilectio stare sine spiritu sancto cum sit dispositio sufficiens et immediata." S II 36 F; Cf. 29 H, 39 H; *Lect.* 77 T; S II 18 I: ". . . [dilectio dei] . . . qua deo bene propter seipsum volumus atque in eius perfectione gaudemus et nos sue voluntati conformare cupimus. Et hic amor dispositio proxima est ad gratiam gratum facientem et ea inexistente ac cooperante meritoria est vite eterne." Cf. IV *Sent.* d 14. q 1. art. 2. concl. 5 U. See Schema I, columns 3 and 4, Chapter Seven.

[79] "Nulla enim opera tanquam bona ad meritum imputantur que non ex radice charitatis procedunt. Hec sola edificium nostrum exornat ut christus inhabitare dignetur." S II 50 G.

[80] "His tribus in christo fundamento unico et solidissimo vivimus, movemur et sumus. Vivimus per fidem, sicut scriptum est 'justus ex fide vivit'" Hab. 2 [:4]. Movemur in eo per spem que sursum sunt desiderantes per quam futuram civitatem

man has to take remains withal the main interest and is sometimes stressed to the point where Biel can say that *through man's decision* to open the door of his heart, *God is converted* and moved to dwell in the soul through the gift of sanctifying grace.[81]

We note that Biel is somewhat loose in his terminology. Here he speaks about the descent of God, in the passage mentioned above about the inhabitation of Christ, most frequently about the gift of the Holy Spirit. When he compares the spiritual birth of Christ *in mente* (!) with the Incarnation, he makes a point of saying that only the second Person of the Trinity came in the flesh, but that in the inhabitation the three Persons are indivisible.[82] If he had left us a more systematic treatment these points would certainly have caught his well-trained eye. As it is, we have to remember that the better part of our sources are sermons written over an extended period of time.

The spiritual birth of the soul is nevertheless presented as a union with the Word through sanctifying grace; it simultaneously implies the descent of Christ *and* the ascent of the soul to union with Christ in love.[83] This union can best be interpreted as *communion* with Christ. Notwithstanding the use of a rather inconsistent but basically theocentric terminology, one is forced to conclude that this communion with Christ is

---

inquirimus non habentes hic mansionem. Heb. 13 [:14]. Sumus in eo per unientem charitatem. . . His nisi firmiter adhereamus frustra de beatitudine speramus. Ille enim tres necessarie sunt ad salutem. . . Omnis qui habet spem hanc in christo sanctificatus est sicut et ille sanctus est. Nemo autem nisi sanctus beatitudinem sortietur quia nihil inquinatum intrabit in illam. . ." *Ibid.*, G/H.

[81] "Converti ad deum — appropinquari deo — aperiri illi est facere quod in se est. Convertitur autem deus ad hominem. Appropinquat ei et intrat habitando in eo et cenando cum illo, per gratiam quam infundit." II *Sent.* d. 27 q 1 art. 2 concl. 4 K. For the early medieval function of these biblical allusions, see A. M. Landgraf, *Dogmengeschichte der Frühscholastik*, vol. I, pt. 1, pp. 241, 249 ff., 253, 261, 263, 267, 278, 290.

[82] "Et quamvis solum verbum natum sit in carne non pater, non spiritus sanctus non tamen solum verbum nascitur in mente quia non solus inhabitat sed et pater et spiritus sanctus." *S* II 12 B.

[83] "Est ergo spiritualis nativitas unio verbi cum natura intellectuali per gratiam gratum facientem . . . Nam per eandem gratiam sive charitatem quam nobis infundendo in nos descendit, sibique unit, etiam elevamur in eum charitative, voluntati sue consentiendo ac per hoc spiritualiter eum gignimus ac nobis unimus." *Ibid.* Usually however, the christus *extra nos* is emphasized: "Quid enim aliud fundamentum posset esse christiano quam christus, cui servire quem imitari, ad cuius regnum necesse est aspirare. . ." *S* II 50 E.

psychological in nature and anthropocentrically determined: it is not an operation of the Holy Spirit but of the spirit of man. Though contrition on its highest level encounters the Holy Spirit, Christ, God or the *gratia gratum faciens*, this is a concomitant appendix to a human act. This human act is indeed brought about by God, but in an indirect way: through the psychological impact of past and future historical acts of God: the Incarnation and the last judgment.[84]

In the present moment of the life of the common Christian, the distance between God and his creature can and has to be bridged by the mental ascent which takes the form of adjustment to the will of God: *consentiendo sue voluntati.*

We mark here that this agreement with the will of God has to be distinguished from the absolute conformity or union with the will of God which is the privilege of the aristocrats of the spirit.

6. "Christ-mysticism" as necessary for salvation

We saw how *lectio* and *meditatio* stimulated the sinner to love God above everything else. It is not clear whether the third stage, *oratio*, is located before or after the moment of infusion of sanctifying grace. Biel shows far less interest in systematization of stages, steps and virtues than, for example his contemporary and friend Wessel Gansfort,[85] or earlier Gerard Zerbold van Zutphen.[86]

As in Biel's understanding the contrition and its concomitant union with Christ is necessary for salvation,[87] he is intent on a simplification of

---

[84] II *Sent.* d 27 q 1 art. 2 concl. 4 K.

[85] "Oratio est ascensus mentis in deum per pium et humilem affectum. Affectus autem preparatur lectione et meditatione. . ." *S* I 47 C.

[86] "Tractatus de cohibendis cogitationibus et de modo constituendarum meditationum, scala meditationis vocatur," in *M. Wesseli Opera* (Groningae, 1614), fol. 194 ff.

[87] *De spiritualibus ascensionibus*, ed. H. Mahien 2 ed. (Bruges, 1941). W. Jappe Alberts' helpful article "Zur Historiographie der Devotio Moderna und ihrer Erforschung" *Westfälische Forschungen* 11 (1958), 51–67, is indicative of the lack of research in the later developments of the *Devotio Moderna*. It would require a special study to establish in detail to what extent Biel is dependent on the piety of the *Devotio Moderna*. Insofar as this movement is far from monolithic, it would be especially revealing to compare Biel with two other leading contemporaries, Wessel Gansfort and Staupitz. The totally different understanding of

traditional ascetic teaching in order to be able to transfer it from the refectory to the pulpit. He grants that the ascent to contrition implies the climbing of a scale of virtues, but he is quick to add that one virtue is all-sufficient: humility.[88]

In view of the fact that the psychological communion with Christ is to be included under the precepts, it does not surprise us to find Biel saying that this decisive and basic virtue is not difficult to acquire. Nobody can excuse himself on grounds that humility would be beyond his reach: a proper consideration of the majesty of God's creation humiliates man sufficiently.[89]

In view of Biel's description of the nature and necessity of contrition, we are now in a position to understand what we earlier called a "strong tendency towards democratization of mysticism." This democratization is due to Biel's emphasis on the psychological communion with Christ as a basic requirement for every Christian. Gerson made a step in this direction by contrasting mysticism with scholasticism as not limited to learned doctors, but including even mere women and simpletons. Gerson makes it clear, however, that the mystical experience marks an advanced stage of sanctity which transcends the level of the beginners. For Biel, one cannot even be a beginner without what he describes as "Christ-mysticism." We spoke only of "a strong tendency," because closer investigation of the use of mystical terminology unmasked what appeared to be "Christ-mysticism" as an eloquent description of a psychological state of mind which can with more right be termed self-justifying piety than mysticism.

---

the relation of contrition and *gratia gratum faciens,* — for both Wessel and Staupitz the temporal aspect of the *gratia predestinationis,* — would be a major point of differentiation; cf. Maarten van Rhijn, *Wessel Gansfort,* p. 238; Ernst Wolf, *Staupitz and Luther,* p. 92 ff. n. 5. The mystical significance of the *act of commemoration* in the Lord's Supper — emphasized esp. by the Sacramentarians and Spiritualists — has not yet been acknowledged. IV *Sent.* d 14 q 2 art. 1. nota *in fine.* A wealth of material has been brought together by the research-studies of W. M. Landeen, which will form the necessary basis for more interpretative analyses. See bibliography of Secondary Sources.

[88] ". . . ut ascendamus virtutum scalam erigamus, cuius etsi multi sunt gradus secundum numerum virtutum, unum tamen et principalem gradum ascendamus qui sufficit nos in altum sustollere, ipse est humilitas ceterarum fundamentum virtutum." *S* I 48 E.

[89] "Et revera facile est humiliari quoniam universa prebent occasionem humilitatis recte consideranti . . . Nullum ergo nobis relinquitur excusationis velamen." *S* I 48 G. Cf. *S* II 23 F.

7. Denial of forensic justification

This term "self-justifying piety," however, should not mislead us; it is only one side of the coin. When the *viator* walks on the paths of the law, oscillating between fear and love, he receives at the very moment that he produces the required act of supreme love for God, sanctifying grace. This infusion is always accompanied by the inhabitation of the Holy Spirit, Christ, or the Holy Trinity. From this point of view, this self-justifying piety can equally well be termed pneumatic piety. The sermons show us again that when Biel in his academic works grants that God *de potentia absoluta* can accept a man to life eternal without inherent grace,[90] but that this is not the case *de potentia ordinata*,[91] he is absolutely serious: the gift of sanctifying grace is necessary for salvation.[92] This grace is a created gift of the Holy Spirit which links the converted sinner in a bond of love with Jesus Christ.[93]

It is important to emphasize this necessity of created grace in view of the widespread misunderstanding according to which the nominalistic doctrine of justification would be essentially forensic. This interpretation is probably due to the term "acceptation" itself. In connection with the theology of Duns Scotus, for whom this term received a new importance,[94] it has often been alleged that justification would not refer to an internal enrichment of the sinner but only to a changed relation with God.[95] The same point has repeatedly been made with respect to Occam and Biel, who are on this point of one mind with Scotus.[96]

---

[90] I *Sent.* d 17 q 1 art. 2 concl. 1; Occam, I *Sent.* d 17 q 2 B; Scotus, *Par.* d 17 q 2 n 5.

[91] I *Sent.* d 17 q 1 art. 2 concl. 2; Occam, I *Sent.* q 3 C; Scotus, *Ox.* d 17 q 3 n 19.

[92] "Omnis actus meritorius necessario presupponit charitatem creatam secundum legem dei ordinatam." I *Sent.* d 17 q 3 art. 2 concl. 1.

[93] "Infundit enim spiritus sanctus dona sua eis quos ad se convertit. Certus sum quod neque mors neque vita . . . poterit nos separare a charitate dei que est in christo iesu domino nostro: et hec necessario est omni homini ad salutem." *S* I 85 C.

[94] Werner Dettloff, *Die Lehre von der Acceptatio Divina bei Johannes Duns Scotus, mit besonderer Berücksichtigung der Rechtfertigungslehre* (Werl Westf., 1954), esp. p. 204 ff.

[95] Karl Werner, *Johannes Duns Scotus*, (Vienna, 1881), p. 424; Reinhold Seeberg, *Die Theologie Joh. Duns Scotus*, p. 312.

[96] Cf. Denifle's judgment on nominalistic theology: "Das ganze Heilswerk wird hier rein äusserlich aufgefasst. Nur Mechanismus, kein Organismus." *Luther und*

One can easily understand that the Scotistic and nominalistic doctrine of sin with its relational emphasis on the obligation to punishment could facilitate a parallel relational understanding of their doctrine of justification. It is indeed true that the major emphasis is not on the created grace but on the act of acceptation, uncreated grace.[97] Against the Thomistic insistence on created grace, the Scotists and nominalists insist on the conditional effectiveness of the habit of grace.

The acceptation by God, however, is not the exterior declaration or *favor dei* of later Protestant orthodoxy; it is the coming of the Holy Spirit himself. In justification, therefore, two gifts are granted: (1) created grace, necessary according to God's revealed will, as the *ratio meriti;* (2) the Holy Spirit, necessary in an absolute sense, as the *ratio acceptationis.*[98]

We are here not so much interested in this structure of thought itself; these data are by no means unknown. But because of the long-standing misconception of the *potentia ordinata* as a nominalistic subterfuge, the nominalistic position has been interpreted either as a mere negative rejection of the Thomist position or, positively, as a proto-Protestant doctrine of justification. In the first point there is some truth, since one senses

---

Luthertum, I, abt. 2 (Mainz, 1906), p. 594. This would be essentially the same view as Luther's: "Nur ein äusserliche [Gnade], die Huld Gottes," *ibid.*, p. 600. Cf. Karl August Meissinger: "Natur und Übernatur klaffen auseinander und sind nur noch mechanisch verklammert. . ." *Der Katholische Luther* (Munich, 1952), p. 108.

Carl Feckes, *Die Rechtfertigungslehre des Gabriel Biel*, p. 80 f. Otto Scheel, *Martin Luther*, II, 174 ff. Wiegand Biel: ". . . annotamus Gabrielem in sensu forensi externo et judiciali justificandi actum sumpsisse. . ." p. 34. Biel explicitly contrasts the forensic justification before the secular judge with justification as transformation in relation to God, the spiritual judge. *Lect.* 31 B.

[97] II *Sent.* d 31 q 1 concl. 1–3.

[98] This distinction makes it possible to reinterpret and save Lombard's thesis that we love God and the neighbor through the Holy Spirit — rejected by the post-Lombardian scholastic tradition: "Nec vult magister negare quin preter illud donum quod est spiritus sanctus etiam aliud donum creatum donetur quod sit habitus inclinans ad diligendum." I *Sent.* d 17 q 3 art. 2 concl. 2. Occam, *ibid.*, B; both depending on Scotus, *Ox.* I d 17 q 3; Lombard, I *Sent.* d 17 c 1. Cf. further Dettloff, pp. 14 f., 154 f. ". . . summus creator . . . dignatur nostram animam sibi templum dedicare in quo nedum in donis sed personaliter vult habitare. . ." S II 53 B. Vignaux has pointed out that the effort to "save" Lombard should not mislead us: ". . . Occam, Pierre d'Ailly, Gabriel Biel ne suspectaient point les catégories du Philosophe; ils en usaient tout naturellement pour situer la vertu de charité dans l'ordre universel." *Luther Commentateur des Sentences*, p. 93.

in the Scotistic and nominalistic criticism a protest against the ontological "Dinglichkeit" of the Thomistic concept of grace.

Our consideration of the mystical elements in Biel's theology — and here we resume our main argument — throws light on the extent of the spiritualization of the process of justification: *the inhabitation of the Holy Spirit is not a special privilege of the aristocrats of the Spirit but is required of every Christian*. The other side of self-justifying piety is pneumatic piety: *acceptation, far from being an exterior imputation of righteousness, is indeed the coming of the Holy Spirit himself to all Christians*. The term *favor* is once used by Biel; not, however, to indicate a forensic declarative act of God, but as a description of the habit of inherent grace.[99]

As we have seen, the *adventus* of the Holy Spirit can very well be described as the incorporation into Christ. Membership in the visible Church is only the incorporation into Christ by *faith*; it is necessary for salvation that one be also incorporated into Christ through faith *active in love*.[100]

One last remark on the connection of justification and mysticism. One

[99] "Dilectio habitualis est aliquod immanens seu favor quidam manens cessante actu voluntatis et cognitionis natum inclinare ad actus dilectionis. . . " *S* I 85 C. As far as I can see this is a remarkably rare use of the word "favor." Peter of Palude uses the word "fautor" indeed in a forensic sense: "Tertia fautoria est facti si quis alimoniam mittat vel liberet . . . Dicuntur credentes qui habent fidem eorum implicitam, non explicitam: reputantes eos bonos et habere bonam fidem." The word can also be applied to the defense by a lawyer of someone against the accusation of heresy by inquisitioners. *IV Sent.* d 18 q 3. This may explain the incorporation of the word in the Protestant dogmatic vocabulary; Cf. Altenstaig, *Vocabularius Theologie*, fol. 86ʳ. Johannes Brinktrine argues that in the doctrine of justification of Occam and Biel e.a. "die Gnade für sich nicht ausreicht, um die Sünde zu tilgen, der favor Dei superadditus ersetzt äusserlich, was die Gnade innerlich nicht zu leisten vermag." *Die Lehre von der Gnade* (Paderborn, 1957), p. 176. He refers probably to the *acceptatio dei* which does not eradicate sin — this is the function of the *gratia creata* — but signifies God's gracious self-commitment to reward the sinless acts performed in state of grace. The meaning of *favor apostolicus* and of technical terms derived from Canon law such as *favor fidei, favor testamenti* and *favor iuris* is discussed by Friedrich Kempf, p. 146 ff.; in this juridical sense employed by Biel *Lect.* 27 K. For the early use of *forensicus*, see Augustine, *De libero arbitrio* III. 10, in *PL* XXXII, 1286.

[100] "Non omnes qui intra ecclesiam fide et numero salutem finaliter consequentur: nam ad vite consecutionem non sufficit christo incorporari fide nisi etiam ei inhereamus gratia, opere et amore." *S* II 48 F. See further *S* II 18 L; *S* II 19 A; *S* II 45 A.

can — and should — stress that the existential meaning of Christ for the *viator* is primarily that of the judge who notes every single act in anticipation of the last judgment. This other aspect, however, of the inhabitation of Christ or his spirit should be seen as its counterpart and completion. Indeed in humility man has to prepare his house and to drive out in fear and trembling the "ass" that polluted this house and made it an uninhabitable stable: Christ the judge is watching every *viator* closely to observe whether he is indeed preparing his soul for his inhabitation. The emphasis on the prior necessity of this self-cleansing activity of the soul gave us reason to speak about "self-justifying piety." But at the very moment that the sinner has completed his preparations, that is, at the moment of his conversion, sanctifying grace is given and the Holy Spirit or Christ takes up his residence in the soul.[101]

This being the case, it does not surprise us that we found no trace of a distinction between justification and sanctification. This does not mean that justification is momentary or complete at the first moment of justification.[102] In this sense we have to understand Biel's three *statuses* of the beginners, the advanced, and the perfect. In actual life there are, of course, many such processes of justification since most *viatores* will lose the inhabitation and sanctifying grace by falling in mortal sin and will need to recover these again by conversion, that is, contrition.

Everything taken into consideration, we may say that the democratization of mysticism noted also throws new light on Biel's doctrine of justification by implying the necessity of inherent grace and inhabitation for all Christians and thus establishing beyond doubt that *this doctrine of acceptation can in no sense of the word be characterized as forensic.*

8. The aristocrats of the Spirit

Notwithstanding the emphasis on the abiding necessity of humility and the central function of the sacrament of penance, the psychological adjustment to the will of God does not generally imply the special operation of the Holy Spirit which proved to be a mark of the penitential mysticism of Jean Gerson. The same does not apply to Biel's description

---

[101] *S* I 48 C–F; *S* I 66 F; *S* I 79 H *in fine.*

[102] ". . . charitas augmentabilis est in viatore per actus ex gratia procedentes meritorie." I *Sent.* d 17 q 4 prop. 9.

of the special union granted only to the most advanced. As this group is only of marginal interest for Biel, who apparently has primarily the average Christian in mind, we can be brief in our discussion.

From sanctification by contrition and confession, Biel distinguishes a special inhabitation of the Holy Spirit which no one can understand who has not experienced it. This leads to a transformation of the soul which is not understood as an essential union, but as a union through love in conformity to the will of God, of higher quality than a mere adjustment to God's will.[103]

It is clear that Biel has now turned from a description of the life of the common Christian under the precepts to a life of renunciation under the counsels. He always takes care to add the words "as far as possible in this world," or the like, to ward off the dangers of extreme asceticism and to remind his listeners of the impossibility of conquering concupiscence; but the shift of focus is clear.[104] The perfect Christian no longer needs psychological stimulation to love God; he lives already in God.[105]

Biel is not always careful to interpret the mystical union as one of conformity with God's will. Though in some cases he makes clear that the perfect transformation is an eschatological experience in which the perfect will share only after the resurrection,[106] when he comes to speak about eucharistic mysticism, he seems to choose exactly the formulations which Gerson had criticized in Ruysbroeck. The soul of the worthy participant is said to be changed into the body of Christ through a most intimate union.[107] The realistic character of this union is underlined

---

[103] "Alius est adventus quo nedum inhabitando animam sanctificat, sed specialiter visitat, perficit ac magnitudine sue dilectionis replet. Atque ipsum quem sic visitat in se transformat, ut secum unus fiat spiritus, non essentia sed voluntatis conformitate. Quam consolationis dulcedinem exprimere nemo potest, nec intelligere inexpertus . . . Ad sic recipiendum spiritum sanctum non sufficit renunciare illicitis mundi . . . sed etiam licitis, quantum status mortalitatis admittit." S I 49 D. Cf. S IV 40 L.

[104] "Perfecti primo habent omnia terrena despicere . . . (quantum hec vita permittit)." S IV 32 L.

[105] "Talis enim non indiget voce exteriore ad devotionem excitandum seu affectum inflammandum. . ." Lect. 62 D.

[106] "In primo, perfectus homo subtrahit se creature, conservat se deo, perdit sese in deo in quo omnia possidet. In secundo se perdit in sua cognitione. In tertio in sua affectione . . . Sic ergo per amorem transformatur in deum . . . In his nos exercentes similes erimus angelis dei in resurrectione." S IV 32 L.

[107] "Ita anima digne accedens . . . convertitur in corpus christi dum ei per intimam et gratiosam unionem incorporatur. . . Sic per hanc conversionem anima

when Biel says that the soul does not merely become a Christbearer, but indeed God, albeit not on grounds of a change of essence. On grounds of his participation in God, the soul is more truly in God than in the body.[108]

One should not expect such mystical experiences every time one takes communion. They are extra gifts *ex opere operantis*, above and beyond the normal sanctification *ex opere operato*. Frequent communion is therefore advisable.[109] One should be grateful for this gift of union when it occurs; but when it does not happen, one should remember that the kingdom of God exists in love and not in the sweet experience of the union.[110]

In his lectures on the Mass, Biel spells out his understanding of mystical deification. In the spiritual eating of the mystical Body of Christ,[111] a deification takes place in which the soul or the essence of the mind remains while its accidents are changed.[112] In this way Biel indeed wards

---

manet in christo et vivit vita gratie que est per christum . . . anima mutatur in christum cum iam fit celestis et ordinatur per hunc cibum in vitam eternam." *S* II. 45 M. Cf. *Lect.* 36 N. This part of *S* II. 45 carries the title "Mysticatio predictorum."

[108] "Unde fit ut non solum participatione huius sacramenti dicatur homo christiferus quasi christum ferens vel habens sed divinus imo deus, non per essentiam sed participatione. . . Cum enim sic per hominem christum anima deo per affectum coniungitur . . . ita ut verius sit in deo quem amat quam in corpore quod animat . . . Verius inquam non essentie permutatione." *S* II 45 O. Cf. Ruysbroeck, *De Ornatu* III. 4.

[109] ". . . prudenter vero qui sibi conscii frequenter accedunt quia que dicta sunt et si conferat quandoque propter opus operantis addit tamen multum virtute operis operati quod non consequuntur qui se substrahunt etiam ex devotione," *S* II 45 U.

[110] ". . . paratus nihilominus ea carere bono animo si non detur, recogitans assidue quia non in sentimento huius dulcedinis sed in charitate est regnum dei," *Lect.* 86 S.

[111] "Corpus christi verum comeditur sacramentaliter i. e. sub specie panis. Corpus christi mysticum comeditur spiritualiter in fide cordis. . ." *Lect.* 36 G.

[112] ". . . In sumptione dum mens in deum transformatur remanet quidem essentia mentis que est anima sed accidentia nova succedunt . . . dici potest quod sunt dii sub humana specie transformati." *Lect.* 86 A. Without acknowledgment Biel paraphrases at length in a sermon the 41st consideration of Gerson's *De Mystica Theologia*: "Plane anima cum devote in hunc cibum convertitur non annihilatur . . . Fuere nonnulli dicentes quod in unione illa perfecta anime cum deo, anima perdit esse suum et redit in ideam propriam quam incommutabiliter et eternaliter habuit in deo, sic quod iam non est creatura, sed ipse deus qui amatur quorum auctor fuit Almaricus hereticus ab ecclesia condemnatus et ab Augustino inter heresiarchas nominatur. Non ergo annihilatur aut deficit anima in suo esse sed similitudinarie transformatur sicut amatorum dicitur esse cor unum et anima una. . ." *S* II 45 N. See for Gerson, notes 48–50 above. The parallel passages in Gerson are indicated

off the danger of such loss of identity as was criticized by Gerson and expressed by Eckhart with the image of the drop that disappears in the sea.

One more point should be made. The experience of *this* union is not merely a matter of proper preparation and reception of the gift of special grace. It depends to a certain degree also on the structure of one's personality in the same way in which some people cry easily.[113]

9. Conclusion: the marriage of mysticism and nominalism

At the end of our investigation we may conclude that there is reason to prefer the title "mystical elements in Biel's theology" to "Biel's mystical theology." The noted inconsistencies in terminology as such are revealing. Biel's major systematic work, his *Sentences* commentary, seems at first sight void of any mystical teaching. It is indeed only on grounds of his *Sermons* and *Exposition of the Mass* that one understands that such terms as "contritio" and "ex opere operantis" for Biel have mystical connotations.

We have seen, however, that most of the inconsistencies can be reduced to a twofold use of mystical terminology: first on the level of contrition, the love for God above everything else, required of all Christians as necessary for their salvation. Secondly, on the level of the chosen few, the perfect ones. Though with respect to eucharistic mysticism, Biel can formulate himself in a way reminiscent of the Eckhartian school of thought, in the total context of his theology his description of the mysticism of the perfect can be characterized as penitential mysticism.

In contrast to the democratic mysticism of the first level — which proved to be in fact self-justifying or pneumatic piety — the mysticism of the second level can be termed aristocratic mysticism, insofar as the

---

by Combes, *Essai . . . I*, 39; *Opera* I, 816. On the reference to Augustine, *ibid.*, I, 531 ff. Biel does not show awareness of the development observed by Combes in Gerson's critique of Almaricus. Cf. *Essai . . .* II, 32, n. 2. On Almaricus see C. Capelle, *Amaury de Bène: Étude sur son panthéisme formel* (Paris, 1932). Cf. Denifle and Chatelain, *Chartularium . . .* I, 71 f.

[113] "Sepe enim contigit quod hi qui maiorem habent dei dilectionem intensive et extensive minus sentiunt se affici ad deum et minus experiuntur dulcorem dulcedinis ad deum quam alii qui sunt minores in dilectione . . . ad quod cooperantur hominis naturalia sic vel sic qualificata. Hinc aliqui mox flent. . ." *S* IV 7 C. For the parallel with Gerson see Stelzenberger, p. 94 f.

personality structure of the chosen few makes them naturally fit to experience the sweetness of the union with God, through love, in conformity to his will.

The abiding eschatological context, due to Biel's understanding of the persistence of concupiscence notwithstanding a progressive sanctification, prevents the transformation or deification of the perfect from transcending the limitations set for the *viator* and thus respects the incommensurability between Creator and creation which is a basic presupposition of the nominalist theologian. Finally, we can return to our point of departure: Gabriel Biel as much as Jean Gerson provides the historian of Christian thought with decisive documentation to prove that mysticism and nominalism are ideal partners in a wholesome "mystical marriage."

Chapter Eleven

HOLY WRIT AND HOLY CHURCH

꧁꧂꧁꧂꧁꧂꧁꧂꧁꧂꧁꧂꧁꧂꧁꧂꧁꧂꧁꧂꧁꧂꧁꧂꧁꧂꧁꧂꧁꧂꧁꧂꧁꧂꧁꧂꧁꧂

I. Nominalism and Extrascriptural Tradition

1. Biblicism or ecclesiastical positivism: clashing interpretations

At the present time there is as little consensus among scholars about the scriptural principle governing late medieval nominalism as there is with respect to the nominalistic doctrine of justification. The diversity in point of view among the different schools of nominalism has been pointed out repeatedly in these pages, especially in connection with Gregory's critical attitude toward the doctrine of justification held by Occam and some of his English disciples. In this chapter our aim is to see whether there are similar variations among nominalists with regard to the authority of the Church and the authority of Holy Scripture. Perhaps in this area, we will find a consensus that can be described as one of the unifying principles of nominalism.

But even if we begin by restricting our investigation to Occam and Biel, it becomes immediately obvious that we are dealing with contradictory research results. Occamistic respect for the authority of Holy Scripture has been stressed at times to the point where it is identified with the *sola scriptura* principle of the Reformation.[1] On the other hand,

---

[1] "So bleibt die Bibel alleinige Autorität," Friedrich Kropatscheck, *Das Schrift-prinzip der lutherischen Kirche*, vol. I: *Die Vorgeschichte: Das Erbe des Mittelalters*, (Leipzig, 1904), 314. Biel teaches "scriptura supra papam" but Occam's "Revolutions-gedanken waren in wenig Generationen verraucht und die Schüler Occams wurden gern von der immer entgegenkommenden Kirche mitsamt ihrem "Schriftprinzip" wieder aufgenommen," p. 326. See Kropatscheck's earlier article "Occam und Luther: Bemerkungen zur Geschichte des Autoritätsprinzips," in *Beiträge zur Förderung christlicher Theologie* 4 (Gütersloh, 1900), 51 ff., esp. 61 f., 71. See also Grabmann: "Die Heilige Schrift, welche irrtumslos ist, steht [für Occam] über

other scholars have passed over this submissive attitude toward Holy Scripture, suggesting rather that the most striking feature of the position of Occam and Biel is their ecclesiastical positivism. Their emphasis on the *fides implicita* is seen then as indicating their attitude of submission to the authority of the Church.[2] Whereas a healthy balance between authority and reason had been the hallmark of medieval thought, such fideism would indeed mark the "journey's end."[3] In this context there is usually a reference to the "logical games" of the Occamists. These are seen to be a natural result of a lack of interest in religious life in general and the theological enterprise in particular. Condemnations like "fideism" and "positivism" are not infrequently accompanied by characterizations like "scepticism" and "naturalism."[4] Depending upon the confessional position of the historian, biblicism is hailed as an evangelical principle or condemned as a form of disintegration; but generally it is seen as

dem Papst und über den Konzilien, welche irren können," *Geschichte der katholischen Theologie*, p. 111.

[2] The most provocative description we found was in Hieronymus Wigand Biel: ". . . Gabriel se in altissimae sordidissimae servitutis profunditate immersum esse, vel nobis tacentibus, orbi literato comprobavit." *De Gabriele Biel celeberrimo papista anti-papista* (Wittenberg, 1719), p. 16. Cf. ". . . hominem papalibus hypothesibus ad vomitum usque inescatum, easdem cum agnitae veritatis iactura servili atque abiecto animo defendentem. . ." [!!], p. 17.

[3] See Etienne Gilson, *History of Christian Philosophy in the Middle Ages*, (New York and London, 1955), p. 498; and M. J. Congar, "Théologie: Étude historique," in *DThC*, vol. XV, col. 405. For the same conclusions see also those of a group of Roman Catholic reformation scholars who emphasize a primarily negative impact of Occamism on Luther. "Dieser Okhamismus war, von der hochmittelalterlichen Schule her gesehen, kein 'System' sondern dessen Leugnung. Er war ein Frage, keine Antwort," Lortz, *Die Reformation in Deutschland*, I, 174. Cf. Louis Bouyer, *Du Protestantisme à l'église* (Paris, 1954), p. 176; English translation: *The Spirit and Forms of Protestantism* (Westminster, Md., 1956), p. 164. Willem H. van de Pol, *Het Wereldprotestantisme*, p. 35 ff. For an extensive presentation of these views see Heinrich Denifle, *Luther und Luthertum* I, abt. 2, (Mainz, 1906), esp. p. 587 ff.

[4] "L'attitude sceptique du nominalisme engendre l'impression que la raison ne peut suivre la foi. Tous ces mouvements d'anticatholicisme. . . " Maurice de Wulf *Histoire de la Philosophie Médiévale*, III (Paris, 1947), 232. For nominalism as fideism, see p. 230. Cf. with this the wish expressed by Albert Lang in his *Die Wege der Glaubensbegründung bei den Scholastikern des 14. Jahrhunderts*: "Es wäre überhaupt zu wünschen, dass gewisse kräftige Verurteilungen des 14. Jahrhunderts und speziell des Nominalismus nicht einfachhin ungeprüft weitergeschleppt würden," in *BB*, vol. XXX, pts. 1–2 (Münster, i.W., 1931) 241, n. 1. See however the words of caution by Robert Guelluy: "On se tromperait également en interprétant le nominalisme d'Ockham comme l'oeuvre d'un esprit positif. . ." *Philosophie et Théologie chez Guillaume d'Ockham*, pp. 224, 363 ff.

neutralized by a practical attitude of ecclesiastical positivism.[5] In sum, regardless of whether biblicism or rather ecclesiastical positivism is stressed, nominalism in either case is accused of holding these two principles in mere juxtaposition, without organic relation.[6]

2. Theses of Paul de Vooght and George Tavard

Two of the most recent studies in this area, however, have given this discussion a new turn by taking up the problem of extrascriptural tradition. Thus late medieval discussions have been more clearly drawn into relation with the decisions of the Council of Trent than had been done before.

After a careful analysis of the relevant sources, Paul de Vooght comes to the surprising conclusion that Occam does not mark the usually alleged point of no return between high scholasticism and total disintegration. On the contrary, in the writings of Occam a new synthesis is achieved between the written and the unwritten Tradition, Scripture and Tradition.[7] Occam himself, according to de Vooght, did not work out this synthesis fully, but he pointed the way that John Wyclif and Jean Gerson would later take. Occam did not understand *sola scriptura* to exclude the possibility of an extra-scriptural tradition.[8] Thus his work marks a turning point in the history of the problem of Scripture and Tradition.[9]

Indeed de Vooght also points to weaknesses of fourteenth-century theology — abstract mental games and uncritical reading of the Bible. He even claims as part of the reason for the emphasis on *sola scriptura* in this period that Holy Scripture itself was not read.[10] Nevertheless,

[5] "Aber so deutlich hier der Gedanke von der ausschliesslichen lehrhaften Autorität der Schrift theoretisch ausgedrückt ist, so wenig haben unsere Autoren mit diesem Gedanken praktisch zu machen gewusst." Seeberg *DG* III, 723. "Die Nominalisten haben der Autorität der Schrift vorgearbeitet, aber sie haben zugleich durch ihren kirchlichen Positivismus ein gewaltiges Bollwerk wider sie aufgebaut. . ." *Ibid.*, p. 724.

[6] "Schrift und Kirchenlehre werden wie unwillkürlich [!]einander gleichgesetzt." Seeberg, *DG* III, 723.

[7] "Ainsi l'Écriture et la tradition, tout comme la théologie et l'Écriture, ne font qu'un," Paul de Vooght, *Les sources de la doctrine chrétienne d'après les théologiens du XIVe siècle et du début du XVe . . ."* (Paris, 1954), p. 245.

[8] De Vooght, pp. 167, 255.

[9] "Occam est la plaque tournante dans l'histoire de la théologie des sources de la doctrine chrétienne," de Vooght, p. 259.

[10] "Sans paradoxe, ils ne plaçaient l'Écriture si haut que parce qu'ils l'ignoraient," de Vooght, pp. 263, 258.

theologians of the period had the insight to relate Scripture and Tradition closely as foundation and interpretation, as conservation and transmission. De Vooght finds in Wyclif and Gerson representatives of this understanding since they hold that Scripture without Tradition is fossilized while Tradition without Scripture leads to arbitrary fantasies.[11]

In a second recent study on the history of the relation of Scripture and Tradition, George Tavard comes to the opposite conclusion.[12] Stressing the continuity of patristic and medieval theology, he claims that until the early decades of the fourteenth century, Scripture and Tradition were seen as mutually inclusive, a view which implies the coinherence of Scripture and Church. Then, however, the synthesis breaks asunder and the organic understanding of the relation of foundation and interpretation is undermined. The disintegration is the result of two new currents of thought: (1) one which opposes Scripture to the Church, thus admitting the possibility that only a remnant in the visible Church would be obedient to Scripture; (2) another which introduces the concept of post-apostolic and oral traditions and raises the Holy See to the dignity of the judge of post-apostolic revelation. "The breaking asunder of that synthesis [the coinherence of Scripture and Church] in the fourteenth century not only made the Church subservient to Scripture or the Scripture ancillary to the Church. It furthermore threw open a door by way of a supposed superiority of the Church over Holy Writ, to the idea that the Church had her own revelation, independent of that which the Apostles recorded in their writings."[13] The extremists of this second group are primarily the canon lawyers who held two distinct revelations and thus departed from "medieval classicism." The extremists of the first group "stood by a restrictive notion of Scripture and paved the way for a complete denial of the Church."[14]

Whereas Tavard — in contrast with de Vooght — agrees with traditional late medieval scholarship in viewing the end of the Middle Ages as

[11] ". . . on hésiterait peu à tenir pour essentiels à toute transmission vivante d'une doctrine vécue: une charte fondamentale, fixée une fois pour toutes (en l'occurrence: la Sainte Écriture) et un organe-interprète, suscité immanquablement par la progression de la vie (dans notre cas: la tradition)," de Vooght, p. 262.

[12] *Holy Writ or Holy Church. The Crisis of the Protestant Reformation* (New York, 1959).

[13] Tavard, p. 36.

[14] "From this to the doctrines of the Reformation there is only a difference of degree," Tavard, p. 40.

364

a period of decline — he accepts nevertheless the more positive interpretation of Occam. What makes his thesis especially relevant to our concern
is that he feels that Biel was not a faithful disciple of Occam on this
point. While Occam stands "between two extremes that are ably contrasted in his *Dialogue*," [15] his disciple Gabriel Biel was "caught between
two conceptions of Scripture. In the first, Scripture is a sufficient rule of
faith, provided that the Church's function of making explicit its implicit
contents be accepted. In the second, Scripture does not suffice: many points
must be believed that derive from Christ apart from what was written." [16]

Jean Gerson, Tavard claims, had a proper understanding of the interrelation of Scripture and Church. Pierre d'Ailly "differs from Gerson
insofar as Scripture, with its right meaning, is not for him the sum
total of the Church's doctrine . . . Post-apostolic revelations have been
made to the Church." [17] Apart from the fact that Wessel Gansfort included hypothetical apostolic tradition within the rule of faith, "Wessel's
orthodoxy is clear," whereas von Wesel is blatantly heretical.[18]

These are only a few of the series of witnesses on whom Tavard has
called. Each of these three pairs — Occam and Biel, Gerson and d'Ailly,
Wessel and von Wesel — highlights the lines of demarcation that divide
orthodoxy from an incipient anti-Catholic disintegration of the unity of
Scripture and Church.

II. Tradition I and Tradition II

1. Scripture and Tradition in the early Church

In view of the variety of new data and opinions recently published,
we will have to proceed with great care in order to come to a fair
evaluation of Biel's position. Descriptions like "synthesis" and "disintegration" are of course value judgments which may reveal more about the
position of the historian than of his historical subject. Therefore we will
rather pose the question whether Biel's concept of Tradition is to be seen

[15] Tavard, p. 31
[16] Tavard, p. 62.
[17] Tavard, p. 55. "This idea of an 'oral tradition' will now stay with us for a
while," p. 56.
[18] Tavard, p. 70; "With Wessel's friend Johann Rucherat von Wesel [c. 1400–
1481] a break has undoubtedly taken place in the pattern of orthodoxy. . . . The
Church is [for him] a mixed body, where error and truth coexist" (p. 71).

as identifying him with a late-medieval, anti-Catholic, proto-Protestant movement or perhaps rather with the fore-runners of the Council of Trent. Even beyond the individual case of Biel, of course, it is important to see what can be said about late medieval nominalism as such on the question of Scripture and Tradition.

If we begin by comparing Biel with Occam, we encounter the difficulty that Occam addresses himself most explicitly to this problem in his *Dialogus inter magistrum et discipulum*,[19] which is indeed a true dialogue. Two views are introduced and defended: (1) Holy Scripture contains all the truths of faith; (2) a complementary unwritten tradition is transmitted through the apostles and their successors. As we will see, however, there is good reason to believe that Occam himself favored the second position.[20]

But the problem Occam raises is deeply rooted in the pre-Occamistic tradition, going back as far as Basil the Great and Augustine. As regards the pre-Augustinian Church, there is in our time a striking convergence of scholarly opinion that Scripture and Tradition are for the early Church in no sense mutually exclusive: kerygma, Scripture and Tradition coincide entirely. The Church preaches the kerygma which is to be found *in toto* in written form in the canonical books.

The Tradition is not understood as an addition to the kerygma contained in Scripture but as the handing down of that same kerygma in living form: in other words everything is to be found in Scripture and at the same time everything is in the living Tradition.

It is in the living, visible Body of Christ, inspired and vivified by the operation of the Holy Spirit, that Scripture and Tradition coinhere. This is not merely to be understood in the one-level sense of the coinherence of source and interpretation. That is certainly the case. But this coinherence is first of all the result of the understanding that both Scripture and

[19] Occam, *Dialogus inter magistrum et discipulum* in *Monarchia romani imperii*, ed. Goldast, II (Frankfort, 1668), 398–957.

[20] See the excellent article by A. Van Leeuwen "L'église, règle de foi, dans les écrits de Guillaume d'Occam," *Ephemerides Theologicae Lovanienses*, 11 (1934), 249 ff.; "Nous ne prétendons pas qu'Occam admet toutes les particularités . . . mais la manière dont il propose les deux hypothèses montre suffisamment qu'il n'attache aucune valeur à la première," p. 256. Since Occam's writings fall into two main periods, before and after his departure from Avignon for the Camp of Louis the Bavarian, we should note that in this chapter we are referring primarily to the "older" Occam, i.e. the writings which postdate 1328.

Tradition issue from the same source: the Word of God, Revelation. They find their common basis therefore in the operation of the Holy Spirit. Through the Holy Spirit the content of the Christian faith, and the act of participation, translation, and thus interpretation by the apostolic Church, the *fides quae creditur* and the *fides qua creditur*, are held together. Scripture and Tradition are substantially — as regards *fides* et *veritas* — coextensive.

This coinherence implies the explicit denial of the extrascriptural Tradition. "To appeal to revelatory truth apart from Scripture is [for Irenaeus] heretical gnosticism." [21] But only within the Church can this kerygma be handed down undefiled. While Clement of Alexandria acknowledged a charismatic apostolic succession independent of the episcopal line,[22] Irenaeus seems to identify the transmission of truth with episcopal succession.[23] Inasmuch as the apostles did not institute other Apostles but bishops, however, the episcopal witness is a derived witness,[24] and its function is to preserve the integrity and totality of the original apostolic witness. To this end the Canon was formed.

Though Scripture and Church coinhere, they do not lose their functional differentiation. On the contrary, the writings of the Apostles which were in the process of being received — not produced by the Church — were understood to contain the original kerygma *in toto*.[25] ·We should

---

[21] E. Flesseman-van Leer, *Tradition and Scripture in the Early Church* (Assen, 1954), p. 191. J. N. Bakhuizen van den Brink has shown in his discussion of Irenaeus "dass die heilige Schrift und die mit ihr idealiter identische kirchliche Verkündigung in der *traditio* sind, die *traditio* also aufgefasst als die lebendige Totalität der ganzen Offenbarung oder des Reichs der Wahrheit"; "Traditio im theologischen Sinne," *Vigiliae Christianae* 13 (1959), 75. See also Bengt Hägglund, "Die Bedeutung der 'regula fidei' als Grundlage theologischer Aussagen," *Studia Theologica* 12 (1958), 1 ff., 17.

[22] *Strom.* VI. 63: VI. 106. It has been suggested that Clement here betrays gnostic influences; G. Bardy, *La théologie de l'Eglise*, vol. I: *De St. Clément de Rome à St. Irenée* (Paris, 1945), 176.

[23] ". . . qui cum episcopatus successione charisma veritatis certum secundum placitum patris acceperunt," *Adv. Haereses* IV, ed. W. Wigan Harvey (Cambridge, Eng., 1857), II, 236.

[24] Oscar Cullmann, "Scripture and Tradition," *SJT* 6 (1953), 116.

[25] J. N. Bakhuizen van den Brink, "Tradition und Heilige Schrift am Anfang des dritten Jahrhunderts," in *Studia Catholica* 9 (1953), p. 109. See J. Geiselmann: "Dass in der Heiligen Schrift nur ein Teil des apostolischen Kerygmas niedergelegt sei, davon weiss wohl die gegen die Reformation gerichtete Kontroverstheologie, davon weiss aber die Theologie der Väterzeit nicht," in *Fragen der Theologie*

therefore beware of thinking in terms of a *de novo* creation of the Canon by the post-apostolic Church in accepting certain writings as apostolic.

The expression "coinherence of Holy Scripture and Holy Church" can only be meaningful when the terms "Scripture" and "Church" are clearly defined. Tavard uses these terms in a variety of ways. Sometimes "Church" stands for this coinherence itself of which Scripture and Tradition are the constitutive elements. More often the apostolic kerygma stands for this coinherence, of which Scripture and Church form the constitutive elements.[26]

Though this lack of clarity would not seem to be disastrous in an analysis of patristic thought where these terms coincide, the increasing functional differentiation of "Church" and "Scripture" in postpatristic history presents problems for which Tavard's usage would leave us conceptually and terminologically ill-equipped.

It is of great import that J. N. Bakhuizen van den Brink has shown that in pre-Augustinian theology, the single term *traditio* actually covers two concepts of tradition. The first is explicitly the *traditio dei* and has a primarily vertical character. The second is the ecclesiastical tradition or traditions which fall in the category of history and therefore have a horizontal character. Whereas the second *can* be the historical expression of the first, it is the first concept of tradition which is the standard of validity for the ecclesiastical tradition.[27] As we in turn approach medieval

heute (Zürich, 1957), p. 97. A. Deneffe employs this terminology in his *Der Traditionsbegriff* (Münster i. W., 1931), p. 71, which seems excellently fitted to express the foregoing. The apostolic witness can then be termed *traditio revelans*, the episcopal witness the *traditio revelationem acceptam praedicans*. This marks the parallel distinction between *traditio constitutiva* and *traditio continuativa*.

[26] Cf. the statement of Yves Congar: "Il [Tavard] semble en effet leur attribuer une position très proche de celle de certains apologistes catholiques du XVI siècle, e.g., pour lesquels c'est *l'Église* qui a discerné les livres inspirés. Mais les Pères anciens faisaient du Canon une tradition apostolique que l'Église gardait et transmettait seulement." "Sainte Ecriture et sainte Eglise," *Revue de Sciences Philosophiques et Théologiques* 44 (1960), 82, n. 8. At one place Church and Scripture are said to be two absolutes according to traditional thought. A few pages later, however, one reads that for the Catholic mind: ". . . the Scriptures and the Church constitute, both together, one absolute," pp. 83, 93.

[27] "Es gibt also zwei Traditionsbegriffe von der frühkatholischen Theologie an, und zwar erstens die *traditio dei* und zweitens die kirchliche Tradition oder Traditionen. Zeigen diese zweiten ihre ganz leicht zu verstehende horizontale oder historische Ausbreitung, die erstere hat vornehmlich vertikalen Charakter. Es ist

sources, we are thus alerted to weigh the use of the term *traditio* in each new context.

2. The Period of Transition: Basil and Augustine

A new concept of tradition was formulated in the East by Basil the Great and was propagated half a century later in the West by Augustine. In Basil's treatise *On the Holy Spirit*, the relation of Scripture and Tradition is discussed in connection with certain liturgical traditions of the Church. We find here for the first time explicitly the idea that the Christian owes equal respect and obedience to written and to unwritten ecclesiastical traditions, whether contained in canonical writings or in a secret oral tradition handed down by the Apostles through their successors.

This Basilean passage is regularly quoted by canonists of the early Middle Ages. The great expert in canon law, Ivo of Chartres, refers to it to insist on equal reverence for scriptural and for extrascriptural oral traditions. More important is the fact that Gratian of Bologna copied this passage from Ivo and incorporated it into his highly influential *Decretum* from where it found its way into the textbooks of both canon lawyers and theologians.[28]

For the canon lawyer, then, the two-sources theory has been established: canon law stands on the two pillars of Scripture and Tradition. The same does not seem to apply to the medieval doctor of theology, however. Theology is understood as the science of Holy Scripture. And notwithstanding the constant and growing temptation to comment on the comments, Holy Scripture is understood to be the authoritative source — the final test of the interpretation of later interpreters.[29] The term *sacra*

---

aber nicht zu leugnen, dass die zweite die Form der ersteren sein kann, während die erstere immer über die Gültigkeit der zweiten zu entscheiden haben wird." J. N. Bakhuizen van den Brink, "Traditio im theologischen Sinne," p. 78.

[28] *De Spiritu sancto* 66 in *PG* XXXII, 188. Basil's *ta men . . . ta de* is rendered here as *alia . . . alia*. For Ivo of Chartres, *PL* CLXI, 283; here instead of *alia . . . alia* we find *quasdam . . . quasdam*. For Gratian *CIC*, Decreti I d XI, c. V; p. 23. Gratian follows Ivo in the use of *quasdam . . . quasdam*.

[29] Thomas, *ST* I q 1 art. 8 ad. 2: "Innititur enim fides nostra revelationi apostolis et prophetis factae, qui canonicos libros scripserunt, non autem revelationi, si qua fuit aliis doctoribus facta."

In addition to the literature quoted in notes 21–25 see on the concept of tradi-

pagina for theology is indeed indicative of this close relation. This unity must not, however, obscure the fact that the medieval theologian — if one may use such a general term — respected the distinction between text and gloss, between Scripture and its interpretation.

Augustine's legacy to the middle ages on the question of Scripture and Tradition is a two-fold one. In the first place, he reflects the early Church principle of the coinherence of Scripture and Tradition. While repeatedly asserting the ultimate authority of Scripture,[30] Augustine does not oppose this at all to the authority of the Church Catholic: ". . . ego vero evangelio non crederem, nisi me catholicae ecclesiae commoveret auctoritas." [31] The Church has a practical priority: her authority as expressed in the direction-giving meaning of *commovere* is an instrumental authority, the door that leads to the fullness of the Word itself.[32]

But there is another aspect of Augustine's thought to be pointed out in which he reflects the Basilean view we have discussed. In contrast with Irenaeus' condemnation of extrascriptural tradition, in Augustine we find mention of an *authoritative* extrascriptural oral tradition. While

---

tion: Johannes Beumer, "Das katholische Schriftprinzip in der theologischen Literatur der Scholastik bis zur Reformation," *Scholastik* 16 (1941) 24 ff.; C. Spicq. *Esquisse d'une histoire de l'Exégèse latin au moyen âge*, Bibliothèque Thomiste 26 (Paris, 1944), 9 ff.; J. de Ghellinck, " 'Pagina' et 'Sacra Pagina': Histoire d'un mot et transformation de l'objet primitivement désigné," in *Mélanges Auguste Pelzer* (Louvain, 1947); Beryl Smalley, *The Study of The Bible in the Middle Ages*, 2 ed. (Oxford, 1952); Gerhard Ebeling, *Evangelische Evangelienauslegung* (Munich, 1942), *Die Geschichtlichkeit der Kirche und ihrer Verkündigung als theologisches Problem* (Tübingen, 1954;). "Hermeneutik," in *RGG*, III, col. 242–262.

[30] ". . . deferens ei [Holy Scripture] culmen auctoritatis." *De Sermo dom. i.m.* I. 11. 32, in *PL XXXIV*, 1245.

[31] *Contra Epistolam Manichaei quam vocant fundamenti liber unus*, 5 in *CSEL* 25. 197, 22. For an analysis of this passage and a survey of its sixteenth-century interpretation, see J.N. Bakhuizen van den Brink, *Traditio in de Reformatie en het Katholicisme in de zestiende Eeuw*, Mededelingen der Koninklijke Nederlandse Akademie van Wetenschappen, Afd. Letterk., n.s. 15.2 (Amsterdam, 1952), 10 ff. Mrs. G. R. Oberman kindly called my attention to a related passage in Augustine, *De beata vita*, I. 4, *CSEL* 63.2,92., which supports a psychological interpretation of *commovere* and *auctoritas:* ". . . illorum [neo-Platonic academicians] auctoritate, qui divina mysteria tradiderunt, sic exarsi ut omnes illas vellem ancoras rumpere, nisi me nonnullorum hominum existimatio commoveret." This latter interpretation is stressed by Gregory of Rimini in the fourteenth century. I *Sent.* d 1 q 1 art. 2 [fol. 3 F].

[32] ". . . credamus divinae auctoritati quam voluit esse in scripturis sanctis de filio suo." Augustine, *De agone christiano* 10, 11; *CSEL* 41.113, 6.

on the one hand the Church "moves" the faithful to discover the authority of Scripture, Scripture on the other hand refers the faithful back to the authority of the Church with regard to a series of issues with which the Apostles did not deal in writing.[33] Augustine refers here to the baptism of heretics. Abelard in the same manner would later treat Mariology, Bonaventura the *filioque* clause, and Thomas the form of the sacrament of confirmation.[34]

3. The Problem of Extrascriptural Tradition: Bradwardine, Wyclif, and Ambrosius of Speier

All these extrascriptural data were inherited by the fourteenth century along with the *sola scriptura* principle. This inheritance contained, therefore, two concepts of Tradition parallel to the two aspects of Augustine's thought mentioned above. These had been unconsciously held together without conscious effort to integrate the two.

If for clarity's sake we call the single-source or exegetical tradition of Scripture held together with its interpretation "Tradition I" and the two-sources theory which allows for an extra-biblical oral tradition "Tradition II," we may say that both Tradition I and Tradition II had their medieval partisans.

Tradition I in the later middle ages should be seen as a protest against the growing acceptance of the Basilean two-sources theory. In

---

[33] "Apostoli autem nihil quidem exinde praeceperunt: sed consuetudo illa . . . ab eorum traditione exordium sumpsisse credenda est, sicut sunt multa quae universa tenet ecclesia, et ob hoc ab apostolis praecepta bene creduntur, quamquam scripta non reperiantur." Augustine *De Baptismo*, 22, 36; *PL* 43.192. See also the justified criticism by W. F. Dankbaar of A.D.R. Polman's *De Theologie van Augustinus: Dogmatische Studies*, vol. I: *Het Woord Gods bij Augustinus* (Kampen, 1955) in his article on "Schriftgezag en Kerkgezag bij Augustinus," *NTT* 11 (1956), pp. 37 ff.

Johannes Beumer points to Tertullian's *De corona militis*, 4, as "der älteste patristische Text, der eindeutig von einer nicht in der Schrift enthaltenen Tradition spricht." "Das Katholische Traditionsprinzip in seiner heute neu erkannten Problematik," *Scholastik* 36 (1961), 220. Tertullian defends here the authority of tradition "ex perseverantia observationis." Cf. however Tertullian: ". . . sed dominus noster Christus veritatem se, non consuetudinem cognominavit." [*De Virg. vel.* 1] and the echo in Cyprian: ". . . quis tam vanus sit ut veritati consuetudinem praeferat. . ." [*Ep.* 75.19.1] as quoted and discussed by J. N. Bakhuizen van den Brink, "Traditio im theologischen Sinne," *Vigiliae Christianae* 13 (1959), 65 ff.

[34] For references see de Voogt, pp. 13–32.

the fourteenth century, at the time of the Western Schism and the final phase of the struggle between Pope and Emperor, the canon lawyer was in high demand. To judge from the many bitter comments by doctors of theology, he not only equaled but surpassed the theologian in status, both at the papal *curia* and at the royal courts. Albeit with varying degrees of eagerness, both curialists and conciliarists drew extensively on the *Decretum* and the decretals. Under the circumstances, therefore, it is not surprising that the canon-law tradition started to feed into the major theological stream in such a way that the Basilean passage became a genuinely theological argument, and the foundation of the position which we have called Tradition II.

Tradition I, then, represents the sufficiency of Holy Scripture as understood by the Fathers and doctors of the Church. In the case of disagreement between these interpreters, Holy Scripture has the final authority. The horizontal concept of Tradition is by no means denied here, but rather understood as the mode of reception of the *fides* or *veritas* contained in Holy Scripture. Since the appeal to extrascriptural tradition is rejected, the validity of ecclesiastical traditions and *consuetudines* is not regarded as "self-supporting" but depends on its relation to the faith handed down by God in Holy Scripture.

Thomas Bradwardine can be pointed out as one of the first outspoken representatives of Tradition I at the beginning of the fourteenth century. Though his references to the problem of Scripture and Tradition are relatively few and scattered, his emphasis on the exclusive and final authority of Holy Scripture is quite explicit. His position on this issue may well underlie his willingness to attack Occamistic Pelagianism despite his feeling that he stood alone over against almost the whole Church, even the *curia*.[35]

John Wyclif was undoubtedly deeply indebted to Bradwardine on this issue. It was Tradition I that provided him with the tools he used to

---

[35] "Totus etenim paene mundus post Pelagium abiit in errorem." (London, 1618), Praefatio 2; "Simon, dormis. . . ?", *De causa Dei*, III. 53. 872 E; "Quis enim Christianus ignorat doctrinam Christi Catholicam omni doctrinae contrariae praeferendam? Et quis nesciat, si Doctores dissentiant magis authenticum in tali materia praeferendum? Et quis in ista materia post Autores sacrae Scripturae authenticior Augustino . . . Quare constat sacram scripturam quam pater sanctificavit et misit in mundum, ratione sui autoris inerrabilis in firmitate et certitudine authenticis omnibus aliis incomparabiliter praeferendam." *De causa Dei*, II. 31.606 C/D; 602 E Cf. my "Tradition and its Authority," in *Bradwardine*, pp. 22–27.

evaluate medieval doctrine critically.[36] As we shall see, Huss and Wessel Gansfort must also be regarded as exponents of Tradition I.

The second concept of tradition, Tradition II, refers to the written *and* unwritten part of the apostolic message as approved by the Church. Here it is not the function of the doctors of Holy Scripture but that of the bishops which is relatively more stressed. The hierarchy is seen to have its "own" oral tradition, to a certain undefined extent independent, not of the Apostles, but of what is recorded in the canonical books. Ecclesiastical traditions, including canon law, are invested with the same degree of authority as that of Holy Scripture. Leading spokesmen for the nominalistic tradition such as Gerson, Occam, d'Ailly — and even more emphatically Biel — will be shown to champion the position of Tradition II.

A very sharp and most succinct formulation of Tradition II in contrast with Tradition I is given, not by a professional canon lawyer, but by Ambrosius of Speier, unfortunately an almost forgotten Carmelite preacher. In a sermon published on the eve of the Reformation, he refers to the formulation of Gratian according to which the responsibilities between the doctors of Scripture and the Pope are divided in such a way that the interpretation of Holy Scripture is to be the task of the theologians, the decision of legal cases that of the papacy.[37] His comment on this is, however, that such an answer should be taken with a grain of salt; then he adds with wry humor: you may rely on the doctors of Scripture in all matters regarding the interpretation of Scripture . . . unless it regards the sacraments and the articles of faith; since the power to interpret a dubious law has been granted not to the theologians but to the Pope.[38] It is clear that he views Scripture as a divine law of which canon law is an integral part.

Until the beginning of the fourteenth century theologians defined their own task in the terms in which we have described Tradition I, while the

[36] Here again de Vooght has shown keen insight: "Prétendre que Wiclif n'admettait pas la tradition . . . c'est lui attribuer gratuitement une opinion dont il n'avait pas l'idée," p. 197, n. 1.

[37] *CIC* D 20. C 1; I. col. 65.

[38] "Sed ponamus quod reperiatur diversitas inter dicta sanctorum approbata ab ecclesia et inter summos pontifices, quibus tunc standum est? . . . Dico secundum doctores quod in expositione scripturarum standum est dictis sanctorum, in decisionibus autem causarum standum est dictis summorum pontificum . . . Et huic responsioni adde unum granum salis quod hoc verum est, sive quod in

enterprise related to Tradition II was more or less an appendix.[39] Yet it was certainly not a sign of "late medieval disintegration" that more and more doctors realized that they had to come to terms with a dual concept of tradition. Rather it indicates theological progress in the period that as a result of their better understanding of the setting and the context of biblical passages,[40] more and more theologians either had to call for a doctrinal reformation or to abandon the claim to a biblical warrant for a particular doctrine. Special significance was thus attached to John

---

expositione scripturarum standum est dictis sanctorum patrum; supple: nisi tractaretur de expositione super sacramentis vel articulis fidei quia tunc standum est pape quia pape et non sanctis data fuit potestas interpretandi legem dubiam." Ambrosius of Speier, *Liber sermonum quadragesimalium de floribus sapientiae*, (Basel, 1516); *Sermo* 37, fol. 265 F (first edition Venice, 1485; first edition north of the Alps, Basel, 1510). Cf. H. Hurter, *Nomenclator literarius theologiae catholicae theologos exhibens aetate, natione, disciplinis distinctos*, II (Innsbruck, 1906), 890 f.; J. H. Zedler, *Universal Lexikon*, 30 (Leipzig, 1743), 1639. Antoninus of Florence is also a representative of Tradition II. He brings up the same issue as Ambrosius in *Summa Theologica* I.xvii.1; col. 821 C. Cf. also his sermon "De assumptione B. Mariae. . .," *Summa* IV.xv.45; col. 1241 ff.

[39] "Pour les scolastiques au XIIe et au XIIIe siècles, ce que le Concile de Trente a appelé les *sine scripto traditiones* se limitaient à quelques exceptions," De Vooght, *Les sources de la doctrine chrétienne*, p. 32.

[40] "Oportet enim semper secundum subiectam materiam sermones accipi et ex circumstantibus scriptura[ru]m verborum significationem colligere. . ." S I 60 F. There is every indication also that Duns Scotus provided late medieval theology with a point of departure for this problem. As Josef Finkenzeller says: "Die Tradition als ursprüngliche und unabhängige Quelle der christlichen Lehre ist in der Zeit, in der Skotus die Sentenzen kommentiert, unbekannt," *Offenbarung und Theologie nach der Lehre des Johannes Duns Skotus. Ein historische und systematische Untersuchung* (Münster i. W. 1960), p. 74. But he goes on to say: "In der Betonung der apostolischen Tradition im Sinne einer über die Hl. Schrift hinausgehenden Überlieferung hat unter den Theologen der Hochscholastik Duns Skotus den entscheidenden Durchbruch gewagt, wenn es ihm auch nicht gelungen ist, die daraus entstehende Frage nach dem Verhältnis von Schrift und Tradition zu beantworten," p. 75.

Finkenzeller is not able to establish the decisive character of Scotus' breakthrough, but we must call attention to the fact that Scotus makes it possible to reconcile the time-honored idea that "holy Scripture contains everything necessary to salvation" with the growing acknowledgment of extra-scriptural truths. The concept of sufficiency of Scripture which for Aquinas is a matter of truths appealing to the intellect tends to become for Scotus a matter of moral precepts appealing to the will. Doctrinal sufficiency develops into moral sufficiency: "Ipsa [doctrina canonis] etiam determinat quae sunt necessaria ad finem, et quod illa sufficiant, quia decem mandata [Math. 19:17]: Si vis ad vitam ingredi serva mandata. . ." *Ox.* Prol. q 2 n 14. Cf. Biel in note 96 below.

20:30: "Now Jesus did many other signs in the presence of the disciples which are not written in this book. . ."

4. Both conciliarism and curialism uphold extrascriptural Tradition

In our search to refine the distinction between Tradition I and Tradition II, we must first reject the possibility that the second would presuppose the understanding of Holy Scripture as divine law and the first would not. Wyclif is as insistent as Ambrosius of Speier on the conception of Holy Scripture as divine law.[41] Thus he can say: ". . . I submit that the gospel of Christ is the body of the law of God . . . Christ, indeed, who directly gave this gospel, I believe to be true God and true man, and in this the law of the gospel excels all other parts of Scripture. . ."[42]

It also proves to be impossible to define the borderline between Tradition I and Tradition II in terms of the contrast between conciliarism and curialism.

We have noted above that Occam makes the distinction between the positions designated as Tradition I and Tradition II explicit in his *Dialogue* and that he seems inclined to accept Tradition II. He indeed distinguishes the task of the doctors of Scripture from that of the papacy and the councils as definition *per modum doctrinae* from the one *per modum auctoritatis*.[43] Contrary to the position taken by Bradwardine and Wy-

---

[41] William Mallard, "John Wyclif and the Tradition of Biblical Authority," *CH* 30 (1961), 56 f. See for further documentation Michael Hurley, S.J., "Scriptura sola: Wyclif and his Critics," *Traditio* 16 (1960), 275 ff. Hurley argues that Wyclif accepted tradition only in theory. *Ibid.*, p. 299. Hurley had however first defined "Tradition" as what we have called Tradition II: "To accept Tradition is to accept the Church's testimony to Christ, not only that original testimony which is Scripture but also that continuous testimony which, when authenticated by the *Magisterium*, is to be received with equal piety and reverence." *Ibid.*, 279. Hurley has not been able to show that Wyclif ever accepted *this* concept of Tradition. When however Tradition is understood as Tradition I, Scripture validly interpreted by the Church, we can agree fully with de Vooght's conclusion: "Personne plus que Wyclif n'a ainsi défendu la tradition. . ." *Les sources de la doctrine chrétienne*, p. 180 f.

[42] Bodleian MS, Mus 86, as quoted in Joseph H. Dahmus, *The Prosecution of John Wyclif* (New Haven, 1952), p. 141. Lechler has pointed out "that on this precise point it was only step by step that Wyclif attained to the truth." *John Wyclif and his English Precursors* (London, 1904), p. 257. With Huss, I have found no such trace of development. De Vooght feels however that one has to stretch the sources to find the "old Huss" in the "young Huss." *L'Hérésie de Jean Huss* (Louvain, 1960), p. 55.

[43] "Contingit enim aliquid definire auctoritate officii et sic definire quae est

375

clif, Occam does not insist that the definition *per modum auctoritatis* should coincide with the one *per modum doctrinae*. The point he makes is that the Pope in defining the boundary between orthodoxy and heresy should *chiefly* rely on Holy Scripture and the theological enterprise therewith connected.[44]

A man's allegiance to conciliarism or curialism therefore does not appear to be a determining factor in his choice of one of the two concepts of tradition. One can as easily be curialist as conciliarist while adhering to Tradition II. The only difference is that in the one case the Pope, in the other the Council has the highest authority in defining extrascriptural Tradition. There is an obvious connection between the defenders of Tradition I and the conciliarists in that both loathe the activities of the canon lawyers. Wyclif and Huss are quite outspoken in their criticism of this group.

But for Wyclif and Huss the battle against curialism is at the same time a battle against Tradition II. Huss says explicitly that those who defend the infallibility of the Pope are pseudo-apostles and antichrists. On closer analysis it appears that it is not primarily this infallibility itself that he opposes but rather the implied addition of the Pope's own law to the law of God, Holy Scripture.[45] To those who accuse him of arbitrary interpretation and "private judgment," Huss answers that indeed the Holy Spirit has to illumine the individual interpreter, but he adds that this gift of understanding has been granted to the holy doctors

---

assertio heretica quae catholica censenda, ad summum pontificem spectat et concilium generale. Aliquando contingit definire per modum doctrinae quomodo magistri in scholis quaestiones definiunt et determinant. . ." *Dial.* I. 1. 1; Goldast, II, p. 399; van Leeuwen, p. 274.

[44] "Summus pontifex debet sacrarum litterarum habere notitiam . . . et eadem ratione in definiendo authentice quae assertio est catholica et quae haeretica reputanda, theologiae principaliter debet inniti." *Dial.* I. 1. 5 Goldast, II. p. 403; van Leeuwen, p. 274.

[45] Huss, *Tractatus de Ecclesia* ed. S. Harrison Thomson (Cambridge, Eng., 1956): ". . . devianti pape rebellare est Christo domino obedire . . . Illi autem doctores qui . . . dicunt quod sit incomprehensibilis potestatis, inpeccabilis, incorrigibilis; et sic quod potest licite facere quicquid libuerit, sunt pseudoprophete et pseudoapostoli Antichristi." Chap. 18 P [p. 169]; ". . . notandum de sede apostolica de qua multi et presertim canoniste multa predicant. . ." Chap. 18 A [p. 157]; "Signum autem defectus pape est si postposita lege dei et devotis ewangelii professoribus tradicionibus attendit humanis . . . permitteret garrire leges humanas in palacio et silere legem Christi, que est lex inmaculata convertens animas." Chap. 18 N. [p. 167].

from whom he does not want to deviate.[46] It is clear that this insistence on the authority of Holy Scripture is not *sola scriptura* in the sense that it would exclude Tradition understood as the ongoing interpretation of Scripture. The *sola* is only restrictive in that the law of God is sovereign and sufficient to determine alone — *without ecclesiastical law* — all cases that have to be tried by the Church.[47]

We may therefore say that apart from the negative characteristic of rejection of extrascriptural Tradition, the positive characteristic of Tradition I is an insistence on a *successio fidei* preserved by the *successio doctorum*, who inherited the charism of truth from the apostles. Such a concept of succession might well go back to Clement of Alexandria.[48] The episcopal succession is not regarded as a guarantee of the validity of the

[46] ". . . non intendimus cum dei auxilio aliter scripturam exponere quam spiritus sanctus flagitat et quam sancti doctores exponunt, quibus dedit spiritus sanctus intellectum." *Ibid.*, Chap. 16 B [p. 133]. Cf. Bradwardine: "Porro de sacra Scriptura audacter pronuntio, quod nulla pars eius realiter alteri contradicit, aut heresi Pelagianae consentit, et si quae sic facere superficialiter videatur, profecto hoc accidit ex defectu oculi minus sani; quare purgandus est oculus, ut possit sincere videre veram mentem Scripturae secundum expositiones Sanctorum. . ." *De Causa Dei*, II 31. 604 E. Cf. Wyclif *De Veritate Scripturae Sacrae* c. 10, 12, 15: "Tradiciones autem morales fundatas in scriptura oportet in perpetuo remanere." Sermo 21.2; ed. Iohann Loserth. *De Sanctis* (London, 1888), p. 156.

[47] ". . . lex sua efficacissima ad causas ecclesiasticas terminandas, cum deus ipsam edidit ad hunc finem." Huss, *Tractatus de Ecclesia* (Cambridge, Eng., 1956), chap. 15 D [p. 121]. Wyclif, *De Civili Dominio*, c. 26.

For a discussion of the twenty propositions drawn from Huss' *De Ecclesia* and censured by Gerson and his Parisian colleagues see Paul de Vooght, *L'Hérésie de Jean Huss*, p. 294 ff. The propositions appear to be of uneven value: "Elles vont d'une objectivité nuancée à l'erreur sans phrases," p. 302. The intimate connection between the rejection of the authority of canon law and a strongly spiritual ecclesiology is apparent throughout. See also Paul de Vooght, *Hussiana* (Louvain, 1960), p. 9 ff. See also note 53.

[48] "Non enim Christus cum sua lege deficit ad regendum ecclesiam, ministrantibus devotis sacerdotibus ipsam legem populo iuxta sanctorum doctorum sentenciam, quam instinctu spiritus sancti ediderunt, ut patet de sanctis Augustino, Jeronimo, Gregorio, Ambrosio, qui post apostolos dati sunt ecclesie ad doctrinam . . . Quomodo ergo illi quatuor sancti doctores non fuerunt vicarii apostolorum et manifesti successores eorum, ymo veriores et cerciores quoad populum quam modernus papa cum suis cardinalibus, qui nec vita sancta fulgent populo nec doctrina? Unde audacter assero quod in quocunque puncto isti sancti quatuor doctores concordant, quod papa cum cardinalibus non potest licite oppositum tamquam fidem populo diffinire." Huss, *Tractatus de Ecclesia* (Cambridge, Eng., 1956), chap. 16 D [p. 121]. This is not the strict boundary of the *consensus quinquesaecularis*: "Et simile est de sanctis aliis, ut de Johanne Cristostomo, Johanne Damasceno, Dyonisio Ariopagita qui

horizontal tradition but is seen as coming from the same source as that from which the *successio doctorum* springs.

5. The position of Occam: two distinct sources

We will now have to investigate whether and to what extent Occam, d'Ailly and Gerson grant the authority of extrascriptural Tradition. As nominalistic conciliarists they have, in common with the upholders of Tradition I described above, an extremely critical attitude toward canon lawyers. Occam states bluntly in the beginning of his *Dialogue* that modern theologians despise the stupid, presumptuous, and wild canonists.[49] D'Ailly is not less fierce in his judgment: the canonists take their decretals for divine Scriptures and hold them in such high respect that some of them are led to commit sacrilege against Holy Scripture itself.[50] He further complains that the Pope selects more prelates from among the canonists than from among the theologians.[51] In the strongest possible

Christi ecclesiam, docti a spiritu sancto, scientia et moribus, illustrarunt." *Ibid.* The same patristic authorities — with the striking omission of pseudo-Dionysius and with addition of Origen and Gregory the Great — are the most often quoted Fathers in Huss, *Sermones de tempore* ed. Anezka Schmidtova (Prague, 1959). For a parallel with Huss see Wyclif: ". . . vocate leges papales quecunque adinvenciones . . . meritorium foret et necessarium ipsas destruere," Sermo 21. 2, pp. 156, 158 f. One may at least wonder whether Melanchthon's concept of the *Ecclesia Doctrix* is necessarily of Erasmian origin. This is the view generally held, cf. Bakhuizen van den Brink, "Traditio in de Reformatie," p. 43, and Adolph Sperl, *Melanchthon zwischen Humanismus und Reformation* (Munich, 1959), p. 41. See also the illuminating analyses by Ernst Benz with regard to the connections between Bohemia and Wittenberg, especially via Melanchthon's Wendic son-in-law Caspar Peucer; *Wittenberg und Byzanz; zur Begegnung und Auseinandersetzung der Reformation und der östlich-orthodoxen Kirche* (Marburg, 1949), pp. 129 ff., 63, 66, 183.

[49] "Imprimis autem volo te scire quod auctores theologi moderni temporis canonistas tamquam non intelligentes, presumptuosos, temerarios . . . despiciunt." Occam, *Dialogus in Monarchia romani imperii*, I. 1. 3.

[50] "Sed reperio iterum in hac schola quosdam juris canonici professores, qui etiam suas decretales epistolas, quasi divinas scripturas accipiunt; et eas taliter venerantur, ut propter hoc eorum aliqui plerumque in divinarum prorumpant blasphemiam Scripturarum . . . apellatione canonicorum librorum solos comprehendens libros divinarum scripturarum et non jurium humanorum. . ." D'Ailly, *Principium in cursum Bibliae praesertim in Evangelicum Marci*, in Gerson, *Opera* I. 614. B/C. Cf. I. 611. C.

[51] "Sedes apostolica plures hodie promovet legistas et canonistas quam theologos ad ecclesiae praelaturas." D'Ailly, *Utrum indoctus in Jure Divino possit juste praeesse*, in Gerson, *Opera* I. 654 B. See also Astrik L. Gabriel, *The College System in the*

terms he accuses Hostiensis of heresy for placing canon law above the divine law of the two Testaments.[52] Gerson, too, attacks the defenders of the curialist cause for taking only their own decretals seriously, as if the divine law (Holy Scripture) were not the law and the standard according to which true law is judged.[53] This attack on the curialistic position is directed in fact against the extreme canonists, but it leads Gerson to stress as Huss does the contrast between divine law and human traditions.[54] This is, however, the extent to which their anticurialistic

---

Fourteenth Century Universities (Baltimore, n.d. [1962]), p. 3. Myron P. Gilmore has called attention to the bitter criticism of the humanist lawyers against the "Bartolist" position, which represents an ahistorical adaptation of the Roman law to feudal and ecclesiastical conditions. "The Lawyers and the Church in the Italian Renaissance," *The Rice Institute Pamphlet*, 46 (1960), 136–154; esp. 137 ff. The interrelation of the anti-"Bartolist" and the anti-Basilean positions deserves further study in view of the (temporary) alliance of the humanists and Reformers.

[52] "Negatur plane et sine ulla reverentia dictum Hostienum tanquam falsum et haereticum si intelligat generaliter, quod Juris scientia sit dicenda scientia scientiarum et omnibus aliis anteponenda: excipienda enim est theologia." D'Ailly, *Utrum indoctus* . . . in *Opera* I. 655 D. Cf. Hostiensis, dist. 19 can. 1; I, p. 58f., *CIC*. On Hostiensis' "non ubi Roma est ibi Papa, sed econverso," see Ernst H. Kantorowicz, *The King's Two Bodies: A Study in Medieval Political Theology* (Princeton, 1957), p. 204.

[53] "Haec irritatio legis nonne manifesta est in eis qui nullam viam pro sedatione schismatis dicunt juridicam, nisi quam libri sui scriptam habent; quasi jus divinum non esset jus, neque via sibi consona dici juridica mereretur. Referrem hic quamplurima super determinationibus et novis irritantibus legem Domini ut de potestate papae sui, quem volunt eximi a quavis humana subjectione, cum jus divinum subjiciat eum omni humanae creaturae propter deum . . . subjiciat et universali ecclesiae tanquam infallibili regulae credendorum simul et agendorum; subjiciat tandem ex dabili casu culpae incorrigibilis, cuique volenti nedum ab eo appellare, sed eundem incarcerare, vel occidere." *Collatio pro facultate decretorium*, Gerson *Opera* IV. 705 D/706 A. Once there is even a hint of a Joachimite ideal of the *ecclesia spiritualis*. Otto von Gierke has pointed to the "Anstaltliche Charakter" of Gerson's ecclesiology. Wyclif and Huss are said to be the first to interiorize "the spiritual state." *Das deutsche Genossenschaftsrecht*, III, 2 ed. (Darmstadt, 1954), 540 ff.

[54] Cf. Gerson, *Opera* III. 16 D. "Quid praeterea (Deus aequissime) sunt tot traditiones, nisi totidem laquei, vincula et retes, pro retinendis implicandisque pedibus humilium ambulare volentium secundum Legem perfectae libertatis quam Christus in paucissimis voluit Sacramentis contineri. Ecclesia rursus quae tota spiritualis esse debuerat tota coelestis, nonne per traditiones hujusmodi fere tota, immo penitus in brutalem sensualitatem miseranda vicissitudine dilapsa est?" Gerson, *Opera* III. 16 D. E. F. Jacob calls attention to the mystical form of Gerson's ecclesiology in connection with his important *Sermo Constantiensis*, *Opera* II, 201 ff., which contains twelve ecclesiological theses (*Ibid.* 205). *Essays in the Conciliar Epoch*, 2 ed. (Manchester, 1953), p. 12.

protestations lead these three nominalists in the direction of *Traditio I*.

Turning now to Occam in particular, we note first on grounds of the evidence available that his attack on the *Canonistae* of his day should not be regarded as a rejection of the authority of canon law as such. Recent research on Occam's use of canonistic materials has clearly established his dependence on the canon lawyers of the thirteenth century.[55] There is no basis for the contention that Occam would pit *sola scriptura* against canon law as such. It is more accurate to say that Occam employed what seemed to him well-established legal tradition against curialistic innovations.

In contrast to upholders of *Traditio I*, Occam does not identify the *successio fidei* with the *successio doctorum*. Final decisions with respect to orthodoxy and heterodoxy must be built "chiefly" on the interpretation of Holy Scripture, the contents of which are defined by theologians *per modum doctrinae*. A definition *per modum auctoritatis* must rely, though only for a small part, also on extrascriptural sources. The rationale of this we find also in the *Dialogue*, a few pages beyond his condemnation of the "wild" canonists. But the form in which the argument is cast is not conducive to seeing the full import of this passage, since Occam asks a question basically different than the one asked by contemporary scholars.

Occam asks whether the Church creates catholic truths *de novo*, that is, declares doctrines true which were not true before. The answer is by no means unexpected. No, the Church merely formulates what truth is in a particular respect since truth is eternal. Occam's rejection of the *de novo* character of definitions *per modum auctoritatis* is essentially the rejection of a biological, immanent evolution of doctrine. The rejection does *not* imply that Occam rejects the concept of development of doctrine as such. His discussion of the Immaculate Conception of the Virgin Mary is evidence of this. The official definition of a doctrine is not the creation of a new truth, but the discernment and acknowledgment of a truth which — we may add in the spirit of Occam — had been "overlooked" by the Church thus far.[56]

---

[55] C. C. Bayley, "Pivotal Concepts in the Political Philosophy of William of Ockham," *Journal of the History of Ideas* 10 (1949), 199 ff. Brian Tierney, "Ockham, the Conciliar Theory, and the Canonists," *Journal of the History of Ideas* 15 (1954), 40 ff.

[56] Occam ends his discussion of the five modes in which truth is received by the Church with the words: "Nihil autem praedictorum ex approbatione . . . veritatis catholica potest fieri, sed per talem approbationem aliquam veritatem fuisse et

While *Occam* is intent on proving this point, *we* are interested in his point of departure. The premise of his argument is that there are five modes possible that lead to the acknowledgment of a doctrine: (1) revealed by God; (2) contained in Holy Scripture; (3) received by the Church universal; (4) conclusions drawn from doctrines received in the first three ways; (5) approved by the Pope.[57]

In his further analysis Occam shows that these *five* possible *modes* can be reduced to *two* different *sources*: the first or the second. The third mode — and this is the point we are most interested in — can be reduced to either (1) or (2) since the Church universal receives a "new" doctrine *either* because it is contained in Holy Scripture *or* because it is otherwise revealed to her by God. This applies then also to (4) and (5): the Pope and the Church have therefore to rely on one of two sources: scriptural and extra-scriptural revelation.[58]

---

esse catholicam *dignoscitur et definitur*." *Dialogus*, I. 2. 12. in *Monarchia romani imperii*, ed. Goldast, II, p. 420. It seems to me that van Leeuwen, in his excellent article "L'Église règle de foi chez Occam," judges Occam's concept of tradition too harshly probably because he compares it with a post-Newman concept of tradition, and thus misses the novelty and significance of these five modes of reception, "Pour lui une définition ecclésiastique est une simple reproduction des vérités révélées: une vérité est objet de la foi catholique avant comme après l'approbation de l'Église ou la proposition par le magistère. Cette accentuation des règles éloignées de la foi aux dépens de la règle prochaine, devrait conduire Occam à la conclusion que le rôle de l'Église et du magistère dans la proposition de la foi est absolument accessoire" (p. 273).

[57] "Si aliqua veritas est catholica aut est dicenda catholica quia a deo revelata, vel quia in scripturis divinis contenta vel quia ab universali ecclesia recepta vel sequitur ex illis vel aliquo illorum quae sunt divinitus revelata et in scripturis divinis inventa et ab ecclesia universali recepta vel quia a summo pontifice approbata." Occam, *Dialogus*, I. 2. 12 in *Monarchia romani imperii*, ed. Goldast, II, 419.

[58] "Si aliqua veritas ideo est catholica quia est a deo revelata . . . approbatio summi pontificis nihil facit ad hoc quod talis veritas sit vere catholica — Si detur secundum . . . talis veritas absque omni approbatione tali est inter veritates catholicas numeranda . . . si tertium detur . . . quaerendum est quare ecclesia universalis talem receperit veritatem. Vel quia sic divinitus approbatur, revelatur vel inspiratur et tunc absque tali receptione ecclesiae vere est catholica . . . aut quia eam in divinis scripturis invenit . . . , si detur quartum . . . per talem approbationem non fit catholica . . . , si detur quintum . . . tunc quaerendum est an summus pontifex innitatur alicui revelationi vel etiam scripturis sacris aut doctrinae ecclesiae universalis; quodcunque illorum detur, sequitur quod summus pontifex per approbationem suam non facit talem veritatem fuisse et esse catholicam." Occam, *Dialogus* I. 2. 12 in *Monarchia romani imperii*, ed. Goldast, II, 419. Holcot also argues from an extrabiblical though apostolic tradition: "Utrum licet christianis aliquas imagines adorare. . . ? Item in canone scripture legitur nihil tale esse con-

We have good reason to believe that Occam is eager to build as strong a case as possible. For he attacks here a basic term "deinceps" used in the *Cum inter nonnullos* of Pope John XXII according to which "from now onwards"[59] it would be heretical to assert that Christ and his disciples had no private or communal property. Considering that the problem of evangelical poverty is never far from Occam's mind,[60] we may well conclude that Occam is not just playing with the two-sources theory but that he indeed believes in the solidity of the argument in its totality.

This conclusion helps us to interpret the more obscure passage in the *Dialogue* to which we have referred where Occam contrasts the *sola scriptura* principle with that of a principle of two doctrinal sources. Here he merely states that some restrict catholic truths to what is implicitly or explicitly contained in Holy Scripture, while *others* hold that there are extrascriptural truths. If our first conclusion is justified, it is clear that this second position is that of Occam himself.[61]

6. The position of Pierre d'Ailly: the law of Christ

Turning now to d'Ailly, we see again that though his attack on the canonists can be violent at times, nevertheless his understanding of the relation of Scripture and Tradition is that of *Tradition II*.

---

cessum ergo superstitiosum videtur tales imagines introducere. Ad oppositum est ritus ecclesie . . . Est autem notandum quod usum imaginum in ecclesia introduxerunt apostoli, licet hoc in canone biblie nullibi exprimatur." *Sap.* Lect. 157 B/C.

[59] ". . . deinceps erroneam fore censendam et haereticam. . ." Denz. 494.

[60] Ph. Boehner, "Ockham's Political Ideas," in *Collected Articles on Ockham* (St. Bonaventure, N. Y., 1958), p. 445.

[61] ". . . multae sunt veritates catholicae quae nec in scriptura sacra continentur explicite, nec ex solis contentis in ea possunt inferri. Et multae etiam sunt veritates aliae, quas oportet certa fide tenere." *Dial.* I. 2. 2; p. 412. We would therefore be less guarded than de Vooght: "A défaut de résoudre la question, Occam a le mérite de l'avoir posée dans toute sa rigueur," p. 167. In *De erroribus Papae Johannis* XXII and in the *Breviloquium de Potestate Papae*, I. 5. 4. [ed. Baudry, (Paris, 1937), p. 135] the limitations of papal authority are clearly indicated. F. Pelster feels that "Ockham vernachlässigt sehr stark das ordentliche Lehramt der Kirche mit dem Papst an der Spitze. . ." "Die indirekte Gewalt der Kirche über den Staat nach Ockham und Petrus de Palude: Eine Übersicht," *Scholastik* 28 (1953), p. 81. Pelster goes on to prove that this entails to some extent the right of private Bible interpretation. Occam's indicated distinction, however, between *per modum auctoritatis* and *per modum doctrinae* throws another light on this issue. We are primarily interested in showing that Occam's explicit reference to *two* sources places him in *Tradition II*; the Church, even if it were understood as the remnant Church, provides the second source.

Like Occam he distinguishes between two forms of definition: the first is the official formulation of a truth *per modum auctoritatis*, the second is the establishment of truth by the exposition of Holy Scripture, *per modum doctrinae*.[62] Though d'Ailly insists on the high authority of the doctor of Scripture,[63] the two modes of definition do not coincide as regards their sources. The difference is not merely that the Pope or the Council promulgates with authority the common findings of the doctors in Holy Scripture; a second difference is that Pope or Council does not rely totally, but only "maxime" on this latter source.[64]

The difference between Occam's "chiefly" and d'Ailly's "as much as possible" does not permit us to construct a contrast between these two. In his treatise on the Holy Trinity, d'Ailly asserts that there are two main categories of truths. There are those contained explicitly in Holy Scripture, the creed and the decisions of the Church and all that can be deduced from these first three modes. Secondly there are truths that are neither explicit nor implicit in any of these. This latter category is not rejected but understood to be open for theological discussion.[65] This does not mean, however, that only Holy Scripture is binding for theologians and that all extrascriptural truth remains undefined, not received by the Church. Next to the Bible there are the decisions of the Church. At this point we see again how important the distinction *per modum doctrinae* and *per modum auctoritatis* is. The Church is not limited in its decisions to the one source of Holy Scripture, but annexed to this divine law are certain basic parts of canon law.[66] This means that in an official decision

[62] "Definitio circa ea quae sunt fidei . . . potest esse dupliciter. Uno modo scholastice et doctrinaliter. Alio modo authoritative et judicialiter." D'Ailly *Apologia*, in Gerson, *Opera* I. 710 A.

[63] See d'Ailly *Tractatus* I, in Gerson, *Opera* I. 723: Occam charges the doctor with the responsibility for "partem [!] quam per sacras scripturas sciunt," *Contra Bened.* fol. 239ᵛ; quoted by van Leeuwen, p. 275; for the whole period see Altenstaig, *Vocabularius Theologie* s.v. "Doctor," fol. 69ᵛ.

[64] "Doctrinalis determinatio vel definitio fidei maxime innititur scripturae sacrae." Quoted — from a treatise not published in the *Opera* but in the *Collectio Judiciorum* of C. Duplessis d'Argentré, vol. I (Paris, 1728), 77; de Vooght, p. 237.

[65] "Quaedam sunt quae in textu sacrae scripturae, vel symboli, aut determinationibus ecclesiae formaliter continentur, vel ex talibus evidenter sequuntur . . . Ideo tales sub nullo sensu vel glossa sunt negandae, vel earum contradictoriae concedendae, sed aliae sunt quae in talibus scripturis expresse non continentur, nec ex eis clare sequuntur et tales disputationi doctorum relinquuntur. . ." *De Tribus suppositis in una natura*, *Opera* I. 627. B.

[66] "Expressa quidem per scripturam authenticam, sicut per authoritatem scrip-

the Church relies not only on the testimony of the doctors of Scripture, but also on that of the canon lawyers.

This explains, then, why the Church, according to d'Ailly, has only to rely "as much as possible" and not altogether on those whose task it is to interpret Scripture. It is clear that d'Ailly belongs to those who uphold Tradition II. However much the authority of the doctor of Scripture may be stressed, the *successio fidei* is only partially established by the *successio doctorum*: the ongoing interpretation of Holy Scripture does for a very important part, but nevertheless only for a part contribute to the development of doctrine, that is, to the ongoing task of the Church to define and receive Catholic truths.

We have to answer one more question before we can turn our attention to Gerson. How shall we understand d'Ailly's attack on the canon lawyers when he does after all acknowledge the importance of their legal contributions to theology? As chancellors of the University of Paris, neither d'Ailly nor Gerson wanted to abolish the faculty of the "two laws"; they merely attacked the extremists among the canonists, such as Hostiensis, by enlisting a more moderate canonist like Gratian in their defense. It is nevertheless important to note that this is not a matter of expediency, an attempt to divide and conquer. The attack on Hostiensis is part of a larger scheme to define the relation of Scripture and canon law; and in the process of placing both in a larger context, not only the authority of canon law, but also that of Holy Scripture becomes relative.

In his treatise on the relation of the Church and the Law, d'Ailly stresses that there is only one law, and that is the law of Christ.[67] This *sola lex* is contrasted with *sola scriptura* by the argument that law can be viewed as a concept, a written document, or a spoken word. Now before there was any written or spoken law, the law itself nevertheless

---

turae divinae vel constitutionem ecclesiae vel bullam apostolicam aut aliam litteram authenticam alicuius personae vel collegii in hoc potestatem habentis. Et sic expresse approbata est doctrina scripturae sacrae novi et veteris testamenti, generalium conciliorum, epistularum Decretalium et quorundam opusculorum sanctorum patrum. . ." D'Ailly, *Apologia*, in Gerson, *Opera* I. 715 C/D. Cf. *ibid.*, 710 C/D. See also d'Ailly's repeated discussion method, *De institutione ecclesie* in *Sacramentale seu Tractatus theologicus de Sacramentis* (Lovanii, 1487), cap. 2 G; 12 T; 13 C, I.

[67] ". . . Lex Christi sola seu doctrina, id est fidei infusae habitus, vel actus quem viator habet de ea, est sibi perfectissima lex creata." D'Ailly, *Utrum Petri ecclesia lege reguletur*, in Gerson, *Opera* I. 664 C.

existed.[68] This argument is first turned against the canonists, Gratian included, since they occupy themselves merely with written law.[69] But it equally counts against the *sola scriptura* principle, since before the New Testament was written, the Church already existed.

The superiority of the Church over Scripture applies of course not to the "present-day Church" alone, but to the faithful of all the generations since the time of Christ.[70] This Church stands above Holy Scripture since the biblical authors were already members of the Church before they had written the books of the Bible. It is not so noteworthy that Augustine's reference to the instrumental authority of the Church is quoted here — this passage is invariably the medieval authority in this context — as that *commovere* in this passage is replaced by *compellere* and interpreted as *approbare*, a term which suggests more of a duality between Scripture and Church than the phrasing of Augustine's text itself.[71]

7. The position of Gerson: the spirit-guided Church

We can now be more concise in our discussion of Gerson's position. Like d'Ailly, Gerson defends the sufficiency [72] of Holy Scripture as containing all the truths necessary for salvation without holding the *sola scriptura* principle in the sense of Tradition I.[73] Gerson distinguishes

[68] ". . . nullo existente scripto vel voce, adhuc lex esset. . ." *Ibid* D.

[69] ". . . Gratianus et alii solum definiunt legem scriptam." *Ibid* 665 A.

[70] "Hoc enim modo ecclesia est majoris auctoritatis quam evangelium sit: quia huius ecclesiae evangelista, seu scriptor evangelii pars existit." *Ibid.* 666 A.

[71] ". . . Evangelio non crederet nisi eum ecclesiae auctoritas compelleret." *Ibid.* Cf. ". . . secundus gradus est veritatum ab ecclesia determinatarum et quae indubitata revelatione apostolorum per successionem continuam devenerunt. Est autem haec ecclesiae auctoritas tanta, ut dixit Augustinus: "In evangelio non crederem si non auctoritas sacrae scripturae impelleret. . ." *Quae veritates sunt de necessitate salutis credendae.* Cod. monac. lat. 5338. fol. 184ʳ quoted by Bernhard Meller, *Studien zur Erkenntnislehre des Peter von Ailly*, Freiburger Theologische Studien 67 (Freiburg i.Br., 1953), p. 183. This MS is, according to Meller, probably from the hand of d'Ailly. The passage quoted by Meller is largely identical with the *Declaratio Veritatum quae credendae sunt de necessitate salutis* edited by Du Pin as a work of Gerson. There is an interesting addition here, however: "Evangelio non crederem nisi me auctoritas ecclesiae catholicae compelleret quamquam vicissim dici possit ecclesiae non crederem sinon auctoritas sacrae scripturae impelleret." *Opera* I. 22 C.

[72] ". . . scriptura nobis tradita est tanquam regula sufficiens et infallibilis. . . ," *Opera* I. 12. D.

[73] ". . . non obligantur credere nisi per miraculum evidens vel scripturam

again the two modes of definition by the Church and the doctors of Scripture.[74] In a treatise directed against the followers of Huss, the importance of the ongoing enterprise of scriptural exposition is stressed.[75] But Scripture cannot be isolated; it has to be understood with the help of Tradition, and this Tradition includes canon law.[76]

In this treatise we see most clearly that though Gerson sees the danger of the extremists under the canonists, he opposes Huss' more restricted concept of Tradition. Gerson's mystical ecclesiology may betray itself in his ideal of the *ecclesia spiritualis*, but this does not lead him to contrast spirit and law. The doctrine of the Church is the final standard; this doctrine has priority not only over the individual doctor, but also over Holy Scripture since it was the Church that separated the canonical from the noncanonical books.[77]

It is important to note that the priority of the Church over Holy Scripture is not only the practical priority of Augustine's *commovere*, but is also a theoretical priority, *approbare*. Along with the catholic truths implicitly or explicitly contained in Holy Scripture, there is a second category of truths that are received by the Church directly from the apostles through apostolic succession.[78]

The same Holy Spirit which Gerson calls the form of the Church and which provides the Church with life and unity[79] also provides the Church

---

sacram et praecipue per ecclesiam detur certitudo." *Ibid.* I. 22. D. Compare further Gerson, *Opera* I. 27 B. with d'Ailly in Gerson, *Opera* I. 666 C.

[74] *Ibid.* 33 C. Gerson agrees with Occam — without naming him — that the unorthodoxy of a heresy is never "deinceps."

[75] *Opera* I. 457 B–458 C. "Scriptura sacra recipit interpretationem ex expositione nedum in suis verbis originalibus, sed etiam in suis expositionibus. . . " *Contra haeresim de communione laicorum. Opera* I. 459 A.

[76] "Scriptura sacra non ita recipienda est nude et in solidum, contemptis aliis traditionibus hominum quin debeat ad intelligentiam veram ipsius habendam, juribus humanis et canonibus et decretis et glossis sanctorum doctorum frequenter humiliter uti." *Opera* I. 458 C.

[77] ". . . nulla auctoritas cuiuscumque scripturae aut doctoris habet efficaciam ad aliquid probandum . . . nisi inquantum doctrinae ecclesiasticae congrueret; aut ab ecclesia approbaretur . . . Non solum doctrinae doctoris sed etiam ipsi canonice praefert [Augustinus] ecclesiam." *Opera* I. 463 A. Gerson's use of the distinction between *interpretatio iuridica* and *interpretatio scholastica* in his *De sollicitudine ecclesiasticorum* is noted by Biel; *Lect.* 28 M refers to *Opera* II. 605 B.

[78] "Secundus gradus est veritatum ab ecclesia determinatarum quae ab indubitata relatione apostolorum per successionem continuam devenerunt." *Opera* I. 22. C.

[79] "Ipse enim spiritus sanctus qui est spiritus christi est etiam suo modo forma

with the proper interpretation of Holy Scripture. The Church as the instrument of the Spirit is the infallible rule in matters of faith.[80] Scripture is the matter, the Spirit and the Church the form: thus is one tempted to characterize Gerson's position. This, however, is still not a complete description. The Spirit not only brings the form but has also inserted some matter into the body of the Church via an extrascriptural revelation given to the apostles and handed down by them to the Church. These truths can be found in Holy Scripture, but not as directly as those implicitly or explicitly contained in a literal-spiritual sense in Scripture.[81]

8. The position of Breviscoxa: the second source

Gerson's position can perhaps best be evaluated in comparison with that of d'Ailly, his predecessor as chancellor of the University of Paris, and Johannes Breviscoxa, who received his theological doctor's degree in 1388,[82] six years later than Gerson. All three were connected with the College of Navarre.

Once in a debate concerning the *plenitudo potestatis*, d'Ailly objected to the use of extrascriptural arguments in theological debate. When criticized by his opponent on grounds of the clearly extrascriptural basis for such orthodox doctrines as those of the Trinity and Transubstantiation, he replied that in regard to the *plenitudo potestatis* no such extrascriptural oral Tradition exists.[83] His reply indicates not only that he — like Occam and Rimini before and Gerson later — would admit only

---

corporis ecclesiae prebens ei vitam, unitatem et motum. . ." *De auferibilitate papae ab ecclesia, Opera* II. 211. B.

[80] "Haec enim est infallibilis regula a spiritu sancto directa qui in his quae fidei sunt nec fallere potest nec falli." *Opera* I. 459 C.

[81] "Primus gradus veritatum credendarum est canon totius scripturae sacrae et singulorum quae in ea litteraliter asserta sunt, sic videlicet quod non stat cum fide ut aliquis dissentiat pertinaciter alicui contento in eadem scriptura ad intellectum spiritus sancti qui est vere et proprie sensus litteralis." *Opera* I. 22 B.

[82] Du Pin, *Opera* I. p. XL.

[83] "Nam multa circa materiam trinitatis et corporis christi tenemur credere quae sacra scriptura non expressit sed per doctrinam vocalem apostolorum et traditiones ecclesiae ad nos pervenerunt." *Opera* I. 675 D. Tavard took this for d'Ailly's own proposition, although it is clear — the text in notes 84 and 85 surround this passage — that d'Ailly is quoting his critic. See Tavard, p. 55. Fritz Hahn quotes this passage even as if it were Gerson's; "Zur Hermeneutik Gersons," *ZThK* 51 (1954), 40.

scriptural evidence in theological debate,[84] but also that he did not deny the *principle* of oral, extrascriptural tradition.[85]

Breviscoxa reports in his treatise *De fide et ecclesia* the same two opinions that Occam contrasted in his *Dialogue*: *some* hold that all catholic truths are implicitly or explicitly contained in Holy Scripture, *others* that there are many truths necessary for salvation which are neither contained in it nor are necessary conclusions from Scripture alone.[86]

Breviscoxa opts for the latter opinion and follows this up with a list of catholic truths which leaves far more room for extrascriptural truths than is the case with Gerson.[87] It appears from Gerson's second category of catholic truths that he agrees with d'Ailly so far as the *principle* of the extrascriptural oral tradition is concerned but that he does not hold Breviscoxa's *application* of this principle. For Gerson *the relation of Scripture and Church is almost that of matter and form*: in the apostolic succession, it is not the separate truths which are handed down but the proper interpretation of Holy Scripture.

[84] "Hic autem dicit quod miratur de modo meo arguendi . . . dicendo: 'hoc non habetur ex scriptura sacra, igitur temerarium est hoc asserere." *Opera* I. 675 D. Here follows the last quote. Cf. Gerson, *Opera* I. 2. B.

[85] "Ad haec respondeo quod in materia de qua loquimur non erat opus de hoc expresse mentionem facere cum sit clarum quod nec ex doctrina vocali apostolorum aut traditione ecclesiae habetur quod. . ." *Opera* I. 675 D.

[86] "Dicunt enim quidam quod illae veritates sunt catholicae et de necessitate salutis credendae quae in canone bibliae explicite asseruntur vel quae ex solis contentis in ea consequentia necessaria et formali possunt inferri . . . Alii dicunt quod pluribus veritatibus quae nec in sacris litteris habentur nec ex solis contentis in eis necessario sequuntur, de necessitate salutis est assentiendum." *Opera* I. 829 B; 830 A.

[87] "Secundum genus est earum quae ab apostolis ad nos per successivam revelationem [sic] vel scripturas fidelium pervenerunt licet in sacris scripturis non innumerantur nec ex eis possunt concludi." *Opera*. I. 821 A. Biel does not use the term "per successivam revelationem," but "per successivam relationem." See note 105, below and its interpretation in note 112. In his "De Jurisdictione Spirituali" Gerson quotes Occam: ". . . ad ostendendum quod aliquae sunt veritates Catholicae quae non sunt in Biblia . . . ut sunt illae quae venerunt ad nos ex relatione successiva Apostolorum." *Opera* II.263 C. The succeeding words establish Gerson's agreement with Occam: "Et puto quod nec etiam apud Graecos hoc vertatur in dubium. . ." Cf. *Opera* I.29 C. In the article cited in note 83 Fritz Hahn did not note that Du Pin published in *Opera* I a number of non-Gersonian treatises. The unfortunate result is that the basic documentation of his article on Gerson rests on Breviscoxa rather than on Gerson. This is especially awkward in view of A. Combes' thesis according to which Gerson in his attack on Ruysbroeck would have had Breviscoxa in mind. *Essai sur la critique de Ruysbroeck par Gerson*, II, 108 ff.

Gerson does not yet define this as precisely as a group of Roman Catholic theologians did recently in their effort to reinterpret the Council of Trent.[88] But here we discover what he really meant in saying that Church and Scripture confirm each other.[89] The literal sense of Scripture is its meaning as intended by the Holy Spirit; this sense is revealed by Christ through his apostles to the Church.[90] But through the ongoing definition of truth by the Church, the canonical boundaries are enlarged and Holy Scripture is materially extended.

While it proved to be characteristic for Tradition I that Tradition was seriously heard but that the canonical books of Holy Scripture were definitely given the final authority in matters of faith, this is not the case with Gerson. For him postcanonical documents of a theological and legal nature, if received by the Church, can without distinction be regarded as expressing the *sensus litteralis* of Holy Scripture itself.[91] Though Gerson holds essentially the same position as d'Ailly, note that they differ in that d'Ailly defines what transcends Holy Scripture as the *law of Christ*, while Gerson defines this as the *Spirit-guided Church*. In both cases the

[88] Josef Geiselmann defines the relation of Scripture and Tradition as "reziprokes Verhältnis": "Die Heilige Schrift des neuen Testaments ist die Norm, an der der Inhalt der apostolischen Tradition in der Form der lebendigen Daseinsweise in der kirchlichen Überlieferung zu prüfen ist. Die kirchliche Tradition aber als das geistgeleitete autoritative Verständnis der apostolischen Tradition ist Norm für das Verständnis der in der Heiligen Schrift enthaltenen apostolischen Tradition." "Die Tradition," in *Fragen der Theologie Heute*, p. 98. With obvious agreement Geiselmann quotes Möhler (*Die Einheit in der Kirche*, 16.8) who defined the relation of Scripture and Tradition essentially as *materia* and *forma*. Through Scripture we possess "den zuverlässigen Stoff," through tradition "den Geist und das Interesse." Through Scripture we know *"wie* der Gottmensch sprach," through tradition we know *"wer* da redete und was er verkündete." The "new" understanding of the problem by a group of such significant theologians as Deneffe, Rahner, Karrer, Congar, Chenu, and Daniélou is, according to Geiselmann, best formulated by A. M. Dubarle in "Mélanges Jules Lebreton" I, *RSR* 39 (1951). "Schrift-Tradition-Kirche, Ein Oekumenisches Problem," in: *Begegnung der Christen. Studien evangelischer und katholischer Theologen*, (Frankfurt, 1959), p. 155.

[89] *Opera* I. 22 C.

[90] "Sensus litteralis sacrae scripturae fuit primo per Christum et Apostolos revelatus. . ." *Opera* I. 3 C.

[91] "Sensus litteralis sacrae scripturae si reperitur determinatus et decisus in decretis et decretalibus et codicibus conciliorum, judicandus est ad theologiam et sacram scripturam non minus pertinere quam symbolum apostolorum, propterea non est spernendus tamquam humana seu positiva constitutione fundatus." *Opera* I. 3 D.

sola scriptura principle functions in the restricted sense of Tradition II.

Gerson indeed acknowledges the important role of the doctor of Scripture, and gives the impression that for him there is a real doctoral succession. In contrast to Huss he makes no sharp differentiation between the first five centuries and later tradition: "In all ages the doctors instructed in Holy Scripture have the authority to expound and proclaim truths which are derived from Scripture just like the ancient doctors."

Nevertheless the operation of the Holy Spirit is not restricted to the illumination of the doctors in their study of Holy Scripture: "the Holy Spirit reveals sometimes to the Church and to later doctors truths or expositions of Holy Scripture which have not been revealed to their predecessors. . ."; "[The feast of] the Nativity of our Lady was ordained by revelation to one single woman." [92]

We cannot be far wrong when we venture to say that Gerson did not impute a tradition of richer content to the episcopal succession than to the doctoral succession, but that for him the Spirit-guided Church contains and transcends both these channels. While Holy Scripture is the largest part of the *norma normata*, it is not so much Tradition — either doctoral or episcopal — but the living Church which is the *norma normans*. "Thus we are able to say that this truth that our Lady was not at all conceived in original sin is among those which are newly revealed or declared, as much by miracles about which we read as well as by the fact that they are held now by the better part of the Holy Church." [93]

9. Tradition I and Tradition II: a fundamental principle of classification

A survey of our findings at this point indicates as a first conclusion that the nominalists we have discussed so far can by no means be praised for, or accused of having reintroduced the *sola scriptura* principle. Though their critical attitude toward what they see as the growing influence of the canon lawyers seems to suggest a common bond with theologians like Wyclif and Huss, such conciliarists as Occam, d'Ailly, and Gerson attack the curialist position, not on grounds of Scripture alone, nor of Scripture as interpreted by the doctors of Scripture, but on

[92] *Six sermons français inédits de Jean Gerson*, p. 421.
[93] *Ibid.*, p. 421.

grounds of the superior authority of the Church which derives its knowledge of revealed truths from two sources: Scripture and Tradition. And we cannot, without qualification, accuse them of ecclesiastical positivism, since the new truths promulgated must rely chiefly or as much as possible on Holy Scripture and must in any case be tested as to their truthfulness by the Church in its entirety.

As regards contemporary research, a second conclusion is that Tavard's thesis of a fourteenth-century disintegration of the classical principle of coinherence of Scripture and Church does not take into account the fact that since Basil and Augustine there had been a growing awareness of extrascriptural tradition. The tension between the sufficiency and "silence" of Holy Scripture as regards the so-called "catholic truths" belongs to the legacy that the fourteenth century inherited.

Furthermore, there is no evidence to support the hypothesis of a demarcation line between orthodoxy and heterodoxy to be drawn between Gerson and d'Ailly. While we still have to investigate in more detail whether Biel deviates from Occam, classified by Tavard along with Wessel Gansfort as "orthodox," it is clear that the difference between Gerson and his predecessor d'Ailly is minute in comparison with the concept of Tradition they hold in common.

Our fourth conclusion is that the decisive late-medieval demarcation line is the one which runs between what we have termed Tradition I and Tradition II. The representatives of the first concept of Tradition by no means isolate Holy Scripture by divorcing it from Tradition understood as the history of interpretation of Scripture. Nor do the upholders of the second concept of Tradition necessarily belong to the curialists and their vocal representatives, the canon lawyers. Critical as they may be of this latter group, both Gerson and d'Ailly stress not only the practical but also the ontological priority of the Church over Holy Scripture as appears clearly from their acknowledgment of authoritative and extrascriptural Tradition.

The issue at stake between curialism and conciliarism has proved thus to be far less significant for the problem of Scripture and Tradition than we have been inclined to think hitherto. Whereas d'Ailly and Gerson contest the curialist thesis of the superiority and unconditional primacy of the See of St. Peter, they accept extrascriptural tradition along with the curialists, though its reception is differently conceived.

For both d'Ailly and Gerson, Holy Scripture is only sufficient inasmuch as one — and we may presume the major — category of catholic truths is contained therein. They are true disciples of Occam in holding that other truths have been revealed and may still be revealed, not as a result of the contributions of the doctors of Scripture but as a result of a handing down of an unwritten oral tradition through the episcopal succession, or even as a result of post-apostolic "new" revelation.

Whereas at places Gerson seems more mindful than d'Ailly of the necessity of alleviating the post-Augustinian tension between Scripture and Tradition in terms that would suggest a matter-form relation, his acceptance of the post-apostolic origin of the doctrine of the Immaculate Conception of the Virgin Mary is particularly indicative of his adherence to the teaching of Occam and d'Ailly. Therefore, if one wishes to doubt the orthodoxy of d'Ailly, he must evaluate Occam and Gerson similarly.

Finally we can conclude that though de Vooght in particular has stimulated contemporary research on the pre-Tridentine and pre-Reformation understanding of the relation of Scripture and Tradition, some of his major conclusions will have to be reconsidered. We have found ample evidence to support his view that the issue of scriptural and extrascriptural tradition clearly became explicit in the post-Occam period. The very fact that the problem itself was brought out in the open enabled theologians like Occam, Wyclif, and Gerson to pay proper attention to it and to work *toward* a synthesis of Scripture and Tradition. We are less inclined than de Vooght to credit these late medieval theologians with having actually reached the point where thesis — Scripture — and antithesis — Tradition — merge into a new synthetic unity.[94] But even if one is willing to admit that Wyclif, Occam, and Gerson do reach this point, the historian of Christian thought proves to be little helped by the application of this Hegelian terminology. On closer consideration we must say that if we want to speak in terms of syntheses, the syntheses of Wyclif and Huss on the one hand and that of Occam, d'Ailly, and Gerson on the other hand differ fully as much as Tradition I differs from Tradition II.

A further investigation may well show that to this problem there are

---

[94] "L'Écriture et la tradition se complètent . . . Elles sont stabilité et mouvement, thèse et antithèse que doit résoudre en synthèse la vie chrétienne vécue." De Vooght, p. 262.

not just two but a number of subtly differentiated solutions suggested by late medieval theologians. We would expect such an investigation to show, however, that these solutions can be divided into the two main categories we have indicated.

De Vooght's observation that according to Occam, Wyclif, and Gerson, Scripture without Tradition would become fossilized while Tradition without Scripture would lead to arbitrary fantasies is certainly well founded, but so generally true that it does not help to establish the exact course of the fundamental demarcation line which can function as a principle of classification of trends in late medieval thought. It is in the analysis of the relation of Scripture and Church that the differences in the understanding of Scripture and Tradition come to the fore. This in turn leads us to point to the difference between Tradition I and Tradition II as the decisive demarcation line. In view of the fact that these two concepts of Tradition entail automatically two different understandings of the theological enterprise as such, it is clear that the significance of this demarcation line transcends that of its narrower doctrinal context. Once theologians were faced with the option between Tradition I and Tradition II, neutrality was to prove impossible.

III. Scripture, Tradition, and Church according to Biel

1. Biel's adherence to Tradition II

Since in this context Biel's most frequently quoted school authorities are Occam, Gerson, and d'Ailly, it is easily understandable that he also holds the Tradition II understanding of the relation of Scripture and Church. However, which of the many possible arguments did he take over, and what is his own final conclusion? Since Biel wrote at a time when conciliarism had lost most of its urgency and canon lawyers were not to the same extent symbols of party politics, would he not have been freer than his conciliar predecessors to accept the idea of an extrascriptural oral tradition handed down through apostolic succession? These are the questions with which we approach Biel's ecclesiology and doctrine of Scripture.

The authority of Holy Scripture is repeatedly stressed by Biel. "Scripture alone" is used as a weapon against the presumption of the individual doctor. Contrary to the statements of any doctor of Scripture, the con-

393

tents of Scripture are self-authenticating in the sense that the truths there expressed are reliable because they are canonical. In a remark probably directed against the Dominican use of the 1323 canonization of Thomas Aquinas, Biel insists on the irrelevance of the personal sanctity of a doctor of Scripture to the reliability of his theological statements. His statements have still to be tested and compared both with Scripture and the probable conclusions drawn from Scripture.[95]

Only Holy Scripture teaches all that is to be believed and hoped and all other things necessary for salvation. Scripture is the Word of God, the very mouth of God, the standard by which we can measure the distance by which we are removed from God or our nearness to Him. This word is instruction, consolation, and exhortation which reaches us through listening, reading, meditation, and contemplation.[96] "It is sufficient for salvation to believe in general that everything revealed by God is true in the sense intended by the Holy Spirit. All these truths of revelation are contained in Holy Scripture." [97]

In this context Biel can speak in terms characteristic of Tradition I: the truth contained in the Gospel has to be understood according to the interpretations of the Fathers.[98] There is also mention of the doctoral succession which we found to be one of the characteristics of Tradition I. From the prophets and John the Baptist to the present day there has been a continuous witness by doctors and preachers to the truth.[99]

[95] "Solum canonicis scriptoribus hic honor est exhibendus ut quecumque dixerint hoc ipso vera esse credantur. Et post modicum alios ita lego ut quantalibet sanctitate quantave doctrina polleant non ideo verum putem quia ipsi ita senserunt sed quia mihi per alios auctores vel canonicas vel probabiles rationes que vero non oberrent persuadere potuerunt." *Lect.* 41 K.

[96] "Per verbum quod procedit de ore dei intelligitur omnis veritatis instructio, omnis consolatio, omnis exhortatio, omnis devotio que ex auditione, lectione, meditatione ac contemplatione divinorum eloquiorum procedit. . . Verbum eterni dei sacra scriptura que ab ore dei procedit ipsius indicat voluntatem sine cuius agnitione nemo recte vivere potest. In hac discimus quantum deo appropinquamus et quantum a deo elongamur . . . que credenda et que speranda et cetera nostre saluti necessaria *que omnia sola docet sacra scriptura.*" *Lect.* 71 G. For the parallel with Scotus see above, note 40.

[97] ". . . sufficit enim ad salutem credere in genere omnia revelata a deo in sensu per spiritum sanctum intento (qualia sunt omnia in canone biblie contenta) esse vera," I *Sent.* Prol. q 1 a 1 nota 3 D.

[98] ". . . veritas in evangelio continetur sane secundum sanctorum expositionem intellecto," *Lect.* 37 J.

[99] "Non solum nobis in scripturis sanctis precursor loquitur, loquuntur et

In one of his sermons Biel explains in a most revealing parable how one should conceive of this form of the development of doctrine. The Holy Spirit is the wind that brings the rain of divine knowledge. This rain first poured mightily down through the clouds of the Apostles and evangelists.[100] But there are also the clouds of the doctors of Scripture and confessors who dispensed the collected water of catholic doctrine of the first clouds by exposition and further clarification whenever the Church was confronted with heresies.[101]

However, even in this context there is a hint that the doctrinal tradition is not solely founded on Holy Scripture and that there is authoritative extrascriptural tradition. The rain did not come all at once since it would have been beyond man's capacity to receive it if God poured forth all his wisdom in the first clouds.[102]

In a sermon on Luke 24:32: "Did not our hearts burn within us while he talked to us on the road, while he opened to us the scriptures," Biel clarifies what it means to "open" Scripture. Christ opens Scripture in four ways: (1) by his historical acts, Christ interprets Scripture typologically — defined by Biel as allegorical exegesis; (2) by his teaching, he expounds Scripture for his disciples historically; (3) by sending the Holy Spirit, he leads his disciples to a further and deeper understanding of Scripture; (4) finally Christ calls forth doctors to illuminate Holy Scripture not only historically and allegorically — as he himself had done — but now also anagogically and tropologically.

When we apply here the well-known rhyme "littera gesta docet, quid credas allegoria, moralis quid agas, quo tendas anagogia," [103] we see that

---

prophete, loquuntur nobis apostoli et evangeliste, loquitur nobis veritas ipsa, loquuntur nobis doctores sancti ac predicatores verbi dei. . . ," *S* IV 1 F.

[100] "He nubes sunt beatissimi apostoli et evangeliste . . . vento celesti permoti velut pluviam grandem efficaciter intulerunt." *S* IV 39 C.

[101] "Sunt quoque nubes doctores sancti et confessores qui aquas catholice doctrine primarum nubium in seipsis collectas prout ecclesie cursus requisivit exponendo, declarando, abiecto hereticorum luto ordinata vicissitudine dispensabant." *Ibid.* D.

[102] "Ne enim aqua divine scientie simul fusa opprimeret potius quam irrigaret mentes humanas eum [sic] ligavit in nubibus. . ." *Ibid.*

[103] "Aperuit autem christus scripturas que de ipso erant quadrupliciter. Primo agendo et pariendo omnia que in scripturis predicta vel figurata erant de ipso. Quia defacili post facta fit applicatio figurarum ad figurata. Secundo ore proprio scripturas discipulis exponendo . . . Tertio per missionem spiritus sancti ipsos discipulos pro scripturarum intellectu extensius et plenius erudiendo. Quarto sus-

Biel finds the peculiar role of the doctor as successor to the biblical authors in their eschatological and moral interpretation of Scripture. One may further conclude that whereas Christ himself is the exegetical key for the historical and allegorical interpretation, his function is less direct in the anagogical and tropological forms of interpretation. In these forms Christ's function is restricted to the sending of the Spirit to provide the understanding of Scripture and to call forth the doctors.

This conclusion is corroborated by the phenomenon that it is not the person nor the historical life of Christ which is seen as the scriptural center, but the truth — sometimes called *veritas*, sometimes *eruditio* — that Christ revealed, that is, the will of God. For Biel the sufficiency of Holy Scripture as teaching everything necessary for salvation refers to Holy Scripture as the will or basic law of God. Furthermore, in accordance with our findings concerning the doctrines of justification and predestination, for Biel the basic theme of Holy Scripture is the truth it conveys about the justice and the love of God, which then together guide the sinner on the path of the law. At one place he states this quite clearly: the power and the mercy of God are the two focal points of biblical instruction to which *all other points* of information are related.[104] At the same time Biel does not leave any doubt that the contents of Holy Scripture do *not* exactly coincide with the body of catholic truths. This appears first of all in the four degrees Biel assumes in revelation: (1) direct revelation in Scripture especially in the Gospels; (2) conclusions drawn from Scripture; (3) conclusions drawn from truths known in these first two ways through apostolic succession, as determined by the Church; (4) special revelations to individual persons.[105]

---

citando doctores qui eas ultimata declaratione elucidarent; non solum historice et allegorice, quomodo per christum aperte fuerunt a principio, sed etiam anagogice et tropologice." *S* II 26 H. See the hermeneutical rhyme cited by Nicholas of Lyra, *Postilla*, in Gal. 4:3.

[104] "Quomodo ergo anima hominis vivere posset vita iusticie et gratie nisi cognosceret dei voluntatem et ea que secundum hanc iusta sunt vel iniusta que agenda et que fugienda, queque amanda et que contemnenda, que timenda et que audenda et que credenda et que speranda et cetera nostre saluti necessaria que omnia sola docet sacra scriptura." *Lect.* 71 G.

[105] "Possunt autem in lege pure divina assignari quattuor gradus. In primo ponuntur leges immediate revelate a deo pro tota communitate hominum aut principaliori parte: scripte in biblia et presertim in evangeliis latis a christo ad consecutionem beatitudinis. In secundo gradu ponuntur leges divine que ex precedentibus solis de-

The third degree of revelation is, of course, the sensitive juncture: from this text it could still be argued that the oral tradition is subsumed under Holy Scripture. As appears from all parallel passages, however, this is not Biel's intention: Scripture and Tradition are two distinguishable sources through which revelation flows.

It is of particular interest that Biel, in his exposition of the thesis that the Church does not create new truths but that she only receives truths which are equally true before the ecclesiastical decision, refers explicitly to the first part of Occam's *Dialogue*.[106] He feels that this makes his own treatment superfluous. Thus when he himself then concludes that there are extrascriptural catholic truths, we find our conclusion that this is indeed Occam's own point of view here corroborated by one who stands relatively closer to him in time and who has obviously studied Occam with dedication.

In a form as explicit as Breviscoxa's, Biel declares that there are many truths which are neither contained in Holy Scripture nor can be derived from Scripture alone. These may have been handed down by the Apostles either through oral tradition or through writings of the Fathers. Some are also of post-apostolic origin, that is, revealed to others than the Apostles. Truths are further defined by councils or popes, truths which are neither necessarily contained in Holy Scripture nor conclusions therefrom. The

---

ducuntur in consequentia evidenti. In tertio gradu ponuntur leges divine ex predictis deducte per successivam relationem apostolorum et aliorum equivalentem scripture canonice. Sicut determinationes ecclesie que spiritu sancto creditur regi. In quarto gradu sunt leges specialiter inspirate et revelate quibusdam singularibus personis pro se aut pro paucis ad hoc electis." III *Sent.* d 37 q 1 art. 1 C. On the Catholic truths see IV *Sent.* d 13 q 2 art. 1 nota 2 D. As his third category of truths indicates, Usingen also holds the Tradition II concept: "Sunt autem credibilia talia: (1) Omnes veritates theologice, canone scripture sacre contente et que ex illis sequuntur in consequentia bona et necessaria. (2) Omnes articuli fidei Catholice, cum sequentibus ex his in bona et necessaria illatione. (3) Omnia que habet ecclesia catholica per apostolorum traditionem et revelationem non scripta in canone biblie. (4) Quecumque definivit et conclusit credenda concilium generale et plenarium, legitime in Spiritu sancto congregatum et procedens, quod catholicam, hoc est universalem ecclesiam representat." *Anabaptismus* . . . Cologne 1529, B 5 c; quoted by Nikolaus Häring, *Die Theologie des Erfurter Augustiner-Eremiten Bartholomaeus Arnoldi von Usingen* (Limburg an der Lahn, 1939), p. 112.

[106] ". . . licet materia ista de heresibus et hereticis latissima sit, et profundissime a venerabili inceptore Guilhelmo Occam in prima parte sui dyalogi disputata tamen hic breviter expediendo." IV *Sent.* d 13 q 2 art. 1 nota 1 A.

most forceful argument for the authority of the Church, thus under-stood, is that it has the promise of the Holy Spirit and so cannot err.

In a passage that could have been transcribed from d'Ailly, Biel dis-cusses all the possible meanings of the word "Church." Like d'Ailly, Biel concludes that the Church stands above Scripture insofar as the term "Church" is defined as referring to all the generations of the faithful after Christ, since the biblical author was a member of the Church of Christ.[107]

2. Biel's further contribution to the medieval dilemma

Biel does not restrict the priority of the Church over Scripture to the practical and historical priority expressed in the Augustinian *commovere*. The use Biel makes of the second principle of Augustine, according to which not only the Church moves the reader to Holy Scripture but Holy Scripture also refers the reader back to the Church, enables him to deal with greater clarity than his predecessors, Occam, d'Ailly, and Gerson, with the problem of the sufficiency of Holy Scripture.

On the one hand, Biel can say, as we saw before, that all the truths necessary for salvation are in some way contained in the Bible. On this ground Biel can assert that papal decrees regarding faith or morals are not binding if contrary to Holy Scripture.[108] This is indeed one aspect of Biel's doctrine of Holy Scripture. In this context he can speak in terms of Tradition I; saving truth is contained in Holy Scripture but has to be interpreted in the light of Tradition, which is understood as the history of biblical exposition.[109] These and similar statements explain why one is often inclined to speak of Biel's "biblicism."

But notwithstanding this clear confession of the sufficiency of Holy Scripture, Biel posits repeatedly an extrascriptural Tradition. Thus when he discusses the sacrament of baptism, he comes to the conclusion that

---

[107] "Hoc enim modo ecclesia maioris est auctoritatis quam evangelium quia huius ecclesie evangelista scriptor evangelii est pars: totum autem maioris auctoritatis est sua parte," *Lect.* 22 D.

[108] "Summi pontificis diffinitiones et precepta si contra scripturam canonicam . . . emanarent, neminem ad sui observantiam obligarent," *Def.* I 8 col. 1.

[109] "Sed hec opinio non acceptatur quia obviat scripture canonice sane intellecte et auctoritatibus sanctorum . . . veritas in evangelio continetur sane secundum sanctorum expositionem intellecto," *Lect.* 37 J.

as regards the time and place of its institution, Holy Scripture is silent. It is not this statement itself but the explanation he offers that is most interesting for our purposes: "many other things that have most certainly to be believed and done are not mentioned in the Bible."[110] Indeed Biel further offers an alternative explanation, which he owes to Duns Scotus, but the principle of extrascriptural Tradition nevertheless has been clearly enunciated.[111]

A second statement removes our last doubts. Combining the conclusions of Thomas and Scotus, Biel acknowledges that neither the form — Thomas — nor the matter — Scotus — of the sacrament of confirmation is prescribed in the Bible. "After all many things not written in Holy Scripture have been handed down to the Church by the apostles and have reached us through episcopal succession."[112] We do not need further proof to show that Biel like Occam, d'Ailly, and Gerson before him adheres to the Tradition II understanding of the relation of Scripture and Church.

While it never becomes clear how Occam and d'Ailly reconcile their acknowledgment of the sufficiency of Holy Scripture with their admission of extrascriptural tradition, and while Gerson also — though trying to solve the riddle by what appears to be a form-matter scheme — accepts

---

[110] "Probabile est igitur quod aliquo actu aut verbis publice coram suis discipulis sacramentum [baptismi] instituit, sed locum et tempus quoad actum scriptura non expressit, sicut multa alia certissime credenda vel agenda tacuit." IV *Sent.* d 1 q 4 a 3 H. Cf. IV *Sent.* d 17 q 1 a 1 G.; *Lect.* 36 A. P. "Hec autem verborum connexio quam canonem [misse]appellamus regulariter partim a christo, partim a sanctis patribus instituta est." *Lect.* 15 C.

[111] "Nec erat necessarium hoc nosse cum sufficienter ipsum sacramentum, materiam, formam usumque necessarium expressit," *ibid.* Cf. Scotus, IV *Sent.* d 3 q 4. " 'Qui vos audit me audit. . . ' [Luke 10:16] . . . In quibus et aliis fundatur potestas diffiniendi, determinandi, statuendi, decernendi precepta, leges, et canones constituendi." *Lect.* 22 K; ". . . non solum ea que ab evangelistis accepimus de christo certa fide tenemus sed etiam ea que apostolica traditione in usum venere ecclesie. . ." *Lect.* 36 P.

[112] "Quod autem tempus institutionis et modus non legitur in scriptura nihil probat: quia multa facit deus que scripta non sunt. Io. 20[:24]. Multa denique tradita sunt ecclesie ab apostolis et per successionem episcoporum ad nos derivata que non sunt scripta in canone biblie." IV *Sent.* d 7 art. 1 nota. 1 D. Cf. Thomas, IV *Sent.* d 7 q 1 art. 1 ad. 1; Scotus, *Ox.* IV d 7 q 1 art. 1. ". . . excepta confirmatione quam sub ista materia et forma qua confertur a christo traditam non legitur . . . sed ipsum sic instituisse ex traditione apostolorum verbali ecclesie sicut nonnulla alia sine ambiguitate creditur." *S* II 13 G.

nonscriptural revelation, Biel formulates the solution for which his predecessors had been searching. The statement "all that the Church believes
is catholic truth" is related to the statement "the Gospel contains the catholic truth" as premise and conclusion. Biel argues this in the following way:
"All that the Church believes contains catholic truth; the Church believes
the Gospel, therefore the Gospel contains catholic truth."[113]

This discussion takes place within the context of a traditional and by
no means a startling discussion on the nature of implicit faith. In the
same fashion Biel speaks about the relation of the statement "everything
contained in Holy Scripture is true" and the statement "God created
heaven and earth"; these two are also related as premise and conclusion.[114]

Church and Scripture can never be contrasted as rivals, but Church
and Scripture support each other in such a way that the Church has an
ontological priority over Holy Scripture. This is Biel's formulation of
the first Augustinian principle, according to which the Church has to
move the faithful to Holy Scripture.

But we find in Biel's work also the second Augustinian principle elaborated, according to which Scripture refers the faithful back to the authority of the Church. From the last words of the Gospel according to St.
Matthew: ". . . I am with you always to the close of the age," [115] Biel
draws two major conclusions: (1) the truth defined and accepted by
the catholic Church has to be believed with the same reverence as if
it were written in Holy Scripture; (2) it is necessary for salvation to
obey the precepts of the Church universal.[116] This emphasis on the function of the Church does not mean, of course, for Biel that a catholic truth
can be created *de novo*.

Biel goes on to mention the five modes of reception as reducible to the

[113] "Nam illa sequitur ex premissa vero coassumpto sic arguendo: Quicquid
credit ecclesia continet catholicam veritatem; evangelium credit ecclesia; ergo
evangelium continet catholicam veritatem." III *Sent.* d 25 q 1 art. 1 cor. 2 E. Cf.
Breviscoxa in *Tractatus de fide* . . . in Gerson *Opera* I.829 A f.
[114] III *Sent.* d 25 q 1 art. 1 nota 2 E.
[115] Mat. 28:20. *RSV*
[116] " 'Ego vobiscum sum omnibus diebus usque ad consummationem seculi'
[Matt. 28:20]. Ex quibus emergunt due fundamentales veritates corollarie . . .
Prima: veritas quam sancta mater ecclesia tanquam catholicam diffinit vel acceptat
eadem veneratione credenda est quasi in divinis litteris sit expressa . . . Secunda:
Preceptis universalis ecclesie cuius perpetua est sanctitas et iustitia, necesse est
fideles quoslibet obedire. . ." *Def.* I 1 col. 3.

two sources of Scripture and extrascriptural Tradition, but since he does not do much more than quote Occam's *Dialogue*,[117] we can omit this. Yet it is interesting to note Biel's comment that Occam marks a new departure with this catalogue of truths and that he was "followed by Gerson and many others." [118] As we saw with respect to Occam, this rejection of the *de novo* character of new truths does not mean a lack of respect for the Church as *regula proxima fidei*! In a number of places, Biel declares theological debates redundant in view of the fact that the Church has already taken a particular decision.[119]

3. Striking absence of attack on canon lawyers

Nevertheless, one different emphasis on Biel's part, in comparison with his fellow nominalists, who are along with him representatives of Tradition II, should not be overlooked. His construction of the relation of Scripture and Church makes it unnecessary to contrast the two forms of definition: *per modum auctoritatis* with *per modum doctrinae*. Unlike Occam, d'Ailly, and Gerson — and *a fortiori* unlike Wyclif and Huss — *Biel nowhere criticizes the canon lawyers or warns against the authority of the canon law.* On the contrary, he goes out of his way to stress, almost in the words of Boniface VIII, that the commands of the Pope have to be obeyed and that papal laws are binding for all the faithful.[120] These laws

[117] III *Sent.* d 25 q 1 art. 3 dub. 3; Occam, *Dialogus* I. 2. 12 in *Monarchia romani imperii*, ed. Goldast, II, 419.
[118] "Que autem veritates sint catholice reputande late in eodem libro [Dialogo] disserit [Occam] quem Gerson et plerique alii in suis scriptis sunt imitati." *Ibid.*
[119] "Olim questio illa poterit esse dubia; sed nunc post determinationem concilii constantiensis, veritatem catholicam determinantis dicere communionem sub utraque specie esse de necessitate salutis omni fideli est heresis. . ." *Lect.* 84. J; Cf. *Lect.* 40 A. Ernst Borchert, however, though at many points freeing himself of a traditional negative evaluation of nominalism, holds nevertheless as characteristic: "Eine weitgehende Ablehnung der Autoritätsauffassung in jeder Form. . ." and again a "unverantwortliche Vernachlässigung des Überlieferungscharakters der Theologie. Die Quellen der Theologie, Heilige Schrift und Tradition bleiben unbeachtet gegenüber der eigenen Spekulation. . ." *Der Einfluss des Nominalismus auf die Christologie der Spätscholastik* (Münster i.W., 1940), p. 9 f. Cf. F. Ehrle, *Der Sentenzenkommentar Peters von Candia*, p. 111.
[120] "Omnes oves christi universi sive fideles: regimini beati Petri tenebantur subesse ac de necessitate salutis vocem eius tanquam veri pastoris sequi, preceptis eius et iussionibus obedire." *Def.* I. 3 col. 1. ". . . beato Petro vite eterne clavigero terreni simul et celestis imperii iura commisit." *Def.* I 5 col. 3.

may not, of course, contradict Scripture, divine and natural law, but even in case of doubt obedience is required.[121]

Ecclesiastical tradition and ecclesiastical law together wtih Holy Scripture constitute the decisive means by which God reveals his will.[122] The individual conscience is also mentioned as one of these means; this is the dictate of right reason which never deviates from divine law, common to Christians and pagans.[123] This voice of natural law in man cannot, however, deviate from divine law as revealed in Holy Scripture, while Holy Scripture in its turn cannot contradict the decisions of the Church since the Church has been promised the abiding assistance of the Holy Spirit. There is, therefore, in Biel's theology, no place for the modern concept of the conscience as the highest tribunal.

The idea that the Church cannot *create* new doctrines is nowhere turned against the authority of the Church to *promulgate* new truths.[124] On the contrary, it proves exactly that *when* the Church accepts a particular doctrine which the individual doctor of Scripture would not have been able to discover in Scripture, it stands obviously on the firm basis of Tradition, written or unwritten.

Biel acknowledges the difficulties involved in finding a scriptural basis for the doctrine of transubstantiation, but then he points to the fact that the Church cannot establish a doctrine *de novo*, by immanent nontranscendental development. This doctrine was not necessarily known by the apostolic Church at the time of the institution of the Eucharist. It may well have been later "discovered," so Biel continues, due to post-apostolic

[121] "Sanctionibus ac decretis apostolicis quas scripture sacre, legi divine et naturali obviare certum non est etiamsi dubium fuerit assensus et obedientia est prestanda." *Def.* I 9 col. 2.

[122] ". . . innotescit dei voluntas per consuetudines rationabiles, institutiones et traditiones universalis ecclesie . . . ex preceptis et constitutionibus eciam patrum et ecclesie prelatorum quorum est divinorum habere scientiam et voluntatem ac legem explicare." *Lect.* 69 B. The *Expositio* shows that Biel is thoroughly acquainted with the canon lawyers, and that he can refer with respect to the "dominos Canonistas." See *Lect.* 9 D.

[123] "Primo per naturalis rationis dictamen et iudicium . . . Dictamen igitur recte rationis manifestatio est legis divine." *Lect.* 69 A.

[124] Cf. his statements with regard to the *Festum Corporis Christi* to establish the Immaculate Conception: "Neque tamen humana devotione inventa est sed spiritus sancti revelatione instituta. . ." *S* III 1 H. "Non tua voluntate beneplacito aut sapientia quia non est fides in sapientia hominum que stulticia est apud deum, secundum apostolum. Sed quia verum hoc esse ecclesia cognovit." *Lect.* 41 L.

revelation to the Church fathers who transmitted it in their writings or due to their intensive study in Holy Scripture.[125]

On the basis of his Tradition II position, Biel can stress the fact that the legal institutional Church and the Church of the creed coincide. Outside the Church no salvation is possible; neither baptism nor good works can avail without submission to the decisions of the Church. The ineradicable center of the Body of Christ, the Church, is the papal see founded on apostolic succession.[126]

4. The hermeneutical problem and tradition

Two occasions in Biel's life make it possible to see how far-reaching were the implications of his understanding of the relation of Scripture and Church. In 1462, at the time of the Mainz interdict, Biel wrote his *Defense of Obedience to the Pope*. In the conclusion of this treatise, Biel indicates the hermeneutical significance of his presuppositions: the meaning of scriptural passages can easily be perverted. Conclusions drawn from Holy Scripture are only probable arguments which are never so clear that they cannot be contradicted by people who want to interpret Scripture in such a way that it suits their own taste. In such a case the papal see has to decide what Holy Scripture really says.[127] While a declaration of submission to the judgment of the Church as such is by no means un-

---

[125] "Sed cur hunc intellectum difficilem sancti dicere et ecclesia determinare elegerunt cum scripture possunt exponi et salvari secundum intellectum facilem de hoc articulo . . . Non enim in potestate ecclesie fuit hunc intellectum verum facere vel non verum sed dei institutis. Intellectum autem hunc a deo verum factum et traditum, ecclesia explicavit, directa in hoc, ut creditur, a spiritu sponsi sui christi . . . Ordinatio autem hec fortasse innotuit ecclesie longo tempore post sacramenti institutionem. Et creditum primum sanctis patribus revelata qui scriptis suis posteros docuerunt vel saltem ipsi per studiosam scripturarum explanationem invenerunt." *Lect.* 41 J.

[126] "Necesse ergo est membrum christi fore quisquis voluerit in celum recipi. Sed quomodo membrum christi esse poterit qui a corpore christi quod est ecclesia separatur? . . ea sola sit quam in sedis apostolice per successiones episcoporum radice constitutam hominum nullorum malicia ullo modo valeat extinguere." *Def.* I. 1. col. 4 f. Cf. *Def.* I. 5. col. 3; *S* IV. 48 A; *Lect.* 24 D.

[127] "Si vero hec mea confessio apostolatus sui iudicio comprobatur quicunque me culpare voluerit se imperitum aut malivolum aut etiam non catholicum sed hereticum comprobabit. Verum quia . . . nihil tam claris probationibus deductum contra quod non possit obiici multaque ex verbis legis et scripture apparentur adduci. Siquidem multa sunt verba in scripturis divinis . . . que possunt retrahi ad eum sensum quem sibi sponte unusquisque presumpsit." *Def.* conclusio.

usual, the form chosen in his peroration indicates that Biel does not so much repeat a traditional formula of orthodox intentions as lay down a general rule of biblical interpretation.

In view of the present-day interest in the history of hermeneutics, it is important to note that Biel does not seem to consider this matter of great importance. This is not too surprising, however, since the hermeneutical problem is not nearly so urgent for one holding to Tradition II as for one who stands for Tradition I. The Church and not Scripture itself forms the link between the literal and spiritual sense of a given passage. The Church has the Spirit and therefore the proper understanding of the truth of God. But since this truth is only partly embedded in Holy Scripture, the interest in the relation of spirit and letter *within* the Scriptures has to give way to the over-arching interest in the relation of written and unwritten truth. Though the present state of research does not permit clear conclusions to be drawn, a more detailed investigation may show that the late medieval interest in hermeneutics proper is most alive in circles of those who hold Tradition I.[128]

And as research progresses, we will have to face the question whether the hermeneutical problem in the later middle ages is the primary issue for which it is generally taken at the present time or rather subsidiary to the decisive issue at stake between Tradition I and Tradition II.[129]

The second event in Biel's life that illustrates his attitude toward the authority of the Church is connected with Sixtus IV's use of the term "per modum suffragii" in 1476, and his further clarification of it the

---

[128] The preoccupation of Gerson with the literal sense of Scripture has led Hahn to assume here an influence by Lyra on Gerson, p. 41 f. Contrary to Lyra, Gerson does not assume a valid two-fold literal sense, but he identifies the literal with the spiritual meaning: "Sensus scripturae litteralis judicandus est prout ecclesia spiritu sancto inspirata et gubernata determinavit. . . ;" in: "De sensu litterali sacrae scripturae," *Opera* I. 3 A. Gerson does not seem to show the great respect of Lyra for the rabbinical tradition: ". . . Judaei litterales judaisant." *Opera* I.459 B. It should be granted that Gerson's position is more progressive than the view Biel expresses in *S* I 102 B: "Scriptura sacra liber est scriptus intus et foris. Intus per allegoriam, foris per historiam. Intus per spiritualem intellectum; foris autem per sensum litere simplicem." For the *duplex sensus litteralis* with Lyra see Gerhard Ebeling, *Evangelische Evangelienauslegung* (Munich, 1942), p. 93.

[129] Wilfrid Werbeck's *Jacobus Perez von Valencia: Untersuchungen zu seinem Psalmenkommentar* (Tübingen, 1959), is a valuable contribution to the field. However, in future studies of the history of hermeneutics a treatment of the relation of Scripture and Church ought to be included, as a necessary preamble. Werbeck accepts Hahn's thesis that Gerson is influenced by Lyra, p. 122.

following year.[130] Pope Sixtus made clear that the Church can reduce purgatorial punishment by issuing plenary indulgences which can then in part be applied by those who acquire them for friends or family already deceased.

Before this statement came into the hands of Biel, he had denied that the Church can remit the sins of those who are in purgatory. Thomas' opinion that there is a certain kind of indulgence transferable to the dead was rejected by Biel on the grounds that the jurisdiction of the Pope is restricted to the living.[131] Biel adds that if Thomas were right, the Pope would be able to liberate whomever he wants from the purgatorial prison and to empty purgatory by issuing plenary indulgences.[132] At that time, however, Biel felt that there was no absolutely convincing solution and that therefore the Church should determine this case.

However, in an appendix to the first imprint (Reutlingen, 1488), and from the second edition (Tübingen, 1499) onwards, inserted after the above-quoted passages, there is an excursus in which Biel completely reverses his position. Now he declares purgatory to belong to the Church militant and therefore to fall under the jurisdiction of the Pope; the Pope cannot empty purgatory since he liberates only those for whom a work of piety has been performed. Not a lack of love on the part of the Pope, but on the part of the faithful keeps the deceased in purgatory.[133]

[130] 1476: ". . . volumus ipsam plenarium remissionem per modum suffragii ipsis animabus purgatorii pro quibus dictam quantitatem pecuniae aut valorem persolverint. . . pro relaxatione poenarum valere et suffragari." Charles H. Lea. *A History of Auricular Confession and Indulgences in the Latin Church*, vol. III (Philadelphia, 1896), p. 585 f. Cf. Walther Köhler, *Dokumente zum Ablassstreit von 1517*, 2 ed. (Tübingen, 1934), no. 24, p. 38.

[131] ". . . meritum persone quantum ad satisfactionem est in potestate facientis . . . ideo potest illud reservare sibi vel dare alteri cui maluerit vivo vel defuncto . . . Sed meritum commune ecclesie cui innituntur indulgentie est in potestate pape ex commissione christi quantum ad eius dispensationem *que limitata est tamen* ad vivos." *Lect.* 57 H. Cf. *Lect.* 56 J; *Lect.* 58 M. Thomas IV *Sent.* d 45 q 6 art. 2. On the pre-Tridentine history of the doctrine of merits for others, see Johannes Czerny, *Das übernatürliche Verdienst für Andere* (Freiburg i Br., 1957), p. 1–53. For Biel p. 49 f.

[132] ". . . sic papa posset liberare quemcunque vellet de purgatorio; immo dando plenarie remissionis indulgentias posset evacuare totum purgatorium . . . Hec autem data est tantum quoad vivos super terram, non ad defunctos qui sunt extra ecclesiam militantem et eius iurisdictionem." *Lect.* 57 H.

[133] "Estimo autem quod in casu huius dubii esset necessaria determinatio ecclesie." *Lect.* 57 H. Cf. *ibid.*, M, N.

405

Biel himself indicates the reason for this turnabout: the statement of Sixtus IV on the significance of the "per modum suffragii" for the dead had come to his attention only after the completion of his lectures, that is, sometime after November 4 and before November 15, 1488, the publication date of the *Expositio*. This settled the case for Biel.[134]

5. Biel as a forerunner of Trent

Biel acts here according to the principle which we have seen operating in all his works. Though he does not take the same critical attitude toward the canon lawyer, his basic position is the same as that of Occam, d'Ailly, Gerson, Breviscoxa, and Ambrosius of Speier. Tradition is not only the *instrumental vehicle of Scripture* through which the contents of Holy Scripture in a constant dialogue comes alive, but Tradition is the *authoritative vehicle of divine truth*, embedded in Scripture but overflowing in extrascriptural apostolic Tradition. In his formulation of this Tradition II principle, Biel comes closer than any of his predecessors to the formulation of the Council of Trent: Scripture and Tradition should be held in equal esteem.[135] The Basilean passage has now been firmly grafted onto the theological tradition.

At this point we must call attention to the fact that the interpretation

[134] "Dum itaque illa scripsi nondum venerat ad manus meas declaratio domini sixti pape novissime de medio sublati [1484] qua declarat indulgentias proficere per modum suffragii etiam animabus in purgatorio existentibus dum ad ipsas per summum pontificem expresse extenduntur." Lect. 57 K. Cf. the final statement in the first edition: "Finitum legendo 4 Novembris anno domini 1488 . . . Impressum . . . feliciterque consummatum . . . anno 1488 . . . 15. die Novembris." At the end of *Lect.* 57 this edition refers to the quoted passage: "Vide additionem necessariam in fine huius operis."

[135] "Et si ad hoc nulla sit auctoritas expressa canonis [scripturae] sufficit ritus et usus ecclesie qui maioris est auctoritatis auctoritate cuiuscumque doctoris particularis: unde beatus Augustinus ex dictis Basilii inquit di. II 'ecclesiasticarum.' Ecclesiasticarum institutionum quasdam in scriptis, quasdam vero apostolica traditione per successores in ministerio confirmatas accepimus, quasdam vero consuetudine roboratas approbat usus: quibus par ritus et idem utrisque debetur pietatis affectus." *Lect.* 2 B. Cf. *CIC*, Canon 5, dist. xi; Friedberg, I, p. 24. Cf. "Sed contra hunc errorem est veritas fidei, scriptura sacra, ac sanctorum dogmata; ecclesie quoque ritus et determinatio atque ratio." *Lect.* 56 H. "Hec autem verborum connexio quam canonem appellamus regulariter partim a christo partim a sanctis patribus instituta est." *Lect.* 15 C. Cf. *Lect.* 35 P. ". . . sed ipsam [matter and form of confirmation] sic instituisse ex traditione apostolorum verbali ecclesie sicut nonnulla alia sine ambiguitate creditur." *S* II 13 G. cf. *Lect.* 14 E.

of the decree of the Council of Trent concerning Scripture and Tradition is currently under discussion. Joseph Geiselmann has found supporters for his view that the Council in its fourth session did not admit the insufficiency of Holy Scripture and the necessity for extrabiblical tradition which this would imply. A full discussion of this issue must be reserved for a forthcoming volume on the relation of late medieval thought to sixteenth century developments. We can only indicate here that there are strong reasons to reject Geiselmann's view.[136]

In view of the usual accusation that nominalism is an anti- or non-

---

[136] For five main reasons it is not possible to accept Geiselmann's thesis.

(1) The partly-partly (*partim-partim*) formula of the original draft of the decree cannot be explained away as a product of nominalistic philosophy as Geiselmann suggests. *Die mündliche Überlieferung*, p. 148; p. 177. Though one has to cede to the nominalistic theologian the honor of having made the two-sources theory ripe for its official reception at Trent, the formulation 'partly-partly' as such is rare and has not yet been traced to a nominalist theologian. The more current translation of the Basilean passage, 'some . . . and others' (*quasdam . . . quasdam*) is used by Gabriel Biel but can be traced back to the early medieval canonists. In view of this textual history, one would be well advised not to give too much weight to the change of the initial 'partly-partly' to the copulative 'and' (*et*). All three formulations render satisfactory St. Basil's own choice of words (*ta men, ta de*). See note 137. Biel uses, of course, *partim-partim* elsewhere; see note 110.

(2) This conclusion is borne out by the statement of the Cardinal legate Cervini who announces on April 6, 1546, after a night spent on the revision of the original draft, that the final version is "in substance" the same: changes have been made, "non tamen in substantia." *CT* V. 76. This would hardly seem compatible with the idea that the Council changed its mind.

(3) The energetic protest against the "partly-partly" formulation which Geiselmann cites as the cause of the alleged change proves to be limited to two representatives, Bonucci and Nachianti. The first stands under suspicion of heresy on points related to Scripture and tradition, and the second was once called (cf. Alois Spindeler, "Pari pietatis affectu. . .", p. 171f.) "avid for novelties" (*CT* I 535; *CT* I 494).

(4) The *Catechismus Romanus* quite clearly interprets 'and' (*et*) as 'partly-partly' (*partim-partim*) when it states that the Word of God is distributed over Scripture and tradition: "Omnis autem doctrinae ratio, quae fidelibus tradenda sit, verbo Dei continetur, quod in scripturam, traditionesque distributum est." *Catechismus Romanus ex decreto sacrosancti Concilii Tridentini iussu S. Pii V Pontificis Maximi editus*, Romae, 1796. *Praefatio*, Sectio 12, p. 7f. This *partim-partim* is of course compatible with *et* whenever one speaks about Scripture and tradition as two sources of proof and confirmation: De quinto articulo, Caput VI, 3, p. 59.

(5) The change from *partim-partim* into *et* is in keeping with nominalistic theology in that the earlier formula could suggest that *equal* parts of the catholic truths reach the Church in Scripture and in tradition. Nominalism stressed rather that Holy Scripture contains the large majority of the catholic truths, whereas some truths are only to be found in tradition.

catholic and non-orthodox movement, it is important to emphasize that *the major representatives of late-medieval nominalism were instrumental in preparing the ground for the decision made on this point at the fourth session of the Council of Trent.*[137]

6. A contrast: Wessel Gansfort as upholder of Tradition I

We have tried to shed light on the significance of Biel's concept of Tradition and the authority of the Church by surveying the treatment of this issue by some of the most important nominalists before Biel. To complete the picture we should like to point to a contemporary of Biel, Wessel Gansfort. Wessel's concept of Tradition can perhaps best be characterized in the following four points:

(1) One is not bound by anything that falls outside the Sacred Canon. No Christian ought "to subscribe to any statement of an assembly against his conscience, so long as it seems to him to assert anything contrary to Scripture." [138] "If therefore one is not bound to believe canons that have been officially published and authoritatively ratified, because they are outside of the Sacred Canon, one is not bound to believe any Pope." [139]

(2) Apostolic traditions not contained in the Canon are only "in the rule of faith," that is, normative, if they make explicit what is contained in the Sacred Canon.

Tavard, who calls Wessel "orthodox" and classifies him with Occam and Gerson, quotes Wessel: "I admit that in this rule of faith I ought to depend on the authority of the Church . . .", but he omits the first part of this sentence in which Wessel explains *why* he admits this point

---

[137] The patristic authority is St. Basil the Great, *Liber de Spiritu Sancto*, 66; *PG* XXXII, 188. Cf. *CIC*, Friedberg, I, 24, n. 30. The various terms used for the description of the relation of the written and the unwritten Tradition such as "alia . . . alia" [Migne translation of St. Basil] "quedam . . . quedam" [Biel], "partim . . . partim" [Trent, first draft] and "et" [Trent, final formulation] are all possible Latin renderings of St. Basil's phrase "ta men . . . ta de."

Cf. our discussion of John Murphy, *The Notion of Tradition in John Driedo* (Milwaukee, 1959) in *Theologische Zeitschrift* 17 (1961), p. 231 ff.

[138] ". . . diligenter inquirere . . . verum intellectum scripturae contra quam ei videtur diffinire sed nunquam contra conscientiam suam sequi multitudinis diffinitionem. . ." "De Sacramento Poenitentiae," Wessel Gansfort, *Opera* (Groningae, 1614), p. 781.

[139] "Si ergo non canonibus jam solemniter publicatis aut authentice roboratis, credere oportet, quia sunt extra sacrum canonem, non papae ulli credere oportet. . ." *Ibid.*, p. 780 f.

in his epistolary discussion with Jacobus Hoeck: "The usual teaching of the Church concerning sacramental confession, *viz.* that it was handed down to the Church by Christ through the apostles, is quite acceptable to you. I believe that *this* opinion of yours is right, *since indeed it is confirmed by the general statements of John in his canonical writings and by the more specific words of James.* Therefore (!) I admit . . ." etc.[140] In accordance with this principle Wessel states that a plenary indulgence is not acceptable.[141] "Do you wish to put the authority of the Pope above the Holy Scriptures?" [142]

(3) The Church's authority is instrumental in character. It has the "passive" task of preserving the *depositum fidei* unadulterated. The words of St. Augustine on the relation of Church and Scripture should not, according to Wessel, be construed as granting the Church a place of superiority over Scripture, but should be understood as a reference to the teaching service of the Church. ". . . Augustine had in mind the beginning of a small and infant faith. He does not compare the authority of the Church with the worth of the Gospel." [143]

(4) Tavard does not see that the key to an understanding of Wessel's doctrine of Church and Scripture is to be found in his distinction between Law and Gospel. The Gospel is not *coextensive* with Holy Scripture but is *in* Holy Scripture. "For in matters of belief we are all primarily under the authority of the Gospel, so that neither an angel from heaven *nor even St. Paul through his epistle is to be believed, if* the teaching of either is at variance with the Gospel." [144] Annexed to this is Wessel's great re-

[140] Tavard, p. 69 f. Compare however Wessel's statement: "De sacramentali confessione mos ecclesiae non admodum tibi displicet, illam a christo traditam ecclesiae per apostolos. Placet mihi haec tua sententia generalibus quidem Ioannis sed specialioribus verbis Iacobi confirmata. Confiteor ergo [!] in hac fidei regula debere me pendere ex ecclesiae auctoritate, cum qua credo non in quam." "Epistolae," *Opera,* p. 888 Wessel comes here very close to the meaning which the term *regula fidei* had for Irenaeus. Bengt Hägglund has pointed out that *fidei* is not to be regarded as a *genitivus objectivus* but as a *genitivus subjectivus.* "Die Bedeutung der 'regula fidei' als Grundlage theologischer Aussagen," *Studia Theologica* 12 (1958), 4 f. Cf. note 153 below.

[141] Gansfort, *Opera,* p. 890 f. Against Antoninus and Gerson, *ibid.,* p. 888 f.

[142] "Numquid vis papae mihi auctoritatem supra scripturam sacram?" Gansfort, *Opera,* p. 892 f.

[143] "Parvulae nascentis adhuc fidei originem texit Augustinus in verbo suo, non auctoritatem ecclesiae cum evangelii dignitate comparat," Gansfort, *Opera,* p. 893. Cf. "De Potestate Ecclesiae," *ibid.,* p. 759.

[144] "Omnesne in credendo primo subjecti sumus evangelio ut neque angelo de

spect for the doctor of Scripture who, if he is a good one, knows the truth better than the untrained prelate.[145]

The Gospel is the truth preached by Jesus and is as such unchangeable. The law is the commandments given by Jesus and important precedents which we are to follow.[146] The Church may change the precedents. "But it has never presumed to change the Gospel. For whenever the Church has believed that a matter of imitation or obedience was subject to change, it has done so for the sake of the unchangeable truth of the Gospel. For the Gospel is a guiding light for obedience and change." [147]

Wessel discerns this "canon within the canon," through what is variously described as love diffused through the Holy Spirit in the hearts of the children of God [148] or the Holy Spirit.[149] When he describes this operation elsewhere as restoring vision to man's blind eyes [150] and as a rule of interpretation of Scripture, it is clear that Wessel bases this on what is known as the *testimonium internum spiritus sancti*.[151]

If one overlooks this distinction between Gospel and Law which considerably qualifies the authority of the Church since it is now subject to the unchangeable Gospel as contained in Scripture, one is bound to miss Wessel's stress on the discriminatory function of the individual Christian: ". . . in case of disagreement every believer should be bound by the example of St. Paul [152] — in defense of the faith — to resist the

---

coelo aliter docenti neque S. Paulo ipsi per epistolam sit credendum?" *Ibid.*, p. 758.

[145] "Hinc jam clare liquet quanto in credendis ad credendum praelato doctor ex officio subiiciatur. Si enim vere doctor est, sicut esse debet . . . debet per exercitatos sensus vel aeque vel magis nosse veritates sacrarum literarum quam non doctores, non exercitati praelati." *Ibid.*, p. 758.

[146] *Ibid.*, p. 758.

[147] "Unde etiam legis praecepta quaedam immutavit; sed evangelium non praesumpsit immutare. Quod enim vel imitando vel obediendo mutabile credidit et mutavit, propter immutabilem evangelii veritatem immutavit. Illa enim lux est ad obediendum et immutandum." *Ibid.*, p. 758.

[148] *Ibid.*, p. 891.

[149] *Ibid.*, p. 891.

[150] "Epistolae," *ibid.*, p. 863.

[151] "Quia in amore tota lex pendet et prophetae utilius erit exercitium charitatis quam studium veritatis non modo ad mercedem verum etiam ad profectum cognitionis. Propterea enim leguntur literae sacrae ut diligatur deus . . . ex diligendo deum sacrae literae planae fiant et apertae. . ." "De Sacramento Poenitentiae," *ibid.*, p. 781. For Wessel's Augustinian-mystical doctrine of justification see Maarten van Rhijn, *Wessel Gansfort* (The Hague, 1917), p. 230 ff.

[152] Gal. 2:11 ff.

Pope to his face and, if necessary, in the presence of all." [153] The Spirit speaks continually to the Church through internal testimony, through Scripture, and through the *magisterium* whenever and insofar as this *magisterium* does not "set aside the commands of God and enjoin their own man-made commands" nor is dominated by "despisers of God," "men who think piety is gain." [154] The unity of the Church is the special task of the Holy Spirit which He does not leave to a Roman Pontiff.[155]

Whereas our investigation of the relation of Gospel and Law in Biel and the major medieval authorities indicated that the Gospel is understood as Law accompanied by the gift of grace, in Wessel a new idea appears on the scene of medieval theology. Now, not only between the Old Law and the New Law but also within the New Testament itself, there is a hierarchical relation established between Law and Gospel. Christ's role as legislator is here viewed as subordinate to His role as the preacher of saving truth. The "Gospel aspect" of the New Law had traditionally been regarded as the infusion of grace, a gift of the Holy Spirit. In Wessel the Holy Spirit reveals the Gospel which is understood as knowledge of redemption, to be ranked above the moral demands of the Decalogue interpreted by the Church.

This means also a new development within the context of Tradition I. Wyclif and Huss had defended the authority of Holy Scripture against Tradition II by employing the concept of the immutable Law, thus denying the Church the authority to introduce any changes. Wessel defends Tradition I against Tradition II by insisting on the immutability not of the Law but of the Gospel. In Holy Scripture the Church is confronted with a standard for faith and life: the Church of the Spirit is the Church of obedience.

There is little need for an extensive comparison between Wessel and Biel. Wessel's understanding of the authority of Scripture, ecclesiastical tradition and the doctor of Scripture shows forth all the characteristics

[153] ". . . in dissidentia fidelis omnis teneatur, exemplo S. Pauli, pro regula fidei contra papam in faciem et si non aliter coram omnibus resistere." Gansfort, "Epistolae," *Opera*, p. 891.

[154] "In deum enim credimus non in ecclesiam catholicam. . . Dico 'periculosis temporibus' . . . quia in illis surgent homines quaerentes semetipsos, contemnentes deum . . . quaestum putantes pietatem." Gansfort, *Opera*, p. 779.

[155] "Unitatem igitur ecclesiae sibi spiritus sanctus fovendam, vivificandam, conservandam retinuit et augendam; non romano pontifici, saepe non curanti, reliquit," *ibid.*, p. 779.

of Tradition I; he stands in the line of Bradwardine, Wyclif, and Huss. A clearer contrast between him and the major representatives of late medieval nominalism is hardly conceivable.[156]

IV. The Pope between Council and Emperor

1. The Pope as vicar of Christ

In this final section two more aspects of Biel's ecclesiology will be investigated: his understanding of the relation of Pope and Council and of the relation of Pope and Emperor, or more realistically Church and State.

In our treatment of the relation of Scripture and Church we pointed out that the promise of the abiding assistance of the Holy Spirit lends the Church the authority to distinguish between orthodoxy and heresy. While this thesis is clear and by no means remarkable or original, there arises a problem as soon as we ask by what means this authority is executed.

In one place Biel leads his audience and readers to believe that the authoritative center of the Church is the Pope, since the rule of the Church has been committed to St. Peter.[157] At other times Biel points explicitly to the Council — more often to the Councils of Constance and Basel than those of Nicaea and Chalcedon[!] — as the magisterial organ to which the promise of the assistance of the Holy Spirit applies.[158] In

---

[156] Kropatscheck's conclusion according to which Wessel's doctrine of Scripture would be inconsistent needs revision. *Das Schriftprinzip der lutherischen Kirche*, I, 314. Kropatscheck bases his judgment on the passage also quoted by Tavard without regard for the context. *Ibid.*, p. 69, see note 130 above. As regards Wessel's relation with the Reformation, see van Rhijn's words of caution, *Studiën over Wessel Gansfort en zijn Tijd* (Utrecht, 1933), p. 45 f. The debate between Gansfort and Hoeck finds nevertheless its close parallel one century later in that between Tyndale and More. Cf. E. Flesseman-Van Leer, "The Controversy about Scripture and Tradition between Thomas More and William Tyndale," *NAK* 43 (1959), 142–164; "The Controversy about Ecclesiology between Thomas More and William Tyndale," *NAK* 44 (1960), 65–86.

[157] "Vana est omnis doctrina et de falsitate suspecta extra Petri naviculam seminata. Navicula hec est catholica ecclesia Petri regimini commissa. . . Omnia alia suspecta habeat quam ecclesie auctoritas non approbavit. Hec enim est que spiritum sponsi habet." *S* I 58 D.

[158] On the 'sub utraque': "Et taliter hodie a cunctis fidelibus observatur per totam ecclesiam occidentalem exceptis paucis schismaticis qui se ab huiusmodi generali observantia subtrahunt . . . contra generales ecclesie determinationes factas in novis-

his discussion of Christ's words 'You are Peter and on this rock I will build my church,'[159] Biel interprets the word "rock" as Christ himself, the primary foundation, while St. Peter is the first of the apostles who form a secondary foundation resting on Christ.[160]

Biel explains the inclusion in the liturgy of the Eucharist of a prayer for the Pope as intended to safeguard him from falling in error and sin, since he can use his power to build as well as to destroy the Church.[161] Such a qualified authority of the Pope can also be seen in Biel's assertion that legal decisions of the Pope are subject to the immutable equity of natural law. Dispensation as such therefore cannot vindicate anyone from sin. "Official papers signed by a prelate will not temper the heat of the fires of Hell."[162]

simis conciliis universalibus Constantiensi et Basiliensi . . . Ea propter merito ut decens, utilis, congruus et rationabilis observabitur, quia impium est cogitare quod christus qui ecclesiam sibi in sponsam suo proprio sanguine copulavit permiserit tam periculose errasse per tanta spacia temporum et annorum." *Lect.* 84 N.

[159] Matt. 16:18.

[160] "Ex quibus patet quod non petrus sed petra in evangelio christi designatur . . . petra autem erat christus quem confessus est simon." *Lect.* 24. E. "Ex quibus concluditur quod christus est fundamentum principale et radicale et primum super quod fundata est ecclesia quia ab eo fides incipit, in eo stabilitur . . . Apostoli vero sunt fundamenta fidei et ecclesie secundaria et minus principalia fundati in fundamento primo." *Ibid.* F. ". . . inter apostolos petrus propter fidei sui soliditatem et constantiam quandoque petra dicitur et pre ceteris apostolis ecclesie fundamentum. . . " *Ibid.* H. Cf. *S* III 25 X.

[161] "Oramus ergo pro papa ut a peccatis et erroribus que tanquam membris capitis infirmitas ecclesie maxime nocet misericorditer preservetur ut quoque iuxta divine legis sanctionem et naturalis iuris equitatem suscepta utatur potestate, non in destructionem sed edificationem ecclesie; paretque domino suo regimine plebem perfectam." *Lect.* 23 O.

[162] "Sed falluntur miseri affectu intellectuque depravati et inaniter sibimet de dispensatione blandiuntur. Potest papa dispensare sed super ius humanum. Equitas autem et naturalis rationis iusticia immutabilis perseverat." *Lect.* 28 Q. "Nec querat excusationem in peccatis superioris auctoritate se muniens per dispensationem, quoniam ut sit recta in executione oportet eam naturali equitate et divinis legibus regulari. Neque idcirco minus ardebit in baratro qui cum licentia prelati demergitur in inferno." *Ibid.* S. Cf. III *Sent.* d 25 q 1 art. 1 n 2 cor. 4 *in fine.* "Ex illo sequitur quod non semper est excommunicandus a deo qui excommunicatur ab homine et prelato. Nec semper habetur ratum in celis quod fit a presidente in terris; sed dumtaxat dum ligat et solvit clave non errante. Non enim commissum est prelatis ligare et solvere iuxta suorum motus capitum et suarum beneplacita voluntatum." *Lect.* 26 O. This restriction is not peculiar to Biel or nominalism but appears for example also in the *Summa Theologica* of the Dominican Antoninus of Florence "Quodsi praelati absque rationabili caussa vel saltem dubia pro sola voluntate licentiam tribuant veniendi contra leges . . . peccabunt ipsi dispensantes

These and similar statements may explain why Biel has been presented as an anti-curialist who saw the highest ecclesiastical power vested in the conciliar representation of the Church and who furthermore rejected the infallibility of the Pope.[163]

At this point we should recall, however, that according to Biel, even those who are in doubt as to the legality of certain papal decretals are obliged to obey. Only in the case that one is absolutely certain that a papal decision is contrary to the will of God is he held to follow the dictate of natural reason. Since this is subject to the divine law expressed in Holy Scripture and since only the Church can interpret the Bible "e mente auctoris," conscientious objection is merely a hypothetical case, except of course when equal ecclesiastical authorities conflict. This problem can therefore be reduced to the question whether one should obey the Council rather than the Pope. It may be true that the rock on which the Church is built is primarily Christ himself; nonetheless the organ of authority is the apostolic succession, centralized in the Pope.[164]

Biel stresses indeed that the Church has not two heads, and that the Pope is only the vicar of Christ.[165] It is in this context that Biel indicates as one of the differences between the Pope and Christ that the former is still a *viator* and subject, therefore, to the vicissitudes of the life of one who is not yet "stabilized in grace." At the same time it should be noted that Biel distinguishes between the function and the person of the Pope and that therefore the admission of the peccability of the person does not imply the admission of the fallibility of papal authority as such.[166]

It would not be proper of course to judge Biel's orthodoxy on grounds of decisions made by a later Council. But it should be granted that while Biel nowhere explicitly distinguishes between doctrinal opinions of the

---

cum dispensatis. . ." I.xvii.1; col. 823 B. Antoninus refers to a series of statements by Canon law authorities.

[163] H. Wiegand Biel, *De Gabriele Biel celeberrimo papista anti-papista* (Wittenberg, 1719), p. 22 ff. Cf. "Ex his evidenter evinci posse putamus Gabrielem . . . nec se induci passum esse ut Pontificis auctoritatem supra oecumenicorum conciliorum potestatem extolleret;" *Ibid.*, p. 25. See also Karl August von Hase, *Lehrbuch der Kirchengeschichte*, 12 ed. (Jena, 1900), p. 200.

[164] "Ex omnibus his patet petrum fuisse caput ecclesie et primatum inter omnes tenuisse; cum autem quilibet papa canonice intrans successor sit Petri, sequitur quod quilibet talis omnem dignitatem, auctoritatem et principalitatem habeat quam habuit Petrus." *Lect.* 23 J.

[165] *Lect.* 23 O.

[166] "Verumtamen et si papa tanquam homo viator nondum in gratia confirmatus quandoque deviat . . . non tamen capitis dignitatem amittit nisi in heresim

Pope as private doctor and official *ex cathedra* definitions,[167] his observation that the Pope as *viator* can not only sin but also err does not necessarily run counter to the decision of the first Vatican Council.[168]

2. Authority of Pope and Council: considerations

While it is clear that Biel has a high regard for the authority of the Pope, this still does not answer our primary question whether the Pope has an absolute authority higher even than that of the Council. If this were the case, we would have discovered a point on which Biel radically deviates from Occam, d'Ailly, and Gerson.[169]

There are two statements in particular which strongly suggest that for Biel the Pope stands above the Council. There is in the first place the section in which Biel unfolds the primacy of the Pope. He adduces three arguments: (1) the Pope forms the highest order in the Church wherein all other orders find their perfection; [170] (2) the Pope has the *plenitudo potestatis*: he has the keys of the empires of heaven and earth; [171] (3) finally the primacy of the Pope appears in the fact that from him stems directly or indirectly the spiritual power of bishops and priests.[172]

---

lapsus extra ecclesiam fieret. . ." *Lect.* 23 K. L. Though Paul Tschackert rejects the idea that Biel was anti-papist, he feels that Biel stood "im allgemeinen auf dem Boden des Constanzer und Basler Konzils . . . wie er auch dementsprechend die persönliche Unfehlbarkeit des Papstes verwarf." *RE, sv* "Biel," III, 209.

[167] Guido Terrenus was the first to distinguish these clearly. Cf. his *Quaestio de magisterio infallibili Romani Pontificis,* ed. Bartholomaeus M. Xiberta, (Münster i.W., 1926).

[168] Denz. 1838, 1839; cf. the historical survey in the articles "Infaillibilité du Pape" by E. Dublanchy, *DThC*, VII, cols. 1638–1717; and Harent, Stéphane, S.J., "Papauté: Infaillibilité pontificale," *Dictionnaire Apologétique de la Foi Catholique,* vol. III (Paris, 1916), cols. 1422–1534.

[169] This would provide the one possible basis for the validity of the second part of Lortz' statement: "Okham war eine fundamental unkatholische Natur. Gabriel Biel . . . hatte ihn kirchlich korrekt zurechtgerückt." *Die Reformation in Deutschland,* I, 176.

[170] ". . . propter ordinem et propinquitatem ad deum ratione officii: quia ipse summus est hierarchia in ecclesia ad quem stat et reducitur tanquam in suum principium omnis ordo ecclesiasticus. . ." *Lect.* 23 M. This hierarchical understanding is organically related to another passage where Biel refers to Pseudo-Dionysius to emphasize the legal character of the New Law, as necessary for salvation: "Lex nova media est inter ecclesiam celestem et statum veteris legis. . ." III *Sent.* d 40 q 1 art. 2 concl. resp. 1.

[171] "Plenitudo autem potestatis petro collata transit in successores," *Lect.* 23 M.

[172] ". . . ab ipso fluit mediate vel immediate omnis potestas spiritualis sive in

In the second place, there is in connection with the issue of the Immaculate Conception of the Virgin Mary a statement in one of his sermons which seems, indeed, to close the case to further discussion. Biel claims there that that issue had already been determined by the Church in 1439 at the Council of Basel, corroborated as it is by the Roman curia, *sub plumbo more romane curie*.[173]

These two elements in Biel's thought on this matter — his emphasis on the primacy of the Pope, and his references to the papal prerogative of confirming conciliar decisions — have led to the assumption that Biel should be viewed, perhaps not as an extreme, but nevertheless as an anticonciliar defender of the curialist cause. But a more complete survey of the available evidence indicates that this conclusion is no more accurate than the one we dealt with above where we have seen Biel categorized as a conciliarist.

The fact that Biel speaks in strong terms about the primacy of the Pope should not be construed as excluding or overshadowing the authority of the Council. In the same series of lectures from which we quoted the three modes in which Biel finds the papal primacy expressed, we find also a discussion of the nature and authority of the Council as the representative body of the militant Church legitimately gathered in the name of the Holy Spirit. "The Fathers are convened from all parts of the world to define and discern catholic truth; in this action they represent the true Church. In this sense of the word the Church is the highest tribunal on earth with authority over every single person, however exalted his status or dignity may be, even if he were the Pope himself."[174]

---

prelatis maioribus, sive in simplicibus presbyteris," *Lect.* 23 M. Cf. *Def.* I. 6. col. 4. C. Ruch draws from this emphasis the conclusion: ". . . l'évêque de Rome a sur l'Église une primauté absolue et universelle, c'est à lui que les questions de foi doivent être soumises et tous les fidèles sont tenus d'accepter ses jugements." Article "Biel," in *DThC* vol. II, col. 818.

[173] "De hac autem veritate olim varie senserunt doctores, sed aliter nunc opinari non licet nec docere postquam super hoc ecclesie determinatio emanavit, facta in concilio Basiliensi in sessione 36 anno domini 1439 . . . quam determinationem vidi sub plumbo more romane curie." *S.* III 1. F. Plitt concluded: "Wo es sich um Wahl zwischen allgemeinem Konzil und Papst handelte, stand ihm der Papst höher," p. 10. Cf. I *Sent.* d 11 q 1 art. 3 dub. 1, where Biel states also with respect to the early Church councils: ". . . auctoritate romani pontificis, cuius auctoritate antiqua concilia congregabantur et confirmabantur."

[174] "[ecclesia militans] uno modo pro congregatione omnium fidelium actu existentium que est ecclesia vera. Alio modo pro ecclesia representativa que est con-

With respect to Biel's understanding of the papal confirmation of the decision of the Council of Basel, there are two more passages which should be taken into consideration. One of these does not mention papal confirmation at all, but mentions in its place confirmation under the seal of the Council itself: *sub blumbo* [sic] *et sigillo concilii generalis*.[175] The parallel to this passage in the *Sentences* stresses the authenticity of the decision of the Council while the authority of the Pope is merely alleged to refute those "impudent ones" who "wildly" claim that the Council was not legally assembled in the 36th session.[176]

The continuation of this same section suggests the direction in which we should look for a solution for what seem to be contradictory statements. Biel there excuses doctors like Bernard, Thomas, and Bonaventura who held an opinion contrary to the decision of the Council of Basel, and he does so on the ground that "at their time there had been no decision taken *either by a council or by the apostolic see*."[177]

3. The middle way between papalism and anti-curialism

If we try now to bring together the results of our investigation on this point, we may say that Biel does not think in terms of *either* the Pope *or* the Council. For him Pope and Council are not rivals but are both representative of the authority of the Church. At the end of the fifteenth century, conciliarism is no longer the same live option as it was in the four-

---

cilium generale in spiritu sancto legitime congregatum . . . convocantur patres de omnibus mundi partibus qui diffiniunt et decernunt: et hec facientes ecclesiam veram representant. Et sic ecclesia est supremum tribunal in terris habens auctoritatem super quamlibet personam singularem cuiuscunque status eminentie aut dignitatis exititerit etiam si papalis. . ." *Lect.* 22. D. The Church as *corpus mysticum*: *Lect.* 22 H; as *ecclesia militans*: S III. 25 X.

[175] "Sic novissime in concilio basiliensi in sessione 36 anno 1439 determinata est hec veritas quod beata et gloriosa virgo originali peccato nunquam subiacuit, quam determinationem sub blumbo et sigillo concilii generalis vidi et manibus tenui." *Lect.* 41 L. The addition of the last two words does admit the conjecture that Biel saw the original copy and perhaps attended the Council of Basel.

[176] "Preterea determinatum est in concilio basiliensi et sub plumbo publicatum in sessione 36 . . . Hec ex originali plumbato . . . Et si qui impudentes ut suam defenderent temeritatem . . . ausi sint [dicere] basiliensem concilium non fuisse legitime congregatum . . . attendant auctoritatem summi pontificis . . ." III *Sent.* d 3 q 1 art. 2 concl. 1 G.

[177] ". . . quoniam eorum tempore hoc licuit quoniam nulla determinatio vel concilii vel apostolice sedis facta fuit." *Ibid.*

teenth century for Occam and in the first decades of the fifteenth century for d'Ailly and Gerson.[178] Biel does not break with this tradition: he holds with them that the Council stands above the Pope in case of conflict.[179]

We noted this same change in climate with respect to the remarkable absence in Biel's writings of any criticism of the canon lawyer. In that connection we saw that this change should not be stressed so as to imply a change of principle. For Biel it has become again the normal situation for Council and Pope to cooperate. The idea of the superiority of the Council has not disappeared but it is no longer the focus of theological interest.[180] The normal situation is that the Pope convenes the Council, the Council decides the issue, whereupon the Pope confirms the decision made. Biel does not hold that the definitions of the Roman Pontiff are "irreformable" as such apart from the consensus of the Church.[181]

But it is significant that he makes use of the Mantua decretal, *Execrabilis*, of Pope Nicolaus V, according to which it is illegal to appeal from the Pope to a future Council, as one of his arguments against Diether of Isenburg.[182] One may well claim that Biel wrote his "Defense" not yet two years after the publication of this decretal and that he was therefore not yet in a position to see that this Mantua decision indeed struck the deathblow to conciliarist theory; but it should be noted that very few outside Rome acknowledged *Execrabilis*.[183]

[178] Cf. the clear analyses by Matthew Spinka, *Advocates of Reform: From Wyclif to Erasmus* (Philadelphia, 1953), p. 13 ff.; 91 ff. See further the unpublished Hartford Seminary Thesis by James K. Cameron, "Conciliarism in Theory and Practice, 1378–1418" (1956).

[179] Gerson, " De potestate eccl.," *Opera* II, 243; Ailly, "De potestate eccl.," *Opera* II, 935, 949 f. P. Tschackert, *Petrus von Ailli* (Gotha, 1877), p. 247 ff. Cf. the survey of Hubert Jedin, *Geschichte des Konzils von Trient,* I: *Der Kampf um das Konzil,* 2 ed. (Freiburg i. Br., 1951), 45 ff.; 489 ff.

[180] Biel represents here the general trend of the time. Cf. Jedin: ". . . die eigentliche konziliare Theorie verliert sichtlich an Einfluss, ohne jedoch zu verschwinden . . . [man kämpft] nicht um die Frage der Oberhoheit des Konzils, sondern darum dass überhaupt ein Konzil stattfindet." *Ibid.* I, 48.

[181] Cf. the final passage of "Pastor aeternus": ". . . Romani Pontificis definitiones ex sese, non autem ex consensu Ecclesiae, irreformabiles esse." Denz. 1839.

[182] "Privat denique constitutio mantuana omnem appellantem contra iura antiqua a summo pontifice ad futurum concilium omni dignitate, si quam habet, ipso facto." *Def.* II 1 col. 2. Cf. for this episode K. Menzel, *Diether von Isenburg: Erzbischof von Mainz 1459–1463* (Erlangen, 1868), p. 103 ff.

[183] "*Execrabilis* war der erste grosse Schlag des Restaurationspapsttums gegen

Though Biel continues to quote Occam and Gerson as his main ecclesiological authorities, he stands at the threshold of the new era in which the authority of the Council as the highest tribunal in matters of faith and morals would be deemphasized in favor of an increasing stress on the papal prerogative to convene a council and confirm its decisions. Indeed if Biel had lived and written half a century earlier, it would have been permissible and possible to adduce some of the passages which we have mentioned as indicative of a curialistic and anti-conciliaristic position. The period between the Council of Pisa (1409) and the publication of *Execrabilis* (1460) was one of far-reaching changes, especially with regard to matters of Church polity. But when we remind ourselves of the fact that Biel holds the Tradition II position and therefore stresses the dynamic element in the development of doctrine, it is understandable that there is no trace of any awareness on his part that he deviates from those who proved in other respects to be his teachers.

An understanding of the overarching importance of the demarcation line between Tradition I and Tradition II should help us to have a more sober estimate of the centrality of conciliarism as a theological issue.

4. *Corpus christianum*

That we should not think in terms of a radical break between Biel and his nominalistic predecessors is apparent also from the fact that with respect to the relation of Church and State, Biel stands squarely in the conciliaristic tradition. He defines ecclesiastical power, like Gerson, as a gift of Christ to the Apostles and their successors to lead the Church militant along the path of evangelical law to life eternal.[184]

The Church cannot be identified with the hierarchy. Biel understands the meaning of the word "Church" in the words of Christ, "if your brother

---

den Konziliarismus. Er hat nicht die erhoffte Wirkung gehabt. Die Bulle stiess in Frankreich und Deutschland auf starken Widerstand und wurde ausserhalb Roms nur sporadisch anerkannt." Jedin, *Geschichte des Konzils von Trient*, I, 52.

[184] "Est [ecclesiastica] potestas a christo supernaturaliter et specialiter collata suis apostolis et discipulis et eorum successoribus legitimis usque in finem seculi ad edificationem ecclesie militantis secundum leges evangelicas pro consecutione felicitatis eterne." *Lect.* 1 C. *Verbatim* quote from Gerson. "Tractatus de Potestate eccl." *Opera* II. 227 A.

sins against you, go and tell him his fault. . . ; if he refuses to listen, tell it to the Church," [185] as not referring solely to ecclesiastical but also to the secular courts. By "Church" is meant the *congregatio fidelium* which encompasses priests *and* laymen.[186] Though, as we have seen, Biel has a high regard for the plenitude of papal power, this does not mean for him that the Pope wields the two swords. The two swords refer to the spiritual power of the Church executed by priests among whom the Pope has supremacy; and to the secular power executed by laymen among whom the head of the State has the highest authority.

Though the spiritual power exceeds the secular power in age, dignity and usefulness, they each have God-given tasks: the State has to preserve the peace and defend the Church; the Church has to render general assistance to the State, especially by way of intercession.[187] The State has not received its authority from God through mediation of the Church, but directly from God to whom alone it is responsible.[188]

It would not be entirely correct to apply here the term *corpus christianum*, as understood by Ernst Troeltsch, since Biel explicitly states that whereas the possession of spiritual power presupposes baptism, secular

[185] Matt. 18:15, 17.

[186] ". . . per illa verba salvatoris non tribuitur aliqua potestas iudicibus ecclesiasticis plus quam secularibus. Nam ibi non accipitur ecclesia pro ecclesiasticis viris qui clerici appellantur tantum, sed pro congregatione fidelium universali vel particulari qui clericos et laicos comprehendit. Dicitur enim quod in tota scriptura divina utriusque testimonii non accipitur nomen ecclesia specialiter pro clericis licet sic sepe in canonibus accipiatur." *Lect.* 75. U. This is the only passage which one could possibly interpret as critical of the Canonists; characteristically enough, not in the context of the discussion of the relation of Scripture and extrascriptural Tradition but in that of the relation of Church and State. Cf. Gerson, *Opera*, II 231 A/B.

[187] "Postquam sacerdos in persona ecclesie oravit pro papa qui est princeps et supremus in potestate ecclesiastica et spirituali; consequenter orat pro rege qui supremus princeps est in potestate terrena et seculari. . . Ita sunt due potestates ecclesiastica videlicet et mundana, una que moderatur spiritualia, alia que corporalia. Ista per clericos, illa regitur per laicos . . . Hec due potestates duo gladii sunt . . . regis interest et secularis potestatis ecclesiam in pace et tranquillitate tutare et defensare. Et quia ecclesia defensionem recipit a regia potestate iure naturali potestatis obligatur ut suffragium, quale potest, maxime spirituale rependat. . . " *Lect.* 23 P. ". . . potestas suprema sacerdotalis excedit regiam antiquitate, dignitate et utilitate. . . " *Ibid.* Q.

[188] "Ab illo est potestas secularis principibus tradita cui ratio usus potestatis est reddenda, sed huiusmodi est deus; ergo a deo est potestas secularis principibus tradita . . . quia ei soli reddenda est ratio. . ." *Lect.* 75 B.

power can also be wielded by non-Christians.[189] Still Biel regards tolerance with respect to faith and morals as heretical; the State has the task to punish those who trespass the divine law. This should not be left to the ecclesiastical courts, but viewed as the direct and special responsibility of the State: kings and judges are the servants of the Kingdom of God.[190]

It is clear that Biel advocates a positive Christian State which is aware of its divine calling and that he rejects the divorce of Church and State propagated in his time and later by large segments of the "Radical Reformation." [191] For Biel, moral integrity and military success are so intimately connected that on this ground already, it is clear that heresy could not possibly be a concern of the Church alone. As soon as transgressions of the divine law are transformed from thought to action, it is in the interest of the State itself to take immediate action.[192] There is no reason to see in the nominalistic understanding of the relation between Church and State a breakdown of the medieval theocracy.[193] We find in Biel —

[189] ". . . potestas secularis contra quam distinguitur potestas ecclesiastica convenit aliis quam christianis." *Lect.* 1 C. Cf. Gerson: "Unde potestas secularis convenit aliis quam christianis baptizatis." *Opera,* II, 227 C. Cf. Ernst Troeltsch, *Die Soziallehren der christlichen Kirchen und Gruppen* (Tübingen, 1912): "Obrigkeit und Kirchengewalt sind zwei verschiedene Seiten der einen ungeschiedenen christlichen Gesellschaft, weshalb . . .die Kirche die ganze Gesellschaft umfasst," p. 523. Cf. the discussion of "die Einheitlichkeit einer kirchlich geleiteten respublica christiana." *Ibid.,* p. 253. Biel uses the term *corpus christianitatis* once in a quote from Ambrose cited in Canon law, as a synonym for *ecclesia. Lect.* 24 H. The quoted passage is found in *CIC* cap. 54 d 50; I, p. 198. Appendix to Augustine's *Sermones,* Serm. 192, C 1; *PL* XXXIX, 2102. Friedberg notes that the passage is variously attributed to Ambrose, Augustine, *et al.*

[190] "Ecce non solum a deo ea potestas regni sed etiam domini est regnum; et omnes reges et iudices ministri sunt regni dei quare regere tenentur ad honorem domini dei sui et per consequens cavere et punire offensas dei . . . Sed hic dicunt heretici et ceteri homines moribus perditi quod nemo cogendus est ad fidem neque ad bonum . . . secularis potestas tenetur publice delinquentes in legem dei congrua cohertione animadvertere. . ." *Lect.* 75. B,H,L.

[191] For the initiative taken by the Archbishop of Mainz in 1477 against the "Drummer of Niklashausen," and his People's Crusade, cf. Norman Cohn, *The Pursuit of the Millennium,* 2 ed. (New York, 1961), p. 241 ff. On the Anabaptist protest against the identification of Church and State, cf. Franklin H. Littell, *The Anabaptist View of the Church,* 2 ed. (Boston, 1958), p. 65 f.

[192] "Ex quibus patet quod inanis est defensio armorum reipublice non correctis vitiis in plebe, quibus correctis haud dubium deus est qui pugnat pro nobis. . ." *Lect.* 75 D.

[193] Marcel Pacaut, *La Théocratie, L'Église et le Pouvoir au Moyen Age,* (Paris, 1957), p. 216 ff.

as in Occam [194] — not the victim of the anticlerical bias of Marsilius of Padua but rather a return in the spirit of Dante [195] to the Gelasian emphasis on the two swords, both entrusted immediately by God, coexisting in a balance of interdependence.

[194] Cf. Adalbert Hamman, O.F.M., "La doctrine de l'Église et de l'État d'après le Breviloquium d'Occam," *FS* 32 (1950), 135 ff.

[195] For parallels with John of Paris and Dante, see Kantorowicz, *The King's Two Bodies*, p. 296. See further Friedrich Kempf, *Papsttum und Kaisertum bei Innocenz III* (Rome, 1954), p. 205 ff.

Postscript

THE CATHOLICITY OF NOMINALISM

ᔐᕙ

IN this final section we do not plan to offer a summary of the results of our investigation. Since we have tried to be as concise as possible in the foregoing exposition by relegating related issues to the footnotes, any further condensation would necessarily lead to distortion. The two schemas in Chapters Seven and Nine, however, may assist by providing a graphic survey.

At this point we should like to comment on the title chosen for this study, which does not, as we realize, reflect the common understanding of the nature of late medieval theology in general and of late medieval nominalism in particular. In this context we must also raise the question of the catholicity or rather the "un-catholicity" or even "anti-catholicity" of nominalism which is said to permeate late medieval theology with stultifying effect.

Throughout this study we have had the opportunity to show that the often-asserted thesis of the "disintegration of late medieval thought" proves to be untenable. It is precisely to call attention to this fact that we have chosen as our title "The Harvest of Medieval Theology."

Though we do not regard this conclusion as the major thesis of this study, it might be useful to meet this contention head on in a final postscript, since it pervades not only the specialized monographs, but also the general textbooks and outlines of the history of Christian thought.

Above we have dealt with the view that Biel exemplifies a late medieval state of theological ignorance and has only a second- and third-hand familiarity with medieval theology.[1] We have seen that this claim cannot be validated in view of Biel's thorough knowledge of the medieval tradition. Even when restricting ourselves to a consideration of his *Expositio,*

[1] See Chapter Five, II, 6.

we find that in this most elaborate of medieval commentaries on the Mass, the whole field of theology is explored with constant reference to the conclusions of the preceding generations. A glance through the apparatus of the critical edition which is now being prepared, and a comparison of the passages quoted by Biel with the corresponding passages in earlier commentaries on the Mass indicate convincingly enough that Biel does not merely copy, but rather goes back to the sources themselves and is amazingly well versed in them. He must have had an enviable library at his disposal, containing the works of all those whom we regard today as the important medieval thinkers.

We have further indicated by way of expositions, quotations, and cross-references to the works of William of Occam that Biel and the Inceptor Venerabilis stand together on all basic philosophical and theological issues.

We have also been searching for deviations from Occam on Biel's part wherever they seem to occur. Our final conclusion in this respect has to be that Biel proves to be a true disciple of Occam, and a faithful preserver of the impressively coherent structure of the Occamistic system.

At the same time we have noted that Biel's emphasis is more explicitly theological than Occam's. Their basic agreement is most clearly apparent in the academic works meant to be read "in scholis." Our documentation for their different emphases has been drawn primarily from Biel's *Sermones* and to a lesser degree from his *Expositio*, which stands halfway between a strictly academic study and a contribution to what one might call pastoral theology. It is works of this genre which are absent from the *corpus occamisticum*. Biel's pastoral works provide us with the evidence that the Occamistic system, preserved with full integrity, is perfectly suited for explicitly theological and pastoral application.

In view of these considerations we have to conclude that there is no basis for the observation made by Joseph Lortz, in his discussion of the nominalistic doctrine of justification, that Biel has corrected Occam's position and has made it acceptable for the Church by a fortunate inconsistency.[2]

This leads us back to the issue of the catholicity of Occam, Biel, and

---

[2] "Diese katholischen Okhamisten [disciples of Biel such as Trutvetter und von Usingen] geniessen lediglich die Früchte einer glücklichen Inkonsequenz. Okham war eine fundamental unkatholische Natur. Gabriel Biel († 1495) hatte ihn kirchlich korrekt zurechtgerückt." *Die Reformation in Deutschland* I, 176. For a discussion of the position of Usingen see Chapter Six, II, 5.

more generally of late medieval nominalistic theology. Now that it proves to be impossible to dissociate Biel from Occam and admit the former's orthodoxy at the expense of the latter, we are confronted with a series of forceful statements in modern scholarship on the problem at hand.

Heinrich Denifle felt not only that late medieval theology marked a period of decay, but also noted in one of his more moderate statements that nominalism lacks the marks of a sound theology.[3] Joseph Lortz states more explicitly that "the occamistic system is radically uncatholic." [4] Whereas the latter has especially the nominalistic doctrine of justification in mind, Maurice de Wulf regards late medieval nominalism more generally as an anti-catholic movement.[5] Willem van de Pol labels Occamism a "caricature of the true content of Catholic truth" and warns against confusing this movement with "the faith and life of the Catholic Church." [6] The most extreme formulation of this position comes from the hand of Louis Bouyer. He imputes to nominalism "what was without doubt most irreparably vitiated and corrupt in Catholic thought at the end of the Middle Ages," and calls attention to "the utter corruption of Christian thought as represented by nominalist theology." [7]

This selection of quotations may indicate that we are not dealing here with a trivial matter or an oblique suggestion of a single scholar. The over-all evaluation of late medieval nominalism and its place in the development of philosophical and theological thought is at stake.

We should like to proceed cautiously in two stages. In view of the danger in trying to determine the degree of orthodoxy of nominalism solely on the basis of doctrinal standards only later developed,[8] we should

[3] *Luther und Luthertum*, I, abt. 2, pp. 522, 536, 587.

[4] "Dieses System des Okhamismus ist wurzelhaft unkatholisch." *Ibid.*, I, abt. 2, p. 473.

[5] *Histoire de la Philosophie médiévale*, vol. III: *Après le treizième siècle*, 6 ed. (Paris, 1947), p. 231 f.

[6] *Het Wereld Protestantisme*, p. 36. The term "caricature" is taken over by F.M. Violet and strengthened by the assertion that Occamism "poisoned all [!] of the philosophical and theological thought of the period." *Verdeelde Christenen in Gesprek* (Hilversum, 1960) p. 79 f.

[7] ". . . ce qu'il y avait sans doute de plus irrémédiablement vicié et corrompu dans la pensée du catholicisme médiéval finissant"; ". . . la corruption foncière de la pensée chrétienne que représente la théologie nominaliste. . ." *Du Protestantisme à l'Eglise* (Paris, 1954), p. 176. Trans. *The Spirit and Forms of Protestantism* (Westminster, Md.), p. 164.

[8] See the thoughtful contribution to a philosophy of history of Christian thought

like first to point out the doctrinal status of nominalism as seen in the context of its own time.

Whereas the late medieval Church, particularly as represented by Pope John XXII, was by no means doctrinally insensitive nor inclined to shy away from more extreme measures such as official condemnations — as the examples of Eckhart and the Fraticelli movement indicate — the censure of the papal committee investigating the writings of William of Occam was never followed up by an official condemnation. The theologians of nominalistic leanings, Nicolaus of Autrecourt and John of Mirecourt, were indeed forced to recant (1347); but the relation of the theses condemned to the main body of Occam's thought was not regarded by the late medieval nominalistic schoolmen as of such intimacy as to affect the status and orthodoxy of the Venerabilis Inceptor. Nominalism remained a valid option in the rapidly growing number of universities.

These condemnations had no more effect on the attitude of the Church toward Occam's thought than did the 1277 condemnation of some Thomistic propositions on the authority of Thomas Aquinas. Though protests were raised by such theologians as Thomas Bradwardine, Gregory of Rimini, and Johannes Capreolus, the late medieval Church did not feel that Occam's position was so "radically uncatholic" that an official condemnation was called for.

If in a second stage of evaluation we now proceed to employ the advantage of historical perspective, and to evaluate Occam's heritage within the larger context of the history of Christian thought, we must come to the conclusion that the discussed propositions regarding the inner structure of the doctrine of justification are to be characterized as at least semi-Pelagian. Durandus, Occam, d'Ailly, Biel, and Usingen, to mention only a few of the theologians we have discussed in the foregoing chapters, held a doctrine of justification which cannot according to any interpretation of the word be termed fully "catholic."

While it seems appropriate to say that this nominalistic doctrine of justification is antiquated [9] by the discussions of the Council of Trent, especially as formulated in the sixth Session, it is improper to see the

---

by Helmut Köster in his discussion of this problem as regards the early Church. "Häretiker im Urchristentum," in *RGG*, vol. III, cols. 17–21.

[9] The nominalistic doctrine of justification "ist heute antiquiert." Johannes Brinktrine, *Die Lehre von der Gnade*, p. 176.

Counter-Reformation in terms of a reaction against nominalism. Luther's earliest opponents, such as Johannes Eck,[10] Bartholomaeus von Usingen,[11] and Kaspar Schatzgeyer,[12] are all deeply indebted to the nominalistic tradition. Jacob Lainez, one of the most influential participants at the Council of Trent and increasingly so in its later stages, pays his respect to Gabriel Biel.[13] The name of Biel and his fellow schoolmen is not only absent from the Trent Index of Forbidden Books; but in an appendix to the 1569 edition of the Index published by the diocese of Munich, Biel's name is included under the suggestive heading: "Most select list of authors from which a complete Catholic library can properly be constituted." [14]

This leads us to the next and final point. The later Middle Ages are marked by a lively and at times bitter debate regarding the doctrine of justification, intimately connected with the interpretation of the works of Augustine on the relation of nature and grace. We have tried to show that the outer structure of the nominalistic doctrine of justification is intended to safeguard the Augustinian heritage and to neutralize the Pelagian dangers of an emphasis on the moral responsibilities of the *viator*. Our conclusion that nominalism has not been able to avoid a Pelagian position should not obscure the fact that nominalism was fully involved in the ongoing medieval search for the proper *interpretation* of Augustine.

For both Occam and Biel, such an interpretation is uncatholic only when it is stubbornly defended against a doctrine which is officially "received" by the Church. Or to put this positively, such an interpretation is Catholic provided it is in accordance with the tradition of the Church, understood as the ongoing formulation of Catholic truths. This concept, together with the aforementioned effort to come to a valid interpretation of Augustine, could of course be nothing more than an instance of a most common phenomenon: the coincidence of subjective orthodoxy and objective heresy. There is, however, more involved here.

[10] See Chapter One, note 43.
[11] See Chapter Seven, note 106.
[12] See Müller, *Die Rechtfertigungslehre nominalistischer Reformationsgegner Bartholomaeus Arnoldi von Usingen O.E.S.A. und Kaspar Schatzgeyer O.F.M. über Erbsünde, erste Rechtfertigung und Taufe*, p. 74 ff.
[13] See Chapter One, note 43.
[14] *Die Indices librorum prohibitorum des sechzehnten Jahrhunderts*, hrsg. von H. Reusch (Nieuwkoop, 1961 [reprint of Tübingen, 1886]), p. 334. Miss Jane Dempsey [Claremont] kindly called my attention to this point.

The nominalistic doctrine of justification, important as it is, should not be identified with its theological system as such. As we have seen in our discussion of the relation of Scripture and Church, a second and as we claim even more important part of the nominalistic system is its doctrine of Tradition and its understanding of the authority of the Church. Though the late medieval discussion of the doctrine of justification has traditionally attracted more attention, it becomes increasingly clear that the relation of Church and Scripture forms a second focus of late medieval theological interest. This second problem has to be regarded as more important for late medieval nominalism than the problem of justification insofar as justification is only an aspect of the Truth which is embedded in the ever-swelling stream of a living Tradition.

On this vital point, and on derivative doctrinal issues such as Mariology, late medieval nominalism can be regarded as the forerunner of the Tridentine formulation of the relation of Scripture and Tradition and is therefore in agreement with beliefs basic and characteristic for what has come to be known as Roman Catholicism. When catholicity is understood in this sense, we are altogether willing to defend the thesis that late medieval nominalism should be viewed as a basically catholic movement.

In a subsequent study, we hope to investigate the relation of nominalistic theology to the beginnings of Reformation theology. There we shall have an opportunity to test late medieval nominalism according to another definition of catholicity.

BIBLIOGRAPHY

ABBREVIATIONS AND PRIMARY SOURCES

SECONDARY SOURCES

BIBLIOGRAPHY

ABBREVIATIONS AND PRIMARY SOURCES

1. PERIODICALS

AHDL   *Archives d'histoire doctrinale et littéraire du moyen âge* (Paris, 1926–)

ALKM   *Archiv für Literatur- und Kirchengeschichte des Mittelalters* (Berlin and Freiburg i. Br., 1885–1900)

ARG   *Archiv für Reformationsgeschichte* (Leipzig and Gütersloh, 1903–)

ASS   *Acta Sanctae Sedis* (Vatican City, 1865–)

CH   *Church History* (Philadelphia, 1932–)

FS   *Franziskanische Studien* (Münster i. W. and Werl, 1914–)

FStud   *Franciscan Studies* (St. Bonaventure, N.Y., 1940–)

HTR   *Harvard Theological Review* (Cambridge, Mass., 1908–)

JEH   *The Journal of Ecclesiastical History* (London, 1950–)

MS   *Medieval Studies* (Toronto, 1939–)

NAK   *Nederlandsch Archief voor Kerkgeschiedenis* (The Hague, 1900–)

NTT   *Nederlands Theologisch Tijdschrift* (Wageningen, 1946–)

RHE   *Revue d'histoire ecclésiastique* (Louvain, 1900–)

RTAM   *Recherches de théologie ancienne et médiévale* (Louvain, 1929–)

SJT   *The Scottish Journal of Theology* (Edinburgh, 1948–)

ZKT   *Zeitschrift für katholische Theologie* (Innsbruck and Vienna, 1877–)

ZThK   *Zeitschrift für Theologie und Kirche* (Tübingen, 1891–)

2. COLLECTIONS, EDITIONS, AND ENCYCLOPEDIAS

BB   *Beiträge zur Geschichte der Philosophie und Theologie des Mittelalters*, founded by Clemens Baeumker (Münster i. W., 1891–).

CC   *Corpus Catholicorum* (Münster i. W., 1919–).

CIC   *Corpus iuris canonici*, ed. Emil Friedberg, 2 vols. (Leipzig, 1879–1881).

431

BIBLIOGRAPHY

CR   *Corpus Reformatorum* (Berlin 1834– ; Leipzig 1906–).

CSEL   *Corpus Scriptorum Ecclesiasticorum Latinorum* (Vienna, 1866–).

CT   *Concilium Tridentinum: Diariorum, actorum, epistolarum, tractatum nova collectio*, ed. Görres-Gesellschaft (Freiburg i. Br., 1901–).

Denz.   Denzinger, H., *Enchiridion Symbolorum*, ed. J. B. Umberg, S.J., 23 ed. (Freiburg i. Br., 1937).

DThC   *Dictionnaire de théologie catholique* (Paris, 1909–1950).

Harnack DG   Harnack, Adolf von, *Lehrbuch der Dogmengeschichte*, 5 ed. (Tübingen, 1932).

PG   *Patrologia Graeca*, ed. J. P. Migne (Paris, 1857–1912).

PL   *Patrologia Latina*, ed. J. P. Migne (Paris, 1844–1890).

RE   *Realencyklopädie für protestantische Theologie und Kirche*, 3 ed. (Leipzig, 1896–1913).

RGG   *Die Religion in Geschichte und Gegenwart*, 3 ed. (Tübingen, 1957–).

Seeberg DG   Seeberg, Reinhold, *Lehrbuch der Dogmengeschichte*, 5 ed. (Leipzig, 1953), 5 vols.

WA   *D. Martin Luthers Werke: Kritische Gesamtausgabe* (Weimar, 1883–).

3. PRIMARY SOURCES — GENERAL

Ailly, Pierre d', *Sacramentale seu Tractatus Theologicus de Sacramentis* (Lovanii, 1487).

—— *Quaestiones super libros Sententiarum* (n.p., 1500).

Alexander of Hales, *Quaestiones disputatae antequam esset frater* (Quaracchi, 1960).

—— *Summa theologica* (Quaracchi, 1924–1948).

Altenstaig, Johannes, *Vocabularius theologie* (Hagenau, 1517).

"Annals of the Wolf Brethren House, the" State Archives, Coblenz, Abt. 701, no. 92.

Anselm of Canterbury, *Monologium*, in *PL*, vol. CLVIII.

—— *Proslogion*, in *PL*, vol. CLVIII.

—— *Cur Deus Homo*, in *PL*, vol. CLVIII.

Antoninus of Florence, *Summa Theologica* (Graz, 1959). A photo-reprint of the Verona edition, 1740 ff.

Aristotle, *Opera*, ed. Academia Regia Borusica (Berolini, 1831–1870).

Augustine, *Opera*, in *PL*, vols. XXXII–XLIII, and in *CSEL* vols. XXV, XXVII–XXVIII, XXXIII–XXXIV, XXXVI, XL–XLIV.

Bernard of Clairvaux, *De diligendo deo; Sermones*, in *PL*, vols. CLXXXII–CLXXXIII.

Bonaventura, *Opera omnia* (Quaracchi, 1882–1902).

Bradwardine, Thomas, *De causa Dei contra Pelagium et de virtute causarum ad suos Mertonenses, libri tres*, ed. H. Savile (London, 1618).

Capreolus, Johannes, *Commentaria in IV Libros Sententiarum* (Venetiis, 1483).

432

Corpus Hermeticum, Texte établi par A. D. Nock et traduit par A. J. Festugière, vol. II (Paris, 1946).

Diehl, W., ed., *Die Schulordnungen des Grossherzogtums Hessen*, Monumenta Germaniae paedagogica, vol. XXVIII (Berlin, 1903).

Duns Scotus, John, *Opera omnia*, Vives ed. (Paris, 1891–1895), vols. VIII–XV: *Opus Oxoniense* = *Quaestiones in IV Libros Sententiarum* [hereafter abbreviated as *Ox.*]; vols. XXII–XXIII: *Opus Parisiense* = *Reportatorum Parisiensum libri IV* [hereafter abbreviated as *Par.*]; vol. XXVI: *Quaestiones quodlibetales*.

Durand de Saint-Pourçain, Guillaume, *Commentaria in IV Libros Sententiarum* (Lugduni, 1562).

Eck, Johann, *Epistola de ratione studiorum suorum*, ed. Johann Metzler, in *Corpus Catholicorum*, vol. II (Münster i. W., 1921).

———*Schutzred ķindtlicher Unschuld wider den Catechisten Andre Hosander* (Aichstet, 1539).

———*Defensio contra amarulentas D. Andreae Bodenstein carolstatini invectiones* (1518), ed. Joseph Greving, *CC*, vol. I (Münster i. W., 1919).

Eckhart, Meister, *Die deutschen Werķe*, ed. J. Quint, vol. I: *Meister Eckharts Predigten* (Stuttgart, 1958).

———*Die lateinischen Werķe*, vol. IV: *Magistri Echardi Sermones*, ed. E. Benz et al. (Stuttgart, 1956).

Gansfort, Wessel, *Opera* (Groningen, 1614).

Geiler, von Kaysersberg, Johann, *Navicula Penitentie* (Augsburg, 1511).

———*Sermones fructuosissimi* (Strassburg, 1519).

Gerson, Jean Charlier de, *Opera Johannis de Gerson* (Argentinae, 1488).

———*Opera omnia*, ed. L. E. Du Pin (Antwerpen, 1706).

———*Six sermons français inédits de Jean Gerson*, ed. Louis Mourin (Paris, 1946).

———*De mystica theologia*, ed. André Combes (Lucani, 1958).

Gregory the Great, *Homiliae in Evangelia*, in *PL*, vol. LXXVI.

Gregory of Rimini, *Super Primum et Secundum Sententiarum* (St. Bonaventure, N.Y.: Franciscan Institute, 1955). A reprint of Venice edition (1522).

Henry of Ghent, *Quodlibeta* (Louvain, 1961). A photo-reprint of Paris edition (1518).

———*Summae quaestionum ordinariarum* (St. Bonaventure, N.Y.: Franciscan Institute, 1953). A photo-reprint of Paris edition (1520).

Henry of Werl, *Opera omnia*, vol. I: *Tractatus de Immaculata Conceptione Beatae Mariae Virginis*, ed. Sophronius Clasen, O.F.M. (St. Bonaventure, N.Y., 1955).

Holcot, Ropertus, O.P., [*Lectiones*] *Super Libros Sapientiae* (Hagenau, 1494). [Abbreviated as *Sap. Lect.*]

———*Quaestiones super IV libros Sententiarum* (Lugduni, 1497).

Huss, John, *Sermones de tempore*, ed. Anezka Schmidtova (Prague, 1959).

———*Tractatus de ecclesia*, ed. S. Harrison Thomson (Cambridge, Eng., 1956).

Johannes de Bassolis, *In IV Sententiarum libros* (Paris, 1516–1517).

Johannes Breviscoxa, *Tractatus de fide et ecclesia, Romano pontifice et concilio generali*, ed. L. E. Du Pin, in *Joannis Gersonii opera omnia* (Antwerpiae, 1706), I, 805–904.

Kaser, K., and E. Schneider, eds., "Württembergisches aus römischen Archiven, II: Auszüge aus den Rechnungsbüchern der apostolischen Kammer für das Gebiet des heutigen Königreichs Württemberg aus den Jahren 1396–1534," *Württembergische Geschichtsquellen* 2 (1895), 357–566.

Lainez, Jacobus, *Disputationes Tridentinae*, ed. H. Grisar, S.J., 2 vols. (Oeniponte, 1886).

Lombard, Peter, *Libri quattuor Sententiarum*, in *PL*, vol. CXCII.

Melhofer von Eriszkilch, Philip, *Offenbarung der allerheimlichisten heymlichkeit der ytzigen Baalspriester durch wölche die Welt langezyt gebendt unde das lyden Christi jhämerlich geschmech worden ist, genannt Canon oder die Styllmes* (Schachen, 1525).

Menot, Michel, *Sermons choisis de Michel Menot*, ed. Joseph Nève (Paris, 1924).

Monumenta conciliorum generalium seculi decimi quarti Concilium Basiliense, 4 vols. (Basel, 1857–1937).

Nicholas of Cusa, *Schriften des Nicolaus von Cues: Predigten 1430–1441*, trans. J. Sikora and E. Bohnenstadt (Heidelberg, 1952).

Nicholas of Lyra, *Glosa ordinaria una cum postilla* (Venetiis, 1485). [Abbreviated as *Postilla*.]

Occam, William of, *Quodlibeta septem una cum tractatu de sacramento altaris* (Argentinae, 1491).

—— *Quaestiones et decisiones in IV libros Sententiarum cum Centilogio theologico* (Lugduni, 1495).

—— *Dialogus*, ed. M. Goldast, in *Monarchiae S. Romani Imperii sive Tractatuum de iurisdictione imperiali, regia, et pontificia seu sacerdotali*, II (Frankfurt a. M., 1668), 394–957.

—— *De Sacramento altaris*, ed. T. Bruce Birch (Burlington, 1930).

—— *Breviloquium de potestate papae*, ed. Léon Baudry (Paris, 1937).

—— *Quaestio prima principalis Prologi in primum librum Sententiarum — cum interpretatione Gabrielis Biel quam ad fidem codicum restituit*, ed. P. Boehner (Paterson, N.J., 1939).

—— *Summa Logicae; Pars Secunda et Tertiae Prima*, ed. Philotheus Boehner (St. Bonaventure, N.Y., 1954).

—— *Centiloquium*, ed. P. Boehner, in *FStud* 1 (1941), pt. 1, p. 58 ff.; pt. 2, p. 35 ff.; pt. 3, p. 62 ff.; vol. 2 (1942), pp. 49 ff., 146 ff., 251 ff.

Pico della Mirandola, Giovanni, *Apologia*, in *Opera omnia*, vol. I (Basiliae, 1572).

Pierre d'Auriole, *Scriptum super primum sententiarum*, ed. E. M. Buytaert (St. Bonaventure, N.Y.; Franciscan Institute, 1953–   ).

Politus, Ambrosius Catharinus, O.P., *Apologia pro veritate catholicae et apostolicae fidei ac doctrinae adversus impia ac valde pestifera Martini Lutheri dogmata* [1520], ed. Josef Schweizer, in *Corpus Catholicorum*, vol. XXVII (Münster i. W., 1956).

Pseudo-Dionysius, *Oeuvres complètes du Pseudo-Denys l'Aréopagite*, ed. M. de Candillac (Paris, 1943).

Quentell, Heinrich, ed., *Expositio himnorum . . . ex quibus possunt faciliter de eisdem sanctis colligi sermones peroptimi* (Colonia, 1494).

Richard de Bury, *Philobiblon: Richard de Bury*, ed. Michael Maclagan (Oxford, 1960).

Richard of Mediavilla, *In IV Libros Sententiarum* (Venetiis, 1507–1509).

Roth, R., *Urkunden zur Geschichte der Universität Tübingen aus den Jahren 1476 bis 1550* (Tübingen, 1877).

Schott, Peter, *Lucubratiunculae Petri Schotti*, ed. J. Wimpheling (Strassburg, 1498).

Spira, Ambrosius, *Liber sermonum quadragesimalium de floribus sapientiae* (Basel, 1516).

Steinbach, Wendelinus, *Gabrielis Biel supplementum in 28 distinctiones ultimas quarti magistri sententiarum* (Parisiis, 1527).

Terrenus, Guido, *Quaestio de magisterio infallibili Romani Pontificis*, ed. Bartholomaeus M. Xiberta (Münster i. W., 1926).

Thomas Aquinas, *Opera omnia iussu impensaque Leonis XIII P.M. edita* (Romae, 1882–1948).

Totting, Henry, of Oyta, *Quaestio de sacra scriptura et de veritatibus catholicis*, ed. Albertus Lang (Münster i. W., 1953).

Usingen, Bartholomaeus Arnoldi von, *Libellus . . . contra Lutheranos* (Erphurdie, 1524).

——— *Sermo de sancta cruce predicatus* (Erphurdie, 1524).

Winckelmann, Johann J., *Gründliche und warhafte Beschreibung der Fürstenthümer Hessen- und Hersfeld* (Bremen, 1711).

Wyclif, John, *Sermones*, ed. Johann Loserth (London, 1887–1890).

Xiberta, Bartholomaeus M., ed. *Enchiridion de Verbo Incarnato: Fontes quos ad studia theologica collegit* (Matriti, 1957).

Zerbold, Gerard, van Zutphen, *De spiritualibus ascensionibus*, ed. H. Mahien (Brugge, 1941).

4. PRIMARY SOURCES — WORKS OF GABRIEL BIEL

Ars Gram.	*Tractatus utilis artis grammatice regiminum, constructionum et congruitatum generalia fundamenta declarans pro iunioribus ex diffusis grammaticorum principiis stilo facili deflorans* (Reutlingen, c. 1486).
De communi vita	*Tractatus magistri gabrielis Byell de communi vita clericorum*, no date. Incip.: "Quesitum est a me. . ." Explic.: ". . . correctioni cuiuslibet sanum sapientis humillime submittenda." Koninklijke Bibliotheek, 's Gravenhage, MS 75.958; fol. 1^r–21^v. Edited by W. M. Landeen in "Appendix. Biel's Tractate on the Common Life," *Research Studies, Washington State University* 28 (1960), pp. 79–95.
Def.	*Defensorium obedientie apostolice* [1462] (Hagenau, 1510).
De Pot.	*Tractatus de potestate et utilitate monetarum* (Oppenheim, 1516). Published under separate cover by Joh. Aquilia, this tract is IV *Sent.* d 15 q 9 of the *Collectorium*. English translation by R. B. Burke (Philadelphia, 1930).
Epist. I	(1462) Incip.: "Gnade und erluchtunge des heyligen geystes. . ." Explic.: ". . . fronefasten anno etc. LXII. Gabriel Byel." Stadtbibliothek Mainz, HS II, fol. 23^r–23^v. Edited by F. W. E. Roth, "Ein Brief des Gabriel Biel, 1462," *Neues Archiv der Gesellschaft für ältere deutsche Geschichtskunde* 35 (1910), 582–585.

BIBLIOGRAPHY

Epist. II	(1470) Incip.: "Gnediger Lieber Junckher. . ." Explic.: ". . . anno etc. LXX. uwer gnade Capplan Gabriel bruder zu sant Maria zu butzspach." Staatsarchiv Darmstadt. Edited by J. Haller, *Die Anfänge der Universität Tübingen 1477–1537* (Stuttgart, 1927) pt. I.
Lect.	*Sacri canonis misse expositio resolutissima* (Basel, 1510).
Noticia Pastoris Boni	*Nomine domini. Amen. Gabriel Byel sacre theologie licentiatus. Prepositus ac capitulum ecclesia sanctorum Marie Andree et Amandi in Urach, constan. dioc.: Omnibus presencium inspectoribus subscriptorum noticiam cum salute litteras apostolicas indulgentiarum plenarie remissionis* (Tübingen, 5 October 1479).
Regula	*Regula puerorum bona et doctrinalis eximii magistri Gabrielis Biel sacre theologie licentiati cum expositionibus diffinitionum donati parcium orationis et rationibus accidentium grammaticalium* (Leipzig, c. 1497).
S I	*Sermones dominicales de tempore* (Hagenau, 1510).
S II	*Sermones de festivitatibus christi* (Hagenau, 1510).
S III	*Sermones de festivitatibus gloriose virginis marie* (Hagenau, 1510).
S IV	*Sermones de sanctis* (Basel, 1519).
S V	*Passionis dominice sermo historialis. . .* (Hagenau, 1510).
SCE	*Sacrosancti canonis misse expositio . . . in Epitomen contracta* (Antverpiae, 1556).
Sent.	*Epithoma pariter et collectorium circa quattuor sententiarum libros* (Tübingen, 1501).

Note: For printed editions see J. H. Zedler, *Universal Lexikon* (Leipzig, 1733) III, 1777 f.; Ludovicus Hain, *Repertorium Bibliographicum* I (Paris, 1826) 3178 ff., supplement II (London, 1898) 1050; *Gesamtkatalog der Wiegendrucke* IV (Leipzig, 1930), 4329–4341.

SECONDARY SOURCES

Alberts, W. Jappe, "Zur Historiographie der Devotio Moderna und ihrer Erforschung," *Westfälische Forschungen* 11 (1958), 51 ff.

Amann, E., and P. Vignaux, "Occam: I. Sa vie, II. Oeuvres, III. Originalité philosophique et théologique, IV. Influence, V. Eglise et la doctrine d'Occam," in *DThC*, vol. XI, cols. 864–904.

Ameri, Hyacinthius, *Doctrina theologorum de Immaculata B.V.M. Conceptione tempore concilii Basiliensis* (Rome, 1954).

Anatriello, Pasquale, *La dottrina di Gabriele Biel sull'Eucaristia* (Milan, 1937).

Andreas, Willy, *Deutschland vor der Reformation: Eine Zeitenwende*, 2 ed. (Berlin, 1934).

Appel, Helmut, *Anfechtung und Trost im Spätmittelalter und bei Luther* (Leipzig, 1938).

Argentré, Charles du Plessis d', *Collectio Judiciorum de novis erroribus* (Paris, 1724–1728), vols. I and II.

Auer, Johann, *Die Entwicklung der Gnadenlehre in der Hochscholastik*, Pt. I:

Das Wesen der Gnade (Freiburg i. Br., 1942), Pt. II: *Das Wirken der Gnade* (Freiburg i. Br., 1951).

Axters, Stephanus, O.P., *Scholastiek Lexicon: Latijn-Nederlandsch* (Antwerp, 1937).

——— *Geschiedenis der Vroomheid in de Nederlanden* (Antwerp, 1956–   ).

Backes, Ignaz, *Die Christologie des heiligen Thomas von Aquin und die griechischen Kirchenväter*. Forschungen zur christlichen Literatur- und Dogmengeschichte, vol. XVII (Paderborn, 1931).

——— "Die christologische Problematik der Hochscholastik und ihre Beziehung zu Chalkedon," in *Das Konzil von Chalkedon: Geschichte und Gegenwart*, vol. II: *Entscheidung um Chalkedon*, ed. Aloys Grillmeier, S.J., and Heinrich Bacht, S.J. (Würzburg, 1953), pp. 923–939.

Bainton, Roland H., "Immoralities of the Patriarchs according to the Exegesis of the Late Middle Ages and of the Reformation," *HTR* 23 (1930), 39–49.

——— "Michael Servetus and the Trinitarian Speculation of the Middle Ages," in *Autour de Michel Servet et de Sebastien Castellion*, ed. B. Becker (Haarlem, 1953), pp. 29–46.

Bakhuizen van den Brink, J. N., *Traditio in de Reformatie en het Katholicisme in de zestiende Eeuw*, Mededelingen der Koninklijke Nederlandse Akademie van Wetenschappen, Afd. Letterk., n.s. 15.2 (Amsterdam, 1952), pp. 27–71.

——— "Tradition und Heilige Schrift am Anfang des dritten Jahrhunderts," *Catholica* 9 (1953), 105–114.

——— "La tradition dans L'Eglise primitive et au XVIe siècle," *Revue d'Histoire et de Philosophie religieuses* 36 (1956), 271–281.

——— "Traditio im theologischen Sinne," *Vigiliae Christianae* 13 (1959), 65–86.

Balić, Karl, O.F.M., *Duns Scoti Theologiae Marianae elementa* (Sibenici, 1933).

——— *Testimonia de assumptione B.V.M. ex omnibus saeculis*, vol. I (Rome, 1948), vol. II (Rome, 1950).

——— "Die Corredemptrixfrage innerhalb der franziskanischen Theologie," *FS* 39 (1957), 218–287.

Bardy, G., *La théologie de l'Église*, vol. I: *De St. Clément de Rome à St. Irénée* (Paris, 1945).

Barnikol, Ernst, *Studien zur Geschichte der Brüder vom gemeinsamen Leben* (Tübingen, 1917).

Barth, Bernhard, O.S.B., "Ein neues Dokument zur Geschichte der frühscholastischen Christologie," *Theologische Quartalschrift* 100 (1919), 409–426; 101 (1920), 235–262.

Baudry, Léon, *Guillaume d'Ockham: Sa vie, ses oeuvres, ses idées sociales et politiques*, vol. I: *L'homme et les oeuvres*, Études de philosophie médiévale XXXIX (Paris, 1949).

——— *Lexique philosophique de Guillaume d'Ockham: Étude des notions fondamentales* (Paris, 1958).

Bauer, Ludwig, "Das Philosophische Lebenswerk des Robert Grosseteste, Bischofs von Lincoln († 1253)" in *Dritte Vereinsschrift der Görres-Gesellschaft für 1910* (Cologne, 1910), pp. 58–82.

——— *Die Philosophie des Robert Grosseteste, Bischofs von Lincoln*, in *BB*, vol. XVIII, pts. 4–6 (Münster i. W., 1917).

Baumgartner, Charles, S.J., ed., "Contemplation," *Dictionnaire de spiritualité, ascétique, et mystique: doctrine et historique*, vol. III (Paris, 1953), cols. 1643–2193.

Bayle, Pierre, *Dictionnaire historique et critique*, vol. IV (Basel, 1739).
Bayley, Charles C., "Pivotal Concepts in the Political Philosophy of William of Ockham," *Journal of the History of Ideas* 10 (1949), 199–218.
Bebermeyer, Gustav, *Tübinger Dichterhumanisten: Bebel, Frischlin, Flayder* (Tübingen, 1927).
Becher, Hubert, S.J., "Gottesbegriff und Gottesbeweis bei Wilhelm von Ockham," *Scholastik* 3 (1928), 369–393.
Beintker, Horst, "Neues Material über die Beziehungen Luthers zum mittelalterlichen Augustinismus," *ZKG* 76 (1957), 144–148.
Benary, F., "Via antiqua und via moderna auf den deutschen Hochschulen des Mittelalters mit besonderer Berücksichtigung der Universität Erfurt," *Zur Geschichte der Stadt und der Universität Erfurt am Ausgang des Mittelalters* (Gotha, 1919).
Benz, Ernst, *Wittenberg und Byzanz: zur Begegnung und Auseinandersetzung der Reformation und der Östlich-orthodoxen Kirche* (Marburg, 1949).
Berlière, U., *L'ascèse bénédictine des origines à la fin du XIIe siècle* (Paris, 1927).
Bernard, P., "Contrition," in *DThC*, vol. III, cols. 1671–1687.
Bess, B., "Gerson, Joh. Charlier," in *RE*, VI, 612–617.
Beugnet, A., "Attrition," in *DThC*, vol. I, cols. 2235–2258.
Beumer, Johannes, S.J., "Das katholische Schriftprinzip in der Literatur der Scholastik bis zur Reformation," *Scholastik* 16 (1941), 24–52.
——— "Der Augustinismus in der theologischen Erkenntnislehre des Petrus Aureoli," *FS* 36 (1954), 137–171.
——— "Die Frage nach Schrift und Tradition bei Robert Bellarmin," *Scholastik* 34 (1959), 1–22.
——— "Das katholische Traditionsprinzip in seiner heute neu erkannten Problematik," *Scholastik* 36 (1961), 217–240.
Biel, H. W., *De Gabriele Biel celeberrimo papista anti-papista* (Wittenberg, 1719).
Bodmann, F. J., *Rheingauische Alterhümer oder Landes- und Regimentsverfassung des Westlichen- oder Niederrheingaues im mittlern Zeitalter* (Mainz, 1819).
Boehner, Philotheus, "A Recent Presentation of Ockham's Philosophy," *FStud* 9 (1949), 443–456.
——— "On a recent Study of Ockham," *FStud* 10 (1950), 191–196.
——— *Ockham: Philosophical Writings* (Edinburgh, 1957).
——— *Collected Articles on Ockham*, ed. E. M. Buytaert (St. Bonaventure, N.Y., 1958).
Bonke, Elzearius, O.F.M., "Doctrina nominalistica de fundamento ordinis moralis apud Gulielmum de Ockham et Gabrielem Biel," *Collectanea Franciscana* 14 (1944), 57–83.
Borchert, Ernst, *Der Einfluss des Nominalismus auf die Christologie der Spätscholastik nach dem Traktat de communicatione idiomatum des Nikolaus Oresme, Untersuchungen und Textausgabe*, in *BB*, vol. XXXV, pts. 4–5 (Münster i. W., 1940).
Bornkamm, Heinrich, "Iustitia Dei in der Scholastik und bei Luther," *ARG* 39 (1942), 1–46.
Bouillard, H., *Conversion et grâce chez S. Thomas d'Aquin* (Paris, 1944).
Bouyer, Louis, *Du protestantisme à l'église* (Paris, 1954). Translated as *The Spirit and Forms of Protestantism*, by A. V. Littledale (Westminster, Md., 1956).

Brady, Ignatius, O.F.M., "The Development of the Doctrine on the Immaculate Conception in the Fourteenth Century after Aureoli," *FStud* 15 (1955), 175–202.

Brandt, E., *Die Mitwirkung der seligsten Jungfrau zur Erlösung nach dem heiligen Antonin von Florenz* (Rome, 1945).

Braun, Wilhelm, *Die Bedeutung der Konkupiscenz in Luthers Leben und Lehre* (Berlin, 1908).

Brinktrine, Johannes, *Die Lehre von der Gnade* (Paderborn, 1957).

Bruch, Richard, "Die Urgerechtigkeit als Rechtheit des Willens nach der Lehre des Hl. Bonaventura," *FS* 33 (1951), 180–206.

Bruin, C. C. de, *Middelnederlandse Vertalingen van het Nieuwe Testament* (Groningen, 1934).

Buescher, Gabriel N., *The Eucharistic Teaching of William Ockham*, The Catholic University of America Studies in Sacred Theology, 44 (Washington, D.C., 1950).

Buschmiller, Robert J., *The Maternity of Mary in the Mariology of St. Albert the Great* (Carthagena, Ohio, 1959).

Butler, Cuthbert, *Western Mysticism*, 2 ed. (London, 1926).

Buytaert, E. M., O.F.M., "The Immaculate Conception in the Writings of Ockham," *FStud* 10 (1950), 149–163.

Cameron, James K., "Conciliarism in Theory and Practice, 1378–1418" (unpub. Hartford Seminary thesis, 1952).

Capelle, C., *Amaury de Bène: Etude sur son panthéisme formel* (Paris, 1932).

Cappuyns, M., "Biel, Gabriel," in *Dictionnaire d'histoire et de géographie ecclésiastique*, vol. VIII (Paris, 1935), cols. 1429–1435.

Carol, J. B., *De Corredemptione B.V.M. Disquisitio Positiva* (Vatican City, 1950).

Chevalier, Irénée, *La théorie Augustinienne des relations Trinitaires* (Fribourg, 1940).

Cohn, Norman, *The Pursuit of the Millennium*, 2 ed. (New York, 1961).

Combes, André, "Jean de Vippa, Jean de Rupa ou Jean de Ripa," *AHDL* 12 (1939), 253–290.

―――― *Jean Gerson: commentateur dionysien* (Paris, 1940).

―――― *Essai sur la critique de Ruysbroeck par Gerson*, vol. I: *Introduction critique et dossier documentaire* (Paris, 1945); vol. II: *La première critique gersonienne du De Ornatu Spiritualium Nuptiarum* (Paris, 1948); vol. III: *L'évolution spontanée de la critique gersonienne* (Paris, 1959).

―――― "La doctrine mariale du chancelier Jean Gerson," *Maria: Etudes sur la sainte Vierge* 2 (Paris, 1952), 865–882.

Congar, Yves M.-J., "Théologie: Etude historique," in *DThC*, vol. XV, cols. 346–447.

―――― "Sainte Ecriture et sainte Eglise," *Revue des Sciences Philosophiques et Théologiques* 44 (1960), 81–88.

―――― *La Tradition et les Traditions: Essai historique* (Paris, 1960).

Connolly, James L. *John Gerson: Reformer and Mystic* (Louvain, 1928).

Copleston, Frederick, S.J., *A History of Philosophy*, vol. II: *Medieval Philosophy: Augustine to Scotus* (Westminster, Md., 1952).

Crehan, J. H., S.J., "Biel and the Mass," *Clergy Review* 43 (1958), 606–617.

Cross, Frank Moore, "Yahweh as Judge" (manuscript in preparation).

Cullmann, Oscar, "Scripture and Tradition," *SJT* 6 (1953), 113–135.

Czerny, Johannes, *Das übernatürliche Verdienst für Andere* (Freiburg i. Br., 1957).

Dacheux, L., *Un réformateur catholique à la fin du XVe siècle: Jean Geiler de Kayserberg* (Paris, 1876).

Dahmus, Joseph H., *The Prosecution of John Wyclif* (New Haven, 1952).

Dankbaar, W. F., "Schriftgezag en kerkgezag bij Augustinus," *NTT* 11 (1956), 37–59.

Day, Sebastian J., *Intuitive Cognition: A Key to the Significance of the Later Scholastics* (St. Bonaventure, N. Y., 1947).

Deneffe, A., *Der Traditionsbegriff: Studie zur Theologie,* Münsterische Beiträge zur Theologie 18 (Münster i. W., 1931).

Denifle, H. S., *Die Universitäten des Mittelalters bis 1400,* vol. I: *Die Entstehung der Universitäten des Mittelalters bis 1400* (Berlin, 1885).

—— *Luther und Luthertum,* vol. I, pt. 1, 2 ed. (Mainz, 1904); vol. I, pt. 2, 2 ed. (Mainz, 1906).

—— *Ergänzungen zu Denifle's Luther and Luthertum,* vol. I: *Quellenbelege: Die Abendländischen Schriftausleger bis Luther über Justitia Dei (Rom. 1:17) und Justificatio* (Mainz, 1905); vol. II: *Lutherpsychologie als Schlüssel zur Lutherlegende: Denifles Untersuchungen kritisch nachgeprüft von Albert Maria Weiss,* O.P., 2 ed. (Mainz, 1906).

—— and E. Chatelain, *Chartularium universitatis parisiensis,* vol. I: *Ab anno MCC ad annum MCCLXXVI* (Paris, 1889); vol. III: *Ab anno MCCCL ad annum MCCCLXXXIII* (Paris, 1894).

Dettloff, W., O.F.M., *Die Lehre von der Acceptatio Divina bei Johannes Duns Scotus: mit besonderer Berücksichtigung der Rechtfertigungslehre* (Werl/Westf., 1954).

Diepenbrock, M., *Heinrich Suso's, genannt Amandus, Leben und Schriften,* 3 ed. (Augsburg, 1854).

Di Fonzo, L., *Doctrina Sanctae Bonaventurae de universali mediatione Beatae Virginis Mariae* (Rome, 1938).

Dillenschneider, Clement, *Marie: au service de notre Rédemption* (Hagenau, 1947).

Dohna, Lothar Graf zu, *Reformatio Sigismundi: Beiträge zum Verständnis einer Reformschrift des fünfzehnten Jahrhunderts* (Göttingen, 1960).

Dorner, J. A., *Entwicklungsgeschichte der Lehre von der Person Christi,* vol. II: *Die Lehre von der Person Christi vom Ende des vierten Jahrhunderts bis zur Gegenwart,* 2 ed. (Berlin, 1853).

Dreher, Bruno, *Die Osterpredigt von der Reformation bis zur Gegenwart* (Freiburg i. Br., 1951).

Dreiling, Raymund, *Der Konzeptualismus in der Universalienlehre des Franziskanererzbischofes Petrus Aureoli,* in *BB,* vol. XI, pt. 6 (Münster i. W., 1913).

Dress, Walter, *Die Theologie Gersons: Eine Untersuchung zur Verbindung von Nominalismus und Mystik im Spätmittelalter* (Gütersloh, 1931).

Dublanchy, E., "Infaillibilité du Pape," in *DThC,* vol. VII, cols. 1638–1717.

—— "Marie: Les privilèges essentiels de la Vierge Marie," *DThC,* vol. IX, cols. 2339–2409.

Dugmore, C. W., *The Mass and the English Reformers* (London, 1958).

Duhem, P., *Etudes sur Léonard de Vinci,* 3 vols. (Paris, 1906–1913).

Duijnstee, X. P. D., *'s Pausen primaat in de latere middeleeuwen en de Aegidiaansche school,* vol. I: *Philips de Schoone* (Hilversum, 1935); vol. II: *Lodewijk de*

Beier (Amsterdam, 1936); vol. III: *Conciliarisme: Pisa — Constanz* (Amsterdam, 1939).

Ebeling, Gerhard, *Evangelische Evangelienauslegung* (Munich, 1942).

—— "Die Anfänge von Luthers Hermeneutik," *ZThK* 48 (1951), 172–230.

—— "Luthers Psalterdruck vom Jahre 1513," *ZThK* 50 (1953), 43–99.

—— "Luthers Auslegung des 14. (15.) Psalms in der ersten Psalmenvorlesung im Vergleich mit der exegetischen Tradition," *ZThK* 50 (1953), 280–339.

—— *Die Geschichtlichkeit der Kirche und ihrer Verkündigung als theologisches Problem* (Tübingen, 1954).

—— "Hermeneutik," in *RGG*, vol. III, cols. 242–262.

Eder, Karl, *Deutsche Geisteswende zwischen Mittelalter und Neuzeit* (Salzburg, 1937).

Ehrle, F., *Der Sentenzenkommentar Peters von Candia, des Pisaner Papstes Alexander V.*, in *FS, Beiheft* 9 (Münster i. W., 1925).

Eichrodt, Walther, *Das Menschenverständnis des Alten Testaments* (Basel, 1944).

—— *Theologie des Alten Testaments*, vol. I: *Gott und Volk*, 3 ed. (Berlin, 1948).

Elie, Hubert, *Le Complexe significabile* (Paris, 1934).

—— *Le Traité 'De l'Infini' de Jean Mair; Nouvelle édition avec traduction et annotations* (Paris, 1937).

Emmen, Aquilin, O.F.M., "Immaculata Deiparae conceptio secundum Guillelmum de Nottingham," *Marianum* 5 (1943), 221–260.

—— "Heinrich von Langenstein und die Diskussion über die Empfängnis Mariens," in *Theologie in Geschichte und Gegenwart: Festschrift Michael Schmaus*, ed. Johann Auer und Hermann Volk (Munich, 1957), pp. 625 ff.

—— "Einführung in die Mariologie der Oxforder Franziskanerschule," *FS* 39 (1957), 99–217.

Espenberger, Johannes N., *Die Elemente der Erbsünde nach Augustin und der Frühscholastik* (Mainz, 1905).

—— *Grund und Gewissheit des übernatürlichen Glaubens in der Hoch- und Spätscholastik* (Paderborn, 1915).

d'Entrèves, Alexander Passerin, *The Medieval Contribution to Political Thought: Thomas Aquinas, Marsilius of Padua, Richard Hooker*, 2 ed. (New York, 1959).

Feckes, Carl, "Die Stellung der nominalistischen Schule zur aktuellen Gnade," *Römische Quartalschrift* 32 (1924), 157–165.

—— *Die Rechtfertigungslehre des Gabriel Biel und ihre Stellung innerhalb der nominalistischen Schule*, Münsterische Beiträge zur Theologie, vol. VII (Münster i. W., 1925).

—— "Gabriel Biel, der erste grosse Dogmatiker der Universität Tübingen in seiner wissenschaftlichen Bedeutung," *Theologische Quartalschrift* 108 (1927), 50–76.

—— "Die religionsphilosophischen Bestrebungen des spätmittelalterlichen Nominalismus," *Römische Quartalschrift* 35 (1927), 183–208.

—— "Biel," in *Lexikon der Marienkunde*, fasc. 5, col. 777 (Regensburg, 1960).

Finkenzeller, Joseph, *Offenbarung und Theologie nach der Lehre des Johannes Duns Skotus: Eine historische und systematische Untersuchung* (Münster i. W., 1960).

Flesseman-van Leer, E., *Tradition and Scripture in the Early Church* (Assen, 1954).

———— "The Controversy about Scripture and Tradition between Thomas More and William Tyndale," *NAK* 43 (1959), 143–164.

———— "The Controversy about Ecclesiology between Thomas More and William Tyndale," *NAK* 44 (1960), 65–86.

Florovsky, Georges, "Cur Deus Homo? The Motive of the Incarnation," in *Festival Volume Hamilcar Alivisatos DD* (Athens, 1957), 3–12.

Fousek, Marianka, "The Perfectionism of the Early *Unitas Fratrum*," *CH* 30 (1961), 396–413.

Franks, Robert S., *A History of the Doctrine of the Work of Christ in its Ecclesiastical Development*, 2 ed. (Edinburgh, 1962).

Franz, A., *Die Messe im deutschen Mittelalter* (Freiburg i. Br., 1902).

Freudenberger, Theobald, *Der Würzburger Domprediger Dr. Johann Reyss* (Münster i. W., 1954).

Friethoff, C., *Die Prädestinationslehre bei Thomas von Aquin und Calvin* (Fribourg, 1926).

Gabriel, Astrik, *The College System in the Fourteenth Century Universities* (Baltimore, n.d. [1962]).

Gandillac, M. de, "Ockham et la 'Via Moderna'" in *Histoire de l'Eglise depuis les origines jusqu'à nos jours*, vol. VIII: *Le mouvement doctrinal du IXe au XIVe siècle* (Paris, 1951), 449–512.

García, M. Fernandez, O.F.M., *Lexicon scholasticum philosophico-theologicum* (Quaracchi, 1910).

Garrigou-Lagrange, R., "St. Thomas et le Néo-Molinisme," appendix to *l'Existence de Dieu*, 4 ed. (Paris, 1923).

Garvens, Anita, "Die Grundlagen der Ethik Wilhelms von Ockham," *FS* 21 (1934), 243–273, 360–408.

Geiselmann, Josef Rupert, "Die Tradition," in *Fragen der Theologie Heute*, ed. J. Feiner, et al. (Zurich, 1957), 69–108.

———— "Das Konzil von Trient über das Verhältnis der Heiligen Schrift und der nicht geschriebenen Traditionen: Sein Missverständnis in der nachtridentinischen Theologie und die Überwindung dieses Missverständnisses," in *Die mündliche Überlieferung*, ed. Michael Schmaus (Munich, 1957), 123–206.

———— "Schrift-Tradition-Kirche: Ein oekumenisches Problem," in *Begegnung der Christen: Studien evangelischer und katholischer Theologen* [Festschrift Otto Karrer], ed. M. Roesle and O. Cullmann (Frankfurt a.M., 1959), 131–159.

———— *Die lebendige Überlieferung als Norm des christlichen Glaubens dargestellt im Geiste der Traditionslehre Johannes Ev. Kuhns* (Freiburg i. Br., 1959).

Gewirth, Alan, *Marsilius of Padua, The Defender of Peace*, vol. I: *Marsilius of Padua and Medieval Political Philosophy* (New York, 1951); vol. II: *The Defensor Pacis* (New York, 1956).

Ghellinck, J. de, "Un évêque bibliophile au XIVe siècle," *Revue d'histoire ecclésiastique* 18 (1922), 271–312; 482–509; 19 (1923), 157–200.

———— "'Pagina' et 'Sacra Pagina': Histoire d'un mot et transformation de l'objet primitivement désigné," in *Mélanges Auguste Pelzer* (Louvain, 1947), 23–59.

Gierke, Otto von, *Johannes Althusius und die Entwicklung der naturrechtlichen Staatstheorien*, 3 ed. (Breslau, 1913).

———— *Das deutsche Genossenschaftsrecht*, vol. III: *Die Staats- und Korporationslehre*

SECONDARY SOURCES

des Altertums und des Mittelalters und ihre Aufnahme in Deutschland, 2 ed. (Darmstadt, 1954).

Gilmore, Myron P., "The Lawyers and the Church in the Italian Renaissance," *The Rice Institute Pamphlet* 46 (1960), 136–154.

Gilson, Etienne, *Introduction à l'étude de Saint Augustin,* 2 ed. (Paris, 1943).

—— *L'esprit de la philosophie médiévale,* 2 vols, 2 ed. (Paris, 1944).

—— *Le Thomisme: Introduction à la philosophie de Saint Thomas d'Aquin,* 5 ed. (Paris, 1947).

—— *Jean Duns Scot: Introduction à ses positions fondamentales* (Paris, 1952).

—— *History of Christian Philosophy in the Middle Ages* (New York and London, 1955).

Glorieux, P., "L'Activité littéraire de Gerson à Lyon: Correspondence inédite avec la Grande-Chartreuse," *RTAM* 18 (1951), 238–307.

—— "L'enseignement universitaire de Gerson," *RTAM* 23 (1956), 88–113.

—— "Thomas Bradwardine," in *DThC,* vol. XV, cols. 765–773.

—— ed., *Jean Gerson. Oeuvres complètes. I. Introduction générale* (Paris, 1960).

Grabmann, M., *Die Geschichte der katholischen Theologie seit dem Ausgang der Väterzeit* (Freiburg i. Br., 1933).

—— *Mittelalterliches Geistesleben: Abhandlungen zur Geschichte der Scholastik und Mystik,* vols. I–III (Munich, 1936).

Grane, Leif, "Gabriel Biels Lehre von der Allmacht Gottes," *ZThK* 53 (1956), 53–75.

Greving, J., *Johann Eck als junger Gelehrter: Eine literar- und dogmengeschichtliche Untersuchung über seinen Chrysopassus Praedestinationis aus dem Jahr 1514* (Münster i. W., 1906).

Guelluy, Robert, *Philosophie et Théologie chez Guillaume d'Ockham* (Paris, 1947).

Guimaraens, F. de, O.F.M., "La doctrine des théologiens sur l'Immaculée Conception de 1250 à 1350," *Etudes Franciscaines* 3 (1952), 181–203; 4 (1953), 23–51, 167–187.

Gwynn, A., *The English Austin Friars in the Time of Wyclif* (Oxford, 1940).

Hägglund, Bengt, *Theologie und Philosophie bei Luther und in der occamistischen Tradition: Luthers Stellung zu der Theorie der doppelten Wahrheit* (Lund, 1955).

—— "Die Bedeutung der 'regula fidei' als Grundlage theologischer Aussagen," *Studia Theologica* 12 (1958), 1–44.

Hagen, K., *Deutschlands literarische und religiöse Verhältnisse im Reformationszeitalter,* vol. I (Erlangen, 1841).

Hahn, Fritz, "Zur Hermeneutik Gersons," *ZThK* 51 (1954), 34–50.

Haller, J., *Die Anfänge der Universität Tübingen, 1477–1537,* vol. I (Stuttgart, 1927); vol. II (Stuttgart, 1929).

Hamman, Adalbert, O.F.M., "La doctrine de l'Eglise et de l'Etat d'après le Breviloquium d'Occam," *FS* 32 (1950), 135–141.

Harent, Stéphane, S.J., "Papauté: Infaillibilité pontificale," *Dictionnaire Apologétique de la Foi Catholique,* vol. III (Paris, 1916), cols. 1422–1534.

Häring, Nikolaus, *Die Theologie des Erfurter Augustiner-Eremiten Bartholomäus Arnoldi von Usingen: Ein Beitrag zur Dogmengeschichte der Reformationszeit* (Limburg an der Lahn, 1939).

Hase, Karl August, von, *Lehrbuch der Kirchengeschichte,* 12 ed. (Jena, 1900).

443

Haubst, Rudolf, *Die Christologie des Nikolaus von Kues* (Freiburg i. Br., 1956).

Haureau, B., *Notices et extraits de quelques manuscrits latins de la Bibliothèque nationale*, vol. III (Paris, 1891).

Heckel, Johannes, "Recht und Gesetz, Kirche und Obrigkeit in Luthers Lehre vor dem Thesenanschlag von 1517: Eine juristische Untersuchung," *Zeitschrift der Savigny-Stiftung für Rechtsgeschichte* 57 (1937), Kanonistische Abteilung 26, pp. 285–375.

———"Initia iuris ecclesiastici Protestantium," (Munich, 1950), *Sitzungsberichte der Bayerischen Akademie der Wissenschaften*, Philosophische-historische Klasse (1949), pt. 15.

———*Lex Charitatis: Eine juristische Untersuchung über das Recht in der Theologie Martin Luthers* (Munich, 1953).

Heerinck, J., *Introductio in theologiam spiritualem, asceticam et mysticam* (Rome, 1931).

Hefele, C. J., and H. Leclercq, *Histoire des conciles*, vols. I–VIII (Paris, 1907–1916).

Hegel, Karl, *Die Chroniken der deutschen Städte vom 14. bis ins 16. Jahrhundert*, vol. XVIII (Leipzig, 1882).

Heim, K., *Das Wesen der Gnade und ihr Verhältnis zu den natürlichen Funktionen des Menschen bei Alexander Halesius* (Leipzig, 1907).

———*Das Gewissheitsproblem in der systematischen Theologie bis zu Schleiermacher* (Leipzig, 1911).

Heppe, Heinrich and Ernst Bizer, *Die Dogmatik der evangelisch-reformierten Kirche*, 2 ed. (Neukirchen, 1958).

Hermelink, H., *Geschichte der theologischen Fakultät in Tübingen vor der Reformation 1477–1534* (Tübingen, 1906).

———*Die Matrikeln der Universität Tübingen*, vol. I (Stuttgart, 1906).

Heynck, Valens, O.F.M., "Die Verteidigung der Sacramentenlehre des Duns Skotus durch den hl. Joh. Fischer gegen die Anschuldigungen Luthers," *FS* 24 (1937), 165–175.

———"Die Verteidigung des Duns Skotus durch den Konzilstheologen Andreas de Vega O.F.M.," pt. III, *FS* 27 (1940), 129–148.

———"Die Reuelehre des Skotusschülers Johannes de Bassolis," *FS* 28 (1941), 1–36.

———"Zur Rechtfertigungslehre des Kontrovers-theologen Kaspar Schatzgeyer O.F.M.," *FS* 28 (1941), 129–151.

———"A Controversy at the Council of Trent concerning the Doctrine of Duns Scotus," *FStud* 9 (1949), 181–258.

———"Zur Busslehre des hl. Bonaventura," *FS* 36 (1954), 1–81.

Hirsch, Emanuel, *Lutherstudien*, 2 vols. (Gütersloh, 1954).

Hochstetter, Erich, *Studien zur Metaphysik und Erkenntnislehre Wilhelms von Ockham* (Berlin and Leipzig, 1927).

———"Nominalismus?" *FStud* 9 (1949), 370–403.

———"Viator mundi: Einige Bemerkungen zur Situation des Menschen bei Wilhelm von Ockham," *FS* 32 (1950), 1–20.

Hödl, Ludwig, *Die Geschichte der scholastischen Literatur und der Theologie der Schlüsselgewalt*, vol. I: . . . *bis zur Summa Aurea*, in *BB*, vol. XXXVIII, pt. 4 (Münster i. W., 1960).

Hoffmann, Fritz, *Die erste Kritik des Ockhamismus durch den Oxforder Kanzler Johannes Lutterell* (Breslau, 1941).

———— *Die Schriften des Oxforder Kanzlers Iohannes Lutterell: Texte zur Theologie des vierzehnten Jahrhunderts* (Leipzig, 1959).

Holl, Karl, *Gesammelte Aufsätze zur Kirchengeschichte*, vol. I: *Luther*, 6 ed., (Tübingen, 1932).

Huizinga, J., *Herfsttij der Middeleeuwen: Studie over levens-en gedachtenvormen der veertiende en vijftiende eeuw in Frankrijk en Nederland*, 6 ed. (Haarlem, 1947). Translated as *The Waning of the Middle Ages* (London, 1955).

Hunzinger, A. W., *Lutherstudien II: Das Furchtproblem in der katholischen Lehre von Augustin bis Luther* (Leipzig, 1906).

Hurley, Michael, S.J., "Scriptura sola: Wyclif and his Critics," *Traditio* 16 (1960), 275–352.

Hurter, H., *Nomenclator literarius theologiae catholicae theologos exhibens aetate, natione, disciplinis distinctos*, vol. II, 3 ed. (Innsbruck, 1906).

Hyma, A., *The Christian Renaissance: A History of the Devotio Moderna* (New York, 1925).

———— *The Brethren of the Common Life* (Grand Rapids, Mich., 1950).

Imbart de la Tour, Pierre, *Les Origines de la Réforme*, 3 vols. (Paris, 1905–1914).

Iodice, Antonio, "L'efficacia del Sacramento della Penitenza negli Scolastici e in Gabriele Biel," *La Scuola Cattolica* 66 (1938), 141–160.

———— "La reviviscenza dei meriti in Gabriele Biel," *La Scuola Cattolica* 66 (1938), 430–442.

———— "La dottrina di Gabriele Biel circa i ministri del potere delle chiavi e la confessione ai laici," *Divus Thomas* 41 (1938), 113–129.

———— "Due curiose opinioni teologiche di Gabriele Biel circa la materia e la forma del sacramento della penitenza e il precetto divino della confessione sacramentale," *Divus Thomas* 44 (1941), 273–292.

Iserloh, Erwin, *Gnade und Eucharistie in der philosophischen Theologie des Wilhelm von Ockham: Ihre Bedeutung für die Ursachen der Reformation*, Veröffentlichungen des Instituts für Europäische Geschichte Mainz, vol. VIII (Wiesbaden, 1956).

———— "Um die Echtheit des 'Centiloquium.' Ein Beitrag zur Wertung Ockhams und zur Chronologie seiner Werke," *Gregorianum* 30 (1949), 78–103; 309–346.

———— *Die Eucharistie in der Darstellung des Johannes Eck: Ein Beitrag zur vortridentinischen Kontroverstheologie über das Messopfer* (Münster i. W., 1950).

———— "Luther-Kritik oder Luther-Polemik," in *Festgabe Joseph Lortz*, ed. E. Iserloh and P. Manns (Baden-Baden, 1958), I, 15–42.

Jacob, E. F., *Essays in the Conciliar Epoch*, 2 ed. (Manchester, 1955).

Janssen, Johannes, *Geschichte des deutschen Volkes seit dem Ausgang des Mittelalters*, vol. I: *Deutschlands allgemeine Zustände beim Ausgang des Mittelalters* (Freiburg i. Br., 1878).

———— *An meine Kritiker: Nebst Ergänzungen und Erläuterungen zu den drei ersten Bänden meiner Geschichte des deutschen Volkes* (Freiburg i. Br., 1882).

Jedin, Hubert, *Geschichte des Konzils von Trient*, vol. I: *Der Kampf um das Konzil*, 2 ed. (Freiburg i. Br., 1951); vol. II: *Die erste Trienter Tagungsperiode 1545/47* (Freiburg i. Br., 1957).

Jellouschek, Carl J., *Die ältesten Wiener Theologen und das Dogma vom Jahre 1950* (Vienna, 1956).

Joret, F. D., *La Contemplation mystique d'àpres S. Thomas d'Aquin* (Lille, 1923).

Jugie, M., and X. Le Bachelet, "Immaculée Conception," in *DThC*, vol. VII, cols. 845–1218.

Kantorowicz, Ernst H., *The King's Two Bodies: A Study in Medieval Political Theology* (Princeton, 1957).

Karrer, Otto and Herma Piesch, *Meister Eckeharts Rechtfertigungsschrift* (Erfurt, 1927).

Kattenbusch, Ferdinand, *Luthers Lehre vom unfreien Willen und von der Prädestination nach ihrem Entstehungsgründe untersucht* (Göttingen, 1875).

Kaup, Julian, O.F.M., "Zum Begriff der iustitia originalis in der älteren Franziskanerschule," *FS* 29 (1942), 44–55.

Kempf, Friedrich, *Papsttum und Kaisertum bei Innocenz III.* (Rome, 1954).

Keuppens, J., *Mariologiae Compendium: Deipara, Mediatrix, Florilegium mariale* (Antwerp, 1938).

Keussen, H., *Die Matrikel der Universität Köln, 1389 bis 1559*, vol. I (Bonn, 1928).

Kidd, B. J., *The Late Medieval Doctrine of the Eucharistic Sacrifice*, 1 ed. (London, 1898); 2 ed. (London, 1958).

Klein, J., *Der Gottesbegriff des Johannes Duns Skotus, vor allem nach seiner ethischen Seite betrachtet* (Paderborn, 1913).

—— "Zur Busslehre des seligen Joh. Duns Skotus," *FS* 27 (1940), 104–113, 191–196.

Knowles, D., *The Religious Orders in England*, vol. II: *The End of the Middle Ages* (Cambridge, Eng., 1955).

Koch, J., *Durandus de Sancto Porciano O.P.*, in *BB*, vol. XXVI, pt. 1 (Münster i. W., 1927).

—— "Philosophische und theologische Irrtumslisten von 1270–1329. Ein Beitrag zur Entwicklung der theologische Zensuren," in *Mélanges Mandonnet* (Paris, 1930), II, 305–329.

—— "Neue Aktenstücke zu dem gegen Wilhelm von Ockham in Avignon geführten Prozess," *RTAM* 7 (1935), 353–380; 8 (1936), 79–93; 168–187.

Koester, Helmut, "Häretiker im Urchristentum," in *RGG*, vol. III, cols. 17–21.

Köhler, Walther, *Dokumente zum Ablassstreit von 1517*, 2 ed. (Tübingen, 1934).

Kokša, Georg, *Die Lehre der Scholastiker des XVI. und XVII. Jahrhunderts von der Gnade und Verdienst der alttestamentlichen Gerechten* (Rome, 1955).

Kölmel, W., "Das Naturrecht bei Wilhelm Ockham," *FS* 35 (1953), 39–85.

—— "Von Ockham zu Gabriel Biel: Zur Naturrechtslehre des 14. und 15. Jahrhunderts," *FS* 37 (1955), 218–259.

Kors, J. B., *La justice primitive et le péché originel d'après S. Thomas* (Kain, 1922).

Koster, M. D., O.P. "Die Himmelfahrt Mariens gleichsam die Vollendung ihrer unbefleckten Empfängnis," *Virgo Immaculata* 10 (1957), 92–115.

Krätzinger, G., "Versuch einer Geschichte des Kugelhauses zu Butzbach," *Archiv für hessische Geschichte und Altertumskunde* 10 (1861), 48–93.

Krautwig, N., *Der Grundlagen der Busslehre des Joh. Duns Scotus* (Freiburg i. Br., 1938).

Kristeller, P. O., *The Philosophy of Marsilio Ficino* (New York, 1943).

—— *Studies in Renaissance Thought and Letters* (Rome, 1956).

Kropatscheck, F., "Occam und Luther: Bemerkungen zur Geschichte des Autoritätsprinzips," in *Beiträge zur Förderung christlicher Theologie* 4 (Gütersloh, 1900), 51–74.

────── *Das Schriftprinzip der Lutherischen Kirche,* vol. I: *Die Vorgeschichte: Das Erbe des Mittelalters* (Leipzig, 1904).

Lagarde, Georges de, *Recherches sur l'esprit politique de la Réforme* (Douai, 1926).

────── *La naissance de l'esprit laïque au declin du Moyen Age* (Paris, 1946).

Lampen, Willibrordus, O.F.M., "Doctrina Guillelmi Ockham de reali praesentia et transsubstantiatione," *Antonianum* 3 (1928), 21–32.

Landeen, William M., "Gabriel Biel and the Brethren of the Common Life in Germany," *CH* 20 (1951), 23–36

────── "The Beginnings of the *Devotio Moderna* in Germany," *Research Studies of the State College of Washington* 19 (1951), 161–202; 221–253.

────── "The *Devotio Moderna* in Germany," *Research Studies* 21 (1953), 275–309; 22 (1954), 57–75.

────── "Gabriel Biel and the *Devotio Moderna* in Germany," *Research Studies* 27 (1959), 135–214; 28 (1960), 21–45, 61–79.

────── "Das Brüderhaus St. Peter im Schönbuch auf dem Einsiedel," *Blätter für Württembergische Kirchengeschichte* 60–61 (1960–1961), 5–18.

Landgraf, A. M., *Dogmengeschichte der Frühscholastik* vol. I, pts. 1 and 2; vol. II, pts. 1 and 2; vol. III, pt. 1 (Regensburg, 1952–1954).

Landmann, Florenz, "Die unbefleckte Empfängnis Mariä in der Predigt zweier Strassburger Dominikaner und Geilers von Kaysersberg," *Archiv für elsässische Kirchengeschichte* 6 (1931), 189–194.

Lang, Albert, *Die Wege der Glaubensbegründung bei den Scholastikern das 14. Jahrhunderts,* in *BB,* vol. XXX, pts. 1–2 (Münster i. W., 1930).

────── *Heinrich Totting von Oyta: Ein Beitrag zur Entstehungsgeschichte der ersten deutschen Universitäten und zur Problemgeschichte der Spätscholastik* (Münster i. W., 1937).

Lappe, J., *Nikolaus von Autrecourt: Sein Leben, seine Philosophie, seine Schriften,* in *BB,* vol. VI, pt. 2 (Münster i. W., 1908).

Laun, Justus F., "Thomas von Bradwardin: Der Schüler Augustins und Lehrer Wiclifs," *ZKG* 47 (1928), 333–356.

────── "Die Prädestination bei Wiclif und Bradwardin," in *Imago Dei: Festschrift für G. Krüger,* ed. H. Bornkamm (Giessen, 1932), 63–84.

Laurent, M. H., "Autour du procès de Maître Eckhart, Les documents des Archives Vaticanes," *Divus Thomas* [Piacenza] 13 (1936), 331–348, 430–447.

Laurentin, René, *Marie: L'Eglise et le sacerdoce* (Paris, 1952).

────── *Court traité de théologie mariale* (Paris, 1953).

Lea, H. Charles, *A History of Auricular Confession and Indulgences in the Latin Church,* vol. III (Philadelphia, 1896).

Lebon, J., "Comment je conçois, j'établis et je défends la doctrine de la médiation mariale," *Ephemerides Theologicae Lovanienses* 16 (1939), 655–744.

Lebreton, Jules, "Contemplation dans la Bible" in *Dictionnaire de spiritualité* vol. II (Paris, 1953), cols. 1643–1716.

Lechler, J., *John Wycliffe and his English Precursors* (London, 1904).

Lechner, Josef, *Die Sakramentenlehre des Richard von Mediavilla* (Munich, 1925).

Leeuwen, A. van, O.F.M., "L'Eglise, règle de foi, dans les écrits de Guillaume d'Occam," *Ephemerides Theologicae Lovanienses* 11 (1934), 249–288.

Leff, G., *Bradwardine and the Pelagians* (Cambridge, Eng., 1957).

—— *Gregory of Rimini: Tradition and Innovation in Fourteenth Century Thought* (Manchester, 1961).

Lella, A. di, O.F.M., "The Immaculate Conception in the Writings of Peter Aureoli," *FStud* 15 (1955), 146–158.

Lengwiler, Edward, *Die vorreformatorischen Prädikaturen der deutschen Schweiz von ihrer Entstehung bis 1530* (Fribourg, 1955).

Lennerz, H., *De Beata Virgine Tractatus Dogmaticus* (Rome, 1957).

—— "Scriptura sola?" *Gregorianum* 40 (1959), 38–53.

—— "Sine scripto traditiones," *Gregorianum* 40 (1959), 624–635.

Lindbeck, George, "Nominalism and the Problem of Meaning as illustrated by Pierre d'Ailly on Predestination and Justification," *HTR* 52 (1959), 43–60.

Linde, Simon van der, *De Leer van den Heiligen Geest bij Calvijn* (Wageningen, 1943).

Link, Wilhelm, *Das Ringen Luthers um die Freiheit der Theologie von der Philosophie* (Munich, 1955).

Linsenmann, F. X., "Gabriel Biel und die Anfänge der Universität zu Tübingen," *Theologische Quartalschrift* 47 (1865), 195–226.

—— "Gabriel Biel, der letzte Scholastiker, und der Nominalismus," *Theologische Quartalschrift* 47 (1865), 449–481 and 601–676.

Littell, Franklin H., *The Anabaptist View of the Church*, 2 ed. (Boston, 1958).

Ljunggren, G., *Zur Geschichte der christlichen Heilsgewissheit von Augustin bis zur Hochscholastik* (Göttingen, 1920).

Loewenich, Walther von, *Luthers Theologia Crucis*, 4 ed. (Munich, 1954).

Longpré, Ephrem, O.F.M., "De B. Virginis maternitate et relatione ad Christum," *Antonianum* 7 (1932), 289–313.

Loofs, J., *Leitfaden zum Studium der Dogmengeschichte*, ed. K. Aland, 5 ed., vol. I (Halle-Saale, 1950), vol. II (Halle-Saale, 1953).

Lortz, Joseph, *Die Reformation in Deutschland*, 2 ed., 2 vols. (Freiburg i. Br., 1941).

—— "Zur Problematik der kirchlichen Missstände im Spätmittelalter," *Trierer Theologische Zeitschrift* 58 (1949), 1–26, 212–227, 257–279, 347–357.

Lottin, Odon, O.S.B., *L'ordre morale et l'ordre logique d'après St. Thomas* (Louvain, 1924).

—— "L'intellectualisme de la morale thomiste," *Xenia Thomistica* 1 (1925), 411–427.

Lubac, Henri de, *Exégèse Médiévale: Les quatre sens de l'Ecriture*, vol. I (Lyons, 1959); vol. II (Lyons, 1960).

Lücker, Maria, *Meister Eckhart und die Devotio Moderna* (Leiden, 1950).

McDonnell, E. W., *The Beguines and Beghards in Medieval Culture* (New Brunswick, 1954).

Maier, Anneliese, *Studien zur Naturphilosophie der Spätscholastik* (Rome, 1949 ff).

—— *Zwischen Philosophie und Mechanik* (Rome, 1958).

Mallard, William, "John Wyclif and the Tradition of Biblical Authority," *CH* 30 (1961), 50–60.

Maltha, A. H., [Review of] A. D. R. Polman's *De Praedestinatieleer van Augustinus, Thomas van Aquino en Calvijn*, *Bulletin Thomiste* 5 (1938–1939), 570–572.

Manser, Gallus M., *Die Geisteskrise des 14. Jahrhunderts* (Freiburg i. Br., 1915).

—— *Das Wesen des Thomismus*, 3 ed., Thomistische Studien V (Fribourg, 1949).

SECONDARY SOURCES

Martin, Gottfried, *Wilhelm von Ockham: Untersuchungen zur Ontologie der Ordnungen* (Berlin, 1949).

Martin, Raymond M., *La controverse sur le péché originel au debut du XIVe siècle* (Louvain, 1930).

McDonnell, E. W., *The Beguines and Beghards in Medieval Culture* (New Brunswick, 1954).

Meissinger, Karl August, *Der katholische Luther* (Munich, 1952).

Meissner, Alois, *Gotteserkenntnis und Gotteslehre nach dem englischen Dominikanertheologen Robert Holkot* (Limburg an der Lahn, 1953).

Meller, Bernhard, *Studien zur Erkenntnislehre des Peter von Ailly*, Freiburger Theologische Studien 67 (Freiburg i. Br., 1954).

Mens, A., *Oorsprong en betekenis van de Nederlandse Begijnen en Begardenbeweging* (Antwerp, 1947).

Menzel, Karl, *Diether von Isenburg: Erzbischof von Mainz 1459–1463* (Erlangen, 1868).

Meyer, O., *Die Brüder des gemeinsamen Lebens in Württemberg 1477–1517* (Stuttgart, 1913).

Michalski, K., "Les courants philosophiques à Oxford et à Paris pendant le XIVe siècle," *Bulletin de l'Académie polonaise des sciences et des lettres* (Cracow, 1921), 59–88.

—— "Les sources du criticisme et du scepticisme dans la philosophie du XIV siècle," *La Pologne au congrès international de Bruxelles* (1924), 241–268.

—— "Le criticisme et le scepticisme dans la philosophie du XIV siècle," *La Pologne au congress international de Bruxelles* (1926), 41–122.

—— "Les courants critiques et sceptiques dans la philosophie du XIVe siècle," *La Pologne au congrès international de Bruxelles* (1927), 192–242.

—— "La physique nouvelle et les différents courants philosophiques au XIVe siècle," *Bulletin de l'Académie polonaise des sciences et des lettres* (Cracow, 1928), 93–164.

—— "La lutte pour l'âme à Oxford et à Paris de XIVe siècle et sa répercussion à l'époque de la Renaissance," in *Proceedings of the Seventh International Congress of Philosophy held at Oxford, September 1–6, 1930* (Oxford, 1931), 508–515

—— *Le problème de la volonté à Oxford et à Paris au XIVe siècle*, Commentariorum societatis philosophicae Polonorum, II (Lemberg, 1937), 233–365.

Michel, A., "Incarnation," in *DThC*, vol. VII, cols. 1445–1539.

Minges, Parthenius, "Die angeblich laxe Reuelehre des Duns Scotus," *ZKT* 25 (1901), 231–257.

—— *Die Gnadenlehre des Johannes Duns Skotus auf ihren angeblichen Pelagianismus und Semi-Pelagianismus geprüft* (Münster i. W., 1906).

—— *Der Gottesbegriff des Duns Skotus auf seinen angeblich exzessiven Indeterminismus geprüft* (Vienna, 1907).

—— *Ioannes Duns Scoti doctrina philosophica et theologica*, 2 vols. (Quaracchi, 1930).

Mitzka, Franz, S.J., "Die Lehre des hl. Bonaventura von der Vorbereitung auf die heiligmachende Gnade," *ZKT* 50 (1926), 27–72; 220–252.

Möller, W., *Andreas Osiander* (Elberfeld, 1870).

Monnerjahn, Engelbert, *Giovanni Pico della Mirandola: Ein Beitrag zur philoso-*

phischen Theologie des Italienischen Humanismus, Veröffentlichungen des Instituts für Europäische Geschichte Mainz: Abteilung für abendländische Religionsgeschichte, vol. 20 (Wiesbaden, 1960).

Morcay, R., *Saint Antonin; Fondateur du Convent de Saint Marc, Archevêque de Florence* (Tours, 1914).

Moody, Ernest A., *The Logic of William of Ockham* (London, 1935).

—— "Ockham, Buridan and Nicholas of Autrecourt: The Parisian Statutes of 1339 and 1340," *FStud* 7 (1947), 113–146.

—— "Ockham and Aegidius of Rome," *FStud* 9 (1949), 417–442.

Mourin, Louis, "Les Sermons français inédits de Jean Gerson pour les fêtes de l'Annonciation et de la Purification," *Scriptorium* 2 (1948), 221–240.

—— *Jean Gerson: Prédicateur français* (Bruges, 1952).

Mückshoff, Meinolf, O.F.M., "Die mariologische Prädestination im Denken der franziskanischen Theologie," *FS* 39 (1957), 288–502.

Müller, A., *Ecclesia-Maria: Die Einheit Marias und der Kirche* (Fribourg, 1951).

Müller, Alphons V., *Luthers theologische Quellen* (Giessen, 1912).

—— *Luthers Werdegang bis zum Turmerlebnis neu untersucht* (Gotha, 1920).

Müller, Otfried, *Die Rechtfertigungslehre nominalistischer Reformationsgegner, Bartholomäus Arnoldi von Usingen O.E.S.A. und Kaspar Schatzgeyer O.F.M. über Erbsünde, erste Rechtfertigung und Taufe,* Breslauer Studien, vol. VIII (Breslau, 1940).

Murphy, John, *The Notion of Tradition in John Driedo* (Milwaukee, 1959). Cf. review in *Theologische Zeitschrift* 17 (1961), 231–234.

Nygren, G., *Das Prädestinationsproblem in der Theologie Augustins* (Göttingen, 1956).

Oakley, Francis, "Medieval Theories of Natural Law: William of Ockham and the Significance of the Voluntarist Tradition," *Natural Law Forum* 6 (1961), 65–83.

Oberman, Heiko A., *Archbishop Thomas Bradwardine: A Fourteenth-century Augustinian: A Study of his Theology in its Historical Context* (Utrecht, 1958).

—— "De Praedestinatione et Praescientia: An anonymous fourteenth-century treatise on predestination and justification," *NAK,* n.s. 43 (1960), 195–220.

—— "Some Notes on the Theology of Nominalism with attention to its Relation to the Renaissance," *HTR* 53 (1960), 47–76.

—— "Thomas Bradwardine: Un Précurseur de Luther?" *Revue d'Histoire et de Philosophie religieuses* 40 (1960), 146–151.

—— "Preaching and the Word in the Reformation," *Theology Today* 18 (1961), 16–29.

—— and J. A. Weisheipl, "The sermo epinicius ascribed to Thomas Bradwardine (1346)," *AHDL* 33 (1958), 295–329.

—— Daniel Callahan, and Daniel O'Hanlon, S.J., eds. *Christianity Divided* (New York, 1961), pp. 223–239.

Oediger, Fr. W., *Über die Bildung der Geistlichen im späten Mittelalter* (Leiden, 1953).

Ortigues, É. "Ecriture et traditions apostoliques au Concile de Trent," *Recherches des sciences religieuses* 36 (1949), 271–299.

Ott, Georg, "Recht und Gesetz bei Gabriel Biel: Ein Beitrag zur Spätmittelalterlichen Rechtslehre," *Zeitschrift der Savigny-Stiftung für Rechtsgeschichte* 69 (1952), Kanonistische Abteilung 38, 251–296.

Ott, Ludwig, "Das Konzil von Chalkedon in der Frühscholastik," in *Das Konzil von Chalkedon: Geschichte und Gegenwart*, vol. II: *Entscheidung um Chalkedon*, ed. Aloys Grillmeier, S.J. und Heinrich Bacht, S.J. (Würzburg, 1953), pp. 873–922.

Pacaut, Marcel, *La Théocratie, l'Église et le Pouvoir au Moyen Âge* (Paris, 1957).

Pannenberg, Wolfhart, *Die Prädestinationslehre des Duns Skotus* (Göttingen, 1954).

Pantin, W. A., *The English Church in the Fourteenth Century* (Cambridge, Eng., 1955).

Pastor, Ludwig von, *Geschichte der Päpste seit dem Ausgang des Mittelalters*, vol. II (Freiburg i. Br., 1886).

Paulus, N., *Der Augustiner Bartholomäus Arnoldi von Usingen: Luthers Lehrer und Gegner* (Strasbourg, 1893).

Pelster, Franz, S.J., "Die indirekte Gewalt der Kirche über den Staat nach Ockham und Petrus de Palude: Eine Übersicht," *Scholastik* 28 (1953), 78–82.

Pelzer, Auguste, "Les 51 articles de Guillaume Occam censurés en Avignon 1326," *RHE* 18 (1922), 240–270.

Petry, Ray C., *Late Medieval Mysticism* (Philadelphia, 1957).

———"Social Responsibility and the Late Medieval Mystics," *CH* 21 (1952), 3–19.

Pfeiffer, Franz, *Meister Eckhart*, 4 ed. (Göttingen, 1924).

Plitt, Gustaf, *Gabriel Biel als Prediger* (Erlangen, 1879).

Pol, William H. van de, *Karakteristiek van het reformatorisch Christendom* (Roermond, 1952).

———*Het Wereldprotestantisme* (Roermond, 1956).

Polman, A. D. R., *De praedestinatieleer van Augustinus, Thomas van Aquino en Calvijn* (Franeker, 1936).

———*Het Woord Gods bij Augustinus*, De Theologie van Augustinus: Dogmatische Studies (Kampen, 1955).

Portalié, E., "Développement historique de l'Augustinisme," in *DThC*, vol. I, col. 2501–2561.

Poschmann, B., *Handbuch der Dogmengeschichte*, vol. IV.3, Busse und letzte Ölung (Freiburg i. Br., 1951).

Post, R. R., *Kerkgeschiedenis van Nederland in de Middeleeuwen*, 2 vols. (Utrecht, 1957).

Prantl, Carl, *Geschichte der Logik im Abendlande*, vol. IV (Leipzig, 1870).

Quispel, G., "L'Évangile selon Thomas et le Diatessaron," *Vigiliae Christianae* 13 (1959), 87–117.

Rad, Gerhard von, *Theologie des Alten Testaments*, vol. I: *Die Theologie der geschichtlichen Überlieferungen Israels* (Munich, 1957).

Rashdall, H., *The Universities of Europe in the Middle Ages*, ed. F. M. Powicke and A. B. Emden (Oxford, 1936).

Raymond, P., O.M.C., "La théorie de l'induction: Duns Scot précurseur de Bacon," *Etudes franciscaines* 21 (1909), 113–126, 270–279.

Renaudet, Augustin, *Préréforme et Humanisme à Paris pendant les premières guerres d'Italie 1494–1517*, 2 ed. (Paris, 1953).

Reusch, H., *Die Indices librorum prohibitorum des sechzehnten Jahrhunderts* (Nieuwkoop, 1961). A reprint of Tübingen (1886).

Rhijn, Maarten van, *Wessel Gansfort* (The Hague, 1917).
───── "Luther en Gregorius van Rimini," *Theologisch Tijdschrift* 53 (1919), 238–259.
───── *Studiën over Luthers rechtvaardigingsleer: Met een nawoord over de nieuwere Erasmus-waardering* (Groningen, 1921).
───── *Studiën over Wessel Gansfort en zijn tijd* (Utrecht, 1933).
Ritschl, Albrecht, "Geschichtliche Studien zur christlichen Lehre von Gott," *Jahrbücher für deutsche Theologie* 10 (1865), 277–318.
───── *Geschichte des Pietismus*, vol. I (Bonn, 1880).
Ritter, Gerhard, *Studien zur Spätscholastik*, vol. I: *Marsilius von Inghen und die ockhamistische Schule in Deutschland*, in Sitzungsberichte der Heidelberger Akademie der Wissenschaften, Philosophische-historische Klasse, 4. Abhandlung (Heidelberg, 1921); vol. II: *Via antiqua und via moderna auf den deutschen Universitäten des XV. Jahrhunderts*, in Sitzungsberichte der Heidelberger Akademie . . . , 7. Abhandlung (Heidelberg, 1922); vol. III: *Neue Quellenstücke zur Theologie des Johann von Wesel*, in Sitzungsberichte der Heidelberger Akademie . . . , 5. Abhandlung (Heidelberg, 1926–1927).
───── "Romantische und revolutionäre Elemente in der deutschen Theologie am Vorabend der Reformation," *Deutsche Vierteljahrschrift* 5 (1927), 342–380.
Rivière, J., "Justification," in *DThC*, vol. VIII, cols. 2042–2227.
Robson, J. A., *Wyclif and the Oxford Schools* (Cambridge, 1961).
Roo, William van, S.J., *Grace and Original Justice according to Saint Thomas* (Rome, 1955).
Roscher, Wilhelm, "Die Blüthe deutscher Nationalökonomik im Zeitalter der Reformation," Sitzung am 12. December 1861 zur Feier des Geburtstages seiner Majestät des Königs, in *Berichte über die Verhandlungen der Königlich Sächsischen Gesellschaft der Wissenschaften*, Philosophische-historische Klasse, 13 (1861), 145–174.
Rosenmüller, Bernhard, *Religiöse Erkenntnis nach Bonaventura* (Münster i. W., 1925).
Roth, D., *Die mittelalterliche Predigttheorie und das Manuale Curatorum des Johann Ulrich Surgant* (Basel, 1956).
Roth, F. W. E., "Ein Brief des Gabriel Biel, 1462," *Neues Archiv der Gesellschaft für ältere deutsche Geschichtskunde* 35 (1910), 582–585.
Ruch, C., "Biel, Gabriel," in *DThC*, vol. II, col. 814–825.
Rückert, Hanns, *Die Rechtfertigungslehre auf dem Tridentinischen Konzil* (Bonn, 1925).
───── *Die theologische Entwicklung Gaspara Contarinis* (Bonn, 1926).
Ruello, Francis, "Etude du terme 'Agathodotis' dans quelques commentaires médiévaux des Noms divins," in *RTAM* 24 (1957), 225–266; 25 (1958), 5–25.
Rupp, E. Gordon, *The Righteousness of God: Luther Studies* (London, 1953).
Saint-Blancat, Louis, "Recherches sur les sources de la théologie luthérienne primitive (1509–1510)," *Verbum Caro* 8 (1954), 81–91.
───── "La théologie de Luther et un nouveau plagiat de Pierre d'Ailly," *Positions Luthériennes* 4 (1956), 61–81.
Sarton, George, *Introduction to the History of Science* (Baltimore, 1947).
Scheel, Otto, *Martin Luther: Vom Katholizismus zur Reformation*, vol. I, 1st and 2nd printing (Tübingen, 1916); vol. I, 3rd and 4th printing (Tübingen, 1921);

vol. II, 1st and 2nd printing (Tübingen, 1917); vol. II, 3rd and 4th printing (Tübingen, 1921).

—— *Dokumente zu Luthers Entwicklung* (*bis 1519*), 2 ed. (Tübingen, 1929).

Schlecht, Joseph, "Dr. Johann Ecks Anfänge," *Historisches Jahrbuch* 36 (1915), 1–36.

Schmidt, Charles, *Histoire littéraire de l'Alsace à la fin du XVe et au commencement du XVIe siècle*, vol. I (Paris, 1879).

Schmücker, R., *Propositio per se nota: Gottesbeweis und ihr Verhältnis nach Petrus Aureoli* (Werl, 1941).

Schneider, Josef, "Die Verpflichtung des menschlichen Gesetzes nach Johannes Gerson," *ZKT* 75 (1953), 1–54.

Schöllgen, Wilhelm, *Das Problem der Willensfreiheit bei Heinrich von Gent und Herveus Natalis* (Düsseldorf, 1927).

Schrohe, H., *Mainz in seinen Beziehungen zu den deutschen Königen und den Erzbischöfen der Stadt bis zum Untergang der Stadtfreiheit* (*1462*), Beiträge zur Geschichte der Stadt Mainz, vol. IV (Mainz, 1915).

Schüler, Martin, *Prädestination, Sünde und Freiheit bei Gregor von Rimini* (Stuttgart, 1934).

Schütz, Ludwig, ed. *Thomas-Lexikon*, 2 ed. (Stuttgart, 1958).

Schwab, J. B., *Johann Gerson: Professor der Theologie und Kanzler der Universität Paris* (Würtzburg, 1858).

Schwamm, Hermann, *Magistri Ioannis de Ripa O.F.M.: Doctrina de praescientia divina, Inquisitio historica* (Rome, 1930).

—— *Das göttliche Vorherwissen bei Duns Scotus und seinen ersten Anhängern* (Innsbrück, 1934).

Seeberg, Erich, *Luthers Theologie: Motive und Ideen*, vol. I: *Die Gottesanschauung* (Göttingen, 1929).

—— *Luthers Theologie in ihren Grundzügen*, 2 ed. (Stuttgart, 1950).

Seeberg, Reinhold, "Bradwardina," *RE*, III, 350–353.

—— *Die Theologie des Johannes Duns Scotus: Eine dogmengeschichtliche Untersuchung* (Leipzig, 1900).

—— "Ockham," *RE*, XIV, 260–280.

—— *Die religiösen Grundgedanken des jungen Luther und ihr Verhältnis zu dem Ockamismus und der deutschen Mystik* (Berlin, 1931).

Seiler, Hermann, *Corredemptrix: Theologische Studie zur Lehre der letzen Päpste über die Miterlöserschaft Mariens* (Rome, 1939).

Sharp, A. B., *Mysticism: Its True Nature and Value* (London, 1910).

Smalley, Beryl, "Some Latin Commentaries on the Sapiential Books in the Late Thirteenth and Early Fourteenth Centuries," *Archives d'histoire doctrinale et littéraire du moyen âge* 18 (1950–51), 117–121.

—— *The Study of the Bible in the Middle Ages*, 2 ed. (Oxford, 1952).

—— "The Biblical Scholar," in *Robert Grosseteste: Essays in Commemoration of the Seventh Centenary of His Death*, ed. D. A. Callus (Oxford, 1955).

—— "Robert Holcot, O.P.," *Archivum Fratrum Praedicatorum* 26 (1956), 5–97.

—— *English Friars and Antiquity in the Early Fourteenth Century* (Cambridge, 1960).

Söll, Georg, "Die Anfänge mariologischer Tradition; Beitrag zur Geschichte der Marienlehre," in *Kirche und Ueberlieferung* [Festschrift Geiselmann], ed. J. Betz und H. Fries (Freiburg i. Br., 1960), pp. 35–51.

BIBLIOGRAPHY

Sperl, Adolf, *Melanchthon zwischen Humanismus und Reformation* (Munich, 1959).

Spicq, P. C., O.P., *Esquisse d'une histoire de l'Exégèse latine au moyen âge*, Bibliothèque Thomiste, vol. 26 (Paris, 1944).

Spindeler, Alois, "Pari pietatis affectu: Das Tridentinum über Heilige Schrift und apostolische Überlieferungen," *Theologie und Glaube* 51 (1961), 161–180.

Spinka, Matthew, *Advocates of Reform from Wyclif to Erasmus* (Philadelphia, 1953).

Spykman, Gordon J., *Attrition and Contrition at the Council of Trent* (Kampen, 1955).

Steenberghen, F., van, *Les oeuvres et la doctrine de Siger de Brabant* (Brussels, 1938).

Stegmüller, F., "Die zwei Apologien des Jean de Mirecourt," *RTAM* 5 (1933), 40–78; 192–204.

——— "Literargeschichtliches zu Gabriel Biel," *Theologie in Geschichte und Gegenwart: Michael Schmaus zum Sechzigsten Geburtstag* (Munich, 1957), pp. 309–316.

Stegmüller, Otto, "Der Immaculata-Traktat des Basler Franziskaners Franz Wiler († 1514)," *Basler Zeitschrift* 60 (1960), 47–64.

Steiff, K., *Der erste Buchdruck in Tübingen, 1498–1534* (Tübingen, 1881).

Stelzenberger, Johann, *Die Mystik des Johannes Gerson* (Breslau, 1929).

Stöckel, Bernhard, *Die Lehre von der erbsündlichen Konkupiszenz in ihrer Bedeutung für das christliche Leibeethos* (Ettal, 1954).

Stöckl, A., *Geschichte der Philosophie des Mittelalters*, vol. II (Mainz, 1865).

Stockums, Wilhelm, *Die Unveränderlichkeit des natürlichen Sittengesetzes in der scholastischen Ethik* (Freiburg i. Br., 1911).

Stratenwerth, Günter, *Die Naturrechtslehre des Johannes Duns Scotus* (Göttingen, 1951).

Strijd, Krijn, *Structuur en inhoud van Anselmus' "Cur Deus Homo"* (Assen, 1958).

Strohl, Henri, *L'évolution religieuse de Luther jusqu'en 1515* (Strasbourg and Paris, 1922).

Stufler, Johannes, *Divi Thomae Aquinatis doctrina de Deo operante* (Innsbruck, 1923).

Sykes, J. G., "A Possible Marsilian Source in Ockham," *English Historical Review* 51 (1936), 496–504.

Tavard, George, *Holy Writ or Holy Church: The Crisis of the Protestant Reformation* (New York, 1959).

Thomson, S. Harrison, "The Philosophical Basis of Wyclif's Theology," *Journal of Religion* 11 (1931), 86–116.

Tierney, Brian, "Ockham, the Conciliar Theory, and the Canonists," *Journal of the History of Ideas* 15 (1954), 40–70.

——— *Foundations of the Conciliar Theory: The Contribution of the Medieval Canonists from Gratian to the Great Schism* (Cambridge, 1958).

Töpke, Gustave, *Die Matrikel der Universität Heidelberg*, vol. I: *Von 1389 bis 1553* (Heidelberg, 1884).

Toner, N., O.E.S.A., "The Doctrine of Justification according to Augustine of Rome," *Augustiniana* 8 (1958), 164–189; 299–327; 497–515.

Trapp, Damasus, O.E.S.A., "Augustinian Theology of the Fourteenth Century," *Augustiniana* 6 (1956), 146–274.

454

SECONDARY SOURCES

——— "Peter Ceffons of Clairvaux," *RTAM* 24 (1957), 101–154.

——— "Clm 27034: Unchristened Nominalism and Wycliffite Realism at Prague in 1381," *RTAM* 24 (1957), 320–360.

Troeltsch, Ernst, *Die Soziallehren der christlichen Kirchen und Gruppen* (Tübingen, 1912).

Tschackert, P., *Peter von Ailli (Petrus de Alliaco): Zur Geschichte des grossen abendländischen Schismas und der Reformkoncilien von Pisa und Constanz* (Gotha, 1877).

——— "Ailli, Peter von," *RE*, I, 274–280.

——— "Biel, Gabriel," *RE*, III, 208–210.

Ueberweg, F. and B. Geyer, *Grundriss der Geschichte der Philosophie*, vol. II: *Die patristische und scholastische Philosophie*, 12 ed. (Berlin, 1951).

Underhill, Evelyn, *Mysticism*, 12 ed. (London, 1930).

Vansteenberghe, E., *'Autour de la 'Docte Ignorance': Une controverse sur la théologie mystique au XV siècle* in *BB*, vol. XIV, pts. 2–4 (Münster i. W., 1915).

Vasella, Oskar, *Reform und Reformation in der Schweiz: Zur Würdigung der Anfänge der Glaubenskrise* (Münster i. W., 1958).

Vereecke, Louis, "Droit et morale chez Jean Gerson," *Revue historique de droit français et étranger* 32 (1954), 413–427.

Vernet, F., *La spiritualité médiévale* (Paris, 1929).

Vetter, F., *Die Predigten Taulers* (Berlin, 1910).

Vignaux, Paul, "Nicolas d'Autrecourt," in *DThC*, vol. XI, cols. 561–587.

——— "Nominalisme," in *DThC*, vol. XI, cols. 717–784.

——— "Occam," in *DThC*, vol. XI, cols. 876–889.

——— *Justification et prédestination au XIVe siècle: Duns Scot, Pierre d'Auriole, Guillaume d'Occam, Grégoire de Rimini* (Paris, 1934).

——— *Luther Commentateur des Sentences* (Paris, 1935).

——— *Nominalisme au XIVe siècle* (Montreal, 1948).

——— "Sur Luther et Ockham," *FS* 32 (1949), 21–30.

——— "Luther: lecteur de Gabriel Biel," *Église et Théologie* 22 (1959), 33–52.

Vollert, Cyril O., *The Doctrine of Hervaeus Natalis on Primitive Justice and Original Sin* (Rome, 1947).

Vonlanthen, Adolf, "Geilers Seelenparadies im Verhältnis zur Vorlage," *Archiv für elsässische Kirchengeschichte* 6 (1931), 229–324.

Vooght, Paul de, *Les sources de la doctrine chrétienne d'après les théologiens du XIVe siècle et du début du XVe . . ."* (Paris, 1954).

——— *Hussiana* (Louvain, 1960).

——— *L'Hérésie de Jean Huss* (Louvain, 1960).

Weijenborg, Reynold, O.F.M., "La charité dans la première théologie de Luther," *RHE* 45 (1950), 617–669. Extensive excerpt reprinted in *Sylloge excerptorum e dissertationibus*, XXI (Louvain, 1950), 615–669.

Weinberg, J. R., *Nicolaus of Autrecourt: A Study in Fourteenth Century Thought* (Princeton, 1948).

Weissenborn, J. C. H., *Akten der Erfurter Universität* (Halle, 1881).

Werbeck, Wilfrid, *Jacobus Perez von Valencia: Untersuchungen zu seinem Psalmenkommentar* (Tübingen, 1959).

Werner, Ernst, *Pauperes Christi: Studien zu sozial-religiösen Bewegungen im Zeitalter des Reformpapsttums* (Leipzig, 1956).

BIBLIOGRAPHY

Werner, Karl, *Die Scholastik des späteren Mittelalters*, vol. II: *Johannes Duns Scotus* (Vienna, 1881); vol. III: *Der Augustinismus in der Scholastik des späteren Mittelalters* (Vienna, 1883); vol. IV: *Der Endausgang der mittelalterlichen Scholastik* (Vienna, 1887).

—— "Der Averroismus in der christlich-peripatetischen Psychologie des späteren Mittelalters," in *Sitzungsberichte der Kaiserlichen Akademie der Wissenschaften*, Philosophisch-historische Klasse 98 (Vienna, 1881), 175–320.

—— "Die nominalisierende Psychologie der Scholastik des späteren Mittelalters," in *Sitzungsberichte der Kaiserlichen Akademie der Wissenschaften*, Philosophisch-historische Klasse 99 (Vienna, 1882).

Wolf, Ernst, *Staupitz und Luther: Ein Beitrag zur Theologie des Johannes von Staupitz und deren Bedeutung für Luthers theologischen Werdegang* (Leipzig, 1927).

—— "Erwählungslehre und Prädestinationsproblem," in *Die Predigt von der Gnadenwahl, Karl Barth zum 10. Mai 1951* (Munich, 1951).

Wolfson, Harry A., "Extradeical and Intradeical Interpretations of Platonic Ideas," *Journal of the History of Ideas* 22 (1961), 3–32.

Wulf, Maurice de, *Histoire de la philosophie médiévale*, vol. III, 6 ed. (Paris, 1947).

Würsdörfer, J., *Erkennen und Wissen nach Gregor von Rimini* in *BB*, vol. XX, pt. 1 (Münster i. W., 1917).

Xiberta, B., O. Carm., "De Magistro Joh. Baconthorp," in *Analecta O.C.* (1927), pp. 3–128; 516–526.

—— *De scriptoribus scholasticis saeculi XIV ex ordine Carmelitarum* (Louvain, 1931).

Zoepfl, Friedrich, *Johannes Altenstaig; Ein Gelehrtenleben aus der Zeit des Humanismus und der Reformation* (Münster i. W., 1918).

Zuidema, Sytse Ulbe, *De Philosophie van Occam* (Hilversum, 1936), vols. I and II.

Zumkeller, Adolar, O.E.S.A., *Hugolin von Orvieto und seine theologische Erkenntnislehre* (Würzburg, 1941).

—— *Dionysius de Montina; ein neuentdeckter Augustinertheologe des Spätmittelalters* (Würzburg, 1948).

—— "Hugolin von Orvieto († 1373) über Urstand und Erbsünde," *Augustiniana* 3 (1953), 35–62; 165–193; 4 (1954), 25–46.

—— "Hugolin von Orvieto über Prädestination, Rechtfertigung und Verdienst," *Augustiniana* 4 (1954), 109–156; 5 (1955), 5–51.

—— "Das Ungenügen der menschlichen Werke bei den deutschen Predigern des Spätmittelalters," *ZKT* 81 (1959), 265–305.

A
NOMINALISTIC GLOSSARY

A NOMINALISTIC GLOSSARY

This glossary presents a selection of central late-medieval concepts, terms, and expressions. It is in no sense final but rather intended as the nucleus of a future more comprehensive glossary. Readers are therefore kindly invited to communicate to the Press or directly to the author their suggestions for changes or additions. For entries at the moment not included, readers should consult the extensive and contemporary theological encyclopedia: Johannes Altenstaig, *Vocabularius theologie* (Hagenau, 1517). For the more strictly philosophical terminology of the period see Léon Baudry, *Lexique philosophique de Guillaume d'Ockham* (Paris, 1958). For the preceding period see Ludwig Schütz, *Thomas-Lexikon*, 2 ed. (Paderborn, 1895; photographic reprint, Stuttgart, 1958); Stephanus Axters, O.P., *Scholastiek Lexicon, Latijn-Nederlandsch* (Antwerp, 1937); M. Fernandez Garcia, *Lexicon scholasticum philosophico-theologicum*. . . [Duns Scotus] (Quaracchi, 1910).

The citations that follow each entry, unless otherwise noted, refer to the most explicit discussion of the concept in the works of Gabriel Biel and thus provide a concise subject index.

Acceptatio Acceptation

The act of God by which out of his freedom [*libertas*] and mercy [*misericordia*] he deigns to grant man the claim to eternal life to which no creature has any inherent or natural right. The term implies the acceptation of the sinner and the works of the justified sinner as fully [*de condigno*] meritorious. This has to be understood in the context of the *potentia absoluta dei*, the *potentia ordinata dei*, the *meritum de congruo* and the *meritum de condigno*.

II *Sent.* d 29 q 1 art. 3 dub. 1.

Acceptio personarum Favoritism

Always negated to emphasize God's impartial judgment. Vulgate texts such as Rom. 2:11: "non enim est acceptio personarum apud Deum" are cited to express God's retributive justice and to warn against presumption on the mercy of God. Cf. II Chron. 19:7; Eccles. 20:24; Eph. 6:9; Col. 3:25; I Tim. 4:9; Jas. 2:1; I Pet. 1:17. The term *acceptatio personarum* has sometimes the same significance, as, e.g., with Gregory of Rimini, II *Sent.* d 26 q 1 art. 3 [fol. 98 I, K].

IV *Sent.* d 15 q 7 art. 1.

Amor amicitiae   The love of friendship

Pure love for something or somebody for its own sake, without an ulterior motive.

III *Sent.* d 27 q 1 art. 2 concl. 2.

Amor concupiscentiae   Possessive love

Love for something or someone as a means to an end. As long as this object is used [*uti*] as a means to reach enjoyment [*frui*] love is *amor sui ordinatus*, a proper form of possessive love.

II *Sent.* d 1 q 5 art. 1 nota 1 A.

Amor dei super omnia propter deum   Unconditional love of God for his own sake

Characteristic of full contrition; attainable by man without the aid of grace [*ex puris naturalibus*].

II *Sent.* d 27 q 1 art. 3 dub. 5 Q.

Asinus   Ass

Symbol of the absurd or of the tenacity of sin. It functions in Christology to expose the absurdity and untenability of the *assumptus* Christology. In theological anthropology the ass refers to the Old Adam or the lower instincts in the *viator*.

III *Sent.* d 1 q 2 art. 1 concl. resp.; *S* I 2 H.

Attritio   Attrition

Repentance for sins out of fear [see *timor servilis*] of punishment by God. In contrast to the Thomistic or Scotistic interpretation, attrition for the nominalist is not a part of contrition nor can it be transformed into contrition.

IV *Sent.* d 16 q 1 art. 3 dub. 1.

Auxilium speciale Special assistance

God's provision of proper disposition for the infusion of sanctifying grace. Also called *adiutorium speciale*.

Posited by Gregory of Rimini, II *Sent.* d 29 q 1 art. 1 [fol. 108 N].

Rejected by Biel, *S* I 87 E; *S* I 39 G.H.I.; *S* I 91 D.

Beati (Comprehensores) The blessed

They have completed their earthly pilgrimage and are *in patria*. The status of the *beati*, in contrast with that of the *viatores*, is characterized by their freedom from the *fomes peccati* and their ability to see directly — no longer *in speculo* or *in enygmate* — most of the mysteries of faith.

Prologi q 1.

Bonitas moralis Moral goodness

Goodness proceeding from virtue which is within reach of man's natural capacities [see *facere quod in se est*]. Used in contrast with *bonitas meritoria* or *dignitas* which implies acceptation or information by grace.

II *Sent.* d 27 q 1 art. 1 nota 1 A.

Captivare [ingenium suum] in obsequium Christi To subdue one's mind in obedience to Christ

While certain catholic truths seem to contradict the evidence of experience or natural reason — e.g. the doctrine of transubstantiation — they are embraced not as knowledge but as acknowledgement of God's wisdom: "belief in the articles of faith does not arise from understanding but understanding from belief in the articles of faith." [See *rationes probabiles*.]

Lect. 41 M, N.

Certitudo naturalis Natural certitude

Certitude based on experience and on demonstrated conclusion.

461

Certitudo probabilis, moralis, civilis or *coniecturalis* Conjectural certitude

That qualified certitude which remains merely probable but is suggested by the better part of the available evidence. Probable certitude of one's worthiness is sufficient for proper reception of the Eucharist.

Lect. 8 A–B; IV *Sent.* d 16 q 3 art. 3 dub. 6.

Certitudo supernaturalis Supernatural certitude

Infallible certitude granted by God, concerning certain contingent catholic truths such as those contained in Scripture and the Creed. Especially used for revelation concerning one's personal salvation.

II *Sent.* d 27 q 1 art. 3 dub. 5 P.

Charitas creata The created gift of the Holy Spirit.

Not really distinct from [see *distinctio realis*]the habit of grace [see *gratia*].

I *Sent.* d 17 passim; II *Sent.* d 27 passim.

Charitas increata The Holy Spirit

Circumscriptive (Commensurative) Local presence

The total thing is present in the whole space it occupies — and nowhere outside of it — every single part of it is in every single part of the space occupied. In contrast, the *definitive* or *terminative* mode designates the presence of a thing in the whole space it occupies — and not outside of it — but this time not a part but the whole is in every part of the space occupied. A third possibility is the *repletive* mode which differs from the *definitive* mode of presence in that the qualification "and not outside of it" is omitted.

I *Sent.* d 37 q 1 art. 1 nota 1 C.

Communicatio idiomatum (Communicatio proprietatum) The interchange of properties

462

In christological discussion, the mutual predication of the concrete properties of the human and the divine nature.

III *Sent.* d 7 q 1 art. 1 nota 1.

Complacentia generalis   General good will

The general unspecified good will of God, the creator, according to which he wants all possible things to be good. To be distinguished from *complacentia specialissima* which is the love of God by which he guides the elect to eternal life.

I *Sent.* d 1 q 3 art. 3 dub. 2.

Comprehensores   See *Beati*

Concupiscentia   Concupiscence

Sensuality not held in check by reason. Used to designate the enjoyment of temporal goods [*fruitio*] which should only be used [*usus*]. Never entirely overcome in the status of the *viator*.

II *Sent.* d 30 q 2 art. 1 nota 1.

Concursus generalis (Influentia generalis)   General concurrence

The cooperation of the first cause — God — with the second cause — creature — indispensable for any action by the second cause irrespective of the presence of grace. [See *ex puris naturalibus.*]

II *Sent.* d 28 q 1 art. 1 nota 2.

Confessio in voto (Confessio in proposito)   The intention to confess

The intention of one fully contrite to avail himself at the first opportunity, of sacramental confession and absolution. The "in voto" condition is the link between the virtue of penance and the sacrament of penance.

IV *Sent.* d 17 q 1 art. 1 nota 2 B.

Conformitas voluntatis   Conformity of the will

The act of adapting one's will to the will of God — characteristic of the nominalistic mystical ideal in contrast to the Eckhartian ideal of essential union with God. More generally it expresses "the golden rule" of nominalistic ethics.

S I 49; *Lect.* 68 H.

Conscientia See *Synderesis*

Contritio Contrition

Repentance for sins out of loving respect [see *timor filialis*] for God. Fundamentally differing from attrition in that it excludes possessive love [see *amor concupiscentiae*] and is rooted in love of friendship [see *amor amicitiae*]. True contrition includes sacramental confession, at least in intention [see *confessio in voto*].

IV *Sent.* d 16 q 1 art. 2.

Coram deo In the eyes of God. In front of God

The term is used in contrast with *coram homine* or *coram hominibus*, and functions especially in the context of penitence and confession [see *forus animae*]. Self-accusation and humility are dangerous when one is confronted with a secular judge but required and even meritorious *coram deo*.

Lect. 31 B.

Credere deo To believe in God

To believe that all of God's words are true and that therefore Holy Scripture is true. This belief is held both by good and evil Christians. [See *fides informis*.]

Credere deum To believe in God

The expression refers especially to the belief that God exists, that he is the highest good, etc. Even the demons believe this. [See *fides demonum*.]

S I 44 G

Credere in deum   To believe in God

The highest form of faith by which one embraces God in knowledge and love. Only possible for those in a state of grace. [See *fides formata*.]

Cf. Altenstaig, *Vocabularius*, fol. 57ᵛ.

Culpa   Guilt

That part of sin which is remitted in the sacrament of penance. Used in contrast with *poena*, punishment for sin, which is transmuted from eternal to temporal by the sacrament of penance.

IV *Sent.* d 4 q 1 art. 1 nota 3 D.

De odio dei   Concerning the hatred for God

A famous test question in late medieval theology is: "Can God command someone to hate him?" Its purpose is to illuminate the relation between God's will and the Decalogue, eternal law and natural law.

I *Sent.* d 42 q 1 art. 3 dub. 1.

Definitive (Diffinitive)   See *Circumscriptive*

Devotio   A movement of the mind toward God

The *devoti* may take the vows of poverty, obedience, and chastity to train themselves to become "singleminded" in devotion. The *devotio moderna*, in origin a lay movement, propagated this form of piety in the fifteenth century.

Lect. 29 D.

Dictamen rationis   The dictate of reason

This is the rule for the will, natural law, which never deviates from the eternal law, the divine reason. Therefore the principles of natural law are immutable [see *synderesis*].

Lect. 69 A.

465

Dignitas actus (*Condignitas actus*)   Worthiness of the act

An act can be said to have worthiness insofar as God has committed himself [see *de potentia ordinata*] to accept the morally good act as meritorious for an eternal reward. [See *meritum de condigno*.] The condition for acceptability *de potentia ordinata* is the habit of grace. However, *de potentia absoluta* no such condition obtains.

I *Sent.* d 17 q 1 art. 1 nota 3 C.

Distinctio [See I *Sent.* d 2 q 11 art. 1.]

Distinctio formalis   Formal distinction

A formal distinction exists when something is one of the things distinguished but not the other; e.g. the Son is of divine essence but he is not the Father, and therefore the Father is formally distinguished from the divine essence.

Distinctio rationis   Rational distinction

It is introduced for purposes of definition and is a product of the mind.

Distinctio realis   Real distinction

A real distinction exists between two things which are different per se.

Dulia   Worship

The honor and reverence which can appropriately be paid to a creature. This is to be distinguished from *latria* which is the honor and reverence due only to God. *Hyperdulia* — a category between *dulia* and *latria* — is due to the Virgin Mary.

S II 51 E; *Lect.* 49 F–50 H.

Electi   The elect

Those who by God's choice of some men and not of others are prepared by grace in this life to take the place of the fallen angels in heaven. [See *praedestinatio, reprobatio*.]

I *Sent.* d 40 q 1 art. 1.

Ex debito iusticiae   Due on grounds of the demands of justice

This phrase is used to describe the unconditional character of God's commitment to his established order, that is, to his *potentia ordinata*. Since God has committed himself to accept good deeds performed in a state of grace, God would do injustice if he failed to act according to his pact. This pact establishes the *dignitas* of an act, the *meritum de condigno*.

Lect. 59 S.

Ex natura rei debita   Due on grounds of the intrinsic value of an act

In contrast to the phrase *ex debito iusticiae*, it refers to the value of a morally good act [*bonitas moralis*]. If it is performed in a state of grace it is meritorius *de condigno*. Even if performed in a state of sin it is meritorius *de congruo*. [See *facere quod in se est*].

II *Sent.* d 27 q 1 art. 1 nota 3.

Ex opere operantis (*Opus operantis*) *per modum meriti* The efficiency of a rite as related to the interior disposition of the administrant or the recipient

It designates the effects of the sacraments of the old law and the *sacramentalia* of the new law. The orthodox interpretation of *ex opere operantis* is that a proper disposition on part of the recipient will provide him with grace above and beyond the amount of grace received *ex opere operato*. The heretical — Donatistic — interpretation of *ex opere operantis* is that a proper disposition on the part of the administrant is required for the validity and efficacy of the rite.

IV *Sent.* d 1 q 3 art. 1 nota 2, 3; *S* II 13 H.

Ex opere operato (*Opus operatum*)   On grounds of the performance of the rite

This designates the efficiency of an exterior rite, performed to signify something, which is derived from its institution. The sacraments of the new law have power in this way to convey grace so long as the recipient does not provide an obstacle [*ponat obicem*] and the administrant has the proper intention.

Lect. 26 G.

Ex pacto divino (Ex institutione divina)   On grounds of the divine pact

This is usually said to be God's pact with the Church. The term functions especially in sacramental theology to designate the Scotistic — nominalistic —view that the fruits of the sacraments are due to God's concomitant action in the administration of the sacraments rather than to the *virtus* of the sacramental signs themselves.

IV *Sent.* d 1 q 1 art. 1.

Ex puris naturalibus   Out of purely natural capacities

This designates acts performed by nature unaided by grace. "Purely natural" excludes grace but not the *influentia generalis*.

II *Sent.* d 28 q 1 art. 1 nota 2.

Facere quod in se est   To do one's very best

To do all that is within one's natural power [see *ex puris naturalibus*] unaided by grace. In this way man is able to love God above everything else [see *amor dei super omnia*] and to earn the infusion of first grace [see *meritum de congruo*].

II *Sent.* d 27 q 1 art. 3 dub. 3 O.

Fides [See III *Sent.* d 23 q 2.]

Fides acquisita (Fides ex auditu)   Acquired faith

The habit of faith acquired by natural means through the *facere quod in se est;* a necessary condition for the reception of the gift of the *fides infusa*.

Fides demonum   Demons' faith

Historical, objective faith held even by the demons. [See *credere deum*.]

Fides explicita   Explicit faith

This faith is the actual conscious assent to a catholic truth, whether it be a general truth or a specific one. Explicit faith is expected of the clergy [*maiores*].

468

Fides formata Faith informed by love

Faith active in love and informed by the habit of supernatural love. By definition this faith is only possible in a state of grace.

Fides implicita Implicit faith

This is the actual or habitual assent to some general proposition which contains many particular truths; as e.g. when one believes what the Church believes. For laymen [*minores*] this is held to be the most prudent form of faith.

Fides informis Faith uninformed by love

That faith which can coexist with mortal sin though not with heresy.

Fides infusa Infused faith

The supernatural habit of faith which, together with hope and love, constitutes the theological triad of virtues, simultaneously infused into the soul at the moment of reception of first grace [see *gratia prima*].

Fides qua The act of faith, that is trust or assent

Fides quae The content of faith, often the articles of faith

Fiducia Confidence

Closely related to the certitude of hope, it is based on the promises of God and the acquisition of merits. Without the latter it is called *vana praesumptio*.

III *Sent.* d 26 q 1 art. 1 nota 2 C.

Fomes peccati The tinder of sin

An inordinate quality — and not a substance — of the body of man; which rebels against the execution of the dictates of right reason. It is not original sin itself but punishment imposed by God because of it and is an abiding characteristic of the *viator* since grace can mitigate but not eradicate it.

II *Sent.* d 30 q 2 art. 3 dub. 2.

Forus animae (*Forus poenitentiae; forus secretissimus*) The courtroom of the soul

Here accusor and accused are the same person standing *coram deo* and dealing with private sins. It is used in contrast with *forus publicus in ecclesia*. This latter term refers to the public responsibility of the Church to exercise the power of the keys and deals with public sins. Confession *in foro ecclesiae* is still needed for those who are already reconciled with God by contrition. [See *confessio in voto*.]

IV *Sent.* d 18 q 2 art. 1 nota 2 C; *Lect.* 7 E.

Gratia gratis data Grace given gratuitously

The supernatural gift of grace for the benefit of the recipient or others. Some scholastic authors use the term to describe a preparatory state before the reception of *gratia gratum faciens*. Others use it to designate a special gift or charisma for the benefit of the whole Church. In both cases, for example the initial vocation by God or the grace of ordination, these gifts can coexist with sin and do not presuppose a state of grace.

II *Sent.* d 26 q 1 art. 1 nota 1 B.

Gratia gratum faciens The grace that makes one a friend of God

This is the habit of justifying grace by which the sinner is made acceptable to God since he is then transposed into a state of grace and inclined to meritorious works. [See *meritum de condigno*.] It is given in the sacraments of baptism and penance.

II *Sent.* d 26 art. 2 concl. 4.

Gratia prima The first grace

This is given to children in baptism and through contrition to adults who have lost their baptismal grace. In the latter case it has to be completed by sacerdotal absolution, at least in intention. [See *confessio in proposito*.]

IV *Sent.* d 18 q 1 art. 2 concl. 2.

Habitus gratiae   The habit of grace

This habit is really indistinct [see *distinctio rationis* and *realis*] from the habit of charity; *de potentia dei ordinata*, it is the necessary condition for divine acceptation.

III *Sent.* d 23 q 1 art. 2; I *Sent.* d 17 passim.

Homo purus (*Humanitas pura*)   Pure manhood or true humanity

This is used in contrast with *deus homo*, the incarnate Son of God, to designate the true humanity of the Virgin Mary.

S III 25 A; *Lect.* 32 B.

Homo verus   Real man

True humanity of Christ according to the Chalcedonian formula.

III *Sent.* d 6 q 1 art. 2 concl. 3.

Hyperdulia   See *Dulia*

Influentia generalis   See *Concursus generalis*

Latria   See *Dulia*

Lex naturalis   Natural law

The natural law is consonant with and a manifestation of the *lex divina* or *lex aeterna*. But whereas divine law is acquired through revelation, natural law is acquired by the natural light of the intellect.

III *Sent.* d 37 q 1 art. 1 nota 1.

Meritum de condigno   A merit meeting the standard of God's justice

"Full merit." An act performed in a state of grace and therefore worthy [see *dignitas*] of divine acceptation. [See *ex debito iusticiae*.]

Meritum de congruo   A merit meeting the standard of God's generosity

"Half merit." An act performed in a state of sin, in accordance with natural or divine law [see *facere quod in se est*] and therefore accepted by God as satisfying the requirement for the infusion of first grace [see *ex natura rei debita*]. In contrast with the *meritum de condigno*, the *meritum de congruo* has no other grounds on which reward is based than the mere generosity [*liberalitas*] of God.

II *Sent.* d 27 q 1 art. 2 concl. 4.

Moderni doctores   Recent doctors

Sometimes this refers to those following the *via moderna*, that is, the school of Occam. Frequently it has the more general meaning of "doctors of the last century." When used in contrast with the *antiqui doctores* — e.g. Augustine, Ambrose, etc. — it refers to the Scholastics generally.

Necessitas absoluta (Necessitas consequentis)   Absolute necessity

This can be applied to creation but not to God.

Necessitas ex suppositione (Necessitas consequentiae)   Conditional necessity

The dialectics of the *potentia dei absoluta* and *potentia dei ordinata* are concerned with this second kind of necessity. *De potentia absoluta*, the necessity like the *necessitas absoluta*, is declared inapplicable to God. The conditional necessity indicates that God, *de potentia ordinata*, has committed himself to his own decrees.

IV *Sent.* d 1 q 2 art. 1 nota 1 A.

Peccatum originale   Original sin

Not only punishment [*poena*] but also guilt [*culpa*]. It is not a positive entity but the absence of original righteousness along with the unfulfilled obligation to possess it. Under the new law this obligation is changed into the requirement to possess the *gratia gratum faciens*. Original sin is always accompanied by the tinder of sin [see *fomes peccati*].

II *Sent.* d 30 q 2 *passim*.

Poena   See Culpa

Potentia dei absoluta   The absolute power of God subject only to the law of non-contradiction, which leaves the actually chosen order out of consideration

Potentia dei ordinata (stante lege; de facto; secundum leges ordinatas et institutas a deo)   The ordained power of God

This is the order established by God and the way in which God has chosen to act in his *opera ad extra*, i.e., over against the contingent order outside him. It is the power which is regulated by the revealed and natural laws established by God. Between the absolute and ordained power of God there is no real distinction but a merely rational distinction. [See *distinctio rationis.*]

I *Sent.* d 17 q 1 art. 3 H.

Praedestinatio ante praevisa merita   Eternal predestination of the elect uncaused by the foreknowledge of their merits

Praedestinatio post praevisa merita   Eternal predestination of the elect on the basis of foreknowledge of their future merits

Praesciti   The reprobate

Those who are foreknown not to accept the offer of grace and thus to die in a state of sin.

I *Sent.* d 41 q 1 art. 2 concl. 1, 2.

Pure credibilia   Beliefs which are held by faith alone

Those articles of faith which even the *beati* do not comprehend, such as the mystery of the Trinity and the eschatological acts of God.

III *Sent.* d 24 q 1 art. 2 concl. 6 H.

Quoad intentionem praecipientis or legislatoris   According to the intention of the lawgiver (God)
Quoad substantiam actus   According to the substance of an act (of man)

The distinction indicates that though the sinner can perform the substance of the acts required by God's law [see *ex puris naturalibus*], these

473

acts are nevertheless not fully meritorious [see *meritum de condigno*] without the presence of the habit of infused grace, since it is God's intention that the law be thus fulfilled.

II *Sent.* d 28 q 1 art. 2 concl. 3.

Ratio acceptationis   The grounds for acceptance

In a strict sense, the *ratio* for acceptance is only the will of God. Functionally, however, the grounds for acceptance by God are provided by the habit of grace [see *gratia gratum faciens*] and the spontaneous good act of the will.

Ratio fidei   The understanding of faith

This functions especially in apologetics, when one has to give a "reason" for one's faith.

S IV 5 D.

Ratio meriti   The grounds for reward [see *acceptatio* and *habitus gratiae.*]

Rationes necessariae   Necessary reasons

These are held by Anselm to be the characteristic structure of God's planning and acting. Nominalists are among those who reject these and replace them with *rationes probabiles*.

Rationes probabiles (Rationes congruentes)   Probable reasons

Given the standpoint of faith, certain creedal statements can be shown — not through demonstration but through persuasion — to be reasonable and in no way contrary to reason.

III *Sent.* d 24 q 1 art. 2 concl. 1.
IV *Sent.* d 6 q 2 art. 3 dub. 1 L.

Removere obicem (Non ponere obicem)   To remove the lock (on the doors of one's heart)

This is the removal of the obstacle to the reception of grace by doing one's very best. [See *facere quod in se est*.]

Repletive   See *Circumscriptive*

Reprobatio   See *Praesciti*

Scintilla conscientiae (*Synderesis, synteresis, sinderesis*)   The spark of the conscience

A natural inclination toward good and away from evil. This is not an act or habit of the will but the voice of natural law speaking through the dictates of right reason.

II *Sent.* d 39 q 1 art. 2 concl. 1.

Securitas   Security

Whereas for Duns Scotus *securitas* resides in the will and *certitudo* in the intellect (IV *Sent.* d 49 q 6), this distinction does not obtain in nominalistic theology. [See therefore *certitudo*.]

Synderesis (*Synteresis, sinderesis*)   See *scintilla conscientiae*

Terminative   See *Circumscriptive*

Testamentum   Testament or will

The new testament of Jesus Christ is the true Christian faith and the law of Christ. The passion and death of Christ validate this testament.

Lect. 53 N.

Timor filialis (*Timor amicalis, timor castus*)   Filial fear
Respect due to God, which stems from true love for God

Timor initialis   Initial fear

This is that quality of fear which stands between *timor servilis* and *timor filialis*, and is partly based on egoistic fear, partly on pure love for God.

III *Sent.* d 35 q 1 art. 1 nota 2 B.

Timor servilis   Servile fear

Awe for God which does not stem from love for God purely for his sake but out of self love. [See *amor concupiscentiae.*] Its motive is avoidance of eternal punishment.

Via antiqua   The old way
Via moderna   The modern way

Terms used in late medieval university statutes to indicate allegiance either to the old doctors of the high Middle Ages — Albert the Great, Thomas Aquinas, Duns Scotus — or to the new doctors, the followers of Occam. [See *doctores moderni.*]

Viator (—— *in via*)   The pilgrim

One who has not yet completed his journey either to the new Jerusalem or to eternal damnation. He has no evident knowledge of God, but is dependent on his sense knowledge and his faith. [See *fides*; see *fomes peccati.*]

Prologi q 1.

Voluntas dei beneplaciti   God's good pleasure

The two aspects of this same will of God, the preceding and subsequent will — *voluntas beneplaciti antecedens* and *consequens* — are not really distinct. [See *distinctio realis.*] The "antecedent will" enables the *viator* to accomplish something or to execute the precepts and counsels given to him by God. The "subsequent will" is the direct will of God which is always executed, whether expressed in general providence [see *concursus generalis*] or in special providence [see *praedestinatio*].

Lect. 68 C, D.

Voluntas dei signi   The signified will of God

This is the declaration or revelation of God's will for his creation which enables man to know the will of God, e.g., the law, but which is certainly not always executed.

I *Sent.* d 46 q 2 art. 2 concl. 1–5.

INDEX OF NAMES
INDEX OF SUBJECTS

INDEX OF NAMES

INDEX OF SUBJECTS